ALL'S WELL THAT ENDS REGISTERED?

EUROPEAN FAMILY LAW SERIES

ALL'S WELL THAT ENDS REGISTERED?

The substantive and private international law aspects of non-marital registered relationships in Europe. A comparison of the laws of Belgium, France, The Netherlands, Switzerland and the United Kingdom

IAN CURRY-SUMNER

intersentia

Antwerp – Oxford

Distribution for the UK:
Hart Publishing
Salter's Boat Yard
Folly Bridge
Abingdon Road
Oxford OX1 4LB
UK
Tel: + 44 1865 24 55 33
Fax: + 44 1865 79 48 82

Distribution for North America:
Gaunt Inc.
Gaunt Building
3011 Gulf Drive
Holmes Beach
Florida 34217-2199
USA
Tel: + 1 941 778 5211
Fax: + 1 941 778 5252

Distribution for Switzerland and Germany:
Stämpfli Verlag AG
Hallerstrasse 7
Postfach
CH-3001 Bern
Switzerland
Tel: + 41 31 300 66 77
Fax: + 41 31 300 66 88

Distribution for other countries:
Intersentia Publishers
Groenstraat 31
BE-2640 Mortsel
Belgium
Tel: + 32 3 680 15 50
Fax: + 32 3 658 71 21

All's well that ends registered?
Ian Curry-Sumner

ISBN 90-5095-532-0
D/2005/7849/90
NUR 822 and 828

ACKNOWLEDGEMENTS

Looking back upon the four years that I have lived in Utrecht and conducted this research , it is clear that this work would not be what it now is without the many people who have made those four years not only possible, but also pleasurable. Many of these people not only helped with my research, but also ultimately made The Netherlands feel like home.

First and foremost, I am deeply indebted to Professor Katharina Boele-Woelki. There are few people in this world who have made such a difference to my life that it is difficult to imagine what my life might have been like if I had not met them. However, Katharina is one of these people. She has provided me with endless opportunities, unparalleled supervision, thought-provoking discussions and the possibility to grow both as an individual and as a researcher. Her sharp, critical, analytical and methodical approach has provided me both with direction and boundaries. It was more than just an honour to have been able to work under her direction. Furthermore, I would also like to thank Professor Ted de Boer, Professor William Duncan, Professor Ewoud Hondius, Dr. Ellen Mostermans and Professor Ingeborg Schwenzer for their willingness to participate as members of my examination committee. Their comments on the original version of this book and their interest in my research have only provided me with further inspiration. I would especially like to thank Dr. Ellen Mostermans for her ever-present willingness to discuss the finer points of my research over the last four years.

Since a substantial portion of the comparative research in this book was conducted abroad at various institutions, I would also like to thank all those who made my visits to the Katholieke Universiteit Leuven, Swiss Institute of Comparative Law, Institute for Advanced Legal Studies and Washburn University School of Law, Topeka possible.

I would also like to thank all my colleagues at the Molengraaff Institute for Private Law, and especially the members of the private international law, comparative law and family law section. Building a life in a foreign country is not easy, but the problem almost solves itself if one is blessed with colleagues like those I have the fortune to work with. In particular I would like to extend my gratitude to Christina Jeppesen, with whom I have had the pleasure to share a room with for four years. Her dedication and ability to make me laugh have made the last four years a joy. Moreover I would especially like to thank Bente Braat, Lieke Coenraad, Harriët Schelhaas, Wendy Schrama and Machteld Vonk, all of whom have read various parts of this research. Additionally, I would like to express special thanks to Machteld Vonk for translating the summary into Dutch.

Without friends I would be a hollow man. Every single one of you has made an impression on me that has changed the way I think, and I thank you for that constant challenge to appreciate the world in a different way. In particular I would like to thank Professors Nancy Maxwell and Caroline Forder for having faith in my ability long before I had the experience to back it up, and thus offering me the chance to prove myself not only to others, but also to myself. Furthermore, I would also like to thank Hans and Eveline Warendorf. Your friendship means more to me than you will ever know. Your openness, generosity and belief in me are a constant source of encouragement. I am also greatly indebted to Janine Bouwman and Bente Braat who have both stood by me as paranymphs throughout this process.

My final words of thanks go to my family and family-in-law. The openness with which I have been welcomed into my American family has been truly spectacular. To Nancy Curry, or "Mom" as I refer to her, thank you for your support, advice and enthusiasm. All people are blessed to have one mother; I therefore feel unbelievably fortunate to have two. My sister, Pamela, to this day surprises me with her endless enthusiasm for life; her inspiration is more than any brother could ever wish for. And of course, my parents. I would like to thank them for their self-sacrifice. Without their support, encouragement and unending zest for the choices that I have made, this PhD would never have been completed and I would not be the person I am today. I thank you both from the bottom of my heart.

And last but not least, I would like to thank Scott; a husband that one can only dream of. I thank you for giving me the courage to strive to achieve my ambitions. You have supplied me with the ability to criticise my own work and the strength to admit when I am wrong. I cannot begin to express my gratitude. It is with great pride that I therefore dedicate this book to Scott, Pamela and my parents.

This research was completed on the 1st September 2005. No account is taken of publications, legislation and case law published after this date.

Ian Curry-Sumner

TABLE OF CONTENTS

PART II: SUBSTANTIVE LAW

CHAPTER III
BELGIUM

CHAPTER IV
FRANCE

CHAPTER V
THE NETHERLANDS

CHAPTER VI
SWITZERLAND

CHAPTER VII
UNITED KINGDOM

CHAPTER VIII
COMPARISON AND EVALUATION

PART III: PRIVATE INTERNATIONAL LAW

CHAPTER IX
CHARACTERISATION: REVISITED

PART IV: APPENDICES

LIST OF ABBREVIATIONS

1 Civ. Ch.	First Civil Chamber (*Premier chambre civile*)
2 Civ. Ch.	Second Civil Chamber (*Deuxième chambre civile*)
3 Civ. Ch.	Third Civil Chamber (*Troisième chambre civile*)
AA	*Ars Aequi*
AC	*Law Reports, Appeal Cases (Court of Appeal and House of Lords)*
AG	Attorney-General
AJCL	*American Journal of Comparative Law*
AJT	*Algemeen Juridische Tijdschrift*
ALR	*Albany Law Review*
Anglo-Am L Rev.	*Anglo-American Law Review*
Arizona JICL	*Arizona Journal of International and Comparative Law*
Arr. Cass.	*Arresten van het Hof van Cassatie*
Art.	Article
Arts.	Articles
ATF	*Arrêts du Tribunal Fédéral*
Appl. No.	Application Number
Belg.	Belgium
Belg. Cass.	Belgian Supreme Court (*Hof van Cassatie*)
Belg. CS	Belgian Council of State (*Raad van Staat*)
Belg. Staatsblad	Belgian Bulletin of Acts and Decrees (*Staatsblad*)
BlZR	*Blätter für Zürcherische Rechtsprechung*
BO	Swiss Official Bulletin (*Bulletin Officiel de l'Assemblee fédérale*)
Brit. HC	British House of Commons
Brit. HL	British House of Lords
Bull. Civ.	*Bulletin des arrêts de la Cour de Cassation*
BYIL	British Yearbook of International Law
CA	Court of Appeal
CBR	*Canadian Bar Review*
CEFL	Commission on European Family Law
CFLQ	*Child and Family Law Quarterly*
Ch	*Law Reports (Chancery Division, High Court)*
CJFL	*Canadian Journal of Family Law*
CLJ	*Cambridge Law Journal*
CLP	*Current Legal Problems*
CLR	*Commonwealth Law Reports*
Col.	Column
Cols.	Columns
Com. Ch.	Commercial Chamber (*Chamber commerciale*)
Conseil Const.	French Constitutional Court (*Conseil Constitutionnel*)
Cornell ILJ	*Cornell International Law Journal*
CP	Civil Partnership
Creighton LR	*Creighton Law Review*
CYIL	*Canadian Yearbook of International Law*
D	*Recueil Dalloz*
DC	District Court

DeuFamR	*Deutsches und Europäisches FamilienRecht*
EB	*Echtscheidings Bulletin*
ECHR	European Convention on Human Rights
ECmHR	European Commission of Human Rights
ECR	*European Court Reports*
ECtHR	European Court of Human Rights
Edin. LR	*Edinburgh Law Review*
EHRLR	*European Human Rights Law Review*
EJ	*Echtscheidingsjournaal*
EJCL	*Electronic Journal of Comparative Law*
EJLR	*European Journal of Law Reform*
ELR	*European Law Review*
Eng.	England & Wales
EPRL	*European Review of Private Law*
et al.	*et alii* (and others)
etc.	*et cetera* (and the rest)
Fam.	*Law Reports (Family Division, High Court)*
Fam Law	*Family Law*
FamPra.ch	*Die Praxis des Familienrechts / La Pratique du Droit de la Famille*
FamRZ	*Zeitschrift für das gesamte Familienrecht*
FF	Swiss Federal Gazette (*Feuille Fédérale*)
FJR	*Tijdschrift voor Familie- en Jeugdrecht*
FLR	*Law Reports, Family Division, High Court*
fn.	Footnote
Fr.	France
Fr. Cass.	French Supreme Court (*Cour de Cassation*)
Fr. Con. C	French Constitutional Court (*Le Conseil Constitutionnel*)
Fr. CS	French Council of State (*Le Conseil d'État*)
Gaz. Pal.	*Gazette du Palais*
Gen. Stadtsbladt	Geneva Bulletin of Acts and Decrees
Ger. CC	German Civil Code (*Bürgerliches Gesetzbuch für das Deutsche Reich*)
Ger. CCIL	Introductory Law to the German Civil Code (*Einführungsgesetz zum Bürgerlichen Gesetzbuche*)
Govt.	Government
Harv. Int. LJ	*Harvard International Law Journal*
HC	*Hague Conference Recueil des Cours*
HR	Dutch Supreme Court (*Hoge Raad*)
ibid	*ibidem* (from the same source)
ICLQ	*International Comparative Law Quarterly*
IFL	*International Family Law*
IJCR	*International Journal of Children's Rights*
IJFL	*Irish Journal of Family Law*
IJLF	*International Journal of Law and the Family*
IJLPF	*International Journal of Law, Policy and the Family*
ILF	*International Law FORUM du Droit International*
IPRax	*Praxis des Internationalen Privat- und Verfahrensrechts*
Ipr.be	*Tijdschrift voor Belgisch Internationaal Privaatrecht*
JBl	*Juristische Blätter*
JBN	*Juridische Berichten voor het Notariaat*
JCP Éd. G.	*La Semaine Juridique Édition Générale*
JCP Éd. N.	*La Semaine Juridique Édition Notarial*

JDI	*Journal de Droit International*
JES	*Journal of European Studies*
JdT	*Journal des Tribunaux (Switzerland)*
JF	*Jura Falconis*
JH	*Journal of Homosexuality*
JL	*Jurisprudence Liège*
JNA	*Journal des Notaires et des Avocats*
JO	*Journal Officiel de la République Française*
JR	*Juridical Review*
JT	*Journal des Tribunaux (France)*
KB / KBD	*Law Reports (King's Bench Division, High Court)*
Lloyd's Rep.	*Lloyds Law Reports*
LLR	*Liverpool Law Review*
LQR	*Law Quarterly Review*
Louisiana LR	*Louisiana Law Review*
MJ	*Maastricht Journal*
MLR	*Modern Law Review*
MP	Member of Parliament (House of Commons)
Neth.	The Netherlands
Neth. Staatsblad	Dutch Bulletin of Acts and Decrees (*Staatsblad*)
Neu. Stadtsbladt	Neuchâtel Bulletin of Acts and Decrees
New LJ	New Law Journal
New Eng. LR	New England Law Review
NI	Northern Ireland
NILQ	*Northern Ireland Law Quarterly*
NILR	*Netherlands International Law Review*
NIPR	*Nederlands Internationaal Privaatrecht*
NJ	*Nederlandse Jurisprudentie*
NJB	*Nederlands Juristenblad*
NJT	*Nieuw Juridisch Tijdschrift*
NLJ	*New Law Journal*
NMRR	Non-marital registered relationship
No.	Number
NTER	*Nederlands Tijdschrift voor Europees Recht*
NYLSJHR	*New York Law Society Journal of Human Rights*
OJ	*Official Journal of the European Communities*
P	*Law Reports, Probate Division, High Court*
PACS	Pacte civil de solidarité
Pas.	*Pasicrisie Belge*
PD	*Law Reports, Probate Division, High Court*
PECL	Principles of European Contract Law
PEFL	Principles of European Family Law
PJA (AJP)	*Pratique Juridique Actuelle*
QB / QBD	*Law Reports (Queen's Bench Division, High Court)*
Rb	Rechtbank (Dutch and Belgian equivalent to district court)
RDIPP	*Rivista di Diritto Internazionale Private e Processuale*
RDS (ZSR)	*Revue de Droit Suisse*
Reg.	Regulation
Rép. Not.	*Répertoire du Notariat Deféńois*
Rev. crit. DIP	*Revue Critique de Droit International Privé*
Rev. crit. jur. belge	*Revue Critique de Jurisprudence Belge*

Rev. Dec. Con. Ct.	*Revue des décisions du Conseil Constitutionnel*
Rev. int. dr. com.	*Revue International de Droit Comparé*
Rev. jur. per. fam.	*Revue Juridique Personnes et Famille*
Rev. not. Bel.	*Revue du Notariat Belge*
Rev. trim. dr. civ.	*Revue Trimestrielle de Droit Civil*
Rev. trim. dr. fam.	*Revue Trimestrielle de Droit Familial*
Rev. trim. dr. eur.	*Revue Trimestrielle de Droit Européen*
RJ Trim. Arr. Niv.	*Recueil Jurisprudence Trimestrielle des Arrêts de Nivelles*
RNRF	*Revue suisse de notariat et du registre foncier*
RO	Swiss Recueil officiel des lois et ordonnances de la confédration suisse
RP	Registered Partnership
RS	Swiss Recueil systématique du droit fédéral
RSDIE (SZIER)	*Revue Suisse de Droit International et de Droit Européen*
RSJ (SJZ)	*Revue Suisse de Jurisprudence*
RW	*Rechtskundig Weekblad*
S	*Sirey (Recueil general des lois et arrêts)*
SA	South African Law Reports
SC	Session Cases
Sch.	Schedule
Scot.	Scotland
S-DC	Sub-District Court
Sec.	Section
Secs.	Sections
SEW	*Tijdschrift voor Europees en Economisch Recht*
SI	Statutory Instrument
SJ	*La Semaine Judiciaire*
SLT	*Scottish Law Times*
Soc. Ch.	Social Chamber (*Chambre Sociale*)
Sp. CC	Spanish Civil Code (*Código Civil*)
SSI	Scottish Statutory Instrument
Sw. FC	Swiss Federal Constitution
Swit.	Switzerland
TBBR	*Tijdschrift voor Belgisch Burgerlijk Recht*
TCR	*Tijdschrift voor Civiele Rechtspleging*
TGI	Tribunal de Grande Instance
TLR	*Times Law Reports*
TPR	*Tijdschrift voor Privaatrecht*
Trib. Féd.	Swiss Supreme Court (*Tribunal Fédéral*)
Vol.	Volume
Vr.	Vredegerecht
WA	*Waarvan Akte*
Web JCLI	*Web Journal of Current Legal Issues*
Will. LR	*Willamette Law Review*
WLR	*Weekly Law Reports*
WPNR	*Weekblad voor Privaatrecht, Notariaat en Registratie*
Yale LJ	*Yale Law Journal*
ZEuP	*Zeitschrift für Europäisches Privatrecht*
ZfRv	*Zeitschrift für Rechtsvergleichung, Internationales Privatrecht und Europarecht*
ZLR	*Zimbabwe Law Reports*
Zur. Stadtsbladt	Zurich Bulletin of Acts and Decrees

NATIONAL AND EUROPEAN LEGISLATION

Belgian Legislation

Belg. CC	Belgian Civil Code (*Burgerlijk Wetboek*)
Belg. CPIL	Belgian Code of Private International Law (*Wetboek van het Internationaal privaatrecht*)
Belg. Cr. C	Belgian Criminal Code (*Strafwetboek*)
Belg. ITC	Belgian Income Tax Code 1992 (*Wet van de inkomstenbelastingen 1992*)
Belg. NC	Belgian Nationality Code (*Wetboek van de Belgische Nationaliteit*)

French Legislation

Fr. CC	French Civil Code (*Code Civil*)
Fr. CPH	French Code on Public Health (*Code de la Santé Publique*)
Fr. CSS	French Code of Social Security (*Code du securité sociale*)
Fr. EC	French Employment Code (*Code du Travail*)
Fr. GTC	French General Tax Code (*Code Général des Impôts*)
Fr. NCCP	French Code of Civil Procedure (*Nouveau Code de Procédure Civil*)

Dutch Legislation

Neth. CC	Dutch Civil Code (*Burgerlijk Wetboek*)
Neth. CCP	Dutch Code of Civil Procedure (*Burgerlijke Rechtsvordering*)
Neth. Cr. C	Dutch Criminal Code (*Wetboek van Strafrecht*)
Neth. PIL(A)A	Dutch Private International Law (Adoption) Act (*Wet conflictenrecht adoptie*)
Neth. PIL(D)A	Dutch Private International Law (Dissolution of Marriages and Judicial Separations) Act (*Wet conflictenrecht echtscheiding*)
Neth. PIL(M)A	Dutch Private International Law (Marriages) Act (*Wet conflictenrecht huwelijk*)
Neth. PIL(N)A	Dutch Private International Law (Names) Act (*Wet conflictenrecht namen*)
Neth. PIL(RP)A	Dutch Private International Law (Registered Partnerships) Act (*Wet conflictenrecht geregistreerd partnerschap*)
Proposed Neth. CPIL	Proposed Dutch Code of Private International Law (*Voorgestelde Wetboek van het Nederlandse Internationaal Privaatrecht*)

Swiss Legislation

Sw. CC	Swiss Civil Code (*Code Civil*)
Sw. CO	Swiss Code of Obligations (*Code des Obligations*)
Sw. CPIL	Swiss Code of Private International Law (*Code du Droit International Privé*)
Sw. Cr. C	Swiss Criminal Code (*Code Pénal*)
Sw OCS	Swiss Ordinance on Civil Status of 28th April 2004 (*Ordonnance du 28 avril 2004 sur l'état civil*)
Sw. RPA	Swiss Registered Partnership Act (*Loi fédérale sur partenariat enregistré entre personnes du même sexe*)

United Kingdom Legislation

A(NI)O 1987	Adoption (Northern Ireland) Order 1987
AA 1976	Adoption Act 1976
ACA 2002	Adoption and Children Act 2002
AEA (NI) 1955	Administration of Estates Act 1955
AEA 1925	Administration of Estates Act 1925
BDR(NI)O 1976	Births and Deaths Registration (Northern Ireland) Order 1976
BDRA 1953	Births and Deaths Registration Act 1953
BNA 1981	British Nationality Act 1981
C(NI)O 1995	Children (Northern Ireland) Order 1995
C(S)A 1995	Children (Scotland) Act 1995
CA 1989	Children Act 1989
CPA 2004	Civil Partnership Act 2004
CSA 1991	Child Support Act 1991
CSA 1995	Child Support Act 1995
DPMCA 1978	Domestic Proceedings and Magistrates' Act 1978
DP(NI)O 1980	Domestic Proceedings (Northern Ireland) Order 1980
EE(SO)R 2003	Employment Equality (Sexual Orientation) Regulations 2003
FAA 1976	Fatal Accidents Act 1976
FHDV(NI)O 1998	Family Homes and Domestic Violence (Northern Ireland) Order 1998
FL(MP)(NI)O 1984	Family Law (Miscellaneous Provisions)(Northern Ireland) Order 1984
FL(NI)O 1993	Family Law (Northern Ireland) Order 1993
FL(S)A 1985	Family Law (Scotland) Act 1985
FL(S)B 2005	Family Law (Scotland) Bill 2005
FLA 1986	Family Law Act 1986
FLRA 1987	Family Law Reform Act 1987
FM(A)A 1988	Foreign Marriage (Amendment) Act 1988
FMA 1892	Foreign Marriage Act 1892
FMA 1947	Foreign Marriage Act 1947
FMO 1970	Foreign Marriage Order 1970
GRA 2004	Gender Recognition Act 2004
H(NI)O 1988	Housing (Northern Ireland) Order 1988
H(S)A 1987	Housing (Scotland) Act 1987
H(S)A 1988	Housing (Scotland) Act 1988
H(S)A 2001	Housing (Scotland) Act 2001
HA 1985	Housing Act 1985
HA 1988	Housing Act 1988
HFEA 1990	Human Fertilisation and Embryology Act 1990
I(PFD)A 1975	Inheritance (Provision for Family Dependents) Act 1975
IA 1986	Insolvency Act 1986
IAA 1999	Immigration and Asylum Act 1999
IEA 1952	Intestates' Estates Act 1952
ITA 1984	Inheritance Tax Act 1984
LGA 1986	Local Government Act 1986
LGA 1988	Local Government Act 1988
LGA 2003	Local Government Act 2003
LGFA 1992	Local Government Finance Act 1992
LPA 1925	Law of Property Act 1925
LR(HW)(S)A 1984	Law Reform (Husband and Wife)(Scotland) Act 1984

LR(HW)A 1961	Law Reform (Husband and Wife) Act 1961
LR(HW)A(NI) 1964	Law Reform (Husband and Wife) Act (Northern Ireland) 1964
LR(PC)(S)A 1986	Law Reform (Parent and Child)(Scotland) Act 1986
M(NI)O 2003	Marriage (Northern Ireland) Order 2003
M(PDR)A 1986	Marriage (Prohibited Degrees of Relationship) Act 1986
M(PDR)A(NI) 1949	Marriage (Prohibited Degrees of Relationship) Act (NI) 1949
M(RGL)A 1970	Marriage (Registrar's General Licence) Act 1970
M(S)A 1977	Marriage (Scotland) Act 1977
M(S)A 2002	Marriage (Scotland) Act 2002
MA 1949	Marriage Act 1949
MA 1983	Marriage Act 1983
MA 1994	Marriage Act 1994
MC(NI)O 1978	Matrimonial Causes (Northern Ireland) Order 1978
MCA 1884	Matrimonial Causes Act 1884
MCA 1973	Matrimonial Causes Act 1973
MFPA 1984	Matrimonial and Family Proceedings Act 1984
MFP(NI)O 1989	Matrimonial and Family Proceedings (Northern Ireland) Order 1989
MH(FP)(S)A 1981	Matrimonial Homes (Family Provision)(Scotland) Act 1981
MR(NI) 2003	Marriage Rules (Northern Ireland) 2003
MWPA 1882	Married Women's Property Act 1882
MWPA 1964	Married Women's Property Act 1964
PA 1995	Pensions Act 1995
PD(S)A 1977	Presumption of Death (Scotland) Act 1977
P(NI)O 1995	Pensions (Northern Ireland) Order 1995
PIL(MP)A 1995	Private International Law (Miscellaneous Provisions) Act 1995
PRSS(S)O 1999	Prior Rights of Surviving Spouse (Scotland) Order 1999
R(NI)O 1977	Rates (Northern Ireland) Order 1977
R(NI)O 1978	Rent (Northern Ireland) Order 1978
R(S)A 1984	Rent (Scotland) Act 1984
RA 1977	Rent Act 1977
RBDM(S)A 1965	Registration of Births, Deaths and Marriages (Scotland) Act 1965
RSA 1953	Registration Services Act 1953
S(S)A	Succession (Scotland) Act 1964
SO(A)A 2000	Sexual Offences (Amendment) Act 2000
SOA 1956	Sexual Offences Act 1956
SOA 1967	Sexual Offences Act 1967
SOA 2003	Sexual Offences Act 2003
SSA 1992	Social Security Administration Act 1992
WA 1837	Wills Act 1837
WAP(NI)O 1994	Wills and Administration Proceedings (Northern Ireland) Order 1994
WRP(NI)O 1999	Welfare Reform and Pensions (Northern Ireland) Order 1999

European Legislation

Brussels I	EC Regulation No. 44/2001 of 22nd December 2000
Brussels II	EC Regulation No. 1347/2000 of 29th May 2000
Brussels IIa	EC Regulation No. 2201/2003 of 27th November 2003
Brussels Convention	EC Convention jurisdiction and the enforcement of judgments in civil and commercial matters

EC Treaty	Treaty establishing the European Community, as amended
Lugano Convention	Lugano Convention of 16th September 1988
Rome Convention	EC Convention on the law applicable to contractual obligations
Rome I	COM (2002) 654: Proposed EC Regulation on applicable law in contractual obligations
Rome II	COM (2003) 427: Proposed EC Regulation on applicable law in non-contractual obligations
Rome III	COM (2005) 82: Proposed EC regulation on applicable law and jurisdiction in divorce

Hague Conference Conventions

1902 Hague MC	Convention of 12th June 1902 relating to the settlement of the conflict of the laws concerning marriage
1902 Hague DC	Convention of 12 June 1902 relating to the settlement of the conflict of laws and jurisdictions as regards to divorce and separation
1970 Hague DC	Convention of 1st June 1970 on the Recognition of Divorces and Legal Separations
1973 Hague LAMO	Convention of 2nd October 1973 on the Law Applicable to Maintenance Obligations
1973 Hague REMO	Convention of 2nd October 1973 on the Recognition and Enforcement of Decisions relating to Maintenance Obligations
1978 Hague MC	Convention of 14th March 1978 on Celebration and Recognition of the Validity of Marriages
1978 Hague MPR	Convention of 14th March 1978 on the Law Applicable to Matrimonial Property Regimes
1985 Hague TC	Convention of 1st July 1985 on the Law Applicable to Trusts and on their Recognition
1993 Hague AC	Convention of 29th May 1993 on the Protection of Children and Co-operation in respect of Intercountry Adoption
1996 Hague CC	Convention of 19th October 1996 on jurisdiction, applicable law, recognition, enforcement and co-operation in respect of parental responsibility and measures for the protection of children

LEGAL LATIN TERMINOLOGY

auctor regit actum	the law of the legal unit that confers a power on a person to perform certain acts in an official capacity governs the formal validity of their act
favor dissolutionis	principle favouring the validity of non-marital registered relationship dissolution
favor divortii	principle favouring the validity of divorces
favor matrimonii	principle favouring the validity of marriages
favor recognitionis	principle favouring the recognition of foreign decisions
favor registrationis	principle favouring the validity of non-marital registered relationships
forum actoris	the court of the applicant's domicile
forum conveniens	a court deems itself to be the most appropriate court to hear the action

forum necessitatis	the court of necessity (in this work, this is synonymous with the place where the relationship was registered)
forum non conveniens	a court has a discretionary power to decline to exercise jurisdiction over a legal issue when it believes that the action may be more appropriately dealt with elsewhere
forum patriae	the court of the party's nationality
forum rei	the court of the respondent's domicile
lex conveniens	most appropriate law in the circumstances of the case
lex domicilli	law of the legal unit where a person is domiciled
lex fori	local domestic law of the legal unit to which a court, wherein an action is brought, belongs
lex loci actus	law of the legal unit where an act takes place
lex loci celebrationis	law of place where marriage is celebrated
lex loci registrationis	law of place where non-marital relationships is registered
lex patriae	law of country to which a person owes national allegiance
lex situs	law of the legal unit where a thing is situated
lex successionis	law of the inheritance (*i.e.* the legal system which determines inheritance rights)
locus regit actum	law of the legal unit where an act takes place governs its form

PART I

INTRODUCTION

"The life of the law has not been logic, it has been experience ... in order to know what it is, we must know what it has been and what it tends to become"

Oliver Wendell Holmes Jr., *The Common Law* (1881) p. 1

CHAPTER I
INTRODUCTION

I.1 PRELUDE

Romeo and Juliet. A story of forbidden love. A story of how society can determine how and when one person may express his or her love for another. A story of names and terminology. Caught in the crossfire of a social order beyond their control, Romeo and Juliet must combat power, politics, and family relationships.

> *'Tis but thy name that is my enemy;*
> *Thou art thyself, though not a Montague.*
> *What's Montague? it is nor hand, nor foot,*
> *Nor arm, nor face, nor any other part*
> *Belonging to a man. O, be some other name!*
> *What's in a name? that which we call a rose*
> *By any other name would smell as sweet.*[1]

Although written in the late 1590s, Romeo and Juliet reminds us of the ever-present impact of social norms on the very private, intimate nature of a couple's relationship. Society's disapproval can quite literally end in the death of a relationship. Yet SHAKESPEARE delves deeper, asking the question whether it is really this love that we despise or simply the name we assign to it. Throughout the play SHAKESPEARE stresses the importance of nomenclature. Was it not for Romeo's name this young couple's love would have known no bounds nor acceptance. The forbidden love depicted by SHAKESPEARE is ubiquitous and evident even in today's modern, and comparably liberal, social order.

The two themes of social norms and nomenclature are indicative of the social debate that has raged for the past few decades surrounding the regulation of same-sex relationships. Homosexuality, once dubbed the "love

---

1 Act II, Scene 2, *Romeo and Juliet.*

that dare not speak its name",[2] has broken free of the shackles of social repugnance and fought those dominant social norms. Yet the way in which we afford recognition to a couple's intimate relationship has been approached very differently around the world. Juliet's question, "what's in a name?", may at first glance seem a rather flippant remark, yet it pinpoints a crucial dilemma facing legislatures today: how can one afford recognition to same-sex relationships without upturning the dominant social order? Can the traditional definition of marriage really be changed?

As well as 1989 being the year that democracy brought the Berlin Wall tumbling, brought an end to a military dictatorship in Chile and saw many students lose their lives in Tiananmen Square, it was also an historic moment for the gay rights movement. In 1989, unaware of the domino effect about to be unleashed, **Denmark** became the first country in the world to grant legal recognition to same-sex couples.[3] Since then not only has **Denmark** granted more rights to same-sex couples and relaxed the initial stringent entry requirements,[4] but other jurisdictions around the world have followed suit. The dawning of a new millennium has also witnessed the dawning of a new era in the recognition of same-sex relationships. For the first time in history, same-sex couples have been afforded the benefit of civil marriage.[5] Yet legal systems are not bubbles floating independently of each other. They are constantly interacting with each other by means of legal transplants, the migration of nationals or the confrontation with foreign systems of law. The impact of these phenomena on the regulation of such new registered relationships cannot be ignored. It is for these reasons that attention must be paid to the international implications of such registration schemes.

In this introductory chapter, it is hoped to delineate the underlying rationale behind this work, both in terms of justification as well as methodology. Numerous factors, both social and academic, have combined and led to the materialisation of this research. These factors will be discussed briefly in **Section I.2. Section I.3** is devoted to explaining the

2 "What is 'the love that dare not speak its name'?" was asked of OSCAR WILDE by the prosecutor during his trial for sodomy. The trial took place between 26th April to 1st May 1895. See H.M. HYDE, *The love that dared not speak its name*, Boston: Little Brown & Co, 1970, p. 1.

3 Act No. 372 of 7th June 1989.

4 Amendments to the original Registered Partnership Act have been realised by virtue of the Act No. 821 of 19th December 1989 and Act No. 360 of 2nd June 1999.

5 See **Appendix 4**.

precise research question addressed, and is followed by an in-depth explanation of the methodology used to conduct this research (**Section I.4**). The accountability of the countries chosen is provided in **Section I.5**.

I.2 SOCIAL AND ACADEMIC SETTING

The justification for this research lies in the culmination of a number of independent, yet interrelated academic and social factors. The increasing number of jurisdictions to have addressed the issues surrounding non-marital relationships by creating registration schemes is testimony to the non-ephemeral character of this phenomenon.[6] Moreover, according to recent statistics more than six million European citizens migrate yearly within the European Union and more than one and a half million third country nationals immigrate into the European Union every year.[7] With these facts in mind, it is foreseeable, as DETHLOFF indicates, that the number of international, cross-border familial relationships is only set to rise.[8]

This increase brings new dilemmas. The variety and diversity of substantive law solutions leads to problems of private international law. At a time when the unification of private international law at European Union level is a prime objective and the harmonisation of substantive family law has rapidly developed from an embryonic state into a fully-fledged academic challenge,[9] the time could not be better to embark upon research into the possibilities for harmonising or unifying the private international law aspects related to non-marital registered relationships in Europe.

The necessity for harmonised or unified legislation has in fact been acknowledged in academic circles for some time. In 1999, ŠARČEVIĆ, among others, called for a re-examination of the possibility to unify the private international law aspects of legally regulated forms of non-marital cohabitation and registered partnerships.[10] In 2001, the same year this research was instigated, these calls were echoed from a very different corner, when WINTEMUTE noted,[11]

---

6 See **Appendices 1-3**.

7 Information gathered in April 2005 from EUROSTAT: http://epp.eurostat.cec.eu.int.

8 DETHLOFF (2003) p. 37-39 and by the European Commission, COM (2004) 254, p. 6.

9 See the list of publications available on the CEFLs website: www.law.uu.nl/priv/cefl.

10 ŠARČEVIĆ (1999). See also BOELE-WOELKI (1999c).

11 WINTEMUTE (2001) p. 767.

> We live in an increasingly mobile and globalising world ... Now that some form of legal recognition of same-sex partnerships has been achieved in a significant number of jurisdictions, the question will increasingly arise as to whether other jurisdictions will recognise the legal status granted to the same-sex couple by their home jurisdiction, either voluntarily, or because of a federal, European or international law obligation to do so. The question is beyond the scope of this conclusion and this book, and will almost certainly be addressed in ... a book entitled *same-sex partnerships and private international law*.

I.3 THE RESEARCH QUESTION

It was the coalescence of the above factors that led to this research. From a mere cursory glance across Europe, there would appear to be absolutely no uniformity of substantive law solution apparent on the issue of non-marital registered relationships. It is, however, important to inventory where these similarities and differences lie, and attempt to find explanations for this situation. Although it is clear that the time is not yet ripe for the unification of family law in Europe,[12] the gauntlet has certainly been picked up in the search for the harmonisation of such rules.[13] Nonetheless, even defenders of harmonisation of family law admit that the field of non-marital registered relationships may well form a formidable opponent.[14] Against this backdrop, and bearing in mind the substantial inroads made into national private international law rules by successive European Regulations, the central question which remains is whether it is desirable, and if so possible, to strive for the harmonisation or unification of private international law rules in the field of non-marital registered relationships.

In attempting to answer this question it is important to notice two different yet interrelated phenomena; namely, on the one hand, the creation of entirely new relationship forms and, on the other, the opening up of civil marriage to same-sex couples. In endeavouring to craft private international law rules with respect to non-marital registered relationships, one is trying to create new rules, albeit based on the rules applicable to marriage. In discussing the private international law questions raised by the opening up of civil marriage to same-sex couples, one is attempting to identify whether existing private international law rules, including international conventions, are applicable to such marriages. The questions posed are

---

12 See **Chapter XIII.1**.

13 See the establishment of the CEFL in 2001: www.law.uu.nl/priv/cefl.

14 Pintens (1999a) p. 242; Jessurun D'Oliveira (2001a) p. 205; Pintens/Vanwinckelen (2001) p. 15 and 23; Pintens (2003) p. 12-16.

therefore of a subtle, yet substantially different nature.[15] Therefore the private international law issues raised by the opening of civil marriage to same-sex couples have not been addressed in this research.[16] A similar restriction has also been made to limit this research to *registration schemes*.[17] Reference will thus not be made to the many forms of regulated, but unregistered cohabitation currently in existence.[18]

I.4 METHODOLOGY AND TERMINOLOGY

I.4.1 STRUCTURE OF THE BOOK

This book is divided into three parts. **Part I**, consisting of **Chapters I and II**, provides an introduction to the topic at hand. One of the most important issues facing the private international lawyer in this field is that of characterisation, which is accordingly placed at the forefront of this work, and will be dealt with after this general introductory chapter. From this theoretical background it will become clear that comparative research into the substantive law solutions is essential, since all characterisation theories rely on some form of comparative law analysis.[19]

Part II, consisting of **Chapters III** to **VIII**, is devoted to the substantive law situation in the seven chosen jurisdictions.[20] After the historical precursors to the respective pieces of legislation have been covered, each chapter will discuss the establishment, legal effects and dissolution of the relationship.

---

15 See, for example, the recent decisions in **Italy** and **Germany** with respect to the recognition of **Dutch** same-sex marriages. In **Italy** the case failed on grounds of public policy (*Tribunale di Latina, Affari Camera di Consiglio*, Case No. 33/05, 31st May 2005), whilst in **Germany** the marriage was recognized as a non-marital registered relationship (see KOOLHOVEN (2005)).

16 *Contra* see JESSURUN D'OLIVEIRA (2001a) p. 2036.

17 The registration of a couple's intent to be regarded as a couple in the eyes of the law removes many of the factual problems associated with unregistered cohabitation. Moreover, the vast differences in approach to the problems raised by unregistered cohabitation were beyond the scope of this research. Nonetheless, although there is nothing to prevent the rules developed in this research from being applied analogously to unregistered cohabitation, that is the subject of a different research proposal!

18 For an overview of the different approaches to issues surrounding non-marital relationships see WOODS (2004), who divides the approaches into four categories; namely, the registration approach, the cohabitation approach, the contractual approach and the proprietary approach.

19 See **Chapter II.2.6**. Further see T. DE BOER (1999a) p. 17-18.

20 For details of the jurisdictions selected and the reasons for this choice see **Section I.5.**

The chapters have been structured to ease comparison. Section 3.4 in the **Belgian** chapter, for example, corresponds to Section 3.4 in the **French**, **Dutch**, **Swiss**, and **British** chapters; thus providing the possibility for simultaneous comparative scrutiny, as well as in-depth domestic analysis. **Chapter VIII** offers a comparison and evaluation of the substantive law solutions in these seven jurisdictions.

Part III, consisting of **Chapters IX** to **XIII**, deals with issues related to private international law. **Chapter IX** returns to the issue of characterisation, and focuses on the characterisation of non-marital registered relationships by applying the theory outlined in **Chapter II** to the substantive law systems analysed in **Part II. Chapters X-XII** deal in turn with the private international law issues associated with the establishment, dissolution and legal effects of non-marital registered relationships. Finally, **Chapter XIII** examines the questions of desirability and feasibility of harmonisation or unification in this field of law.

I.4.2 COMPARATIVE METHODOLOGY

The comparability of the institutions chosen is crucial to this research.[21] The research question posed attempts, in part, to establish whether a *tertium comparationis* actually exists in the jurisdictions studied with respect to the institutions created. In assessing whether this commonality is present, a number of different factors need to be studied.[22] As KOKKINI-IATRIDOU has identified, this commonality may lie in the function, structure[23] or consequences of the legal institutions.[24]

The presence of these variables may differ from subject to subject. Nevertheless, an attempt has been made to identify the existence of such common features, which has in turn determined part of the structure of the national reports in **Chapters** III to VII. Particular attention has been paid to the historical precursors to the introduction of legislation in this field. In identifying the social spurs that sparked legislative activity, one is better

---

21 It is a presupposed criterion that "comparative law" exists. For more on this discussion see W.J. KAMBA, "Comparative law. A theoretical framework", *ICLQ*, 1974, p. 485-519 at 487, and O. KAHN-FREUD, "Comparative law as an academic subject", *LQR*, 1996, p. 40-651 at 41.

22 PINTENS (1999a) p. 49-51.

23 Seen from a morphological point of view, in the sense of the "form" of these institutions.

24 KOKKINI-IATRIDOU (1986) p. 165.

able to fully appreciate the social functions of the institution itself.[25] The structure and form of the institution is best understood in terms of the formalities associated with its formation and its dissolution.[26] Finally, the legal effects of entering into such a relationship will also be dealt with extensively.[27] These variables have thus formed the framework upon which the substantive law research is based. Furthermore, three stages of any comparative study must be distinguished: analysis, synthesis and evaluation.

1. *Analysis.* KOKKINI-IATRIDOU distinguishes between two methods that can be used in this first stage of research: simultaneous or successive comparison.[28] Both of these methods will be utilised for the purposes of this research. The successive method, whereby an individual report is provided covering all of the legal problems on each legal system, has been used in **Part II: Substantive Law**. Such an approach is supported by ZWEIGERT and KÖTZ, who, in sketching the parameters of comparative law, talk of the preparation of separate reports, "offered for each legal system or family of legal systems" which should be "objective ... free from any critical evaluation, though containing all significant qualifications or modifications".[29] The research question posed in this book is focused on the possibilities for harmonising, or possibly unifying, the private international law rules in this field of law;[30] it is not intended to provide a complete synthesis of the substantive law rules in this field, save for when this is to the advantage of, or necessary for, the attainment of the abovementioned objectives. A solid grounding in the substantive law solutions offered by particular countries provides the necessary fuel to drive the private international law machinery. Without the knowledge of domestic substantive law solutions, a private international lawyer is left floundering.

The simultaneous method, on the other hand, whereby a report is provided divided per legal question, has been utilised in **Part III: Private International Law**. As already stated, this research is focused on the desirability and feasibility of harmonisation or unification possibilities in the field of private international law, and as a result the simultaneous

25 **Chapters III.3**, **IV.3**, **V.3**, **VI.3** and **VII.3**.

26 **Chapters III.4**, **III.6**, **IV.4**, **IV.6**, **V.4**, **V.6**, **VI.4**, **VI.6**, **VII.4** and **VII.6**.

27 **Chapter III.5**, **IV.5**, **V.5**, **VI.5** and **VII.5**.

28 KOKKINI-IATRIDOU (1988) p. 187-188.

29 ZWEIGERT/KÖTZ/WEIR (1998) p. 43.

30 As to the desirability of unified or harmonized rules see **Chapter XIII.3**.

method enucleates the differences and similarities in both approach and result in a clear and systematic manner.

2. *Synthesis.* This involves a comparative synthesis of the differences and similarities between the legal systems chosen. Both the successive and simultaneous methods of comparative law have also been used in completing the second stage of the comparisons. In **Part II**, the comparative synthesis has been undertaken separately and produced in **Chapter VIII**. In contrast, in **Part III** the comparative synthesis forms an integral part of each chapter.

3. *Evaluation.* On the basis of this synthesis, one is able to complete the third and final stage of the comparison, namely evaluation.[31] In a field where the link between the cultural environment and the law is still strong,[32] the point of departure in the search for harmonised or unified rules has been the *common core approach.*[33] The so-called *better law approach*[34] has only been applied as a subsidiary method. Nonetheless, the evaluation criteria enunciated are applied even when a common core is found. In this way, all solutions have been measured against the same yardstick.

I.4.3 SPECIAL CASE OF NORTHERN IRELAND

Private international law in **Northern Ireland** is a complex area, not least because of the uncertainty that surrounds the precedent of **English** decisions in **Northern Ireland**.[35] The vast majority of private international law in **England & Wales** is still based on common law precedent. The question therefore arises when, and to what extent, this is also applicable in **Northern Ireland**. In order to answer this question each rung of the judicial ladder must be taken in turn. As the highest court in **Northern Ireland**, it is clear that House of Lords' decisions are binding on all other **Northern Irish** courts. However, although strictly speaking, as is the case in **Scotland**, this is only true of decisions originating in **Northern Ireland**, in practice all of its

---

31 T. de Boer (1999b) p. 15; Kokkini-Iatridou (1986) p. 176; Pintens (1999a) p. 91-92, §102.

32 Pintens (1999b) p. 238-239; De Oliveira (2000) p. 272; Boele-Woelki (2002a) p. 17; Antokolskaia (2003c) p. 37-44.

33 Boele-Woelki *et al.* (2004) p. 2.

34 Antokolskaia (2002c) p. 6-7; Antokolskaia (2003b) p. 173-178 and 180-181.

35 Dickson (2001) p. 89. See further R. Byrne and J.P. McCutcheon, *The Irish legal system*, Shannon: Butterworths Ireland, 1996, 3rd Edition, p. 319-409, especially p. 347-353.

decisions are treated with the greatest respect. It has even been said that should a conflict arise between a House of Lords' decision originating from **England & Wales** or **Scotland** and a **Northern Irish** Court of Appeal case, the House of Lords decision should be followed.[36] With respect to Court of Appeal decisions, **Northern Irish** courts are not strictly bound by decisions of the **English** Court of Appeal. However, in practice such decisions are treated with the greatest respect and are generally followed unless there are serious reasons to depart from such authority.[37] It therefore follows that the private international law of **Northern Ireland**, as a predominantly common law area, will be the same as that of **England & Wales** unless otherwise stated. Hence, it is proposed to regard the term **England & Wales** as including the jurisdiction of **Northern Ireland** for the purposes of private international law, unless otherwise provided.

I.4.4 TERMINOLOGY

A number of terminological choices have been made throughout this research. Firstly, reference has been made to the term "domicil" when referring to the British notion of domicile. This aids in distinguishing between the vastly different concepts. Secondly, the term "non-marital registered relationship" has been selected to describe all the different forms of national legislation.[38] A neutral, overarching term has thus been created in which every individual State can find solace. Terms such as "registered partnership", "civil union" or "domestic partnership" have been avoided so as to prevent confusion with any particular national system. In choosing such an all-embracing term, care has been taken to ensure that the phrase adequately reflects the notions inherent in domestic substantive legislation. Hence, the term consists of three independent, yet equally important facets.

- "Non-marital". This serves to indicate that a distinction has been drawn between marital relationships and other forms of regulated relationships. Same-sex marriages do not, therefore, fall within the scope of this research.
- "Registered". This indicates that unregistered forms of cohabitation prevalent in many societies are not included.
- "Relationship". Although somewhat obvious, this term highlights the loving, familial nature of each party's commitment to the other.

---

36 DICKSON (2001) p. 88.

37 DICKSON (2001) p. 89.

38 KOKKINI-IATRIDOU (1986) p. 94-95; PINTENS (1999a) p. 90, §100.

Together, these three terms form the overarching phrase used throughout this research to describe the various forms of domestic, substantive legislation (*i.e.* the *wettelijke samenwoning*, *pacte civil de solidarité*, *geregistreerd partnerschap*, *partenariat enregistré* and civil partnership).

It is also important to note the distinction between the terms harmonisation and unification. Harmonisation implies a concern to reconcile differences on the basis of similarities. It is a non-coercive method based on dialogue without attempting to force a uniform solution on all parties. Unification, on the other hand, means the voluntary or imposed "uniformisation" of different systems and thus often entails a greater sacrifice.[39] This difference is important to bear in mind when one is attempting to propose common solutions. The feasibility and desirability of harmonising or unifying the rules in this field is necessarily dependent upon the topic under discussion.[40] It is for this reason that the criteria which have been used to determine whether such possibilities exist have been explained in each chapter individually. Nonetheless, a number of general, overarching principles have formed the keystone to this evaluation. Any rule should serve to promote co-operation in the field of international recognition of decisions. In the field of relationship recognition, this is supplemented with the aim to prevent limping relationships. Keeping these general objectives in mind, combined with the necessity for any rule to adequately reflect the parties' expectations, one is able to begin to answer the research question posed.

I.5 JURISDICTIONAL ACCOUNTABILITY

The selection of legal systems necessarily depends on the subject chosen, the aims of the research and the accessibility of the legal systems to the comparatist. However, a number of selection criteria were conceived in order to distil the exponentially increasing wealth of material. These criteria are summarised below.

Firstly, the aim of this research was to identify whether the rules in this field of law could be harmonised or unified in Europe. A geographical restriction was thus imposed in the research question itself. However, such a restriction must not be confused with a restriction to Member States of

39 MEULDERS-KLEIN (2003) p. 106.

40 For the extent to which the distinction between harmonisation and unification is relevant for this research see **Chapter XIII.1**.

the European Union. Secondly, it was decided that the countries eventually chosen must have legislated for a domestic form of non-marital registered relationship. In those countries where non-marital registered relationship legislation has not yet been enacted, the ensuing private international law questions are very different than in those where a domestic solution has already been carved out. Those countries without domestic substantive law legislation are thus confronted with a legal institution unknown to their national legal system, raising issues of characterisation and public policy. Although these issues also arise with respect to countries where domestic legislation has already been enacted, the existence of a domestic framework radically alters any ensuing analysis. As a result of these two criteria, the countries to be studied had to be selected from: **Belgium**, **Denmark**, **Finland**, **France**, **Germany**, **Iceland**, **Luxembourg**, **The Netherlands**, **Norway**, **Sweden**, **Spain**,[41] **Switzerland** and the **United Kingdom**.[42]

Turning one's attention to the function of these particular legislative enactments, one is immediately confronted with two different sorts of legislation. On the one hand there are registration schemes open to couples regardless of sex (**Belgium**, **France**, **Luxembourg**, **The Netherlands** and **Spain**) and, on the other, those restricted to same-sex couples (**Denmark**, **Finland**, **Germany**, **Iceland**, **Norway**, **Sweden**, **Switzerland** and the **United Kingdom**). It was decided to ensure that the countries selected were representative of both approaches. Furthermore, a brief glimpse into the literature published on this field, indicates a sliding scale of rights and duties afforded to those registering such a relationship. As far as possible, jurisdictions were selected covering the entire spectrum.[43]

An added complication to the entire field is the opening of marriage to same-sex couples (**Belgium**, **The Netherlands** and **Spain**). Although, as already stated, these relationships fall outside the scope of this research, their impact on non-marital registered relationship legislation cannot be overestimated. It was thus decided to ensure that the countries represented

---

41 Wherever reference in this section has been to **Spain** the reader must note that this only refers to the eleven regions of **Spain** which have introduced forms of non-marital registered relationships.

42 See **Appendices 1** and **2**.

43 Although it is impossible here to categorise the various countries with any degree of accuracy, it must be noted that it is generally accepted that **Belgium** has provided one of the weakest forms of non-marital registered relationship, whilst **The Netherlands** and the **Scandinavian** countries have created some of the strongest.

both those jurisdictions where marriage is restricted to different-sex couples, as well as those countries were this prohibition has been lifted.

Turning one's attention to the more traditional selection criteria, there are as many legal systems as there are attempts to divide them into groupings. Although from the very outset of this research this author has questioned the usefulness of such a division for the purposes of this topic,[44] attention must nonetheless be paid to these categorisations. Therefore, although not ultimately determinative, countries have, as far as possible, been selected to be representative of the traditional legal families present in Europe, *i.e.* Romanistic (**France**, **Belgium**, **Luxembourg**, **The Netherlands**,[45] **Spain**), Germanic (**The Netherlands**, **Germany**, **Switzerland**), Anglo-American (**United Kingdom**) and Nordic (**Denmark**, **Finland**, **Iceland**, **Norway** and **Sweden**).[46]

Since this research is focused on the possibility of harmonising or unifying private international law rules, it is also important to appreciate the distinct methods utilised in various European countries in dealing with the topic of private international law. In some countries, codification of the rules of private international law has taken place (**Belgium**, **The Netherlands** to some extent, **Switzerland**), whereas in the vast majority of countries in this field reference is still made to a wealth of case law and statutory materials.

In analysing all these various facets[47] it was decided to study the laws of **Belgium**,[48] **France**,[49] **The Netherlands**,[50] **Switzerland**[51] and the **United**

---

44 See, for example, PINTENS (1999a) p. 89, who signals the limited usefulness of such classifications for micro-comparisons.

45 The Dutch legal system although historically based on the French legal system has, over the course of time, shown more resemblance to the German legal system. It is therefore placed in both groupings.

46 ZWEIGERT/KÖTZ/WEIR (1998) p. 63-73; PINTENS (1999a) p. 65 *et seq.* Reference has also been made to the modern classifications of MATTEI and HUSA, see further HUSA (2004). In this field it is perhaps more noticeable that the instance of legal transplants is exceedingly high. See, for example, JÄNTERÄ-JAREBORG (2003a) and ANTOKOLSKAIA (2005) Chapter 4.

47 The exclusion of **Germany** and a **Nordic** country, primarily on the basis of linguistic ability, has not affected the representative nature of the countries selected, which embrace all aspects of the chosen criteria. Furthermore, as will be shown in **Chapter VIII**, the grouping into legal families is certainly not decisive in this field of law.

48 An EU country, with a weak registration scheme open to both same-sex and different-sex couples, as well as to couples within the prohibited degrees of marriage. Same-sex marriage is permitted and a codification of private international law has recently entered into force. Belgium represents the *Romanistic* legal tradition.

Kingdom.[52] These countries provide the broadest possible coverage of the various divisions outlined above within the restrictions imposed by virtue of the author's language ability and time constraints.[53] No comparison to be carried out by an individual researcher within a restricted period of time can wish to include all available jurisdictions; a selection has to be made.

---

[49] An EU country, with a weak registration scheme open to both same-sex and different-sex couples. Same-sex marriage is not currently permitted in **France** and a private international law remains heavily dominated by case law. France represents the *Romanistic* legal tradition.

[50] An EU country, with a strong registration scheme open to both same-sex and different-sex couples. Same-sex marriage is permitted and a codification of private international law is currently in preparation. **The Netherlands** represents an interesting mix of *Romanistic* and *Germanic* legal traditions. Reference to **The Netherlands** only refers to the Kingdom in Europe, thus excluding the Netherlands Antilles and Aruba. The *Gemeenschappelijk Hof van Justitie van de Nederlandse Antillen en Aruba* has recently held that same-sex marriages celebrated in The Netherlands must be registered in the population registers in Aruba: *Aruba v. Oduber*, 23rd August 2005, Registration No. EJ2101/04 – H 12/05.

[51] A non-EU country, with a strong registration scheme restricted to same-sex couples, and same-sex marriage is not permitted. Private international law was codified in 1987. **Swiss** law represents a *Germanic* legal family tradition.

[52] An EU country, with a strong registration scheme restricted to same-sex couples. Marriage is currently restricted to different-sex couples and private international law remains heavily dominated by case law. Although the **UK** represents a *common law* legal tradition, **Scots** law is often identified as a *mixed* legal system.

[53] PINTENS (1999a) p. 49 and 52-53.

CHAPTER II
CHARACTERISATION: THE PROBLEM

II.1 INTRODUCTION

In the same way that humans organise everyday facts, experiences and knowledge into groups and categories, legal systems classify and categorise legal issues.[1] Every legal system confers a particular legal character on, or assigns a particular legal category to, every legal issue.[2] The determination of the most appropriate legal category for a given legal issue is known as "characterisation".[3] This chapter will focus on the theoretical aspects of this process.

The problem of characterisation was first discussed, at the turn of the twentieth century, by the French scholar BARTIN and subsequently by the German jurist KAHN.[4] It was later introduced to Americans by LORENZEN in 1920[5] and to English lawyers by BECKETT in 1934.[6] BECKETT averred that,

> In every case which involves a question of private international law the court is called on to decide whether a given state of facts, or a rule of law and the right resulting therefrom, falls into one or other of these conceptions or categories of analytical jurisprudence. It is this process – involved in every case – which I describe by the English word 'classification' and which in French legal literature is described by the word 'qualification'.[7]

---

1 GRAVESON (1974) Chapter 2.

2 WOLFF (1977) Chapter 13.

3 English jurists tend to use the word characterisation whilst continental European jurists tend to use English terms such as qualification or classification. The core issue at stake is that which in French is termed *qualification*, in Dutch *kwalificatie* and in German *Qualifikation*. The term characterisation has been used throughout this text. See further FALCONBRIDGE (1954) p. 55.

4 KAHN (1891) and BARTIN (1897a), (1897b), (1897c).

5 LORENZEN (1920).

6 BECKETT (1934).

7 BECKETT (1934) p. 46.

Since decisional harmony can only be achieved if all states involved are in agreement as to the assignment of a legal issue to a particular legal category, the problem of characterisation cannot be ignored.[8] The challenge posed by characterisation is both common and much discussed,[9] and has certainly been noticed with respect to the new forms of non-marital registered relationships.[10] However, before one can discuss the problem of characterisation with respect to these relationships, it is first important to delineate the nature of the process a court is confronted with in this area.

Anton v. Bartolo

A Maltese couple, domiciled in Malta prior to 1870, ultimately settled in Algeria, at that time a French colony, where the husband acquired land and subsequently died in 1889. As a result of living in Algeria both parties acquired a French domicile. After her husband's death, the deceased's widow claimed – besides one half of the common matrimonial property, about which there seems to have been no dispute – a usufruct over one quarter of the property left by the deceased. The claim was brought in France where the question arose whether this was an issue related to matrimonial property law or the law of succession.[11]

The delineation of the nature of the process of this issue depends on the characterisation of the legal issue raised. According to **French** private international law, the two choice of law categories and their associated choice of law rules were clear: matrimonial property law was governed by the first matrimonial domicile (*i.e.* **Maltese** law) and the law of succession was governed by the last matrimonial domicile (*i.e.* **French** law). According to **French** law the claim was unfounded whereas according to **Maltese** law the claim was well founded.[12] This case thus illustrates that characterisation is the name given to the process by which a judge assigns a particular legal issue to a particular legal category. This legal category consists of a choice of

---

8 JUENGER (1993) p. 71.

9 **English:** LORENZEN (1920); COOK (1924); BECKETT (1934); UNGER (1937); ROBERTSON (1940); LEDERMAN (1951); FALCONBRIDGE (1954) Chapters 3-5; BLAND (1957); RABEL (1958) p. 47-72; GRAVESON (1974) Chapter 2; LEVONTIN (1976) Chapter 5; WOLFF (1977) Chapter 13; KAHN-FREUD (1980) Chapter 9; NORTH/FAWCETT (1999) Chapter 3; COLLINS (2000) p. 33-45; JUENGER (1993) p. 71-74; STONE (1995) p. 385-391; FORSYTH (1998); LIPSTEIN (1999). **French:** ARMINJON (1923); RABEL (1933); RIGAUX (1956); BATIFFOL/LAGARDE (1993) p. 474-491, §291-298; AUDIT (2000) p. 171-185, §191-206; LOUSSOURAN/BOUREL (2004) p. 231-246, §183-196; KNOEPFLER *et al.* (2005) p. 144-153, §277-303; **Dutch:** SALOMON (1933); KOSTERS (1962) Chapter 8; ERAUW (1985) p. 95-99.

10 *E.g.* JESSURUN D'OLIVEIRA (2003a); DEVERS (2004) p. 35 *et seq*; FULCHIRON (2000) p. 900.

11 (1891) *JDI* 1171. See also ANCEL/LEQUETTE (2001) p. 73-81, Case *No.* 9.

12 The **French** court eventually decided that the case related to matrimonial property and thus applied the matrimonial property law of **Malta**.

law rule with a connecting factor. By application of this choice of law rule to the facts of a given case, one is able to identify the applicable law in the dispute at hand.

Characterisation also plays an important role outside of choice of law rules. The rules on jurisdiction often differ substantially depending upon the legal category to which a particular legal issue is assigned.[13] Furthermore, in the field of recognition of foreign judgments it is often necessary for a judge to first characterise the foreign institution in order to determine whether it is eligible to be recognised. A Dutch judge, for example, would have to determine whether a polygamous marriage celebrated in India is consistent with the definition of marriage according to Dutch private international law before he is able to recognise such a marriage.[14] Problems associated with characterisation can thus transpire owing to a number of crucial factors:[15]

- Different legal systems may contain ideas and concepts completely unknown to one another. For example the Swiss notion of *pacte successoral* or *Erbvertag*[16] has no equivalent under English law, whilst the English notion of a *trust* has no exact legal counterpart in Switzerland.[17]
- Different legal systems assign problems of a common nature to different branches of the law. According to German law, the nature of the remedy for breach of promise to marry is considered tortious,[18] whereas under old English law the remedy was considered contractual.[19]
- Different legal systems attach different meanings to the same legal terms. The term *domicile*, for example, has different meanings in England and in France.

---

13 See, for example, **Chapters XI** and **XII** with respect to the rules on jurisdiction with respect to non-marital registered relationships.

14 This question would be answered with reference to Art. 5, Neth. PIL(M)A.

15 For a fascinating overview of the various situations in which an issue of characterisation may arises see LIPSTEIN (1999) p. 9-27.

16 A sort of inheritance contract regulated by Arts. 468, 494, 512-515 Sw. CC.

17 **Switzerland** is, in fact, not alone in not having an equivalent to the trusts, since no continental system has an equivalent.

18 If the engagement is broken off, any gifts exchanged may be reclaimed according to the rules of unjust enrichment: §§1301, Ger. CC. If the fiancé(e) provokes the break-off of the engagement without good cause he/she is liable for damages: §§1298 and 1299, Ger. CC.

19 The remedy was considered contractual up until its abolition as a result of Sec. 1(1), Law Reform (Miscellaneous Provisions) Act 1970.

II.2 THEORIES OF CHARACTERISATION

Although there have been as many theories postulated as there are commentators,[20] the various ideas espoused can be divided into four general approaches. The first stresses that when a court is confronted with the issue of characterisation, the court should refer to its own system of law: a *lex fori* approach (**Section II.2.2**). The second approach maintains that disputes should be characterised according to the system of law that will ultimately decide the case: the *leges causae* approach (**Section II.2.3**). The third theory refers the case to analytical jurisprudence and comparative law principles: a *comparative law* approach (**Section II.2.4**).[21] The fourth and final approach aims to achieve a compromise between these various methods: a *via media* approach (**Section II.2.5**).[22] Each of these methods will be discussed in turn.

II.2.1 IGNORANCE OR INCOMPREHENSION OF THE PROBLEM

The dispute surrounding characterisation has raged for many years and left many judges bemused. Some courts cede to conceptualism,[23] others to overcomplicated and almost futile analysis,[24] and yet others attempt to stretch the given rules to achieve a required result.[25] The **French** Supreme Court, for example, upheld a judgment of a lower court in which it had been decided that the question of domicile was merely a question of fact and that a conflict with respect to the definition of domicile was by analogy

---

20 For an overview of the various approaches on this topic up until 1956, see RIGAUX (1956).

21 ROBERSTON (1940) p. 25.

22 This category is not really heterogeneous. However, all these commentators share a rejection of all other options proffered in favour of a hybrid system.

23 In *Maynard v. Eastern Air Lines Inc.* (1949) 178 F.2d 139, 2d.Cir, the Second Circuit Federal Court held that a characterisation in the field of tort mandated the application of a ceiling on wrongful death recovery imposed by the *lex loci deliciti.*

24 *MacMillan Inc. v. Bishopsgate Investment Trust plc. (No. 3)* [1996] 1 WLR 387.

25 For common law lawyers, it is important to note that such an approach has been adopted in the **United States of America**. In *Haumschild v. Continental Casualty Co.* (1959) 7 Wis.2d 130, 95 N.W.2d 814, the Wisconsin Supreme Court characterised interspousal immunity as a rule of "family law" in order to permit the wife to recover damages in tort from her negligent husband, and in *Levy v. Daniels 'U-Drive Auto Renting Co.* (1928) 108 Conn. 333, 143 A.163, the Connecticut Supreme Court characterised a suit for personal injury arising out of a car accident as a rule of contract in order to apply Connecticut law and thus allow recovery despite the contributory negligence of the driver. This decision has however been the subject of extensive criticism: SCOLES/HAY/BORCHERS/SYMEONIDES (2001) p. 69, §2.16; CURRIE/KAY/KRAMER (2001) p. 43-47, §2.1.

also a question of fact; as a result, the question of characterisation did not arise.[26]

II.2.2 *LEX FORI* APPROACH

Originally postulated by KAHN, BARTIN has become widely recognised as the foremost advocate of a *lex fori* approach to characterisation. LORENZEN summarises this approach, saying,

> This writer maintains that whenever the application of the internal law of the forum or that of another country depends on the nature of a particular juridical relationship, it is the law of the forum which must decide what the nature of the relationship is.[27]

BARTIN reasons that whenever a court decides to apply foreign law it will, as a result, be restricting its own sovereignty. If the court decides for itself what legal institutions and at what times it will apply foreign law then the court has limited its own sovereignty itself.[28] However, if the foreign jurisdiction is permitted to determine this question, then the restriction on the forum's sovereignty will be at the mercy of the foreign jurisdiction and the forum court will no longer "be master in its own home".[29] BARTIN'S reasoning for a *lex fori* approach to the issue of characterisation rests therefore on the principle of sovereignty,[30] perceiving disparate characterisations as differing expressions of sovereignty.[31] When the court is confronted with two different characterisations of the same legal issue, BARTIN regards these as two distinct expressions of sovereignty. Consequently, the court must follow the characterisation that results from its own notion of sovereignty *i.e.* its own form of characterisation.[32] Although KAHN made a distinction between the "collisions in point of

---

26 Fr. Cass., 22nd October 1900 (1900) *JDI* 964. Such a view is also supported by some academics namely A.A. EHRENZWEIG. For EHRENZWEIG'S views see, NADELMANN/VON MEHREN/HAZARD (1961) p. 406 *et seq.* In contrast, FALCONBRIDGE (1954) p. 70-72.

27 LORENZEN (1920) p. 259.

28 BARTIN (1897a) p. 236-239.

29 ROBERSTON (1940) p. 26.

30 NIBOYET labels this the *raison juridique* as opposed to the *raison pratique*, which he encapsulates as: "Il y a nécessité, en fait, parce que si on ne consulte pas la *lex fori* l'on s'enferme dans un cercle vicieux": NIBOYET (1928) p. 499.

31 BARTIN (1897b) p. 469-470.

32 BARTIN concedes two exceptions to this rule. Firstly, the *lex situs* should apply to the determination of the distinction between movables and immovables (BARTIN (1897a) p. 250-253) and secondly, in the field of contracts the *lex loci contractus* should be determined by the law applicable to the case (BARTIN (1897b) p. 476).

contact" and "latent conflict of laws",[33] he remained of the opinion that in both cases the *lex fori* should determine questions of characterisation.[34] LORENZEN, a champion of BARTIN'S theory,[35] uses the **English** cases of *Ogden v. Ogden*[36] and *In Re Martin*[37] to support the idea that according to Anglo-American law,[38]

> [L]egal transactions ... are governed in general by the strictly internal law of the forum, the principal exception to the rule being that the character of property as moveable or immovable is controlled by the law of the situs.[39]

Furthermore, LORENZEN avers that since foreign law is not applied on the basis of a "binding necessity" but instead by virtue of a willingness to appreciate and accept the validity of foreign law, as well as to adhere to principles of comity, the characterisation from which the application of foreign law results must similarly depend upon the law of the forum.[40] In the editorial comments in the 1918/1919 edition of the *Yale Law Journal*, LORENZEN comments on the question of characterisation,

> Asides from some existing system, of positive law – constitutional, statutory or judge-made – it seems clear that there is no inherent reason why the law of any sovereign nation – England, for example – may not, if the sovereign English Parliament or the appropriate English court so decrees, attach any legal consequences whatever to any state of facts whatever, including acts done in other countries, even by persons not citizens or residents of England.[41]

Some four years later, COOK pragmatically concurred, encapsulating the support for the *lex fori* approach, by contending that,

> In making a choice between such rules, it is obvious that here as elsewhere the basis must be a pragmatic one – of the effect of decision one way or the other in giving a practical working rule. In this connection it may be suggested that in many cases it

33 The categorisation of characterisation problems into three categories is central to KAHN'S theory but irrelevant to the current discussion. For further explanation see KAHN (1891) p. 91 and 99; SALOMON (1933) Chapter 1; FALCONBRIDGE (1954) p. 54-55.

34 KAHN (1891) p. 91 and 99.

35 Other supporters of BARTIN'S theory include KOSTERS (1962) p. 146; MULDER (1947). Contrast with GEMMA (1899) Sec. 91 *et seq.*; BUZZATTI (1899) p. 16.

36 (1908) P 46.

37 (1900) PD 211 at 227.

38 He also shows in contraction to *In Re Martin* that the English courts have not always been consistent in the field of domicile when applying the *lex fori* approach: *In Re Johnson* (1903) 1 Ch 821 and *In Re Bowes* (1906) 22 TLR 711.

39 LORENZEN (1920) p. 268.

40 LORENZEN (1920) p. 269.

41 LORENZEN (1918) p. 69.

> makes little difference which rule is adopted, so long as it is reasonably simple and definite ... [42]

This approach has found academic, legislative and judicial favour in a number of legal systems around the world,[43] including **The Netherlands,**[44] **Switzerland,**[45] **France,**[46] **Belgium,**[47] and the **United Kingdom.**[48] Nonetheless, this theory has also been the subject of fierce and sustained attack, resulting in a number of alternative theories having been proposed. WOLFF, an ardent supporter of the comparative law approach, is especially critical of the solution proposed by KAHN and BARTIN, questioning the logical basis upon which the *lex fori* approach is founded.[49] Although agreeing that *Ogden* seemingly opposes any other approach, WOLFF argues that *Ogden* is an incorrect application of the law, citing academic disparagement[50] as well as offering a possible public policy based explanation of the *Ogden* decision.[51]

II.2.3 *LEGES CAUSAE* APPROACH

One of the earliest proponents of the *leges causae* approach was DESPAGNET, who advanced the proposition that the law governing a legal issue must also control its characterisation.[52] He argued that when a court deems a foreign law to be applicable in a given case, it must be understood as *including* the application of the organisational system of such a law. According to DESPAGNET, a court must accept the characterisation adopted by the foreign

42 COOK (1924) p. 488. He goes on to argue that attempting to apply a simple and definite rule, it is thus better to apply one's own law.

43 See HERNÁNDEZ-BRETON (2004).

44 Hof Arnhem, 1st October 1986, NJ 1987, 96; Rb Middelburg, 19th September 1996, NJ 1997, 217; HR, 12th November 2004, Case *No.* C03/149HR, annotated by POLAK in AA 2005, p. 38 at 40, §2.

45 Trib. Féd., 29th January 1970 (1970) 96 II *ATF* 79, §7; Trib. Féd., 1st July 1974 (1974) 100 II *ATF* 200, §2; Trib. Féd., 9th July 1985 (1985) 111 II *ATF* 276 at 278; Trib. Féd, 18th November 1986 (1986) 112 II *ATF* 450 at 452; Trib. Féd., 17th April 2001 (2001) 127 III *ATF* 390 at 393; Trib. Féd., 5th April 2002 (2002) 128 III *ATF* 295, §2c. See also, PATOCCHI/GEIZINGER (1995) Art. 13, Sw. CPIL and KNOEPFLER *et al.* (2005) p. 149-150, §294-298.

46 LOUSSOUARN/BOUREL (1999) p. 208, §190; BATIFFOL/LAGARDE (1993) p. 477, §292; Fr. Cass., 1 Civ. Ch., 22nd June 1955 (1956) *D* 73, annotated CHAVRIER.

47 HEYVAERT (2002) p. 114, §255 and references.

48 **Scot:** ANTON/BEAUMONT (1990) p. 69; **Eng:** NORTH/FAWCETT (1999) p. 38; in relation to torts, Sec. 9(2), PIL(MP)A 1995; **UK:** *Ogden v. Ogden* [1908] P 46.

49 WOLFF (1977).

50 WOLFF (1977) p. 153, fn.2.

51 WOLFF (1977) p. 154, fn.1.

52 DESPAGNET (1898) p. 253.

law in order to apply the latter in conformity with the rules of private international law sanctioned by its own law.

LORENZEN criticises DESPAGNET'S approach, stating that the basis upon which it is founded is "idealistic"[53] and that it "rests wholly upon a fiction".[54] LORENZEN, quoting STORY, believed private international law to be founded upon the "mutual convenience of nations as understood and applied by the courts of the forum".[55] As a result it is simply not pragmatic to believe that courts will adopt characterisations of legal issues according to the law of some other nation. HECKE, furthermore, illustrates the vicious circle nature of the *leges causae* approach in his introduction to **Belgian** private international law.[56] Although, of the jurisdictions studied in this book, this approach has found express judicial support in both **England**[57] and **Belgium**,[58] the theoretical objection to such a characterisation rests on the fact that since characterisation is part of the process whereby meaning is given to a choice of law rule of the *lex fori*, it would seem remarkable if some other law could be used to determine how restrictively or broadly that rule was to be interpreted. Practically speaking, the task is also almost impossible. Even the "most cosmopolitan of judges will more readily understand issues from the point of view of their own legal system".[59]

II.2.4 A COMPARATIVE LAW APPROACH

Rising against this background is the third possible solution, argued first by RABEL[60] and later by BECKETT,[61] that characterisation should be founded on comparative law and analytical jurisprudence. The theory postulates developing a system of internationally accepted analytical concepts that would provide a framework for the characterisation of the question. BECKETT argues that characterisation is simply an interpretation or

---

53 LORENZEN (1920) p. 269.
54 LORENZEN (1920) p. 270.
55 STORY (1857) p. 32.
56 HECKE/LENAERTS (1989) p. 140-142. See also STRIKWERDA (2002) p. 46 and KNOEPFLER *et al.* (2005) p. 151, §299.
57 *In Re Maldonado* [1954] P 223.
58 Belg. Cass., 28th March 1952, (1952) I *Pas.* 483, criticised by LOUSSOUARN in (1953) *Rev. Crit. DIP* 133. This theory has also received support from certain Belgian authors: VANDER ELST/WEBER (1983) p. 312, §73.2; HECKE/LENAERTS (1989) p. 140-142.
59 FORSYTH (1998) p. 152.
60 RABEL (1933); RABEL (1958) Chapter 2.
61 BECKETT (1934) p. 46.

application of rules of private international law. Since private international law is based upon analytical jurisprudence, it follows that characterisation should also take place on the basis of analytical jurisprudence.

> These conceptions are borrowed from analytical jurisprudence, that general science of law, based on the results of the study of comparative law, which extracts from this study essential general principles of professedly universal application – not principles based on, or applicable to, the legal system of one country only.[62]

Although admitting that such analytical jurisprudence will always be flavoured by national interpretation, BECKETT goes on to assert that this approach is far less nationalistic than the pure *lex fori* approach suggested by KAHN and BARTIN.[63] Nonetheless, this approach has also been the subject of criticism. WOLFF does not undermine the fact that such comparative and analytical work is being undertaken,[64] but pragmatically asks that when an inherent difference appears between two systems of law,[65]

> How could the most erudite 'comparer' of laws or the most incisive 'analyst' remove such differences of classification without thereby altering the law?[66]

II.2.5 *VIA MEDIA* APPROACH: RULES IN CONTEXT

Sympathising with RABEL'S views yet unable to accept this idealistic approach, many have distinguished two tasks facing a court confronted with a problem of characterisation.[67] Firstly, the judge is charged with the task of identifying the scope of the categories available. Once this task has been completed, the court is obliged to examine the legal issue in order to identify under which category it may best be subsumed. RAAPE argued that the first task is one for the forum judge to ascertain whereas in performing the second task, the judge is being asked to examine the foreign issue in its own context and thus apply a *leges causae* approach to this task.[68]

---

62 BECKETT (1934) p. 59.

63 BECKETT (1934) p. 59-60.

64 See also STRIKWERDA (2002) p. 46: "De autonome of rechtsvergelijkende opvatting is vanuit een internationalistische visie op het IPR aantrekkelijk, maar te hoog gestemd. De praktische problemen bij toepassing van deze opvatting zijn immers groot".

65 In his example, WOLFF outlines the different approach taken under **French** and **Italian** law in relation to the making of joint wills. **French** law regards this as a rule of form, whilst **Italian** law regards it as a rule related to the intrinsic validity of the will.

66 WOLFF (1977) p. 154.

67 RAAPE (1934).

68 RAAPE (1934) p. 477 *et seq.*

FALCONBRIDGE, KAHN-FREUD, LIPSTEIN and NIEDERER have added further nuance to this approach.[69] This approach has thus been appended with the principle that the categories of the *lex fori* which the judge is charged with identifying during the first stage of the process are those of the private international law of the forum,[70] and thus need not necessarily correspond directly to those of domestic, internal law.[71] KAHN-FREUD argues that,

> It has been frequently pointed out ... that the concepts of the *lex fori* used in order to classify a question or issue or – if one likes – legal or social relation, are not always and should not always be identical with the analogous concepts used for purely internal purposes.[72]

He argues that the gradual evolution of this differentiation would reduce the dispute between the adherents of the *lex fori* approach and those of the comparative law approach. KAHN-FREUD's theory presupposes that legislatures will develop and adopt useable concepts for private international law.[73] KAHN-FREUD admits this theory will never eliminate the problem of characterisation altogether but may "in the fullness of time, greatly reduce its size".[74] ANTON has also noted that this two-pronged approach is probably the one most closely attuned to judicial practice in the **United Kingdom**.[75] He argues that Lord ANDERSON'S dicta in the **Scottish** Court of Session case of *Higgins v. Ewing's Trustees* and UTHWATT J.'s dicta in the **English** High Court *Re Cohn* illustrate this point.[76] ODERKERK has also noted that in **The Netherlands** it is generally agreed that the category to

69 FALCONBRIDGE (1954) Chapter 3-5 (*via media* approach); NIEDERER (1940); KAHN-FREUD (1980) p. 228-229 (enlightened *lex fori* approach); LIPSTEIN (1981) p. 94-104.

70 This approach has been supported in **English** case law: *Re Bonacina* [1912] 2 Ch 394 (contract without consideration), *Srini Vasan v. Srini Vasan* [1946] P 67 (polygamous marriage recognised for granting a nullity decree), *R v. Sagoo* [1975] QB 855 (polygamous recognition does not entail offence of bigamy), *Bamgbose v. Daniel* [1955] AC 107 (polygamous marriage recognised for succession), and in statutes: Sec. 47, MCA 1973, as amended by Sec. 5(2), PIL(MP)A 1995. FALCONBRIDGE'S via media approach has also been followed by courts in **South Africa** (*Laurens v. von Hünhe*, 1993 (2) SA 104 (W), *Kunhe & Nagel AG Zürich v. APA Distributors (Pty) Ltd*, 1981 (3) SA 536 (W), *Laconian Maritime Enteprises Ltd v. Agromar Lineas Ltd*, 1986 (3) SA 509 (D) at 539D-E, *Minister of Transport Transeki v. Abdul*, 1995, (1) SA 509 (N) at 369F-G; in **Lesotho** (*Ngheku Mohopi v. Agens Motleleng* as referred to in NEELS (1989)) and **Zimbabwe** (*Coutts & Co. v. Ford & Anor*, 1997 (1) ZLR 440 (H).

71 This approach has been supported by LIPSTEIN: LIPSTEIN (1981) p. 94-104.

72 KAHN-FREUD (1980) p. 228-229.

73 See **Chapter IX.5** for examples of practical application of this theory.

74 KAHN-FREUD (1980) p. 229.

75 ANTON/BEAUMONT (1990) p. 70-71.

76 (1925) SC 440.

which the domestic judge assigns a legal issue is defined according to domestic private international law rules.[77] Authors in **Switzerland** also advocate this approach.[78] BUCHER and BONOMI argue that although the forum court is ultimately responsible for the process of characterisation, the legal categories to which a particular legal issue are assigned are not simply replicas of domestic private law, but are influenced by foreign law.[79] **Belgian** author, RIGAUX, has also suggested a *via media* approach of his own is his book *Droit International Privé*, although this closely resembles many of the approaches already outlined in this sub-section.[80] Even **French** case law can be cited to support the idea that a term has to have a different interpretation at the private international law level than that adopted in purely domestic situations.[81] In an excellent analysis of the current approach taken in **France**, ELHOUEISS also comes to the conclusion that one can no longer talk of a pure mutual exclusive relationship between these two categories.[82]

II.2.6 EVALUATION

Despite the apparent common core of opinion for a pure *lex fori* approach, authority exists in all jurisdictions studied for not applying a strict *lex fori* approach to the process of characterisation. Whether one accepts that the private international law rules with respect to the new forms of non-marital registered relationship are suitable for harmonisation, or whether this is even desirable, it is submitted that strict adherence to the *lex fori* approach in this field of law is undesirable.

Furthermore, it appears to be almost universally accepted in the seven jurisdictions studied that an enlightened *lex fori* approach or a *via media* approach is more suitable to the process of characterisation. In differentiating the two tasks facing a court confronted with a problem of characterisation, one is able to pacify proponents of both the *lex fori* and *leges causae* approaches. In doing so, one also respects the inherent differences in domestic substantive law by providing for a private international law characterisation, which takes into account the variety of domestic solutions to a particular problem.

---

77 ODERKERK (2004) p. 64, fn. 20; STRIKWERDA (2002) p. 45.

78 DUTOIT (2005) p. 42, Art. 13, *No.* 3 and KNOEPFLER *et al.* (2005) p. 151, §300.

79 BUCHER/BONOMI (2004) p. 144, §533.

80 RIGAUX (1987) p. 323-326, §475-479.

81 Cour d'Appel Paris, 10th January 1970 (1971) *Rev. crit. DIP* 525; LIPSTEIN (1999) p. 7, §19.

82 ELHOUEISS (2005) p. 287, §10 and p. 299-305.

However, regardless of the characterisation theory to which one subscribes in the field of private international law, one should, in general, consider legal systems outside one's own system of law.[83] As a result, the process of characterisation is always dependent on comparative law, the extent of which depends upon which theory one endorses.[84] By conducting extensive research into the substantive law rules of those jurisdictions to have enacted legislation creating a form of non-marital registered relationship, a private international lawyer will be better equipped to deal with those issues relating to characterisation, which arise in all areas of private international law.

Whilst the forum court may well perform the procedural mechanism of characterisation, the legal category to which the forum court assigns a particular legal issue is the domain of domestic private international law, not of domestic substantive law. Moreover, the domestic private international law concept is sometimes an autonomous one,[85] originating at an international, interregional or supranational level. This is true, for example, when one considers the rules on jurisdiction and recognition and enforcement of civil and commercial matters across the European Union. Taking this perspective into account, AUDIT states,

> On entend limiter l'incidence des conceptions propres à chaque système juridique national sur leur interprétation et, par suite, éviter des disparités dans leur mise en œuvre.[86]

In interpreting the increasingly extensive legislation emanating from the European Union, the ECJ has opted to interpret European legislative terms autonomously.[87] Instead of obliging a court to identify an appropriate legal

---

83 Apart from the case where one subscribes to a *stricto senu lex fori* approach. However, adherence to such an approach brings into question the entire *raison d'être* for private international law.

84 See also JESSURUN D'OLIVEIRA (2003a) p. 31-32.

85 JESSURUN D'OLIVEIRA (2003a) p. 32.

86 AUDIT (2004) p. 792.

87 The first of such cases came in 1964, ECJ, *Unger,* Case *No.* 75/63 [1964] ECR 347. Such an approach has also been upheld in the field of private international law. See, for example, ECJ, *LTU Lufttransportunternehmen GmbH & Co. KG v. Eurocontrol,* Case *No.* 29/76, [1976] ECR 1541 on the interpretation of Art. 1, Brussels Convention; ECJ, *Gourdain v. Nadler,* Case *No.* 133/78, [1979] ECR 733, the ECJ held "the concepts used in Article 1 of the Convention (Brussels 1968 Convention) which serve to indicate its scope must be regarded as independent concepts which must be interpreted by reference, first, to the objectives and scheme of the convention and, secondly, to the general principles which

category by selecting a particular approach, the court is simply obliged to identify the appropriate legal category by applying autonomous European concepts. Such an approach is also evident with respect to the Rome Convention.[88]

> The need for uniform application of Community law and the principle of equality require that the terms of a provision of Community law which makes no express reference to the law of the Member States for the purposes of determining its meaning and scope must normally be given an autonomous and uniform interpretation throughout the Community.[89]

The increasing mobility of citizens in the European Union, the diversity of forms of non-marital registered relationships and the impact of such schemes in the field of EU law, especially in relation to the free movement of persons, require uniformity of approach to the issue of characterisation. Non-marital registered relationships strike the heart of an individual's personal status.[90] The universality of such concepts should be upheld as far as possible. In striving towards the harmonisation or unification of private international law rules in the field of non-marital registered relationships, or at the very least towards the harmonisation of the characterisation of such relationships, one must simultaneously undertake extensive research into the substantive law rules in the countries involved. By analysing this legislation and identifying the functions, aims and consequences thereof, the true ambit of any autonomous concept will be easier to delineate. As CHESHIRE has said,

> The fact that a rule has been classified, or that it ought properly to be classified, in a particular way for a domestic transaction containing no foreign element, does not preclude an entirely different approach when a question of private international law is involved.[91]

To analogise, when one hears the word "house", an image is immediately conjured; perhaps a building on its own piece of land, generally with a roof,

---

stem from the corpus of the national legal systems. For further examples see AUDIT (2004) p. 792-794.

88 ECJ, *SPRL Arcado v. Haviland,* Case *No.* 9/87 [1988] ECR 1539 at 1555.

89 ECJ, *The Queen v. Secretary of State for the Home Department, ex parte Nana Yaa Konadu Yiadom,* Case *No.* 357/98 [2000] ECR 9265, §26. See also, "Communication from the Commission to the Council and the European Parliament on European contract law", 13th September 2001, *OJ,* C-255/1, p. 6-7.

90 See further **Chapter IX.2.2**.

91 NORTH/FAWCETT (1999) p. 41.

perhaps a lawn and usually a number of rooms, including a living room, bathroom, kitchen and bedroom. Although there are quite literally thousands of different types, styles and sizes of houses, there are features that houses have in common, hence unifying them under the heading of "house". However, before one is able to understand the common characteristics in these disparate constructions, one must first identify the individual characteristics of each of these structures in order to understand what they have in common and where they differ. The same is true of the characterisation of non-marital registered relationships. It is crucial to be fully aware of the domestic legislation creating these registration schemes in order to characterise legal issues stemming from such laws. **Chapters** III-VII will therefore present the results of detailed research with respect to the substantive law rules of seven European countries, highlighting the domestic legislation regarding non-marital registered relationships.

Yet, to continue the analogy, before one can begin building a house, architectural plans must be commissioned to ensure that the structure of the house is sturdy. Once the plans have been authorised, emphasis shifts to laying the foundations. Ensuring that the foundations are stable and dependable prevents problems occurring at a later stage. Only once all this groundwork has been completed, can one begin erecting the frame of the house, eventually filing in details such as plumbing, electricity and insulation. This chapter provides the plans from which one can begin to lay the substantive law foundations (**Chapters** III-VII). **Chapter** IX will provide the framework around which the private international law rules themselves (**Chapters** X-XII) will be built.

PART II

SUBSTANTIVE LAW

"If the prime responsibility of the Church today is to communicate something of a vision, the possibility of fully committed, faithful same-sex relationships, or covenanted partnerships, will, I believe, strengthen rather than undermine what is at the heart of the Christian faith, as it is reflected in the marriage covenant"

Lord Bishop of Oxford, House of Lords, 22nd April 2004
During the debate on the Civil Partnership Act 2004

CHAPTER III
BELGIUM

III.1 INTRODUCTION

On the 1st January 2000, Belgium created the so-called *wettelijke samenwoning* or *cohabitation légale*, joining the ranks of other European nations to have introduced a form of non-marital registered relationship.[1] The most recent available statistics concerning the number of statutory cohabitations registered will be presented in **Section III.2**. After a brief description of the precursors to the enactment of this legislation in **Section III.3**, **Section III.4** will shift attention to the analysis of how a statutory cohabitation can be established, the legal effects of such a relationship (**Section III.5**) and the methods for its dissolution (**Section III.6**).[2]

III.2 EMPIRICAL EVIDENCE AND STATISTICS

Current statistics show a surprisingly large number of registrations in Flanders after 2001, coinciding with the extension of tax benefits to statutory cohabitants in that region.

Table 1: *Number of marriages celebrated (as of January 2005)*[3]

Year	**2000**	**2001**	**2002**	**2003**	**2004**	**Total**
Marriages	45,123	42,110	40,434	41,805	*TBA*	169,472

1 Royal Decree, 14th December 1999, *Belg. Staatsblad,* 23rd December 1999.

2 On the 1st June 2003, Belgium went one step further and opened civil marriage to couples of the same-sex. However, as already stated in **Chapter I**, the rules relating to same-sex marriage will not be addressed in this book. Brief reference has however been made to the passage of this legislation, see **Section III.3.6.**

3 Statistics obtained from http://statbel.fgov.be/home_nl.htm. Unfortunately no accurate data is maintained on the number of same-sex marriages that have been celebrated.

Table 2: *Number of statutory cohabitations registered (as of January 2005)*[4]

	Regions			
	Flanders	*Wallonia*	*Brussels*	*Total*
2000	3,845	1,061	238	5,144
2001	19,846	1,289	292	21,427
2002	3,920	4,422	616	8,958
2003	4,790	4,903	1,570	11,263
2004	8,008	8,240	2,250	18,498
Total	**40,409**	**19,915**	**4,966**	**65,290**

Key: F: *Flanders*; W: *Wallonia*; B: *Brussels Capital Region*; T: *Total*

Since details relating to the parties' relationship are not requested, no statistics are available on the number of statutory cohabitations between couples within the prohibited degrees of relationship.

III.3 HISTORICAL PERSPECTIVE

Two proposals regarding the introduction of statutory cohabitation were submitted to the Chamber of Representatives, the first in 1993 (the Socialist Proposal), and the second in 1994 (the Coalition Proposal). Both proposals found inspiration from proposed partnership laws in **France**, especially the *contract d'union civile*.[5]

III.3.1 SOCIALIST PROPOSAL

The first proposal, introduced by Flemish Socialist Representative SWENNEN,[6] was promulgated on the 20th July 1993. This proposal, later resubmitted to the Senate and the Chamber of Representatives,[7] distinguished between cohabitation contracts and governmentally regulated schemes for cohabitants. Only the latter, regulated schemes were to provide for *statutory institutions* for cohabitants. Under this proposal, the statutory institution would have introduced a "love menu" (*menukaart voor de liefde*)

---

4 Statistics obtained from the external relations department of the *Rijksregister*.

5 SENAEVE/COENE (1998b) p. 125. See **Chapter IV.3** on the French proposals.

6 *Belgian Chamber*, 1992-1993, No. 1143/1 (20th July 1993).

7 *Belgian Senate*, 1995-1996, No. 172/1; *Belgian Chamber*, 1995-1996, No. 372/1 (17th January 1996).

offering a series of options to cohabitants intending to regulate their relationship:[8]

- *Unregulated cohabitation*: No specific form of legal regulation.
- *Cohabitation contract*: A conventional contract with respect to the consequences of the cohabitation.
- *Statutory regulation*: A regulatory cohabitation scheme aimed at providing a flexible, minimalist institution: a *union civile*.[9]
- *Marriage*: A formalistic and traditional statutory institution.

This proposal aimed to introduce the second and third options in this four-tiered system; the fourth already existing and the first requiring no action on the part of the legislature. Parties wishing to enter into a cohabitation contract would first had to have satisfied the conditions of contractual competency as laid down in Arts. 1123 and 1124, Belg. CC.[10] Thus, the proposal would have allowed every natural, contractually competent person to enter into a cohabitation contract. Although not expressly stated in the proposal itself, it is clear from the explanatory notes that this love menu would have been available regardless of the sex of the parties involved.[11] A cohabitation contract would have been prohibited if a person was already committed by another cohabitation contract, a marriage or a *union civile*, and likewise if the parties were related to each other up to and including the second degree.[12]

With regard to *unions civiles*, similar prohibitions were included with respect to those who had not fully terminated either another *union civile* or a previous marriage.[13] The aim, it seems, was to allow those who were able to sign a cohabitation contract the opportunity to enter into a statutorily regulated cohabitation scheme. Competency for registration would have rested with the Registrar of Births, Deaths and Marriages (hereinafter the Registrar) of the residency of one of the parties.[14] The Registrar would have been responsible for registration of the parties' joint declaration in a new

---

8 *Belgian Chamber*, 1992-1993, No. 1143/1, p. 14 (20th July 1993).

9 According to the Dutch text an *instapregeling voor samenwonenden*, whilst in French it was regarded as a *union civile*. For purposes of this text the French term has been used.

10 SENAEVE/COENE (1998b) p. 127.

11 *Belgian Chamber*, 1992-1993, No. 1143/1, p. 10-11.

12 In **Belgian** law, the point of computation begins with either of the persons in question and is then counted upwards to the common ancestor and then downwards to the other person.

13 Thus excluding those persons who were only judicially separated.

14 Proposed Art. 311-*quarter*, *Belgian Chamber*, 1992-1993, No. 1143/1, p. 18.

register.[15] A number of rights and duties would have been granted upon registration, except in the fields of parentage, social security and immigration. In relation to property, the parties would have been able to choose between a separation of property with a community of gains or a complete separation of property.[16] In relation to inheritance, existing spousal intestate succession rules would have been extended to partners who had cohabited for more than two years.[17]

In terms of dissolution of the partnership, a unilateral request submitted to the Registrar of the place where the original declaration was registered would have been sufficient to terminate the relationship.[18] The Registrar would then have been required by means of a bailiff's summons to inform the other party of the termination of the partnership. Upon terminating, a partner who was able to demonstrate his or her hardship to the satisfaction of the court could have been awarded maintenance, which would have had to have been paid by the other partner.[19] The duration of the maintenance would have been equal to the duration of the partnership. If special economic circumstances had been proven, the court would have had the power to reduce or extend this duration.[20] Despite intense discussions in the Chamber of Representatives, the Socialist proposal failed to achieve widespread support.

III.3.2 COALITION PROPOSAL

Representatives of the French-speaking socialist party, the Ecological Party and the Democratic Front for French Speakers jointly submitted the second proposal on the 2nd March 1994.[21] Shortly after the parliamentary elections, this proposal was resubmitted to the Senate unaltered by Senators BOUTMANS and JONCKHEER.[22] Meanwhile, Representatives of both Dutch and French speaking parties submitted a slightly altered version of this proposal to the Chamber of Representatives.[23] It is this last proposal that

---

15 The same register would also be used to register declarations ending partnerships.

16 Title V, Book III, Belg. CC.

17 Proposed Art. 745-*octies*, *Belgian Chamber*, 1992-1993, No. 1143/1, p. 19.

18 Proposed Art. 311-*sexies*, *Belgian Chamber*, 1992-1993, No. 1143/1, p. 18.

19 Proposed Art. 311-*sexies* (3), *Belgian Chamber*, 1992-1993, No. 1143/1, p. 18.

20 Proposed Art. 311-*sexies* (4), *Belgian Chamber*, 1992-1993, No. 1143/1, p. 18.

21 *Belgian Chamber*, 1993-1994, No. 1340/1 (2nd March 1994).

22 *Belgian Senate*, 1995-1996, No. 1-114/1 (3rd October 1995).

23 *Belgian Chamber*, 1995-1996, No. 170/1 (23rd October 1995). French-speaking Socialists (*Parti Socialiste*), French-speaking Greens (*Écologistes confédérés pour l'Organisation de*

will be analysed in this section. The proposal used the Dutch term *samenlevingscontract* and the French term *contrat de vie commune* to describe the institution to be created.[24] According to the proposal, every contractually competent person of age would have been allowed to enter into a *samenlevingscontract*.[25]

The coalition proposal allowed for same-sex and different-sex couples to enter into a *samenlevingscontract*, although relatives in the ascending and descending line would not have been able to benefit from such a scheme.[26] The proposal also provided for the creation of a new register, whereby the Registrar in the residency of one of the partners would have been competent, and obliged, to make a declaration that the parties had consented to the *samenlevingscontract*.[27] Compared with the socialist proposal, the coalition proposal went further in terms of the consequential rights and obligations imposed on the partners. It would have introduced a new Art. 228-*sexties* (1), Belg. CC, which would have imposed a duty of aid and assistance on both parties.[28] Further rights would also have been granted in respect of rented property,[29] property owned by one of the partners,[30] liability for debts,[31] immigration law,[32] inheritance law[33] and inheritance tax.[34] With respect to the termination of the partnership, the coalition proposal stated that the *samenlevingscontract* could be terminated on a party's unilateral request. The termination would then have been

Luttes originales); Dutch-speaking Greens (*Anders Gaan Leven*) and the Democratic Front for French Spakers (*Front democratique des Francophones*).

24 In this book the Dutch term *samenlevingscontract* has been used.

25 Proposed Art. 228-*bis*, *Belgian Chamber*, 1995-1996, No. 170/1, p. 4

26 In the explanatory notes reference was also made to eldery couples as beneficiaries: p. 2.

27 Proposed Art. 76-*bis*, Belg. CC, *Belgian Chamber*, 1995-1996, No. 170/1, p. 7. A diplomatic or consular service would also have been competent.

28 Art. 221, Belg. CC would thus have been extended to those involved in a *samenlevingscontract* obliging the partners to contribute, as far as their means allow, to the costs of the partnership.

29 Proposed Art. 228-*septies* (2), Belg. CC, *Belgian Chamber*, 1995-1996, No. 170/1, p. 7.

30 Proposed Art. 228-*decies* (3)(3), Belg. CC, *Belgian Chamber*, 1995-1996, No. 170/1, p. 8.

31 Proposed Art. 228-*octies* (5), Belg. CC, *Belgian Chamber*, 1995-1996, No. 170/1, p. 8.

32 A rule concerning immigration was proposed and would have allowed the foreign partner of a Belgian with a *samenlevingscontract* a right to a residence permit, as well as amending Art. 16(2) of the Act of 28th June 1984 concerning some aspects of the situation of foreigners and concerning the introduction of the Belg. NC.

33 Proposed Art. 745-*octies*, *Belgian Chamber*, 1195-1996, No. 170/1, p. 8, would have extended the scope of Art. 745-*bis* up to and including Art. 745-*septies*, Belg. CC.

34 The proposal stated that spouses and those having signed a *samenlevingscontract* should be treated in the same manner.

recorded in the Population Register, and would have been valid two months after registration by the Registrar.[35] Upon termination of the *samenlevingscontract,* both parties would have had a right to maintenance; equivalent, at most, to the length of the *samenlevingscontract.*

III.3.3 PROPOSAL FOR STATUTORY COHABITATION

Both proposals outlined above ignited a political firestorm that, although smouldering in 1995, had not really been set alight. The political parties were unable to agree on a number of crucial issues and it seemed as though an insurmountable deadlock had been reached. The breakthrough came in June 1997 when the Flemish majority parties, the Christian People's Party and the Socialist Party,[36] agreed upon a compromise in the fields of inheritance tax for non-married cohabitants, the introduction of a civil law status for non-married couples and the removal of discrimination between married and unmarried couples.[37] On the 9th July 1997, the Chamber of Representatives held a special sitting with professors from various Belgian universities. Although all seemed agreed on the need to introduce a new institution for two cohabitating people outside of the institution of marriage, there was at that time no firm agreement as to the eventual character of such an institution. A Commission was subsequently established consisting of representatives of the abovementioned political parties and a compromise text was proposed whereby the new institution of "statutory cohabitation" would be created within the confines of the Belgian Civil Code. For political reasons this compromise text was submitted as an amendment to the original coalition proposal, completely replacing the original text of that proposal.[38] In comparison to the lengthy process preceding the introduction of the Bill, subsequent discussions in Parliament were succinct. On the 19th March 1998, the Chamber of Representatives approved the proposed introduction of statutory cohabitation, as did the Senate on an amended version, on the 16th July 1998, which was subsequently approved by the Chamber of Representatives on the 29th October 1998.[39] A little less than a month later, the approved

---

35 Proposed Art. 228-*nonies*, Belg. CC.

36 The *Christelijke Volkspartij* and the *Socialistische Partij.*

37 Some of these aims were in the meantime fulfilled in the Flemish District: Flemish Parliament Decree, 1st October 1997, p. 25865. See later for more detail: **Section III.5.8.**

38 *Belgian Chamber*, 1997-1998, No. 170/2, (LANDUYT, VISER, DUQUESNE and WILLEMS).

39 The proposal was not without its opponents. A case was submitted to the Court of Arbitration requesting the annulment of the Act of 23rd November 1998. The Court rejected the case on the ground that the there was a justification for treating the different

text was published in the Belgian Bulletin of Acts and Decrees, and came into force on the 1st January 2000.[40]

III.3.4 REGISTERED PARTNERSHIP PROPOSAL

At the same time Parliament was grappling with political compromises in the field of statutory cohabitation, the academic world was pondering solutions to the problems raised by same-sex couples on the one hand and the legal position of cohabiting different-sex couples on the other. Since October 1996, the Institute for Family Law at the Catholic University of Leuven had been investigating the possibility of introducing a registered partnership scheme for same-sex couples.[41] The published research report concluded with an elaborate proposal partially inspired by the legal systems of **Denmark**, **Norway**, **Sweden**, **Iceland** and **The Netherlands**.[42] The research report stated there was a lacuna in substantive **Belgian** law due to same-sex couples' inability to marry. It concluded that such couples had no possibility to benefit from the rights and obligations that were exclusively restricted to couples of different sex through the institution of marriage.

In the opinion of the research team, the fact that two parties who wish to live with each other are of the same-sex or of different-sex was, from an ethical-anthropological viewpoint, of absolutely no relevance.[43] To draw a distinction was an instance of direct discrimination, not because marriage is inaccessible to partners of the same-sex but because the law offers partners of the same-sex no other opportunity to gain access to the allotted rights and obligations offered by marriage.

The report suggested that two people of the same sex should have the possibility to register their relationship in a civil ceremony and receive exactly the same legal consequences in the private and public law spheres as if they were married.[44] In this way, marriage could retain its traditional form and remain available only to different-sex couples, whilst same-sex couples could find similar legal protection in another institution. The report

---

groups differently: Arbitragehof, 23rd February 2000, Case No. 23/2000, Role No. 1616, *Belg. Staatsblad* 18th March 2000, p. 8602.

40 *Belg. Staatsblad*, 23rd November 1998.

41 SENAEVE/COENE (1998b).

42 SENAEVE/COENE (1998b) Chapter 4, p. 145-226.

43 SENAEVE/COENE (1998b) p. 19.

44 SENAEVE/COENE (1998b) p. 229.

also suggested that not only should the requirements for this new institution be the same as those for marriage, but that the same rights, duties and obligations should be imposed on the parties. Registered partners should, according to the authors, also be placed on an equal footing in the fields of anti-discrimination, consumer law and inheritance. It was also argued that the dissolution procedures for ending a registered partnership should be the same as those available for marriage, *i.e.* divorce on the ground of fault, on the ground of separation for at least five years or mutual agreement.[45] In other words, a parallel institution would have been created, working side-by-side marriage.

The researchers also found no evidence to suggest that children raised in a family with two women or two men were any worse off than those raised in a two parent different-sex family. However, it was noted that there is nonetheless one important difference between a child raised by same-sex parents and a child raised by different-sex parents, namely that in same-sex relationships, a third person will always be involved in the child's conception either by means of sperm, embryo or egg donation, or surrogacy.

III.3.5 SAME-SEX MARRIAGE

Although individual members of the Chamber of Representatives had made numerous proposals with modest success,[46] the Federal Government introduced a Bill on the 14th March 2002 to open marriage to couples of the same-sex.[47] The Bill was subsequently passed on the 30th January 2003.[48] From 1st June 2003,[49] same-sex couples have been able to celebrate civil marriages in Belgium, with the majority of the consequences of a different-sex civil marriage being attached.[50] Unlike SENAEVE who believes that same-sex marriage and non-marital registered relationships should be analysed as one institution,[51] it is this author's opinion that same-sex marriage and non-

---

45 SENAEVE/COENE (1998b) p. 235.

46 *Belgian Chamber*, 1996-1997, No. 932/1; *Belgian Chamber*, 1998-1999, No. 2208/1 and 1999-2000 No. 692/1 (G. VERSNICK); *Belgian Chamber*, 1999-2000, No. 485/1 (29th Feburary 2000) (F. VAN DEN EYNDE); *Belgian Chamber*, 1999-2000 No. 861/1 (K. GRUAWLES); *Belgian Chamber*, 2000-2001, No. 1011/1 (P. VANELTHOVEN).

47 *Belgian Chamber*, 2001-2002, No. 1692/1 (14th March 2002). Also SENAEVE (2002) p. 50.

48 *Belgian Chamber*, 2002-2003, No. 2165/3 which resulted in the Act of 13th February 2003, *Belg. Staatsblad*, 28th Feburary 2003. For a discussion of this Act see RENCHON (2003).

49 Act of 13th February 2003, *Belg. Staatsblad*, 28th February 2003. See SENAEVE (2003d).

50 Differences in the field of paternity and adoption are still present (**Section III.5.9**).

51 SENAEVE (2003c) p. 19, §1489-2.

marital registered relationships should, and must, be analysed as different forms of registered relationships.[52] Initially, same-sex marriages were restricted to **Belgians** and **Dutch** nationals, due to the corresponding application of **Belgian** private international law rules to same-sex marriages.[53] This private international law rule has, however, subsequently been amended.[54] Same-sex married couples are still prevented from jointly adopting children, and children born to a female same-sex marriage are not regarded as the legal children of both parties; the presumption of paternity thus not being extended to encompass same-sex marriages.[55]

III.4 ESTABLISHMENT

III.4.1 POSITION OF THE INSTITUTION

The Belgian Civil Code is divided into three books, each dealing with a different area of private law. Book I deals with issues related to the law of persons, Book II with issues related to goods and the restrictions imposed on property and Book III with issues related to the manner in which property can be obtained. The Act of 23rd November 1998, which created the institution of statutory cohabitation,[56] introduced five new articles under Title Vbis, Book III, Belg. CC, immediately after the provisions on matrimonial property law.[57] In order to fully accentuate Parliament's intent that this law, unlike marriage, was not to impose a change in the partners' lives,[58] but was only to regulate property and financial matters, the new institution was created in Book III and not Book I, Belg. CC.[59] Hence, it is profoundly clear from the positioning of this law that this new institution's ambitions are significantly lower than those of the previous proposals outlined in **Section III.3**.

---

52 For further explanation of this opinion see **Chapter I.3**.

53 See **Chapter X** for explanation of Belgian marital private international law rules.

54 See SCHIMDT (2004); ERAUW (2004) p. 126-127; Art. 47(2), Belg. CPIL.

55 PERTEGÁS SENDER (2003) p. 257-280.

56 BAURAIN (1998); RENCHON (1998).

57 Arts. 1475-1479, Belg. CC.

58 *Belgian Chamber*, 1995-1996, No. 170/8, p. 62 (DUQUESNE) and p. 63 (WILLEMS).

59 SENAEVE (2003c) p. 28 *et seq*, §1510-1 *et seq*.

III.4.2 EXCLUSIVITY

The "principle of exclusivity" consists of two important, distinguishable yet interrelated facets. Firstly, parties to a non-marital registered relationship may only be involved in one institutionalised relationship at any one time (*i.e.* either a form of non-marital registered relationship or a marriage). Secondly, this relationship may only be registered between two people. Both of these facets will be discussed in turn in order to assess whether the forms of non-marital registered relationship adhere to the same principles as marital relationships.[60]

Replicating the rules of marriage, a statutory cohabitation can only be registered between two persons.[61] Objections were raised during parliamentary discussions with respect to this condition. Representative LAEREMANS stated that such a requirement would in effect introduce a new form of discrimination. He believed that this requirement was discriminatory towards those in relationships with more than two people and thus would be liable to be held unconstitutional by the Court of Arbitration.[62] In response, it was noted that there was absolutely no social pressure to introduce legislation to regulate the organisation of relationships involving more than two people.[63]

Persons wishing to register a statutory cohabitation will be prevented from doing so if one or both of them is already married or involved in a statutory cohabitation.[64] In contrast, those wishing to marry are only prevented from doing so if one or both of them is already married.[65] The existence of a statutory cohabitation is thus no bar to a marriage. However, the statutory cohabitation is terminated by operation of law upon celebration of the marriage, thus adhering to the principle of exclusivity.[66]

---

60 This analysis will likewise be applied in **Chapters IV.4.2**, **V.4.2**, **VI.4.2** and **VII.4.2**.

61 **Marriage**: Art. 146, Belg. CC; **Statutory Cohabitation**: Art. 1475(1), Belg. CC.

62 *Belgian Chamber*, 1995-1996, No. 170/8, p. 61.

63 *Belgian Chamber*, 1995-1996, No. 170/8, p. 61.

64 Art. 1475(2)(1), Belg. CC.

65 Art. 147, Belg. CC. Bigamy is also a criminal offence: Art. 391, Belg. Cr. C.

66 See **Chapter III.6.8**.

III.4.3 SEX OF THE PARTIES

Prior to June 2003, those wishing to marry had to be of a different sex.[67] However, as a result of amendments to the Belgian Civil Code, Belgium became the second country in the world to permit same-sex couples to marry.[68] Since this date statutory cohabitation and marriage have been open to both different-sex and same-sex couples. Although the sex of the parties to a statutory cohabitation is irrelevant, the legislation does not expressly provide for this.[69] According to SENAEVE this was so evident that the legislature saw no need to provide for its explicit regulation.[70] As a result no problems arise in relation to either marriage or statutory cohabitation should one of the parties undergo gender reassignment surgery. Sexual orientation is also irrelevant in determining a person's eligibility to celebrate a marriage or register a statutory cohabitation.[71]

III.4.4 MINIMUM AGE

Since the 19th January 1990, the minimum age at which one can marry has been equalised and fixed at eighteen,[72] thus bringing the marriageable age into line with the age of majority.[73] This legislation also approved the introduction of a legal procedure, granted by the Youth Court,[74] to allow those who have not attained the age of eighteen to enter into marriage. With respect to statutory cohabitation, only those over the age of eighteen are allowed to enter into such a relationship.[75] The procedure at the Youth Court for those who have not attained the age of eighteen is not extended to minors who wish to enter into a statutory cohabitation. This lack of such a procedure thus imposes a minimum age limit of eighteen to statutory cohabitation in all cases.[76]

---

67 Rb Antwerp, 27th January 1999 (1999) *EJ* 50, annotated UYTTERHOEVEN.

68 For literature on the subject see: KOTTERMAN-VAN DE VOSSE (2001); SENAEVE (2002).

69 Art. 1475(1) Belg. CC. See also SENAEVE (2003d).

70 SENAEVE (2003c) p. 34, §1522-1.

71 *Belgian Chamber*, 1995-1996, No. 170/8, p. 59.

72 Art. 144, Belg. CC. Prior to this statutory amendment, the legal minimum age to marry was set at eighteen for men and fifteen for women. See COMM. PERS. (SENAEVE).

73 Art. 488, Belg. CC.

74 Art. 145(1), Belg. CC.

75 **Marriage:** Art. 144, Belg. CC; **Statutory Cohabitation:** Arts. 1123 and 1124, Belg. CC.

76 See SENAEVE (2003c) p. 32-33, §1516-1517.

III.4.5 RESIDENCY

In order to register a statutory cohabitation,[77] the parties must have a common habitual residence in Belgium at the time the partnership is to be registered.[78] If the parties satisfy this requirement, Art. 1476(1), Belg. CC states that the registration documentation is to be delivered to the Registrar of the municipality of their common domicile.[79] Although the law imposes no further requirements, no exception to these rules is provided for. Accordingly, this rule is more restrictive than the equivalent rules for celebrating a marriage, where the required connection to the municipality where the instrument of intent to marry must be registered is much weaker. As a result of Art. 44, Belg. CPIL, a marriage may be celebrated in Belgium if either of the spouses are Belgian, have their domicile in Belgium or has had their habitual residence in Belgium for at least three months.[80] Even the places where the marriage may be registered if one of these conditions is satisfied are broader than the respective requirements for statutory cohabitation.[81]

III.4.6 PROHIBITED DEGREES OF RELATIONSHIP

Unlike marriage, which is forbidden between all blood relatives in the direct ascending and descending line, and relatives in the indirect ascending

---

77 In the original version of the coalition proposal, Art. 28 dealt would have amended Art. 16(2) of the Act of the 28th June 1984 concerning some aspects of the situation of foreigners and concerning the introduction of the Belgian Nationality Code, thus allowing a non-Belgian to enter into a statutory cohabitation.

78 Art. 59(2), Belg. CPIL.

79 In the original proposal accepted by the Belg. CR, reference was made to residence. See also ERAUW/VERHELLEN (1999) p. 152. The term "domicile" needs thus to be read in the sense of Art. 102, Belg. CC.

80 For Belgians living abroad the possibility is provided for registration either in the Belgian consular or diplomatic representation abroad or in Brussels: ERAUW/VERHELLEN (1999) p. 152; *Belgian Chamber*, 1995-1996, No. 170/1 p. 4-5. See **Chapter X.4**.

81 Art. 44, Belg. CPIL and Art. 63, Belg. CC. Firstly, the parties may register their instrument of intention to marry in the municipality where one of them is registered in the population register, aliens' register or register for candidates for refugee status (Art. 63(1), Belg. CC. COMM. PERS. (D'HONDT/VERSCHELDEN); SENAEVE (2003a) p. 86-89, §185-190). Secondly, a number of exceptions to this rule are provided for (Art. 63(2), Belg. CC. COMM. PERS. (D'HONDT/VERSCHELDEN) See also Govt. Circular, 17th December 1999, *Belg. Staatsblad*, 31st December 1999). Thirdly, Art. 63(3), Belg. CC regulates those situations where two Belgian nationals not registered in Belgium wish to marry.

and descending line up to and including the third degree,[82] statutory cohabitation is allowed between all relatives.[83] For this reason, questions regarding marriages between relatives related in the fourth degree do not apply to statutory cohabitations since such a prohibition does not exist.[84] As a result of adoption,[85] marital obstacles are created between the adopter and the adoptee.[86] These are not extended to statutory cohabitation. Adoptive parents are accordingly allowed to enter into a statutory cohabitation with their adopted children.[87]

III.4.7 COMPETENCY AND CONSENT

Those persons competent to register a statutory cohabitation and those competent to celebrate a marriage are virtually identical, despite differences in the sources of the applicable legal provisions. Only those deemed contractually incompetent will be prohibited from registering a statutory cohabitation.[88] Minors, those declared incompetent, and all those unable to determine their will due to mental disturbance, alcohol or drugs will be forbidden from registering a statutory cohabitation. Despite the fact that these contractual competency provisions are not *mutatis mutandis* applicable to marriage, those unable to determine their own will are also prohibited from celebrating a marriage.[89] Consequently, although the rules are to be found in different sections of the Belgian Civil Code, the outcome

---

82 Art. 161, Belg. CC is also applicable to those related by virtue of adoption since Art. 370(1), Belg. CC places those adopted by means of full (or strong) adoption in exactly the same position as those related by familial legal ties. COMM. PERS. (WILLEKENS).

83 Arts. 161-163, Belg. CC with respect to prohibitions in the field of marriage. In Belgian law, family law degree is calculated by climbing from the person in question to the common ancestor and then descending to the relative: Art. 738, Belg. CC. For criticism see *Belgian Chamber*, No. 170/8, p. 18 (MULDERS-KLEIN). A prohibition on the basis of affinity would be introduced by virtue of *Belgian Chamber*, 2002-2003, No. 110/1, p. 21.

84 Some fourth degree marriages are accepted *e.g.* between cousins. Others have, however, caused problems *e.g.* a great-uncle and grandniece: SENAEVE (2003c) p. 36, §1527.

85 Two forms of adoption are allowed: weak adoption and strong adoption. The rules described in this section apply to weak adoption. In terms of strong adoption, a child retains its links with its original family (Art. 370(1)(2), Belg. CC). Thus marital prohibitions also exist with respect to the adopted child's original family.

86 Art. 363, Belg. CC.

87 Since Arts. 1475-1479, Belg. CC do not elucidate whether people related to each other by means of familial bond are prohibited from entering into a statutory cohabitation, they are by default permitted to do so: SENAEVE (2003c) p. 38, §1533(1).

88 Art. 1475(1), Belg. CC in conjuction with Arts. 1123 and 1124, Belg. CC.

89 SENAEVE (2003c) p. 40, §1539-1540; Belg. Cass., 28th May 1958 (1957-1958) *RW* 2105. This prohibition also includes minors: Art. 144, Belg. CC.

is the same. This is, however, not the case when one turns one's attention to the requirements for valid consent, where the rules on statutory cohabitation differ from those applying to marriage. With respect to marriage, the grounds for proving lack of consent are more restrictive than those for ordinary contractual obligations,[90] which are in turn applicable to statutory cohabitation.[91]

III.4.8 FORMAL VALIDITY

A statutory cohabitation is brought into being by means of a "declaration of statutory cohabitation".[92] This declaration, a written document, needs to be submitted to the Registrar of the municipality of the common domicile of the parties.[93] It has not been determined whether both parties need to be present at the handing over of this text.[94] The document must contain a wide range of information.[95] After receiving this document, the Registrar must establish whether both cohabitees have satisfied the requirements for entering into a statutory cohabitation. If the Registrar is satisfied that the conditions have been fulfilled, he or she must record this on the Register of Births, Deaths and Marriages. If the Registrar is not satisfied that the conditions have been met then he or she may refuse to note the statutory cohabitation on the register. At this point, the parties may commence legal proceedings against the Registrar with the aim of eventually being able to enter into a statutory cohabitation. Unlike marriage, persons wishing to enter into a statutory cohabitation do not have to wait fourteen days after the note is entered in the Register of Births, Deaths and Marriages before being allowed to enter into a statutory cohabitation.[96] Nevertheless, a limited form of publicity is provided for, in that the declaration of statutory cohabitation must be registered in the abstracts of the Population Register.[97]

---

90 Art. 180 and 181, Belg. CC.

91 Arts. 1109-1118, Belg. CC. See **Section V.6.6** for information on this interplay.

92 VERBREEK (2000) p. 121: Some couples sign the declaration during a formal ceremony.

93 Art. 1476(1), Belg. CC.

94 COMM. PERS. (SENAEVE).

95 These formalities would be abolished by virtue of *Belgian Chamber*, 2003-2004, No. 110/1 (15th July 2003) (MAINGAIN and PAYFA). Instead, a statutory cohabitant would be deemed to have been concluded if the parties had lived together for two years, had had a child together or signed a contract regulating the proprietal aspects of their cohabitation (Proposed Art. 1475(1), *Belg. CC*).

96 Art. 165(1), Belg. CC.

97 Art. 4(1), Royal Decree of 16th July 1992 concerning the obtaining of information from the Population Register and Aliens Register. See also Govt. Circular, 1st December 1999, *Belg. Staatsblad*, 7th December 1999.

III.5 LEGAL EFFECTS

III.5.1 GENERAL

Upon the creation of a statutory cohabitation, Belgian law imposes a number of rights and duties on the parties concerned, both with respect to each other and with respect to third persons. In order to ascertain the purview of these rights, it is vital that one also establish the respective rights and duties imposed on spouses, thus enabling a sound comparison to be made between marriage and statutory cohabitation.[98]

III.5.2 CIVIL STATUS

As explained in **Section III.4.8**, the formal procedure for registering a statutory cohabitation is different from celebrating a marriage. These procedural differences give rise to different effects in relation to the respective consequences on the parties' civil status. Only those instruments recorded in the Register of Births, Deaths and Marriages will have an effect on a person's civil status.[99] Although the parties must deposit their declaration of statutory cohabitation with the Registrar, the Registrar may not subsequently prepare a deed (*akte*) in the Register of Births, Deaths and Marriages, as is the case for marriage,[100] but is instead obliged to make an announcement (*melding*) of the declaration (*verklaring*) in the Population Register.[101] As a result, registration of a statutory cohabitation has no effect on a person's civil status.

The Population Register exists alongside the Register of Births, Deaths and Marriages and concerns the administrative registration of identity details, such as information related to a person's nationality, date and place of birth, parentage, marital status, and the composition of their family.[102] As a result of the enactment of the statutory cohabitation legislation and by virtue of

---

98 For further explanation of this argument see **Chapter I.4.1**.

99 Arts. 34-40, Belg. CC.

100 All deeds of civil status are made in duplicate: Art. 40, Belg. CC. The second deed is handed over on a yearly basis to the district court: Art. 43, Belg. CC.

101 Art. 1476(1)(3), Belg. CC. The difference between an "announcement" and a "deed" can be found in the different methods used to alter information in the registers. The difference in terminology is more than purely symbolic and is further evidence of the Government's intention that this institution was to have no effects on one's civil status.

102 Art. 1, Royal Decree of 16th July 1992 concerning the determination of information that must be entered into the Population Register and the Aliens Register.

the Royal Decree of 30th December 1999, a number of amendments were effected with regard to the information that must be recorded in the Population Register. Prior to 1st January 2000, only marital contracts and contracts relating to matrimonial property needed to be recorded in the register. Since that date contracts signed after the declaration of a statutory cohabitation also need to be registered.[103] Furthermore, a termination of statutory cohabitation must also be recorded in this register.[104]

III.5.3 NATIONALITY

The Belgian Nationality Code (Belg. NC) distinguishes two ways Belgian nationality can be granted: by attribution or by acquisition.[105] Belgian nationality can be acquired by people above the age of eighteen by means of a declaration of nationality, a choice of nationality, a declaration by a (foreign) spouse of a Belgian national, or by possession of a legal status and naturalisation.[106]

Since the enactment of the Belg. NC, marriage no longer results in the spouse of a Belgian national automatically acquiring Belgian nationality.[107] Instead, the spouse of a Belgian national has a right to a special procedure used to obtain Belgian nationality, thus preserving the legislature's wish to maintain the unity of nationality within the family unit.[108] Statutory cohabitants, on the other hand, are denied access to this speedier and simpler procedure and must utilise other methods to acquire Belgian nationality, most importantly by means of a declaration of nationality or by the naturalisation procedure. Acquiring Belgian nationality by means of a declaration is a recent addition to the other methods, being introduced by the Act of 13th June 1991. This procedure, although requiring an extended period of residence in Belgium,[109] does not require the party to undertake judicial steps in order to gain Belgian nationality. In contrast, the naturalisation procedure, although requiring the completion of a formal, legal procedure, does not require as extended a period of residence.

---

103 Art. 1(10), *ibid*, as amended by Royal Decree of 30th December 1999.

104 Art. 1(27) and 1(28), *ibid*.

105 Art. 1, Belg. NC.

106 Arts. 12-bis, 13-15, 16, 17, 19-21, Belg. NC respectively.

107 Art. 16(1), Belg. NC. See VERWILGHEN (1985) p. 337, §618.

108 This method of obtaining Belgian nationality is independent of the way in which the spouse acquired Belgian nationality. Thus is does not matter whether Belgian nationality was *attributed* to the spouse or that he or she *acquired* Belgian nationality.

109 Seven years according to Art. 12-*bis*, Belg. NC.

In order to be eligible for naturalisation, the foreigner must have attained the age of eighteen, have had his or her main place of residence in Belgium for at least three years prior to beginning the naturalisation procedure and have had his or her place of residence in Belgium during the entire procedure.[110] The term "main place of residence" is defined neither in the Belg. NC nor in ancillary legislation. Instead, resort must be made to the term's natural and common meaning.[111]

If one thus compares a statutory cohabitant to his or her married counterpart, one sees that, all things being equal *i.e.* should neither have Belgian parents nor have been born on Belgian territory, a spouse of a Belgian national is required to wait at least three years before being able to acquire Belgian nationality, and a statutory cohabitant is required to wait either three years and begin a naturalisation procedure or wait seven years and make a declaration of Belgian nationality.[112] Furthermore, evidence of a statutory cohabitation could perhaps be used in proving that a person's "main place of residence" is the common domicile of the parties, thus aiding in the determination of whether a foreigner is entitled to utilise the naturalisation procedure.

III.5.4 NAME LAW

Marriage has no automatic effect on a person's surname; both spouses thus retain their pre-marital surname after marriage.[113] However, on the basis of legal custom, confirmed by case law, each person has the right to use the surname of his or her spouse.[114] This possibility is not open to statutory cohabitants and as a result statutory cohabitants are forbidden from using the surname of their partner.[115] A statutory cohabitant who wishes to

---

110 Arts. 19-21, Belg. NC. In the original text a five-year residency period was imposed on applicants. By virtue of the Act of 1st March 2000, this has been reduced to three years.

111 Rb Nivelles, 1 Civ. Ch., 8th November 1955 (1955) *RJ Trim. Arr. Niv.* 23. See further VERWILGHEN (1985) p. 309, §557

112 There is, however, no difference between the treatment afforded to statutory cohabitants and unmarried, unregistered couples.

113 PINTENS (1981) p. 39.

114 Belg. Cass., 6th February 1967 (1967-1968) *RW* 1071. Each spouse possesses a right and therefore neither spouse is obliged to take the name of his or her partner: SENAEVE (2003a) p. 106; Belg. Cass., 29th March 1965 (1964-1965) *RW* 2017. One must however distinguish between the right to use one's spouse's surname in day-to-day life and in a professional sphere: SENAEVE (2003a) p. 106-107, §227-232; COMM. PERS. (ROODHOOFT).

115 To do so would probably be regarded as a crime of using a false name according to Art. 231, Belg. Cr. C and Belg. Cass., 6th February 1967 (1967-1968) *RW* 1071. This crime can

change his or her surname may nevertheless still do so under certain restricted circumstances.[116] Anyone may submit a request to the Minister of Justice to change his or her surname for any reason.[117] This right is only permitted if "it is supported by serious reasons".[118] Such reasons have included the wish to replace a ridiculously sounding or strange name,[119] the wish to perpetuate a name that is at risk of dying out,[120] and the wish to give a child the name of its legal father who cannot pass on his name in the normal manner.[121] Although to this author's knowledge no case has yet arisen to decide this matter with respect to statutory cohabitants, it is clear from the aforementioned case law that the mere fact that a statutory cohabitation has been registered will almost certainly not provide sufficient cause for a name change to be granted, thus preventing statutory cohabitants from being able to alter their surnames to match that of their partner.

III.5.5 TAXATION, SOCIAL SECURITY AND PENSIONS

As part of the original coalition proposal discussed above,[122] the differences in the field of social security law between married couples and cohabiting couples would have been removed entirely.[123] This seems to have been a step too far for the Belgian legislature, and as a result statutory cohabitants received no privileged status in the field of social security. For many benefits in the field of social security, the marital status of the applicant is not relevant: for example, unemployment benefits, invalidity and sickness benefits, family allowance, health insurance and calculation of a person's subsistence level are all awarded without reference to the marital status of

---

be punished with a prison sentence of between eight days to three months and/or a monetary fine of between €125 and €1500 (the current euro-inflation factor is 5).

116 This is contained in the Act of 15th May 1987 concerning surnames and forenames. The unchangeable nature of the surname remains the starting point and thus the alteration of a person's surname remains, according to this Statute, an exception: Art. 3(2).

117 Art. 2(1), Act of 15th May 1987.

118 Art. 3(2), *ibid.*

119 For an overview of cases in which a person's surname has been changed see, PINTENS (1981) p. 68-69. Examples include Anus (Ministry of Justice, Change of Name, 1973, No. 25), Lavatori (Ministry of Justice, Change of Name, 1971, No. 60) and Lemort (Ministry of Justice, Change of Name, 1973, No. 10).

120 PINTENS (1981) p. 74.

121 Arbitragehof, 14th July 1994 (1996) *TBBR* 214-223.

122 See **Section III.3.3.**

123 SENAEVE/COENE (1998a) p. 134.

the applicant.[124] However, in relation to pensions, work-related accident benefits, profession related illness benefits, secured income for elderly persons and compensation for handicapped persons, a person's marital status is relevant and leads to different treatment. In contrast, registration of a statutory cohabitation does not impact one's social security assessment; cohabitants are treated as though they were single.

Even so, certain benefits may well *indirectly* accrue to some statutory cohabitants. For example, in determining the subsistence level of an applicant, any person with whom the applicant cohabits and forms a "factual family" must be taken into account.[125] Although this situation is restricted to heterosexual cohabitants,[126] the simple fact that the applicant has entered into a statutory cohabitation with his or her partner will lead to the fulfilment of the "factual family" condition, thus resulting in the income of his or her partner being taken into account in order to assess the applicant's subsistence level.[127]

With respect to tax law, the situation is somewhat different. When the law creating the institution of statutory cohabitation was enacted, statutory cohabitants were treated no differently than their unmarried counterparts. A distinction was thus made between unmarried couples, including statutory cohabitants, on the one hand and married couples on the other (often to the financial disadvantage of married couples). This distinction was endorsed in a wide variety of tax matters, including the income-tax free portion of the couples' salary and housing tax-credit.[128] However, due to recent developments in the field of tax law this situation has been radically altered.[129]

---

124 For further information see: http://mineco.fgov.be/.

125 SENAEVE (2000) p. 451-452.

126 Art. 13(1)(2), Royal Decree of the 30th October 1974.

127 SENAEVE (2000) p. 451. As seen in **Section III.2** in fact the vast majority of statutory cohabitations are in fact concluded by different-sex couples.

128 A housing tax-credit or *woningaftrek* is the sum of money that can be deducted from the total income received as a result of immoveable property. Thus if property has an assigned value (this is known as the *kadastraal inkomen* and involves a complicated mechanism for determining how much a house would be worth if it were to be rented) of €5,000, each unmarried person has a housing tax-credit of €3,000, and they have bought the house together, then their net income from immoveable property would be assessed as zero. See VAN DE WOESTEYNE (2001) p. 152.

129 *Belgian Chamber*, 2000-2001, No. 1270/1. The law was subsequently enacted in the form of the Act of 10th August 2001 relating to the reform of income tax law. A number of cases have already been brought before the Court of Arbitration to repeal some of the

Since 2005, statutory cohabitants have been placed on an equal footing with their married counterparts.[130] Art. 2(2), Belgian Income Tax Code (Belg. ITC) now explicitly states that statutory cohabitants are to be treated in the same manner as married partners.[131] Although this equalisation of the terms "statutory cohabitant" and "spouse" does not occur throughout the whole of the Belg. ITC, Art. 2(2) must be read as having corresponding application wherever necessary.[132] As a result of this equalisation, statutory cohabitants are able to benefit from a number of advantages that, until the passage of this Act, were the exclusive domain of married couples. For example, both may now benefit from the application of a "marriage" quotient,[133] the attribution of a benefit or advantage to the co-working spouse, compensation for the loss of one's occupation, and the signing of a life insurance policy or pension plan with the statutory cohabitant as a beneficiary.[134]

One of principal aims of the legislature was to equalise all forms of cohabitation, thus making the fiscal system marriage neutral.[135] Prior to this reform, non-married persons were able to benefit from €4,095 tax-free salary. Those who merely cohabited (with or without a declaration of statutory cohabitation) were both able to enjoy a tax-free level of €4,095.[136] The tax-free level for married couples, on the other hand, was set at €3,250 for each partner. The Act of the 10th August 2001 raised this tax-free level

provisions of the law, see namely, Arbitragehof, 5th June 2003, Case No. 95/2002, Role No. 2394, *Belg. Staatsblad*, 22nd June 2002, p. 28510; Arbitragehof, 14th May 2003, Case No. 63/2003, Role No. 2395, *Belg. Staatsblad*, 5th June 2003, p. 30633.

130 Art. 2(2), Act of 10th August 2001, amends Art. 1, Belg. ITC.

131 As a result of Art. 2, Act of 10th August 2001 concerning the reform of income tax law.

132 *Belgian Chamber*, 2000-2001, No. 1270/1, p. 8. This change also means that a dissolution of a statutory cohabitation is equivalent to a divorce; a surviving statutory cohabitant as equivalent to a surviving spouse and so on.

133 A calculation which is applied to married couples whereby 30% of the income of the higher earning spouse is attributed to the other spouse and is taxed accordingly: Arts. 87-89, Belg. ITC.

134 *Belgian Chamber*, 2000-2001, No. 1270/1, p. 8.

135 *Belgian Chamber*, 2000-2001, No. 1270/1, p. 3.

136 Income tax is levied on income derived from the following categories: (a) income earned by the spouse, after the deduction of the marriage quotient and attribution of income to the co-working spouse; (b) various sources of income as listed in Art. 90(1)-(4), Belg. ITC; (d) income other than that mentioned in (a) or (b), which is his or her own property on the basis of property law; (d) all other sources of income.

for married persons to €4,610 each from 2004, and to €5,660 from 2005 onwards (thus equal to that of cohabiting couples and individuals).[137]

Changes have also been made in relation to housing tax-credit. Prior to 2005, unmarried persons who were the owner of a house in which they lived enjoyed a right to a housing tax-credit to the value of €2,975.[138] If the couple lived together outside the institution of marriage, then both retained the full value of this tax-credit, whilst if they were married they were entitled to €2,975 in total, plus €288 due to the fact that they were married. A married couple was thus heavily disadvantaged.[139] As a result of the Act of 10th August 2001, married couples have, since 2005, been treated identically to cohabitants, with both groups receiving a housing tax-credit of €4,017 per person on any income derived from immoveable property.[140] These changes have also resulted in immoveables no longer being assigned to the highest earning spouse, but instead being assigned to the person in whose name the property is registered.[141]

III.5.6 RIGHTS AND DUTIES OF THE PARTNERS TO EACH OTHER

Although at first glance some of the compulsory rules applicable to married couples regardless of their matrimonial property system appear to be equally applicable to statutory cohabitees, the actual benefits statutory cohabitees derive from these provisions is limited. One of the reasons the rights and duties imposed on spouses by the so-called *primair stelsel/régime primaire* are of such importance is due to the fact that a marriage is difficult to terminate, thus protecting the weaker party.[142] A statutory cohabitation, on the other hand, can be terminated on the unilateral will of one of the parties, thus leaving but a hollow shell of the essential protection offered to spouses.[143] Nonetheless, the following rights and duties that the partners

---

137 The original figures were agreed upon in 2001. Due to periodic, inflation-related increases, these figures have changed each year since the passing of the Act in 2001. In 2001 these figures were set at €3390 for 2004, €4,095 for 2005. By 2004 these figures had increased to €4,610 for married couples and €5,570 for unmarried couples.

138 This is the approximate equivalent value of 120,000 BEF.

139 If spouses had children then the housing tax-credit was increased by €250. From 2005, this tax-credit will also be *mutatis mutandis* available to statutory cohabitants.

140 Art. 16(6), Belg. ITC. If the spouses have children then the housing tax-credit is increased by €335, which from 2005 which also be applied to statutory cohabitants.

141 As is the case for unmarried couples, see VAN DE WOESTEYNE (2001) p. 153.

142 LELEU (1999) p. 124.

143 An opinion supported by DEBUSSCHER (1999) p. 167.

owe to each other, whether by virtue of celebrating a marriage or a statutory cohabitation, are mandatory in nature and cannot be contracted out of.[144] With respect to married couples these rights can be found in Chapter VI, Title V, Book I, Belg. CC, whilst reference to Title Vbis, Book III, Belg. CC must be sought in order to assess the full ambit of these rights and duties with respect to statutory cohabitants. From the outset it must be noted that these provisions only apply to a marriage or statutory cohabitation, respectively, so long as it is in existence.[145]

III.5.6.1 Duty to cohabit

Art. 213, Belg. CC, imposes a duty on spouses to live with each other and conduct a communal life together. This duty it to be executed at the marital abode (*echtelijke verblijfplaats/résidence conjugale*),[146] which in turn is to be determined by the spouses themselves.[147] Although application of Art. 213, Belg. CC, is not *mutatis mutandis* applicable to statutory cohabitants, one could argue that such a condition is in fact evident in terms of the establishment of a statutory cohabitation. A statutory cohabitation can only be established if the two persons live together (*samenleven/vie commune*). The question thus arises whether the obligation to live together in Art. 1476, Belg. CC can be seen equivalent to the duty imposed on spouses. Due to the fact that statutory cohabitants are required to state their common domicile on the declaration of statutory cohabitation,[148] it can be argued that the parties could be under a duty to cohabit. Other arguments can also be tendered to support such a proposition. Firstly, all the rights and obligations bestowed on statutory cohabitants involve the protection of a common household. If the parties were not under a duty to live together, such rights and duties would be of little use to either party, thus negating the importance of the statutory cohabitation scheme. Secondly, the institution is identified by the term *wettelijke samenwoning* or *cohabitation*

---

144 PINTENS/VAN DER MEERSCH/VANWINCKELEN (2002) p. 47.

145 **Marriage:** Art. 212(1), Belg. CC; **Statutory Cohabitation:** Art. 1477(1), Belg. CC.

146 The marital abode is not to be confused with the parties' residence. The marital abode is in principle agreed upon between the parties themselves (Art. 214(1), first sentence, Belg. CC). However, if the parties are not in agreement with each other the *vredesrechter* (sub-district court judge) has competence to determine where this may be (Art. 214(1), second sentence, Belg. CC). In this case, the judge can decide that one of the possible abodes is the marital abode (Rb Leuven, 8th February 1991 (1991-1992) *RW* 475).

147 Art. 214(1), Belg. CC, unless one of the spouses cannot express his or her opinion, in which case the marital residence is determined by the other: Art. 214(2), Belg. CC.

148 Art. 1476(1)(3), Belg. CC.

légale and thus even includes the phrase "living together" in its title. The fact that Art. 213, Belg. CC, is not *mutatis mutandis* applied to statutory cohabitants does not therefore completely rule out parties to a statutory cohabitation being under a duty to cohabit.

Conversely, it can also be argued that statutory cohabitants are not subject to a duty to cohabit. The parties to a statutory cohabitation are under a duty to contribute to the burdens and obligations of the relationship.[149] However, this duty is terminated the moment the statutory cohabitants cease to live together, tending to suggest that the parties are not subject to a duty to cohabit.[150] In summary, it would appear that despite the fact that the element of cohabitation underpins the notion of statutory cohabitation parties who have signed and registered such a declaration are not under an express duty to cohabit. If statutory cohabitants are not subject to this duty, then statutory cohabitants are not entitled to claim any of the sanctions available to married couples for a failure to perform this duty.[151]

III.5.6.2 Duty of fidelity

Art. 213, Belg. CC also imposes a duty of marital fidelity on spouses. On the basis of this duty, a spouse is obliged to ensure that he or she only has sexual contact with his or her spouse. Any form of explicit sexual expression with a third party is thus also prohibited although not penalised.[152] SENAEVE indicates that this duty of marital fidelity coupled with a wide interpretation of the duty to cohabit also imposes a duty that the spouses "remain" sexually active.[153] There is no corresponding duty imposed on statutory cohabitants, which is both understandable and reasonable. Statutory cohabitants may, as has already been explained in **Section III.4.6**, be concluded between those within the prohibited degrees of marriage. If a duty of sexual activity or fidelity were imposed on statutory cohabitants then this would be completely incongruous with Belgian public policy.[154]

---

149 Art. 1477(3), Belg. CC.

150 SENAEVE (2003c) p. 101, §1695-2.

151 These sanctions include the right to claim to defer the assistance which one spouse must provide the other, a right to claim enforcement of emergency, provisional measures, divorce, and judicial separation. See further SENAEVE (2003c) p. 92, §1667.

152 SENAEVE (2003c) p. 96, §1678.

153 SENAEVE (2003c) p. 93, §1668. This is turn implies that a sexual relationship between the spouses must be present at the beginning of the relationship (p. 96, §1678). The same obligation is also imposed on same-sex marriages (p. 93, §1668).

154 COMM. PERS. (WILLEKENS).

III.5.6.3 Duty to provide support and assistance

Each spouse is obliged to provide support and assistance to the other during the course of the marriage.[155] The duty to provide assistance necessitates that each spouse ensures for the well being of his or her spouse as well as the avoidance of acts that could be harmful to his or her spouse. The duty to provide support complements the duty to provide assistance by ensuring that the financially stronger spouse is obliged to share his or her living standard with his or her partner, regardless of need.[156] This duty is thus much broader than the right to spousal maintenance.[157] Nonetheless, in a similar vein to the other facets of Art. 213, Belg. CC., neither of these duties are applicable to statutory cohabitants.[158]

III.5.6.4 Duty to contribute to household expenses

Like spouses, statutory cohabitants are obliged to contribute to the costs of the relationship in proportion to their means.[159] This duty encompasses the efforts and expenses that the spouses incur as a result of the material needs of the living together in a familial bond.[160] LELEU has argued that if the statutory cohabitation involves an affective, sexual relationship, then the term "costs of the cohabitation" could be seen to be synonymous with "costs of the marriage".[161] Others believe this to simply be a fact requiring no further explanation.[162] Whatever the case may be, authors agree that the courts should adopt an identical standpoint with regards the interpretation of Art. 1477(3), Belg. CC as they have done with Art. 221(1), Belg. CC.

Although the extension of Art. 221(1), Belg. CC, provides the parties with a basic level of protection during the existence of their statutory cohabitation, it does have limitations. If one of the statutory cohabitants is unable to

---

155 Art. 213, Belg. CC.

156 Belg. Cass., 18th October 1963 (163-1964) *RW* 1862.

157 Arts. 205-211, Belg. CC. See Belgian answers in PINTENS/TORFS, in: BOELE-WOELKI/BRAAT/SUMNER (2003a). See COMM. PERS. (ROODHOOFT).

158 SENAEVE (2003c) p. 100-101, §1695(1).

159 **Marriage:** Belg. Cass., 26th June 1995 (1996) *EJ* 5, annotated ROODHOOFT; **Statutory Cohabitation:** Art. 1477(3), Belg. CC.

160 Obviously, this term has been considerably examined in terms of its precise meaning. For further details see SENAVE (2003c) p. 98, §1686-1687; PINTENS/VAN DER MEERSCH/VANWINCKELEN (2002) p. 370-371.

161 LELEU (1999) p. 127.

162 PINTENS/VAN DER MEERSCH/VANWINCKELEN (2002) p. 370, §774.

provide for the costs of the common household and the partner proceeds to the sub-district court, the party unable to meet his or her obligation may simply terminate the statutory cohabitation.[163] According to some authors, Art. 1477(3), Belg. CC, does, nonetheless, provide the parties with a possibility to claim overdue arrears.[164] Another possibility is for the judge to impose emergency, provisional measures for a period of up to one year.[165]

If one of the spouses fails to fulfil his or her obligation, the sub-district court judge is competent, in accordance with Art. 221(2), Belg. CC, to hear any ensuing dispute. This provision has not however been correspondingly extended to statutory cohabitants. The absence of the *mutatis mutandis* application of Arts. 221(2) to 221(6), Belg. CC,[166] was debated during the parliamentary proceedings. However, since these provisions are based on maintenance claims, which statutory cohabitants are not entitled to, it was felt inappropriate to apply these Articles to statutory cohabitants.[167]

III.5.6.5 Duty to contribute to the repayment of debts

Both statutory cohabitants and spouses are under a duty to contribute to the repayment of debts incurred in connection with the relationship.[168] The fact that Art. 222, Belg. CC is not *mutatis mutandis* applied should not detract from its analogical function. Art. 222, Belg. CC and Art. 1477(4), Belg. CC, pose the principle for division of the debts incurred by the spouses or cohabitants with respect to the maintenance of the relationship and children during the relationship.[169] The debts include any debts incurred as a result of caring and raising the children, irrespective of whether the

---

163 As already stated the rights and duties granted to statutory cohabitants only last for "as long as a statutory cohabitation is in existence": Art. 1477(1), Belg. CC.

164 LELEU (1999) p. 127; PINTENS/VAN DER MEERSCH/VANWINCKELEN (2002) p. 371, §776.

165 According to Art. 1479(1), Belg. CC, Art. 223, Belg. CC is *mutatis mutandis* applicable. The district court judge is able to order emergency, provisional measures, relating to the common residence, the person and goods of the statutory cohabitants and any children, as well as the statutory and contractual obligations of both parties.

166 Arts. 221(3) to (6), Belg. CC, regulate disputes brought on the basis of Art. 221(2).

167 *Belgian Chamber*, 1997-1998, No. 170/8, p. 101.

168 **Marriage:** Art. 222, Belg. CC. COMM. PERS (TORFS); **Statutory Cohabitation:** Art. 1477(4), Belg. CC.

169 It is interesting to note, that although the legislature saw no need to introduce rules relating to the possibility for statutory cohabitants to adopt children, or exercise parental authority over children, it nonetheless introduced rules relating to the responsibility of the partners for debts incurred by the parties as a result of caring and raising children.

children were biological children of the parties to the relationship.[170] This rule provides a creditor recourse, from either of the spouses or statutory cohabitants, for a debt incurred in relation to the maintenance of the house or children, so long as the debt is not excessive, despite the fact that only one party entered into the obligation.[171] The duty to contribute to the repayment of past debts is one of the few measures not affected by the termination of the statutory cohabitation.[172] Should the parties to a statutory cohabitation cease to cohabit, the problematic question arises as to whether Art. 1477(4), Belg. CC, still applies. Until recently opinions were divided on this issue with respect to married couples, but since the 15th October 1999, it is clear that Art. 222, Belg. CC, continues to apply even if the spouses have ceased to cohabit.[173] It is hoped that such an analysis will also be applied to statutory cohabitants when applying Art. 1477(4), Belg. CC.[174]

III.5.6.6 Protection of the home

(a) *Owned property*: From the analogous application of Arts. 215, 220(1) and 224(1)(1), Belg. CC,[175] identical protection is afforded to statutory cohabitees and spouses in relation to owned property.[176] As a consequence, one person cannot act alone concerning the common abode or household goods.[177] If a person who possesses rights over an abode transgresses the

---

170 Art. 203, Belg. CC.

171 This not only includes contractual obligations but also non-contractual obligations which are beneficial to the maintenance of the relationship and children. See, for example, Fr. Cass., 1 Civ. Ch., 7th June 1989 (1990) *D* 21, annotated MASSIP.

172 LELEU provides two reasons for such a rule. (1) These debts are incurred prior to the termination of the statutory cohabitation and (2) this provision is aimed at protecting creditors. See further: LELEU (1999) p. 128-129.

173 Belg. Cass., 15th October 1999 (1999) *Arr. Cass.* 536.

174 LELEU (1999) p. 128; PINTENS/VAN DER MEERSCH/VANWINCKELEN (2002) p. 371.

175 In the original proposal only the provisions of Art. 215 were extended to statutory cohabitants: *Belgian Chamber*, 1997-1998, No. 170/12. The report submitted by VANDENBOSSCHE and LOZIE on behalf of the *Commissie voor de Justitie* brought the Chamber's attention to the fact that Arts. 220(1) and 224(1)(1), Belg. CC had not, yet should have been, correspondingly extended to the statutory cohabitation scheme: *Belgian Chamber*, No. 170/15, p. 2, §3. See also BRAT (1998) p. 123.

176 For an extensive analysis of the content of these rules see COMM. PERS. (TOBBACK: Arts. 215 and 224) and COMM. PERS. (DE WOLF: Art. 220).

177 In Art. 215(1), Belg. CC the phrase "on immoveable property that serves as the main home of the family" (*op het onroerend goed dat het gezin tot voornaamste woning dient*) is used in order to describe the home which is protected. This must however, with respect to statutory cohabitants, be understood to simply mean the main home of the statutory cohabitants, since not all statutory cohabitants will necessarily form a "family".

prohibitions laid out in these provisions, the resulting deed can be declared null and void at the request of the other party.[178] In relation to Art. 224, Belg. CC it is perplexing that only Art. 224(1)(1), Belg. CC, has been extended to statutory cohabitants without further reference to Art. 224(2), Belg. CC. Art. 224(1)(1), Belg. CC provides a party with a possibility to nullify a transaction performed by the other party which transgresses the prohibition laid out in Art. 215, Belg. CC. It thus seems logical that Art. 224(2), Belg. CC should also apply *mutatis mutandis*, since it is here that a one-year limitation period is established.[179]

(b) *Rented property*: Art. 215(2), Belg. CC protects the spouses or a tenant who does not possess any rental rights over the immoveable property.[180] In a similar fashion to the situation with respect to owned property, this provision has also been *mutatis mutandis* extended to statutory cohabitants.[181] The law obliges the landlord to provide both parties with all relevant documents.[182] LELEU has expressed his concern about the ability of the statutory cohabitants to conceal their relationship from their landlord, and subsequently contest a termination of the rental contract due to the fact that it has only be sent to one of the statutory cohabitants.[183] During the parliamentary proceedings, Representative JEANMOYE noted that similar problems had been solved with respect to married couples by ensuring that a spouse of a tenant must inform the landlord or landlady that he or she is married to the tenant in order to enable him or her to make use of this provision.[184]

III.5.7 PROPERTY LAW

Upon celebration of a marriage and in the absence of a pre-nupital agreement, the property of the parties automatically becomes subject to the

---

178 Even if the third party acts in good faith: LELEU (1999) p. 125. However, if the party refuses to co-operate without good reason then the district court can avoid application of this provision: LELEU (1998) p. 53-65

179 That is to say, one year since the party has become aware of the transaction. This limitation period is also subsequently extended to the heirs of the deceased, should that party die before the limitation period expires: Art. 224(2)(2), Belg. CC.

180 LELEU (1999) p. 126.

181 Art. 1477(2), Belg. CC.

182 This has since been tempered by the decision of the Belg. Cass., 22nd March 1991 (1991) I *Pas.* 602; (1991-1992) *RW* 846.

183 LELEU (1999) p. 126.

184 *Belgian Chamber*, 1997-1998, No. 916/5.

rules of the statutory community of property.[185] This community of property is limited to marital gains. According to this statutory community of property, all assets and credits acquired prior to the celebration of a marriage are the separate property of the spouses.[186] Gifts, *inter vivos* legacies, income by way of inheritance and any personal items are also deemed to remain outside the scope of the community of property.[187] In a similar fashion, debts contracted prior to the marriage and debts burdening gifts, legacies and inheritances are deemed to be separate debts.[188] Separate debts are listed exhaustively in Arts. 1406 and 1407, Belg. CC. As a result of this presumption, debts that are not separate in accordance with these Articles are deemed to be communal debts.[189] With respect to the applicable property regime for statutory cohabitants and in contrast to the statutory community of property regime applicable to spouses, the legislature opted for observance of the legal customary principle of the separation of property, and thus assimilated it to factual cohabitation.[190] The following sections thus outline the principles of the property regime applicable to statutory cohabitants.

III.5.7.1 Separate Property

Property, including any income derived therefrom, and any profits accumulated as a result of work remain the property of each partner separately, if a statutory cohabitant can prove that he or she is the legal owner of the property. If a statutory cohabitant cannot prove that he or she is the legal owner of the property, then such property will be deemed to be held jointly by both statutory cohabitants.[191] Some authors believe that the express provision of such a rule in Art. 1478(1) is unnecessary since it adds nothing new to the current legal customary rules.[192] On the other hand, the express articulation of the separation of property elucidates a situation that is often misconstrued, thus bringing with it increased legal certainty and clarity.[193] Furthermore, one of the formal requirements imposed on the Registrar is that he or she must inform future parties to a statutory

185 Art. 1391, Belg. CC.

186 Art. 1399(1), Belg. CC.

187 Arts. 1399(1), 1400 and 1401 Belg. CC.

188 Art. 1406, Belg. CC.

189 Art. 1408, Belg. CC.

190 Art. 1478(1), Belg. CC. PINTENS/VAN DER MEERSCH/VANWINCKELEN (2002) p. 374.

191 Art. 1478(2), Belg. CC.

192 SENAEVE/COENE (1998a) §22; LELEU (1999) p. 129; COMM. PERS. (SENAEVE).

193 An opinion shared by the Belgian Senate: *Belgian Senate*, 1997-1998, No. 916/5, p. 30-31.

cohabitation of the content of Arts. 1475-1479, Belg. CC, and thus must inform the parties of the absence of a community of property regime.[194] This is important since, unlike Art. 1477, Belg. CC,[195] the parties may contract out of the provisions governing the statutory property regime for statutory cohabitants.[196]

III.5.7.2 Community of Property

A community of property is not excluded simply because of the statutory separation of property. On the contrary, goods to which a statutory cohabitant cannot prove ownership as well as those goods which a statutory cohabitant voluntarily places in a community of property will need to be shared upon the termination of a statutory cohabitation. This is done in accordance with the rules of co-ownership in Art. 577(2), Belg. CC. If the statutory cohabitation is ended due to the death of one of the partners, then the communal goods will be regarded as a gift subject to contrary evidence.[197]

III.5.8 INHERITANCE LAW

Statutory cohabitants, unlike spouses, are not privileged by the rules of intestate succession. If the person dies intestate, two criteria are of the utmost importance in determining who will inherit:[198] the degree of familial relationship and the marital bond.[199] If the deceased leaves behind a surviving spouse and no other descendants or blood relatives, then the spouse will inherit the entire estate in full ownership.[200] If the deceased leaves behind descendants, the surviving spouse will receive a usufruct over the entire estate, with the descendants receiving their share in bare ownership.[201] If a person pre-deceases some of his or her blood relatives as

---

194 Art. 1476(1)(2)(5), Belg. CC.

195 See **Section III.5.6.**

196 Laid down in Art. 1478, Belg. CC.

197 Art. 1478(3), Belg. CC.

198 Art. 732, Belg. CC. No distinction is made between the various goods of the inheritance.

199 PINTENS/VAN DER MEERSCH/VANWINCKELEN (2002) p. 598, §1255. The position of the surviving spouse as intestate successor has continued to gain importance. As a result of the Act of 14th May 1981, the spouse was eventually placed on an equal footing with those entitled to inherit by virtue of their legal familial ties to the deceased, despite the fact that the spouse does not, as such, belong to the family of the deceased.

200 Art. 745-*bis* (1)(3), Belg. CC.

201 Art. 745-*bis* (1)(1), Belg. CC, whether the children are a result of the marriage or not.

well as a surviving spouse, the inheritance of the surviving spouse will depend upon the matrimonial property regime in which the parties were married. If communal property is present, the surviving spouse has an absolute interest over such property, exercising a usufruct over any property that belonged wholly to the deceased.[202] None of these rules have been correspondingly applied to statutory cohabitants.

In order for a surviving statutory cohabitant to inherit from his or her deceased partner's estate, the deceased must have left a last will and testament. Nonetheless, the testator does not possess total testamentary freedom. A testator is prohibited from disinheriting his or her children, or ascendants.[203] Although a spouse is also entitled to certain protection,[204] a spouse may still be disinherited under certain conditions.[205] Statutory cohabitants have not been assimilated to this position and as a result a statutory cohabitant can be disinherited by her or her partner.[206]

In the original coalition proposal, inheritance law provisions in the case of intestate succession were granted to statutory cohabitants, although the right to receive maintenance at the cost of the estate was not included.[207] A surviving statutory cohabitant is also prohibited from making a maintenance claim against the estate of the deceased.[208] This situation has been criticised in Belgian literature as having created unreasonable situations with respect to the surviving partner.[209] One can imagine for example a situation whereby a partner has given up his or her occupation in order to look after the common children, and upon the death of his or her partner receives no right to claim maintenance from the devolved estate of the deceased.

---

202 PINTENS/VAN DER MEERSCH/VANWINCKELEN (2002) p. 603, §1268. Act of 14th May 1981 extended the opportunity for a spouse to convert a usufruct into an absolute interest, a monetary sum or a valued or indexed interest: Art. 745-*quarter* (1), Belg. CC.

203 VERBEKE (2000a).

204 VERBEKE (2000a). Act of the 14th May 1981 extended the rights of forced inheritance to surviving spouses, but merely granted a surviving spouse a right to a two-fold forced share to usufruct. Article 915-*bis*, Belg. CC.

205 Art. 915-*bis* (3), Belg. CC. See further VERBEKE (2002a) p. 30-31.

206 This would also be changed should a current proposal pending before the Chamber of Representatives be accepted: Proposed amendment to Art. 915-*bis* (2), *Belgian Chamber*, 2003-2004, No. 846/1, (25th February 2004) (BOURGEOIS).

207 See **Section III.3.3.**

208 Art. 205-*bis*, Belg. CC.

209 For criticism see PINTENS/VAN DER MEERSCH/VANWINCKELEN (2002) p. 377, §793.

The quest to equalise the position of spouses and statutory cohabitants has not ceased. In 2000, Representatives GIET and MAYEUR submitted a proposal to the Chamber of Representatives aimed at rectifying this situation.[210] In the explanatory note, the proposers elucidated that the law needed to be changed in order to guarantee a minimum level of protection for statutory cohabitants.[211] The proposal aimed at ensuring that statutory cohabitants were equally entitled to a usufruct over immoveable property that the parties to the statutory cohabitation had used up until the moment when the estate devolved, as well as over any household goods in the house at that time.[212] Despite this proposal's failure to become law, the ongoing struggle to extend inheritance rights to statutory cohabitants has not diminished. On the 15th July 2003, Representatives MAINGAIN and PAYFA resubmitted a proposal to the Chamber of Representatives that, amongst other changes, called for the extension of intestate inheritance law to statutory cohabitants.[213] On the 25th February 2004, Representative BOURGEOIS submitted another proposal to extend the rules of intestate succession to cohabitants.[214] Although the proposal chooses not to opt for an equalisation of all inheritance rights between married couples and cohabitants,[215] a cohabitant would in actual effect be placed in an almost identical position as his or her married counterpart.

Inheritance tax is levied on all inherited property, regardless of how one inherits such property. Competency in this field rests with the three Belgian Regions.[216] In 1997, the Flemish Regional Council considerably reduced inheritance taxes for cohabitants.[217] However, prior to 30th June 2000, in

---

210 *Belgian Chamber*, 1999-2000, No. 661/1 (GIET and MAYEUR).

211 Explanation to the proposal, *Belgian Chamber*, 1999-2000, No. 661/1, p. 3.

212 Proposed Art. 745-*bis* (3), Belg. CC. If the house was rented, there would have been no inheritance law consequences, apart from the usufruct over the household goods.

213 *Belgian Chamber*, 2002-2003, No. 110/1 (15th July 2003) (MAINGAIN and PAYFA); *Belgian Chamber*, 2002-2003, No. 2135/1 (21st November 2002) (MAINGAIN).

214 *Belgian Chamber*, 2003-2004, No. 846/1, p. 7. Proposed Art. 745-*octies* (1), Belg. CC. This aims at extending these rules to statutory cohabitants as well as factual cohabitants.

215 For the not so convincing reasons why such a solution has been opted for, see *Belgian Chamber*, 2003-2004, No. 846/1, p. 8.

216 Belgium consists of three regions: the Flemish Region (*Vlaamse Gewest/Région Flamande*), the Wallonian Region (*Waalse Gewest/Région Wallonne*) and the Brussels Capital Region (*Brussels Hoofdstadgewest/Région de Bruxelles-Capitale*). The regions have exclusive competency in the fields of local facilities such as land use regulation, environment, accommodation, transport and employment.

217 Flemish Regional Council Decree, 15th July 1997, *Belg. Staatsblad*, 1st October 1997. The levels were set at: <€75,000: 10%; €75,000-€125,000: 35%; >€125,000: 50%.

order to enjoy these reduced rates of taxation the cohabitants had to have lived together for at least three continuous years and have maintained a common household. On the 30th June 2000, these conditions were abolished for statutory cohabitants,[218] and since the 1st January 2001, full equality between the statutory cohabitants and their married counterparts has been achieved.[219] These legislative enactments in the Flemish Region have since been echoed in the Brussels Capital Region and the Wallonian Region, thus achieving full equality between statutory cohabitants and married couples in the field of inheritance tax.[220]

III.5.9 CHILDREN

III.5.9.1 Parentage

Maternity is proven according to one of three methods.[221] The child's mother is normally determined according to the *mater semper certa est* axiom, in that the woman who gives birth to a child and is recorded as such on the birth certificate is deemed to be the legal mother.[222] Although Art. 312(1), Belg. CC, does not oblige the birth mother to record her name on the birth certificate, this must be read in conjunction with Art. 57(2), Belg. CC, which states that it is compulsory that the surname, first name and residence of the mother are mentioned on the birth certificate. The combination of Arts. 57(2) and 312(1) means that the mother must always

---

218 Flemish Regional Council Decree, 30th June 1997, *Belg. Staatsblad*, 17th August 2000.

219 Flemish Regional Council Decree, 1st December 2000, *Belg. Staatsblad*, 11th January 2000. Since this date, statutory cohabitants are therefore entitled to the following rates of inheritance tax: <€50,000: 3%; €50,000-€250,000: 9%; >€250,000: 27%. The same decree has also reduced the length of cohabitation for unregistered couples to one year.

220 In the Brussels Capital Region the bands are set at: <€50,000: 3%; €50,000-€100,000: 8%; €100,000-€175,000: 9%; €175,000-€250,000: 18%; €250,000-€500,000: 24%; >€500,000: 30%. In the Wallonian Region those rates are set at: <€12,500: 3%; €12,500-€25,000: 4%; €25,000-€50,000: 5%; €50,000-€100,000: 7%; €100,000-€150,000: 10%; €150,000-€200,000: 14%; €200,000-€250,000: 18%; €250,000-€500,000: 24%; >€500,000: 30% (Decree of 14th November 2001 concerning inheritance tax between statutory cohabitants, *Belg. Staatsblad*, 29th November 2001). In the Wallonian Region, only statutory cohabitants who have registered their statutory cohabitation at least one year prior to the death of their partner, will be entitled to benefit from such reduced rates (Art. 48, Wallonian Code on Inheritance Tax)

221 The removal of marriage as a keystone in parentage laws stems from the ECtHR decision: ECtHR, *Marckx v. Belgium*, Appl. No. 6833/74, 13th June 1979.

222 Art. 312(1), Belg. CC and Art. 57(2), Beg. CC

be identified.[223] Should it be the case that no name is mentioned on the birth certificate then two other methods for the determination of maternity exist: recognition[224] and from research conducted to determine biological maternity.[225] According to Art. 57(2), Belg. CC, it is compulsory that these rules are completely independent of the marital status of the woman, and thus women involved in a statutory cohabitation are treated identically to the spousal equivalents.

In terms of determining paternity, three methods are recognised in Belgium: paternity by reason of marriage, recognition and the judicial determination of paternity.[226] If the parties are involved in a different-sex marriage then the principle of *pater is est quem nuptiae demonstrant* is applied and the legal father is deemed to be the man to whom the legal mother is married.[227] This rule only applies to different-sex marriages and has no equivalent outside of this situation. Recognition and judicial determination are, however, available to unmarried couples, same-sex married couples and statutory cohabitants.

The person who wishes to recognise a child need by no means prove that he is the genetic father of the child, and thus there are many instances whereby a non-genetic father recognises a child.[228] Only in a case where there is manifest improbability that the man is the genetic father of the child will a Registrar or notary be able to refuse to draw up a declaration of recognition. Recognition is nonetheless understood to be a "voluntary legal act by a man who wishes to create a legal parental bond with a child" and thus is not open to women.[229] It is therefore impossible for a female partner in a statutory cohabitation to become the legal mother of her partner's child

---

223 The Belgian Supreme Court does not, however, exclude the fact that a birth certificate may be without a mother's name, in which special procedures are recognised for the determination of motherhood: Belg. Cass., 29th January 1993 (1993) *Arr. Cass.* 129.

224 If the maternity of a child is not legally settled by virtue of the birth certificate, then a woman can legally recognise a child as her own: Art. 313(1), Belg. CC. VERSCHELDEN (2004) p. 104-117, §116-144.

225 As a last resort, a district court is also competent to judicially determine motherhood on the basis that she has given birth to the child: Art. 314(1), Belg. CC. VERSCHELDEN (2004) p. 118-142, §145-209.

226 Arts. 315-318 (*marriage*), Arts. 319-321 (*recognition*), and Arts. 322-325, Belg. CC (*judicial determination*).

227 Art. 315, Belg. CC.

228 SENAEVE (2003b) p. 47, §803-843.

229 VERSCHELDEN (2004) p. 182, §287.

by means of recognition.[230] It is also impossible for both men in a same-sex statutory cohabitation to be deemed legal fathers of the child.[231] Although a child may be recognised by more than one person of the same-sex, if a child is recognised by two people of the same-sex, only the first will be deemed valid until this recognition is declared null and void.[232] If, however, the statutory cohabitation involves a different-sex couple, the couple will be placed in an identical situation to an unmarried cohabiting different-sex couple; the statutory cohabitation having no effect on their respective parentage rights.

III.5.9.2 Parental Responsibilities[233]

Belgian law only allows parental authority to be exercised by those who have already been determined to be a child's legal parents.[234] A statutory cohabitation is thus irrelevant in determining whether a person is vested with parental authority.[235] A couple of proposals have however been submitted to both Chambers of the Belgian Parliament in order to rectify this situation.[236]

III.5.9.3 Adoption

Belgian law allows for two kinds of adoption: adoption and full adoption.[237] Belgian law also permits both single and joint adoption applications. In the latter case, an order may not be made upon the application of more than one person unless the applicants are of the different sex and either married

---

230 This is also the case for female same-sex marriages.

231 Again, this is also the case for male same-sex marriages.

232 Art. 329, Belg. CC.

233 The term "parental responsibilities" has been used since this accords to the terminology of the Council of Europe (in their White Paper of 15th January 2002 on the principles concerning the establishment and legal consequences of parentage) and the recently published results of the CEFLs questionnaire on parental responsibilities. See PINTENS/PIGNOLET, in: BOELE-WOELKI/BRAAT/CURRY-SUMNER (2005).

234 Arts. 371 *et* seq, Belg. CC. SENAEVE (2003b) p. 136 *et seq*, §1065 *et seq*; PINTENS/PIGNOLET, in: BOELE-WOELKI/BRAAT/CURRY-SUMNER (2005) p. 265.

235 Arts. 373 and 374, Belg. CC state that the legal parents exercise parental authority jointly regardless of whether they live together or not. PINTENS/PIGNOLET in BOELE-WOELKI/BRAAT/CURRY-SUMNER (2005) p. 78-79, 345 and 390.

236 *Belgian Senate*, 2003-2004, No. 167/1; *Belgian Chamber*, 2003-2004, No. 393/1; *Belgian Chamber*, 2003-2004, No. 815/1. These proposals have also been echoed by the Arbitragehof, 8th October 2003 (2004) *Rev. trim. dr. fam.* 185-201, annotated RENCHON.

237 **Adoption:** Arts. 345-367, Belg. CC; **Full Adoption:** Arts. 368-370.

or cohabiting.[238] This therefore means that same-sex statutory cohabitants are prevented from adopting the same child.[239] Furthermore, step-parent adoption is prohibited unless the adoptive parent is married to the legal parent and of a different sex.[240] Those involved in a statutory cohabitation can, however, adopt individually, although this depends on the individual adoption service, since many automatically reject homosexual adoptive parents.[241]

III.5.9.4 Artificial Reproductive Techniques

In Belgium, it is the medical world and not the legal world that determines the rules on permission or denial of the availability to artificial reproductive techniques. As a result, a gynaecologist or fertility treatment centre is entitled to determine on a case-by-case basis whether or not to allow women to undergo fertility treatment and under what conditions.[242]

III.6 DISSOLUTION

III.6.1 GENERAL

Married couples do not possess a monopoly on relationship breakdown; relationships between statutory cohabitants break down too. Unlike marriage, where judicial proceedings are the only method available to couples wishing to terminate their relationship,[243] those wishing to terminate a statutory cohabitation must avail themselves of an administrative procedure; Art. 1476(2), Belg. CC does not provide a mechanism for the judicial termination of a statutory cohabitation. Although at first glance it might seem somewhat idiosyncratic that a legal institution regulating the relationship between two people cannot be judicially terminated, it is a logical result of the ways in which a statutory cohabitation may be terminated. Art. 1476(2), Belg. CC, provides for the

---

238 Arts. 343(1) Belg. CC, as amended by Act of 24th April 2003, *Belg. Staatsblad,* 16th May 2003. On law prior to this amendment see SENAEVE (2003b) p. 83, §905. This Act is, however, at the date of writing not yet in force.

239 SENAEVE (2003b) p. 84, §907.

240 SENAEVE (2003b) p. 86, §918. In this case, a number of special rules indicate that step-parent adoption is actually stimulated in Belgium: Art. 345(2), Belg. CC.

241 BORGHS (2004a) p. 297-298.

242 BORGHS (1998); BORGHS (2004a) p. 295-297.

243 Art. 227, Belg. CC.

unilateral, administrative termination of a statutory cohabitation.[244] Due to the fact that all rights and duties created by virtue of the statutory cohabitation are immediately terminated upon the dissolution of the statutory cohabitation,[245] and that the partners to a statutory cohabitation owe each other no duty of maintenance,[246] the other partner will gain nothing from resorting to judicial proceedings, thus rendering such a procedure redundant.

III.6.2 JUDICIAL: JOINT PETITION

As stated above, no judicial proceedings are possible.

III.6.3 JUDICIAL: UNILATERAL PETITION

As stated above, no judicial proceedings are possible.

III.6.4 ADMINISTRATIVE: JOINT DECLARATION

According to Art. 1476(2)(2), Belg. CC, a statutory cohabitation can be terminated when the parties make a joint declaration that they wish their statutory cohabitation to be terminated. The joint declaration must be made in writing and handed to the Registrar in the municipality where both parties have their common domicile or, if the parties do not have a common domicile, to the Registrar of the municipality where one of them has their domicile.[247] In the latter situation, the Registrar to whom the declaration is handed must send a signed letter of notification to the Registrar of the municipality of the other party's residence within eight days.

Moreover, the joint declaration must comply with certain conditions. The document must state the date of the declaration, the first name, surname, place and date of birth of both parties, the signature of both parties, the domicile of both parties, and a statement that the parties wish to end their statutory cohabitation.[248] No reason need be mentioned on the declaration as to why the partnership is to be terminated,[249] and any costs associated

244 See **Section III.6.5** for more details.

245 See **Section III.6.9** for more details.

246 SENAEVE (2003c) p. 218, §2059-5.

247 Art. 1476(2)(3), Belg. CC. See also DE KEZEL (1999) p. 137.

248 Art. 1476(2)(2), Belg. CC. See also DE BUSSCHERE (1999) p. 20-21.

249 SENAEVE (2003c) p. 218, §2059(4)-2059(5).

with the declaration must be borne equally by both parties.[250] If all the abovementioned conditions are satisfied, then the Registrar must make a note of the termination of the statutory cohabitation in the Population Register.[251]

III.6.5 ADMINISTRATIVE: UNILATERAL DECLARATION

Art. 1476(2), Belg. CC, also provides for the unilateral declaration by either one of the parties to terminate the statutory cohabitation.[252] In a similar fashion to the joint declaration, a unilateral declaration must be delivered to the Registrar of the common domicile of parties or if the parties do not have a common domicile, to the Registrar of one of their domiciles. The Registrar must give notice by means of a bailiff's summons (*exploit d'huissier de justice*) to the other party within eight days. He or she must also inform the Registrar of the domicile of the other party. The formal requirements are identical to those required for the submission of a joint declaration as stated above. Any costs associated with the declaration must be borne by the requesting party.[253] If all the abovementioned conditions are satisfied, then the Registrar must make a note of the termination of the statutory cohabitation in the Population Register.[254]

III.6.6 ANNULMENT PROCEEDINGS

A marriage may only be annulled on one of the grounds listed in Arts. 180 and 181, Belg. CC.[255] These grounds are more restrictive than those applicable to ordinary contracts, in that threats, misrepresentation as to character and injury do not suffice as grounds for the annulment of a marriage.[256] Annulment proceedings for statutory cohabitation, on the other hand, are regulated by the ordinary rules on the annulment of contractual obligations, thus providing a broader possible range of annulment grounds.[257] Furthermore, unlike marriage, where special rules allow for

---

250 Art. 1476(2)(5), Belg. CC. De Kezel (1999) p. 137.

251 Art. 1476(2)(6), Belg. CC.

252 Senaeve (1998) p. 257. This would be abolished according to Proposed Art. 1476(2), *Belg. CC, Belgian Chamber*, 2002-2003, No. 110/1, p. 27.

253 Art. 1476(2)(6), Belg. CC. De Kezel (1999) p. 137.

254 Art. 1476(2)(6), Belg. CC.

255 Two types of nullity: Absolute and relative. Senaeve (2003c) p. 55-57, §1574-1577.

256 Senaeve (2003c) p. 42-44, §1545-1549.

257 Misrepresentation, threats and injury are permitted: Arts. 1109-1118, Belg. CC.

third parties to prevent the celebration of a marriage, no such provisions apply to statutory cohabitation.[258]

III.6.7 DEATH AND PRESUMPTION OF DEATH

Art. 1476(2)(1), Belg. CC, provides for the termination of a statutory cohabitation by virtue of the death of one of the partners, along identical lines as the dissolution of a marriage by virtue of death.[259] The date of death is recorded as the date upon which the statutory cohabitation is terminated.[260] It should be noted that according to Belgian law, the absence of one of the spouses never leads to the termination of the marriage.[261] This rule has also been preserved in relation to statutory cohabitees, thus preventing a spouse or statutory cohabitee from remarrying or entering into another statutory cohabitation. Nonetheless, should a new statutory cohabitation nonetheless be registered and a bigamous relationship entered into, only the absent statutory cohabitee is authorised to request for an annulment of the (subsequent) statutory cohabitation.[262]

III.6.8 ENTRY INTO MARRIAGE / CONVERSION

A statutory cohabitation is brought to an end when either one or both of the parties enters into a marriage, whether with the other party to the statutory cohabitation or with a third party.[263] Spouses, on the other hand, cannot terminate their marriage by entering into a statutory cohabitation.[264] Since the 1st June 2003, this is option is also open to the couples of the same-sex.[265] The statutory cohabitation is terminated by operation of law and occurs at the moment of celebration of the marriage.[266] It was seen to be unnecessary and superfluous for a couple already in a statutory cohabitation, to first end their statutory cohabitation before celebrating a marriage.

---

258 SENAEVE (2003c) p. 61, §1590(1)-1590(3).

259 Art. 227(1), Belg. CC elucidates the same rule for the ending of a marriage.

260 The number of missing people declared is extremely low at around 5 per annum, despite the relatively high number of people who disappear. SENAEVE (2003c) p. 218, §62.

261 This is a result of the Belgian principle that absence does not have consequences upon the personal status of the absent person. See further, SENAEVE (2003a) p. 44, §62.

262 Art. 139, Belg. CC applied analogously. See further, SENAEVE (2003a) p. 44, §62.

263 Art. 1476(2)(1), Belg. CC. A conversion procedure was never discussed.

264 See **Section III.4.2**.

265 PERTEGÁS SENDER (2003) p. 261.

266 SENAEVE (1998) p. 257.

III.6.9 EFFECTS OF DISSOLUTION

A statutory cohabitation is deemed to have ended the day on which: a person dies, on which either one or both of the parties celebrate a marriage or on which the Registrar receives a declaration of termination.[267]

III.6.9.1 Maintenance

Unlike upon the termination of a marriage, where depending upon the ground for divorce, spouses are entitled to a maintenance claim,[268] statutory cohabitants are not entitled to claim maintenance, even if this is necessary and irrespective of the length of the statutory cohabitation.[269] This maintenance claim may however only be claimed on the basis that he or she cannot attain the same standard of living after the divorce as he or she enjoyed during the marriage.[270] A statutory cohabitant is also prevented from making a maintenance claim against the devolved estate should he or she be pre-deceased by his or her partner.[271]

III.6.9.2 Effects with respect to children

Since the declaration of a statutory cohabitation has no legal effect on any children involved in the relationship, all legal ties present upon the ending of the relationship will also remain intact. If either one or both of the parties were deemed to be the legal parent(s) of the child, then this will remain unaffected by the termination of the statutory cohabitation. If either one of the parties had been vested with parental authority, then once again such rights and obligations will continue unaffected.[272]

---

267 No waiting period is provided for this final method of termination, which includes a unilateral declaration of termination as well as a joint declaration.

268 Accordingly, if the counterclaim of the respondent spouse is successful, neither spouse is entitled to maintenance since they are both considered to be guilty: Belg. Cass., 5th February 1965 (1965) I *Pas.* 569. For further information see PINTENS/TORFS, in: BOELE-WOELKI/BRAAT/SUMNER (2003b) p. 41-42.

269 Divorce on grounds of fault: guilty spouse must pay; Divorce on the ground of separation: applicant must pay maintenance; Divorce on grounds of consent: depends on spousal agreements. SENAEVE (2003c) p. 218, §2059-4.

270 Art. 301(1), Belg. CC.

271 Non-application of Art. 205-*bis*, Belg. CC. See **Section III.5.8.** Nonetheless, if the statutory cohabitants are related to each other, they will indeed be able to make a maintenance claim against the other party: Arts. 205 and 207, Belg. CC.

272 PINTENS/PIGNOLET, in: BOELE-WOELKI/BRAAT/CURRY-SUMNER (2005) p. 276-277.

III.6.9.3 Effects with respect to property

Art. 1477(1), Belg. CC states that the rights afforded to statutory cohabitants by virtue of Art. 1477 are only amenable while the statutory cohabitation is still in existence. The termination of the statutory cohabitation thus brings to an end the protection of the "family home" at the time when that protection is probably most needed.[273] Nonetheless, a person previously involved in a statutory cohabitation who loses his or her rights over the "family home", does still retain his or her right to file a claim to the sub-district court judge on the basis of emergency, provisional measures, although the application of these regulations is limited to one year and the statutory cohabitant must bring their action within three months of the termination of the statutory cohabitation.[274]

[273] For further criticism see **Section III.5.6.**

[274] Art. 1479(3), Belg. CC.

CHAPTER IV
FRANCE

IV.1 INTRODUCTION

In 1999, France joined the ever-increasing list of countries to legislate for non-marital registered relationships. Legislation to introduce the so-called *pacte civil de solidarité* (hereinafter the PACS) was the result of more than a decade of parliamentary debate and political activity. This chapter will follow the same structure as the preceding chapter, dealing in turn with the most recent statistics on the number of PACSs to have been registered (**Section IV.2**), the historical precursors to the introduction of the PACS legislation (**Section IV.3**), how a PACS can be established (**Section IV.4**), the legal effects thereof (**Section IV.5**) and the procedures for the termination of a PACS (**Section IV.6**).

IV.2 EMPIRICAL EVIDENCE AND STATISTICS

PACSs are, in general, concluded between young, different-sex couples wishing to profit from the fiscal abatements provided for in the PACS legislation.[1] It is also true that the PACS is sometimes preferred since it is less complicated than remarrying (in relation to the termination procedures available) yet provides more protection than *concubinage*.[2] As a result of the passing of the Act of 6th August 2004, district courts are required to collate biannual statistics concerning the number of PACSs concluded within their territorial competency.[3] These statistics must include the number of PACSs dissolved, making note of the average length of the PACS and the average age of the parties concerned. Statistics on PACSs concluded before this date, compiled by the Ministry of Justice, were subject to a prohibition on recording the sex of parties. Nonetheless, one is able to discern that the sex of the parties varies substantially depending on the

---

1 FESTY (2001) p. 369. For tax implications, see further **Section IV.5.5** and **Section IV.5.8**.

2 FESTY (2001) p. 369.

3 Art. 16, Act of 6th August 2004, No. 2004-801 inserting Art. 14(1) the into Act of the 15th December 1999, No. 99-944.

municipality in which the PACS is registered; more same-sex PACSs are concluded in metropolitan districts than in rural areas.[4]

Table 3: *Number of marriages celebrated (as of July 2005)*

Year	Marriages
1999	286,191
2000	297,922
2001	288,255
2002	279,087
2003	275,963
2004	259,400
Total	**1,686,818**

Table 4: *Number of PACSs registered (July 2005)*[5]

Year	Registrations
1999	6,139
2000	22,108
2001	19,410
2002	24,979
2003	20,858
2004	37,605
Total	**131,099**

IV.3 HISTORICAL PERSPECTIVE

IV.3.1 EARLY HISTORY

In 1989 two important cases came before the French Supreme Court.[6] In the first case, *Secher v. Air France*, a male flight attendant sought a reduced-price plane ticket for his same-sex partner, as would have been available if his partner had been of different sex. The Court of Appeal in Paris held that expressions such as *conjoint en union libre, agent et sa concubine* and *vie maritale* could only be interpreted so as to cover the exclusive situation of

4 Rubellin-Devichi (2001) p. 419, §116; Rault (2003).

5 Statistics available from www.ined.fr/population-en-chiffres/france/index.html.

6 Fr. Cass., Soc. Ch., 11th July 1989, *Bull. civ.*, Vol. 311, No. 514 and *Bull. civ.*, Vol. 312, No. 515.

one man and one woman living together as though they were husband and wife. The expressions were intended to be based upon marriage and as such could not be extended to same-sex couples.[7] In the second case, *Ladijka v. Caisse primaire d'assurance maladie de Nantes*,[8] a woman was denied the benefit of her female partner's public health and maternity insurance cover, again coverage which would have been granted had her partner been of a different sex. The Court of Appeal in Rennes once again held that the concept of *vie maritale*, used in the applicable social security legislation, could only be applied to unmarried different-sex couples. The French Supreme Court affirmed both decisions.[9]

At the same time as the French Supreme Court's decisions, a perceptible movement was taking shape in France aimed at reforming conjugal life and eliminating the discrimination faced by non-married couples. Despite the generality of its stated aim, the primary goal was legal recognition of the union between two persons of the same sex.[10] Indeed, it was mainly groups concerned with defending the rights of homosexuals and those active in the ever continuing and increasing fight against AIDS who advocated law reform and rallied around the various parliamentary initiatives.

IV.3.2 CONTRAT DE PARTENARIAT CIVIL

In light of the repeated refusal by the French courts to recognise same-sex relationships, new legislation seemed to be the only way to find a suitable solution to the precarious legal situation of such couples. A catalogue of parliamentary proposals began in 1990 with a proposal submitted by Senator MÉLENCHAN concerning a *contrat de partenariat civil* (hereinafter the CPC).[11] Inspired by the suggestions of *Gaie pour les libertés* and *Homosexualité et Socialisme*, the CPC aimed at granting cohabitees the same social advantages offered to spouses. Its approach was universal, being open not only to couples involved in an intimate relationship but also to siblings and mere friends. This proposal was, however, never debated in the French Parliament and its impact was, at the very most, modest.

---

7 Cour d'Appel Paris, 1 Civ. Ch., 11th October 1995, on appeal from Conseil de prud'hommes de Paris, 14th November 1984, Case No. 8546.008/R (1986) *D* 380.

8 Cour d'Appel Rennes, 27th November 1985, on appeal from Commission de première instance de sécurité sociale de Nantes, 19th January 1984 (1986) *D* 380.

9 For discussion of the decisions, see annotated case by MARCEL DORWLING-CARTER (1990).

10 BORRILLO (2001a) p. 476.

11 *French Senate*, 25th June 1990 (Socialist), Act No. 422.

IV.3.3 CONTRAT D'UNION CIVILE

In 1992, National Assemblyman AUTEXIER and seven other members of the Socialist party presented a legislative proposal entitled the *contrat d'union civile* (hereinafter the CUC).[12] The initiative permitted an unmarried individual to enter into a CUC with any other unmarried individual regardless of the sex of the parties, so long as the parties were not related in the ascending or descending line. Although the Bill was never discussed in its entirety, two areas of the proposal, namely the rules on social welfare benefits and tenancies, were debated in detail. As a result of these discussions, amendments to allow for the availability of social welfare benefits to a dependent cohabitee regardless of the sex of the partner were adopted by the Parliament, effectively overturning the *Ladijka* decision.[13] Furthermore, the provisions that restricted the assignment of a lease to cohabitee of a different sex were subsequently declared unconstitutional.[14]

The lack of debate on the CUC proposal and the accompanying right-wing political shift as a result of the 1993 general election created an unsuitable climate for the discussion of the rights of same-sex couples.[15] Nonetheless, another similar CUC proposal was submitted in late 1993 by National Assemblymen MICHEL, CHEVÈNEMENT and SARRE.[16] The proposal was identical to the previous one apart from the areas of parental authority and social security, but once again failed to be discussed.

In the light of growing public apathy for the plight of same-sex couples and the Government's refusal to address the issue, the HIV/AIDS organisation, *Aides*, took an active role in pushing the debate forwards. In 1995, *Aides* proposed new legislation which would have introduced a *contrat de vie sociale*, attempting to eradicate many of the forms of discrimination endured by those most affected by the AIDS epidemic.[17] The proposal was aimed at the regulation of a couple's life and made reference to the same

---

12 *French National Assembly*, 25th November 1992 (Socialist), Act No. 3066.

13 Act of 27th January 1993, No. 93-121. For reference to *Ladijka* decision see fn. 8.

14 Conseil Const., 21st January 1993 (1993) *Rev. Dec. Con. Ct.* Decision No. 93-317.

15 The 1988 elections had produced the following results: *Rassemblement pour la République (RPR)*: 129 seats, *Parti Socialiste (PS)*: 262 seats and *Union pour la Démocratie Française (UDF)*: 130 seats. In 1993, the political claimate changed dramatically and the results were *Rassemblement pour la République (RPR)*: 247 seats, *Parti Socialiste (PS)*: 54 seats and *Union pour la Démocratie Française (UDF)*: 213 seats.

16 *French National Assembly*, 23rd December 1993 (Movement of Citizens), Act No. 880.

17 BORRILLO (2001a) p. 479.

prohibited degrees of marriage as listed in the French Civil Code. In 1995, the Mayor of Saint-Nazaire added momentum to this movement by declaring that he would begin issuing so-called "certificates of communal life" to any couple, regardless of sex.[18] By the end of the 1990s, more than 300 districts had adopted similar symbolic certificates.

IV.3.4 CONTRAT D'UNION SOCIALE

Even if the political climate was not suitable for progress to be made in protecting the rights of same-sex couples, activity in this field did not cease. On the 19th June 1996, Socialist Senators introduced a Bill aimed at broadening the right to transfer a lease after the death or desertion of the tenant to any person who had lived with the tenant for at least one year, regardless of the sex of the tenant.[19] Three days later, *Le Monde* published an appeal, co-signed by former Prime Minister ROCARD and six future Ministers, entitled "Towards a better citizenship: The CUS." On the 23rd January 1997, a group of socialists deposited a proposal to introduce a *contrat d'union sociale* (CUS).[20] A similar Bill was also introduced on 19th March 1997 in the French Senate.[21] The apparent discriminatory distinctions proposed in the field of immigration sparked fierce criticism from gay rights organisations and the Bill proceeded no further.[22] A proposal by the communist party aimed at improving the rights for unmarried couples also failed to achieve widespread support.[23]

IV.3.5 CONTRAT D'UNION CIVILE ET SOCIALE

The change in political power as a result of the 1997 general election in favour of the left presented the socialists with a window of opportunity.[24] On the 23rd July 1997, a group of parliamentarians, headed by National Assemblyman MICHEL presented a legislative proposal to the French

---

18 *Le Nouveau Observateur*, 27th September 1995.

19 *French Senate*, 19th June 1996 (Socialist), Act No. 454.

20 *French National Assembly*, 23rd January 1997 (Socialist), Act No. 3315.

21 *French Senate*, 19th March 1997 (Socialist), Act No. 274

22 *Aides Fédération Nationale*, 10th February 1997, "Une avancée pour le droit des personnes: le contrat d'union sociale à l'Assemblée nationale."

23 *French National Assembly*, 20th February 1997 (Communist), Act No. 3367.

24 1997 election results produced a resounding victory for the socialists: *Rassemblement pour la République (RPR)*: 134 seats; *Parti socialiste (PS)*: 241 seats; *Union pour la Démocratie Française (UDF)*: 108 seats.

National Assembly to create a *contrat d'union civile et sociale* (CUCS).[25] On the same day, the Socialists reintroduced the CUS in the French Senate for the second time.[26] The CUCS intended to create a second type of marriage, with the Registrar of Births, Deaths and Marriages (hereinafter the Registrar) being competent to register the contract. The principal objective of the CUCS was equality; granting same-sex partners the rights already offered to different-sex spouses. In many aspects the CUCS was, as its name suggests, a compromise between the CUC and the CUS.

The CUCS expressly avoided any reference to adoption or artificial reproduction techniques. The partners were not obliged to be faithful, nor were they obliged to live together. They were only obliged to perform the terms of the contract concluded by them, which could be ended by common agreement or by means of a judicial procedure. The CUCS sustained extensive criticism.[27] The essential objective of this contract was to achieve solidarity between the partners, without any mention of fidelity. In this respect some critics saw inconsistency.[28] The proposal was rejected by groups who repudiated the possibility of same-sex cohabitees being considered as a "pretended form of family". The ground for these allegations was that, *inter alia,* same-sex couples cannot procreate, therefore they can never constitute a family in the traditional sense. Such critics also considered homosexuals the negation of the family order.[29]

In light of increasing pluralism characterising French family law, many saw that the law should function not only to support marriage but also to support a variety of other relationships that people choose for themselves.[30] Thus the basic tenets of pluralism on the one hand and personal autonomy on the other should, it was argued, be reflected in the law itself.[31] Nonetheless, in view of the criticisms of the CUCS, the proposal was sidelined. Meanwhile, the communist party stepped up the debate in the National Assembly and the Senate with proposals to improve the rights of

---

25 *French National Assembly*, 23rd July 1997 (Radical/Movement of Citizens), Act No. 88.

26 *French Senate*, 23rd July 1997 (Socialist), Act No. 94.

27 For criticism of the CUS and CUCS see LEVENEUR (1997); MALAURIE (1997a) No. 35; CALAIS-AULOY (1998); GAUDU (1998); ROLAND (1998); CABRILLAC (1999). For support of the schemes: MOUTOUH (1998).

28 BEIGNIER (1999a).

29 MALAURIE (1997b) No. 35.

30 MOUTOUH (1998).

31 For an overview of the arguments see STEINER (2000).

unmarried couples, including same-sex couples.[32] Although the CPC, CUC, CUS and CUCS received varying degrees of support, none of the proposals were passed. In the spring of 1998, the Government commissioned two reports which were published before the summer of that year. The reports proposed yet two more solutions to the problems faced by couples living outside the protected ambit of marriage.[33]

IV.3.6 PACTE D'INTÉRÊT COMMUN

One of the reports, namely the HAUSER Report, proposed the introduction of a *pacte d'intérêt commun* (hereinafter the PIC). The most important difference between the CUCS and the PIC was that the new plan did not profess any comparison with marriage. By avoiding all reference to sexual and emotional relationships and providing more of an open agreement, the HAUSER Report aspired to avoid the ideological discussion which had thwarted the passage of the CUCS. The PIC was to have been created by a notarial act and could also have been created for a certain period of time.

The second report, effectuated by THÉRY, was more ambitious in its analysis. Submitted just a few weeks after the HAUSER report, it went beyond property issues and addressed the fundamental matters raised by those who called for the recognition of same-sex relationships. In point-blankly refusing to open civil marriage to couples of the same-sex and refusing to allow same-sex couples to jointly adopt, THÉRY argued for the maintenance of the symbolic order of western culture. The author proposed insertion of a sex neutral definition of unregistered cohabitation in the French Civil Code, but yet again, these proposals came under fierce attack. Homosexual lobby groups saw this as a weak comprimise, since it provided little acknowledgement of same-sex relationships. They argued, and rightly so in this author's opinion, that the acceptance of *de facto* cohabitation does not imply legal acceptance of same-sex relationships on any kind of par as that offered to different-sex couples. For many, unregistered cohabitation could not, under any circumstances, be reagrded as an institution, and thus the proposals were seen as too modest.

---

32 *French National Assembly*, 30th September 1997 (Communist), Act No. 249; *French Senate*, 1st December 1997 (Communist), Act No. 138.

33 HAUSER (1998) and THÉRY (1998).

IV.3.7 PACTE CIVIL DE SOLIDARITÉ

By the summer of 1998, the Government, now already firmly embarrassed by the apparent lack of support for a non-marital regulatory institution, invited two National Assemblymen, BLOCHE and MICHEL, to prepare a report which ultimately became law: the *pacte civil de solidarité* (PACS).[34] The proposed Bill was first presented for debate in the National Assembly on 9th October 1998. However, poor representation by the left-wing parties during the debate allowed the right-wing to call for a motion of unconstitutionality.

The unified condemnation of homosexuality by the right-wing parties had a counter-effect and unified those on the left against such homophobic tendencies. The palatability of the Bill was further enhanced by opening the PACS to different-sex couples as well.[35] When the Bill was reintroduced one month later,[36] a number of important amendments had been made, most notably that the PACS would be concluded not before the mayor but before the court clerk of the district court. New ambiguities were also introduced with the removal of an obligation of fidelity and cohabitation. Commentators argued as to whether the PACS would be able to be celebrated between close friends and whether it would be a legal union or a simple contract.[37]

These ambiguities indicated the political anxiety of the Socialist party in relation to legislating on the issue same-sex relationships. Yet although the majority of socialist MPs were openly hesitant about the aspirations of the PACS, socialist politicians also saw the need to maintain a unified stance against the conservatives and consequently espoused the proposal. The eventual debate lasted more than seventy hours and emotions ran extremely high.[38] Despite the countless amendments made in the ensuing months, the

---

34 BORRILLO (2001a) p. 481.

35 STEINER (2002) p. 1.

36 This was actually in response to five private members bills registered immediately after the vote of *exception d'irrecevabilité* on 9th October 1998.

37 SERIAUX (1998). Although SÉRIAUX highlights the legal ambiguities in relation to the CUC, many of the same legal ambiguities were raised with respect to the PACS.

38 Comments during the debate reaffirmed the homophobic sentiments of some members of the National Assembly. On 8th November, upon the announcement by the Minister of Justice that the PACS would not give same-sex couples the right to adopt, conservative deputy LALOUCHE shouted "so sterilise them!" and the conservative catholic deputy DE VILLIERS added "Your innovation, the PACS, is simply a return to barbarism."

Bill's first reading eventually ended on the 10th December 1998 with a majority of the deputies voting in favour.[39]

However, this was but a mere drop in the ocean compared to the political quagmire that ensued. A subsequent conflict between the French National Assembly and the Senate ended with the Senate removing the original essence of the National Assembly's Bill. The Senate instead introduced an article providing for a legal definition of unregistered cohabitation as an alternative to the PACS. Upon the return of the Bill, the National Assembly restored the majority of the provisions relating to the PACS,[40] although the amended provision on cohabitation was retained. When the Bill returned to the Senate for its second reading, the Senate simply refused to discuss it. Faced with this impasse, a cross-party commission was established in May 1999 in order to find a compromise. The commission could not find a compromise and instead sent the Bill back to the National Assembly for a third reading. On 30th June 1999, on the final day of the parliamentary session, the Senate refused to adopt the Bill at third reading.[41]

On 13th October 1999, the final vote took place in the National Assembly and the PACS was adopted by 315 votes to 249, with four abstentions. On the same day, 213 deputies and 115 Senators filed an application with the French Constitutional Court declaring the PACS legislation to be unconstitutional.[42] On 9th November 1999, the French Constitutional Court declared the law consistent with the Constitution,[43] and, after being signed by President CHIRAC on 15th November 1999, it was published in the Official Journal the following day.[44] It was only a matter of days before the first couples were able to register their partnerships under this new legislation.

---

39 On the second vote on the PACS, 300 Assemblymen voted in favour with 243 voting against. In the Senate, 216 voting resulted in an almost mirror image with 216 voting against and only 97 voting in favour of the proposal.

40 The provisions on the application of the law to the French overseas territories and the extension of certain consequences of the PACS to siblings were, however, not restored.

41 According to Art. 45, French Constitution, after three transmissions between the Senate and National Assembly, the National Assembly has the final say on the Bill.

42 Arts. 61 and 62, French Constitution allow for a majority of the Senate to challenge the constitutionality of an Act of Parliament (in order to compensate the effects of Art. 45).

43 For further discussion of the decision see **Chapter IX.**

44 Act of 15th November 1999, No. 99-944. Procedures relating to the PACS are detailed in Decrees No. 99-1089, 99-1090 and 99-1091, 21st December 1999 and Decrees No. 2000-97 and 2000-98, 3rd February 2000.

IV.4 ESTABLISHMENT

IV.4.1 POSITION OF THE INSTITUTION

The French Civil Code consists of three books: Book I (Persons), Book II (Property and methods for the modification of ownership) and Book III (Methods by which ownership can be acquired). A twelfth chapter, entitled "The PACS and cohabitation", was inserted into Book I.[45] In doing so, the French legislature established a third type of conjugal relationship located, in terms of legal importance, somewhere between marriage and pure, factual cohabitation. The placement of the PACS legislation signifies an intention on the part of the Government that this new institution was to be regarded as affecting the family life of those involved. Although, as will be discussed later, the celebration of a PACS does not explicitly create a new civil status, the situating of this legislation in Book I, Fr. CC is nonetheless of fundamental importance to the familial character of the PACS.

IV.4.2 EXCLUSIVITY

Like marriage, a PACS may only be concluded between two people.[46] Persons wishing to register a PACS will be prevented from doing so if either one of them is already married or already involved in a PACS.[47] As regards marriage, neither party may already be involved in another marriage. There is thus no prohibition on celebrating a marriage if one or both of the parties are involved in a PACS. Nonetheless, a PACS is brought to an immediate end by operation of law upon the celebration of a marriage.[48] As a result of this termination procedure, the principle of exclusivity is maintained, with these two institutions remaining legally exclusive.[49]

IV.4.3 SEX OF THE PARTIES

The signing of a PACS is open to two people, whether of a different or the same sex, with no reference made to the sexual orientation of the parties.[50]

---

45 *Concubinage* has been translated throughout this book as cohabitation. From time to time however, for ease of reading the French word *concubinage* has been retained.

46 **Marriage:** Art. 147, Fr. CC; **PACS:** Art. 515-1, Fr. CC.

47 Art. 515-2(2) and 515-2(3) Fr. CC.

48 Art. 515-7(3), Fr. CC.

49 For discussion of this method of dissolution, see **Chapter IV.6.8**.

50 Art. 515-1, Fr. CC.

Marriage, on the other hand, is still viewed in a traditional sense and can only be concluded between one man and one woman.[51] A marriage celebrated between two people of the same sex is null and void.[52] Since sex is irrelevant in determining the validity of a PACS, the problems raised by gender reassignment surgery with respect to marriages do not create similar problems with respect to the PACS legislation.[53]

IV.4.4 MINIMUM AGE

Unlike when registering a PACS where both parties must have attained the age of eighteen,[54] a woman wishing to marry need only to have reached the age of fifteen whilst a man must be eighteen.[55] The reason for the distinction is grounded in the perceived difference between the progression of men and women through puberty.[56] Nevertheless, with parental consent and consent of the *Procureur de la République* it is possible to dispense with this age requirement for aspirant spouses.[57] Moreover, minors who wish to marry are required to obtain parental consent.[58] No comparable exemption is allowed for in the PACS legislation.[59]

---

51 Classical interpretation of Art. 144, Fr. CC. See also CARBONNIER (2002) p. 419; GUIHO (1993) p. 38-40. The mayor of Bégles (a small town just outside Bordeaux) was in fact suspended for one month from the 15th June 2004 for performing a wedding ceremony for a couple of the same-sex: http://www.liberation.fr/page.php?Art.=226609. The marriage was, however, subsequently annulled. See further AGOSTINI (2004) and TGI Bordeaux, 27th July 2004.

52 According to nineteenth century doctrine, this ground of nullity would have led to a declaration of nullity as well as a declaration that the marriage never existed. Since 1953, this has been altered and now non-satisfaction of this condition leads to the nullification of the marriage: RUBELLIN-DEVICHI (2001) p. 68, §170-171.

53 For further references on the problem of transsexual marriages in France, see RUBELLIN-DEVICHI (2001) p. 25, §52.

54 Article 515-1, Fr. CC.

55 Art. 144, Fr. CC. For criticism of this distinction see HOUSERAND/HUET-WEILLER (1993) No. 132 *et seq.*

56 RUBELLIN-DEVICHI (2001) p. 26, §54.

57 Art. 145, Fr. CC. It must be proved that the parties have in fact reached puberty even though they have not reached the legal minimum age to celebrate a marriage, RUBELLIN-DEVICHI (2001) p. 26, §54.

58 Art. 146 *et seq*, Fr. CC. This consent is personal and non-replaceable. The person from whom consent is required differs depending on familial situation. For a full overview of competent persons see, CARBONNIER (2002) p. 429. Obviously these provisions only apply to women.

59 A minor even if emancipated cannot conclude a PACS: ROY (2002) p. 762.

IV.4.5 RESIDENCY

In order to register a PACS both parties must be resident in the same French municipality.[60] No exception to this rule is allowed. If the parties to a future PACS do not possess a common residence it is impossible for them to register a PACS.[61] The residency rules for those wishing to celebrate a marriage on the other hand are less restrictive. As long as one of the future spouses is domiciled in France or has been resident in France for at least one month on the date of publication of the celebration of the marriage, they will be allowed to celebrate their marriage.[62] Despite the relative flexibility of the law, an attempt has been made to ensure that at least one of the parties has a real connection to the place where the marriage is to be celebrated.

IV.4.6 PROHIBITED DEGREES OF RELATIONSHIP

A marriage is prohibited between ascendants and descendants in the direct line whether legal or natural. Although the same restriction applies to the registering of a PACS, the law is silent as to whether the relatives mentioned must be legal or natural relatives.[63] The French Constitutional Court has however reasoned that the objectives behind these prohibitions are identical.[64] As a result, the prohibition in the PACS legislation extends to legal and natural relatives.[65] Moreover, relatives in the indirect ascending or descending line up to and including the third degree are prevented from celebrating either a PACS or marriage.[66] During the parliamentary discussions, the same reasons for these general prohibitions were given as are used for the incest prohibitions elucidated for celebration of a

---

60 Art. 515-3, Fr. CC in conjunction with Art. 1, Decree of 21st December 1999, No. 99-1089. A person's residency is understood as a "stable and habitual bond" with reference to Cour d'Appel Dijon, 4th February 1986 (1987) *JNA* 452, annotated DE LA MARNIERRE; Fr. Cass., 1 Civ. Ch., 16th March 1999 (1999) V *JCP Éd. G.* 1887.

61 CARBONNIER (2002) p. 737. Nonetheless, this residence does not have to be a person's main place of residence. A secondary common residence in France is sufficient: REVILLARD (2000) p. 343, No. 21; MIGNOT (2001) p. 629.

62 Art. 74, Fr. CC.

63 **Marriage**: Art. 161, Fr. CC; **PACS**: Art. 515-2(1), Fr. CC.

64 Conseil Const., 9th November 1999, Decision No. 99-149, *JO* 16th November 1999, §§25 and 28.

65 Brothers and sisters are also prohibited from celebrating a marriage or a PACS on the basis of Art. 162, Fr. CC (**Marriage**) and Art. 515-2(1), Fr. CC (**PACS**).

66 **Marriage**: Art. 162 and 163, Fr. CC; **PACS:** Art. 515-2(1), Fr. CC.

marriage.[67] Therefore, even though expressed somewhat differently, it is submitted that the prohibitions in terms of the PACS are identical, or at the very least must be interpreted to be identical, to those imposed on future spouses.[68]

Marriages between ascendants and descendents as a result of adoption are prohibited without possibility for dispensation.[69] Art. 366(3) and 366(4), Fr. CC do, however, allow for the granting of an exemption from the prohibition for adopted brother and sisters. Since Art. 515, Fr. CC, is silent on the issue of whether Art. 366, Fr. CC, is *mutatis mutandis* applicable to those registering a PACS, one must assume that persons related by virtue of adoption are not prevented from registering a PACS.[70]

IV.4.7 COMPETENCY AND CONSENT

In order to register a PACS, the parties must satisfy the legal conditions of contractual competency laid down in Arts. 1109 *et seq.*, Fr. CC. These requirements state that both parties must provide valid consent for the contract to be enforceable. If a party's consent was furnished in error, extorted under duress or misrepresentation then the PACS will be null and void.[71] Similarly, both parties to a marriage must also validly consent to their marriage.[72] The complete absence of consent will lead to the annulment of the marriage.[73] Moreover, if the consent was not free, a spouse may apply to have the marriage annulled.[74]

A person subject to such a *tutelle* guardianship[75] may not celebrate a marriage without the express consent of his or her parents and, failing that, the express consent of the family council specially convened for this purpose.[76] In either case, the opinion of a medical physician is required.[77]

67 RUBELLIN-DEVICHI (2001) p. 421, §1171.

68 BATTEUR (2000).

69 Art. 366(1), Fr. CC.

70 BENABENT (2001) p. 258, §437.

71 Art. 1109, Fr. CC.

72 Art. 146, Fr. CC.

73 CORNU (2003) p. 308, §188.

74 Although the grounds for the annulment of the marriage are more restrictive than for the PACS, see **Section IV.6.6** for further details.

75 A *tutelle* guardianship is imposed permanently on any adult suffering from an alteration in their mental faculties by reason of sickness, infirmity, or age: Arts. 492-507, Fr. CC.

76 Art. 506(1) and (2), Fr. CC.

77 Art. 506(3), Fr. CC. TERRÉ/FENOUILLET (1996) p. 283, §357.

Parties subject to *tutelle* guardianship may not register a PACS, however, under any circumstances.[78] If, once a PACS has been concluded, a person subsequently becomes subject to a *tutelle* guardianship order, then the other partner, the family council or judge of guardianships may request that the PACS be brought to an end.[79]

According to Art. 514, Fr. CC, a person subject to a *curatelle* guardianship[80] is able to celebrate a marriage if he or she has the consent of his or her guardian, or, failing that, the judge of guardianships. However, the PACS legislation remains silent on whether a person subject to a *curatelle* guardianship is able to register a PACS. Commentators are nonetheless agreed that a person under a *curatelle* guardianship is subject to the same conditions as those imposed on someone wishing to marry.[81]

IV.4.8 FORMAL VALIDITY

The formalities that need to be met prior to the celebration of a marriage and the registration of a PACS are entirely different. Although at times the PACS legislation seems to have drawn inspiration from the marriage ceremony, there are few similarities to be found.[82] This section will thus focus on the formalities for the registration of a PACS.

IV.4.8.1 Preparatory phase

The basic PACS agreement must be made in writing, and it is here that the first differences with respect to marriage occur. Due to the PACSs contractual nature, the preliminaries to the registration of a PACS resemble more the formalities prior to the signing of a contract than the formalities prior to the celebration of a marriage. Although Art. 515-3, Fr. CC, lays down stringent criteria for the formal registration of the PACS agreement, no criteria are imposed on the content of such an agreement.[83] Nonetheless, it is clear that any provisions agreed upon cannot run counter to the very

---

78 Art. 506-1(1), Fr. CC states that parties must be natural persons of age. This Article implies that the parties are therefore not subject to a *tutelle* guardianship: see RUBELLIN-DEVICHI (2001) p. 420, §1170; CORNU (2003) p. 105.

79 Art. 506-1(2) and 506-1(3), Fr. CC. RUBELLIN-DEVICHI (2001) p. 61, §144 and p. 431 §1185; PILLEBOUT (2000) p. 82, §172. See **Section V.6.6.** RUBELLIN-DEVICHI (1999) p. 1909.

80 The *curatelle* guardianship, is used for temporary situations: Arts. 508-515, Fr. CC.

81 FRENSEL (2001); BÉNABENT (2003) p. 291, §436; GRANET/LÉCUYER (1999/2001) No. 40-43.

82 RAULT (2003).

83 BRAAT (2000) p. 77.

essence of the PACS legislation.[84] The Ministry of Justice has however recommended that those wishing to register a PACS do so after consultation with a notary or lawyer.[85] Whatever provisions are eventually drawn up in the agreement, the agreement must be made in duplicate.[86] The law does not impose the requirement, as was proposed during the parliamentary proceedings, that a notarial deed be drafted.[87] The agreement can thus be drafted by means of a private simple agreement in the form of an authentic instrument or by notarial deed.[88]

IV.4.8.2 Registration phase

For the PACS to acquire public law effects and be effective against third parties, French law requires that the PACS be publicly accessible.[89] Accordingly, once the agreement has been concluded the partners must register it by means of a joint declaration at the district court of the partners' common residence.[90] No prescribed form of celebration is necessary.[91] The parties must simply supply the necessary documentation,[92] and have the agreement made in duplicate.[93] The district court clerk can only register the declaration if he or she is satisfied that all the necessary formal conditions have been fulfilled.[94] Once all the formalities have been

---

84 Conseil Const., 9th November 1999, Decision No. 99-149, *JO*, 16th November 1999.

85 MINISTRY OF JUSTICE, "Pacte civil de solidarité (PACS). Mode d'emploi", available on the internet at: http://www.justice.gouv.fr/justicef/pacs2.html.

86 Art. 515-3(4), Fr. CC.

87 *French National Assembly*, 8th November 1998 (MICHEL), p. 8506.

88 VIVIER (2001) p. 31, §27; COMBRET (1999).

89 Art. 515-3(6), Fr. CC. RUBELLIN-DEVICHI (1999).

90 Art. 515-3, Fr. CC in conjunction with Decree of 21st December 1999, No. 99-1089. For the reasons why the PACS is not registered at the same place as marriages, see earlier, **Section V.3.7**.

91 Celebration of the marriage must be public, and the parties must first celebrate a civil marriage prior to any religious celebration: *Loi du 11 germinal an XI* imposed this sanction and any minister who celebrates a religious wedding prior to a civil service is guilty of a crime according to Art. 433-21, Fr. Cr. C. See further, CARBONNIER (1981) p. 1007.

92 Decrees No. 99-1089 and 99-1090, 21st December 1999.

93 RUBELLIN-DEVICHI (2001) p. 431 §1185; PILLEBOUT (2000) p. 421, §1172.

94 CORNU (2003) p. 110. Unlike a PACS, a marriage is concluded by the mayor. The symbolic nature is thus emphasised by the presence of a State official adorned with a French tricolour.

discharged, the district court clerk must register the agreement in the specified register.[95]

According to Art. 515-3, Fr. CC, the PACS is legally binding on third parties only after it has been registered by the district court clerk.[96] This provision has, however, caused considerable disagreement amongst legal scholars. BEIGNER, a staunch supporter of the view that the PACS is an institutional contract,[97] envisages problems with this provision if the PACS has been created by means of a notarial deed. A notarial deed becomes binding when it is signed, whereas according to the widely supported view, the PACS only becomes binding once it has been registered by the district court clerk of the place of birth of the parties. A problem therefore arises with respect to the date upon which a PACS created by notarial deed becomes effective. Nonetheless, the French Minister of Justice has reaffirmed that the PACS agreement will only become binding from the date of registration by the district court clerk.[98]

IV.4.8.3 Administrative phase

The third and final stage of the registration of a PACS requires the district court clerk to send the agreement without delay to the district court of the place of birth of each of the partners, where it is also registered.[99] The district court clerk must ensure that each of the agreements is dated and stamped and must then return them to the parties.[100] The registration process only provides for the compulsory registration of the existence of a PACS, and does not provide for the registration of the agreement itself. This places third parties in a weak position. This position is made even weaker by the advice of the *Commission Nationale de l'Informatique et des*

---

95 This register is maintained in chronological order: "Circulaire relative aux modalités de l'enregistrement des déclarations de pacte civil de solidarité dès le promulgation de la loi". Available on the internet at: http://www.justice.gouv.fr/publicat/cirpacs/html.

96 Art. 515-3(6), Fr. CC.

97 As opposed to marriage which is a contractual institution: BEIGNER (2001) p. 232-236.

98 "It is the registration by the district court clerk which gives the contract its date and makes it enforceable against third parties, not the date on which the PACS was drafted or registered with a notary": *Réponse ministérielle*, 23rd October 2000, *JO*, No. 47664, p. 6134, *JCP Éd. N.*, 2000, p. 1724. See also Art. 515-3(6), Fr. CC. In contrast, see GRIMALDI (2001) p. 931, §4404.

99 Art. 515-3(2), Fr. CC. In the case of a person not having a place of birth in France, the agreement is sent to the district court of Paris. The register in the birth-place is maintained alphabetically.

100 Art. 514-3(4), Fr. CC.

Libertés, stating that access to the register should remain extremely restricted to protect the privacy of those concerned.[101] The reason for this restriction was founded in the Commission's opinion that although the PACS legislation bore witness to the changing moral attitude of society, prejudices had not completely disappeared.[102] Furthermore, a PACS agreement may be modified any at time. The parties must make a joint declaration to that effect before the clerk of the district court where they registered their initial PACS agreement. The same procedure applies to the modification as to the original declaration of the PACS.[103]

IV.5 LEGAL EFFECTS

IV.5.1 GENERAL

The main difference between the PACS and the other forms of non-marital registered relationship discussed in this book is that the PACS is an open agreement. The parties can choose to regulate the areas they wish and create the outcomes they desire, so long as the agreements reached remain within the scope and aim of the law. The parties are prohibited from contracting out of certain rights and duties, which will be discussed in **Section IV.4.6.1**.

IV.5.2 CIVIL STATUS

The notion of civil status or *d'état civil*, according to French law, stems from the separation of church and State after the French Revolution.[104] Prior to this separation, the church was responsible for the registration of births (baptisms), marriages and deaths (burials). When the church and State were eventually separated, the State saw the need for the regular and consistent registration of such information and thus introduced the concept of *l'état civil*.[105] According to Art. 35, Fr. CC, only those details contained in Title II, Book 1, may be registered by the Registrar, including births, deaths

---

101 Opinion of the *Commission Nationale de l'Informatique et des Libertés*, 25th November 1999.

102 Similar arguments were also used with respect to the collection of data on the number of PACSs being registered. See also **Section IV.2**.

103 RUBELLIN-DEVICHI (2001) p. 421, §1172.

104 PLASSCHAERT (2002) p. 3.

105 This was introduced into the French Civil Code on the 20th September 1792.

and marriages.[106] Accordingly, only information which is registered by the Registrar is capable of having an impact on the civil status of the parties involved.

Unlike marriage, which entails a change in the civil status of the parties involved, a PACS involves no change of the parties' civil status. The marriage ceremony is extremely formalistic, with the Registrar obliged to read aloud the provisions in Arts. 212-215, Fr. CC. He or she must also request for the verbal confirmation of both spouses and their parents, should this be required. Once all these formalities have been completed, the Registrar can pronounce the parties man and wife according to the law and effect a change in their civil status.[107] All of these formalities are notable in their absence from the PACS legislation. One of the original reasons espoused by the drafters of the legislation for refusing to allow the PACS to affect one's civil status was that of privacy.[108] All the records of civil status in France are public and as such open to public inspection. The drafters of the legislation, wishing to protect the privacy of some couples who might not have wanted others to know that they had signed a PACS, opted for a scheme which would have no effect on one's civil status, thus removing the associated privacy problems. The French Constitutional Court highlighted the absence of an effect on the parties' civil status, "*la conclusion d'un pacte civil de solidarité ne donne lieu à l'établissement d'aucun acte d'état civil, l'état civil des personnes qui le concluent ne subissant aucune modification*".[109]

However, despite the fact that the PACS is not registered by the Registrar as is the case in marriage,[110] and despite the fact that the French Constitutional Court has already stated that the signing of a PACS has no bearing on one's civil status, the PACS legislation does create a quasi-marital, registered, institutionalised scheme for the registration of relationships. It is argued that despite not having direct, tangible effects on one's *civil status*, the PACS does, at the very least, affect one's personal status or *le statut*

106 The Registrar is also competent to register name changes, the recognition of a child *etc.*

107 CARBONNIER (2002) p. 451-452.

108 RAULT (2003).

109 Conseil Const., 9th November 1999, Decision No. 99-149, *JO*, 16th November 1999, §29.

110 Arts. 75(6) and 76, Fr. CC. Art. 75(6) states that an instrument of civil status must be drawn up immediately, whereas Art. 76 lays down the requirements concerning the information which must be included in the instrument.

personnel. This concept is crucial at the private international law level and will be discussed in **Chapter IX.2**.

IV.5.3 NATIONALITY

French nationality can be acquired, as opposed to attributed, in one of four ways: by reason of marriage, by reason of birth and residence in France, by reason of a declaration of nationality, or by reason of a decision of the Government (hereinafter the naturalisation procedure).[111]

Although marriage, as of itself, does not affect one's nationality, it can have an indirect effect on some of the other methods of acquiring French nationality.[112] If a person marries a French national, then he or she is entitled to acquire French nationality as long as the marriage has subsisted for two years and a number of other conditions are satisfied.[113] The spouse must make a declaration of nationality and at the time of making this declaration the spouses' *communauté de vie* must be effective.[114] One spouse must possess French nationality and the spouse wishing to acquire French nationality must have a sufficient knowledge of the French language. If the spouse cannot prove that he or she has lived in France for a uninterrupted period of one year since the date of the marriage, then the probationary period is increased to three years from the date of the marriage.[115]

The naturalisation procedure in contrast is much longer and arduous. Six conditions must be satisfied before a person may be able to acquire nationality using this procedure. The applicant must be ordinarily resident in France at the time of the application, have been habitually resident in France for the previous five years, be at least eighteen years of age, not have been sentenced for serious criminal offences, be of good character and be able to demonstrate that he or she is now assimilated into French society (*e.g.* proficiency in the French language).[116] The five-year residence period required of persons wishing to acquire French nationality can however be

---

[111] Art. 21-1 to 21-25(1), Fr. CC.

[112] Art. 21-1, Fr. CC.

[113] Art. 21-2, Fr. CC as amended by the Act of 26th November 2003, No. 2003-1119.

[114] This provision has been introduced to prevent the acquisition of French nationality by those involved in so-called "sham marriages".

[115] Arts. 21-4 and 26-3, Fr. CC deal with those situations when the Minister of Justice or other competent authority may refuse to grant nationality on this basis. Non-linguistic assimilation is not one of those grounds: Art. 21-4, Fr. CC.

[116] Art. 21-16 to 21-24, Fr. CC.

reduced to two-years if the applicant has successfully completed two years of university education in view of obtaining a diploma conferred by a French university or establishment of higher education, if the applicant can show that owing to his or her talents he or she can provide significant services to France.[117]

In terms of the PACS, no changes to the law on nationality were effected. Accordingly, even if a PACS has been registered, the non-French national(s) will not be permitted to exploit the swifter nationality acquisition procedure provided for spouses, and must thus apply as an individual according to the naturalisation procedure.[118] This obviously places those foreigners involved in a PACS at a disadvantage compared to their married counterparts, since they must be resident in France for at least five years instead of two. Nonetheless, the PACS does provide an "element of appreciation" for obtaining a French residence permit.

IV.5.4 NAME LAW

French law recognises two types of surnames: *le nom transmis* and *le nom d'usage*. The *nom transmis* is a name connected to one's parentage, and is immutable.[119] As a result it is detached from the marital status of an individual or the existence of a PACS. Although a person is always entitled to change their *nom transmis* to parallel that of their partner, it is virtually inconceivable that such a procedure would be successful.[120]

The *nom d'usage* is not transmittable but can be affected by one's marriage as well as by parentage.[121] This situation has however remained unaffected with the passing of the PACS legislation and as a result persons who have registered a PACS are not entitled to change their *nom d'usage*. According to French tradition, the wife has always taken the name of her husband.[122] This tradition has since been confirmed in both case law and scholarly

---

117 Art. 21-18, Fr. CC.

118 Bénabent (2001) p. 266, §455.

119 Terré/Fenouillet (1996) p. 127, §153.

120 Terré/Fenouillet (1996) p. 142-143, §174. A change of surname is only allowed under very restricted circumstances should a legitimate interest be proven by the applicant (Art. 61(1), Fr. CC), such as the possible extinction of an existing surname (Art. 61(2), Fr. CC).

121 This position has been affirmed by Art. 2.3.1 of a circular issued by the Prime Minister on the 26th June 1986: "*la nature juridique du nom d'usage exclut toute mention à l'état civil et sur le livret de la famille*".

122 Rubellin-Devichi (2001) p. 87, §246.

writing,[123] and continues to thrive in French society today.[124] Although a wife make take her husband's surname entirely, or affix his surname to her own, either before or after her own surname, a husband is only permitted to append his wife's surname to his own, whether before or after his own surname.[125] Hence, although a wife may use her husband's surname to entirely replace her own surname, such an option is not available to a male spouse.[126] The parties to a PACS, on the other hand, are prohibited from benefiting from such privileges.[127]

IV.5.5 TAXATION, SOCIAL SECURITY AND PENSIONS

Although in principal the parties to a PACS are deemed to be a joint fiscal unit assimilated to the degree of a married couple for the purposes of income tax and local taxation,[128] a distinction between them must be made. Although joint taxation for spouses commences the day of celebration of the marriage,[129] three years must first have elapsed before parties to a PACS will be deemed eligible for joint taxation.[130] Once this time period has elapsed partners having registered a PACS and those having celebrated a marriage are treated for all intents and purposes as identical in these two fields of taxation. In terms of wealth tax, those having entered into a PACS are

---

123 Fr. Cass., 1 Civ. Ch., 16th March 1941 (1941) I *D* 210; Fr. Cass., 1 Civ. Ch., 6th November 1985 (1986) *D* 168; TGI Nîmes, 15th December 1810 (1811) *S* 260: "*Les pères seuls, en qualité de chefs de famille, transmettent leur nom à leurs enfants et les mères, perdant le leur dans le mariage, sont privées dur droit de le transmettre à l eurs descendants*"; DEKEUWER-DEFOSSEZ/DECOUX (2002) Étude 271; RUBELLIN-DEVICHI (2001) p. 87 *et seq*, §246 *et seq*.

124 According to recent statistics more than 91% of women take their husband's surname after marriage: VALETAS (2001) p. 2. This is compared with United Kingdom: 94%, The Netherlands: 55%, and Belgium: 22%.

125 The ability of the husband to put his wife's name first is only recent development and prior to Govt. Circular, 26th June 1986, the husband was only allowed to take his wife's name after his own: (1986) *D* 393, §2.2.1 and §2.3.2.

126 DEKEUWER-DEFOSSEZ/DECOUX (2002) Étude 269-67; RUBELLIN-DEVICHI (2001) p. 87 *et seq*, §247; CORNU (2003) p. 47.

127 TGI Briey, 30th June 1966 (1967) II *JCP Éd. G.* 15130; GRANET/LÉCUYER (1999/2001) No. 46. Including for artistic reasons: Cour d'Appel Paris, 17th April 1989 (1989) *D* 160.

128 GRANET/LECUYER (1999/2001) No. 89.

129 **Income tax:** Art. 6(1)(2), Fr. GTC; **Local Tax:** DIBOS-LACROUX (2001) p. 43.

130 Art. 6(1)(3), Fr. GTC inserted by virtue of Art. 4, Act of 15th November 1999, No. 99-944. It must also be noted that this is not an option; once three years have elapsed the parties to a PACS are obliged to submit joint tax returns. This joint tax return concerns their wages and other sources of income. Art. 6, Act of 15th November 1999 added an extra paragraph to Art. 885-A, Fr. GTC.

treated in exactly the same manner as their spousal counterparts from the moment the PACS becomes binding.[131]

Health and maternity insurance are also extended equally to spouses and PACS partners.[132] In various other areas, the rights of married couples have been extended to parties who have registered a PACS, namely in terms of joint civil service job transfers,[133] simultaneous holiday leave[134] and bereavement leave.[135] In the field of pensions, no change has resulted from the passage of the PACS legislation. The ability of the surviving spouse to claim the pension of his or her deceased spouse has thus not been correspondingly extended to those involved in a PACS.

IV.5.6 RIGHTS AND DUTIES OF THE PARTNERS TO EACH OTHER

As already stated, the main difference between the PACS and the other forms of non-marital registered relationship discussed in this book lies in the fact that the French PACS is an open agreement. The parties to a PACS are able to choose to regulate those issues which they wish to regulate, so long as the agreements reached remain within the ambit of the law.[136] As a result, the PACS legislation is in fact more noticeable for the absence of duties and rights imposed on the parties than the opposite. The majority of the rights and duties imposed on spouses are clearly absent with respect to the PACS. However, a number of rights and duties cannot be avoided by those wishing to register a PACS agreement. The inalienable nature of these particular rights and duties will be explored in more detail in this section.

---

131 See earlier under **Section IV.4.8.2** for the date on which the PACS becomes binding. Goods used for professional purposes, such as industrial, commercial, artistic or agricultural goods are, by virtue of Art. 885N, Fr. GTC, excluded from the scope of this provision. By virtue of a memo sent on the 6th January 2000, parties to a PACS are also assimilated to their married counterparts should this exclusion be applied.

132 A benefit which had already been granted to cohabitants if they were "effectively, totally and permanently dependent" on the partner, Act of 27th January 1993, No. 93-121.

133 GRANET/LECUYER (1999/2001) No. 107.

134 Art. L-223-7, *in fine*, Fr. EC grants those working for the same employer a right to have simultaneous holidays.

135 Art. L-226-1(4), Fr. EC grants 2 days leave in the case of the death of a PACS partner.

136 CORNU (2003) p. 106.

IV.5.6.1 Duty to cohabit

The duty imposed on spouses to maintain a *communauté de vie*, encompassing a number of interrelated elements, is not extended to parties who have registered a PACS.[137] However, the PACS is aimed at the regulation of the parties' *vie commune*. Despite the obvious difference in the terminology used, it is difficult to comprehend a difference in the content of these duties. In fact, CORNU uses the phrases *communauté de vie* and *vie commune* synonymously.[138] By virtue of the duty to maintain a *communauté de vie*, spouses are obliged to share the same home and thus the same place of residence: a duty of factual cohabitation.[139] The French Constitutional Court has held that as a result of the obligation to register their agreement in their common residence, the parties to a PACS are equally subject to the obligation to cohabit.[140]

The spousal *communauté de vie* also touches upon the more basic needs of the marital pair, thus demanding that the pair work at maintaining the harmonious nature of the marriage: a duty of spiritual cohabitation.[141] This is also evident in the PACS legislation by virtue of Art. 515-4(1), Fr. CC, in that the parties are obliged to provide each other with mutual and material support.[142] The final element of the spousal duty to maintain a *communauté de vie* is the duty to maintain a sexual relationship, even though such a duty is unenforceable at law: a duty of sexual cohabitation.[143] This duty is inextricably intertwined with the principle of marital exclusivity[144] and adultery as a factor to be taken into account in fault based divorce proceedings.[145] Despite the similarities between the PACS and marriage in

---

137 Art. 215, Fr. CC.

138 CORNU (2003) p. 50, §25.

139 Even if the parties' central places of business are different or their domiciles are different, they are still obliged to cohabit: CORNU (2003) p. 50, §25; RUBELLIN-DEVICHI (2001) p. 92-93, §257. The place of cohabitation is now called the "common residence" (*résidence commune*) and not the "marital domicile" (*domicile conjugal*).

140 Conseil Const., 9th November 1999, Decision No. 99-149, *JO* 16th November 1999; BRAAT (2000) p. 75 at 77.

141 CORNU (2003) p. 52, §26.

142 See **Section IV.5.6.3.**

143 RUBELLIN-DEVICHI (2001) p. 91-92, §256. This duty harks back to the days of canonical law, which stated that the definition of marriage included the *copula carnalis:* CORNU (2003) p. 51, §25. In etymological terms, this is where the word "couple" derives from.

144 See **Section IV.3.2.**

145 Divorce law has been radically altered by the enactment of the Act of 26th May 2004. Prior to this Act, adultery could be taken into account if it could be described as an act

relation to the other two elements of this duty, it is with respect to the duty of sexual cohabitation that the comparison stops, since this was clearly not the intention of the French Parliament.[146]

IV.5.6.2 Duty of fidelity

Art. 212, Fr. CC, imposes a duty of spousal fidelity; a duty almost inseverable from the duty to cohabit. This duty has not, however, been correspondingly applied to those involved in a PACS; infidelity is thus without sanction for parties to a PACS. In relation to marriage, the duty of fidelity and the duty to cohabit have formed the backbone of French marriage laws since the introduction of the Napoleonic Codes.[147] The provision imposes an obligation to have monogamous sexual relations with one's spouse, avoiding any form of sexual intercourse with third parties, including acts preliminary to sexual intercourse.[148] Regardless of its importance, this duty is not applicable to the PACS legislation. Nonetheless, this too has recently been thrown into doubt.[149]

IV.5.6.3 Duty to provide support and assistance

Although spouses are subject to a duty to provide support and assistance to each other,[150] parties to a PACS are not subject to an identical obligation.[151] Despite the apparent blank slate upon which parties to a PACS are able to draw up their agreement, the partners are not allowed to derogate from the obligation to provide each other with mutual and material assistance.[152] The French Constitutional Court stressed the obligatory nature of this provision. It held that the particular nature of the assistance must be specified in a

---

that led to a serious or renewed breach of marital duties (Art. 242, Fr. CC). See further LEMOULAND (2004).

146 A situation which was absolutely not the intention of the French Parliament. This is no more noticeable than in the absence of a duty of fidelity. See **Section VI.4.8.1.B.**

147 It is true, however, that these duties have not always been equally imposed on both spouses. Art. 215, Fr. CC previously stated: "*La femme est oblige d'habiter avec son mari, le mari est tenu de recevoir sa femme.*" Amended by the Act of 4th June 1970, No. 70-459.

148 Case law in France has concluded that adultery consists of not only a material element but also an element of intention: Fr. Cass., 2 Civ. Ch., 3rd May 1995 (1995) *Bull. Civ,* No. 130. See also RUBELLIN-DEVICHI (2001) p. 89-91, §253-254.

149 TGI Lille, 5th June 2002, annotated LABBÉE (2003) *D*519.

150 Art. 212, Fr. CC.

151 Art. 515-4, Fr. CC.

152 Art. 515-4, Fr. CC.

PACS agreement; the parties to a PACS are not allowed to avoid the application of such a requirement altogether.[153]

It must also be noted that spouses are under a duty to provide moral and material guidance "for the family",[154] whilst parties to a PACS are only under a duty to provide for the mutual and material support "of each other".[155] The unwillingness to refer to children in the PACS legislation coupled with a number of compromises settled in 1998, has led to ambiguity surrounding the extent to which parties to a PACS are subject to the same duties imposed on spouses with respect to the provision of support and assistance for children. It would appear from the wording of this provision that spouses and parties to a PACS are subject to an identical duty with respect to each other, but are also subject to the same duty in relation to their children.

IV.5.6.4 Duty to contribute to household expenses

Both spouses are equally obliged to contribute to the expenses of the marriage in proportion to their means.[156] The obligation to contribute applies even if the other spouse is not in need of such contribution, differing substantially from the law of maintenance, and cannot be contracted out of.[157] Despite the absence of an explicit reference to Art. 214, Fr. CC some commentators have argued that Art. 515-4(1), Fr. CC imposes the same obligation on parties to a PACS.[158] CARBONNIER, for example, has argued that the absence of a direct reference to Art. 214, Fr. CC simply made the legislation more palliative and in effect the duty is encompassed in the duty to provide "material assistance".[159]

IV.5.6.5 Duty to contribute to the repayment of debts

Art. 220, Fr. CC provides that each spouse is jointly and severely liable for all debts incurred in connection with the upkeep of the marital home and

---

153 Conseil Const., 9th November 1999, Decision No. 99-149, *JO*, 16th November 1999, §31. If a dispute arises as to the form of assistance, the matter may be resolved by the courts: VIVIER (2001) p. 32, §28.

154 Art. 213, Fr. CC.

155 Art. 515-4(1), Fr. CC.

156 Art. 214, Fr. CC.

157 Fr. Cass., 1 Civ. Ch., 23rd June 1970 (1971) *D* 162, annotated LARROUMET.

158 RUBELLIN-DEVICHI (2001) p. 424, §1177 and references.

159 CARBONNIER (2002) p. 739.

the education of the children.[160] Although parties to a PACS are held jointly and severely liable for the debts incurred by one of them with respect to the needs of everyday life and the expenses related to the common household by virtue of Art. 515-4(2), Fr. CC, it is unclear whether this duty covers the same scope as that imposed on spouses.[161] Firstly, it is unclear whether "*l'entretien du mariage*" and "*les besoins de la vie*" are to be interpreted in a similar fashion. Secondly, it is unclear whether the duty imposed on parties to a PACS equally extends to the education of children. Art. 220, Fr. CC states this explicitly whereas Art. 515-4(2), Fr. CC is silent on the matter. Since Parliamentary intent was very clear that the PACS was to have no impact on children, it would seem difficult to justify extending this duty to the education of children. It is also unclear, as ALLEAUME acknowledges, whether parties to a PACS are protected from manifestly excessive purchases, as is the case with spouses.[162] Regardless of whether the parties are entitled to such protection, the French Constitutional Court has stated that despite the uncertainty, parties to a PACS are always entitled to resort to tortious liability.[163]

IV.5.6.6 Protection of the home

(a) *Rented property*: Like spouses,[164] those involved in a PACS and not named on the tenancy are protected should the tenant abandon the "familial" home or die prematurely.[165] Furthermore, the lessor may terminate the tenancy under certain conditions either for his or her benefit or for the benefit of his or her spouse or PACS partner.[166] However, unlike spouses, parties to PACS are not protected from the unilateral decisions of the tenant.[167] Hence, the tenant is permitted to terminate the tenancy without the prior authorisation of his or her PACS partner. Furthermore, in

---

160 Conseil Const., 9th November 1999, Decision No. 99-149, *JO*, 16th November 1999, §25.

161 GRIMALDI (2001) p. 933, §4411.

162 ALLEAUME (2000) p. 453.

163 Conseil Const., 9th November 1999, Decision No. 99-149, *JO*, 16th November 1999, §25; RUBELLIN-DEVICHI (2001) p. 426, §1179.

164 Art. 1751(3), Fr. CC.

165 Art. 14, Act No. 89-462 of 6th July 1989, as amended by Act No. 99-944 of 15th November 1999. See further GRANET/LÉCUYER (2001) §164.

166 Art. 15, Act No. 89-462 of 6th July 1989, as amended by Act No. 99-944 of 15th November 1999. See further GRANET/LÉCUYER (2001) §165.

167 Art. 1751, Fr. CC states that the right to a lease of premises used by both spouses, even if the lease was concluded before the marriage, is, regardless of their matrimonial regime or any agreements made, considered to belong to both spouses.

the cases of separation, a party to a PACS is not entitled to benefit from the attribution of the property.[168]

(b) *Owned Property*: If the property is listed in the name of one of the parties, the other party to a PACS, unlike the other party to a marriage,[169] is unprotected since the owner can dispose of his or her property freely. If, on the other hand, the parties own the property together, then one must proceed in accordance with the presumptions laid down by the relevant rules of familial property law.[170]

IV.5.7 PROPERTY LAW

In the absence of a pre-nuptial agreement, the French Civil Code ordains the applicability of a statutory matrimonial community of property regime.[171] The regime is one of a community of gains, whereby only property acquired during the marriage other than by means of gift or inheritance is held jointly.[172] Property belonging to the community belongs to both spouses jointly and is administered by both spouses on equal terms.[173] This statutory community of property is not however applied to those involved in a PACS. In contrast, a distinction is made between two categories of property: movable furnishings and any other property. Both of these categories are subject to slightly different partnership property regimes.

IV.5.7.1 Movable furnishings

Upon signing a PACS, all *meubles meublants* (literally translated as "furnishing furniture") are subject to a *régime de l'indivision*.[174] However, two categories of goods are excluded from the scope of the regime. Firstly, all goods acquired prior to the conclusion of the PACS, as well as those goods whose date of acquisition cannot be established, will not be subject to

---

168 DIBOS-LACROUS (2001) p. 37.

169 Art. 215, Fr. CC. Furthermore, a spouse may be able to obtain a judicial lease on the basis of Art. 285-1, Fr. CC

170 See **Section IV.5.7**.

171 Arts. 1400-1496, Fr. CC regulate the general community of property regime.

172 Art. 1401, Fr. CC. For more information on French matrimonial property law see, CORNU (1997); CARBONNIER (2000); TERRÉ/SIMLER (2001); CABRILLAC (2004).

173 Arts. 225 and 1421, Fr. CC, since the passing of Act of 23rd December 1985, No. 85-1372.

174 Art. 515-5(1), Fr. CC.

this provision.[175] Secondly, all goods inherited or received gratuitously will also fall outside the scope of this presumption.[176] According to the French Constitutional Court, it would appear that such a presumption cannot be circumvented by either of the partners unless they are able to produce an agreement stating that they have explicitly excluded the application of this regime.[177]

In order for this agreement to be valid it must be made in duplicate before a court clerk and prior to the conclusion of the PACS. This condition thus raises the question of whether a future modification to the original PACS agreement can amend the initial presumption with respect to *meubles meublants*.[178] The French Constitutional Court seems to have answered this question in the affirmative, although their reasoning is somewhat unclear. The court stated that when an agreement is made at the time the PACS is concluded the agreement concerns future goods *i.e.* goods that are acquired after the conclusion of the PACS. Obviously, another option is to insert a clause into the act of acquisition of the *meuble meublant* at the time of purchase.[179]

In order to ascertain the full extent of the category of *meubles meublants* reference must be made to Art. 534, Fr. CC, which states that this phrase only includes those movable furnishings intended for use and ornamentation of the home comprising tapestries, beds, seats, mirrors, clocks, tables, china and other articles of this kind. The list in Art. 534 is not exhaustive and has been updated as a result of technological advances through case law, and accordingly includes electric household appliances, TVs, computers and stereos *etc.*[180]

IV.5.7.2 Other property

On first reading of Art. 515-5(2), Fr. CC, it would seem that the presumption applied to all other property is the same as that applied to *meubles meublants*.[181] However, the presumption is different and leads to

175 Art. 515-5(1), Fr. CC: *ils feraient l'acquisition ... postérieurement à la conclusion du pacte.*

176 Art. 515-5(1), Fr. CC: *ils feraient l'acquisition à titre onéreux.*

177 Conseil Const., 9th November 1999, Decision No. 99-149, *JO*, 16th November 1999, §32.

178 For further information on the modification of the PACS, see **Section IV.4.8.3**.

179 HAUSER (2000) p. 411.

180 RUBELLIN-DEVICHI (2001) p. 425, §1178.

181 FULCHIRON (2001a) p. 960.

various problems. All other property bought for value[182] and not falling within the boundaries of the abovementioned category, is regulated in accordance with Art. 515-5(2), Fr. CC.[183] All such property is subject to a presumption of *indivision par moitié*, unless the act of acquisition or subscription provides otherwise.[184] In practice, this means that each partner will receive an equal right to one half of such property. The French Constitutional Court has held that,

> Considérant que, de même, la présomption d'indivision par moitié pour les autres biens dont les partenaires deviennent propriétaires à titre onéreux postérieurement à la conclusion du pacte ne peut céder que devant la production d'un acte d'acquisition ou de souscription qui en dispose autrement.[185]

This rule has sustained fierce attack and criticism from academics and practitioners alike, many stating that it contravenes the very essence of the PACS legislation.[186] Many believe that the Court confused two separate questions, namely the scope of the presumption and the force of that presumption. If property is purchased in the joint names of the parties and there is no mentioned exclusion of the presumption of *indivision par moitié*, then this presumption will apply to such property. This is also the case should the goods be bought by one party but placed in the name of both parties. Problems arise, however, when the property is purchased by one party and placed in that party's name. There are two possible schools of thought on the application of the presumption of *indivision par moitié* to such property, namely a narrow reading or a wide reading.

A narrow reading of Art. 515-5(2), Fr. CC would lead to the conclusion that a good purchased by one party in their own name is subject to the simple presumption of the separation of goods, subject to evidence provided by the

---

182 This condition thus excludes all goods received gratuitously either by virtue of being a gift or by virtue of succession.

183 HAUSER has raised questions as to the exact boundaries of this category, questioning whether this includes incorporeal property (HAUSER (2000) p. 411). The answer to this question must surely be affirmative, since Art. 515-5 is quite clear that *everything* other than *meubles meublants* is subject to the presumption in Art. 515-5(2), Fr. CC. This thus includes the income of both parties: FLOUR (1999) p. 284.

184 Art. 515-5(2), Fr. CC.

185 Conseil Const., 9th November 1999, Decision No. 99-149, *JO*, 16th November 1999, §32.

186 See for example: FLOUR (1999) p. 284 ; LEMOULAND (1999) p. 484; FULCHIRON (2001a) p. 960. FLOUR suggests that this joint ownership regime is, in principle, a means of managing provisional situations that tend to disappear once one of the co-owners requests division.

other party to the contrary.[187] This point of view is further supported by the fact that a purchase in a partner's sole name could be sufficient to satisfy the condition that the act of acquisition states that the presumption of *indivision par moitié* is excluded.

Alternatively, a wide reading of Art. 515-5(2), Fr. CC, would lead one to conclude that, as with matrimonial community of property, goods acquired under title of one of the parties during the PACS will be subject to the presumption of *indivision par moitié*.[188] Furthermore, this would result in a coherent reading of Art. 515-5, Fr. CC in its entirety, in that *meubles meublants* acquired in the name of one party are also not excluded from the respective presumption applicable to them. One can also refer to the aim of the legislature to apply a regime similar to that of the matrimonial community of property. The legislature thought that such an exclusion would provide an alternative mechanism for acquiring title, such that the acquisition by a partner does not paralyse the community of property presumption. Some commentators, of whom FULCHIRON is the most candid, argue that the only way sense can be made of Art. 515-5(2), Fr. CC is to read it in conjunction with Art. 1538, Fr. CC.[189] This Article provides that a spouse may use any means he or she has to prove that he or she possesses exclusive ownership rights to the disputed property. FULCHIRON argues that Art. 515-5(2), Fr. CC, proposes the principle and not the exception to the rule. The act of acquisition or the subscription allows for determination of ownership of the property. In default thereof, the property is presumed to be subject to *indivision par moitié*, regardless of whether the property was purchased using money from both parties or not; the presumption only applies if the act of acquisition or subscription indicate so.[190]

IV.5.8 INHERITANCE LAW

It can be seen from the parliamentary discussions surrounding the introduction of the PACS that the benefits afforded to the surviving spouse of the deceased will be the last bastion of marital benefits to be removed

---

187 HAUSER (2000) p. 413.

188 RUBELLIN-DEVICHI (2001) p. 575, §1551; GRIMALDI (2001) p. 932, § 4407.

189 FULCHIRON (2001a) p. 962-963.

190 This approach has also been supported in a ministerial response, *Réponse ministérielle,* 23rd November 2000, *JO,* No. 23816, *JCP Éd. N,* 2000, p. 1769.

from the exclusive ambit of the institution of marriage.[191] The exclusive rights granted to a surviving spouse in the case of intestacy,[192] include:

- If the deceased spouse leaves surviving issue, the surviving spouse is entitled to choose between a usufruct over the whole of the deceased's estate or bare ownership of one-quarter of the deceased's estate, if the children are born of the marriage;[193]
- If the deceased spouse leaves no surviving issue but the parents survive, the surviving spouse is entitled to bare ownership of one half of the deceased's estate;[194]
- If the deceased spouse leaves only one parent, the surviving spouse receives three-quarters of the deceased's estate;[195]
- If there are no surviving issue or blood relatives, the estate passes to the surviving spouse absolutely.[196]

In contrast, those involved in a PACS have absolutely no privileged position in relation to intestate succession. The surviving partner in a PACS is unable to benefit from the protection to which a surviving spouse is entitled. In the absence of intestate protection, it is therefore necessary that the parties to a PACS draw up a last will and testament in order to effectuate their wishes after their death. Nevertheless, a person is not entitled to total testamentary freedom. A defined proportion of the estate, *réserve legale*, must be given to specified categories of heirs, *héritiers réservataires*.[197] As a result, a testator only has the freedom to dispose of that portion of his or her estate that he or she is entitled to, known as the *quotité disponible*.[198] If there are no surviving ascendants or descendants and the surviving spouse was still the legal spouse of the deceased at the time of death, the surviving spouse will be entitled to a *réserve légale*.[199] Parties to a PACS are also excluded from the protection offered by this provision.

---

191 The law on inheritance was completely revised in 2001 by virtue of the Act of 3rd December 2000, No. 2001-1135. RUBELLIN-DEVICHI (2001) p. 427, §1180. REPONSE MINISTERIELLE, No. 44056, 22nd May 2000 (2000) *JCP Éd. N.* 1046. For a brief overview of the impact of marriage on inheritance law see TERRÉ/LEQUETTE (1997) p. 70-74, §72-75 (It must however be noted that this overview was written prior to the 2001 reform).

192 Arts. 756-767, Fr. CC deal with the rights of a spouse entitled to inherit.

193 Art. 757, Fr. CC. If the children are not born of the marriage then the surviving spouse is only entitled to ownership of one quarter of the estate of the deceased.

194 Art. 757-1, Fr. CC.

195 Art. 757-1(2), Fr. CC.

196 Art. 757-2, Fr. CC. Subject to the exception provided for in Art. 757-3, Fr. CC.

197 TERRÉ/LEQUETTE (1997) p. 501-503, §622-2.

198 See further TERRÉ/LEQUETTE (1997) p. 504-511, §623-629.

199 Art. 914-1, Fr. CC.

In terms of inheritance tax, distinctions between the treatment of spouses and parties to a PACS are also evident. If a spouse inherits from the estate of his or her deceased spouse or receives a gift, he or she is exempt from paying tax on the first €76,000 of this inheritance or gift.[200] If a party in a PACS inherits from his or her deceased partner or receives a gift, only the first €57,000[201] is exempt.[202] However, this abatement does not apply to gifts between parties to a PACS if the PACS has not been registered for at least two years.[203] In relation to spouses, once this abatement has been reached, tax is levied according to one of seven categories on a sliding scale up to a maximum of 40% on sums in excess of €1,700,000.[204] With respect to parties to a PACS, the first €15,000 in excess of the abatement is subject to a 40% tax, after which everything is taxed at 50%.[205] In order for these tax concessions to apply, the property must either have been inherited or, if the property was a donation, the PACS must have been registered for at least two years.[206] If this is not the case, then the parties to a PACS are taxed at the same rate as unmarried couples.[207]

IV.5.9 CHILDREN

French law distinguishes between natural parentage (**Section IV.5.9.1**) and other forms of parentage *i.e.* parentage established by means of adoption (**Section IV.5.9.3**) or by use of artificial reproductive techniques (**Section IV.5.9.4**). Parental authority issues will be dealt with in **Section IV.5.9.2**.

IV.5.9.1 Parentage

Despite statutory amendments to the law on parentage in 1972 and 1993,[208] the French Civil Code retains a distinction between legitimate and natural children. Children born to a marriage are regarded as legitimate, whilst

200 Art. 779-I, Fr. GTC.

201 Before 1st January 2002, this sum was set at €46,000: Art. 779-III(1), Fr. GTC.

202 Art. 779-III(1), Fr. GTC.

203 Art. 779-III(2), Fr. GTC.

204 On sums less than €7,600 the surviving spouse pays 5%, between €7,600-€15,000: 10%, €15,000-€30,000: 15%, €30,000-€520,000: 20%, €520,000-€850,000: 30%, €850,000-€1,700,000: 35%, and on sums over €1,700,000, 40%: Art. 777, Table II, Fr. GTC.

205 Art. 777-*bis*(1), Fr. GTC.

206 Art. 777-*bis*(2), Fr GTC.

207 Abatement of €1,500 after which all sums are taxed at 60%. Art. 777, Table III, Fr. GTC.

208 Act of 8th January 1993, No. 93-22. This law radically amended the French law on parentage. The 1972 Act confirmed the principle of equality between legitimate and natural (or illegitimate) children. Amended by Act of 4th March 2002, No. 2003-304.

children born outside of wedlock are termed natural children.[209] It is necessary to compare those procedures available to parents of legitimate children as opposed to those of natural children. In dealing with legitimate children, unlike many other European jurisdictions, legal motherhood is not granted automatically by reason of giving birth to a child; the principle *mater semper certa est* is thus not applicable in France. Maternity is instead proved *voluntarily* by virtue of a birth certificate,[210] *tacitly* by virtue of the apparent possession of a legal status,[211] or *contentiously* by means of a judicial procedure.[212] The birth certificate is made before the Registrar and must be made within three days of the birth.[213] This declaration must be made by the father and in the absence thereof by the doctor, midwife, health official or anyone else present at the delivery.[214] The second method of proof of parentage is that of the possession of an apparent legal status that results from a sufficient collection of facts indicating a bond of parentage between a child and the family to which he or she is said to belong.[215] If both these forms of proof are present, *i.e.* birth certificate and an apparent possession of a status, then maternity cannot be contested.[216] However, should neither of these forms of proof be present, a judicial procedure to determine maternity may be initiated if there is enough evidence to support the commencement of proceedings.[217]

For a child born to a marriage, paternity is determined by operation of law in accordance with the adage *pater is est quem nuptaie demonstrant*.[218] If

---

209 The number of children born outside of wedlock is, however, on the increase. In 1981, 12.7% of children were born outside of wedlock, in 1986 this had risen to 21.9%, in 1991 to 31.9%, in 1996 to 39.3% and in 2001 to 43.7%: *Population et Sociétés. Bulletin de l'INED*, March 1998, No. 333. For more information see TERRÉ/FENOUILLET (1996) p. 577, §697.

210 Art. 319, Fr. CC. This is by far the most common method for the establishment of maternity: CORNU (2003) p. 358, §218; TERRÉ/FENOUILLET (1996) p. 581, §702.

211 Art. 320, Fr. CC.

212 Arts. 323 and 328, Fr. CC.

213 Not including the date of birth: Art. 55, Fr. CC.

214 Art. 56, Fr. CC. CORNU (2003) p. 358, §218.

215 Art. 311-1, Fr. CC.

216 Art. 322, Fr. CC. RUBELLIN-DEVICHI (2001) p. 512, §1392. Unless swapping of the child took place prior to the birth certificate being drawn up: Art. 322-1, Fr. CC.

217 Art. 323, Fr. CC.

218 Art. 312(1), Fr. CC. This presumption can, of course, be challenged by father on the basis that he is not the father of the child: Art. 312-2, Fr. CC. See further, CORNU (2003) p. 362-366, §220-223; RUBELLIN-DEVICHI (2001) p. 497-510, §1351-1385.

the parents of a child marry subsequent to the child's birth, the child will be legitimised retrospectively.[219]

In contrast, children born to unmarried couples are deemed to be natural children. Parentage can be established in one of three ways: *voluntarily* by means of recognition, *tacitly* by the possession of an apparent legal status or *contentiously* by means of a judicial determination. With respect to the last two methods, the rules applicable to legitimate children also apply to natural children. As a result, neither of these methods allow for two persons of the same sex to possess legal parental status over the same child at the same time.

Recognition, on the other hand, is only available to parents of natural children. Recognition is regarded as a voluntary act undertaken either by the mother or father of the child.[220] In terms of maternity, if the mother has her name registered on the birth certificate and is able to corroborate this with the possession of an apparent legal status, these two factors are sufficient to satisfy the conditions for recognition.[221] In the absence thereof, and with respect to paternity, recognition can only take place should an authentic instrument be drawn up.[222]

None of the above mentioned methods of establishing parentage draw any distinction between non-married couples and those involved in a PACS.[223] Accordingly, whatever methods are accessible to an unmarried person for establishing parentage are equally available to a person involved in a different-sex PACS. For example, if a different-sex couple have registered a PACS agreement and conceive a child naturally, both parents will have to initiate steps before the child's parentage can be established. By virtue of Art. 338, Fr. CC, as long as recognition is not contested in court, recognition by one person renders the contradictory establishment of another's

---

219 Art. 331, second sentence, Fr. CC. Since the Act of 1972, a child can also be legitimised by reason of a judicial decision: Art. 330, Fr. CC. See further, CORNU (2003) p. 382-387, §239-243; GUIHO (1993) p. 261, §347; TERRÉ/FENOUILLET (1996) p. 602-613, §727-736.

220 Outlined in Art. 334(8), Fr. CC. For more information on the detail of the recognition see, TERRÉ/FENOUILLET (1996) p. 602-613, §727-736; GUIHO (1993) p. 301-305, §396-402; CORNU (2003) p. 395-399, §252-254.

221 Art. 337, Fr. CC. RUBELLIN-DEVICHI (2001) p. 493, §1327.

222 This includes an instrument of civil status, a notarial deed or a declaration before a judge: TERRÉ/FENOUILLET (1996) p. 608, §732.

223 The Government has also noted that there are also no plans to change this position in the future: *Réponse ministérielle*, 3rd March 2005, *JO*, No. 94187, p. 615.

parentage inadmissible. As a result of this provision, persons in a same-sex relationship are not both allowed to recognise the same child.[224]

IV.5.9.2 Parental Responsibilities

Parents of legitimate children are vested with joint parental authority over their children by operation of law.[225] In relation to natural children, if both father and mother have already established their legal parentage in relation to the child, both parents will be vested with joint parental authority.[226] If, on the other hand, the parents are unmarried (and hence those registered in a PACS) and parentage has only been established with respect to one parent, only this parent will be vested with automatic parental authority.[227] Obviously, with respect to same-sex couples only one of the couple may be vested with parental authority, as a result of the fact that only one of them may be deemed to be the child's legal parent. Although in a recent case a same-sex couple was awarded joint parental authority, this is to be seen, according to the French Minister of Justice, as an exceptional case.[228] The granting of such a declaration for different-sex couples involved in a PACS would place them in exactly the same legal position to the child as their married counterparts. Nonetheless, regardless of the need for couples involved in a PACS to undertake steps to gain parental authority over the children of their partner, a parent loses the single parent's right to child benefits upon the registration of his or her PACS.[229]

---

224 See CARBONNIER (2002) p. 292.

225 Art. 371-1(2), Fr. CC; FERRAND, in: BOELE-WOELKI/BRAAT/CURRY-SUMNER (2005) p. 268.

226 Art. 372-1, Fr. CC; FERRAND, in: BOELE-WOELKI/BRAAT/CURRY-SUMNER (2005) p. 340.

227 Art. 372-2, Fr. CC.

228 The case involved a female same-sex couple. One of the partners gave birth to a child as a result of artificial reproductive techniques. After the child's birth, the mother's partner adopted the child by means of a weak adoption (*adoption simple*). Due to a change in the law in 2002 (Act of 4th March 2002, N° 2002-305), the couple were entitled to request that they be awarded joint parental authority. The request was allowed by the District Court in Paris on the 7th July 2004. *Le Monde*, 22nd September 2004, "La justice reconnaît pour la première fois une famille homoparentale". In contrast to the French Minister of Justice's comments, there appears to be a growing trend in French courts to allow the same-sex partner of a parent, irrespective of whether they have formalised their relationship or not, to obtain part of the package of parental responsibilities through the delegation of parental responsibilities by the parent. For further information see FERRAND, in: BOELE-WOELKI/BRAAT/CURRY-SUMNER (2005) 654-655 and 664-665.

229 Art. L-524-2, Fr. SSC. see for example "*le demande d'allocation de parent isolé*".

IV.5.9.3 Adoption

Two types of adoption exist in France: strong adoption (*l'adoption plénière*) and weak adoption (*l'adoption simple*). Despite the difference in consequences attached to these types of adoption, the vast majority of requirements are identical.[230] According to French law, an application for adoption may be made jointly by a married couple,[231] or individually.[232] Although the law does not, in principle, permit successive adoption, a successive adoption may be ordered either after the death of one or both of the adopters, or after the death of one of the two adopters if the new request is made by the new spouse of the survivor.[233] The PACS legislation has not altered this situation; although the possibility for single-parent adoption remains open to same-sex or different-sex unmarried couples, the possibility of joint parent adoption remains the exclusive domain of married couples.[234] Married persons are also afforded the opportunity to adopt their spouse's child;[235] an option, once again, not open to those involved in a PACS.[236]

Even if single-parent adoption remains open to those involved in a PACS, the European Court of Human Rights decision in the case of *Fretté v. France*, gives no aid to homosexuals wishing to adopt.[237] By a majority of four votes to three, the Court upheld the decision of the French *Conseil d'État* whereby an adoption order was refused, *inter alia*, on grounds of the applicant's homosexuality. The majority held that despite the fact that the decision was decisively based on the applicant's homosexuality,[238] France

---

230 RUBELLIN-DEVICHI (2001) p. 590, §1609. The main exception to this rule can be found in the requirement that strong adoption can only take place should the child be under the age of fifteen, whereas weak adoption can take place regardless of the child's age: Art. 345, Fr. CC.

231 Art. 343, Fr. CC. As long as the couples have either been married for at least two years or both parties have attained the age of twenty-eight.

232 Arts. 343-1, Fr. CC. As long as both of the parties have reached twenty-eight.

233 Art. 346-2, Fr. CC.

234 Art. 343, Fr. CC is not *mutatis mutandis* applicable to the PACS legislation.

235 Art. 345-1, Fr. CC. This is only allowed if: (1) parentage has been legally established with regard to that spouse; (2) the parent other than the spouse has been totally deprived of parental authority; (3) the parent other than the spouse is dead and has left no ascendant to the first degree or where the latter obviously took no further interest in the child.

236 DIBOS-LACROUX (2001) p. 52; RUBELLIN-DEVICHI (2001) p. 594, §1619.

237 ECtHR, *Fretté v. France*, Appl. No. 36515/97, 26th February 2002.

238 In previous cases, the ECtHR had held that the defendant State must prove particularly convincing and weighty reasons if discrimination on the basis of sexual orientation was at issue: ECtHR, *Lustig-Prean and Beckett v. United Kingdom*, Appl. No. 31417/96 and

had pursued a legitimate aim, *i.e.* the protection of the health and rights of children involved in adoption procedures. Furthermore, in determining whether France had proven that they had an "objective and reasonable justification" for this discriminatory treatment, the majority felt that owing to the lack of consensus on the issue,[239] the State must be afforded a wide margin of appreciation. As a result the Court held that France had indeed proved an objective and reasonable justification for the discriminatory treatment and found no violation of Art. 8, ECHR.[240] This decision has thus allowed French authorities to continue to refuse single parent adoptions on grounds of the applicant's homosexuality.

IV.5.9.4 Artificial Reproductive Techniques

Access to artificial insemination remained unmodified by both the PACS legislation and the wide-ranging revision of the French Code for Public Health (Fr. CPH) in 2000.[241] The French Constitutional Court in judging the constitutionality of the PACS legislation also stated,

> La loi n'a pas d'effet sur la mise en œuvre des dispositions légales relatives à l'assistance médicale à la procréation, lesquelles demeurent en vigueur et ne sont applicables qu'aux couples formés d'un homme et d'une femme.[242]

The refusal to modify the legislation governing artificial insemination has thus maintained the ban on same-sex couples utilising such artificial reproductive techniques. Art. L-2141(2), Fr. CPH, limits the use of artificial insemination treatment to a one-man, one–woman couple who have lived together for a period of at least two years.[243] Although a PACS could serve as possible evidence for a different-sex couple of their two-year period of cohabitation, it does not in any way assist a same-sex couple in their attempts to conceive a child.

32377/96, 27th September 1999, ECtHR, *Smith and Grady v. United Kingdom,* Appl. No. 33985/96 and 33986/96, 27th September 1999 and ECtHR, *Salgueiro da Silva Mounta v. Portugal,* Appl. No. 33290/96, 21st December 1999.

239 ECtHR, *Fretté v. France*, Appl. No. 36515/97, 26th February 2002, §41.

240 ECtHR, *Fretté v. France*, Appl. No. 36515/97, 26th February 2002, §§42 and 43.

241 Act of 16th December 1999, No. 99-944 and Ordinance of 15th June 2000, No. 2000-548.

242 Conseil Const., 9th November 1999, Decision No. 99-149, *JO*, 16th November 1999, §29.

243 Art. L-2141(2)(3), Fr. CPH, Art. L-152(2), Old Fr. CPH. RUBELLIN-DEVICHI (2001) p. 482, §1307.

IV.6 DISSOLUTION

IV.6.1 GENERAL

Contractual liberty, that is to say the ability for the parties to end a contract at any time, is one of the founding principles of the PACS.[244] Although in theory this founding principle remains true, the law nonetheless prescribes time periods that must first be satisfied before the partnership can be dissolved.[245] These periods vary according to the method of dissolution requested and will thus be discussed in the relevant sub-sections below. In all cases of dissolution, the clerk of the district court does not register the reason for the dissolution unless the PACS is ended by reason of the death of one or both of the partners.[246]

A marriage can only be dissolved by reason of the death of one of the spouses, by judicial separation or by divorce.[247] Although the death of one of the parties to a PACS also brings a PACS to an end,[248] the rules on judicial separation do not apply to the dissolution of a PACS. Despite the wide-ranging reforms to French divorce law,[249] a divorce decree must still be sought through judicial channels; the option of administrative divorce does not exist.[250] On the other hand, the option for the judicial dissolution of a PACS does not exist. The absence of judicial proceedings can be explained by the fact that a PACS may be dissolved unilaterally by either party, thus negating the need to provide for a judicial procedure for the termination of a PACS.

IV.6.2 JUDICIAL: JOINT PETITION

A PACS may not be dissolved judicially.

---

244 VIVIER (2001) p. 109.

245 See Art. 515-7(3), Fr. CC.

246 Advice from the *Commission Nationale d'Informatique et des Libertés*, 25th November 1999.

247 Despite French divorce law undergoing substantial reform in 2004 these methods remain the only possibilities.

248 See **Section V.5.7** for further details.

249 Act of 26th May 2004, No. 2004-439. For the legislative history to this reform see FERRAND, in: BOELE-WOELKI/BRAAT/SUMNER (2003a) p. 58-60.

250 FERRAND, in: BOELE-WOELKI/BRAAT/SUMNER (2003a) p. 118.

IV.6.3 JUDICIAL: UNILATERAL PETITION

A PACS may not be dissolved judicially.

IV.6.4 ADMINISTRATIVE: JOINT DECLARATION

Similar to the absence of judicial procedures to terminate a PACS, there is a complete lack of administrative procedures available to dissolve a marriage. A PACS can, however, be dissolved upon a joint declaration of the parties to the effect that they wish to dissolve their PACS.[251] In this case, the parties must file a joint, written document with the clerk of the district court where at least one of them resides at the time they request the dissolution. The clerk must then register the document of dissolution in the Register and send a copy of the dissolution to the clerk of the district court where the initial PACS declaration was received.[252] The clerk of the district court who received the initial PACS declaration must then also ensure that the dissolution is recorded in the margin of the original PACS instrument. The clerk who receives the joint declaration to terminate the PACS must also ensure that a copy of the document of dissolution is sent to the clerk of the district court of the place of birth of each party.[253] The clerk of this latter district court must ensure that the termination of the PACS is recorded in the margin of the register mentioned in Art. 515-3(5), Fr. CC. If either or both of the parties were born abroad then the court clerk of the District Court in Paris will be competent hereto.[254] It is important to note that the competent district court is thus the court in a party's residence and not the clerk where the initial declaration was made. Only when a record is made in the margin of the original instrument creating the PACS will the PACS be deemed to have been terminated.[255]

IV.6.5 ADMINISTRATIVE: UNILATERAL DECLARATION

A PACS may also be terminated on the unilateral will of one of the parties, without consulting the other party.[256] Although at first glance this

---

251 Art. 515-7(1), Fr. CC.

252 Art. 515-7(5), Fr. CC.

253 Art. 515-7(5), second sentence, Fr. CC.

254 If the parties live abroad then the declaration should be filed with the French Embassy or Consult of the country in which they are resident: PILLEBOUT (2001) p. 79.

255 Art. 515-7(7)(1), Fr. CC.

256 Art. 515-7(2), Fr. CC.

dissolution may look to be a simple formality, certain conditions must be fulfilled before this declaration may become effective.[257] Should one of the parties to a PACS wish to terminate the relationship, he or she must serve notice of his or her decision on the other and send a copy of that notice to the court clerk of the district court which received the initial instrument creating the PACS. The notice must be served by means of a bailiff's summons on the other party. The apparent brutality of this method of dissolution is alleviated or tempered somewhat by a three-month delay before the PACS will be deemed to have been terminated.[258] This method for terminating the PACS has encountered fierce attack, being compared by some commentators to the much castigated divorce reform of 1975.[259] However in justifying the constitutionality of this provision, the French Constitutional Court referred to Art. 4, Declaration of the Rights of Man 1789. In recalling the contractual nature of the PACS, the court stated that a private law contract for an undetermined period of time can always be ended upon the unilateral will of one of the contracting parties.[260] The notice requirements imposed on the party wishing to terminate and the possibility of damages arising out of the breach of the conditions of the contract being awarded to the other party, led the court to believe that the principle of contractual immutability would be guaranteed.[261]

IV.6.6 ANNULMENT PROCEEDINGS

The contractual nature of the PACS is no more evident than with respect to annulment proceedings. In the same way that non-observance of certain formal conditions can lead to the *a posteriori* annulment of a marriage, non-observance of certain formal conditions for the registration of a PACS can also lead to the annulment of the PACS agreement. However, unlike marriage where two types of annulment are available, *nullité relative* and *nullité absolue*,[262] only one type of annulment procedure is available in relation to the PACS.[263] Due to the absence of any further explanation of the term annulment in the opening sentence of Art. 515-2, Fr. CC, the French

---

257 Carbonnier (2002) p. 741; Cornu (2003) p. 108; Rubellin-Devichi (2001) p. 431-432, §1186.

258 Art. 515-7(7)(2), Fr. CC.

259 Carbonnier (2002) p. 741.

260 Conseil Const., 9th November 1999, Decision No. 99-149, *JO*, 16th November 1999, §61.

261 Conseil Const., 9th November 1999, Decision No. 99-149, *JO*, 16th November 1999, §§62 and 63.

262 See further Malaurie (1998) p. 112, §201; Lemouland (1999) p. 485.

263 Rubellin-Devichi (2001) p. 68-79, §169-200.

Constitutional Court has held that the term must be interpreted as only referring to *nullité absolue*.[264] As a result, a PACS may be annulled as a result of non-adherence to the rules on exclusivity or incest, whilst a marriage may also be annulled should the rules of age, sex, publicity, competence of the Registrar and consent not be adhered to.[265] Another difference between these two institutions lies in the fact that if the parties continue to live together or if the woman is found to be pregnant, a marriage may no longer be annulled, whilst these facts form no hindrance for the annulment of a PACS.[266]

Moreover, a marriage may only be annulled on one of the grounds listed in Arts. 180 to 184, Fr. CC.[267] These grounds are more restrictive than those applicable to ordinary contracts, since misrepresentation is not sufficient as a ground for the annulment of a marriage. Annulment proceedings for the PACS, on the other hand, are regulated by the ordinary annulment rules on contractual obligations, thus providing a broader possible range of annulment grounds.[268] The absence of misrepresentation as a ground for the annulment of a marriage is intentional. The stability of the institution of marriage is considered more important than the need to protect individual spouses from possible misrepresentation. Thus a marriage is not allowed to be annulled on the basis of an error made by one of the spouses as to his or her wealth, intelligence, character or race. A PACS, on the other hand, may be annulled on the basis one of these grounds, since the stability of the PACS is not regarded as more important than the mistake itself.[269]

IV.6.7 DEATH AND PRESUMPTION OF DEATH

Art. 515-7(4), Fr. CC, states that upon the death of one of the partners, the PACS will be deemed to have been terminated. The surviving partner, or

---

264 Conseil Const., 9th November 1999, Decision No. 99-149, *JO*, 16th November 1999, §27. Some commentators still disagree with the opinion of the Conseil Const., see ROY (2002) p. 759-786.

265 Art. 184, Fr. CC.

266 Art. 181 and 185(2), respectively, Fr. CC.

267 TERRÉ/FENOUILLET (1996) p. 299, §372; CARBONNIER (2002) p. 423-424: "*Le seul fait que le mariage ait été déterminé pour des manœuvres mensongères ne suffit pas à entraîner sa nullité*".

268 Arts. 1109 *et seq*, Fr. CC.

269 The absence of misrepresentation as a ground for the annulment of a marriage gives added credence to the proposition that the PACS should be characterised as a contract; marriage is afforded a special status and treated differently to a normal contract, whereas the PACS is treated in exactly the same way as any other.

any other interested party, must provide the court clerk of the district court where the PACS was originally registered with the deceased's death certificate.[270] The court clerk must mention the date of death in the register of their place of residence and send a true copy to the court clerk of the district court of the birthplace of each of the parties.[271] The PACS will be deemed to have ended on the day upon which the deceased died, in the same way as with marriages.[272] Art. 112, Fr. CC states that when a person has ceased to appear at his or her residence or domicile and has not been heard from, the judge of guardianships can, on the application of any interested party, establish a presumption of absence. If ten years have elapsed since this presumption was established, then the district court may issue a declaration of absence.[273] This declaration has exactly the same consequences as a declaration of death, thus terminating any marriage or PACS in existence.[274] It is expressly provided for that the spouse of an absentee may remarry,[275] which by analogous application to the conditions laid down for the PACS with respect to bigamy, suggests that a party involved in a PACS may also enter into a new PACS or marry.[276]

IV.6.8 ENTRY INTO MARRIAGE / CONVERSION

The PACS may also be ended by marriage, either by one of the parties to a third person or of the parties to each other. If the PACS should be terminated by the marriage of one of the parties to another, the party who celebrates a marriage should send notice of his or her decision to the other by means of a bailiff's summons. A true copy of that notice must also be sent to the clerk of the district court who received the original PACS declaration.[277] A birth certificate upon which mention of the marriage has been made or a marriage certificate must also be sent along with this notice. The clerk is then obliged to note this marriage on the register in the parties' place of residence.[278] The clerk must then ensure that the clerk of the place of birth of both parties also receives a true copy of the marriage certificate,

---

270 Art. 515-7(4), Fr. CC.

271 Art. 515-7(5), Fr. CC. If the parties were born abroad then this must be sent to the court clerk of the district court in Paris: Art. 515-7(6), Fr. CC.

272 Art. 515-7(7)(3), Fr. CC.

273 Art. 227(1), Fr. CC.

274 Art. 122(1), Fr. CC.

275 Art. 128(3), Fr. CC

276 See **Section IV.4.2** for the rules on the exclusivity of marriage and the PACS regime.

277 Art. 515-7(3), Fr. CC.

278 Art. 515-7(5), Fr. CC.

which must be mentioned in the margin of the register of the district court of the place of birth of both parties.[279] The PACS is deemed to have come to an end by operation of law on the date of celebration of the marriage.[280]

IV.6.9 EFFECTS OF DISSOLUTION

IV.6.9.1 Maintenance

As a result of the divorce reform of 2004,[281] the previous distinction between *pension alimentaire* (payable to a claimant who claimed divorce on the basis of six years separation or mental illness)[282] and *prestation compensatoire* (payable to compensate for the disparity between the spouses' living conditions as a result of the divorce)[283] has been abolished. In principle, any spouse will now be entitled to maintenance if he or she satisfies the means criteria, regardless of the type of divorce and the allocation of fault.[284] Nonetheless, in cases of a divorce based on fault, the judge will have discretion to refuse such maintenance awards if the circumstances so justify.[285] Regardless of these legislative changes, the position of those involved in a PACS remains unlatered and neither party is entitled to a maintenance claim.

A spouse is also entitled to claim for compensation or damages for which two legal provisions exist. Art. 266, Fr. CC allows for a claim to be made by the innocent spouse should a divorce be decreed on a grounds of fault, whilst Art. 1382, Fr. CC allows a more general compensation claim if a spouse can prove that the other spouse was at fault (thus removing the requirement that the fault be entirely the responsibility of one spouse). This latter option is of course also open to those involved in a PACS. Moreover, in the special case of a PACS being terminated by means of a unilateral declaration, the partner served with the notice of the termination may file for tortious damages.[286] The parties may not contract out of this possibility

---

279 If the parties were born abroad, then the court clerk of the *tribunal de grande instance* in Paris is competent hereto: Art. 515-7(6), Fr. CC.

280 Art. 515-7(7)(3), Fr. CC.

281 Act of 26th May 2004, No. 2004-439 concerning divorce.

282 Art. 281 (old), Fr. CC in conjunction with Arts. 237 and 238, Fr. CC.

283 Art. 270 (old), Fr. CC. See further, CARBONNIER (2002) p. 610-611.

284 Art. 270(1), Fr. CC as a result of the Act of 26th May 2004, No. 2004-439.

285 Art. 270(2), Fr. CC as a result of the Act of 26th May 2004, No. 2004-439.

286 Art. 515-7(8), Fr. CC.

in their original PACS declaration.[287] Although the PACS legislation provides no guidance on how this claim is to be made, one is to assume that no special procedure is required and reference instead should be made to the ordinary law on contracts. With reference to the case law on unmarried cohabitants prior to the PACS legislation, it may also be argued that Art. 266, Fr. CC, may be analogously applicable.[288]

IV.6.9.2 Effects with respect to children

Unlike a marriage, which affects the relationship of children to a marriage, a PACS has no effect on the relationship between a party to a PACS and any children of the family. As a result, the termination of a PACS has no effect on the exercise of parental authority or on the parentage of the child.[289]

IV.6.9.3 Effects with respect to property

Although the impact of the presumptions of *indivision par moitié* appear to have the same effect on the parties' property as the matrimonial community of property regime,[290] parties to a PACS must resolve their own property disputes upon the dissolution of their relationship. Of course, the parties may have already agreed upon rules for the settlement of property disputes in their original PACS agreement. If, however, the parties have made no prior agreement and/or they cannot reach a consensus on the settlement of these issues, the district court is competent to decide the property consequences of the termination.[291] It will also be for the judge to decide issues in relation to a person's property should one of the parties to a PACS die or be placed under guardianship. As a result, the judge will need to look to the original PACS document and divide the goods accordingly. A party may also request that certain goods be preferentially assigned to him or her.[292]

---

287 CORNU (2003) p. 109.

288 CARBONNIER (2002) p. 722-724.

289 FERRAND, in: BOELE-WOELKI/BRAAT/CURRY-SUMNER (2005) p. 416-417.

290 FULCHIRON (2001) p. 968.

291 Art. 515-7(8), Fr. CC.

292 Art. 832, Fr. CC *mutatis mutandis* applicable. Only agricultural land holdings are excluded from the application of Art. 832, Fr. CC. An exclusion which is difficult to justify, despite its obvious minor importance: GRANET/LÉCUYER (1999/2001) No. 87.

CHAPTER V
THE NETHERLANDS

V.1 INTRODUCTION

The Netherlands was the first country in the world to allow for same-sex couples to legally marry, not more than three years after the introduction of registered partnership in 1998.[1] As with other Chapters, after providing the most recent statistics on the number of partnerships registered (**Section V.2**), attention will be paid to the legislative process prior to enactment of the Registered Partnership Act (**Section V.3**). **Section V.4** will focus on how a registered partnership can be established, **Section V.5** on the legal effects of registering such a partnership and **Section V.6** on how one may terminate the partnership once it has been celebrated.

V.2 EMPIRICAL EVIDENCE AND STATISTICS

Although an empirical study has been conducted in The Netherlands to analyse, *inter alia*, the reasons for entering into the agreement,[2] due to the small numbers involved in the registration process at the time of the survey the analysis of the data is of little statistical value.

Table 5*: Number of marriages celebrated in The Netherlands (as of July 2005)*[3]

Year	Male-Male	Female-Female	Male-Female	Total
2001	1,339	1,075	79,677	82,091
2002	935	903	83,970	85,808
2003	727	759	81,135	82,621
2004	552	590	74,914	76,056
2005	198	208	24,994	25,400
Total	**3,751**	**3,535**	**344,690**	**351,976**

1 As was the case with **Belgium**, the passage of legislation introducing same-sex marriage will only be mentioned in passing: see **Chapter V.3.9**.

2 SCHERF (1999) p. 19-20.

3 Statistics available on http://www.cbs.nl. Up to and including the figures for May 2005.

Table 6: *Number of partnerships registered in The Netherlands (as of July 2005)*[4]

Year	Male-Male	Female-Female	Female-Male	Total
1998	1,686	1,324	1,616	4,626
1999	894	863	1,500	3,257
2000	815	785	1,322	2,922
2001	285	245	2,847	3,377
2002	358	382	7,581	8,321
2003	446	453	9,074	9,973
2004	432	527	10,190	11,149
2005	109	119	4,270	4,498
Total	**5,025**	**4,698**	**38,400**	**48,123**

V.3 HISTORICAL PERSPECTIVE

V.3.1 DUTCH COURT DECISIONS

The legal journey resulting in the legislative enactment of registered partnership was not smooth. Around the beginning of the 1990s, two cases brought the legal problems facing same-sex couples to the forefront of judicial awareness. In 1989, the District Court in Amsterdam decided the first case (involving two men)[5] and in 1989 the Dutch Supreme Court eventually decided the second case (involving two women).[6] Both courts held against the petitioners, with the Dutch Supreme Court holding that,

> Civil marriage is since time immemorial understood to be an enduring bond between a man and a woman to which a number of legal consequences are attached, which partly relate to the difference in sex and the consequences connected therewith for the descent of children. Marriage has these characteristics not only in The Netherlands but in many countries. Moreover, it cannot be said that the general opinion in the legal community has developed such that the considerations just mentioned do not justify the distinction in treatment on the grounds of sexual orientation, which can manifest itself in the impossibility to enter a relationship-like marriage with a person of the same sex as oneself.[7]

4 Statistics available on http://www.cbs.nl. Up to and including the figures for May 2005.

5 Rb Amsterdam, 13th February 1990 (1990) *NJCM* 456-460. For the situation prior to 1990, see BOELE-WOELKI/TANGE (1989).

6 HR, 19th October 1990, NJ 1992, 192. For earlier decisions see Rb Rotterdam, 5th December 1988; Hof The Hague, 2nd June 1989, NJ 1989, 871.

7 HR, 19th October 1990, NJ 1992, 192 (translated FORDER in: MAXWELL (2001) p. 147).

Nonetheless, although the Dutch Supreme Court held that it was not discriminatory to deny same-sex couples the *possibility* to get married,[8] it made no ruling on whether the denial of the *legal effects* of marriage was discriminatory. The court insinuated that this scrutiny was a task for the legislature and not for the judiciary.

V.3.2 FIRST KORTMANN COMMITTEE

The insinuation by the Dutch Supreme Court for parliamentary scrutiny was duly heeded and led to the formation of the First Kortmann Committee. The committee published its report, *Leefvormen* ("Lifestyles"), on the 20th December 1991. It suggested the introduction of one of two schemes: a registration scheme at the local city council (so-called "light registration") or a registration at the Registry of Births, Deaths and Marriages (so-called "heavy registration"). The report also suggested that any scheme should be open to same-sex and different-sex couples as well as within the prohibited degrees of marriage. After initial research conducted by the *Instituut voor onderzoek naar Overheidsuitgaven* (Institute for Review of Public Expenditure), only the latter proposal for a "heavy" registration scheme was maintained.[9] Even so, the Bill submitted to Parliament in 1994 did not provide for the registration of different-sex couples,[10] instead limiting registration to same-sex couples and those within the prohibited degrees of marriage. However, in view of an influential memorandum published in September 1995, the possibility of registering was again opened to both different-sex couples and same-sex couples (although not to couples within the prohibited degrees of marriage).[11] It was hoped that this amendment would meet complaints raised principally from the COC (Dutch homosexual lobby group) that registered partnership was in essence a second-class marriage.[12] Others, including many academics, were nonetheless extremely critical of the move.[13]

Meanwhile, as the First Kortmann Committee was discussing a national system of partnership registration, municipalities all over The Netherlands

---

8 "In 1990 besliste de Hoge Raad dat een huwelijk tussen personen van hetzelfde geslacht niet mogelijk is", in: HR, 19th October 1990, NJ 1992, 192.

9 BOELE-WOELKI (1999a) p. 3.

10 *Dutch Second Chamber*, 1993-1994, 23761, No. 3, p. 2.

11 *Dutch Second Chamber*, 1994-1995, 22700, No. 5 (*Notitie Leefvormen*).

12 *Dutch Second Chamber*, 1994-1995, 22700, No. 5, p. 5 and 23761, No. 7, p. 10. For more discussion of the influence of the COC see **Chapter IX**.

13 VAN MOURIK (1997); HOEVENAARS (1997); KOPPEN/LEKKERKERKER (1992a) p. 774.

were already tackling the problem first hand. According to Dutch law, municipalities are allowed to maintain an unlimited number of registers. As a result, a number of city councils began to create registers for same-sex relationships, despite the fact that these registrations had no legal consequences. In 1991, the town of Deventer registered the first same-sex relationship. In the following years more than 130 municipalities also established such a register.[14]

V.3.3 SECOND KORTMANN COMMITTEE

Despite the political activity of the early 1990s, the pressure to allow same-sex couples to marry in the same manner as different-sex couples continued to intensify.[15] A majority of the Parliament was in favour of opening civil marriage to couples of the same-sex.[16] In April 1996, this pressure led the Dutch Second Chamber of Parliament to adopt two non-binding resolutions submitted by VAN DER BURGH and DITTRICH demanding the swift introduction of same-sex marriage.[17] The Government, wary of unleashing an anti same-sex marriage backlash in neighbouring countries, decided instead to appoint a committee to examine the issues surrounding the introduction of same-sex marriage. As a result the Second Kortmann Committee was established on the 28th May 1996, with the aim of investigating whether the institution of marriage should also be open to same-sex couples. In the meantime, passage of the Registered Partnership Bill continued and was eventually enacted in 1997.[18]

In October 1997, the Second Kortmann Committee published its report. The Committee agreed that whatever the eventual result was to be, only one institution should exist and registered partnership should be abolished.[19] A second area of consensus was that no familial legal ties should be created by operation of law as a result of celebrating a same-sex marriage since this

---

14 H. VAN VELDE, *The long road to civil marriage* (1st April 2001, Gay Krant).

15 For an English overview see MAXWELL (2001).

16 Those parties which supported the opening of civil marriage to same-sex couples were: the Labour Party (*Partij van de Arbeid*), Democrats 1966 (*D66*), Green Left (*Groen Links*) and the Party for Democracy and Freedom (*Volkspartij voor Vrijheid en Democratie*).

17 *Dutch Second Chamber*, 1995-1996, 22700, No. 18 and 14; *Handelingen, Dutch Second Chamber*, 1995-1996, p. 4883. These resolutions were supported with 81 votes to 60.

18 *Neth. Staatsblad*, 1997, No. 324 tot wijziging van Boek 1 van het Burgerlijk Wetboek en van het wetboek rechtsvordering in verband met opneming daarin van bepalingen voor het geregistreerd partnerschap.

19 KORTMANN (1997) p. 24, §5.5.

would involve too great an abstraction from the biological reality that same-sex couples cannot conceive children naturally.[20] It was here, however, that the unanimity of the Committee floundered. Only five of the eight members supported the opening of civil marriage to same-sex couples. Three discernible categories of arguments were forwarded by the members of the Committee on both sides. The first category concerned arguments related to the principle of equality; the second, the social meaning of the marital bond and finally the international repercussions of such a move. The majority of the Committee recognised the flexible and continually evolving nature of marriage and stressed the importance of the principle of equality above all other issues. The minority did not see equality as an issue, believing instead that same-sex and different-sex couples were not equal since same-sex couples were unable to reproduce naturally. It was noted by all members that international recognition of such an institution could cause problems for those couples wishing to have their partnership recognised abroad, but the majority indicated that such couples would be aware of the difficulties and eventually the opening of civil marriage in The Netherlands could have a positive rather than negative effect on international recognition.[21]

The Cabinet, led by Prime Minister KOK, felt that the scales were not tilted in favour of opening civil marriage to same-sex couples, although the Cabinet did agree to allow same-sex couples to adopt Dutch children. Nonetheless, after the 1998 general elections and the reappointment of the "purple coalition",[22] the Cabinet agreement stated that it would submit a proposal to Parliament before the 1st January 1999 calling for the opening of civil marriage to same-sex couples. In the meantime, such a proposal was sent to the Council of State along with a proposal to allow same-sex couples to adopt children. Less than two years later both Chambers accepted the proposals. On the 1st April 2001, The Netherlands became the first country in the world to allow for same-sex civil marriage.[23]

---

20 KORTMANN (1997) p. 23, §5.4.

21 KORTMANN (1997) p. 17-21, Chapter 4.

22 The Cabinet was called the "purple coalition" because when the colours of the main political parties in the Cabinet are mixed, purple is the result.

23 There were of course those academics who were against the opening of marriage to same-sex couples, although these commentators represented a minority in Dutch literature: *e.g.* NUYTINCK (1996).

V.4 ESTABLISHMENT

V.4.1 POSITION OF THE INSTITUTION

The Dutch Civil Code is divided into eight books, each dealing with a different area of private law. Book 1 deals with all issues related to family law and the law of persons. The Act of 5th July 1997 created the institution of registered partnership under a new Title 5A in Book 1. The positioning of the institution of registered partnership in this book signifies Parliament's intention to regard this as an institution akin to that of marriage, affecting family life and having consequences for one's civil status.

V.4.2 EXCLUSIVITY

Like marriage, a person may only be involved in *one* registered partnership with *one* other person at any one time, whether of the same or different sex.[24] Although both or either of the parties to a marriage or registered partnership may have already been married or involved in a registered partnership, they must be legally separated before they will be allowed to enter into a (another) registered partnership.[25] If the parties have previously been registered or married then a statement with the name of the previous partner/spouse must be delivered to the Registrar of Birth, Deaths, Marriages and Registered Partnerships (hereinafter the Registrar) in the place of residence of one the parties.[26] Registration is therefore only possible if the parties are not registered and not married at the time of registration, whether with each other or with a third party.

The celebration of a polygamous marriage is a criminal offence in The Netherlands.[27] This prohibition is likewise extended to registered partnerships.[28] Criminal sanctions are also imposed on any Registrar who knowingly co-operates in the celebration of a bigamous marriage.[29] This liability is extended to a Registrar who knowingly celebrates a "bigamous"

---

24 **Marriage:** Arts. 1:33 and 1:42, Neth. CC; **RP:** Art. 1:80a(1) and (2), Neth. CC.

25 Legally separated must be distinguished from judicially separated. Legal separation involves the legal dissolution of a registered partnership/the termination of a marriage.

26 Art. 1:80a(4), Neth. CC.

27 Art. 237, Neth. Cr. C.

28 Art. 237, in conjunction with Art. 90-*octies*, Neth. Cr. C.

29 Art. 379, Neth. Cr. C.

registered partnership or a registered partnership if he or she knows that one or both of the parties are already married (or vice-versa).[30]

V.4.3 SEX OF THE PARTIES

Since the 1st April 2001, marriage is no longer confined to persons of a different sex.[31] According to Art. 1:80a(1), Neth. CC, a person can enter into a registered partnership with another person irrespective of his or her sex. Mirroring the provisions for marriage, Dutch law makes no reference to the partners' sexual orientation.[32] A homosexual man is therefore allowed to enter into a registered partnership with a heterosexual man. Since registered partnership and marriage are open to both different-sex and same-sex couples and sexuality is not an issue, the problems raised due to transsexual registered partnerships and marriages are also obsolete.

V.4.4 MINIMUM AGE

In line with the conditions for marriage, a registered partnership can only be celebrated if both of the parties have attained the age of majority, currently set at eighteen.[33] If serious reasons exist, the Minister of Justice can remove this age impediment on request.[34] In addition, minors need the permission of their parents in order to enter into a registered partnership or a marriage.[35] This permission is not required should the mental capacity of the parents be so severely impaired that they are not in a fit state to determine their own will or to understand the meaning of the declaration.[36]

V.4.5 RESIDENCY

When the Registered Partnership Act was first introduced in 1997, many members of the Dutch Parliament expressed concern that The Netherlands would become a haven for sham registrations and wished to prevent the

---

30 Art. 379 in conjunction with Art. 90-*octies*, Neth. Cr. C.

31 Art. 1:30, Neth. CC.

32 For the complete absence of any discussion on a person's sexual orientation in a marriage see, NIEUWENHUIS (2004) p. 65-66, Inleiding and Art. 1:30.

33 Art. 1:80a(6) in conjunction with Art. 1:31, Neth. CC.

34 Art. 1:31(3), Neth. CC. An appeal to the district court is also possible should such a request be refused. A further appeal is also allowed to the Administrative Division of the Council of State. NIEUWENHUIS (2004) p. 67-68, Art. 1:31.

35 Art. 1:80a(6) in conjunction with Art. 1:35(1), Neth. CC.

36 Art. 1:80a(6) in conjunction with Art. 1:35(2), Neth. CC.

onset of "registration tourism".[37] As a result, the residency requirements imposed on the registration of partnerships were more stringent than the equivalent rules with respect to marriage. Old Art. 1:80a(2), Neth. CC, required *both* parties to either:

- possess Dutch nationality; or
- possess the nationality of a EU of EEA country;[38] or
- have a valid residence title.[39]

In 2001, the Government, at the same time as enacting legislation to allow for same-sex civil marriages, amended these conditions.[40] The Act harmonised the residency rules with respect to the eligibility criteria for entry into a marriage and a registered partnership. Accordingly, for a registered partnership or a marriage to be validly celebrated, only *one* of the parties needs to satisfy one of the following conditions. The person:

- must possess Dutch nationality; or
- must have his or her domicile in The Netherlands;[41] or
- must have permanent residency in The Netherlands.

In order to be granted permanent residency in The Netherlands one must comply with the conditions laid down in the Aliens Act 2000.[42]

V.4.6 PROHIBITED DEGREES OF RELATIONSHIP

Marriages and registered partnerships are prohibited between relatives in the direct ascending or descending line.[43] Marriages and registered partnerships between brothers, sisters or between a brother and sister are

---

37 *Dutch Second Chamber*, 1996-1997, 23761, No. 3 p. 5; No. 7, p. 15; No. 11, §§22-26. It was stated that a tourist visa is not enough to satisfy the conditions and that one also needs to fulfill Arts. 9, 9a and 10, Aliens Act 2000.

38 According to old Art. 1:80a(1), Neth. CC, an EU or EEA citizen also needed to be in possession of a valid residency title (a *verblijfstitel*) since he or she was required to be registered with the Basic Municipality Administration (*Gemeentelijke Basis Administratie*).

39 The phrase "residence title" must be understood with reference to old Arts. 9, 9a and 10, Aliens Act 2000, *Dutch Second Chamber*, 1996-1997, 23761, No. 11, p. 7.

40 *Neth. Staatsblad*, 2001, No. 11.

41 Domicile is explained with reference to Title 3, Book 1.

42 *Neth. Staatsblad*, 2000, No. 454.

43 Art. 1:80a(6) in conjunction with Art. 1:41, Neth. CC; *Dutch Second Chamber*, 1995-1996, 23761, No. 5.

also prohibited.[44] However, the Minister of Justice may lift prohibitions between adoptive brothers and sisters if serious reasons exist.[45] As is the case for marriage, persons not related in the direct ascending or descending line *i.e.* aunts, uncles, nephews, nieces and cousins, are permitted to register their partnerships.[46]

V.4.7 COMPETENCY AND CONSENT

A person incapable of determining his or her free will or of understanding the meaning of his or her declaration to marry will not be allowed to celebrate a marriage.[47] These rules are *mutatis mutandis* applicable to registered partnerships.[48] If such a person is not under guardianship then the Registrar must make this decision.[49] With respect to the required consent, the law distinguishes between four different groups of people who must obtain the consent of third parties in order to marry or register their partnership. The first group, consisting of minors, requires the consent of both of the minor's parents.[50] The second group, consisting of minors placed under guardianship, requires the consent of the guardian in addition to both of the minor's parents.[51] Persons placed under a guardianship due to alcohol abuse or being a spendthrift require the consent of their guardian,[52] whilst those under guardianship due to mental disorder must obtain the consent of the sub-district court judge.[53]

V.4.8 FORMAL VALIDITY

Prior to the celebration of a marriage or registration of a partnership, information must be submitted to the Registrar in the place of residence of

---

44 Art. 1:80a(6) in conjunction with Art. 1:41, Neth. CC. This includes half-brothers and half-sisters: Rb Middelburg, 21st December 1956, NJ 1957, 226.

45 Art. 1:80a(b) in conjunction with Art. 1:41(2), Neth. CC. For further historical information see J. DE BOER (2002) p. 123, §123; VAN DER BURGHT/DOEK (2002) p. 65, §143.

46 As a result of the lifting of the prohibition in 1983: *Neth. Staatsblad*, 1983, No. 290.

47 Art. 1:80a(6) in conjunction with Art. 1:32, Neth. CC.

48 Art. 1:80a(6), Neth. CC.

49 VAN DER BURGHT/DOEK (2002) p. 60, §132.

50 Art. 1:35(1), Neth. CC. This may be replaced by the judge: Art. 1:36, Neth. CC.

51 Art. 1:35(3), Neth. CC. This may be replaced by the judge: Art. 1:36, Neth. CC.

52 Art. 1:37(1), Neth. CC. Art. 1:37(2) states that this consent may be replaced by the *kantonrechter* (sub-district court judge) if the guardian's consent is not obtained.

53 Art. 1:38, Neth. CC. VAN DER BURGHT/DOEK (2002) p. 62, §138.

one of the parties.[54] If both parties have a place of residence outside of The Netherlands, this information must be given to the Registrar in The Hague.[55] The Registrar is under a legal duty to then prepare an instrument of registration unless he or she believes that making such an instrument would be against public policy.[56] A number of documents must be lodged with the Registrar pursuant to Art. 1:44, Neth. CC. These are the same as those documents required for a marriage.[57] The parties are entitled to select a different municipality for the celebration of the marriage or registration of the partnership than that where the information has been deposited.[58] This is known as a *keuzegemeente* or a "municipality of choice". If the registration is not fully completed within a year of the date of the instrument then a new instrument must be drawn up.[59]

Once the instrument has been deposited with the Registrar, the parties must wait fourteen days.[60] This period allows the Registrar to determine whether there are any important reasons why the registration should not take place, *e.g.* one of the conditions of registration has not been fully satisfied.[61] The registered partnership ceremony itself closely resembles that of marriage, apart from two important differences.[62] Firstly, the future parties to a registered partnership, as with parties to a future marriage, must declare that they consent to the registration. However, with registered partnerships, the parties do not need to give this consent in any particular prescribed format.[63] The second difference is that registered partners may celebrate a religious ceremony before the civil ceremony takes place,[64]

---

54 **Marriage**: Art. 1:43(1), first sentence, Neth. CC; **RP**: Art. 1:80a(4), first sentence, Neth. CC.

55 **Marriage**: Art. 1:43(1), second sentence, Neth. CC; **RP**: Art. 1:80a(4), second sentence, Neth. CC.

56 Art. 1:80a(4), in conjunction with Art. 1:18b(2), Neth. CC.

57 This includes a birth certificate of each of the parties and a certified true copy of their registration in the personal records database, an instrument of consent to the marriage if required, a death certificate all of those whose consent would have been required, evidence proving previous marriages or registered partners have been properly terminated, and an instrument of declaration to marry.

58 Art. 1:80a(4), in conjunction with Art. 1:43(2), Neth. CC.

59 Art. 1:80a(4), in conjunction with Art. 1:46, Neth. CC.

60 VLAARDINGERBROEK (2004) p. 103, §3.9.1.

61 Art. 1:80a(6), in conjunction with Art. 1:62, Neth. CC.

62 Although the law requires no specific form for the registration of the partnership, such form can be provided: VLAARDINGERBROEK (2004) p. 117-118, §4.3.5.

63 Art. 1:67, Neth. CC is not applicable to registered partnerships. See **Section V.5.2**.

64 Art. 1:68, Neth. CC is not applicable to registered partnerships. Art. 449, Neth. Cr. C, stipulates that the celebration of a religious wedding prior to a civil wedding will be fined

whereas future spouses are prohibited from doing so.[65] The reasoning for the fact that Art. 449, Neth. Cr. C is not extended to registered partners lies in the fact that registered partnerships are not celebrated in church.[66]

V.5 LEGAL EFFECTS

V.5.1 GENERAL

The Registered Partnership Adjustment Act effected changes in more than one-hundred existing statutes, thereby equating registered partnership with marriage.[67] The two institutions are treated exactly the same with respect to public law (*e.g.* taxation and social security) and are effectively treated the same for private law issues as well.[68] This section will discuss some of those rights and duties in-depth.

V.5.2 CIVIL STATUS

Along lines similar to marriage, a registered partnership modifies the civil status of the parties concerned, although minor differences in the procedure are evident. As regards marriages, the Registrar must prepare a marriage certificate immediately upon the solemnisation of the marriage.[69] All details listed in Arts. 36, 38, 40 and 57 of the Royal Decree on Civil Status must be included in the marriage certificate.[70] Once all the formalities have been concluded, the marriage certificate is issued and subsequently registered in the Register of Births, Deaths and Marriages.[71] The future spouses must both

up to a maximum of €2,250. Art. 90-*octies*, Neth. Cr. C, states that the term "marriage" must be interpreted to include "registered partnerships" throughout the Neth. Cr. C except in Art. 449. For more information on the relationship between Arts. 1:68 and 1:80a, Neth. CC and Art. 449, Neth. Cr.C see LOONSTEIN (2005).

65 Some authors have called for the repeal of the prohibition on religious marriages prior to civil marriages: ROES (2001) p. 111-113; PLASSCHAERT (2002) p. 654; LOONSTEIN (2005).

66 *Dutch Second Chamber*, 2001-2002, 28078, No. 2, p. 2, SUMNER/FORDER (2003) p. 266.

67 *Neth. Staatsblad*, 1997, No. 660.

68 Art. 1:80b, Neth. CC.

69 Art. 1:67(2), Neth. CC.

70 *Neth. Staatsblad*, 1994, No. 160. PLASSCHAERT (2002) p. 760-762.

71 If the formalities concerning the provisions of Art. 1:67(1), Neth. CC are not fulfilled then no marriage will be deemed to have taken place. If however after the reading of Art. 1:67(1), Neth. CC the certificate is not signed by the parties due to unforeseen and disastrous circumstances, then the marriage is still deemed to have taken place, even though the certificate is not registered in the Register. In this case, Art. 1:24, Neth. CC allows for a judicial addition to the Register to be made.

declare, in the presence of a competent Registrar and witnesses, their desire to enter into a marriage with each other and abide by all the rights and duties connected therewith. Immediately after this declaration, the Registrar declares that they are joined together as spouses. It is by means of this declaration that the marriage is deemed to have been celebrated and produces an effective alteration in the parties' civil status; the parties henceforth being regarded as "spouses".

With respect to registered partnerships, slight differences are apparent in the manner in which and time at which an alteration of the parties' civil status occurs. The certificate of registered partnership is free of form, apart from a few restrictions as mentioned in the Royal Decree on Civil Status.[72] Due to the fact that Art. 1:67, Neth. CC, is not *mutatis mutandis* applicable to the registration of a registered partnership, a registered partnership comes into existence upon the drawing up of the certificate of registered partnership.[73] Thus, should an instrument of registered partnership not be signed, the registered partnership will not have been established.[74] This formal disparity between the moments at which modification to a person's civil status occurs does not, however, detract from the identical consequences on the parties' civil status itself. Solemnisation of a marriage and registration of a registered partnership are in this respect treated identically.[75]

V.5.3 NATIONALITY

The ability to acquire or lose Dutch nationality is regulated by the Kingdom of The Netherlands Nationality Act.[76] Dutch nationality can either be acquired or attributed. If one is not attributed Dutch nationality by virtue of birth, recognition, adoption, or by choice (used by foreigners born in The Netherlands),[77] then one must undergo a process of naturalisation in order to acquire Dutch nationality.[78] Alongside the requirements that there are no objections to an unlimited stay in The Netherlands and that one has

---

72 Arts. 36, 38, 40, 55a and 57a, Royal Decree on Civil Status lay down a number of conditions that must be satisfied before a certificate of registered partnership is deemed to be valid.

73 Namely upon the moment that the certificate is signed by both parties and the Registrar.

74 PLASSCHAERT (2002) p. 957.

75 PLASSCHAERT (2002) p. 957-960.

76 Act of 19th December 1984, *Neth. Staatsblad,* 1984, No. 628 and 629.

77 Arts. 3(1), 4(1), 4(2), 5 and 6, respectively, Kingdom of The Netherlands Nationality Act.

78 Arts. 7-13, Kingdom of The Netherlands Nationality Act.

attained the age of majority,[79] the applicant is required to have lived in The Netherlands for five years immediately prior to the application.[80] If, however, the applicant is married or in a registered partnership with a Dutch national, then the spouse or registered partner need only have lived three years in The Netherlands to be entitled to apply.[81] Since 1998, all people seeking naturalisation are required to satisfy the conditions of the Act on the current rules with respect to the naturalisation of newcomers in Dutch society.[82] By virtue of these provisions, all newcomers older than eighteen years are required to follow an integration course (*inburgering*) before the process of naturalisation can be completed.[83]

V.5.4 NAME LAW

In principle, the celebration of a registered partnership, as with a marriage, brings no change in the surname of the parties.[84] As with married couples, registered partners gain the right and competency to use each other's surnames if they should wish to do so.[85] This competency is retained after the dissolution of the registered partnership so long as the partner does not re-register or marry anew.[86] As a result of these rules, four possibilities are available to registered partners and spouses alike, regarding their possible post-marital and post-registered surname. The parties can retain their own surname, adopt the surname of their partner, retain their own surname and affix their partner's surname thereafter or retain their own surname and affix their partner's surname before.[87] Use of a name to which one is not entitled is punishable according to Art. 1:8, Neth. CC.[88]

---

79 Art. 233, Neth. CC. Currently set at eighteen.

80 Art. 8, Kingdom of The Netherlands Nationality Act.

81 Furthermore, cohabitation is not required. The requirement is, however, imposed on unmarried and unregistered couples: VLAARDINGERBROEK (2004) p. 36, §2.2.2.D.

82 *Neth. Staatsblad,* 1998, No. 261, Wet houdende regels met betrekking tot de inburgering van nieuwkomers in de Nederlandse samenleving, Wet van 9 april 1998.

83 Learning about the Dutch language and society are included. The municipalities are responsible for the organisation of the training.

84 VLAARDINGERBROEK (2004) p. 63, §2.4.7; VAN DER BURGHT/DOEK (2002) p. 18, §29.

85 Art. 1:9(1), Neth. CC. This use of the surname of the spouse does not lead to a change of surname, but can be registered in the registers of the Municipal Administrative Personal Details: Art. 80, Act concerning the Municipal Administrative Personal Details.

86 Art. 1:9(3), Neth. CC.

87 VLAARDINGERBROEK (2004) p. 64, §2.4.7. For use of a hyphen see DE GROOT (2002) Arts. 1:9-1:13.

88 Art. 6:162, Neth. CC states that such a use is tortuous and allows for a claim to be made even if no damage was sustained, although the claimant must be able to prove a sufficient interest in bringing the claim: Art. 3:303, Neth. CC.

V.5.5 TAXATION, SOCIAL SECURITY AND PENSIONS

General amendments to a plethora of fiscal legislation have placed registered partners in an identical position to their spousal counterparts with regard to the collection of various taxes.[89] Due to the changes made by the Registered Partnership Adjustment Act,[90] the definition of "child" for taxation purposes has also been changed to include the child of a registered partner.[91] In the field of social security, registered partners are also treated identically to married persons.[92] However, upon the death of a registered partner, although the surviving registered partner will be entitled to a pension, that pension may, in certain circumstances, be smaller than that paid out to a widow or widower.[93]

V.5.6 RIGHTS AND DUTIES OF THE PARTNERS TO EACH OTHER

The provisions of Title 6, Book 1, Neth. CC, are applicable regardless of the matrimonial property regime applicable for the spouses, although certain rights can be avoided by terms agreed upon in a marital contract.[94] Art. 1:80b, Neth. CC, states that Title 6 is *mutatis mutandis* applicable to registered partner.

---

89 Art. 2(5), General Revenue Act; Art. 2(4), Revenue Collection Act 1990; Arts. 2(2), 17(2), 45(1), 46, 55(5), Income Tax Act 1964; Art. 11 and 22, Salary Tax Act 1964; Art. 2(2) and 26(1), Property Tax Act 1964; Arts. 4(b) and 5(b), Company Tax Act 1969; Art. 15(1)(b), Legal Transaction Taxes Act; Arts. 13a(4) and 32(6), Inheritance Tax Act.

90 *Neth. Staatsblad*, 1997, No. 660.

91 In **Dutch** law, the point of computation of degree begins at either of the persons in question and is then counted upwards to the common ancestor and then downwards to the other person.

92 Amendments were thus made to numerous social security Acts including the Sickness Act, Insurance for Inabaility to Work Act, General Inability to Work Act, Unemployment Benefit Act, Social Security (Amendment) Implementation Act, General Survivors Benefits Act, General Support Act, Handicapped Persons Benefits Act, as well as the Pensions and Saving Funds Act.

93 As a result of the introduction of Art. 2c(1), Pensions Funds Act only periods since the implementation of the Act will be taken into account in attempting to calculate the level of the pension. However, Art. 2c(2), Pensions Funds Act states that previous periods of participation may be taken into account.

94 NIEUWENHUIS (2004) p. 113, Inleiding.

V.5.6.1 *Duty to cohabit*

Prior to the Act of 31st May 2000,[95] spouses and registered partners were obliged to live together.[96] During the debate on the introduction of registered partnership, it was questioned whether this Article was outdated.[97] Despite the repeal of Art. 1:83, Neth. CC, the practical situation has changed little.[98] Even prior to the repeal, spouses and registered partners were entitled to avoid living together,[99] and non-performance of this obligation was very rarely sanctioned.[100] Nonetheless, some commentators have questioned the ideology behind the removal of this provision, due to the often-made assumption that spouses or registered partners do in fact live together.[101] Despite the absence of a duty to cohabit, it is often assumed, as reference to Art. 1:84, Neth. CC proves, that the spouses or registered partners do in fact live together. The absence of a general duty to cohabit does not, therefore, detract from the specific obligation to cohabit in order to obtain certain benefits.[102]

V.5.6.2 *Duty of fidelity*

Art. 1:81, Neth. CC, states that spouses owe each other a duty of fidelity (*getrouwheid*). This duty is *mutatis mutandis* applicable to registered partners.[103] The duty lasts as long as the marriage or registered partnership is in existence. Although non-adherence to this duty can be an important factor in the eventual determination of the irretrievable breakdown of the marriage, its scope with respect to registered partnerships is unclear.[104] Do registered partners owe each other a duty of "registered monogamy"? Unlike marriages where the irretrievable breakdown of the marriage needs

---

95 *Neth. Staatsblad*, 2001, No. 275.

96 Art. 1:83, Neth. CC.

97 *Dutch Second Chamber*, 1995-1996, 23761, No. 6, p. 17.

98 VAN DER BURGHT/DOEK (2002) p. 116, §222. LAT-marriages (living-apart-together marriages) are now legalised: VERSTAPPEN (2002) p. 309. Calls for the abolition of the judicial separation procedure have since increased as one of the main consequences of the procedure is to remove the obligation to cohabit: FORDER (2001) p. 308.

99 Art. 1:85(2) (old), Neth. CC.

100 J. DE BOER (2002) p. 169, §190.

101 VAN DER BURGHT/DOEK (2002) p. 116, §222; VAN MOURIK/NUYTINCK (1998) p. 74, §81; J. DE BOER (2002) p. 169, §190.

102 J. DE BOER (2002) p. 169, §190.

103 Art. 1:80b, Neth. CC. Adultery is however no longer criminal since the enactment of the Act of 6th May 1971, *Neth. Staatsblad*, 1971, No. 291.

104 Art. 1:151, Neth. CC (divorce) and Art. 1:169, Neth. CC (judicial separation).

to be proven for a divorce to be granted,[105] registered partnerships can be ended without being irretrievably broken down, thus negating the somewhat limited value of this provision.[106] Nonetheless, although possibly meaningless in terms of a legally enforceable obligation, the duty of fidelity says more about the essence of what it means to be involved in a registered partnership.[107]

V.5.6.3 Duty to provide support and assistance

Art. 1:81, Neth. CC, also imposes a duty on spouses to provide support and assistance to their partner, and is once again correspondingly applicable to registered partners.[108] The phrase "support and assistance" (*hulp en bijstand*) has been interpreted to be broader than financial obligations, and thus includes the multitude of other material obligations that exist between spouses or registered partners.[109] Spouses, and thus registered partners, are also obliged to provide for each other's needs.[110] This phrase has also been interpreted rather broadly, obliging spouses and registered partners to provide for each other's needs in proportion to their own means, so that the more financially well-off spouse or registered partner will have a greater obligation than his or her comparatively less financially well-off registered partner.[111] This duty only applies during the existence of the marriage or registered partnership. Upon the dissolution of the relationship, the obligation is dealt with in accordance with the law on maintenance.[112]

Spouses and registered partners are also placed in an identical situation in relation to their mutual duty to care for any minor children who form part of the family.[113] This Article can be seen as a complement to Art. 1:247, Neth. CC which imposes an obligation on those vested with parental authority to care and raise the children under their care.[114] According to the Dutch Supreme Court, the duty imposed by way of Art. 1:82 is terminated

---

105 Art. 1:151, Neth. CC.

106 See **Section V.6** for methods of dissolving a registered partnership.

107 This is also, to a certain extent, true of spouses: VAN MOURIK/NUYTINCK (1998) p. 72, §78.

108 Art. 1:80b, Neth. CC.

109 VAN DER BURGHT/DOEK (2002) p. 108, §218.

110 Art. 1:81, *in fine*, Neth. CC.

111 See further HR, 10th May 1974, NJ 1975, 183.

112 HR, 4th December 1987, NJ 1988, 678, annotated by LUIJTEN. See **Section V.6.9.1**.

113 Art. 1:82, Neth. CC. The text of Art. 1:82, was amended as a result of the Act of 31st May 2000, *Neth. Staatsblad*, 2001, No. 275. See further: FORDER (2001) p. 307.

114 VAN DER BURGHT/DOEK (2002) p. 115, §222.

upon the termination of the marriage.[115] Since Art. 1:82, Neth. CC is analogously applied to registered partnerships,[116] this duty is also terminated upon the dissolution of the registered partnership.

V.5.6.4 Duty to contribute to household expenses

Art. 1:84, Neth. CC elaborates on the duty to provide for each other's needs as expounded in Art. 1:81, Neth. CC. Spouses are, as a result, under a duty to contribute to the costs of maintaining the household, including the cost of caring for and raising children.[117] This duty can, however, be reduced to zero by means of a marital contract[118] or written agreement.[119] Despite attempts to amend the current regime, Dutch law still provides for a complicated set of rules for the defrayment of household expenses.[120] This duty is nonetheless *mutatis mutandis* applicable to registered partners.[121] The term "household costs" relates to those costs incurred for the interests of the common household.[122] Regardless of the sort of household expense, all such expenses are to be paid from the income of the spouses or registered partners; first from joint income and thereafter from the private income of each of the spouses or registered partners in proportion to their income.

Read in conjunction with Art. 1:82 and Title 17, Neth. CC, costs incurred as a result of all children who are part of the family are covered by this obligation.[123] If either of the spouses or registered partners fails to fulfil his or her obligation under this provision, or if there is a dispute with respect to the purview of the duty, the judge of the district court is competent to hear the case.[124] Since the repeal of the duty to cohabit, the question has arisen as to how this duty is to be applied to those spouses or registered partners who

---

115 HR, 23rd May 1975, NJ 1976, 412.

116 Art. 1:80b, Neth. CC.

117 Art. 1:84, Neth. CC. For the care and raising of children, see **Section V.5.6.3.**

118 VAN DER BURGHT/DOEK (2002) p. 108, §218; WORTMANN/VAN DUIJVENDIJK-BRAND (2002) p. 66, §46. See also HR, 17th November 1961, NJ 1962, 46.

119 In existence since 22nd June 2001 (Act of 31st May 2001, *Neth. Staatsblad*, 2001, No. 275).

120 *Dutch Second Chamber*, 1999-2000, 27084, No. 4, p. 6-11. FORDER (2001) p. 310.

121 Art. 1:80b, Neth. CC.

122 NIEUWENHUIS (2002) p. 116, Art. 1:84; J. DE BOER (2002) p. 173-183, §202-217.

123 J. DE BOER (2002) p. 178-179, §208.

124 Art. 1:84(4), Neth. CC.

do not live together. The Dutch Supreme Court has held that the answer to this question depends on the reasons why the parties do not live together.[125]

V.5.6.5 Duty to contribute to the repayment of debts

In principle, each spouse or registered partner is liable for any obligations entered into by him or her.[126] In terms of those liabilities and obligations entered into for the "ordinary running of the household", Art. 1:85, Neth. CC provides an important exception to that rule.[127] For these obligations spouses and registered partners are equally liable. Reference to case law must be made in order to ascertain the exact extent of this category of obligations.[128] It is, however, clear that the boundaries of this category are identical regardless of whether a person is involved in a marriage or a registered partnership.

V.5.6.6 Protection of the home

In accordance with Art. 1:88, Neth. CC, both spouses and registered partners are entitled to identical protection with respect to their marital or familial home. Accordingly, a spouse or registered partner requires the consent of the other with respect to any contract for the disposal, encumbrance or the giving in use and legal transactions for the discontinuation of the use of a dwelling in which the spouses or registered partners live jointly, or in which the other spouse or registered partner is living alone.[129] The restriction laid down in Art. 1:88, Neth. CC only restricts a person's capacity to enter into legal transactions of a certain nature, and the general rule is that a spouse or registered partner's freedom to enter into contracts is unfettered by this restriction.[130]

---

125 If the parties live apart as a result of an agreement (for whatever reason), then Art. 1:84 still applies: HR, 25th June 1971, NJ 1972, 58. If, however, the parties do not cohabit for serious reasons, only the duty encompassed by Art. 1:81, Neth. CC is applicable.

126 VAN DER BURGHT/DOEK (2002) p. 117, §223; J. DE BOER (2002) p. 185, §227; NIEUWENHUIS (2002) p. 118-119, Art. 1:85; VAN MOURIK/NUYTINCK (1998) p. 77, §88.

127 VAN DER BURGHT/DOEK (2002) p. 128, §237; J. DE BOER (2002) p. 186-188, §228-231; NIEUWENHUIS (2002) p. 118-119, Art. 1:85.

128 VAN DER BURGHT/DOEK (2002) p. 129, §238.

129 Art. 1:88(1)(a), Neth. CC in conjunction with Art. 1:80b, Neth. CC.

130 NIEUWENHUIS (2002) p. 120-126, Art. 1:88.

V.5.7 PROPERTY LAW

As a result of the introduction of registered partnership, Dutch matrimonial property law has been the subject of intense debate and revision.[131] The third of a series of three bills aimed at reforming the legal relationship of spouses and registered partners,[132] still awaiting enactment,[133] deals specifically with provisions related to matrimonial property.[134] If the future parties to a registered partnership do not draw up a registered partnership contract, their property will be regulated according to the rules on the statutory community of property scheme for registered partners or the so-called *gemeenschap van geregistreerd partnerschap.*[135] Since the law is identical with respect to spouses and registered partners, reference here will only be made to registered partners. According to the present law, when the parties register their partnership, in principle, all property which the parties have at that time and acquire in the future during the registered partnership, forms part of their community of property. Four exceptions to this rule are provided for: inherited property, property connected to one of the registered partners,[136] pension rights,[137] and rights provided for in accordance with Art. 4:28 and 4:30, Neth. CC.[138] This community also includes the partners' debts.[139] All debts are treated as community debts, although exceptionally a debt will be deemed to be a private debt if

131 VERSTAPPEN (2002) p. 307. For general information on matrimonial property see SOONS (1999); JOPPE (2003); KRAAN (2003).

132 **First Bill**: Act on Rights and Duties of Spouses and Registered Partners, *Neth. Staatsblad*, 2001, No. 275 (See FORDER (2001) p. 306-312; SUMNER/FORDER (2003) p. 269-270). **Second Bill**: Act on Contractual Participation Clauses, *Neth. Staatsblad*, 2002, No. 370 (See SUMNER/FORDER (2003) p. 270-276).

133 *Dutch Second Chamber*, 2002-2003, 28867, No. 1-6. For general commentary see, *inter alia*, M.J.A. VAN MOURIK, "De omvang van de nieuwe wettelijke gemeenschap van goederen", *WPNR*, 2003, Vol. 6545, p. 637-644; A.J.M. NUYTINCK, "De derde tranche van de herziening van het huwelijksvermogensrecht", *FJR*, 2003, p. 150-156; H.C.F. SCHOORDIJK, "Modernising van ons huwelijksvermogensrecht. Het concept regeringsontwerp derde tranche", *NJB*, 2003, p. 218-222; C.G. BREEDVELD-DE VOOGD and W.G. HUIJGEN, "Naar een beperkte gemeenschap? Niet doen!", *WPNR*, 2004, Vol. 6562, p. 43-50.

134 Thus also to registered partners by virtue of analogous application to registered partnerships: Art. 1:80b, Neth. CC.

135 Art. 1:93, Neth. CC.

136 The *Hoge Raad* has strictly interpreted the term "connected to" with respect to spouses. This restrictive interpretation is thus correspondingly applicable to registered partners.

137 Pension Rights Equalisation (Separation) Act.

138 Art. 1:94, Neth. CC.

139 Art. 1:94(2), Neth. CC.

inextricably connected to a private asset of one of the partners. The registered partner from whose side the asset came from is, during the existence of the registered partnership, entitled to deal with and dispose of that asset.[140]

The proposals for reforming the statutory community of property contemplate a number of pressing problems facing Dutch matrimonial property law. The most far-reaching proposal in the Bill would exclude assets acquired and debts incurred before the celebration of the marriage or registration of the partnership.[141] In order to deal with some of the evidential problems associated with such a scheme, proposed Art. 1:94(8), Neth. CC, would provide that if it cannot be proved that an asset belongs to one or other spouse or registered partner it would be presumed to belong to them both. The proposal also attempts to address the disadvantageous position of the person who does not work outside the home, with respect to the control and management of the community of property. A distinction is thus made between, on the one hand, goods for which title has been registered or goods used in the business of one of the spouses or registered partners and, on the other, all other goods. The first category of goods can be dealt with and disposed of by the spouse in whose name the goods are registered.[142] With respect to all other goods, a new rule has been proposed which allows either spouse to deal with or dispose of such property.[143]

If the parties, however, decide that they would prefer to opt-out of the statutory community of property scheme, they are free to do so, but are required to draw up a contract of registered partnership property with a public notary.[144] This choice may be made before or during the registered partnership.[145] The parties may opt for one of the statutory schemes provided for in the Neth. CC, or one of the many standard non-statutory schemes, including a total separation of property. If the parties decide to

---

140 Art. 1:97(1), Neth. CC.

141 Proposed Art. 1:94(1), Neth. CC. As a result *inter vivos* and testamentary goods would always be excluded from the community of property: Proposed Art. 1:94(2)(a), Neth. CC. *Dutch Second Chamber*, 2002-2003, 28867, No. 2, p. 2 and No. 3, p. 20-21.

142 Proposed Art. 1:97(1), first sentence, Neth. CC. For those goods used in the business of a registered partner, the law remains unchanged.

143 Proposed Art. 1:97(1), second sentence, Neth. CC.

144 An "akte van partnerschapsvoorwaarden": Art. 1:115, Neth. CC.

145 Art. 1:114, Neth. CC.

terminate their community of property, they must do so by agreement or by means of a court order.[146]

V.5.8 INHERITANCE LAW

After a forty-five year discussion, inheritance law in The Netherlands was finally revised with the introduction of a new Book 4 to the Neth. CC.[147] According to Art. 4:8, Neth. CC, the surviving registered partner is treated in exactly the same way as the surviving spouse.[148] According to Art. 4:10(1), Neth. CC and in the absence of a will, the surviving registered partner and the children of the deceased are entitled to inherit first.[149] The surviving registered partner will, by operation of law, immediately acquire his or her deceased partner's estate.[150] Before administering the estate the surviving registered partner is under a duty to satisfy all the debts of the estate.[151] However, before any division of the estate can take place, it is necessary to assess the value of the estate.[152] If the registered partner dies having left a last will and testament, the estate will be divided in accordance with the deceased's wishes.[153] Although, according to Dutch inheritance law, a person is unable to completely disinherit his or her children, the provision does not apply to a spouse or registered partner.[154] Nevertheless, a number of other rights are granted to the surviving partner, none of which can be avoided by means of a will. The surviving registered partner has the right to remain for a period of six months in the residence where he or she lived at the moment of the deceased partners' death.[155] During that period he or she also has the right to claim that the other next-of-kin co-operate in the granting of a right to use the residence and the contents of that residence.[156] Moreover the surviving partner may claim a right to use the other goods of the deceased, insofar as he or she can demonstrate that these

---

146 Arts. 1:99-1:113, Neth. CC.

147 *Neth. Staatsblad*, 2002, No. 430. For a translation see SUMNER/WARENDORF (2005).

148 Equivalent to the old Art. 4:879a, Neth. CC.

149 This is followed by the deceased's parents, brothers and sisters; his or her grandparents; and finally by his or her great-grandparents. However, as a restriction only those related to the deceased up to the sixth degree can allowed to inherit: Art. 4:12(3), Neth. CC.

150 Art. 4:13(1) and 4:13(2), first sentence, Neth. CC.

151 Art. 4:7 and 4:13(2), second sentence, Neth. CC.

152 Art. 4:65, Neth. CC.

153 Art. 4:42, Neth. CC.

154 Art. 4:63, Neth. CC.

155 Art. 4:28, Neth. CC.

156 Art. 4:29, Neth. CC.

goods are necessary for his or her care.[157] If the partner dies intestate and there are no ex-spouses, ex-registered partners or children, then the surviving partner will inherit everything.[158] The situation will differ if there are other statutory heirs involved.

Art. 19(1), Inheritance Law Act 1956, allows a child who is subject to joint parental authority to fall within the group of persons who can inherit from the co-parent and vice versa.[159] By virtue of Art. V of the Registered Partnership Act,[160] this provision has also been extended to children raised in a registered partnership. This amendment, however, only has consequences regarding the co-parent, and not the extended family. As a result of further changes to the Inheritance Law Act 1956, registered partners also pay inheritance tax at the same rate as spouses,[161] and receive the benefit of the higher tax free portion of the inherited share.[162]

V.5.9 CHILDREN

Thirty years ago, questions of parentage and parental authority were answered according to general, clear and simple rules.[163] Children born to married couples were regarded as the legal children of spouses. As a result both spouses were vested with parental authority. Today, this situation has changed radically and Dutch law provides for one of the most complicated systems in the world with respect to the rules on parentage and parental

---

[157] Art. 4:30, Neth. CC.

[158] By simple application of Art. 4:10(1), Neth. CC.

[159] FORDER (1999a) p. 19.

[160] *Staatsblad* 1997, No. 324.

[161] As a result the surviving registered partner receives the following advantageous percentages: <€21,212: 5%; €21,212-€42,419: 8% (minimum €1,060); €42,419-€84,829: 12% (minimum €2,756); €84,829-€169,650: 15% (minimum €7,845); €169,650-€339,293: 19% (minimum €20,568); €339,293-€848,219: 23% (minimum €52,800); >€848,219: 27% (minimum €169,852). Those inheriting in a capacity other than one mentioned in Art. 24(1), Inheritance Tax Act 1956 are taxed at the following rates: <€21,212: 41%; €21,212-€42,419: 45% (minimum €8,696); €42,419-€84,829: 50% (minimum €18,239); €84,829-€169,650: 54% (minimum €39,444); €169,650-€339,293: 59% (minimum €85,247); €339,293-€848,219: 63% (minimum €185,336); >€848,219: 68% (minimum €505,959).

[162] Spouses and registered partners do not have to pay tax on the first: €496,324 whereas unrelated heirs must pay tax on the share above €1,839.

[163] For an overview of the law in relation to parental authority, see DOEK (2000). The number of children born outside of wedlock has risen dramatically since the turn of the 1980s: in 1981 the percentage of children born outside of wedlock stood at 4.8%, in 1986 at 8.8%, in 1991 at 12.0%, in 1996 at 17.0% and in 2001 at 27.1% (figures from www.cbs.nl). See also BOELE-WOELKI/BRAAT/CURRY-SUMNER (2005) p. 93-95.

authority.[164] The ever-increasing removal of marriage as the keystone in family law has gained momentum since the 1980s and can be traced in numerous legislative changes in this field.[165]

Despite the continuing debate surrounding parentage and parental authority, the question of how to deal with the relationship between registered partners and their children was left unanswered with the enactment of the Registered Partnership Act. Since then sporadic amendments have been endorsed which have liberalised the law and yet at the same time made it increasingly complex, intricate and inconsistent. It is now necessary to distinguish between different-sex married couples, female same-sex married couples, male same-sex married couples, different-sex registered partners, male same-sex registered partners and female same-sex registered partners. Children raised by two people, neither of whom are the child's legal parents add further complexities. Since this work does not attempt to provide a comprehensive and exhaustive account of Dutch law in relation to children, an overview of the current situation will be given in relation to registered partnership, providing information where necessary on the relevant subtle distinctions made by the Dutch legislature.[166]

Nevertheless, before one can begin to analyse the rules themselves, it is first necessary to clarify the terminology used. In deciding upon the correct translations for the Dutch legislation, one must bear in mind that the Dutch legislation itself has often been drafted in a very inconsistent and inadequate manner.[167] The terms referred to in this book are: legal parent (*juridische ouder*),[168] parental authority (*ouderlijk gezag*) and co-parent (*sociale ouder*).[169]

---

164 SCHRAMA (2002).

165 For example joint parental authority is no longer connected with the existence of a marriage, HR, 4th May 1984, NJ 1985, 510. For further examples and explanation see the introduction to WORTMANN (2001) p. 231.

166 For a sample of the research currently being conducted on this field, see VONK (2004).

167 A wealth of literature has now been published on this topic, amongst others see DOEK (2000); WORTMANN (2001); NUYTINCK (2002); DE GRAAF (2003); DOEK (2004).

168 In Title 14, Book 1, Neth. CC reference is always made to the *ouder*. This has been interpreted to mean the *juridische ouder*, thus the legal parent.

169 For the reasoning behind certain translations see SUMNER/WARENDORF (2003) p. v-vi.

V.5.9.1 Parentage

The legal mother of a child is always the woman who gives birth to the child.[170] Even if the woman who gives birth to the child is not the genetic mother of the child, she will still be deemed to be the legal mother.[171] If the legal mother of the child is involved in a regulated same-sex relationship, whether it is a same-sex marriage or a same-sex registered partnership, then her female partner will not automatically be deemed to be the "legal parent" of the child.[172] The only way for a same-sex female partner of the legal mother to gain legal parenthood is by means of adoption.[173] Although current Dutch law does not allow for a woman to recognise a child, criticism has nonetheless been levied at such a situation.[174]

Determination of legal paternity is a somewhat more difficult proposition. If the child is born to a different-sex married couple, then the male spouse of the legal mother, *i.e.* the woman who has given birth to the child, is deemed to be the legal father.[175] This presumption has not been extended to same-sex married couples or registered partners (regardless of sex).[176]

---

170 Art. 1:198, Neth. CC. Recently reinforced: Rb Groningen, 20th July 2004, LJN No. AQ8757.

171 This scenario is typical in cases of surrogacy, where the birth mother is implanted with genetic material from the commissioning parents, or from (anonymous) donors. NIEUWENHUIS (2004) p. 233, Art. 1:198. This has nonetheless come under fierce criticism. BROEKHUIJSEN-MOLENAAR, for example, is convinced that the possibility should exist for the legal mother to deny maternity or for the recognition of a child by the mother: BROEKHUIJSEN-MOLENAAR (1999) p. 39-40. DE RUITER has also proposed that maternity should be determined according to genetics: DE RUITER (1993) p. 99.

172 See further HENSTRA (2002). With the introduction of same-sex marriage the question was raised in the Second Chamber. The legislature rejected the extension of the presumption of paternity in such a case believing that it would detract too far from the reality and would not sit correctly with the fundamental ideology of parentage law that a child has a mother and can have a father, *Dutch Second Chamber*, 1999-2000, 26 673, No. 5, p. 20.

173 Open to same-sex couples since the 1st April 2001: *Wet adoptie door personen van hetzelfde geslacht, Neth. Staatsblad*, 2000, No. 10. For further details see **Section V.5.9.3**.

174 LOENEN (1995) p. 95; WAALDIJK (2000a) p. 178; HENSTRA (2002) p. 185.

175 Art. 1:199(a), Neth. CC. This presumption is also extended, by virtue of Art. 1:199(b), to the man who was married to the woman who gave birth to the child, if the marriage was ended as a result of death within 306 days prior to the child's birth, even if the mother has remarried. This also seems to coincide with the biological truth since 90% of children born within marriage are the biological children of the mother's husband: VLAARDINGERBROEK (2004) p. 171, §6.5.2.

176 In the Official Report by the Kortmann Commission, this limitation was justified by the argument that " ... otherwise the gulf between reality (there is no parentage) and the law (legal parentage exists) ..." would become too great: KORTMANN (1997) p. 5.

When the institution of registered partnership was introduced in 1998, the presumption of paternity was not extended. An extension of the presumption was considered too problematical since it would have required the implementation of a complicated dual regime for extending the presumption to different-sex couples only, since the registered partnership scheme was open to both same-sex and different-sex couples.[177] However, since 2001 marriage has been open to couples of the same-sex and thus this argument no longer holds true.[178] The question, as yet unanswered, remains as to why one regime exists for different-sex married couples and a different regime operates for same-sex married couples and registered partners, regardless of sex. Nevertheless, at the time of writing the presumption of paternity has not been extended to registered partners.[179]

Accordingly, in order for the male registered partner of the legal mother to be regarded as the legal father of the child he must recognise the child,[180] have his paternity judicially determined[181] or adopt the child.[182] If, on the other hand, the legal father of the child is already known or has already

[177] ANTOKOLSKAIA (2002a) p. 786-787.

[178] HENSTRA has argued for this presumption to be extended to the female partner of the mother; automatically if they are married and by means of an ability to recognise if they are involved in a registered partnership or cohabiting: HENSTRA (2002) p. 185.

[179] Art. 1:199(a), Neth. CC is not extended to registered partnerships.

[180] A long discussion has developed surrounding the aim of the recognition. Should it be the case that the recognition is a legal act aimed at establishing a legal paternal link with a child, irrespective of the biological reality, or on the other hand, is the recognition simply an acknowledgment of an already existing biological link? See VLAARDINGERBROEK (2004) p. 181-182, §6.11.2. The current Dutch solution is a mismatch of the two standpoints. A man is able to recognise a child even if he is not the child's biological father, although this may, at a later stage, be contested due to the fact that he is not the biological father: Art. 1:205(1), Neth. CC.

[181] Art. 1:207, Neth. CC provides for the possibility of the judicial establishment of paternity. A substantial amount of case law has now been developed in terms of DNA-testing. As a result of a Supreme Court decision, a man can be ordered to submit to DNA-testing. If the man refuses to the test, adverse conclusions can be drawn: HR, 22nd September 2000, NJ 2001, 647. See HEIDA (2002) p. 122-129; SUMNER/FORDER (2003) p. 282-285.

[182] If a man wishes to recognise the child, he must first obtain the permission of the legal mother. Since the 1st April 1998, the permission of the mother can now be replaced by the *rechtbank* if the recognition would not prejudice the interests of the mother in an undisturbed relationship with the child or the interests of the child and the man who fathered the child is the begetter of the child" (Art. 1:204(3), Neth. CC). The Hoge Raad has recently allowed the recognition of a child regardless of the relationship between the father and the mother and child: HR, 16th February 2001, NJ 2001, 571.

been ascertained,[183] a male registered partner may only become the legal father of the child by means of adoption.[184] If one of the parties to a same-sex registered partnership already possesses legal parentage over the child, either by means of birth (maternity) or by means of recognition, judicial determination or adoption (paternity), the other partner may only become a legal parent of the child by means of adoption.[185] Once the male registered partner has been granted legal fatherhood, he may also be vested with parental authority.[186]

V.5.9.2 Parental Responsibilities

Parents can be vested with parental authority either automatically by operation of law or on their request.[187] A person vested with parental authority has a duty to care for and raise his or her child.[188] The precise ambit of the rights and duties encompassed by the notion of parental authority is, however, not listed.[189] Yet although the legislature has given those vested with parental authority a somewhat loose rein, certain statutory limits are imposed.[190] The term co-parent has been used when describing a registered partner who is neither a legal parent nor someone vested with parental authority. A distinction needs to be drawn between those situations whereby parental authority is awarded by operation of law and those in which one or both of the parties must undertake steps to acquire parental authority over their child.

---

183 If a child has already been recognised, a judicial determination of parentage is not subsequently allowed, even if by the same man. This may be advantageous since nationality can be attributed from a man to a child if he is judicially determined to be the father, whereas this is not the case if he has recognised the child: Rb Breda, 13th May 2004, LJN No. AP1163.

184 An adoption can only take place if the legal father has no objections: Art. 1:228(1)(d), Neth. CC. This has also been extended to those who have "family life" with the child: Hof The Hague, 25th April 2001, LJN No. AB1581.

185 VONK (2004) p. 105-107.

186 Art. 1:252, Neth. CC.

187 The rules of parental authority are listed in Title 14, Book 1, Neth. CC.

188 Art. 1:247, Neth. CC. Art. 1:247(2), Neth. CC explains that this is inclusive of the mental and corporal well being of the child, as well as the promotion of the development of his or her personality. This includes not only clothing, food and accommodation but also education, medical treatment *etc.* NIEUWENHUIS (2004) p. 294-295, Art. 247.

189 VAN TEEFFLEN (2001) p. 137; BOELE-WOELKI/BRAAT/CURRY-SUMNER (2005) p. 125-126, 166-168, 196, 203, 214, 233-234, 246 and 261.

190 *E.g.* Compulsory Education Act 1994 (*Neth. Staatsblad*, 1994, No. 255) states that parents have a duty to send their children to school as soon as they attain the age of five.

A. By operation of law

Prior to the enactment of the Registered Partnership Act, only married couples could exercise joint parental authority;[191] a same-sex partner was thus unable to share parental authority over the child of his or her partner. Although unmarried couples were prevented from acquiring parental authority by operation of law, the Dutch Supreme Court had held that the district court could grant parental authority to the other parent.[192] By virtue of the Act of 4th October 2001,[193] this situation was radically altered. Two new articles were inserted into the Neth. CC: Arts. 1:253aa and 1:253sa. As a result of Art. 1:253aa, if the male partner of the legal mother has recognised the child prior to its birth, such that both parties to the registered partnership are the legal parents of the child,[194] both parties to the registered partnership will be automatically vested with parental authority.[195] This Article is dependent on the legal parentage of the child having been determined *prior* to the child's birth.[196] The provision does not apply to a male partner who has not recognised the child before its birth or same-sex registered partnerships since the partner is not entitled to recognise the child.[197]

Nonetheless, if the partner of the legal mother is not the legal parent of the child, and so long as there is no other legal parent, the partner of the legal mother will be vested with automatic parental authority by virtue of Art. 1:253sa, Neth. CC.[198] If the child has another legal parent, the parties to the registered partnership (or same-sex marriage) must undertake steps in order to be vested with parental authority.

---

191 Art. 1:251(1), Neth. CC.

192 HR, 21st March 1986, NJ 1986, 585.

193 *Neth. Staatsblad*, 2001, No. 468.

194 SCHRAMA (2002) p. 277-303.

195 Art. 1:253aa, Neth. CC. In reality a woman must be involved in the relationship, *i.e.* a registered partnership between a man and a woman or between two women.

196 That is to say that the father must have recognised the child prior to birth: Art. 1:2, Neth. CC states that an unborn child will be considered to be born if it is in his or her best interests to be so regarded. It is deemed to be in his or her best interests in this case: J. DE BOER (2002) p. 516, §719.

197 This provision is never applicable to the position of a male registered partnership since the child can never be born "to" the relationship.

198 See also BOELE-WOELKI/BRAAT/CURRY-SUMNER (2005) p. 347.

B. On request

A number of options are available to those couples who are not vested with parental authority by operation of law. The options available, once again, depend on the nature of their relationship, as well as the existence of a legal parent not involved in the relationship.

- *Registration: Child recognised after birth*: In accordance with Art. 1:252(1), Neth. CC, if the child is recognised after its birth, the parents may register with the clerk of the district court as having joint parental authority. The Registrar only has a limited competency and cannot determine whether the parental authority order is in the best interests of the child.[199]
- *Court decision: Child has not been recognised*: By virtue of the Joint Parental Authority and Guardianship Act, a co-parent has the right, should the legal parent consent, to request a district court judge to vest him or her with parental authority alongside that of the legal parent.[200] This request can only be granted if the legal parent is the sole holder of parental authority rights.[201] If the judge vests the co-parent with parental authority, Art. 1:245(5), Neth. CC stipulates that this parental authority shall be exercised jointly.

As soon as the co-parent is awarded parental authority, he or she is under a duty to support the child.[202] The co-parent, with the consent of the legal parent, is also entitled to request that the name of the child be changed to the co-parent's name.[203] According to the law as it stands, two women who have a child during a registered partnership are allowed to use the surname of the non-mother, whereas two women who have a child during a marriage can only use the name of the birth mother.[204] If the co-parent is a

---

[199] SCHRAMA (2002) p. 277-303.

[200] Art. 1 :253t, Neth. CC. This requires a close personal relationship with the child.

[201] Art. 1:253t(1), Neth. CC. See further SCHRAMA (2002) p. 277-303. It could happen that the father of the child has recognised the child as his own, and therefore this would prevent the application of the provision. However, this will seldom occur since recognition requires permission of the biological mother: Art. 1:204(1)(c), Neth. CC. Although this can, and often is, substituted by the consent of the district court: Art. 1:204(3), Neth. CC.

[202] Art. 1:235w, Neth. CC.

[203] Art. 1 :235t(5), Neth. CC.

[204] By virtue of Art. 1:253sa(3), Neth. CC, Art. 1:5(4), 1:5(5) and 1:5(6) apply *mutatis mutandis* to registered partners and not to married couples. Art. 1:253sa applies when a legal parent is vested with parental authority over a child with a non-legal parent. In this case the non-legal parent, if they are joined in a registered partnership, is able to use her

Dutch national, it is also possible for a non-Dutch national child to obtain Dutch nationality through the Dutch co-parent.[205] The co-parent is also entitled to apply to the district court to resolve any such dispute.[206]

However, there remain differences between a co-parent who exercises joint parental authority and a parent who is the child's legal or adoptive parent.[207] Differences in legal consequences are evident, especially in the field of the administration of property,[208] as well as a striking difference in terms of the language used to describe the partner's relationship towards the child.[209] However, although these differences remain, their effect is of less importance now that same-sex couple adoption is permitted.[210]

V.5.9.3 Adoption

When the Registered Partnership Act was passed in 1998, the prohibition on same-sex adoption remained. However, on the 1st April 1998, the law was changed to allow for adoption by single adults and unmarried different-sex couples who had lived together for a minimum of three continuous years immediately preceding the adoption application.[211] The disparity between different-sex and same-sex relationships was subsequently challenged before the Neth. SC. In 1998, two mothers petitioned the court for joint adoption rights over each other's children.[212] The two women had a committed relationship, were living together and had each given birth to children conceived with the sperm of the same donor father.[213] The Dutch Supreme Court decided that this was not a question for the judiciary but

surname for the child's surname: ADVIESBUREAU (2003) p. 390. This mistake is now soon to be altered by virtue of *Dutch Second Chamber*, 2003-2004, 29353, No. 6.

205 *Neth. Staatsblad*, 2000, No. 618, Art. 6(1).

206 Art. 1:253v, Neth. CC.

207 WORTMANN (1998).

208 BOELE-WOELKI/BRAAT/CURRY-SUMNER (2005) p. 261.

209 Book 1, Title 14, §3A, Neth. CC (which deals with joint parental authority) reads "gezamenlijk gezag van een ouder met een ander dan een ouder" or translated "joint parental authority of a parent with a person other than a parent".

210 Although currently restricted to internal adoptions, step-parent adoption is permitted: see **Section V.5.9.3.**

211 *Neth. Staatsblad*, 1997, No. 772. See also VLAARDINGERBROEK (2000).

212 HR, 5th September 1997, NJ 1998, 686.

213 The donor had signed an instrument before a notary public stating that he would not exercise any rights nor have any duties or responsibilities towards the child.

should instead be determined by the legislature.[214] The Dutch Supreme Court did, however, recognise that "more elaborate legal recognition than is now the case in national law" is required in order to respect the rights of same-sex couples with children.[215]

The Second Kortmann Committee, referring to the decision of the Dutch Supreme Court, recommended that it should be possible for one partner in a same-sex couple to adopt the child of the other partner, but stressed that this should be implemented with caution. The Committee thought adoption should only be allowed if the relationship between the child and the other biological parent was of no significance, and was not expected to become one of any significance.[216]

The CDA faction in the Second Chamber thought the proposal unnecessary, in light of the possibility for an application for joint parental authority.[217] Moreover questions were raised as to whether this was actually in the best interests of the child or more for the improvement of the position of same-sex couples.[218] The strict Protestant factions raised similar criticisms.[219] When the Bill was sent to the First Chamber, all the Christian parties disapproved, stating that it was not in the best interests of the child to be raised in a same-sex environment.[220] The Bill eventually passed through the First Chamber with ease; only the Christian Democrats, the strict Protestant parties and two members of the liberal left faction voted against the Bill. On the 1st April 2001, the legislation opening up adoption to couples of the same-sex came into force.[221] The Adoption (Same-Sex Couples) Act enables two people of the same sex to adopt a Dutch child[222] or the child of their

214 In a similar line to the decisions of the *Hoge Raad* with respect to the opening up of marriage to same-sex couples, see **Section V.3.3.**

215 HR, 5th September 1997, NJ 1998, 686 at 687. See also MAXWELL (1999).

216 VLAARDINGERBROEK (2004) p. 246-247, §7.10.

217 Christen Democratisch Appèl (Christian Democrats).

218 *Dutch Second Chamber*, 1999-2000, 26673, No. 4, with reference being made to Art. 1:227 (old), Neth. CC. This is now in a more explicit form in Art. 1:227(3), Neth. CC.

219 *Gereformeerd Politiek Verbond-fractie* (GPV) and *Reformatorische Politieke Federatie-fractie* (RPF).

220 *Handelingen, Dutch First Chamber*, 2000-2001, 14606, 19th December 2000.

221 *Neth. Staatsblad*, 2001, No. 145. Art. 1, Act on the Placing of Foreign Children for Adoption, *Neth. Staatsblad*, 1988, No. 566 states that the term "aspirant adoptive parents" is to be understood as "spouses of different sex." (*Neth. Staatsblad*, 2001, No. 128).

222 Despite the legal possibility to adopt, VONK discusses the practical difficulties in realising such wishes: VONK (2004) p. 108-109.

partner.[223] The situation with respect to the adoption of foreign children is somewhat more complicated.[224] Prior to 1st January 2004, same-sex couples wishing to adopt a child from abroad from a State not party to the 1993 Hague AC had to undergo two separate procedures involving a minimum waiting period of four years.[225] For different-sex couples (regardless of whether they are married, registered or unregistered) joint adoption of a child from a State not party to the 1993 Hague AC can take place by means of one procedure after one year.[226] A current bill before Parliament seeks to redress these differences, by permitting same-sex couples to adopt foreign children, as well as removing the one-year period for which a step-parent must have cared for the child.[227] Moreover, the three year period during which the adopter must have cared for and raised the child wil be reduced to one year.[228]

V.5.9.4 Artificial Reproductive Techniques

Since the 1st November 1993, commercial surrogacy has been illegal in The Netherlands.[229] There is no legislation in The Netherlands restricting access to assisted reproduction services to married couples. Female same-sex registered partners are therefore eligible for artificial insemination treatment, unless, just as with different-sex married couples, there are specific reasons against the provision of such treatment.[230] If a child is born in a female same-sex relationship, the same provisions with regard to parentage will apply as those outlined in **Section V.5.9.1**.[231] However, a registered partner who is pregnant by means of donor insemination cannot

---

223 KOENS (2001) p. 27. See also *Dutch Second Chamber,* 1998-1999, 26673, No. 3, p. 3.

224 A joint application to adopt a foreign child is thus prohibited if the couple is of the same-sex. See Art. 1, Act on the Placement of Foreign Children for Adoption (*Wet opneming buitenlandse pleekinderen*).

225 One of the parties first had to ensure that he or she was the legal parent, either by operation of law, recognition, judicial determination or adoption. The second step was for the partner of the legal parent to then begin a single parent adoption procedure (step-parent adoption). In order for a step-parent adoption to be granted the parties must have cared for the child for at least one year: Art. 1:228(1)(f), third sentence, Neth. CC. The partner msut also have lived together for at least three years: Art. 1:227(2), Neth. CC.

226 SIMONS (2004) p. 152-155.

227 Press Release from the Ministry of Justice, www.justitie.nl/nieuws/50624homoparen.asp.

228 Nieuws, "Regeling voor interlandelijke adoptie door homoparen", *NJB,* 2005, p. 1376.

229 Introduction of Arts. 151b and 151c, Neth. Cr. C; *Neth. Staatsblad,* 1993, No. 486.

230 Hospitals are, however, free to make their own policies. See www.freya.nl.

231 The female same-sex partner cannot recognise the child, but is able to adopt.

require her female partner, even if she had consented to the insemination, to pay for the child's care and upbringing.[232]

The possibilities for male same-sex registered partners to have a child via artificial reproduction are absent. For biological reasons, such a partnership always requires the involvement of a female person, *i.e.* a surrogate mother, and since Dutch law presupposes that the birth mother is the legal mother,[233] the situation of male registered partners will always be very different to that of female or different-sex registered partners.[234]

V.6 DISSOLUTION

V.6.1 GENERAL

The termination of a registered partnership is governed by Arts. 1:80c-1:80g, Neth. CC. For the most part, these methods have been inspired by the methods available to married couples to terminate their marriage.[235] However, judicial separation, available to married couples wishing to terminate their marriage, is not available to registered partners.[236] The majority of spouses using the judicial separation procedure often do not wish to divorce for religious reasons.[237] The Government, believing that those involved in a registered partnership would not have such religious convictions, saw no reason to extend the possibility of such a judicial separation procedure to registered partnership.[238] This reasoning can, however, be challenged,[239] and some commentators have called for an extension of the rules on judicial separation to registered partners.[240]

---

232 HR, 10th August 2001, LJN No. ZC3598.

233 Art. 1:198, Neth. CC.

234 For current Dutch law on surrogacy, see BROEKHUIJSEN-MOLENAAR (1999).

235 Art. 1:149, Neth. CC.

236 For detailed information see BOELE-WOELKI/BRAAT/SUMNER (2003a) p. 121-126.

237 J. DE BOER (2002) p. 477, §667. *Dutch Second Chamber*, 1993-1994, 23761, No. 3, p. 9; No. 7, p. 20.

238 HEIDA (2000) p. 41.

239 Judicial separation brings to an end the community of property and up until the abolition of the duty of cohabitation, also brought such a duty to an end (Art. 1:83 (old), Neth. CC). The judicial separation also affects certain provisions with respect to children, maintenance and the use of the common household.

240 See, for example, WAALDIJK (2000) p. 177-178.

V.6.2 JUDICIAL: JOINT PETITION

Judicial proceedings for the termination of a registered partnership may only be initiated upon receipt of a petition filed by one of the parties, thus excluding the possibility of a joint petition.[241] Marriage, on the other hand, may be terminated either by means of a joint petition or a unilateral petition.[242] As a result, all provisions with respect to a joint petition for divorce are not correspondingly applicable to registered partners.[243] Questions have been raised as to the desirability of a joint petition procedure for registered partners. Parliament's intentions were, however, clear: the creation of a two-track system. Those wishing to terminate their registered partnership jointly were to make use of the administrative procedure, whilst those wishing to terminate the relationship unilaterally were to make use of the judicial procedure. Questions can, and will, however, be raised with respect to the final outcome of the administrative dissolution of registered partnerships.[244]

V.6.3 JUDICIAL: UNILATERAL PETITION

Like marriage, the judicial dissolution of a registered partnership can be requested by one of the parties and is effective when the court's judgment is recorded in the Register of Births, Deaths, Marriages and Registered Partnerships.[245] Unlike the problems that arise in relation to the administrative dissolution of a registered partnership,[246] Art. 1:80e, Neth. CC stipulates that all provisions relating to court proceedings for divorce are *mutatis mutandis* applicable to the judicial dissolution of a registered partnership.[247] If the parties fail to register the judgment within six months of the final order being given, the judgment will no longer be effective from that date onwards.[248] The judicial procedure is identical in all aspects to a unilateral petition for divorce,[249] except with respect to children.[250]

---

241 Art. 1:80c(d), Neth. CC. J. de Boer (2002) p. 489, §688e.

242 Joint petition (*gemeenschappelijk verzoek*) and unilateral petition (*eenzijdig verzoek*).

243 For example, Art. 819, Neth. CCP.

244 See **Section V.6.4.**

245 **Marriage:** Art. 149, Neth. CC; **Registered Partnership:** Art. 1:80e(2), Neth. CC.

246 See **Section V.6.4.**

247 Art. 1:80e(1), states that Arts. 1:151, 1:153, 1:155, 1:157-1:160, 1:164, 1:165, Neth. CC are all applicable.

248 Art. 1:163(3), Neth. CC.

249 All the relevant rules detailed in Title 9 with respect to the dissolution of a marriage by means of divorce are *mutatis mutandis* applicable to registered partnerships, apart from

V.6.4 ADMINISTRATIVE: JOINT DECLARATION

Unlike marriage, registered partnerships may be terminated by means of an administrative procedure devoid of judicial intervention. The registered partnership in this case must be terminated by a mutual agreement. A distinction must be drawn between the agreement to terminate (*beëindigingsovereenkomst*) and the declaration to terminate (*beëindigingsverklaring*).

V.6.4.1 Agreement to Terminate

Art. 1:80d, Neth. CC, provides the necessary framework to accompany the ground for dissolution expounded in Art. 1:80c(c), Neth. CC, namely the dissolution of a registered partnership by mutual consent. Both partners must have agreed that the relationship has irretrievably broken down and that they wish to terminate their relationship.[251] A number of provisions applicable to divorce are *mutatis mutandis* applicable to registered partners utilising this procedure.[252] Problems have nevertheless arisen due to the absence of the *mutatis mutandis* application of a number of other provisions, relating to the power:

- of the court to order maintenance to be paid by one partner;[253]
- of the parties to reach agreements regarding maintenance, notably a number of protective provisions regarding dissolution of the registered partnership;[254] and
- of the court to regulate the use of the former dwelling.[255]

Art. 154 (dealing with joint petitions), Art. 1:163(1) (which is paraphrased in Art. 1:80e(2)) and Art. 1:163(2) (dealing with joint petitions).

250 A judge is unable to order ancillary provisions with respect to minors in judicial proceedings to terminate a registered partnership: Art. 1:253aa(2), Neth. CC and Art. 828, Neth. CCP; Rb Leeuwarden, 12th November 2003, LJN No. AN8913. In contrast, see Rb Maastricht, 8th January 2004, LJN No. AO3414 where the court held that Art. 828, Neth. CCP does not conform with Art. 8, ECHR since the extension of parental authority to registered partners in 2002, and declared such a request admissible.

251 Art. 1:80d(1), Neth. CC.

252 Art. 1:80d(2) states that Arts. 1:155, 1:159(1) and (3), 1:159a, 1:160 and 1:164, Neth. CC are all *mutatis mutandis* applicable to the termination of a registered partnership by means of mutual consent

253 Art. 1:157, Neth. CC. Some commentators believe that this provision should have, however, been correspondingly applicable: VERSTAPPEN (1997) p. 277.

254 Art. 1:158, Neth. CC.

255 Art. 1:165, Neth. CC.

The position of children in a registered partnership also need not have been discussed upon dissolution of the registered partnership by means of a joint declaration.[256] This position could have been justified when registered partnership was first introduced due to the fact that registered partnership had no effect on the parties' relationship with any children. However, this situation has since been amended and registered partners are now granted joint parental authority over any children born to the registered partnership.[257] This amendment to the legislation therefore negates such arguments and requires that this lacuna be filled.[258]

The absence of rules relating to maintenance and the use of the former dwelling of the partners has been compensated for in Art. 1:80d(1), where it is stated that the agreement to terminate the registered partnership must deal with the following matters:

- Maintenance payments for the support of the registered partner who lacks sufficient means to support him or herself, and cannot reasonably be expected to do so;
- Agreement as to which of the partners is to be the tenant of their main residence hitherto, or which of the partners shall be entitled to use the dwelling and its contents belonging to one or both of the partners, or which one or both of the partners enjoys use-rights, and for how long such entitlement is to continue;
- The division of any community entered into by the partners on the registration of partnership or the compensation agreed pursuant to the conditions in Title 8, Book 1, Neth. CC.
- The equalisation or compensation of superannuation rights.[259]

The last five words of the second sentence of Art. 1:80d, "*evenwel niet op straffe van nietigheid*" (translated as "without this being a condition of its

---

256 Such a rule is also not required with respect to marriage, since joint parental authority continues automatically upon divorce: Art. 1:251(2), Neth. CC. It would appear that since the introduction of joint parental authority for registered partners (Arts. 1:253aa and 1:253sa, Neth. CC), parental authority also continues unhindered upon the termination of a registered partners, unless the parties request otherwise (HR, 28th March 2003, LJN No. AF2688). See further VONK (2003) p. 125-126. See also **Section V.5.9.2**.

257 Arts. 1:253aa and 1:253sa, Neth. CC.

258 If one looks to the material published on this topic prior to the statutory amendments of 2001 (*i.e.* before joint parental authority was extended to registered partners), the majority of commentators noted that agreements with respect to children where not necessary, since registered partnership had no consequences on any children: WORTMANN/VAN DUIJVENDIJK-BRAND (1998).

259 Art. 1:80d(1)(a) to (d), inclusive, Neth. CC.

validity") have been afforded considerable attention in Dutch literature, with opinions divided as to the compulsory character of this provision.[260] It is submitted here that the parties do not need to reach an agreement on the individual issues raised but must be able to state that they have at the very least addressed the issues mentioned. Regardless of whether this sentence is compulsory in nature or not, the legislature believed that since the parties are attempting to regulate the termination of their partnership themselves, the State should remain, as far as possible, outside any negotiations. It therefore falls for the notary or lawyer to advise the parties as to the questions raised concerning the interrelationship of Art. 1:80d, Neth. CC, and the other provisions of Book 1, Neth. CC.[261]

V.6.4.2 Declaration to Terminate

Once the parties have drawn up their agreement to terminate, whether they have received legal assistance or not, they are obliged to register the agreement with the Registrar. It must be dated and signed by both parties and one or more lawyers or notaries. According to Art. 1:80d(3), Neth. CC, the declaration referred to in Art. 1:80c(d), Neth. CC, must be registered by the Registrar within three months of the agreement being entered into. Once the agreement is registered in the Registry, the registered partnership is deemed to have been terminated.

V.6.5 ADMINISTRATIVE: UNILATERAL DECLARATION

A unilateral, administrative dissolution procedure for terminating a registered partnership does not exist in The Netherlands.

V.6.6 ANNULMENT PROCEEDINGS

In the same way that a marriage may be annulled due to the non-satisfaction of one of the formal marital requirements, a registered partnership may also be annulled for identical reasons.[262] The only

260 For arguments for the **non-compulsory** nature of the Art. 1:80d matters see: HOEVENAARS (1997); VERSTAPPEN (1997) p. 277; WORTMANN (2002) p. 167. For commentators supporting the **compulsory** nature see, KRAAN (1997) p. 4; MELLEMA-KRANENBURG (1997) p. 2; WAALDIJK (2000) p. 168; J. DE BOER (2002) p. 487, §688c.

261 FORDER (1999a) p. 22.

262 *I.e.* non-satisfaction of Arts. 1:31-1:42, Neth. CC. The rules on annulment contained in Section 5, Title 5, Neth. CC are *mutatis mutandis* applicable (except for Art. 1:77(2)(a)).

exception to this rule is the non-corresponding application of Art. 1:77(2)(a), Neth. CC, to the annulment of a registered partnership. Art. 1:77(2), Neth. CC, provides for an exception to the rule that the annulment of the registered partnership has retrospective effective to the date when the registered partnership was registered.[263] As a result of Art. 1:77(2)(a), not being applicable to registered partners, the annulment of a registered partnership also has retrospective effect with respect to children. Therefore, in principle, if either of the parties to a registered partnership was vested with parental authority as a result of the existence of the registered partnership,[264] which is subsequently annulled, such parental authority will be revoked.[265] Due to the fact that registered partners may, since 2002, be vested with joint parental authority either by operation of law or upon request, this situation is unacceptable and Art. 1:77(2)(a), Neth. CC should thus be declared *mutatis mutandis* applicable to the annulment of a registered partnership.[266]

V.6.7 DEATH AND PRESUMPTION OF DEATH

Art. 1:80c(a) and (b), Neth. CC, provides for the termination of a registered partnership by the death or presumed death of a registered partner, along identical lines to the dissolution of a marriage by death or presumption of death.[267]

V.6.8 ENTRY INTO MARRIAGE / CONVERSION

The conversion procedure,[268] as laid down in Art. 1:80g, Neth CC, states that if both registered partners notify the Registrar that they wish to convert their registered partnership into a marriage, the Registrar of the residency of one of the parties may draw up an instrument of conversion. It would seem that the Registrar is granted a discretionary competence to refuse to draw up such a document; however that is not the case. The Registrar is only allowed to refuse to draw up such an instrument on those

---

263 Art. 1:77(1), Neth. CC.

264 By virtue of Arts. 1:253aa or 1:253sa, Neth. CC.

265 *Contra* VLAARINDERBROEK (2004) p. 117-118, §4.3.5.

266 This position is shared by NUYTINCK (2004).

267 Arts. 1:412-425, Neth. CC are therefore applicable to missing persons and Arts. 1:426-430, Neth. CC are applicable to presumed dead persons.

268 For a detailed discussion of the Parliamentary proceedings, see SUMNER (2004a).

grounds listed in Art. 1:18b, Neth. CC.[269] Furthermore, the future spouses must live in The Netherlands, although not necessarily together or one of them must possess Dutch nationality.[270] In the latter case, the conversion must take place at the Registry in The Hague.

The conversion constitutes a termination of the registered partnership and causes the marriage to commence on the date the deed of transformation is registered in the Register of Marriages. Moreover, this Article also states that the conversion does not alter any pre-existing parentage relationship with children born prior to the conversion.[271] The mirror procedure to convert a marriage into a registered partnership is elucidated in Art. 1:77a, Neth. CC. Although the conversion of a registered partnership into a marriage has, as yet, not caused significant problems domestically, the conversion of a marriage into a registered partnership has instigated considerable discussion.[272]

In a number of cases, problems have arisen with respect to instruments of conversion having been prepared without the parties actually being aware of the related consequences. In a case before the District Court in Alkmaar,[273] a woman requested a divorce on the 27th February 2002. She requested that the judge make ancillary orders on the basis of Art. 827, Neth. CCP.[274] Her husband also submitted a request for the court to make judgment with respect to Art. 827, Neth. CCP. An oral hearing was scheduled for the 30th September 2002. During the oral hearing, it appeared that the parties had converted their marriage into a registered partnership before the Registrar on the 20th August 2002.[275] This conversion thus prevented the district court judge from making ancillary orders under Art. 827, Neth. CCP since their marriage had already been dissolved. This case illustrates the inadequacy of the current system. There are two "competent

---

269 Including when the parties fail to submit the documents listed in Art. 1:18(2), the Registrar considers the submitted documents inadequate, or the Registrar is of the opinion that the drawing up of an instrument would be against Dutch public policy.

270 WORTMANN (2002) p. 165-172.

271 Art. 1:80g(3), Neth. CC.

272 For an overview of academic articles on the topics see, SUMNER (2003) p. 21-22.

273 Rb Alkmaar, 10th October 2002 (2003) *EB* 12.

274 Ancillary provisions in relation to maintenance, property division, parental authority, contact, care and upbringing of children *etc.* Art. 828, Neth. CCP states however that the Arts. granting the judge the power to order ancillary provisions with respect to minor children are not applicable to registered partnerships.

275 Further examples see HEIDA (2003) p. 113.

authorities" involved in the termination of marriages. On the one hand, the Registrar is responsible for the conversion of marriages into registered partnerships, and the district court, on the other, is responsible for divorce proceedings. As illustrated in the above-mentioned case, whilst the judicial procedure was already underway, the parties' marriage was converted into a registered partnership without the knowledge of the district court, since the Registrar is not obliged to inform the district court that such a procedure has taken place. The parties were therefore unaware of the consequences that converting their marriage into a registered partnership could have on their case before the district court, possibly believing that they were in fact making their divorce "easier".[276]

The combination of the procedure for converting a marriage into a registered partnership and the possibility to subsequently terminate the registered partnership administratively, gives rise in effect to a possible administrative divorce or a so-called "lightning divorce" procedure.[277] This phenomenon has received widespread attention[278] and figures indicate that there were 5,000 "lightning divorces" in 2004.[279] However, two proposals currently before the Dutch Second Chamber and due to be discussed later this year propose the abolition of the possibility to convert a marriage into a registered partnership.[280]

V.6.9 EFFECTS OF DISSOLUTION

V.6.9.1 Maintenance

Depending on the method used to dissolve the registered partnership, a registered partner may be entitled to maintenance.[281] If the parties dissolve their partnership by joint declaration, they must ensure that they have

---

276 By virtue of conversations with district courts in Alkmaar, The Hague, Utrecht, Leeuwarden, Amsterdam and Maastricht it is clear that it is not exceptional for some couples to "reconvert" their registered partnership into a marriage, in order to allow for the judge to make ancillary orders on the basis of Art. 827, Neth. CCP. If "reconversion" is indeed on the increase, then one can certainly question whether the Government was indeed erudite in conceiving such procedures.

277 See BOELE-WOELKI (2003a) p. 121.

278 FORDER (1999b); WORTMANN (2002); REINHARTZ (2002a); BOELE-WOELKI (2003b) p. 49.

279 CBS, "Flitsscheiding blijft populair" (www.cbs.nl). This has been fiercely attacked and is due to be abolished. For information on the proposals see **Chapter VIII.3.3**.

280 *Dutch Second Chamber*, 2004-2005, 29676, No. 2, Art. I.B, p. 2 (LUCHTENVELD proposal) and *Dutch Second Chamber*, 2004-2005, 30145, No. 2, Art. I.B, p. 1 (DONNER proposal).

281 For instances when a registered partner may not be entitled see SUMNER (2004a).

regulated the payment of maintenance.[282] The parties are, however, entitled to agree that no maintenance will be paid upon termination of their registered partnership. If one of the parties files for the registered partnership to be judicially terminated, then all the provisions related to maintenance between former spouses are *mutatis mutandis* applicable to maintenance between former registered partners.[283] Upon the dissolution of a registered partnership or a marriage, Dutch law grants the judge the power to award a former spouse or registered partner maintenance at his or her request, if he or she does not have sufficient income to maintain himself or herself and cannot be reasonably expected to be able to gain such income.[284] The court enjoys a wide discretion according to Art. 1:157(1), Neth. CC, in awarding maintenance, in that it has the freedom to take into account "all the circumstances of the case".[285] It has been held that the duration of the marriage (and thus registered partnership) and the behaviour of the person entitled to maintenance can be taken into account.[286] Since 1994, maintenance claims have also been statutorily limited, signalling the end of the "life-long" duty to provide maintenance.[287] If a marriage or registered partnership has not lasted for more than five years and no children have been born to the relationship, the duty to maintain ends upon the expiry of the period equivalent to the period of the marriage or registered partnership.[288]

V.6.9.2 Effects with respect to children

By virtue of Art. 1:251(2), Neth. CC, spouses vested with parental authority continue to exercise such authority after a divorce has been decreed.[289] Despite this Article not being *mutatis mutandis* applicable to registered partners, registered partners vested with parental authority continue to exercise such authority after the dissolution of their registered

282 See **Section V.6.4.1** for further discussion of the problems associated with this rule.

283 Art. 1:80e(1), Neth. CC.

284 Art. 1:157(1), Neth. CC. It must be noted that the judge is not obliged to award maintenance but merely may grant an award of maintenance.

285 HR, 20th December 1991, NJ 1992, 180.

286 Boele-Woelki/Braat/Sumner (2003b) p. 135-136.

287 *Neth. Staatsblad*, 1994, No. 570. Vlaarinderbroek (2004) p. 357. This duty is limited in principle to 12 years: Art. 1:157(3) to 1:157(6), inclusive. Although this 12 year period is not a maximum and parties are allowed to agree to a period longer than twelve years.

288 Art. 1:157(6), Neth. CC.

289 Art. 1:251(2), Neth. CC.

partnership.[290] Although this has not been expressly stated, this can be inferred from a decision of the Dutch Supreme Court.[291] The Court noted that the method by which the parents were vested with parental authority was not important in determining the termination of parental authority. As a result, unmarried couples who have acquired parental authority by means of a judicial decision should be treated identically to those couples who were vested with parental authority by operation of law. This principle is thus equally applicable to the termination of such parental authority and results in parental authority remaining intact after the separation of unmarried couples. It can thus be inferred from the analysis of the Dutch Supreme Court that such a rule applies with respect to registered partners.[292]

Upon the dissolution of their marriage or registered partnership, parents are obliged to pay maintenance for the care and upbringing of their children. With respect to the care and upbringing of the child, this duty is terminated as soon as the child attains the age of eighteen;[293] with respect to education and maintenance this age is set at twenty-one.[294] Although step-parents are obliged to provide maintenance to minor children of their spouse or registered partner who are treated as children of the family until the child has attained the age of majority, this duty ends upon the termination of the marriage or registered partnership.[295]

V.6.9.3 Effects with respect to property

If the registered partnership is terminated by means of a joint declaration, Art. 1:80d(b) and 1:80d(c), Neth. CC, obliges the parties to have included agreements for the division of any community of property as well as for the allocation of accommodation which served as their principal residence in their agreement to terminate their registered partnership. If the registered partnership is terminated judicially, the court is entitled to apply any of the provisions applicable to the division of matrimonial community property to

---

290 VONK (2003) p. 126; BOELE-WOELKI/BRAAT/CURRY-SUMNER (2005) 368-369.

291 HR, 28th March 2003, LJN No. AF2688.

292 HR, 28th March 2003, LJN No. AF2688, §3.4.1-3.4.3.

293 Art. 1:392, Neth. CC. An exception is granted to children who have attained the age of majority and have not received money due for the costs of care and upbringing, despite such sums being due, HR, 11th December 1987, NJ 1988, 723.

294 Art. 1:395a, Neth. CC.

295 Art. 1:395, Neth. CC. In this case, the maintenance rules of Arts. 1:253w and 1:394, Neth. CC are both nonetheless applicable.

the property of registered partners.[296] According to current matrimonial property law, the community of property is terminated as soon as the divorce becomes final.[297] However, current proposals before the Dutch Second Chamber will alter this situation if enacted. Proposed Art. 1:99(b), Neth. CC, provides that the community property between registered partners would be brought to an end upon the filing of a petition for the termination of the registered partnership.

---

296 Art. 1:80b, Neth. CC states that all the provisions of Titles 7 and 8, Neth. CC are *mutatis mutandis* applicable to registered partnerships.

297 Art. 1:99(a), Neth. CC.

CHAPTER VI
SWITZERLAND

VI.1 INTRODUCTION

In a procedure characterised by cross-party support, a form of registered partnership (*le partenariat enregistré, eingetragene Partnerschaft*,[1] *unione domestica registrata*) was eventually introduced in 2005.[2] Due to the fact that the Swiss Registered Partnership Act (Sw. RPA) will enter into force on the 1st Janaury 2007, there are currently no statistics available on the number of partnerships registered. As a result, only the most recent statistics with respect to the number of marriages celebrated can be provided in **Section VI.2**. This is followed by an account of the legislative history surrounding the introduction of registered partnership (**Section VI.3**), information on how a registered partnership can be established (**Section VI.4**), the rights and duties attached to such a partnership (**Section VI.5**) and the manner in which such a partnership may be terminated (**Section VI.6**).

VI.2 EMPIRICAL EVIDENCE AND STATISTICS

***Table 7**: Number of marriages celebrated in Switzerland (July 2005)*[3]

Year	Total	Year	Total
1998	38,683	2002	40,213
1999	40,646	2003	40,056
2000	39,758	2004	39,460
2001	35,987	**Total**	**274,803**

1 A number of German speaking parties objected to the name *registrierte Partnerschaft* since the word was commonly used during the 1960s when homosexuals were registered by local police, see PLANT (1986). For more details see FF 2003, p. 1192 at 1213 (§1.6.1).

2 FF 2004, p. 2935, RS 211.231.

3 http://www.statistik.admin.ch/eindex.htm.

VI.3 HISTORICAL PERSPECTIVE

VI.3.1 EARLY PARLIAMENTARY HISTORY

Prior to 1994 there is scant record of any parliamentary time having been allocated to questions concerning non-marital cohabitation, let alone issues related to same-sex cohabitants.[4] However, in 1994 the Council of States was forced, for the first time, to consider the legal problems faced by same-sex couples,[5] when State Councillor PETITPIERRE posed a parliamentary question on the 15th March 1994 asking the Federal Council to report on the implications for Switzerland of the newly adopted registered partnership legislation in Denmark and Norway.[6] On the 11th May 1994, the Federal Council replied to this question stating that at that time it had no intention of introducing a special regulatory framework for the registration of same-sex couples. Nonetheless, the Federal Council did agree to undertake a comprehensive consultation procedure with all interested parties.

In the same year, National Councillor GRENDELMEIER submitted a proposal demanding that same-sex relationships be placed on an equal footing with marriage.[7] On the 9th January 1995, the Commission for Same Rights for Same-Sex Couples gathered 85,181 signatures to a petition also entitled "Same rights for same-sex couples".[8] It was admitted that an improvement in the legal situation of homosexual couples would require extensive federal and cantonal legislative change.[9] The petition went on to highlight other instances of legal discrimination in areas as wide-ranging as health benefits and paternity. Later that year on the 6th September 1995, the Federal Democratic Union (FDU) submitted a counter-petition entitled "For a

---

4 In 1975 the matter was discussed in relation to joint parental authority being extended to non-married cohabitants: *Swiss National Council,* BO 1975, 1780, as well as in 1983 in relation to the revision of matrimonial property law: *Swiss National Council,* BO 1983, 708. Previous debates in the Swiss Parliament in relation to homosexuality had always centred on the homosexual as an individual and not on the problems faced by homosexual couples.

5 The Swiss Parliament consists of two chambers: the Council of States (*Conseil des Etats/Ständerates/Consiglio degli Stati*) and the National Council (*Conseil national/Nationalrates/Consiglio nazionale*). The Swiss Executive is known as the Federal Council (*Conseil fédérale/Bundesrat/Consiglio federale*).

6 *Swiss Council of States,* BO 1994, No. 94.1027, 778.

7 *Swiss National Council,* BO 1994, No. 94.3439, Proposal.

8 *Swiss Council of States,* BO 1997, No. 96.2011, 701, Petition.

9 MINISTRY OF JUSTICE (1999) p. 40.

healthy family and against legal equality for homosexual couples".[10] Although the petitioners accepted that homosexuals were entitled to respect, it was an unacceptable claim, in their eyes, that their relationships should obtain the same legal status as the "natural couple". It was added that the promotion of the healthy family is a vital investment for the future of the State and therefore the State should clearly privilege the family both legally and financially.[11]

VI.3.2 MOUNTING PARLIAMENTARY PRESSURE

In February 1996, the National Council's Commission for Legal Affairs deliberated both petitions. After an intensive and lively discussion, the Commission demanded that the Federal Council examine the possibilities to eliminate the legal problems faced by same-sex couples as a result of the refusal to grant them the rights and obligations afforded to married couples.[12] On the 13th June 1996 the National Council voted in favour of communicating this demand to the Federal Council.[13] This demand thus enjoined the Swiss Federal Government to devise a plan to eliminate the forms of legal discrimination faced by same-sex couples and to offer same-sex couples a formal partnership registration procedure akin to marriage. On the same day, the National Council also considered the FDU petition and sent these demands to the Council of States.[14]

On the 16th March 1998, the Liberal Party submitted an alternative proposal to the National Council demanding that the Federal Council undertake a detailed examination of the legal situation of homosexual couples.[15] In light of the speeches already made on this topic and the ongoing work by the Ministry of Justice, the Federal Council accepted the proposal.[16] On the 30th November 1998, National Councillor GROS deposited a parliamentary initiative co-signed by twenty-one other parliamentarians aimed at the introduction of registered partnership for same-sex and different-sex couples.[17] On the 9th December 1998, State Councillor SPOERRY submitted

---

10 *Swiss Council of States*, BO 1997, No. 96.2012, 702, Petition.

11 In the eyes of the petitioners, family could only be used with reference to a heterosexual situation.

12 MINISTRY OF JUSTICE (1999) p. 4.

13 68 votes to 61, 1 abstention and 70 absentees: *Swiss National Council*, BO 1996, 911.

14 *Swiss Council of States*, BO 1997, No. 97.3252, 700.

15 See FREIBURGHAUS (2001); PICHONNAZ (2004) p. 392-398.

16 *Swiss National Council*, BO 1998, No. 98.3104, 1530.

17 *Swiss National Council*, BO 1998, No. 98.443, 1821.

an ordinary question demanding the Federal Council to inform the Council of States when it intended to present its findings concerning the legal problems faced by same-sex couples.[18] Further fuel was added to the fire when National Councillor GENNER deposited an initiative allowing for same-sex civil marriages.[19]

VI.3.3 REPORT OF THE MINISTRY OF JUSTICE

In response to this increasing pressure, the Federal Council announced on the 1st March 1999 that it would publish a report on the legal problems faced by homosexual couples.[20] As promised, the Ministry of Justice published its report in the summer of 1999.[21] The report was divided into three main sections. The first dealt with the legal situation abroad, with an overview of the legislative developments around the world concerning the implementation of forms of non-marital registered relationships. The second provided a detailed analysis of the legal position of same-sex couples in Switzerland and was followed by the third and final section expounding four possible solutions to the problems identified.[22]

According to the report, the problems outlined in the second section of the report could be solved by means of specific legislative intervention.[23] Alternatively, a second avenue of redress would have been to legislate for the introduction of a partnership contract.[24] In the third option, two different alternatives were considered, namely a registered partnership scheme with limited rights and benefits or alternatively a registered partnership scheme akin to marriage.[25] The fourth possible option was the opening of civil marriage to same-sex couples.[26]

---

18 *Swiss Council of States*, BO 1998, No. 98.1186, Ordinary Question (SPOREY).

19 *Swiss National Council*, BO 1998, No. 98.453, Parliamentary Initiative (GENNER).

20 For press releases see http://www.ofj.admin.ch/f/eazw-index.html.

21 MINISTRY OF JUSTICE (1999).

22 Some commentators state that the Ministry of Justice endorsed 5 solutions. This confusion arises due to the fact that variant 3 consisted of two possible solutions: SANDOZ (2001a).

23 MINISTRY OF JUSTICE (1999) p. 40. This option would have taken many years to implement and would have required the consent of all cantons. See DESSEMONTET/ANSAY (2004).

24 A view supported by SANDOZ (2001a) p. 61. In this article, SANDOZ proposes a new Title I-*bis*, Title 9, Sw. CC, inserting Arts. 330a to 330p. This proposal would create a partnership contract along similar lines to the proposals outlined by the Ministry of Justice. See also SANDOZ (2000a).

25 MINISTRY OF JUSTICE (1999) p. 43-44.

26 See HANGARTNER (2001). The results of the consultation procedure indicate that there were no cantons in favour of such an approach and only three political parties. Such an

VI.3.4 CANTONAL CHANGE

Once the report was published, the Government opened a consultation procedure with all those interested parties. Despite the fact that the federal wheels had started rolling, cantons began to ease the difficulties faced by same-sex couples by enacting their own cantonal forms of registered partnership.[27] Although these cantonal solutions were less extensive than their federal counterpart, they provided the necessary impetus for action to be taken at the federal level, as well as providing an indication of the increasing tolerance towards homosexuality in Swiss society.[28] The problems faced by same-sex couples were not always within the corrective competency of the cantons and thus cantonal partnership legislation only had a limited effect.[29] The future of these registration schemes has now, of course, been thrown into doubt since the passing of the Sw. RPA.[30]

In a number of other cantons, namely Aargau, Basel District, Basel Town, Lucerne, Ticino, and Valais, proposals have been put forward aimed at

---

approach was bound to fail, and therefore the Government opted for a proposal that was less radical in its aims, and thus accordingly more likely to succeed. See MINISTRY OF JUSTICE (2000) p. 10-11. Marriage is normally defined as "l'union de deux personnes physiques de sexes différents célébrée selon les formes de la loi civile": WERRO (2000) p. 30; PICHONNAZ (2004) p. 392; COTTIER (2005) p. 187-189.

27 **Geneva**: Act on Registered Partnership of 15th February 2001 (*Loi sur le partenariat du 15 février 2001*), *Gen. Stadtsblatt*, 15th February 2001, No. 7611 (in force as of 5th May 2001). **Zurich**: Act on the registration of same-sex couples of 21st January 2002. Accepted as a result of referendum of 2nd April 2002 (*Gesetz über die Registrierung gleichgeschlechtlicher Paare vom 21. Januar 2002. Ablauf der Referendumsfrist 2. April 2002*), *Zur. Stadtsblatt*, 1st February 2002, No. 5. The first registered partners in Zurich were ERNST OSTERTAG and ROBI RAPP. After a forty-seven year relationship, they were finally able to celebrate their relationship in a public ceremony. I am heavily indebted to them for the historical background provided on the situation in Switzerland (in force as of 22nd May 2001). **Neuchâtel**: Act on Registered Partnership of 6th February 2004 (*Loi sur le partenariat enregistré du 6 février 2004*) *Neu. Stadtsblatt*, 17th March 2004, No. 10 (in force as of 6th February 2004).

28 As was pointed out by the Ministry of Justice, MINISTRY OF JUSTICE (1999) p. 40.

29 MINISTRY OF JUSTICE (1999) p. 40. This option would have taken many years to implement and would have required the consent of all cantons. See DESSEMONTET/ANSAY (2004).

30 The question arises whether couples who have registered such partnerships will be able to register federally. Furthermore, the schemes in Geneva and Neuchâtel are also open to different-sex couples, thus creating problems in attempts to abolish these systems entirely. See also PICHONNAZ (2004) p. 430-431. It has however been noted that the federal legislation is broader than the cantonal legislation, thus necessitating new legislation in these three cantons: *Swiss National Council*, 2003-2004, BO 2003, 1826.

introducing forms of registered partnership in various guises.[31] However, most of these cantons had placed such discussions on hold until the Federal Government had voted on the Sw. RPA. As result of the subsequent enactment of the Sw. RPA, the need for these proposals has ceased and they all have since been removed from their respective cantonal Parliamentary agendas.

VI.3.5 CONSULTATION PROCEDURE AND BEYOND

On 27th September 1999, and thus before the consultation procedure on the Ministry of Justice report was complete, the National Council voted in favour of National Councillor GROS'S motion proposing to draft a registered partnership bill.[32] By the beginning of 2000, the academic community had also recognised the significance of these developments and three individual colloquia were held in Lausanne, Zurich and Bern, respectively, to discuss the various issues related to the introduction of a registered partnership scheme for same-sex couples.[33]

In August 2000, the Ministry of Justice published the results of the consultation procedure.[34] Twenty-five cantons, ten political parties and twenty-five organisations participated, as well as 178 non-official contributors. On the 25th October 2000, the Federal Council took notice of the results of the consultation procedure and instructed the Federal Ministry of Justice to prepare a proposal for the introduction of registered partnership for same-sex couples. This therefore follows the second alternative of the third option proposed by the Government.[35]

---

31 **Aargau:** Auszug betreffend rechtliche Situation gleichgeschlechtlicher Paare (5th March 2002); **Basel Dsitrict:** Gleichstellung gleichgeschlechtlicher Partnerschaften (14th March 2002); **Basel Town:** Überweisung eines Auszugs durch den Grossen Rat an den Regierungsrat zur Prüfung der Übernahme des Zürcher Gesetzesentwurfs über die registrierte Partnerschaft (9th January 2002); **Lucerne:** Über eine rechtliche Grundlage für registrierte Partnerschaften von homosexuellen Paaren (5th June 2002); **Ticino:** Introduzione di una riforma legislative cantonale volta a riconoscene le unioni registrati di coppie omosessuali (28th January 2002); **Valais:** Loi sur le partenariat enregistrée (3rd October 2002), the bill has however since rejected by the Cantonal government.

32 *Swiss National Council,* BO 1999, No. 98.443, 1821. The vote was 105 to 46.

33 **Lausanne:** 23rd Feburary 2000: *Cohabitation non maritale. Évolution récente en droit suisse*; in **Zurich:** 4th November 2000: NETWORK symposium and **Bern:** 10th November 2000: *Schweizerische Gesellschaft für Internationales Recht.*

34 MINISTRY OF JUSTICE (2000). For a good overview of the interest groupd having taken part in the consultation procedure, see COTTIER (2005) p. 185-187.

35 See **Section VI.3.3.**

This mandate was accepted and on the 14th November 2001, the Ministry of Justice published its proposal.[36] Consultation on the proposal opened immediately, and the results were published in February 2002.[37] On the 26th June 2002, the Federal Council took notice of the results of the consultation and instructed the Ministry of Justice to prepare a detailed, legislative proposal before the end of the year. On the 29th November 2002, a legislative proposal for the introduction of registered partnership for same-sex couples was submitted to the Swiss Federal Assembly.[38] Debate on the proposal began in the National Council on the 2nd December 2003.[39] After a number of minor amendments, the final text of the proposal was eventually adopted on the 18th June 2004.[40] Despite being accepted by both chambers in Parliament, the Bill was subject to a nationwide referendum on the 5th June 2005.[41] The Act will finally enter into force on the 1st January 2007.[42]

VI.4 ESTABLISHMENT

VI.4.1 POSITION OF THE INSTITUTION

The Sw. RPA does not create a regulatory institution within the ambit of the Sw. CC.[43] Only a small minority during the consultation procedure demanded that the Act be integrated into Book II, Sw. CC.[44] Instead, the thirty-eight article Act creates a separate regulatory instrument for registered partnerships, as well as amending numerous others pieces of

---

36 MINISTRY OF JUSTICE (2001).

37 MINISTRY OF JUSTICE (2002).

38 FF 2003, p. 1192.

39 *Parl. Doc., Sw. NC,* BO 2003, No. 02.090, 2nd December 2003, 3rd December 2003, 10th June 2004, 18th June 2004. *Parl. Doc., Sw. CS,* BO 2003, No. 02.090, 3rd June 2004, 18th June 2004. The final proposal was approved by 112 votes to 51 in the National Council and 33 to 5 (4 abstentions) in the Council of States.

40 FF 2004, p. 2935.

41 FF 2004, p. 5511. In the referumdum (5th June 2005) 1,557,671 people (58%) voted for the legislation and 1,126,578 people (42%) voted against.

42 Press Release, Department of Justice, 5th June 2005, available at www.admin.ch/ch.

43 The Swiss Civil Code consists of five books: Book I (Law of Persons); Book II (Family Law); Book III (Inheritance Law), Book IV (Property Law) and Book V (Obligations).

44 The Cantons of Lucerne and Zurich and eight officially invited organizations: Juristes Démocrates de Suisse, Lesbenorganisation Schweiz, NETWORK, Pink Cross Antenne Gaie Suisse, Fédération Suisse des Avocats, Union syndicale suisse, Rechtswissenschaftliche Fakultät Universität Luzern and the Faculté de droit, Université de Neuchâtel: MINISTRY OF JUSTICE (2002) p. 10.

legislation.[45] Although not affecting the essential legislative force of the legislation, the refusal to amend the Sw. CC is of significant symbolic value, since the registered partnership scheme remains outside the scope of codified Swiss family law.[46]

VI.4.2 EXCLUSIVITY

Like current Swiss law on marriage,[47] a registered partnership can only be celebrated between two people.[48] Registration of a partnership is also prohibited if either one or both of the parties are already involved in another registered partnership or marriage.[49] Any person wishing to marry must also prove that any previous marriage has been dissolved or declared null and void according to Swiss law.[50] Although this Article has not been amended by the passage of the Sw. RPA, Art. 26 of that Act prevents the celebration of a marriage if either one of the parties is already involved in a registered partnership.[51]

VI.4.3 SEX OF THE PARTIES

Unlike marriage, which must be celebrated between two people of a different sex,[52] a registered partnership can only be celebrated between two

---

45 *Loi du 29 septembre 1952 sur la nationalité* (RS 141.0); *Loi fédérale du 26 mars 1931 sur le séjour l'établissement des étrangers* (RS 142.20); *Loi fédérale du 26 juin 1998 sur l'asile* (RS 142.3); *Loi fédérale du 21 mars 1997 sur l'organisation du gouvernement et de l'administration* (RS 172.010); *Loi fédérale du 20 décembre 1968 sur la procédure administrative* (RS 172.021); *Code civil* (RS 210); *Code des obligations* (RS 220); *Code pénal* (RS 311.0) and *Loi fédérale du 18 novembre 1987 sur le droit internationale privé* (RS 291).

46 However, if one examines the *Recueil Systématique* it is very clear that the Sw. RPA affects issues of family law due to its placement at 211.231 of the systematic collection.

47 WERRO (2000) p. 75, §292.

48 Art. 2(1), Sw. RPA.

49 Art. 4(1), Sw. RPA.

50 Art. 96, Sw. CC. WERRO (2000) p. 75, §293. The dissolution must be valid according to Swiss law, which thus rules out dissolutions pronounced by ecclesiastical courts or institutions: Trib. Féd., 30th September 1980 (1980) 106 II *ATF* 180.

51 Polygamous marriages and registered partnerships are not only deemed null and void but also lead to criminal sanctions: Art. 105(1) Sw. CC and Art. 215, Sw. Cr. C, as amended.

52 Art. 94(1), Sw. CC states that a marriage can only be celebrated between a man and a woman. This was recently interpreted by the Tribunal Fédéral as meaning a marriage may be celebrated between one man and one woman: Trib. Féd., 3rd March 1993 (1993) 119 II *ATF* 264. This case has however been heavily criticised since the court discussd in issue of recognition, without first noting that the "marriage" was null and void by virtue of Danish law and therefore was not eligible for recognition in Switzerland: SCHWANDER (1993) p.

people of the same sex.[53] Since Swiss law recognises changes to one's original birth sex, this phrase must be understood as referring to one's current sex as indicated on one's birth certificate.[54] However, no special procedure is provided for those couples involved in a marriage where one party undergoes sex reassignment surgery to "convert" their marriage into a registered partnership. As a result, the marriage must first be annulled before the parties will be permitted to enter into a registered partnership. The question obviously arises whether a person involved in a different-sex non-marital registered relationship abroad will be prohibited from entering into a registered partnership or celebrating a marriage in Switzerland. This obviously depends on whether Swiss private international law would recognise different-sex, non-marital registered relationships.[55]

As with the law on marriage, the law on registered partnership makes no reference to the parties' sexual orientation. However, since Art. 2(2), Sw. RPA states that the couple must share a common life and assume responsibility for one another's rights and duties stemming from the partnership, one could argue that being homosexual is an implicit condition. In the explanatory notes to the legislation, it was highlighted that the aim of Art. 2(2), Sw. RPA is to grant a legal framework to the affectionate and sexual bond that exists between two men or two women, thus underlining the homosexual nature of the relationship.[56] The title of the 1999 report by the Ministry of Justice stressed the Government's search for a legal solution to the problems experienced by homosexuals, and therefore adds further weight to the argument that although the law is silent as to the sexual

---

1265; HONSELL/VOGT/SCHNYDER (2002) Art. 43-45, No. 17-21; BUCHER (1994) §3; OTHENIN-GIRARD (1999a) p. 442-443; WERRO (2000) p. 31, §61-62.

53 Art. 2(1), Sw. RPA.

54 Tribunal Neuchâtel (1946) I *JdT* 122 where it was stated: "it is not the body alone which determines a person's sex, it is also his soul ...". Amendments to the birth certificate rest with the judiciary and since this ruling, there have been no associated problems with birth certificate amendments. This stance is thus in conformity with ECtHR case law: ECtHR, *Goodwin v. United Kingdom*, Appl. No. 28957/95, 11th July 2002. Furthermore, the Tribunal Saint-Gall concluded that in the case where one party changes their sex during a marriage, and the other party consents, the original marriage must continue since the change of sex does not form a ground for annulling the marriage not a ground for divorce ((1997) *AJP* 340). This decision received fierce criticism and led to a circular from the Federal Office of Civil Status stating that no birth certificate should be amended if a person is married, unless this is accompanied by a decree of nullity ot the death certificate of the spouse. See also Trib. Féd., 3rd March 1993 (1993) 119 II *ATF* 264.

55 See further **Chapters IX.6** and **X.3.3.3**. BUCHER (2004a) p. 189, §259; SCHWANDER (2001) p. 350-356.

56 FF 2003, p. 1192 at 1233.

orientation of the future partners, it is assumed that the partners are homosexual. Regardless, the result is the same as with marriage: non-adherence to this requirement has no effect on the legality of the partnership.[57]

VI.4.4 MINIMUM AGE

Until recently, the age of majority in Switzerland was obtained once one had attained the age of twenty. As of 1st January 1996 the age of majority has been lowered to eighteen.[58] This legislative change removed the previous rule that a man had to have reached the age of twenty and a woman the age of eighteen before they could celebrate a marriage.[59] Although at the time this reduction in the age of majority drew mixed feeling, a similar bone of contention was not evident in the debates on registered partnership.[60] As a result, all those having attained the age of eighteen are entitled to form a registered partnership or celebrate a marriage.[61]

VI.4.5 RESIDENCY

Swiss authorities are competent to celebrate a marriage or register a partnership if either of the future spouses have their domicile in Switzerland or possess Swiss nationality.[62] If neither party is domiciled in Switzerland or has Swiss nationality, they may nonetheless marry or register their partnership in Switzerland if they have their habitual residence in Switzerland.[63] An exception to these rules is, however, offered to aspirant spouses, although not to registered partners, should neither one of them possess Swiss nationality nor be domiciled or habitually resident in Switzerland. In this case, the parties will be permitted to marry in Switzerland if the State of both parties' domicile or of their nationality

---

57 WERRO (2000) p. 93-95, §387-402.

58 RO 1995, p. 1126.

59 Art. 96(2), Old Sw. CC replaced by Art. 94(1), Sw. CC.

60 WERRO (2000) p. 68, §250-251; GUILLOD (1997) p. 491.

61 Art. 3(1), Sw. RPA.

62 **Marriage:** Art. 43(1), Sw. CPIL; **RP:** Art. 65a, Sw. CPIL.

63 Art. 20(2), Sw. CPIL. BUCHER (2004a) p. 38, §77 and p. 188, §524; BUCHER/BONOMI (2004) p. 161, §583.

would recognise any subsequent Swiss marriage.[64] The absence of such an exception in relation to registered partnership can be traced to the Ministry of Justice's desire to prevent "registration tourism".[65] Corresponding application of the marriage provisions would have allowed those individuals with absolutely no connection to Switzerland to travel to Switzerland and register their partnership.

VI.4.6 PROHIBITED DEGREES OF RELATIONSHIP

The list of those people prohibited from entering into a registered partnership by virtue of their familial relationship is identical to the prohibitions imposed on those wishing to marry.[66] Registration of a partnership is, as a consequence, not permitted between relatives in the direct ascending or descending line to any degree,[67] nor between relatives in the indirect ascending or descending line to the second degree (*i.e.* between brothers and sisters whether of whole or half blood).[68] These same rules apply regardless of whether the relationship is established naturally or by means of adoption.[69]

As a result of the passing of the Sw. RPA, changes have also been made to the Sw. CC in relation to marriages celebrated between *alliés*.[70] Although the prohibitions had been based on the preservation of peace in the family home, it had been noted that in modern Swiss society there are few problems associated with *alliés* living together outside of wedlock.[71] Due to the outdated aims of this provision, the Federal Council argued that such an impediment should not be extended to registered partnerships, although did not propose the abolition of these requirements with respect to marriage.[72]

---

64 Art. 43(2), Sw. CPIL. This is understood to mean that either both parties' State of domicile or both parties' State of nationality or one parties' State of domicile and the other's State of nationality: BUCHER (2004a) p. 39, §82.

65 FF 2003, p. 1192 at 1259.

66 **Marriage:** Art. 95(1) and (2), Sw. CC; **RP**: Art. 4(1), Sw. RPA.

67 WERRO (2000) p. 73, §279.

68 By virtue of a statutory amendment the previous prohibition of marriages between relatives in the third degree (*i.e.* between an uncle and niece, nephew and aunt) has been repealed: Art. 100(1)(1), Old Sw. CC.

69 FF 2003, p. 1192 at 1232.

70 Arts. 95(1)(2), Sw. CC. The definition of *allié* is to be found in Art. 21(2), Sw. CC: a bond that exists between a person and the relatives of his or her spouse or registered partner.

71 Art. 95(1)(2), Sw. CC. WERRO (2000) p. 72, §270; FF 2003, p. 1192 at 1233.

72 FF 2003, p. 1192 at 1233.

In heeding the advice of many,[73] the Council of States proposed to abolish this prohibition with respect to marriage,[74] which was subsequently seconded by the National Council.[75] As a result, these prohibitions no longer apply to aspirant spouses or registered partners.

Adoption does not eliminate the marital impediments imposed on a person resulting from the relationship between such a person and his or her descendants, on the one hand, and the family into which this person was born, on the other.[76] This provision, although still in force has never caused a marriage to be prohibited. The Ministry of Justice saw the miniscule possibility that such a scenario could occur reason enough to avoid express prohibition in the Sw. RPA.[77]

VI.4.7 COMPETENCY AND CONSENT

Anyone subject to legal guardianship by reason of their incapacity requires the consent of their legal representative before being able to enter into either a marriage or registered partnership.[78] Persons requiring legal guardianship are those who "*pour cause maladie mentale ou de faiblesse d'esprit, est incapable de gérer ses affaires, ne peut se passer de soins et secours permanents ou menace la sécurité d'autrui*".[79] In the original proposal promulgated for consultation,[80] the possibility for the legal representative's refusal to be substituted by a court was not correspondingly applicable to registered partnerships.[81] Due to criticism levied, in the main

---

73 See, for example, Trib. Féd., 6th December 2001 (2002) 128 III *ATF* 113 at §5a.

74 *Swiss Council of States*, 3rd June 2004, BO 2004, 234. State Councillor LEUMAN, on the other hand, felt that this was not the correct time to introduce such changes.

75 *Swiss National Council*, 10th June 2004, BO 2004, 992. As a result respective amendments have been made to Arts. 95 and 105(3), Sw. CC.

76 Art. 95(2), Sw. CC. This provision thus prevents, for example, an adopted child from marrying the descendants of his birth parents.

77 FF 2003, p. 1192 at 1233.

78 **Marriage**: Art. 94(2), Sw. CC; **RP**: Art. 3(2), Sw. RPA. The only difference being that Art. 94(2), Sw. CC is worded in the negative: A person under legal guardianship may *not* consent to marriage without the consent of his or her legal representative, whereas Art. 3(2), Sw. RPA is phrased positively: A person under legal guardianship *must* possess the consent of his or her legal representative.

79 Art. 369, Sw. CC.

80 MINISTRY OF JUSTICE (2001) p. 23.

81 This power is provided for in the case of marriage in Art. 94(2), second sentence, Sw. CC.

by homosexual lobby groups,[82] this situation was rectified and this possibility extended to registered partners accordingly.[83]

Despite the similarities between marriage and registered partnership with respect to issues of competency,[84] the law with respect to consent is starkly different. Although parties wishing to celebrate a marriage or register a partnership must both consent freely, the grounds for challenging this consent are different. In relation to marriage, the grounds for proving lack of consent are more restrictive than those for ordinary contractual obligations,[85] which are in turn applicable to registered partnerships.[86]

VI.4.8 FORMAL VALIDITY

VI.4.8.1 Preparatory Phase

Both those wishing to register their partnership and those wishing to celebrate a marriage must submit their application to the Registrar in one of their respective domiciles.[87] For Swiss nationals not domiciled in Switzerland, the Registrar of the district where the marriage is to take place is competent to accept their application.[88] It is as yet unclear whether the same rules will apply to registered partners.[89] The parties must appear personally thus prohibiting the possibility of marriages or registered partnerships by proxy.[90] However, if the parties can prove that, for serious reasons, they cannot attend personally they will be allowed to execute the preparatory procedure in written form.[91] The parties are also obliged to

---

82 FF 2003, p. 1192 at 1233.

83 Art. 3(2), Sw. RPA. The competent court is determined according to Art. 44(b), Federal Act on Judicial Organisation (*Loi fédérale d'organisation judiciaire*).

84 Both parties must state their desire to marry, freely and openly: Art. 71, Sw. OCS.

85 Art. 107(2), Sw. CC.

86 Arts. 10(1), Sw. RPA. See further **Section VI.6.6.**

87 **Marriage:** Art. 98(1), Sw. CC; **RP:** Art. 5(1), Sw. RPA.

88 Art. 73(2), Sw. OCS. In this case, the declaration must be accompanied by a declaration that the marriage will be recognised in the State of domicile of both parties or in the State of nationality of both parties, as well as all documents designated in Art. 64, Sw. OCS.

89 According to an e-mail received from the Swiss Ministry of Justice, this will have to be determined by practice but will either be determined according to the choice of the parties or the place of origin of one or both of the parties.

90 **Marriage:** Art. 98(2), first sentence, Sw. CC; **RP:** Art. 5(2), first sentence, Sw. RPA.

91 **Marriage:** Art. 98(2), second sentence, Sw. CC; **RP:** Art. 5(2), second sentence, Sw. RPA.

personally deliver all the required documents to the competent Registrar.[92] At the same time, they must declare that they have satisfied all the required conditions for entry into a marriage or registered partnership respectively.[93]

With respect to aspirant spouses, once the Registrar has received the application, he or she is obliged to examine the documents to ensure that the parties have met the required conditions for entry into a marriage, that the application has been submitted in the correct manner and that the identity of both parties can be established.[94] With respect to registered partnerships, this duty is more restrictive. The Registrar is only entitled to verify that the conditions are satisfied and that no impediments to the registration exist, and is thus not entitled to verify the identity of the parties nor the procedure by which the application had been received.[95] No explanation has been provided for the absence of these provisions. In the original explanatory report published on the 29th November 2002, Art. 6, Sw. RPA had provided the Registrar with the possibility to refuse the application if the only reason for the registration of the partnership was to avoid the requirements of immigration.[96] However, during the debate in the National Council on the 2nd December 2003, these provisions were deleted without discussion.[97] In the Council of States, State Councillor MARTY noted that the removal of these safeguards was a question of form rather than essence.[98]

In relation to marriage, if the relevant conditions in Art. 99(1), Sw. CC are satisfied, the Registrar must communicate the completion of the preparatory procedure to the future spouses and inform them of the necessary waiting

---

92 **Marriage:** Art. 64, Sw. OCS. This Art. states that the parties must submit (a) a certificate indicating their current domicile, (b) documents relating to their birth, sex, name, parenting and civil status and (c) documents concerning the birth, sex, name and parents of any children. **RP:** Art. 8, Sw. RPA. The documents required are to be determined by the Federal Council, but it is expected that these documents will be mirrored on those required for entry into a marriage.

93 **Marriage:** Art. 98(3), Sw. CC in conjunction with Art. 65, Sw. OCS; **RP:** Art. 5(3), Sw. RPA.

94 Art. 99(1), Sw. CC.

95 Art. 6, Sw. RPA.

96 MINISTRY OF JUSTICE (2001) p. 24.

97 *Swiss National Council*, 2nd December 2003, BO 2003, 1821, Art. 6(2) and 6(3) deleted by 114 votes to 63.

98 *Swiss Council of States*, 3rd June 2004, BO 2004, 233. Such a safeguard is provided for in Art. 45(2), Sw. CPIL analogously applicable by virtue of Art. 65a, Sw. CPIL.

period as stipulated by law.[99] If the conditions are not satisfied or there are serious doubts as to whether these conditions are satisfied, the Registrar must refuse to celebrate the marriage. The waiting periods imposed on future spouses are, however, not applicable to future registered partners.[100] Instead, those wishing to register their partnership are entitled to do so as soon as the Registrar has scrutinised the documentation and ensured fulfilment of the relevant criteria.

VI.4.8.2 Celebration Phase

Unlike a marriage ceremony, which is based on the exchange of vows during a public ceremony before two witnesses,[101] a registered partnership is concluded at the moment when both parties sign the declaration of registered partnership.[102] Despite the absence of a compulsory ceremony, registered partnerships must be declared publicly and anyone may attend unless the Registrar imposes a limit for reasons of public order.[103]

VI.5 LEGAL EFFECTS

VI.5.1 GENERAL

Upon the registration of a registered partnership, Swiss law imposes a number of rights and duties on the parties concerned, both with respect to each other and with respect to third persons and the State. It is vital that one establish a suitable point of reference in order to assess the extent of these rights and duties. Accordingly, the rights and duties imposed on registered partners will be compared to the equivalent rights and duties imposed on spouses.

---

99 Art. 100(1), Sw. CC in conjunction with Art. 68(1), Sw. OCS. These Articles state that the marriage must be celebrated at least ten days but no more than three months since completion of the preparatory phase. The ten-day waiting period can however be avoided in urgent cases: Art. 100(2), Sw. CC in conjunction with Art. 67(2), Sw. OCS.

100 Art. 67(2), Sw. OCS.

101 WERRO (2000) p. 74, §288.

102 *Cf.* **Marriage:** Art. 117(1), Sw. CC; **RP:** Art. 7(1), Sw. RPA.

103 Art. 7(2), Sw. RPA.

VI.5.2 CIVIL STATUS

In contrast to marriage, registered partnership is not based on a long-standing tradition. However, the aim of the Swiss legislature was clear; the formation of a registered partnership is to have identical consequences on the parties' civil status as the celebration of a marriage.[104] In order to guarantee legal security and ensure uniform terminology, a new civil status has been expressly established by virtue of the Sw. RPA.[105] This new civil status is explicitly stated in the Act itself and not by means of a separate ordinance. Once registered the partners will be deemed to be *lié par un partenariat enregistré*. Nevertheless, the requisite documentation necessary to afford a change in civil status is not explicitly ordained in the legislation.[106]

VI.5.3 NATIONALITY

Three different forms of nationality need to be distinguished: Swiss nationality (*nationalité suisse*), cantonal nationality (*indigénat*) and a communal nationality (*droit de cité* or *bourgeoisie*). The law on Swiss nationality is regulated by the Federal Act on the Acquisition and Loss of Swiss Nationality (Sw. ALSN).[107] By virtue of a special procedure, spouses of Swiss nationals are granted special rights with respect to the acquisition of Swiss nationality. According to Art. 27(1), Sw. ALSN, the spouse of a Swiss national may be granted Swiss nationality if they satisfy a number of conditions, namely that have lived in Switzerland for five years, have been married for at least three years prior to the application and have resided in Switzerland for at least one year prior to the request for naturalisation.[108] If the foreign spouse does not live in Switzerland, then the couple must have been married for at least six years and the foreign spouse must have "close connections" with Switzerland.[109]

In contrast, the ordinary procedure for obtaining Swiss nationality, dealt with in Art. 15, Sw. ALSN, requires that a foreigner has resided in Switzerland for at least twelve years and at least three of the previous five

---

104 FF 2003, p. 1192 at 1232.

105 Art. 2(3), Sw. RPA; PICHONNAZ (2004) p. 409.

106 Art. 64, Sw. OCS. See further fn. 94.

107 RS 141.0.

108 Arts. 27 and 28, Sw. ALSN are based on Art. 38(1), Sw. FC.

109 Art. 28(1), Sw. ALSN.

years prior to the submission of the naturalisation application.[110] The new Swiss Registered Partnership Act has amended Art. 15, Sw. ALSN, stating that a foreign registered partner of a Swiss national will be allowed to acquire Swiss nationality if he or she has lived in Switzerland for a period of five years, the parties have been registered for three years prior to the application and the foreign partner has lived in Switzerland for at least one year prior to the application.[111] Although the amendments have been made to Art. 15, Sw. ALSN, the resemblance to Art. 27(1), Sw. ALSN is self-evident and in practice treats registered partners in exactly the same way as their married counterparts. Nonetheless, it does indicate a reluctance on the part of the Swiss legislature to provide for direct corresponding application of the provisions on marriage to registered partnership, despite the indication that registered partnerships and marriages are to be treated identically.

In determining the attribution and acquisition of *le droit de cité* and *l'indigénat* a distinction must be made between the acquisition of these forms of nationality by men and women.[112] Neither marriage nor registered partnership has any impact on the *l'indigénat* or *le droit de cité* of a man.[113] In contrast, a woman acquires the *l'indigénat* and *le droit de cité* of her husband as a result of marriage, but not as a result of a registered partnership.[114] With respect to registered partners, the Federal Council noted that, in this area, Swiss law did not guarantee for the equal treatment of men and women. As a result, in creating modern legislation for registered partners,[115] and in light of the different nature of a same-sex relationship,[116] it could not be justified to impose this inequality on registered partners.

---

110 Art. 15, Sw. ALSN.

111 Art. 15(5) and (6), Sw. ALSN.

112 According to Art. 22(2), Sw. CC, *droit de cité* is regulated by public law.

113 **Marriage:** Trib. Féd., 23rd March 1999 (1999) 125 III *ATF* 209; **RP:** FF 2003, p. 1192 at 1216.

114 Art. 161, Sw. CC, as amdened by Federal Act of 23rd March 1990, *BO*, 1991, p. 1034 at 1043. For further explanation of the precise acquisition by women see Trib. Féd., 17th November 1988 (1988) 114 II *ATF* 404. A woman acquires the *indigénat* and *droit de cité* of her husband in addition to her own.

115 FF 2003, p. 1192 at 1214-1215.

116 Application of the current law on *le droit de cité* with respect to registered partnerships would have led to a situation where parties to a female registered partnership both acquired each other's *droit de cité* whereas the *droit de cité* of parties to a male registered partnership remained unchanged.

VI.5.4 NAME LAW

In contrast to the celebration of a marriage, where the husband's surname is declared to be that of both spouses,[117] the surname of parties to a registered partnership remains unaltered as a result of registration. In the explanatory note accompanying the registered partnership proposal, the Federal Council noted that a person's surname plays an important role not only in terms of identification but also in terms of a person's identity.[118] In relation to marriage it was added that the common familial surname helps to protect and maintain the stability and unity of the family home.[119] Furthermore, it was noted that current Swiss law treated men and women differently, and therefore, for the same reasons as espoused above in relation to *le droit de cité,* the Federal Council saw no reason to extend such discriminatory provisions to registered partners. Although, other options are available to those intending to marry to avoid the automatic use of the husband's surname,[120] no option for the alteration of a registered partner's legal name is provided for by virtue of the new legislation.[121]

Swiss customary law also provides for a *nom d'alliance*,[122] which is linked to but independent from one's legal name.[123] A *nom d'alliance*, unlike a legal name, is not transmittable but is mutable. Bearing in mind the importance

---

117 Art. 160(1), Sw. CC. By virtue of Art. 270(1), Sw. CC all children take the name of the family, and thus the husband. This is based on the principle of unity of the surname in the family: DESCHENAUX *et al.* (2000) p. 76, §80; Trib. Féd., 19th March 1982 (1982) 108 II *ATF* 161.

118 FF 2003, p. 1192 at 1217.

119 FF 2003, p. 1192 at 1217; WERRO (2000) p. 125-126, §559-560.

120 *A man to take the surname of his wife:* Art. 30(2), Sw. CC in conjunction with Art. 12(2), Sw. OCS. *Wife wishes to retain her own surname after that of her husband:* Art. 160(2), Sw. CC in conjunction with Art. 12(1), Sw. OCS. If she already has a double-barrelled surname then she is only allowed to place the first of these two names in front of her husband's surname: Art. 160(3), Sw. CC; DESCHENAUX *et al.* (2000) p. 82-86, §97-106. Proposals have been made to change this situation, but have failed: FF 1999, p. 4565; *Swiss National Council,* BO 1999, No. 94.434, 1570.

121 A person's legal surname may be amended in accordance with Art. 30(1), Sw. CC, should *justes motifs* be found. It is unlikely that the Swiss Federal Supreme Court will regard a registered partnership as constituting *justes motifs* in terms of Art. 30(1) since this would effectively circumvent the intentions of Parliament. Case law has stated that the phrase *justes motifs* must be understood in accordance with the rules of law and equity (Trib. Féd., 19th December 1973 (1973) 99 Ia *ATF* 561). For further explanation see SCYBOZ/GILLIERON (1999) p. 53-4, Art. 30(1).

122 This is also different from the *nom d'usage* which is used by artistics, writers, journalists *etc.* in their professional life: See NÄF-HOFMANN/NÄF-HOFMANN (1998).

123 DESCHENAUX *et al.* (2000) p. 78, §83.

of a persons's surname in terms of identifying him or herself with his or her partner, the Federal Council thought it more suitable to allow for registered partners' to make use of their partner's *nom d'alliance*. As a result and in the same way as marriage, upon registering a partnership either partner may take the surname of their partner in its entirety or use their own surname in combination with that of their partner. In the latter case, the family name must be placed first followed by a hyphen. Despite the fact that the *nom d'alliance* does not have an official character and cannot be registered in the registers of civil status,[124] it may be used on a person's passport.[125]

VI.5.5 TAXATION, SOCIAL SECURITY AND PENSIONS

Both married couples and registered partners are taxed jointly, that is to say that their incomes are added together in accordance with the prevailing principle of family taxation. As a result of the progressive taxation rates, dual-income couples were placed at a disadvantage compared to single income couples, despite certain corrective measures.[126] In order to eliminate these disadvantages, a Commission of Experts drafted a report on the existing system of family taxation for the Federal Finance Department, setting out the present defects and putting forward proposals for a new approach.[127] One of the fundamental decisions taken by the Commission was that married and cohabiting couples in the same financial situation should be subject to the same tax burden. In its report, the Commission took the lasting partnership between a man and woman as its starting point and saw no need to take same-sex partners into account, especially since at that time such couples were ignored by the civil law.[128] This has however been rectified by the passage of the Sw. RPA. By virtue of amendments to the Federal Act on Direct Tax[129] and the Federal Act on the Harmonisation of Direct Cantonal and Communal Tax,[130] the position of registered partnerships in the field of federal and cantonal tax law is equated to that applicable to married couples.[131]

124 Trib. Féd., 29th May 1984 (1984) 110 II *ATF* 97.
125 STETTLER/GERMANI (1999) p. 35-36, §40.
126 HEGNAUER/BREITSCHMID (2000) p. 34, §2.32; MINISTRY OF JUSTICE (1999) p. 33.
127 LOCHER (1998).
128 LOCHER (1998) p. 63.
129 RS 642.11.
130 RS 642.14.
131 A change that was in principle not contested during the consultation procedure.

The notions of marriage and registered partnership are also equated across a wide range of statutory pension and social security schemes,[132] including elderly person and survivorship insurance,[133] invalidity insurance,[134] sickness insurance,[135] accident insurance,[136] military insurance,[137] insurance for agriculture families[138] and unemployment insurance.[139] Nonetheless, due to inequality between men and women in the field of social security, complete equality in treatment between registered partners and spouses is, according to the Ministry of Justice, impossible. In the event of the death of one's spouse, the rules for entitlement differ depending on the sex of the surviving spouse. Due to this inequality, the Ministry of Justice saw fit to equate the situation of registered partners with that of widowers.[140]

VI.5.6 RIGHTS AND DUTIES OF THE PARTNERS TO EACH OTHER

VI.5.6.1 Duty to cohabit

Like marriage, there is no mention in the Sw. RPA of future registered partners being under a duty to cohabit.[141] Non-cohabting same-sex couples are therefore entitled to register their partnership in the same way that non-cohabiting different-sex couples are entitled to a celebrate a marriage. However, in the absence of an express duty to cohabit, it must not be overlooked that Swiss law assumes that the couple will, in principle, live together after the celebration of their marriage or the registration of their

132 Art. 13a, *Loi fédérale sur la partie générale du droit des assurances sociales*, RS 830.1. According to Art. 13a(1), this rule is consequently applicable in all federal social security schemes apart from *la loi fédérale sur la prévoyance professionnelle* (RS 831.40) and *la loi fédérale sur le libre passage* (RS 831.42) where seperate amendements have been made.

133 *La loi fédérale sur l'assurance-vieillesse et survivants* (RS 831.10) and corresponding provisions in *la loi fédérale sur les prestations complémentaires à l'assurance-vieillesse, survivants et invalidité* (RS 831.30).

134 *La loi fédérale sur l'assurance-invalidité* (RS 831.20) and *la loi fédérale sur les prestations complémentaires à l'assurance-vieillesse, survivants et invalidité* (RS 831.30).

135 *La loi fédérale sur l'assurance maladie* (RS 832.10).

136 *La loi fédérale sur l'assurance-accidents* (RS 832.20).

137 *La loi fédérale sur l'assurance militaire* (RS 833.1).

138 *La loi fédérale sur les allocations familiales dans l'agriculture* (RS 836.1).

139 *La loi fédérale sur l'assurance-chômage* (RS 837.0). Although according to British-English usage, the term unemployment benefit is more widespread, the EU and the majority of other English language nations around the world refer to unemployment insurance.

140 See **Sections VI.5.3** and **VI.5.4**; FF 2003, p. 1192 at 1222. To treat female and male registered partners differently would have only introduced new inequalities.

141 Art. 2(2), Sw. RPA: FF 2003, p. 1192 at 1232. GRÜTTER/SUMMERMATTER (2004) p. 453.

partnership.[142] This assumption is no clearer in relation to spouses than the fact that in a number of rights and benefits determine the parties' *demeure commune* (common residence)[143] or *logement de la famille* (family home) to be crucial.[144] The Federal Council noted in the explanatory notes accompanying the Sw. RPA that since the legislation implementing registered partnership does not provide the possibility for registered partners to found a family,[145] reference to a *logement de la famille* would not be suitable.[146] Instead the phrase *logement commun* (common home) has been used for registered partners.[147] Nonetheless, the same result is achieved with respect to registered partners and it is, in principle, assumed that registered partners will live together.

Unlike marriage where the spouses are under a duty to choose their *demeure commune* jointly, no corresponding provision has been drawn up with respect to registered partners.[148] However, the historical background to the enactment of Art. 162, Sw. CC, aids in explaining this irregularity.[149] Nonetheless, once a *logement de la famille* or a *logement commun* has been established, Art. 14(1), Sw. RPA provides for a literal replication of Art. 169(1), Sw. CC.[150] Accordingly, a registered partner is not allowed to terminate a tenancy, relinquish the common residence, nor limit the rights over the common residence by other legal acts without the express consent of his or her partner.[151] In the absence of a *logement commun*, registered

---

142 DESCHENAUX *et al.* (2000) p. 101, §160.

143 The phrase *demeure commune* has been held to mean the place of residence where the spouses live together: HEGNAUER/BRIETSCHMID (2000) p. 181, §17.09. DESCHENAUX *et al.* (2000) p. 101, §160.

144 It is equally crucial to understand the difference in Swiss law between the phrases *demeure commune*, *domicile* and *logement de la famille*. The general rule is that the spouses have a *demeure commune* at the place of their *logement de la famille*, which is equally the *domicile* of each of the parties: Trib. Féd., 17th October 1997 (1997) 123 I *ATF* 289 at 293.

145 See later **Section VI.5.9**.

146 FF 2003, p. 1192 at 1239.

147 As used in Art. 14, Sw. RPA.

148 Art. 162, Sw. CC.

149 Art. 160(2), Old Sw. CC stated that the marital home was determined by the husband alone. Art. 162, Sw. CC was therefore introduced in order to rectify this situation. Art. 162, Sw. CC, thus serves a corrective purpose which was not necessary with respect to registered partnerships.

150 Obviously subject to the substitution of *logement commun* for *logement de la famille*.

151 If it is not possible to obtain the consent of the other, or if it is refused without legitimate cause then the interested registered partner may proceed to the judge: Art. 14(2), Sw. RPA, reproducing the terms of Art. 169(2), Sw. CC.

partners are not able to benefit from the protection afforded by Art. 14, Sw. RPA.[152]

To even further complicate the matter, spouses, unlike registered partners, are under an express duty to maintain a *vie commune* during their marriage.[153] If during their *vie commune*, a spouse fails to pay maintenance to the other spouse, fails to compensate the other spouse for the care of the home, children or work done in the spouse's business, then the court may order that a certain monetary sum be paid.[154] However, provision is made in the Sw. RPA, for the case when a registered partner wishes to terminate their *vie commune*.[155] It is therefore logical to assume that since identical protection is offered to a registered partner as that offered to a spouse upon the termination of the *vie commune*,[156] both groups of couples must also be under an obligation to maintain a *vie commune* during their relationship. This argument is further supported by the fact that parties to a registered partnership are under a duty to maintain a *vie de couple*.[157] It will thus have to be seen whether the Swiss Federal Supreme Court will interpret the phrase *vie de couple* in the same manner as it has interpreted the phrase *vie commune*.

VI.5.6.2 Duty of fidelity

Although for a long time this duty focused on the sexual relationship of the spouses, nowadays reference is made to a much broader understanding of

---

152 PICHONNAZ (2004) p. 410. This is identical to the situation of spouses: NÄF-HOFMANN/NÄF-HOFMANN (1998) No. 72; HAUSHEER/REISSER/GEISSER (1999) Art. 169, No. 17. This only applies to childless married couples who do not cohabit. There are however those authors who believe that the presence of two separate *logements* does not necessarily rescind one's right to the protection afforded by Art. 169, Sw. CC, as long as the spouses are able to prove that their *vie commune* is established in both locations: DESCHENAUX *et al.* (2000) p. 116, §201.

153 Arts. 171-179, Sw. CC. See also GRÜTTER/SUMMERMATTER (2004) p. 455.

154 Art. 173(1) and (2), Sw. CC.

155 Art. 17(1), Sw. RPA, GRÜTTER/SUMMERMATTER (2004) p. 455-457.

156 **Marriage:** Art. 175, Sw. CC. DESCHENAUX *et al.* (2000) p. 69, §61. See also Trib. Féd., 16th June 1995 (1995) 121 III *ATF* 149 (sham marriage) and Trib. Féd., 22nd February 1995 (1995) 121 III *ATF* 49 (maintenance). **RP:** Art. 17(1), Sw. RPA. The wording of Art. 17, Sw. RPA is not entirely identical, in that a registered partner need only prove "justes motifs", whilst a spouse must prove that for a long period of time "sa personnalité, sa sécurité matérielle ou le bien de la famille sont gravement menacés". See further, FF 2003, p. 1192 at 1241; PICHONNAZ (2004) p. 411.

157 Art. 2(2), Sw. RPA.

the term.[158] However, regardless of the scope of this duty, this provsion is not *mutatis mutandis* applicable to registered partners. The duty imposed on spouses safeguards not only the affective interests of each spouse but also his or her material interests, forcing both parties upon the solemnisation of their marriage to renounce all relationships, sexual and otherwise, that could place their marriage in jeopardy.[159] Although some participants during the consultation procedure recommended the imposition of a duty of fidelity on registered partners, the Federal Council regarded the express imposition of such a duty as unnecessary. Instead registered partners owe each other a "duty of respect".[160] The Federal Council noted that this has effect not only with respect to the parties themselves but also in relation to third parties. This provision emphasises Parliament's intent that both parties must recognise and understand that the registration of a partnership is a serious undertaking.[161] Honesty and loyalty are elements singled out for specific mention, as is the preservation of the intimacy of the partnership in relation to third parties.[162] Despite the difference in nomenclature, the duty of respect in combination with the duty to provide assistance (see **Section VI.5.6.3**) covers the same scope as the spousal duty of fidelity.[163]

VI.5.6.3 Duty to provide support and assistance

Spouses and registered partners are both subject to an identical obligation to provide assistance to their partner in proportion to their means.[164] The duty is, however, not always easy to differentiate from the duty of fidelity imposed on spouses and the duty of respect imposed on registered partners.[165] Regardless of these difficulties, the duty imposed on spouses and registered partners embraces both a material and moral aspect, or proprietal

---

158 Art. 159(3), Sw. CC.

159 STETTLER/GERMANI (1999) p. 14, §19; DESCHENAUX *et al.* (2000) p. 66, §55.

160 Art. 12, Sw. RPA.

161 *Cf.* Art. 159(3), Sw. CC with respect to marriage.

162 FF 2003, p. 1192 at 1237-8. It is here that one is able to see the almost identical scope of this duty as compared with the spousal duty of fidelity.

163 The only exception to this being the duty to maintain a sexual relationship: FF 2003, p. 1192 at 1237.

164 **Marriage:** Art. 159(3), Sw. CC; **RP:** Art. 12, Sw. RPA; GRÜTTER/SUMMERMATTER (2004) p. 451. Swiss law makes no distinction between a duty to provide support (*Hilfe/aide*) and assistance (*Beistand/assistance*). For more detail on the assessment of what is "in proportion to their means", see DESCHENAUX *et al.* (2000) p. 221-222, §477-478.

165 HEGNAUER/BREITSCHMID (2000) p. 198, §19.07; HAUSHEER/REUSSER/GEISER (1999) Art. 159, No. 26; FF 2003, p. 1192 at 1237.

and non-proprietal duty.[166] One such example of the proprietal duty imposed on both groups of couples is the duty to provide support to one's spouse or registered partner in the exercise of his or her professional activities.[167] On the other hand, the extent of the non-proprietal duty has been understood as a duty to allow one's partner to "blossom in his or her private life".[168] Furthermore, the duty also entails a level of economic assistance, which is subsequently expounded upon in Art. 163, Sw. CC (See **Section VI.5.6.4**). Although this duty of assistance is identical in both marriage and registered partnership between the partners themselves, the extent of this duty is not so clear when it comes to children in a registered partnership.[169] However, as at least one author has already indicated, Art. 27(1), Sw. RPA does impose a duty on a registered partner to provide support for any child raised in the registered partnership.[170] The question is thus left open in how far the judiciary will interpret these duties as identical.

IV.5.6.4 Duty to contribute to household expenses

Parties to a marriage are subject to an obligation to provide maintenance for the *famille*.[171] Parties to a registered partnership, on the other hand, are subject to an obligation to provide maintenance for the *communauté*.[172] The duty thus imposed on spouses extends beyond that imposed on registered partners since it envelops the provision of maintenance of any children.[173] The Sw. RPA is devoid of almost any reference to children and thus it would appear that the choice of the word *communauté* instead of *famille* indicates Parliament's intention that registered partnership is to have no

---

166 *E.g.* Trib. Féd., 11th July 1991 (1991) 117 II *ATF* 218 at 228.

167 STETTLER/GERMANI (1999) p. 19-21, §27; DESCHENAUX *et al.* (2000) p. 67, §56.

168 This can include the desire to have children (BRÄM/HASENBÖHLER (1998) Art. 159, No. 152) as well as support during daily life and in cases of familial or extraneous difficulty such as sickness (BRÄM/HASENBÖHLER (1998) Art. 159, No. 123) or unemployment (BRÄM/HASENBÖHLER (1998) Art. 159, No. 118-121).

169 For this duty in relation to spouses see, BRÄM/HASENBÖHLER (1998) Art. 159, No. 152; DESCHENAUX *et al.* (2000) p. 67, §57; FF 2003, p. 1192 at 1223-1227.

170 PICHONNAZ (2004) p. 409.

171 Art. 163(1), Sw. CC. This is regarded as a supplement to the broad duty to foster the prosperity of the marriage: Art. 159(2) and (3), Sw. CC. Provision is also provided for those cases should recourse be needed to the court: Art. 13(2), Sw. RPA replicates the provisions of Art. 173(1) and (3), Sw. CC, and Art. 13(3), Sw. RPA with Art. 177, Sw. CC.

172 Art. 13(1), Sw. RPA. Art. 159(2), Sw. CC, is however not accordingly extended to registered partners: GRÜTTER/SUMMERMATTER (2004) p. 451.

173 DESCHENAUX *et al.* (2000) p. 216-219, §464-470.

consequences for children. However, the exclusion of the duty to provide maintenance for children is not as simple as it first appears, since Swiss case law has provided for non-financial contribution to be taken into account when determining a party's contribution to the household expenses, on the basis that this non-financial contribution is often performed due to the presence of children. The question thus arises whether a registered partner's contribution to the household will be treated in the same way, even in the absence of common children.

However, as already highlighted, Art. 27(1), Sw. RPA does state that if one of the parties to a registered partnership has a child, the other registered partner is obliged to assit appropriately in the accomplishment of the maintenance obligation.[174] This provision is equivalent to the maintenance duty imposed on spouses.[175] This provision could thus be used to extend the maintenance obligation imposed on spouses by virtue of Art. 163 (and further expounded in Arts. 276 to 278, Sw. CC) to registered partners. Despite this uncertainty, the explanatory note to the Act does not shed any further light on whether the existing case law on Art. 159(2), Sw. CC will be used as the basis for the interpretation of this Article.

Further concerns can also be raised with the exclusion of Arts. 164 and 165, Sw. CC, with respect to registered partners.[176] Adopted by the legislature in 1984, Art. 164, Sw. CC allows one spouse to claim an equitable sum from the other to be placed at his or her free disposal for any work done as listed in Art. 164(1), Sw. CC. This sum is aimed at compensating a spouse for his or her non-financial contribution to the maintenance of the household.[177] The Federal Council acknowledged that many people during the consultation procedure had called for the analogous application of this provision to registered partners.[178] However, in light of the developments that have taken place since 1984, it was thought unnecessary to extend this provision to registered partners, especially in view of the fact there are no

---

174 GRÜTTER/SUMMERMATTER (2004) p. 452 and 463-465, where it is stated that Art. 27(1), Sw. RPA acts as a supplement to Art. 13, Sw. RPA.

175 Art. 159, Sw. CC. See FF 2003, p. 1192 at 1245; GRÜTTER/SUMMERMATTER (2004) p. 463. Furthermore, this duty is copied from that imposed on step-parents (Art. 299, Sw. CC) and on spouses with respect to children born before the marriage (Art. 273, Sw. CC).

176 FF 2003, p. 1192 at 1216. GRÜTTER/SUMMERMATTER (2004) p. 453.

177 DESCHENAUX *et al.* (2000) p. 231, §504. This thus includes unpaid care and upbringing of the children, household work and unpaid work and assistance in the spouse's profession. Art. 165, Sw. CC may apply in cases where such work is paid.

178 FF 2003, p. 1192 at 1216.

common children in registered partnerships.[179] The Federal Council nevertheless noted that registered partners have the possibility to draw up contracts in order to regulate the situation where one partner provides unpaid work for the other's business.[180]

Similar arguments were also espoused for not extending application of Art. 165, Sw. CC to registered partners. Art. 165(1), Sw. CC permits a spouse to claim an equitable sum when the value of his or her contribution to the profession of his or her spouse is considerably greater than the sum of his or her maintenance claim under Art. 163, Sw. CC.[181] This Article aimed at bringing an end to the debate on whether Art. 320, Sw. CO applied in this sort of situation.[182] Once again, however, this rule has not been correspondingly applied to registered partners. The parties to a registered partnership are of course entitled to reach an agreement independently of these provisions, in a similar fashion to Art. 165(3), Sw. CC, in order to regulate their individual situation in relation to such contributions.[183]

VI.5.6.5 Duty to contribute to repayment of debts

Neither the celebration of a marriage nor the registration of a partnership has any affect on a person's debts.[184] As a result, a spouse or registered partner who owes a debt to third party is also ultimately responsible for its repayment. However, due to the manner in which a spouse represents the conjugal unit,[185] and a registered partner represents the *communauté*,[186] a debt entered into by one spouse on behalf of the conjugal unit or a

---

179 FF 2003, p. 1192 at 1216.

180 Art. 320(2), Sw. CO.

181 Art. 165(1), Sw. CC. Art. 165(2) provides that the same is also true where the contribution is a result of income or wealth. See further: DESCHENAUX *et al.* (2000) p. 243-245, §537-542.

182 Trib. Féd., 6th October 1987 (1988) 114 II *ATF* 414. The Tribunal Fédéral stated that where a person's work for his or her spouse's profession is not sufficiently rewarded in an corresponding increase in his or her standard of living, then such work can be reimbursed if it should exceed his or her obligation to provide assistance: 114 II *ATF* 414 at 415.

183 FF 2003, p. 1192 at 1217. Art. 165, Sw. CC is, however, aimed at precisely the opposite situation, namely when no agreement has been reached.

184 **Marriage:** Art. 203(1), Sw. CC and DESCHENAUX *et al.* (2000) p. 481, §1180; **RP:** Art. 23, Sw. RPA and GRÜTTER/SUMMERMATTER (2004) p. 460; GREMPER (2004) p. 502.

185 Art. 166(1), Sw. CC. DESCHENAUX *et al.* (2000) p. 480-489, §1177-1198.

186 Art. 15(1), Sw. RPA. This is almost a word-for-word replica of Art. 166, Sw. CC. Art 15(4), Sw. RPA, is a rewording of the power provided to a judge to remove or partially remove a spouse's power to contract on behalf of the conjugal unit: Art. 174, Sw. CC.

registered partner on behalf of the *communauté*, is equally enforceable against the other.[187]

VI.5.6.6 Protection of the home

By virtue of Art. 169, Sw. CC and Art. 14, Sw. RPA, both spouses and registered partners are entitled to identical protection with respect to the familial or common home. Accordingly, neither spouse nor registered partner is allowed to terminate the tenancy, to alienate the marital home or familial apartment, nor limit his or her partner's rights to the family home by other legal acts without his or her partner's express consent to that effect.[188] This provision thus protects a person from the unilateral acts of his or her partner with respect to the marital or familial home.[189] The original registered partnership proposal had stated that the parties possessed a *demeure commune*, whilst the final Act coins the phrase *logement commun*, aligning it still closer to the phrase utilised for the marital home, namely *logement familial*.[190] Despite this difference in terminology, the Federal Council noted that these provisions should be interpreted identically. Accordingly, a house will be deemed to be a *logment commun* if, by virtue of the will of the parties, it is destined to be used by them and their minor children.[191] The protection offered to spouses by virtue of Art. 169(1), Sw. CC and registered partners by virtue of Art. 14, Sw. RPA, is complemented by Arts. 266l to 266n, Sw. CO.[192] These Articles have thus also been accordingly amended as a result of the passing of the Sw. RPA.

---

187 DESCHENAUX *et al.* (2000) p. 482, §1181. This duty is imposed as long as this "*n'excède pas ses pouvoirs d'une manière reconnaissable pour les tiers*": DESCHENAUX *et al.* (2000) p. 200, §419. If a spouse or registered partner does exceed their power of representation, the court is empowered to remove such powers: Art. 174(1) and (3), Sw. CC, replicated in Art. 15(4), Sw. RPA. GRÜTTER/SUMMERMATTER (2004) p. 454.

188 **Marriage:** Art. 169(1), Sw. CC; **RP:** Art. 14, Sw. RPA.

189 DESCHENAUX *et al.* (2000) p. 109-143, §184-276.

190 Art. 169, Sw. CC.

191 Trib. Féd., 3rd November 1992 (1992) 118 II *ATF* 489 at 490 (in defining the nature of *logement de la famille*). DESCHENAUX *et al.* (2000) p. 113, §193

192 DESCHENAUX *et al.* (2000) p. 126, §228 and p. 131, §240-243. Further rights are also extended including those encapsulated in Arts. 271a and 273a, Sw. CO. If, however, the *logement de la famille* includes an agricultural enterprise then the household will not be covered by Art. 266n, Sw. CO: Trib. Féd., 14th September 1999 (1999) 125 III *ATF* 425.

VI.5.7 PROPERTY LAW

As a result of the overhaul of Swiss matrimonial property law in 1988, three different statutory matrimonial regimes exist. A regime of *la participation aux acquêts* (regime of contribution to jointly acquired property) became the default matrimonial regime and replaced the old regime of *l'union des biens.*[193] Two other statutory schemes, namely *la communauté de biens* (community of property)[194] and *la séparation des biens* (separation of property), were also created. These latter two statutory schemes must be contracted into for them to become applicable.[195] During the debates on the introduction of registered partnership, the Swiss Federal Council noted that during the existence of a marriage, the regime of contribution to jointly acquired property is almost indiscernible from a regime of separation of property, and only upon the dissolution of the relationship do the two regimes become distinguishable.[196] However, the separation of property regime owes its appeal to its simplicity and clarity. Furthermore, the Federal Council noted that the majority of the benefits, rights and obligations imposed on the parties by virtue of a community of property can actually be achieved by virtue of contractual agreements. However, in determining the most suitable property regime for spouses, the Federal Council noted that leaving everything to the contractual will of the parties could be to disadvantage of the economically weaker party, who, traditionally speaking, was the female partner who stayed at home to care for and raise the children. As a result, for marital situations, a separation of property regime could have led to unjust results when the parties separated, and thus a regime of contribution to jointly owned property was introduced.

With respect to registered partners, the Federal Council believed that the same arguments did not hold true. The Federal Council assumed that the majority of same-sex couples consist of two wage-earning parties (and thus financially independent) and felt that the aim of protecting a financially weaker party was not as valid in relation to registered partners.[197] Both registered partners are therefore free to pursue their economic goals

---

193 Arts. 181 and 196, Sw. CC. See also BRAAT (2004).

194 Art. 221, Sw. CC. Within this category various possibilities exist. The spouses are entitled to opt for a universal community of property, a community of assets or any other form of community of property which they desire, so long as it remains within the confines of the law: Art. 222(1), Sw. CC.

195 Art. 247, Sw. CC.

196 FF 2003, p. 1192 at 1220.

197 FF 2003, p. 1192 at 1220.

without the risk of the profits of such an enterprise accruing to the other and thus being lost upon dissolution of the partnership.[198] Moreover, the Federal Council stated that since registered partnerships do not involve children, the reasons espoused for the application of a community of property are not evident.[199] As a result, the property of each party to a registered partnership is unaffected by registration of their partnership.[200]

The scheme would operate in exactly the same manner as the separation of property regime for spouses.[201] If the registered partners are unable to prove ownership of particular property then, and only then, will such property be considered to be co-owned by the registered partners.[202] However, the Federal Council also realised that, although such a scheme would be adequate in the majority of cases, there would be some instances were the provisions applicable to the statutory regime of contribution to jointly acquired property would be more favourable.[203] Therefore, Art. 25(1), Sw. RPA provides the partners with an opportunity to opt-into the regime of contribution to jointly acquired property.[204] Such an agreement must be presented in the form of an authentic instrument signed by both parties and their legal counsel.[205]

For the parties who opt into the statutory regime of contribution to jointly acquired property and in an identical fashion to marriage, four categories of property will exist: each partner's own property and each partner's assets acquired during the registered partnership. In principle, the parties retain ownership of and administration over their own property during the registered partnership. A party's own property consists of four separate categories of goods:[206] (a) the personal effects of the registered partner for

---

198 A somewhat cynical approach when one enters a partnership, it must be said. Surely part of the concept of entering into a registered partnership is to share in the spoils and tribulations of the relationship, to assist in the maintenance of the relationship and to respect one's partner. It would seem that the idea of retaining ones profits from a business venture runs counter to these goals and would fuel economically selfish goals of one partner to the disadvantage of the other.

199 FF 2003, p. 1192 at 1220.

200 Art. 18, Sw. RPA.

201 Arts. 247-251, Sw. CC. GRÜTTER/SUMMERMATTER (2004) p. 457.

202 Art. 19(2), Sw. RPA. *Cf.* Art. 248, Sw. CC.

203 FF 2003, p. 1192 at 1221.

204 Laid down in Arts. 196-219, Sw. CC. Arts. 185-193, Sw. CC are equally applicable to such a declaration. GRÜTTER/SUMMERMATTER (2004) p. 461-462.

205 Art. 25(3), Sw. RPA. In this case, Arts. 185-193 are *mutatis mutandis* applicable.

206 Art. 198, Sw. CC.

his or her exclusive use,[207] (b) the goods which a registered partner brings to the registered partnership or which he or she acquires by means of inheritance or gratuitously during the registered partnership, (c) compensation for certain tortious acts, and (d) goods acquired to replace personal property.[208] Property acquired during the registered partnership that does not fall into one of the above-mentioned categories is known as *les acquêts*. Unlike in relation to party's own property, where the legislature has specifically provided an exhaustive list of categories, the Swiss Civil Code only provides a list of examples of *les acquêts*.[209] Such property thus includes income from work, personal and occupational pensions, benefits derived from invalidity benefits, income from goods categorised as a party's own property, as well as property whose aim is to replace another *l'acquêt*.[210] Each registered partner retains the administration over his or her own property as well as his or her *acquêts*.[211]

VI.5.8 INHERITANCE LAW

By virtue of Art. 36, Sw. RPA and the Annex thereto, Art. 462, Sw. CC has been amended to place registered partners in an identical position to spouses with respect to inheritance law. Accordingly, in the absence of a will, the size of the inheritance share of a spouse or registered partner varies according to which other relatives are surviving. Swiss law classifies statutory heirs into three groups. If the descendant should leave relatives in the first category of heirs, namely descendants *i.e.* children, grandchildren, great-grandchildren *etc.*, the surviving spouse or registered partner will receive one-half of the deceased's estate.[212] If the deceased should leave relatives in the second category of heirs, namely his or her mother, father or their descendants *i.e.* brothers, sisters, nieces, and nephews of the deceased, the surviving spouse or registered partner will receive three quarters of the entire estate.[213] In all other cases, the surviving spouse or registered partner

---

207 See for further explanation FF 1979, p. 1179, *Message du Conseil fédéral concernant la révision du code civil Suisse (effets généraux du mariage, régimes matrimoniaux et successions)*.

208 DESCHENAUX *et al.* (2000) p. 397, §984, p. 401, §994, p. 399, §990 and p. 405, §1005.

209 Art. 197(1), Sw. CC.

210 For further explanation of exact boundaries of these categories see DESCHENAUX *et al.* (2000) p. 430 *et seq*, §1065 *et seq*.

211 Art. 201(1), Sw. CC. See further, DESCHENAUX *et al.* (2000) p. 475-480, §1161-1176.

212 Art. 462(1), Sw. CC, as amended by the Sw. RPA. DESCHENAUX *et al.* (2000) p. 732, §1922.

213 Art. 462(2), Sw. CC, as amended by the Sw. RPA. DESCHENAUX *et al.* (2000) p. 733, §1925.

is entitled to inherit the entire estate.[214] Although a person is entitled to make a testamentary disposition to dispose of his or her property,[215] or a *pacte successoral*,[216] certain statutory heirs, namely the deceased person's descendants, father, mother and surviving spouse cannot be totally disinherited.[217] By virtue of an amendment to Art. 470(1), Sw. CC, the surviving registered partner has been inserted into this list and is subject to identical treatment as a spouse.[218]

The levying of inheritance tax lies with the competency of the cantons, or in some instances with the cantonal communities. The propensity of rules is therefore great.[219] However, the cantons are increasingly in the process of eliminating inheritance tax altogether, at least for descendants. Prior to the passage of the Sw. RPA, if a canton imposed inheritance tax, relief was often not afforded to same-sex couples, who were thus liable to pay inheritance tax of up to 40%.[220] An example of an exception is the Canton of Bern, which operates a reduced rate of inheritance tax applicable in the case of partnerships lasting more than ten years.[221] The Sw. RPA nonetheless assimilates the position of registered partners to that of spouses for the purposes of all taxation. However, by virtue of the Swiss Federal Constitution, the cantons possess exclusive competency in this field and thus the Federal Government is unable to force those cantons that deviate from this rule to change their law.

VI.5.9 CHILDREN

The debate concerning children and registered partnership centred on whether extension of the rules in the field of parentage, parental authority, adoption and artificial insemination was in fact in the best interests of the child.[222] It was felt by many that allowing same-sex couples to adopt or

---

214 Art. 462(3), Sw. CC, as amended by the Sw. RPA. DESCHENAUX *et al.* (2000) p. 734, §1926.

215 Art. 467, Sw. CC.

216 Art. 468, Sw. CC.

217 Art. 470, Sw. CC.

218 Art. 471, Sw. CC.

219 At present inheritance tax rates tend to oscillate between 6 and 15%: FF 2003, p. 1192 at 1230.

220 BAUR (2001) p. 531.

221 Art. 10(1)(2), Act concerning Inheritance and Gift Tax. The partners must have a family household (*Hausgemeinschaft*) or a common household (*Wohngemeinschaft*).

222 For a detailed discussion of the issues surrounding children in same-sex relationships see FF 2003, p. 1192 at 1223-1227.

utilise artificial reproductive techniques would lead to a distortion of the biological reality of the situation that same-sex couples cannot conceive children naturally.[223] Even homosexual lobby groups admitted that it was too early to begin fighting for such rights in Switzerland.[224] It was thought by many that although the time might have been ripe for the recognition of same-sex partnerships, Switzerland's society was still adamantly against the recognition of same-sex families.

VI.5.9.1 Parentage

The birth mother is deemed to be the legal mother of the child by operation of law.[225] The birth of a child must be declared within three days of its birth[226] and must be registered in the Register of Births, Deaths and Marriages.[227] Thus, if a woman in a female registered partnership gives birth, irrespective of how she conceived in the first place, she will be deemed to be the legal mother of the child upon the child's birth.

The father of a child is established by reason of marriage, recognition, judicial decree or adoption.[228] If the child is born during marriage, then the adage *pater est quem nuptiae demonstrant* applies and the husband of the legal mother is deemed to be the legal father.[229] This rule has not been correspondingly extended to registered partnerships. If the mother is unmarried or the husband has successfully denied paternity,[230] the father of the child may apply to recognise the child.[231] The Swiss Federal Supreme Court has held that only the biological or natural father is allowed to recognise the child.[232] Any interested party may oppose the recognition by the man, but it must be based on the fact that the man is not the biological

---

223 FF 2003, p. 1192 at 1224.

224 For example, in the petition "Same rights for same sex couples" no reference was made to the situation with regards children: *Swiss Council of States*, BO 1997, No. 96.2011, 701.

225 Art. 252(1), Sw. CC.

226 Art. 49(1), Sw. CC.

227 Art. 9(1), Sw. OCS.

228 Art. 252(2) and (3), Sw. CC. For adoption see **Section VI.4.8.3** for further details

229 Art. 255(1), Sw. CC. The vast majority of cases in Switzerland are governed by this rule: STETTLER (1987) p. 25. In 2003, only 12.4% of children were born outside of marriage. An extremely low figure in comparison with statistics in **France** (**IV.4.8.1**) and **The Netherlands** (**V.4.8.1**).

230 Art. 256, Sw. CC allows for the husband or the child to apply to the court for the presumption of paternity to be set aside.

231 Art. 260, Sw. CC.

232 Trib. Féd., 23rd September 1982 (1982) 108 II *ATF* 344.

father of the child.[233] Once again this has not been altered as a result of the passing of the Sw. RPA and as a result it is impossible for the female registered partner of the legal mother to recognise the child. The final option, apart from adoption, for determining paternity is for the mother or child to ask the court to determine paternity.[234] As a result of these provisions the situation with respect to registered partners is evident; registered partners are treated in the same way as unmarried persons. The main difficulty is that for registered partners to conceive a child, a third party will always be involved, whether it be the surrogate mother, a begetter, a sperm donor, an egg donor or a combination of any one or more of these.[235] As a result of the current law, only those persons biologically related to a child will be able to avail themselves of the position of legal parent.

VI.5.9.2 Parental Responsibilities

Only legal, and thus (presumed) biological, parents are able to exercise parental authority over their children.[236] If the parties are married then parental authority is exercised jointly and by operation of law.[237] In contrast, if the parties are unmarried or in a registered partnership, the mother is vested with sole parental authority,[238] unless the father has recognised the child or his paternity has been judicially determined.[239] The fact that the mother is homosexual has been held by the Swiss Federal Supreme Court not to be a ground for the removal of parental authority.[240] As a result, in a registered partnership it is impossible for both parties to possess parental authority over the same child. In a female registered partnership, one female may be vested with parental authority by virtue of

---

233 Art. 260b(1), Sw. CC.

234 Art. 261(1), Sw. CC. This procedure is normally only requested in order to retrieve some financial sum from the natural father.

235 STETTLER (1987) p. 38.

236 Title VIII, Sw. CC lists the effects of the establishment of the parent-child relationship. The French text talks of *l'authorité parentale*, the Italian of *autorità parentale* and the German of *elterliche Sorge*.

237 Art. 297(1), Sw. CC; HAUSHEER/ACHERMANN-WEBER/WOLF, in: BOELE-WOELKI/BRAAT/CURRY-SUMNER (2005) p. 273.

238 Art. 298(1), Sw. CC. Unless the mother is a minor under guardianship in which case Art. 298(2), Sw. CC applies and the guardian appoints a guardian for the child or transfers parental authority to the father.

239 HAUSHEER/ACHERMANN-WEBER/WOLF, in: BOELE-WOELKI/BRAAT/CURRY-SUMNER (2005) p. 407.

240 Trib. Féd., 23rd September 1982 (1982) 108 II *ATF* 369 at 371.

the birth of the child, whilst in a male registered partnership one man may be vested with parental authority either by having recognised the child[241] or having had his paternity judicially determined.[242]

VI.5.9.3 Adoption

Swiss law allows for joint adoption as well as step-parent and single parent adoption. Joint adoption is, however, restricted to married couples who have been married for at least five years prior to the adoption application.[243] This situation has not been amended as a result of the Sw. RPA, and accordingly registered partners are not permitted to apply for joint adoption.[244] Step-parent adoption is allowed, but again restricted to married couples.[245] In refusing to extend the possibility of step-parent adoption to same-sex couples, the Federal Council referred to the position of different-sex step-parent adoptions. In these cases, it was only considered to be in the best interests of the child to allow such adoptions when:

- parental authority is vested solely in one parent and economic difficulties and long-term stress are alleviated with the arrival of a new partner; and
- a child is younger than eight and treats the new parent as his or her parent, both psychologically and socially.

The Federal Council noted that children in Swiss society regarded the roles of mother and father as being satisfied by people of different sex. As a result it could not be seen to be in the best interests of a child to allow for step-parent adoption for same-sex couples. With respect to the former situation, the stigmatisation and discrimination that the child would suffer at the hands of his or her peers, could not justify the acceptance of step-parent adoption for registered partners. In fact, the vast majority of those consulted during the consultation procedure actually supported this standpoint.[246]

Single parent adoption is allowed in accordance with Art. 264b, Sw. CC, as long as the party has reached the age of thirty-five. Although the homosexual orientation of the party is not an explicit ground for the refusal

---

241 Arts. 260-260c, Sw. CC.

242 Arts. 261-263, Sw. CC.

243 Art. 264a(1) and (2), Sw. CC.

244 Art. 28, Sw. RPA. GRÜTTER/SUMMERMATTER (2004) p. 466.

245 Art. 264a(3), Sw. CC inserted as Federal Act of 26th June 1998, RO 1999, No. 1118.

246 FF 2003, p. 1192 at 1223.

of the adoption order, it is unlikely that a person in a registered partnership would succeed in applying for single parent adoption since in granting the adoption order, the competent authority must take into account the child's need to have a mother and father.[247]

VI.5.9.4 Artificial Reproductive Techniques

On the 17th May 1992, the Swiss people approved a constitutional amendment giving power to the Federal Government to legislate on genetics and artificial reproductive techniques.[248] The new Federal Constitution exploits that right and only permits artificial reproductive techniques if a person's "infertility cannot be remedied in any other way".[249] Debate has since surrounded the interpretation of this phrase. If understood in a broad sense, the mere absence of a male partner in a female same-sex registered partnership or a female partner in a male same-sex registered partnership could satisfy this requirement. This argument has not, however, found support in Swiss literature. The mere absence of a male or female partner will not be deemed enough to satisfy this provision, thus denying same-sex couples, registered or not, access to artificial insemination techniques.[250]

In order to further plug any possible legal loophole, and further protect the interests of children *la loi fédérale du 18 décembre sur la procréation médicalement assistée* lays down certain principles with respect to the access to artificial reproductive techniques.[251] Art. 3(2) of that Act stipulates that only couples are entitled access to artificial reproductive techniques. Furthermore, these couples must be able to show that a bond of parentage is able to be established between them and the child, with reference to the provisions of Arts. 252-263, Sw. CC.[252] Moreover, sperm donation is limited to married couples.[253] These provisions therefore restrict artificial reproduction to married couples and different-sex cohabitants, preventing registered partners from access to such medical techniques.[254] This is (as if needed) furthermore reinforced by the Sw. RPA, which expressly prohibits

247 HEGNAUER (1984) p. 470, §4; HONSELL/VOGT/GEISER (2002) p. 1394-1396.

248 GUILLOD (1997) p. 492-493.

249 Art. 119(2)(c), Sw. FC.

250 MINISTRY OF JUSTICE (1999) p. 35.

251 FF 1998, p. 4992.

252 Art. 3(2)(a), Federal Act of 18th December on medically assisted reproduction.

253 Art. 3(3), Federal Act of 18th December on medically assisted reproduction.

254 FF 1996, p. 245.

registered partners from being authorised to make use of artificial reproductive techniques.[255]

VI.6 DISSOLUTION

VI.6.1 GENERAL

Divorce law was the focal point of the major revision of Swiss family law which entered into force on the 1st January 2000.[256] The legislation overhauled the existing provisions of the Swiss Civil Code on divorce which dated from 1907.[257] One of the main aims of this legislation was to induce spouses, as far as possible, to submit a joint petition for divorce. Whilst stressing the importance of maintaining judicial divorce proceedings, emphasis was placed on encouraging the spouses to reach an agreement with respect not only to their divorce but also with the effects thereof.[258] The timing of this reform provides an excellent focal point in endeavouring to ascertain the precise difference in the philosophy behind the institution of marriage on the one hand and registered partnership on the other. The wholesale reform of Swiss divorce law has not be mirrored in the Sw. RPA, despite the almost contemporaneous nature of these debates. The difference in result cannot therefore be explained with reference to the traditions emblazoning marriage, and must instead be justified with reference to the fundamental disparity between these institutions themselves.[259] Furthermore, the judicial separation procedure available to spouses is not extended to registered partners.[260]

VI.6.2 JUDICIAL: JOINT PETITION

Like the possibilities provided for spouses to terminate their marriage by means of a joint petition,[261] registered partners are equally entitled to submit

255 Art. 28, Sw. RPA. GRÜTTER/SUMMERMATTER (2004) p. 466.

256 Federal Act of 26th June 1998 (FF 1996, p. 1).

257 See further HAUSHEER/WOLF, in: BOELE-WOELKI/BRAAT/SUMNER (2003a) p. 53.

258 FF 1995, p. 29-30.

259 FF 2003, p. 1192 at 1225.

260 Due to the non-application and non-replication of Art. 117-118, Sw. CC. GRÜTTER/SUMMERMATTER (2004) p. 467.

261 Arts. 111 and 112, Sw. CC. The option to divorce by joint petition is not, however, a mere formality. The parties must prove to the court that their marriage has irretrievably broken down and that they therefore wish to terminate it. See further, HAUSHEER (1999) p. 7; HAUSHEER/WOLF, in: BOELE-WOELKI/BRAAT/SUMNER (2003a) p. 97-98.

a joint petition requesting the termination of their registered partnership.[262] However, unlike the divorce procedure, no distinction is drawn between a petition accompanied by an agreement on all the consequences thereof and a petition accompanied by a partial agreement or no agreement at all.[263] The Federal Council, in justifying this procedural disparity, referred to the absence of common children in registered partnerships.[264] Nonetheless, since the registration of a registered partnership is based upon the desire of both parties to be involved in a *vie de couple*, as soon as this desire ceases to exist, the registered partnership loses its basis, thus providing the rational behind a consensual dissolution procedure.[265]

Despite the similarities in the termination procedure for registered partners and the Art. 112 divorce procedure, the wording of the relevant provisions of the Sw. RPA is almost identical to the wording of Art. 111, Sw. CC.[266] However, like the Art. 112 divorce procedure, registered partners wishing to dissolve their partnership need only reach an agreement on the principle of dissolution and need not reach an agreement as to the consequences thereof.[267] In those areas where disagreement as to the consequences of the dissolution persists, the parties must submit to the jurisdiction of the judge to make orders on those issues.[268]

The competency of the court to ensure that any agreements reached between the spouses are exhaustive, clear and neither contrary to the law nor manifestly unreasonable, is likewise extended to the judge in areas

262 Art. 29, Sw. RPA.

263 **Marriage:** Arts. 111 (joint petition with agreement on all effects) and 112 (joint petition without agreement), Sw. CC; **RP:** Art. 29, Sw. RPA.

264 FF 2003, p. 1192 at 1228. The Federal Council argued that the presence of children in marriages, or at least the possible presence of children in marriages, justifies operating a dual system. The absence of children in registered partnerships therefore removes this necessity.

265 GRÜTTER/SUMMERMATTER (2004) p. 468; FF 2003, p. 1192 at 1225.

266 The agreement according to Art. 111, Sw. CC, must deal with the dissolution of the matrimonial community of property (Art. 120(1), Sw. CC), the attribution of the marital home (Art. 121, Sw. CC), the adjustment of pension benefits under occupational pension schemes (Arts. 122-124, Sw. CC), the payment of maintenance (Arts. 125-132, Sw. CC) and contain proposals on those matters relating to any children (Art. 145(1), Sw. CC). With respect to the proposals reached in relation to children, the court must scrutinise these facts *ex officio* and has complete discretion to reach its own conclusions after considering all the facts of the case.

267 GRÜTTER/SUMMERMATTER (2004) p. 467-468.

268 Art. 29(3), Sw. RPA, *cf.* Art. 112(1), Sw. CC. WERRO (2000) p. 115, §508 and 116, §512.

where the registered partners have been unable to reach agreement.[269] Furthermore, the judge must also ascertain whether the filing of the petition has taken place willingly and after careful consideration,[270] although the judge is not allowed to inquire as to the reasons for the dissolution.[271] The duty imposed on the judge in an Art. 111 procedure to hear the parties separately and jointly[272] is not expressly imposed on the judge in hearing the dissolution of a registered partnership.[273] Whether the duty imposed on the judge to hear the parties will be interpreted as imposing a duty to hear the parties separately and jointly on issues in which they have reached an agreement, as is the case for the Art. 112 procedure,[274] is yet to be seen. Furthermore, from a literal reading of the Sw. RPA, the court need only assess whether the parties have freely consented to the dissolution, and thus need not, unlike in a divorce procedure, research whether the parties have also consented to the agreements reached.[275] Unlike an Art. 111 procedure where the parties must wait for the completion of a two-month reflection period prior to the pronouncement of a final dissolution order,[276] the dissolution of a registered partnership can take effect immediately, as is the case with an Art. 112 procedure.[277]

If during the joint petition proceedings for a divorce, either under Article 111 or 112, it becomes clear that the procedural conditions have not been met, *i.e.* that the parties are no longer in agreement that their marriage has irretrievably broken down and that they wish to terminate it, the proceedings may be converted to unilateral proceedings for divorce should

---

269 **Marriage:** Art. 140(2), Sw. CC; **RP:** Art. 35, Sw. RPA, in conjunction with Art. 140(2), Sw. CC.

270 **Marriage:** Arts. 111(1) and 112(1), Sw. CC; **RP:** Art. 29(1), Sw. RPA. See further WERRO (2000) p. 110, §481.

271 WERRO (2000) p. 113, §498 and p. 115, §507.

272 Art. 111(1), Sw. CC.

273 Art. 29(1), Sw. RPA.

274 Art. 112(1), Sw.CC. WERRO (2000) p. 115, §150.

275 GRÜTTER/SUMMERMATTER (2004) p. 468. However, due to the analogous application of the procedural divorce rules to the dissolution of a registered partnership (Art. 35, Sw. RPA), the court must be ensure that such consent is present (Art. 140(2), Sw. CC).

276 Arts. 111(2) and 112(3), Sw. CC. GRÜTTER/SUMMERMATTER (2004) p. 469.

277 Art. 29(2), Sw. RPA, *cf.* Art. 112(3), Sw. CC.

one of the parties still wish to pursue a divorce.[278] This possibility has, however, not been extended to registered partners.[279]

VI.6.3 JUDICIAL: UNILATERAL PETITION

Both marriages and registered partnerships may be dissolved upon the unilateral petition of one of the parties submitted to the court.[280] This petition must however be supported by the existence of certain facts before a divorce decree or decree of dissolution will be prounced. In order to obtain a divorce decree, a petitioning spouse must be able to prove a two-year period of separation.[281] This period will however be reduced should the petitioning spouse be able to show that the continuation of the marital bond would be unreasonable.[282] Despite the fact that the law on divorce was amended in 2000, two proposals were submitted in 2001 calling for the reduction of the then four-year separation period for filing a unilateral petition to two years.[283] These proposals succeeded in sparking parliamentary debate, and the law was subsequently amended to allow for divorce after a two-year period of separation.[284]

In outlining the proposals for the unilateral termination of a registered partnership, the Federal Council noted that marriage, as the foundation stone of society and the keystone to the family unit, has the express protection of the State by virtue of Art. 14, Sw. FC.[285] Furthermore, the Federal Council observed that since this constitutional protection is not afforded to registered partners, the lengthy period of separation required of

---

278 Art. 113, Sw. CC. This option is not open to registered partners.

279 No explanation for this was provided for in the explanatory note: FF 2003, p. 1192 at 1227-1228. GRÜTTER/SUMMERMATTER (2004) p. 469 also note the absence of such a possibility.

280 **Marriage:** Arts. 114 and 115, Sw. CC; **RP:** Art. 30, Sw. CC.

281 Art. 114, Sw. CC. The previous four-year period began at the moment the legislation was enacted (Trib. Féd., 10th July 2000 (2000) 126 III *ATF* 401, §2) and thus by analogy this two-year period commenced on the date when the legislative amendment was enacted.

282 Art. 115, Sw. CC. The Sw. SC has held that although Art. 114 should be interpreted broadly, Art. 115 should be given a restrictive interpretation: Trib. Féd., 10th July 2000 (2000) 126 III *ATF* 401, §§4b, 4c, 5b. See also Tribunal Basel, 31st March 2000, *Fam.Pra.Ch*, 2000, 692, No. 54 and Tribunal Zurich, 2nd March 2000, *Fam.Pra.Ch*, 2000, 530, No. 38.

283 *Swiss National Council*, BO 2001, No. 01.408, Parliamentary Initiative (NABHOLZ) and *Swiss National Council*, BO 2001, No. 01.3645, Motion (THANEI MINORITY).

284 RO 2004, No. 2161.

285 FF 2003, p. 1192 at 1225.

married couples prior to submitting a unilateral petition for divorce need not be applied to registered partners.[286] As a result, the possibility for a reduction in the period of separation, as is provided for in the divorce procedure, was deemed unnecessary for registered partnerships. As a result a petitioning registered partner need only prove a one-year period of separation in order to obtain a dissolution of his or her registered partnership.[287]

VI.6.4 ADMINISTRATIVE: JOINT DECLARATION

As is the case with proceedings to terminate a marriage, administrative procedures are not available for the dissolution of a registered partnership.

VI.6.5 ADMINISTRATIVE: UNILATERAL DECLARATION

See **Section VI.6.4.**

VI.6.6 ANNULMENT PROCEEDINGS

In the same way that non-observance of one of the conditions laid down in **Sections VI.3.2** to **VI.3.7** with respect to marriage can lead to the annulment of the marriage, non-observance of certain conditions for entering into a registered partnership can also lead to the annulment of the relationship. Two categories of reasons for annulling a marriage can be discerned: *les causes absolues* and *les causes relatives.* The absolute causes for the annulment of a marriage have been extended to registered partnerships in their entirety.[288] These causes include that either one or both of the parties at the moment of celebrating their marriage or registered partnership were already validly married or involved in a registered partnership to another,[289]

---

286 The argument stated in the *message* that "*le droit matrimonial s'est développé au cours de nombreux siècles et qu'il est marqué par la tradition*" is thus not valid in this situation (see FF 2003, p. 1192 at 1214).

287 Art. 30, Sw. RPA.

288 When the registered partnership proposal was first submitted to Parliament, an extra ground was available for the annulment of a registered partnership, in anticipation of changes to the laws on marriage (FF 2002, p. 3469 at 3591) on the ground that the partnership was registered in order to avoid the provisions of immigration law. However, this was eventually removed in the belief that registered partnership should mirror marriage law as currently in force: PICHONNAZ (2004) p. 419.

289 **Marriage:** Arts. 96 and 105(1), Sw. CC; **RP:** Arts. 4(2) and 9(1)(b), Sw. RPA. See further **Section VI.3.2.**

that the spouses or registered partners were related to each other within the prohibited degrees of relationship,[290] or that at the time of celebration or registration one of the parties was subject to long-term incapacity.[291]

Despite the identical nature of the absolute causes for annulling a marriage, differences are discernible in relation to the relative causes for annulment. With respect to the relative causes for annulling a marriage, four categories can be distinguished: the temporary incapacity of one of the spouses, mistake on the part of one of the spouses, misrepresentation or fraud.[292] In relation to registered partnerships, the relative causes for annulment are summarised in one category referring to the respective parties' lack of consent (*vice du consentment*).[293] As a result of Art. 7, Sw. CC, which states that all the general provisions on the law of obligations with respect to the conclusion, effects and termination of contracts are also applicable in civil law matters, the term lack of consent must thus be understood with reference to the law of obligations. Accordingly, three general grounds exist for the annulment of a registered partnership, namely error,[294] misrepresentation[295] and substantial fear.[296] As a result of this difference in treatment, registered partnerships will be easier to annul than marriages since the general law of obligations provides for wider annulment grounds than those provided for in Art. 107, Sw. CC, with respect to marriage.[297] In both cases, the annulment of a marriage or registered partnership, the action must be commenced within six months of the discovery of the lack of consent or within five years of the registration of the partnership or celebration of the marriage.[298] In justifying this difference in treatment, the Government argued that there was no public interest in maintaining a registered partnership if a lack of consent can be proven.

---

290 **Marriage:** Arts. 95 and 105(3), Sw. CC; **RP:** Art. 9(1)(a), Sw. RPA. See further **Section VI.3.6.**

291 **Marriage:** Arts. 94 and 105(2), Sw. CC; **RP:** Arts. 4(1) and 9(1)(b), Sw. RPA. See further **Section VI.3.7.**

292 Art. 107, Sw. CC. See further **Section VI.3.7.**

293 Art. 10(1), Sw. RPA.

294 Art. 24(1), Sw. CO.

295 Art. 28, Sw. CO.

296 Art. 29, Sw. CO.

297 FF 2003, p. 1192 at 1237. PICHONNAZ (2004) p. 421.

298 **Marriage:** Art. 108(1), Sw. CC; **RP:** Art. 9(2), Sw. RPA.

VI.6.7 DEATH AND PRESUMPTION OF DEATH

In the same way that the death of either or both of the spouses automatically brings a marriage to an end, so too does the death of one or both of the registered partners.[299] Art. 31(1), Sw. CC, deals with the moment upon which death is determined. Furthermore, Art. 38(1), Sw. CC allows for a declaration of absence to be pronounced if a person has disappeared for a prolonged period of time.[300] By virtue of Art. 38(3), Sw. CC, this has the effect of dissolving the marriage but has not unfortunately been analogously extended to registered partners. It is hoped that either the Swiss judiciary or legislature will rectify this situation as soon as possible. There is also no principle of the presumption of death according to Swiss law.

VI.6.8 ENTRY INTO MARRIAGE / CONVERSION

Due to the fact that marriages are restricted to different-sex couples and registered partnerships to same-sex couples, the option of converting a registered partnership into a marriage does not exist, unless one of the parties undergoes gender reassignment surgery.[301]

VI.6.9 EFFECTS OF DISSOLUTION

VI.6.9.1 Maintenance

Like marriage, each partner upon the dissolution of the registered partnership is entitled to maintenance.[302] Art. 34(4), Sw. RPA analogously applies the rules regulating maintenance after divorce to the dissolution of a registered partnership.[303] Nonetheless, Art. 125(2), Sw. CC is not analogously applied to registered partners with the effect that the statutory criteria list for determining maintenance is not applicable. However, the principle of equitable maintenance contribution requires that all the relevant circumstances be taken into account, most notably the duration of the relationship, the division of the duties during the relationship and the

---

299 WERRO (2000) p. 88, §359.

300 HEGNAUER/BREITSCHMID (2000) p. 52, §6.03; WERRO (2000) p. 85, §347.

301 See earlier **Section VI.3.3.**

302 **Marriage:** HAUSHEER/WOLF, in: BOELE-WOELKI/BRAAT/SUMNER (2003b) p. 54; **RP:** Art. 34(1), Sw. RPA.

303 Arts. 126-132, Sw. CC.

living standard during the registered partnership.[304] Furthermore, if one of the parties, by reason of the division of duties during the registered partnership, has limited or not exercised his or her right to employment, he or she can demand equitable maintenance contributions from his or her partner.[305]

VI.6.9.2 Effects with respect to children

Since it is not possible for a same-sex couple to be vested with joint parental authority over a child, the possibility for disagreement has therefore been removed. If one of the partners does, however, have parental authority over a child, this remains unaffected as a result of the dissolution of the registered partnership.[306] Art. 27(2), Sw. RPA does, however, state that in the case of suspension of the *vie commune* or in the case of a dissolution of the registered partnership, the partner who does not have parental authority over the child may request the court to become the child's guardian by virtue of Art. 274a, Sw. CC. This provision states that where extraordinary circumstances exist, the right to personal contact with a child can also be given to other persons, in particular relatives, provided it is in the best interests of the child.[307]

VI.6.9.3 Effects with respect to property

As is the case upon the moment a divorce decree is issued, from the moment of the dissolution of the registered partnership, the registered partners cease to be the legal heirs of one another.[308] According to the Ministry of Justice's reasoning for the introduction of a separation of property, same-sex couples are more likely to consist of two wage-earning parties, which therefore negates the reasons to protect the financially weaker party.[309] As with spouses who opt for the separation of property regime, registered partners who remain in the default statutory regime will be subject to the same procedural rules as those that apply to those spouses and unmarried cohabitants. With respect to the separation of property, the

---

304 FF 2003, p. 1192 at 1249-1250.

305 **Marriage:** Art. 125(2)(1), Sw, CC; **RP:** Art. 34(2), Sw. RPA.

306 Upon divorce, the judge retains a discretion to decide what must be done with respect to the parental authority exercised over any children: Art. 156, Sw. CC.

307 *I.e.* step-parents and grandparents: see HONSELL/VOGT/GESIER (2002) p. 1474-1476.

308 Art. 31(1), Sw. RPA in accordance with an identical provision with respect to marriage to be found in Art. 154(2), Sw. CC.

309 FF 2003, p. 1192 at 1220.

Sw. CC does not provide for any rules except for goods regarded as the joint property of the parties.[310] Since each party is the sole owner of all other goods, there is no matrimonial property settlement as such. If the parties to a registered partnership, on the other hand, opt for the default matrimonial property regime of contribution to jointly acquired assets, the same rules will apply to the dissolution of their property as apply to spouses married in this regime.[311]

Regardless of the applicable property regime, the pension-sharing provisions applying at the time of divorce are equally applicable to registered partners.[312] This not only refers to Arts. 122-124, Sw. CC but also to Art. 30c(6), *la loi fédérale sur la prévoyance professionnelle vieillesse, survivants et invalidité*[313] and Arts. 22, 22b to 22c, 24(2), 24(3), 25a, 26(3) of *la loi le libre passage*.[314] The assignment of the *logement de la famille* in the case of spouses or the *logement commun* in the case of registered partners is also identical.[315] As a result the case law established on the basis of Art. 121, Sw. CC is equally applicable to the interpretation of Art. 32, Sw. RPA.[316]

310 DESCHENAUX *et al.* (2000) p. 726, §1914.

311 See further DESCHENAUX *et al.* (2000) p. 507-594, §1245-1485.

312 Art. 33, Sw. RPA.

313 RS 831.42.

314 RS 831.40. FF 2003, p. 1192 at 1248.

315 **Marriage:** Art. 121, Sw. CC; **RP:** Art. 32, Sw. RPA.

316 PICHONNAZ (2004) p. 426.

CHAPTER VII
UNITED KINGDOM

VII.1 INTRODUCTION

This chapter will deal with three different legal jurisdictions: **England & Wales**, **Scotland** and **Northern Ireland**.[1] The three legal systems have been dealt with simultaneously since their historical backgrounds lend themselves to such an analysis. The fact that the Civil Partnership Act 2004 (CPA 2004) has been dealt with in a UK-wide legislative enactment further strengthens this argument. Together these three countries form the territory of the **United Kingdom**, with territory-wide legislation referred to as **British** law.[2] Reference to **Great Britain** only refers to **England & Wales** and **Scotland**. It must nevertheless be stressed that the applicable laws differ in many areas. **England & Wales** and **Northern Ireland** are common law systems whilst **Scotland** is a mixed civil and common-law jurisdiction,[3] thus demanding that these three jurisdictions often be examined independently. Finally, one must remember that when one talks of **English** law this necessarily includes the territory of **Wales**.

Despite their similarities and differences, it is crucial that should **Scots** law fall to be applied by an **English** court, it is nonetheless **Scots** law that will be applied, even though it may be identical.[4] At the end of the 1990s, separate

---

1 These countries are territorially defined by the Preamble and Part 1, Union with Scotland Act 1706; Art. 1, Union with England Act 1707; Sch. 2(5), Interpretation Act 1978.

2 It must be noted that the phrase **United Kingdom** does not include the independent jurisdictions of the **Channel Islands** nor the **Isle of Man**. Although there are at present no plans, as far as this author is aware, to introduce similar legislation in the **Channel Islands**, a public consultation has been launched in the **Isle of Man** as to the possibility of introducing similar legislation. See further, ISLE OF MAN GOVERNMENT/REILTYS ELLAN VANNIN), *Possible Civil Partnership bill. Public consultation document*, Douglas: General Registry, April 2005 (available at www.gov.im/registeries).

3 See, for example, HUSA (2004) especially at p. 31 and SMITS (2003).

4 Although in *Attorney General for New Zealand v. Ortiz* [1984] AC 1, the House of Lords seemed to apply English case law to the interpretation of New Zealand statutes. Thus where the law is identical, English judges, even though in theory should apply the law of

legislative bodies for **Scotland** and **Northern Ireland** were created in a process known as devolution.[5] Whilst in **Northern Ireland** those areas of law subject to the remit of the **Northern Irish** Parliament are known as "transferred matters", throughout this book reference will be made to the term "devolved matters" as an all-encompassing term for both **Scotland** and **Northern Ireland**.[6]

The same structure is used in this chapter as in the other substantive law chapters. **Section VII.2** will focus on the most recent marriage statistics available in the three jurisdictions. This is followed by an account of the legislative history surrounding the introduction of civil partnership (**Section VII.3**), followed by information on how a civil partnership can be established (**Section VII.4**), the rights and duties attached to such a partnership (**Section VII.5**) and the manner in which such a partnership may be terminated (**Section VII.6**).

VII.2 EMPIRICAL EVIDENCE AND STATISTICS

The CPA 2004 is not due to come into force until 5th December 2005. As a result, only the most recent statistics with respect to the number of marriages celebrated in the **United Kingdom** can be provided.

***Table 8**: Number of marriages celebrated regionally since 1998 (July 2005)*

	England & Wales		**Scotland**		**Northern Ireland**	
Type	*Civil*	*Religious*	*Civil*	*Religious*	*Civil*	*Religious*
1998	163,072	104,231	12,898	16,770	1,854	5,972
1999	162,679	100,836	12,434	17,506	1,833	5,795
2000	170,800	97,161	12,079	18,288	1,910	5,674
2001	160,238	88,989	11,487	18,134	1,881	5,400
2002	168,530	85,870	11,449	17,377	2,113	5,486
2003	*TBA*	*TBA*	13,861	16,896	*TBA*	*TBA*
Total	**825,319**	**477,087**	**63,908**	**104,971**	**9,591**	**28,327**

the land which has been deemed applicable, will often make reference to English law should the law be identical. See further COLLIER (2001) p. 366-367.

5 Created as a result of the Scotland Act 1998 and the Northern Ireland Act 1998 respectively. Although Wales also received its own legislative body, namely the Welsh Assembly by virtue of the Government of Wales Act 1998, this has little competency in the fields of law discussed in this book.

6 This choice has been made for no reason other than ease of reading.

VII.3 HISTORICAL PERSPECTIVE

VII.3.1 LEGISLATION PRIOR TO THE CPA 2004

As the new millennium dawned, so too did a new era for homosexuals in the **United Kingdom**. Although the battle for the equalisation of the age of consent between heterosexual and homosexual sex resurfaced, this was by no means a sudden or drastic change of policy. In fact, as early as 1994 an attempt had been made to equalise the age of consent at sixteen. This was, however, defeated in the House of Commons.[7] Nevertheless, the age of consent was reduced to eighteen by Sec. 145, Criminal Justice and Public Order Act 1994. In 1997 the European Commission of Human Rights condemned the United Kingdom for maintaining a discriminatory age of consent.[8] This situation was further criticised by the European Parliament in its Annual Report on Human Rights in the European Union adopted initially by the Committee on Citizens' Freedoms and Rights and subsequently by the Parliament as a whole.[9] In response, the House of Commons introduced the Sexual Offences (Amendment) Bill on the 28th January 2000 with the aim of equalising the age of consent at sixteen in **England & Wales** and **Scotland**, and seventeen in **Northern Ireland**. It received three consecutive defeats at the hands of the House of Lords, before the House of Commons used the power invested in it by the Parliament Acts and enacted the Sexual Offences (Amendment) Act on the 30th November 2000. The Act came into force on the 8th January 2001.[10]

In 2000, attempts were also made by the Government to repeal the infamous Sec. 28, Local Government Act 1988 (LGA 1988).[11] This provision prevented local councils from promoting or encouraging homosexuality through publications, campaigns or in schools. Although no local authority

---

7 BARLOW (1999) p. 37. See further INGLIS (2001a) and (2001b).

8 ECtHR, *Sutherland v. United Kingdom*, Appl. No. 25186/94, 1st July 1997, §67.

9 Annual Report on Human Rights in the European Union in 1998 and 1999, *OJ*, C-377, 29th December 2000, p. 344, §56.

10 **Eng and NI:** Sec. 7(3), SO(A)A 2000 (Commencement No. 1) Order 2000, SI 2000/3303; **Scot:** SO(A)A 2000 (Commencement No. 2) (Scotland) Order 2000, SSI 2000/452.

11 *House of Commons*, Vol. 343, Cols. 685 (28th January 2000), *House of Commons*, Vol. 344, Cols. 432-501 (10th February 2000), *House of Commons*, Vol. 345, Cols. 127-131 (28th February 2000).

had ever been prosecuted under Sec. 28, LGA 1988[12] it has been invoked more than thirty times to prevent projects from going ahead.[13] The repeal process was more successful in the devolved **Scottish** Parliament, where the **Scottish** version of Sec. 28, LGA 1988,[14] was successfully repealed on the 21st July 2000. On the 24th July 2000, legislation to repeal Sec. 28 in **England & Wales** was passed in the House of Commons in a free vote during the passage of the LGA 2003.[15] The repeal became effective on the 18th November 2003.

The removal of discriminatory provisions was further enhanced with the enactment of the Sexual Offences Act 2003 (SOA 2003). This Act was the end result of a major review of sexual offences, which had begun in 1999.[16] On the 18th November 2003, the SOA 2003 was passed, repealing the homosexual offences of buggery and gross indecency.[17] The Act also removed the previous ban on same-sex sexual activity between more than two persons.[18] However, despite these legislative amendments some associated offences remain, including "solicitation or importuning in a public place for immoral purposes".[19]

VII.3.2 SPECIFIC PARTNERSHIP LEGISLATION

The torrent of legislative equalisation with respect to private sexual activity was mirrored with an increasing judicial trend towards broader recognition of cohabiting couples that lived together "as husband and wife".[20] However,

---

12 In May 2000 the Christian Institute unsuccessfully took Glasgow City Council to court for funding an AIDS support charity which the Institute alleged promoted homosexuality: *The Independent*, 18th May 2000, p. 13.

13 *BBC News*, 25th July 2000, http://news.bbc.co.uk.

14 Namely Sec. 2A, Local Government Act 1986.

15 The LGA 1988 never applied to **Northern Ireland**: Sec. 42(2), LGA 1988.

16 HOME OFFICE (2000).

17 Sec. 12, SOA 1956 (buggery) and Sec. 13, SOA 1956 (gross indecency). Following HOME OFFICE (2000) p. 101, §44.

18 This had been challenged before the ECtHR, *ADT v. United Kingdom,* Appl. No. 35765/97, 31st July 2000.

19 Sec. 32, SOA 1956. In 2003/2004, 1,939 men were convicted of this crime. See further www.homeoffice.gov.uk.

20 The phrase "living as husband and wife" is used in more than eighty statutes covering a wide range of topics. In the case of *Harrogate BC v. Simpson* [1986] 2 FLR 91 tenancy rights were extended to cohabiting couples, "living as husband and wife", but at the same time restricted to different-sex couples. This trend has recently been halted with the landmark House of Lords decision in *Ghaidan v. Mendoza* [2004] UKHL 30. See also ANDERSEN (1997) for a pre-CPA 2004 view.

although this trend had been far-reaching with respect to different-sex cohabiting couples, such recognition had generally not been afforded to same-sex couples.[21] Nonetheless, despite this lack of recognition by the Government and judiciary, in the late 1990s a number of local authorities across **England & Wales** began to introduce forms of non-legally binding commitment ceremonies.[22] The development of such civil ceremonies culminated in the move by the Greater London Authority to create a partnership register.[23] Although both same-sex and different-sex couples may sign the register, the parties derive no legal benefits therefrom. Even so, it was seen as the "first step" on the road to full equality.[24] By the time civil ceremonies began taking place in **Scotland**, a number of legislative amendments had already been passed that offered recognition to committed, same-sex relationships, regardless of whether the relationships had been registered.[25]

VII.3.3 HOUSE OF COMMONS

On 24th October 2001, GRIFFITHS (MP for Reading East) sought the leave of Parliament to introduce a Bill that would have allowed any couple, same-sex or different-sex, to register their relationship. The House of Commons approved the motion, introduced under the ten minute rule in which an MP is allowed to deliver a speech lasting ten minutes in support of a proposal.[26] Although the Bill was scheduled for second reading on the 10th May 2002, the debate was postponed and the Bill was subsequently dropped.[27] Although the Bill in itself is relatively insignificant, the mere fact that the Bill was tabled, coupled with its timing, deserves mention.[28]

---

21 See, for example, the FAA 1976 and the RA 1977.

22 At present civil ceremonies are possible in almost all counties in **Great Britain**. For more information see www.civilceremonies.co.uk.

23 http://www.london.gov.uk/mayor/partnerships/index.jsp.

24 A. MASON, Executive Director of Stonewall, *Stonewall Press Release* (5th September 2001).

25 Sec. 87(2), Adults with Incapacity (Scotland) Act 2000; Sch. 3(2), Housing (Scotland) Act 2001; Sec. 1(2)(c), Mortgage Rights (Scotland) Act 2001; Protection from Abuse (Scotland) Act 2001; Reg. 4, Civil Legal Aid (Scotland) Amendment Regulations 2003; Sec. 71, Agricultural Holdings (Scotland) Act 2003; Mental Health (Care and Treatment)(Scotland) Act 2003.

26 The vote cast was 179 votes for to 59 votes against.

27 *House of Commons*, Vol. 373, Col. 327 (24th October 2001); *House of Commons*, Vol. 375, Col. 640 (23rd November 2001).

28 SUMNER (2002b) p. 24. Also noted during the debate on the CPA 2004: *House of Commons*, Vol. 425, Col. 204 (12th October 2004).

VII.3.4 HOUSE OF LORDS

On the 9th January 2002, Lord LESTER submitted a Bill to the House of Lords for first reading.[29] In the explanatory notes accompanying the Bill, it was stated that the Bill was "designed to remedy the lack of protection for cohabiting couples (regardless of sex) in English law and to give them the opportunity to register a civil partnership."

On the 25th January 2002 the Bill received a lengthy and emotional debate in the House of Lords.[30] Emphasis was placed upon upholding, supporting and strengthening the institution of marriage, but at the same time many Peers acknowledged the weaknesses in the current legal protection afforded to same-sex couples. Particular emphasis was placed upon the inability of cohabiting couples to take advantage of inheritance tax exemptions, as provided for married couples. In response to those who opposed the Bill on the basis that it would undermine the institution of marriage,[31] Lord LESTER retaliated arguing that this Bill would in actual effect support marriage by allowing couples to enter into a civil partnership as a prelude to marriage.[32]

In dealing with the issue of children,[33] Lord LESTER believed that this would be better dealt with through specific child orientated legislation.[34] It was also recognised, and indeed highlighted, that Parliament must look beyond the borders of the **United Kingdom**.[35] As a result of the Government's promise to address the issues raised by the Civil Partnership Bill, Lord LESTER agreed to drop the Bill on the understanding that should the Government fail to act the Bill would be reintroduced.

---

29 *House of Lords*, Vol. 630, Col. 561 (9th January 2002).

30 *House of Lords*, Vol. 630, Cols. 1691-1746 (25th January 2002).

31 *House of Lords*, Vol. 630, Cols. 1736-1740 (25th January 2002) Baroness BUSCOMBE.

32 *House of Lords*, Vol. 630, Col. 1744 (25th January 2002).

33 Many Peers opposed the Bill because it failed to provide adequately for children *e.g.* *House of Lords,* Vol. 630, Col. 1704 (25th January 2002) Lord BISHOP OF WINCHESTER, and *House of Lords*, Vol. 630, Col. 1714 (25th January 2002) Lord ELTON.

34 For example, by means of the CA 1989.

35 Special attention was given to the situation in **The Netherlands**, where it was noted registered partnership has been available for different-sex and same-sex couples since 1998, and since 2001 marriage has also been opened to same-sex couples. See **Chapter V**.

VII.3.5 GOVERNMENT BILL AND THE CONSULTATION PROCESS

In June 2003,[36] the Department of Trade and Industry, on behalf of the British Government, announced its intent to create an institutionalised, registration scheme for the legal recognition of committed same-sex couples. A consultation procedure was initiated in **England & Wales**,[37] which was subsequently mirrored in **Scotland**[38] and **Northern Ireland**.[39] By March 2004 all three consultation procedures had been completed[40] and legislative proposals were submitted to the House of Lords.[41] The initial aim of the legislation was clear,

> The Government has no plans to allow same-sex couples to marry. The proposals are for an entirely new status of legal partnership. Same-sex partnership registration schemes already operate alongside opposite-sex marriage in some countries.[42]

In **England & Wales** and **Scotland**, the majority of respondents were supportive of the aims outlined in the consultation procedure.[43] The situation in **Northern Ireland**, however, was the complete opposite, with 86% of respondents opposed to the introduction of civil partnership.[44] Nonetheless, the Northern Ireland Office of Law Reform pressed ahead with the proposals stating that,

> The Government remains convinced of the strong equality and social justice imperatives behind the civil partnership proposal. There is significant unfairness and inequality caused by the fact that, although many committed same-sex couples live in partnership, and to all intents and purposes, as families, they experience serious social disadvantages due to the absence of any legal recognition of their partnerships.[45]

---

36 Only six months after the publication of the LAW COMMISSION'S paper "Sharing Homes" which, *inter alia*, addressed the issue of non-marital registered relationships. See LAW COMMISSION (2002).

37 WOMEN AND EQUALITY UNIT (2003a).

38 SCOTTISH EXECUTIVE (2003a).

39 NORTHERN IRELAND OFFICE OF LAW REFORM (2004a).

40 WOMEN AND EQUALITY UNIT (2003b); SCOTTISH EXECUTIVE (2004a); NORTHERN IRELAND OFFICE OF LAW REFORM (2004b).

41 *House of Lords*, 2003-2004, Bill N°. 53.

42 WOMEN AND EQUALITY UNIT (2003b) p. 14.

43 83% of respondents were in favour in **England & Wales**, and 86% in **Scotland**. WOMEN AND EQUALITY UNIT (2003b) p. 9; SCOTTISH EXECUTIVE (2004a) p. 5.

44 NORTHERN IRELAND OFFICE OF LAW REFORM (2004b) §1.6, p. 5.

45 NORTHERN IRELAND OFFICE OF LAW REFORM (2004b) §2.1.3, p. 8.

As a result of the devolution process of the late 1990s, a number of aspects of the civil partnership scheme fell to the sole competency of the **Scottish** Parliament or the **Northern Irish** Assembly. However, by virtue of a Sewell motion, the **Scottish** Executive granted Westminster the power to legislate on these issues. Such a move is a result of the complicated devolution procedure enshrined in the Scotland Act 1998. The **Scottish** Parliament may legislate in any area unless the Westminster Parliament has reserved that area. However, at the same time as devolving power, the Scotland Act 1998 also allows for the **Scottish** Parliament to grant Westminster the power to legislate on devolved matters should the Scottish Executive agree.[46] With respect to **Northern Ireland**, the situation was even more complicated and was the subject of fierce debate in the House of Commons.[47] In the end, on the advice of the Northern Ireland Law Reform Office,[48] the provisions applicable to **Northern Ireland** were included in a single **United Kingdom**-wide Civil Partnership Act.[49] The end result was that Westminster initiated a Bill containing provisions for all three countries.[50] The Bill was eventually passed on the 17th November 2004, received Royal Assent on the 18th November 2004 and entered into force on the 5th December 2005.

VII.4 ESTABLISHMENT

All areas of the registration process, both capacity requirements and the formal registration procedure, are devolved matters that are to be dealt with by the regional legislative bodies in **Scotland** and **Northern Ireland**. However, although Westminster has been granted legislative competency in this field, one must be aware of the legal differences between these three jurisdictions.

---

46 For further explanation of the technical mechanism of the Sewell Convention and its present usage, see BURROWS (2002) and NORRIE (2003a).

47 *British House of Commons,* Vol. 425, Cols. 176, 222-223, 235-237 (12th October 2004).

48 On the 14th October 2002, the Secretary of State for Northern Ireland announced that the devolved institutions were to be suspended. The Assembly was formally dissolved on the 28th April 2003. Since this time the Secretary of State for **Northern Ireland** has assumed responsibility for the direction and control of the Northern Irish Departments.

49 NORTHERN IRELAND OFFICE OF LAW REFORM (2004a) p. 16, §3.17. A number of groups in the consultation procedure voiced concerns about introducing UK wide legislation. However, as was noted, "... once devolution is restored then the Northern Ireland Executive and Assembly are able to decide on transferred matters so they could choose then what to do on the issues within their remit. At present, however, there is no Assembly so these decisions have to be taken under direct rule and legislation taken forward at Westminster": NORTHERN IRELAND OFFICE OF LAW REFORM (2004b) p. 32, §8.2.

50 *British House of Lords,* Vol. 659, Col. 1176 (30th March 2004).

VII.4.1 POSITION OF THE INSTITUTION

The CPA 2004 creates a new legal status throughout the entire **United Kingdom** entitled "civil partnership".[51] In creating such an opt-in system the Government noted that the scheme supports individual choices and does not impose responsibilities on those who do not wish to acquire them.[52] As part of the consultation procedure, parties were asked to express their views on the nomenclature of such a partnership scheme. In answer to a request for alternative nomenclature, a number of possibilities were offered including partner, life partner, dedicated partner, partner-in-life, MATE (married and together) and the German term *Lebensabschnittsmitfahrer*![53] As a result of the common law background to the **British** legal system, and in a similar manner to all forms of legislation enacted in the **United Kingdom**, the civil partnership scheme has been expanded upon in an Act of Parliament, namely the CPA 2004.

VII.4.2 EXCLUSIVITY

Like marriage,[54] the CPA 2004 enacts legislation to prevent a couple from entering into a civil partnership if they are already married (whether with each other or with a third party) or involved in another civil partnership (whether with each other or with a third party).[55] If persons succeed in celebrating multiple registrations or a mutually concurrent civil partnership and marriage, then an offence similar to the offence of perjury will have been committed.[56] It is also provided that a civil partnership may only be

---

51 In how this would be incorporated in the ongoing changes of the Registry of Births, Deaths and Marriages see the OFFICE FOR NATIONAL STATISTICS (2003).

52 WOMEN AND EQUALITY UNIT (2003a) p. 17.

53 WOMEN AND EQUALITY UNIT (2003b) p. 31.

54 **Eng:** LOWE/DOUGLAS (1998) p. 30; HERRING (2003) p. 43; CRETNEY *et al.* (2003a) p. 47, §2-020; **Scot:** THOMPSON (1996) p. 29; CLIVE (1992) p. 76-77; EDWARDS/GRIFFITHS (1997) p. 256, §9.15; **NI:** O'HALLORAN (1997) p. 13-14. Specific statutory amendments have also been introduced to ensure that bigamous marriages are void: **Eng:** Sec. 11(b), MCA 1973; **Scot:** Sec. 5(4)(b), M(S)A 1977; **NI:** Art. 13(1)(d), MC(NI)O 1978. See **Section VII.6.6.**

55 **Eng:** Sec. 3(1)(b), CPA 2004; **Scot:** Sec. 86(1)(d), CPA 2004; **NI:** Sec. 138(1)(b), CPA 2004.

56 **Eng:** Sec. 32, CPA 2004. The Perjury Act 1911 codified the law on perjury in England & Wales. The maximum sentence for perjury is seven years and through a series of Court of Appeal cases it can be discerned that a custodial sentence is nearly always recommended. **Scot:** Sec. 100, CPA 2004; **NI:** Sec. 158, CPA 2004. The punishments imposed by virtue of these sections are however different, by virtue of the differences with respect to the punishments imposed in the field of marriage

celebrated between two persons at any one time,[57] thus upholding the second facet of the principle of exclusivity, which is also to be found in **British** law with respect to marriage.[58]

VII.4.3 SEX OF THE PARTIES

Despite numerous attempts made in both the House of Lords and House of Commons, which aimed at opening civil partnership to certain persons within the specified degrees of family relationships regardless of their sex,[59] the CPA 2004 only allows for the registration of same-sex relationships.[60] Obviously these requirements are clearly different to the law on marriage, where only different-sex couples are allowed to celebrate a marriage.[61]

As a result of these restrictions certain problems arise with respect to transsexuals. As a result of the Gender Recognition Act 2004 (GRA 2004),[62] a person of either gender who has applied and successfully been granted a gender recognition certificate in accordance with this Act will be recognised for all purposes as having the acquired gender.[63] In **England & Wales** and **Northern Ireland**, if a person is married at the time a gender recognition certificate is requested and the Gender Recognition Panel grants an application, then an interim gender recognition certificate must be granted.[64] As a result of this interim gender recognition certificate, the marriage becomes voidable.[65] As soon as a court pronounces the marriage void and issues a full gender recognition certificate, the parties may apply to

---

57 **UK:** Sec. 1(1), CPA 2004; **Eng:** Sec. 2(1), CPA 2004; **Scot:** Sec. 85(1), CPA 2004; **NI:** Sec. 137(1), CPA 2004.

58 **UK:** *Hyde v. Hyde* (1866) LR 1 P&D 130 (although an English case, this is used in Scottish and Northern Irish courts as precedent).

59 *E.g. British House of Lords*, Vol. 662, Cols. 1362-1391 (24th June 2004), Baroness O'CATHAIN. However the Government announced almost immediately that it intended to reverse the amendments made in the House of Lords: *British House of Commons*, Vol. 425, Col. 175 (12th October 2004).

60 **UK:** Sec. 1(1), CPA 2004; **Eng:** Sec. 3(1)(a), CPA 2004; **Scot:** Sec. 86(1)(a), CPA 2004; **NI:** Sec. 138(1)(a), CPA 2004.

61 *Hyde v. Hyde* (1866) LR 1 P&D 130.

62 The GRA 2004 applies, subject to limited exceptions, to the entire **UK**: Sec. 28, GRA 2004. The GRA 2004 was passed after numerous court decisions condemning the UK for not recognising sex reassignment surgery for the purposes of birth certificates. See, for example, *Bellinger v. Bellinger* [2003] UKHL 21 and ECtHR, *Goodwin v. UK*, Appl. N°. 28957/95, 11th July 2002, (2002) 35 EHRR 18. See further NICOL (2004).

63 Sec. 9(1), GRA 2004.

64 Sec. 4(3), GRA 2004.

65 **Eng:** Sec. 12(g), MCA 1973, amended by Sch. 2, GRA 2004; **NI:** Art. 14(h), MC(NI)O 1978.

the court, without delay, to be registered as civil partners.[66] In **Scotland**, if a person is married at the time a gender recognition certificate is requested and the Gender Recognition Panel grants an application, the parties must apply to be divorced before a full gender recognition certificate can be issued.[67] *Vice versa*, a civil partnership will be voidable in **England & Wales** and **Northern Ireland**, and be able to be terminated in **Scotland**, on the ground that one of the parties to the civil partnership has been issued with an interim gender recognition certificate.[68]

VII.4.4 MINIMUM AGE

In a manner identical to marriage,[69] both parties to any civil partnership must have attained the age of majority on the date of registration of the civil partnership, which is currently set at sixteen.[70] Persons under the age of eighteen in **England & Wales**[71] and **Northern Ireland**[72] are also required to gain written parental consent (from each parent who has parental responsibility and each guardian, all those in possession of a residence or care order, or the court should the child be a ward of court) before being allowed to register a civil partnership or solemnise a marriage. However, such rules are not duplicated in the **Scottish** provisions on civil partnership, as is consistent with the **Scottish** rules on marriage.[73]

---

66 **Eng:** Sec. 5(2) and Sch. 3, CPA 2004; **Scot:** Sec. 96, CPA 2004; **NI:** At present there is no legislative, expedited route available in such situations in **Northern Ireland**. However, after personal contact with the **Northern Ireland** Law Reform Office, it is clear that the aim is to introduce such an expedited, in both directions, under the power granted to the **Northern Irish** Assembly under Sec. 159, CPA 2004, to enact regulations which it appears necessary or expedient.

67 Sec. 1(1)(b), D(S)A 1977, as inserted by §6, Sch. 2, GRA 2004.

68 **Eng:** Sec. 50(1)(d), CPA 2004; **Scot:** Sec. 117(2)(b), CPA 2004; **NI:** Sec. 174(1)(d), CPA 2004.

69 **Eng:** Sec. 2, MA 1949; **Scot:** Sec. 1(1), M(S)A 1977; **NI:** Art. 6(6)(c), M(NI)O 2003.

70 **Eng:** Sec. 3(1)(c), CPA 2004; **Scot:** Sec. 83(1)(c), CPA 2004; **NI:** Sec. 134(1)(c), CPA 2004.

71 **Marriage:** Sec. 3, MA 1949; **CP:** Sec. 4, CPA 2004. The need for sixteen and seventeen year olds to obtain parental consent prior to celebrating this partnership is, however, a duplicate of the rules on marriage. See LOWE/DOUGLAS (1998) p. 37-38; HERRING (2003) p. 41; CRETNEY *et al.* (2003a) p. 12-14, §1-006 to §1-010. This requirement has however been severely criticised by the LAW COMMISSION (1988) §7.11.

72 **Marriage:** Art. 22, M(NI)O 2003; **CP:** Sec. 141, CPA 2004.

73 **Marriage:** EDWARDS/GRIFFITHS (1997) p. 247; THOMSON (1996) p. 22-23.

VII.4.5 RESIDENCY

VII.4.5.1 England & Wales

The rules in relation to the civil marriage ceremonies have recently been changed and unified.[74] For two people to register their civil partnership or celebrate a civil marriage they must provide notice of their intent to the registration authority. The rules are slightly different with respect to those intending to marry and those intending to register a civil partnership. Although both sets of parties must have lived in an **English** or **Welsh** registration district for at least seven days immediately prior to delivering their notice,[75] the Marriage Act 1949 (MA 1949) determines to which registration district this notice must be submitted,[76] whereas for the registration of a civil partnership this is left completely open.[77] In practice this allows a couple wishing to register a civil partnership to give notice of their civil partnership to a registration district in Manchester whilst they live in a registration district in London. In this example, those wishing to marry, on the other hand, are only able to give notice in London. This possibility is expressly excluded for those intending to marry, except in exceptional circumstances. [78]

Provision is provided for those cases in which residents of other parts of the **United Kingdom** wish to register a civil partnership in **England & Wales.**[79] In these cases, the non-English resident may give notice regardless of the requirement of residency, and the English resident must also obtain a certificate of non-impediment according to the relevant provisions.[80]

---

74 Prior to the far-reaching reforms of the IAA 1999, two separate procedures existed in England & Wales for the solemnisation of a marriage: a certificate procedure (with a 21 day waiting period) and a licence procedure (with a 1 day waiting period). This has since been abolished and harmonised into the current system (Sec. 160, IAA 1999).

75 **Marriage:** Sec. 27(1)(a), MA 1949; **CP:** Sec. 8(1)(b), CPA 2004.

76 If the aspirant spouses live in the same registration district then the notice must be submitted to this registration district (Sec. 27(1)(a), MA 1949) and if not, then to their respective registration districts (Sec. 27(1)(b), MA 1949).

77 Sec. 8(1), CPA 2004.

78 Secs. 34 and 35, MA 1949. Nonetheless, under the proposals in OFFICE FOR NATIONAL STATISTICS (2003) the same will also be true of marriages.

79 Sec. 20, CPA 2004. Provision is also made for those serving in the armed forces.

80 **Scot:** Sec. 97, CPA 2004; **NI:** Sec. 150, CPA 2004.

VII.4.5.2 Scotland and Northern Ireland

Since the passing of the Marriage (Scotland) Act 1977 (M(S)A 1977), there have been no residence requirements imposed on parties wishing to marry in **Scotland**.[81] As a result, provided there is no legal impediment to marry, anyone is entitled to marry in **Scotland**. The notice requirements that must be satisfied prior to a marriage can be sent by post by someone resident abroad. It is nevertheless necessary for both parties to be present at the ceremony. As a result of the CPA 2004, the absence of residency requirements also holds true for those wishing to register a civil partnership.[82] As of the 1st January 2004, no prior residency is required in **Northern Ireland** in order to register a civil partnership or celebrate a marriage.[83]

VII.4.6 PROHIBITED DEGREES OF RELATIONSHIP

As a result of the passage of the CPA 2004, and despite the attempts made in both Houses,[84] the laws of all three jurisdictions with respect to the prohibited degrees of relationship are identical, save a few exceptions, for those wishing to register a civil partnership[85] or celebrate a marriage.[86] Three categories can thus be discerned in all three jurisdictions: relationships prohibited by virtue of consanguinity (proximity of relationships derived from blood ties), by virtue of affinity (proximity of relationships derived from marriage), and by virtue of adoption. A common feature in all three countries is that the lists are exclusive. As a result, if the relationship is not mentioned in the relevant legislation the parties may validly marry or register a partnership.[87]

---

81 However, this has not always been the case: CLIVE (1992) p. 8.

82 SCOTTISH EXECUTIVE (2003a) p. 22, §6.13.

83 See www.groni.gov.uk and NORTHERN IRELAND LAW REFORM OFFICE (2004a) p. 41, §9.1.

84 See **Section VII.4.3**.

85 **Eng:** Sec. 3(1)(d), CPA 2004 with reference to Part 1, Sch. 1, CPA 2004; **Scot:** Sec. 82(1)(b), CPA 2004 with reference to Sch. 10, CPA 2004; **NI:** Sec. 132(1)(d), CPA 2004 with reference to Sch. 12, CPA 2004.

86 **Eng:** Sec. 1 and Sch. 1, MA 1949, as amended by M(PDR)A 1986; **Scot:** Sec. 2 and Schs. 1 and 2, M(S)A 1977, as amended by the M(PDR)A 1986; **NI:** M(PDR)A(NI) 1949, as amended by Art. 18, FL(MP)(NI)O 1984.

87 Naturally, subject to the relevant private international law rules.

With respect to consanguinity, in addition to the prohibitions set forth in **English** and **Northern Irish** law,[88] **Scottish** law also prohibits civil partnerships and marriages between a person and his or her great-grandparent or his or her great-grandchild.[89] All three jurisdictions, provide for restrictions based on the affinity between the parties,[90] although these prohibitions may be lifted if both parties have attained the age of twenty-one and the latter was not at any time before reaching the age of eighteen a "child of the family" in relation to the other.[91] Marriages and civil partnerships are also prohibited between persons and their adoptive child or former adoptive child, adoptive parent or former adoptive parent in all three jurisdictions.[92]

VII.4.7 COMPETENCY AND CONSENT

Although all three jurisdictions require all aspirant civil partners or spouses to provide free and valid consent, due to the differences in national marriage law, the three jurisdictions have used different wording with respect to civil partnership.

In **Scotland**, both parties must possess the capacity to understand the nature of the undertaking and provide true consent.[93] If either of these is lacking, the marriage or civil partnership will be deemed void.[94] The classic headings under which this issue arises are mental incapacity, error and fraud, intoxication, jest, force and fear, and sham marriages.[95] The question of capacity to consent often surfaces in relation to those with a mental incapacity. For example, in *Long v. Long*,[96] it was held that even though a woman had been subject to supervision in an institution for long periods of

---

88 **Eng:** Part 1, Sch. 1, CPA 2004; **NI:** Sch. 12, CPA 2004.

89 **Scot:** Cols. 1 and 2, Sch. 10, CPA 2004.

90 The **Scottish** rules are slightly more restrictive than those in rest of the UK.

91 For a definition of "child of the family", see **Eng:** Sec. 2(2), Sch. 1, CPA 2004; **Scot:** Sec. 101(7), CPA 2004; **NI:** Sec. 2(2), Sch. 12, CPA 2004.

92 **Eng:** Sch. 1, MA 1949, as amended by M(PDR)A 1986 (marriage) and §1(1), Sch. 1, CPA 2004 (CP); **Scot:** Sec. 3, Sch. 1, M(S)A 1977, as amended by the M(PDR)A 1986 (marriage) and Sec. 86(1), CPA 2004 which amended Sec. 41, A(S)A 1978 (CP); **NI:** M(PDR)A(NI) 1949, as amended by Art. 18, FL(MP)(NI)O 1984 (marriage) and §1(1), Sch. 12, CPA 2004 (CP).

93 **Marriage:** Sec. 5(4)(d), M(S)A 1977; **CP:** Sec. 86(1)(e)(i), CPA 2004.

94 **Marriage:** Sec. 5(4)(d), M(S)A 1977; **CP:** Sec. 123(b), CPA 2004

95 EDWARDS/GRIFFITHS (1997) p. 256-262, §9.16-9.26; THOMSON (1996) p. 32-38; CLIVE (1992) p. 84-95. By analogy this would thus include sham civil partnerships.

96 (1950) SLT 32.

time due to her mental state, she was nonetheless capable of understanding the nature of marriage, and giving her consent thereto.

In **England & Wales** and **Northern Ireland**, a distinction is drawn between those cases where consent is totally absent and those cases where at the time of its formation, though capable of giving a valid consent, a person was suffering from a mental disorder of such a kind or to such an extent as to be unfit to register a marriage or civil partnership.[97] In both cases, the applicable rules for civil partnerships are identical to the rules on marriage.

VII.4.8 FORMAL VALIDITY

Since issues of formal validity are questions that have been devolved to the **Scottish** Parliament and **Northern Irish** Assembly respectively, each country maintains its own system of registration of civil partnerships and the celebration of marriages. Although these have over the course of time been harmonised, it is important to maintain the distinction between these three countries. Furthermore, in order to compare marriage and civil partnerships, one must first be aware that religious marriages are permitted throughout the **United Kingdom** and are binding without the celebration of a subsequent civil ceremony.[98] Civil partnerships, on the other hand, provide a secular alternative to marriage for same-sex couples.[99] It is important here to compare like with like. Hence the rules on civil partnership will be compared to the rules on civil marriages.

VII.4.8.1 England & Wales

Unlike civil marriages, where a distinction is drawn between registry offices and approved premises,[100] civil partnerships may be registered anywhere so long as they do not take place in "religious premises" and the place of

---

97 **Eng:** Sec. 12(c) and (d), MCA 1973 (marriage) and Sec. 50(1)(a) and (b), CPA 2004 (CP); **NI:** Art. 14(c) and (d), MC(NI)O 1978 (marriage) and Sec. 174(1)(a) and (b), CPA 2004 (CP).

98 **Eng:** LOWE/DOUGLAS (1998) p. 38-43; CRETNEY *et al.* (2003a) p. 14-15, §1-011; **Scot:** EDWARDS/GRIFFITHS (1997) p. 269-271, §9.38, THOMSON (1996) p. 11-12; **NI:** O'HALLORAN (1997) p. 8-9.

99 See for example the comments of Deputy Minister SMITH, *British House of Commons,* Vol. 425, Col. 177 (12th October 2004). In fact civil partnerships are prohibited from being registered in religious premises as defined by the CPA 2004. **Eng:** Sec. 6(b), CPA 2004; **Scot:** Sec. 93(2), CPA 2004; **NI:** Sec. 137(5), CPA 2004.

100 CRETNEY *et al.* (2003a) p. 22-25, §1-031 to §1-034.

registration has been specified in the notice of the proposed civil partnership.[101] However, for civil marriages in a register office, civil marriages in approved premises and civil partnerships, the notice and registration procedure are identical.[102] For both civil marriages and civil partnerships, alternative procedures also exist for house-bound persons, detained persons and those who are seriously ill.[103] This book only deals with the standard procedure.[104]

In order for two people to register a civil partnership or celebrate a civil marriage, they must give notice of their proposed civil partnership or civil marriage to a registration authority.[105] Along with the notice, the parties must also provide the necessary declaration that the parties believe there to be no impediment of "kindred or alliance or other lawful hindrance to" the marriage or the formation of a civil partnership.[106] The registration authority to which notice of marriage or civil partnership has been given must affix the "relevant information" in a conspicuous place for fifteen successive days[107] after the day on which the notice was recorded.[108] As soon as this waiting period has expired, the registration authority in whose district registration of the marriage or civil partnership is due to take place is obliged to issue a "civil partnership schedule" or a "marriage certificate"

---

101 **Marriage:** Secs. 45 and 46A, MA 1949; **CP:** Sec. 6(1), CPA 2004. The registration authority in whose area the civil partnership is to take place must also agree: Sec. 6(3)(b), CPA 2004.

102 This difference between marriages in approved premises and marriage in register offices lies in the fact that permission must first be sought for the marriage to be conducted in approved premises whereas this is not the case in a register office.

103 **Marriages:** Sec. 26(1)(bb), MA 1949, as inserted by MA 1994 (standard procedure in approved premises), Sec. 26(1)(dd), MA 1949, as inserted by MA 1983 (house-bound and detained persons); M(RGL)A 1970 (seriously ill persons); **CP:** Secs. 8-17, CPA 2004 (standard procedure); Secs. 18-19, CPA 2004 (house-bound and detained persons); Secs. 21-27, CPA 2004 (seriously ill persons).

104 The other procedures are virtually identical, save for reductions in the waiting periods.

105 **Marriage:** Sec. 27(1), MA 1949, as amended by the IAA 1999; **CP:** Sec. 8(1), CPA 2004. For marriages, this is subject to the British Subjects (Facilities) Acts 1915 and 1916 in which British or Commonwealth citizens resident in the following countries are allowed to give notice in that country: Bahamas, Barbados, Belize, Bermuda, Botswana, Canada (Newfoundland only), Cyprus, Dominica, Fiji, the Gambia, Ghana, Gibraltar, Grenada, Guernsey, Isle of Man, Jamaica, Jersey, Kenya, Leeward Islands, Lesotho, Malawi, Malaysia, Mauritius, New Zealand, Nigeria, St. Lucia, St. Vincent, Seychelles, Sierra Leone, Singapore, Sri Lanka, Swaziland, Tanzania, Uganda, Zambia and Zimbabwe. This exception has not been extended to civil partnerships.

106 **Marriage:** Sec. 28(1), MA 1949; **CP:** Sec. 8(4), CPA 2004.

107 This period may be reduced for marriages (Sec. 31(5^A), MA 1949) and for civil partnerships (Sec. 12, CPA 2004) if there are exceptional circumstances.

108 **Marriage:** Sec. 31(1), MA 1949; **CP:** Sec. 11, CPA 2004.

respectively.[109] The parties are then under an obligation to ensure that the civil partnership schedule is signed or marriage is solemnised on the basis of the marriage certificate within twelve months.[110]

Unlike marriages where a ceremony is required,[111] the CPA 2004 provides for no such requirement, although parties are entitled to make use of a ceremony if permitted by the local council.[112] Nonetheless, both parties must be present in both instances. Upon the invitation of, and in the presence of, the civil partnership registrar and in the presence of two witnesses and each other, each of the civil partners must sign the civil partnership schedule.[113] After both parties have signed the schedule, both witnesses and the civil partnership registrar must also add their signatures.[114] Once everyone who is obliged to sign the civil partnership schedule has done so, the civil partnership registrar is obliged to ensure that the relevant information is recorded in the register as soon as practicable.[115]

VII.4.8.2 Scotland

Scotland has not escaped the legislative changes that have swept across the **United Kingdom** in the field of marriage registration. Although this section will only deal with civil marriages,[116] it must also be noted that although the Marriage (Scotland) Act 1939 abolished two of the three irregular forms of marriage in **Scotland**,[117] it did not abolish marriage by cohabitation with habit and repute.[118] This phenomenon is something peculiar to **Scots** law. The couple must prove that there has been cohabitation,[119] this cohabitation

---

109 **Marriage:** Sec. 31(2), MA 1949; **CP:** Sec. 14(1), in conjunction with Sec. 14(5), CPA 2004.

110 **Marriage:** Sec. 33, MA 1949; **CP:** Sec. 17(2), CPA 2004.

111 Secs. 44(3) (registered buildings), 44(5) (register office), 46[B](3) (approved premises), MA 1949. The words read: "I do solemnly declare that I know not of any lawful impediment why I, *AB*, may not be joined in matrimony to *CD*" and each of them shall say to each other: "I call upon these persons here present to witness that I, *AB*, do take thee, *CD*, to be my lawfully wedded wife [*or* husband]."

112 Sec. 2(1), CPA 2004.

113 Sec. 2(1), CPA 2004.

114 Sec. 2(3), CPA 2004.

115 Sec. 2(4), CPA 2004.

116 **Scotland** also allows for religious marriages, and as has been indicated in **Section VII.2**, religious marriages account for more marriages in **Scotland** than civil marriages.

117 Sec. 5, M(S)A 1939 abolished marriage by declaration *de praesenti* and marriage by promise *subsequente copula*.

118 EDWARDS/GRIFFITHS (1997) p. 271-274, §9.40.

119 Mere sexual intercourse is not enough. THOMPSON (1996) p. 17.

must have been as husband and wife,[120] the cohabitation must have taken place in **Scotland,**[121] and the cohabitation must have been for a sufficiently long enough period for the court to be able to infer that the parties tacitly agreed to marry.[122] This possibility has not been extended to same-sex couples and thus a similar civil partnership by habit and repute has not been created.

In order to celebrate a marriage or register a civil partnership in **Scotland**, each of the intended partners must deliver notice of their intention to celebrate a marriage or register a civil partnership to the District Registrar.[123] The parties are not obliged to deliver this notice in person and can thus deliver notice by post.[124] This notice must nonetheless be accompanied by a number of documents, as provided for in Sec. 88(2) and (3), CPA 2004. Upon receipt of the notice, the District Registrar must enter such particulars as may be prescribed in the so-called "marriage book" or "civil partnership book".[125] The notice must then be publicised for a minimum period of fifteen days prior to the civil partnership or marriage being allowed to take place.[126] When the Registrar is satisfied that there is no legal impediment to the marriage or civil partnership, he or she will prepare a marriage schedule or civil partnership schedule respectively.

VII.4.8.3 Northern Ireland

Recent changes to the formal procedure for celebrating a marriage in **Northern Ireland** have also been reflected in the civil partnership legislation. As a result those intending to celebrate a civil marriage or those intending to register a civil partnership need to give notice of their intention to marry or register a partnership to the Registrar.[127] This notice must be presented in person.[128] A number of documents, identical regardless

---

120 This cohabitation can thus not be as man and mistress. Although in the case of *Nicol v. Bell* (1954) SLT 314, it was proven that a relationship which began in such a way could in fact develop into such a relationship.

121 THOMPSON (1996) p. 17.

122 At one point in time this was thought to be one year (*Campbell v. Campbell* (1866) 4 M 867; *Wallace v. Fife Coal Company Ltd* (1909) SC 682.

123 **Marriage:** Sec. 3(1), M(S)A 1977; **CP:** Sec. 88(1), CPA 2004.

124 SCOTTISH EXECUTIVE (2003a) p. 22, §6.13.

125 **Marriage:** Sec. 4, M(S)A 1977; **CP:** Sec. 89, CPA 2004.

126 **Marriage:** Sec. 6(4), M(S)A 1977; **CP:** Sec. 90(2), CPA 2004.

127 **Marriage:** Art. 3(1), M(NI)O 2003; **CP:** Sec. 139(1), CPA 2004.

128 **Marriage:** Art. 3(4)(a), M(NI)O 2003; **CP:** Sec. 139(3), CPA 2004.

of the type of relationship one wishes to register, must also be submitted along with the notice.[129] Once notice has been delivered to the Registrar, the parties have twelve months in which to celebrate their marriage or register their civil partnership.[130] However, the parties must also wait at least fourteen days after giving notice before celebrating the marriage.[131] If the Registrar is satisfied that there is no legal impediment to the formation of a marriage or civil partnership, he or she must complete a marriage or civil partnership schedule.[132]

If the parties intend to marry, then the Registrar will then ensure that this schedule is available for signature during the ceremony.[133] During this ceremony both parties to the marriage, both witnesses to the marriage and the person who solemnised the marriage must sign the marriage schedule.[134] It is at this moment that the marriage is deemed to have been celebrated,[135] and not the time at which the marriage schedule is registered with the General Registry. A ceremony is, on the other hand, not required in a civil partnership. Instead, a civil partnership is deemed to have come into existence as soon as both parties to the civil partnership have signed the civil partnership schedule in the presence of each other, two witnesses and the registrar.[136] Once the civil partnership schedule has been signed, both witnesses and the registrar must also sign it,[137] although if this should not take place, it does not lead to the civil partnership being void.[138]

VII.5 LEGAL EFFECTS

VII.5.1 GENERAL

As soon as a marriage or civil partnership is deemed to have been formed, a plethora of rights and responsibilities are automatically incumbent on both parties to the relationship. This section will compare and contrast the most

---

129 **Marriage:** Art. 5(3), M(NI)O 2003; **CP:** Sec. 141(3), CPA 2004.

130 **Marriage:** Art. 5(3), M(NI)O 2003; **CP:** Sec. 141(3), CPA 2004.

131 Art. 3(2), MR(NI) 2003. It is certain that the same time periods will also be set for civil partnerships, likewise in secondary legislation.

132 **Marriage:** Art. 7(1), M(NI)O 2003; **CP:** Sec. 143(a), CPA 2004.

133 Art. 19(1)(a), M(NI)O 2003.

134 Art. 20(1), M(NI)O 2003.

135 Art. 25, M(NI)O 2003.

136 Sec. 137(1), CPA 2004.

137 Sec. 137(3), CPA 2004.

138 Sec. 137(2), CPA 2004.

important rights and duties imposed on those involved in a marital relationship with those imposed on persons involved in a civil partnership. It will also be made clear in each section which Parliamentary body in the **United Kingdom** is competent for legislating on each topic.

VII.5.2 CIVIL STATUS

Although legislative responsibility for civil registration has been devolved to the **Scottish** Parliament and **Northern Irish** Assembly, legislative competency for **Wales** remains with the **United Kingdom** Government at Westminster.[139] As has been noted by the *Commission Internationale d'État Civil*,[140] there is no exact, direct equivalent of the term *l'état civil* or *burgerlijke stand* in common law countries. However, recent proposals for modernising the civil registration system in **England & Wales** have made reference to the term *civil status*, which will thus be adhered to throughout this section.

Civil registration in **England & Wales** began in 1837 and is regulated by the Marriage Act 1949 (MA 1949), the Births and Deaths Registration Act 1953 (BDRA 1953) and the Registration Services Act 1953 (RSA 1953).[141] At present civil registration in **England & Wales** is undergoing widespread modernisation.[142] When these changes are enacted[143], they will substantially reform the formal workings of civil registration in **England & Wales** and create a so-called "through life record".[144] Since all these policy papers were published prior to the enactment of the CPA 2004, civil partnerships are not referred to. Similarly, since this policy framework had not resulted in legislative enactments prior to the enactment of the CPA 2004, no reference to such proposals could be made. Although the technical aspects of the registration of a civil partnership is not regulated in the CPA 2004, Secs. 28 to 30, CPA 2004 make it abundantly clear that the responsibility for

---

139 The **Welsh** Assembly does, however, need to be consulted on any regulatory reform order which affects Wales: OFFICE FOR NATIONAL STATISTICS (2003) p. 4

140 See www.ciec1.org.

141 In **Scotland**, civil registration of births, deaths and marriages began in 1855. In **Northern Ireland** registration of births and deaths began in 1864 and marriages in 1845.

142 In September 1999, the Registrar General for **England and Wales** published a consultation document, REGISTRAR GENERAL (2002). The responses to this consultation paper were used to develop a new policy framework for the civil registration service. See OFFICE FOR NATIONAL STATISTICS (2002) and (2003).

143 A Regulatory Reform Order is currently awaiting debate before the House of Commons.

144 OFFICE FOR NATIONAL STATISTICS (2003) p. 81, §5.

registering civil partnerships lies with the same district registration authorities responsible for registering marriages, and that the Registrar General of **England & Wales** is ultimately responsible.[145] Any reform of the registration of civil marriage will thus also affect the registration of civil partnerships.

Despite differences in the method of achieving the result, the situation in **Scotland** is identical to that in **England & Wales**.[146] The Registrar General for Births, Deaths and Marriages for **Scotland** is responsible for appointing a number of district registrars who, as well as being responsible for the administration of the registration of marriages, are also responsible for administering the registration of civil partnerships. The district registrars operate out of the same registration offices as those responsible for marriages.[147] Similarly in **Northern Ireland**, responsibility for the registration of marriages and civil partnerships rests with the district registrars.[148] In summary, it is clear that despite the substantial modernisation currently underway in this field of law, the Government's intention, as has been represented legislatively, is that marriages and civil partnerships are to be treated in exactly the same manner with regard to registration and the effect on the parties' civil status, regardless of any possible changes to the manner in which such relationships are registered.

VII.5.3 NATIONALITY[149]

The power to legislate on issues of nationality was not devolved to the **Scottish** Parliament nor to the **Northern Irish** or **Welsh** Assemblies.[150] The

---

145 Secs. 28 and 30(1), CPA 2004.

146 A similar reform to the one which has taken place in England & Wales also took place in Scotland (SCOTTISH REGISTRAR (2001)) and resulted in the M(S)A 2002.

147 **Marriage:** Sec. 8(1), RBDM(S)A 1965; **CP:** Sec. 135, CPA 2004.

148 The twenty-six district councils are known as the local registration authorities (Sec. 151(1), CPA 2004) and the Registrar General with respect to civil partnerships is the Registrar General for Northern Ireland (Sec. 160, CPA 2004).

149 Uncertainty exists concerning the distinction between the term "nationality" and "citizenship". See DE GROOT (2004) p. 2-5 for further discussion. It is, however, argued that in the UK the term "nationality" is a term used to describe all those connected to a particular State. The term "citizenship" is then used to further differentiate between different types of nationals, those with citizenship and those without.

150 It must be noted that persons born in **Northern Ireland** are also entitled to **Irish** nationality, by virtue of the Irish Citizenship and Nationality Act 1956. For the effect of this rule see ECJ, *Chen and Others*, 19th October 2004, Case N°. 200/02. This is obviously not affected by the passing of the CPA 2004.

British Nationality Act 1981 (BNA 1981) came into force on the 1st January 1983 and replaced all previous nationality laws. In doing so, it created three main types of British nationality: British Citizenship,[151] British Overseas Territories Citizenship[152] and British Overseas Citizenship.[153] This distinction is important when one examines the rules on the acquisition of British citizenship on the basis of one's marriage or civil partnership.

One of the more radical amendments made by the BNA 1981 was the removal of a woman's entitlement to acquire British citizenship as a result of marrying a man with British citizenship.[154] At the same time, men and women were placed on an equal footing, resulting in the rule that if a person who is not a British citizen marries a British citizen and wishes to acquire British citizenship, he or she must apply for naturalisation, unless he or she qualifies for registration.[155]

Like spouses, civil partners are entitled to a swifter naturalisation procedure.[156] If the Secretary of State is satisfied that on the application of a person who is of full age and capacity, who on the date of the application is

---

151 Part I, BNA 1981. Aimed at people closely connected with the United Kingdom, the Channel Islands and the Isle of Man (Sec. 1(1), BNA 1981).

152 Part II, BNA 1981, as amended by the British Overseas Territories Act 2002. Aimed at people connected with the British Overseas Territories (Sec. 15(1), BNA 1981). British Overseas Territories as of 1st January 2005 were: Anguilla, Bermuda, British Antarctic Territory, British Indian Ocean Territory, Cayman Islands, Falkland Islands, Falkland Islands' Dependent Territories (*i.e.* South Georgia and South Sandwich Islands, up until 3rd October 1985 and then of their own right from 4th December 2001), Gibraltar, Hong Kong (up until 1st July 1997), Montserrat, Pitcairn, Henderson, Ducie and Oeno Islands, St. Christopher and Nevis (up until 19th September 1983), St. Helena and Dependencies, the Sovereign Bases of Akrotiti and Chekelia, Turks and Caicos Islands, and the British Virgin Islands (Sch. 6, BNA 1981)

153 Part III, BNA 1981. Aimed at those citizens of the United Kingdom and Colonies without connections with either the United Kingdom or the British Overseas Territories (Sec. 26, BNA 1981).

154 Upon marrying a British citizen, a woman simply had to register her new citizenship. Unlike naturalisation which involves a discretionary procedure, registration is a matter of right. Any British Overseas Territories Citizen, British Overseas citizen, British subject under the BNA 1981 or British protected person, who has been in the United Kingdom for five years, is entitled to be registered as a British citizen provided that they are not in breach of the immigration laws: LOWE/DOUGLAS (1998) p. 71.

155 THOMPSON (1996) p. 43; LOWE/DOUGLAS (1998) p. 70-71; CRETNEY *et al.* (2003a) p. 92-93, §3-045.

156 Sec. 6(2), BNA 1981 as amended by Sch. 27, CPA 2004.

either married to or the civil partner of a British citizen,[157] and fulfils the requirements in Sch. 1, BNA 1981, he or she may grant that person a certificate of naturalisation. Sch. 1, BNA 1981 states that for such an application to be made, the person who applies must have been in the **United Kingdom** at the beginning of three years ending with the date of the application, and that the number of days on which he or she was absent from the **United Kingdom** in that period does not exceed 270 days.[158] This period is thus two years shorter than the five-year period imposed on those not married to **British** citizens.[159]

VII.5.4 NAME LAW

A person's name is simply a label for identification in the eyes of a **British** lawyer. What an individual's name is at any particular time is a matter of fact rather than law, and there is usually little difficulty in changing it if the person so requires.[160] The general rule according to **English**, **Scots** and **Northern Irish** law is that a person is entitled to change his or her name at will.[161] The acquisition of a new name is therefore most commonly effected by use and reputation. This is sufficient and provides just as much evidence as more formal methods such as deed poll.[162] Traditionally, upon getting married a woman usually takes her husband's surname and retains it regardless of the marriage having been terminated by virtue of a divorce, an annulment, a separation order or the death of her spouse. One will have to wait and see whether the same tradition will also be true of civil partners.

VII.5.5 TAXATION, SOCIAL SECURITY AND PENSIONS

Although social security and tax credit legislation passed in Westminster only extends to **Great Britain**, the vast majority of this legislation is also immediately extended to **Northern Ireland**. The amendments contained in Sch. 24, CPA 2004 equate the status of civil partner to that of spouse across a wide range of fields that can be divided into a number of distinct

---

157 It is important to note that being married to a person who possesses British Overseas Territories Citizenship or British Overseas Citizenship does not qualify.

158 Para. 3(a), Sch. 1, BNA 1981.

159 Para. 1(2)(a), Sch. 1, BNA 1981.

160 MEAD (1995) p. 1.

161 *R v. Smith* (1865) 4 F&F 1099, per WILLES J.

162 Deed poll is a formal method for changing one's name in the **United Kingdom**. For more information see MEAD (1995) Chapter 7 and www.ukdps.co.uk.

categories.[163] Parts 3 to 6 and 11 to 12, Sch. 24, CPA 2004, equalise the position of civil partner to that of spouse with respect to all income related benefits, including income support, income-based jobseekers allowance, housing benefit as well as council tax benefit, child benefit and guardian's allowance, bereavement benefits, and adult dependency increases.[164] As a result and in an identical fashion to spouses, when a civil partner claims an income-related benefit (other than pension credit), the other civil partner may be required to make payments which offset some or all of the benefit paid until the civil partnership ends. The same equality has also been achieved with respect to child support legislation in **Great Britain** and **Northern Ireland**,[165] as well as with respect to job seeker's allowance from joint couples,[166] tax credits[167] and pension credits.[168] In terms of taxation, Sec. 103, Finance Act 2005 grants the Treasury the power to enact regulations to ensure the equal treatment of civil partners and spouses in the fields of income tax and capital gains tax.[169]

VII.5.6 RIGHTS AND DUTIES OF THE PARTNERS TO EACH OTHER

The comparison of the rights and duties imposed on spouses and civil partners is possibly one of the most complex fields of law in this Chapter.[170] The majority of the rights and duties imposed on spouses stem from common law principles and are as such not necessarily applied analogously.

---

163 A distinction has thus been made between income-related benefits, non-income related benefits, child support legislation, taxation and pensions.

164 **Eng. and Scot.:** Consequential amendments made to the Social Security Contributions and Benefits Act 1992 and Social Security Administration Act 1992; **NI:** Consequential amendments made to the Social Security Contributions and Benefits (Northern Ireland) Act 1992 and Social Security Administration (Northern Ireland) Act 1992. See further CRETNEY *et al.* (2003a) p. 188-194, §7-013 to §7-026, especially p. 191, §7-018 to §7-023.

165 **Eng. and Scot:** Consequential amendments made to the CSA 1991 and CSA 1995; **NI:** Consequential amendments made to the Child Support (Northern Ireland) Act 1991 and Child Support (Northern Ireland) Order 1995.

166 **Eng and Scot:** Consequential amendments made to the Jobseekers Act 1995; **NI:** Consequential amendments made to the Jobseekers (Northern Ireland) Order 1995.

167 **UK:** Tax Credits Act 2002. By virtue of Sec. 69(2), Tax Credits 2002, this Act applies automatically to the entire territory of the United Kingdom.

168 **Eng and Scot:** Consequential amendments made to State Pension Credits Act 2002; **NI:** Consequential amendments made to State Pension Credits (Northern Ireland) Order 2002.

169 Sec. 255 CPA 2004 and the accompanying order made in the form of Civil Partnership (Amendment of provisions relating to contracted-out occupational and appropriate personal pensions schemes)(surviving civil partner) Order 2005 and the consultation paper published in March 2005 by the Department of Work and Pensions.

170 CRETNEY *et al.* (2003a) p. 69, §3-001.

It is therefore important to first delineate the scope of the duty imposed on spouses before determining whether this right is also imposed on civil partners. This in itself poses great difficulty due to uncertainty surrounding the extent of such rights in **English**, **Scots** and **Northern Irish** marriage law. Furthermore, when considering the legal effects produced by marriage at common law, it is important to bear in mind three principles: the doctrine of unity, the notion of consortium and the common law duty for a husband to maintain his wife. It is by virtue of these three common law principles that one is able to discern the majority of the rights and duties imposed on spouses, and the equivalent duties applicable to civil partners.

VII.5.6.1 Duty to cohabit

In the absence of statutory provisions in this field, it is necessary to analyse some of the main principles that have been developed at common law. The law has always required that a couple should have the intention of living together as husband and wife when they enter into a marriage,[171] or as it is known in **Scotland**, adhere to each other.[172] Nonetheless, neither party is able to force a right to cohabit upon the other.[173] Although this choice of a home traditionally rested with the husband, like many other areas of domestic life, this decision is now one that the spouses must agree upon.[174] Both spouses have an equal say in where they eventually decide to live, or whether they live together at all.[175] Although the original Civil Partnership Bill submitted to the House of Lords by Lord LESTER attempted to impose an additional cohabitation requirement on those wishing to register a civil partnership,[176] this did not find favour in the eventual CPA 2004. However, despite the absence of an express duty to cohabit, the aim of the Act is clear, namely that the civil partners are expected to live together, irrespective of

---

171 CRETNEY (2003b) p. 143; O'HALLORAN (1997) p. 28. See, furthermore, the rather bizarre application of this rule in *Weldon v. Weldon* (1883) 9 PD 52.

172 EDWARDS/GRIFFITHS (1997) p. 277, §10.03; CLIVE (1992) p. 155; *e.g. MacKenzie v. MazKenzie* (1895) 22 R (HL) 32 at 40.

173 *R v. Jackson* [1891] 1 QB 671. In **England & Wales** this right was abolished by the MCA 1884.

174 LOWE/DOUGLAS (1998) p. 57; CLIVE (1992) p. 155; O'HALLORAN (1997) p. 28. In **Scotland**, this was abolished by means of statute: Sec. 4, LR(HW)(S)A 1984.

175 *Dunn v. Dunn* (1949) P 98 at 103 *per* Lord DENNING; *McGowan v. McGowan* [1948] 2 All ER 1032 applying *Dunn v. Dunn*.

176 Sec. 2(1)(c), Civil Partnership Bill [HL] submitted to the House of Lords by Lord Lester stated that the couple must have lived together "for the period of six months ending, with the date of the application for registration of the civil partnership (otherwise than merely by reason of one of them being the other's employee, tenant, lodger or border)".

whether this duty is enforceable. Thus, in an identical fashion to marriage, should the parties not live together or have no intention of living together they will not be barred from registering their civil partnership.

VII.5.6.2 Duty of fidelity

Although some authors believe that it would be going to far to say that spouses are under a duty to have sexual intercourse with each other, in **England & Wales** and **Northern Ireland** each spouse is under a duty to consummate the marriage and the incapacity or willful refusal of the respondent to do so will entitle the petitioner to a decree of nullity.[177] The effect of allowing a marriage to be declared voidable on this basis therefore implies that the parties are not under a duty to have sexual intercourse, unless one of the parties wishes to. However, regardless of whether there is a duty to have sexual intercourse, sexual relations outside the marital bond will suffice as a ground for divorce across the **United Kingdom**.[178] This ground is not, however, extended to the dissolution of a civil partnership.[179] Nonetheless, infidelity in a civil partnership is not without consequence, since the Government's intention is that such behaviour will be able to be brought under the term "unreasonable behaviour" as a ground of dissolution.[180] As a result, it would appear that irrespective of whether the parties to a marriage or civil partnership are under a continuing duty to have sexual intercourse during their relationship, they are both under an identical duty to remain sexual faithful to their partner, at the risk of dissolution of the relationship.

VII.5.6.3 Duty to provide support and assistance

Stemming from the doctrine of unity, a husband was traditionally under a common law duty to maintain his wife.[181] This duty is now governed by

---

177 See **Section VII.6.6.** In **Scotland**, impotency is a ground for a marriage to be declared voidable and the wilful refusal of sexual intercourse by either spouse over a sufficiently long period of time may constitute behaviour justifying divorce: *H v. H* (1968) SLT 40, *Lennie v. Lennie* (1950) SC (HL) 1. See further CLIVE (1992) p. 155; EDWARDS/GRIFFITHS (1997) p. 381, §14.09.

178 See **Section VII.6.3.1.**

179 See **Section VII.6.3.1.**

180 WOMEN AND EQUALITY UNIT (2003b) p. 36.

181 CLIVE (1992) p. 162; EDWARDS/GRIFFITHS (1997) p. 286; CRETNEY (2003b) p. 90-94. If as a result of the marriage all the wife's property transferred to husband, then it was logical that the husband be under a duty to ensure that he supported his wife. Although since

statute and may be claimed by either spouse. In **England & Wales** and **Northern Ireland**, spouses and civil partners are under an identical duty to provide reasonable maintenance to each other.[182] If the court, having considered all those matters to be taken into account,[183] deems that a spouse or civil partner has failed in this duty, the court can issue a periodical payments order or lump sum order not exceeding £1,000. The same is also true of the power granted to the county or High Court although such orders may be made without financial limit.[184]

In **Scotland**, both spouses and civil partners are subject to an identical duty to owe "aliment" to the other for the duration of the marriage or civil partnership.[185] The obligation to provide aliment aims to provide a party with such support as is reasonable in the circumstances with regard to those needs and the resources of the parties.[186] Although spouses and civil partners are entitled to draw up aliment agreements themselves, such agreements may be subsequently challenged in court on the statutory ground that they were not fair and reasonable in all the circumstances at the time they were made.[187]

VII.5.6.4 Duty to contribute to household expenses

Civil partners, like spouses, are under no duty to contribute to household expenses. However, rules have been developed with respect to spouses if one spouse pays a "household allowance" to the other. One of the harshest

---

1882 a woman's property has no longer vested in her husband (Sec. 1(1), MWPA 1882), this duty was not made reciprocal until 1978.

182 **Eng.:** *Marriage:* Sec. 2, DPMCA 1978 (magistrates) and Sec. 27, MCA 1973 (county/High court); *CP:* §1, Sch. 6, CPA 2004 (magistrates) and §39, Sch. 5, CPA 2004 (county/High court); **N.Ire:** *Marriage:* Art. 3, DP(NI)O 1980, as amended by MFP(NI)O 1989 (magistrates) and Art. 29, MC(NI)O 1978 (county/High court); *CP:* §1, Sch. 16, CPA 2004 (magistrates) and §34, Sch. 15, CPA 2004 (county/ High court).

183 **Eng.:** *Marriage:* Sec. 3(2), DPMCA 1978 (magistrates) and Sec. 27(3), MCA 1973 (county/ High court); *CP:* §5, Sch. 6, CPA 2004 (magistrates) and §43(2), Sch. 5, CPA 2004 (county/High court); **N.Ire:** *Marriage:* Art. 5, DP(NI)O 1980 as amended by MFP(NI)O 1989 (magistrates) and Art. 27, MC(NI)O 1978 (county/High court); *CP:* §38(1), Sch. 15, CPA 2004 (magistrates) and §5, Sch. 16, CPA 2004 (county/High court).

184 LOWE/DOUGLAS (1998) p. 757; O'HALLORAN (1997) p. 545; CRETNEY *et al.* (2003a) p. 78-84, §3-011 to §3-026; HERRING (2003) p. 131-132.

185 **Marriage:** Sec. 1(1)(a) and (b), FL(S)A 1985; **CP:** Sec. 1(1)(bb), FL(S)A 1985, as amended by §10, Sch. 28, CPA 2004.

186 Sec. 4(1), FL(S)A 1985. See further EDWARDS/GRIFFITHS (1997) p. 286-293, §10.15-10.25; CLIVE (1992) p. 162-181.

187 Sec. 7(1), FL(S)A 1985. This only applies to spousal aliment or civil partner aliment.

consequences of the system of separate property was where, for example, a husband had provided his wife with a housekeeping allowance, but the woman saved such money. Since the husband had intended the money to be used for the household, no donation could be implied and as a result the money remained his own.[188] Legislation was passed in the 1960s to rectify this situation.[189] In **England & Wales** and **Northern Ireland** these provisions are only applicable to money provided by a husband to his wife and not vice versa,[190] whilst in **Scotland** this discriminatory element has been removed.[191] Although amendments to the **Scottish** legislation have been made by virtue of the CPA 2004,[192] no consequential amendments have been made to the legislation in force in **England & Wales** or **Northern Ireland**. Logically speaking, since the same general property rules apply to civil partners as to married couples, it must be assumed that a civil partner is placed in exactly the same position as a spouse prior to the legislation of the 1960s, *i.e.* that a civil partner providing the household allowance remains the owner of such an allowance should it not be used for household maintenance. However, the importance of this statute should not be overemphasised. In the four decades which it has been on the statute book, it has rarely been used.[193]

VII.5.6.5 Duty to contribute to repayment of debts

Throughout the United Kingdom, a spouse or civil partner incurs absolutely no liability for debts incurred by his or her spouse or civil partner.[194] An exception to this general rule does however apply to the repayment of council tax in **Great Britain** and rates in **Northern Ireland**.[195] On the other hand, the law in relation to insolvency and bankruptcy requires a delicate balance to be struck between the rights of the family and the rights of the creditors.[196] Therefore, creditors are offered protection against possible

---

188 THOMSON (1996) p. 71. See also *Blackwell v. Blackwell* [1943] 2 All ER 579; *Hoddinott v. Hoddinott* [1949] 2 KB 406 in which the husband was entitled to retain winnings from a horserace, the stake for which had been paid by the wife out of her housekeeping allowance.

189 **Eng and Scot:** Sec. 1, MWPA 1964; **Scot:** FL(S)A 1985; **NI:** Art. 3, LR(HW)A(NI) 1964.

190 LOWE/DOUGLAS (1998) p. 122; O'HALLORAN (1997) p. 481; CRETNEY *et al.* (2003a) p. 104, §4-005.

191 Sec. 26, FL(S)A 1985.

192 Sec. 26, FL(S)A 1985, as amended by §29, Sch. 28, CPA 2004.

193 CRETNEY *et al.* (2003a) p. 163, §6-002.

194 Secs. 1(1) and 2(1), LR(HW)A 1962.

195 **Eng:** Sec. 9, LGFA 1992; **Scot:** Sec. 77, LGFA 1992: **NI:** R(NI)O 1977.

196 See the wise words from *Re Citro* [1991] Ch 142 at 147: "Melancholy consequences of debt and improvidence with which every civilised society has been familiar".

bankrupts transferring all their property to their spouses. For example, if a wife or civil partner whose business is failing transfers some shares into her husband's or civil partner's name without adequate consideration, this transaction can be set aside.[197] Nonetheless, the "innocent" spouse or civil partner is not left entirely unprotected since his or her matrimonial home rights or occupancy rights will bind a subsequent trustee.[198]

VII.5.6.6 Protection of home

Legal and beneficial ownership of land carries with it a *prima facie* right of occupation.[199] The common law right of a wife to occupy the matrimonial home by virtue of her right to her husband's consortium has now become a statutory right, which has since been gender neutralised, as well as extended to civil partners.

(a) *Statutory occupational rights:* In **England & Wales** and **Northern Ireland**, a spouse or civil partner with "matrimonial home rights",[200] if in occupation, has the right not to be evicted or excluded from the dwelling-house[201] by the other spouse or civil partner except with the leave of the court.[202] If the spouse or civil partner is not in occupation then he or she has the right with the leave of the court to enter and occupy the dwelling-house.[203] Identical protection is also offered to spouses and civil partners in **Scotland** by virtue of their "occupancy rights".[204]

---

197 In **England & Wales**, for example, Sec. 423, IA 1986, as amended by the CPA 2004. Similar provisions also apply in **Scotland** and **Northern Ireland**.

198 HERRING (2003) p. 154 and, for example, in **England & Wales**: Sec. 336(2), IA 1986, as amended by §57, Sch. 8, FLA 1996.

199 Ownership of property as a result of celebrating a marriage or registering a civil partnership is dealt with **Section VII.5.7**.

200 Sec. 30(1), FLA 1996, as amended by Sch. 9, CPA 2004 and Art. 4(1), FHDV(NI)O 1998, as amended by Sch. 19, CPA 2004: (a) one spouse or one civil partner ("A") is entitled to occupy a dwelling-house by virtue of (i) a beneficial estate or interest or contract; or (ii) any enactment giving A the right to remain in occupation; and (b) the other spouse or civil partner ("B") is not so entitled.

201 **Eng:** As defined in Sec. 63, FLA 1996, as amended by Sch. 9, CPA 2004; **NI:** Art. 2, FHDV(NI)O 1998, as amended by Sch. 19, CPA 2004.

202 **Eng:** Sec. 30(1)(a), FLA 1996, as amended by Sch. 9, CPA 2004; **NI:** Art. 4(2)(a), FHDV(NI)O 1998, as amended by Sch. 19, CPA 2004. Matrimonial home rights only arise if one of the spouses/civil partners is entitled to occupy the dwelling-house.

203 **Eng:** Sec. 30(1)(b), FLA 1996, as amended by Sch. 9, CPA 2004; **NI:** Art. 4(2)(b), FHDV(NI)O 1998, as amended by Sch. 19, CPA 2004.

204 **Marriage:** Sec. 22, as read in conjunction with Secs. 1(1) and (4), MH(FP)(S)A 1981; **CP:** Sec. 135, as read in conjunction with Secs. 101(1) and (4), CPA 2004.

(b) *Rented property:* This area of law is extremely complex and technical and for the purposes of this book is unnecessary to describe in detail. Instead is it important to note that a distinction is made between private rented property and public sector tenancies. With respect to private rented property, tenancies granted prior to the 15th January 1989 are governed by the applicable Rent Act,[205] and are known as *regulated tenancies,*[206] whilst those granted after that date are governed by the applicable Housing Act[207] and are either known as *assured tenancies* or *assured shorthold tenancies.*[208] Public sector tenancies, on the other hand, are governed by the relevant Housing Act, and are known as *secure tenancies.*[209] Accordingly, and like spouses,[210] if one civil partner has a regulated tenancy but the other is in occupation of the premises by virtue of his or her matrimonial home rights, the occupier is to be regarded as though his or her occupation is by the tenant him or herself.[211] The same equality in treatment between civil partners and spouses has also been achieved by granting the surviving civil partner protection against eviction upon the death of the civil partner in whose name the tenancy was signed.[212]

VII.5.7 PROPERTY LAW

Unlike continental European systems, the **United Kingdom** does not have specific rules for dealing with matrimonial property law.[213] The celebration

---

205 **Eng:** RA 1977; **Scot:** R(S)A 1984; **NI:** R(NI)O 1978. In Northern Ireland, tenancies are still covered by the provisions of the R(NI)O 1978.

206 A holder of one of these tenancies is a *protected tenant* if the lease is contractual, or a *statutory tenant* if the lease has expired yet he or she remains in occupation.

207 **Eng:** HA 1988; **Scot:** H(S)A 1988.

208 BARLOW (2001) p. 44-46, §3.05-3.10; LOWE/DOUGLAS (1998) p. 172-177.

209 **Eng:** HA 1985; **Scot:** H(S)A 1987 and 2001. This is especially important since same-sex couples had previously been denied access to such beneficial provisions: *Harrogate Borough Council v. Simpson* [1986] 2 FLR 91.

210 LOWE/DOUGLAS (1998) p. 173.

211 **Eng:** Sec. 30(4)(a), FLA 1996, as amended by §1, Sch. 9, CPA 2004; **Scot:** Sec. 13, MH(FP)(S)A 1981; **NI:** Art. 4(4), FHDV(NI)O 1998, as amended by §3, Sch. 19, CPA 2004. As a result of registering a partnership, parties will be protected under the statutory scheme without having to rely on the decision in *Fitzpatrick v. Sterling Housing Association* [2000] 1 FLR 271. See ROBERTS (2000), BAILEY-HARRIS (1999) and INGLIS (2001a) and (2001b).

212 See further LOWE/DOUGLAS (1998) p. 881-884.

213 This was, however, not always the case, and previously all the wife's property was deemed to be vested in the man by operation of law at the moment of marriage: CLIVE (1992) p. 231; *Fraser v. Walker* (1872) 10 M 837 at 847. Statutorily enacted in **Eng:** MWPA 1882; **Scot:** Sec. 24, FL(S)A 1985; **NI:** reference.

of a marriage or the registration of a civil partnership has absolutely no impact upon the ownership of the partners' property. Neither spouse nor civil partner acquires a right to own or administer the property of the other upon marriage or civil partnership. This statement is true with respect to the property acquired prior to the registration of the relationship, as well as with property acquired after such registration. Only upon termination of the relationship is a judicial corrective mechanism provided for.[214] As a result, whenever ownership of family assets during the marriage or civil partnership is litigated, recourse must be made to the ordinary rules governing property law.[215] Accordingly, if a dispute does arise during the marriage or recourse to the courts is necessary, legal ownership of any property will first need to be determined followed by the determination of equitable or beneficial ownership.

Nevertheless, it has been recognised that in applying pure property law to spouses one essentially forgets the "family element" in their relationship.[216] Consequently, special property rules of law have been introduced which are specifically applicable to spouses, and subsequently extended to civil partners, and do not treat them as strangers. Firstly, as already seen above in **Section VII.5.6.6**, there are special rules for spouses and civil partners in which they are entitled to matrimonial home or occupancy rights.[217] Secondly, spouses and civil partners are also entitled to a statutory right to succeed in certain tenancies on the death of a tenant.[218] Thirdly, although the income of either partner remains his or her own property,[219] if the income is placed in a common fund, it would appear that they both acquire a joint interest in the whole fund.[220] Property subsequently bought using money from this common fund belongs solely to one partner if the object bought is for his or her sole use, but is owned by the parties jointly if the object is for their joint use. Possibly the most important exception to the separate property rule concerns household goods. Due to the difficulty of

214 See **Sections VII.6.9.1** and **VII.6.9.1.**

215 *Pettitt v. Pettitt* [1970] AC 77 and *Gissing v. Gissing* [1971] AC 866. See WRAGG (1996).

216 THOMPSON (1996) p. 62.

217 And to a limited extent cohabitants, but that is outside the realm of this book.

218 See LOWE/DOUGLAS (1998) p. 881-884.

219 See, for example, *Heseltine v. Heseltine* [1971] 1 All ER 952, where income from a wife's investments was deemed to be her own property.

220 *Jones v. Maynard* [1951] Ch 572 at 575.

determining the exact ownership of household goods,[221] such goods are presumed to be owned by the parties in equal shares.[222]

VII.5.8 INHERITANCE LAW

VII.5.8.1 England & Wales and Northern Ireland

In contrast to the manner in which amendments have been made in other areas of the law as a result of the passage of the CPA 2004, in the field of intestate succession, amendments have been made to the primary legislation instead of replicating the relevant provisions in the CPA 2004 itself.[223] As a result, references to the term "husband or wife" in Sec. 46, AEA 1925 and Sec. 7, AEA (NI) 1955 have been replaced by the phrase "spouse or civil partner".[224] The interest that the surviving spouse or civil partner takes over and above the personal chattels[225] depends upon the remaining issue. Sec. 46, AEA 1925 and Sec. 7, AEA (NI) 1955, provide that should the surviving spouse or civil partner leave no issue and no parent, sibling of whole or half blood, then the residuary estate will be held in trust for the surviving spouse or civil partner.[226] If the deceased leaves a parent or a sibling of whole or half blood but no issue, then the surviving spouse or civil partner takes a statutory legacy of £200,000[227] and an absolute interest in one half of the residue.[228] If the deceased leaves any children or remoter issue, then the

---

221 **Scot:** Sec. 25(3), FL(S)A 1985, as amended by §28, Sch. 28, CPA 2004. As a result, goods used by one spouse alone are clearly excluded since the goods must be used for "joint domestic purposes". In **England & Wales** and **Northern Ireland**, reference tends instead to be made to express, resulting and constructive trusts: *Rowe v. Prance* [1999] 2 FLR 787.

222 **Scot:** Sec. 25(1), FL(S)A 1985, as amended by §28, Sch. 28, CPA 2004; In **Scotland**, special rules also exist in relation to furniture and plenishings in the matrimonial home by virtue of Sec. 3(2), MH(FP)(S)A 1981. These rights are equally applicable to civil partners by virtue of Sec. 103(2), CPA 2004.

223 **Eng:** Sch. 4, CPA 2004; **NI:** Sch. 14, CPA 2004.

224 **Eng:** Sec. 46, AEA 1925, as amended by §7, Sch. 4, CPA 2004; **NI:** Sec. 7, AEA (NI) 1955, as amended by §10, Sch. 14, CPA 2004.

225 The term "personal chattels" is defined by Sec. 55(1)(x), AEA 1925 (**Eng**) and Sec. 45(1), AEA (NI) 1955 (**NI**).

226 **Eng:** Sec (1), Table, Sec. 46(1)(i), AEA 1925, as amended by §7, Sch. 4, CPA 2004; **NI:** Sec. 7, AEA (NI) 1955, as amended by §10, Sch. 14, CPA 2004.

227 **Eng:** Sum set by the Family Provisions (Intestate Succession) Order 1993 (SI 1993/2906). Interest is set according to orders set by the Lord Chancellor, which is currently set at 6%; **NI:** Sum set by the Administration of Estates (Rights of Surviving Spouse) Order (Northern Ireland) 1993.

228 **Eng:** Sec (3), Table, Sec. 46(1)(i), AEA 1925, as amended by §7, Sch. 4, CPA 2004; **NI:** Sec. 7, AEA (NI) 1955, as amended by §10, Sch. 14, CPA 2004.

surviving spouse or civil partner will take a statutory legacy of £125,000[229] and a life interest in half of the residue.[230] The surviving civil partner is also placed in an identical position as the surviving spouse with respect to the matrimonial home.[231]

Equality is also achieved in the field of testate succession in both jurisdictions.[232] According to these provisions the spouse or civil partner of the deceased and the former spouse or former civil partner of the deceased are entitled to bring a claim under the I(PFD)A 1975 or the I(PFD)(NI)O 1979.[233] This is a significant improvement on the law prior to the enactment of the CPA 2004, when same-sex couples were prevented from making a claim under either of these Acts.[234] In order for the applicant's claim to be successful, the applicant must show that the provision of the deceased's will or the law relating to intestacy are not such as to make "reasonable financial provision" for him or her.[235] In determining the scope of reasonable financial provision, the judge will apply a different test to surviving spouses and civil partners than he or she would apply to all other categories of applicant.[236]

---

229 **Eng:** Sum set by the Family Provisions (Intestate Succession) Order 1993 (SI 1993/2906). Interest is set according to orders set by the Lord Chancellor, which is currently set at 6%; **NI:** Sum set by the Administration of Estates (Rights of Surviving Spouse) Order (Northern Ireland) 1993.

230 **Eng:** Sec (2), Table, Sec. 46(1)(i), AEA 1925, as amended by §7, Sch. 4, CPA 2004. A spouse or civil partner is however entitled to redeem this life interest for the capital value, if he or she so wishes: Sec. 47A, AEA 1925, as amended by §9, Sch. 4, CPA 2004; **NI:** Sec. 7, AEA (NI) 1955, as amended by §10, Sch. 14, CPA 2004.

231 In **England & Wales** these rules are laid down in the Intestate's Estate Act 1952, which has been accordingly amended by the CPA 2004.

232 **Eng:** §15-27, Sch. 4, CPA 2004; **NI:** §16-28, Sch. 14, CPA 2004.

233 **Eng:** Sec. 1(1)(a), I(PFD)A 1975, as amended by §15, Sch. 4, CPA 2004; **NI:** Art. 3(1), I(PFD)(NI)O 1979, as amended by §17, Sch. 14, CPA 2004.

234 BARLOW (2003) p. 100, §5.08; *Fitzpatrick v. Sterling Housing Association* [1997] 4 All ER 705. However, this rule has not been tested since the House of Lords decision in *Ghaidan v. Godin-Mendoza* [2004] UKHL 30, appealed from [2001] EWCA Civ. 1533.

235 **Eng:** Secs. 1(1) and 2(1), I(PFD)A 1975; **NI:** Art. 1(1) and 2(1), I(PFD)(NI)O 1979.

236 See further LOWE/DOUGLAS (1998) p. 890; CRETNEY *et al.* (2003a) p. 209, §8-021. The crucial distinction is thus that in determining "reasonable financial provision" for a spouse or civil partner the judge will decide what it would be reasonable in all the circumstances of the case for the spouse or civil partner to receive, whether or not that provision is required for his or her maintenance: Sec. 1(2), I(PFD) 1975 and Art. 1(2), I(PFD)(NI)O 1979.

VII.5.8.2 Scotland[237]

Civil partners in **Scotland** are placed on an equal footing to their married counterparts by virtue of amendments to the Succession (Scotland) Act 1964 (S(S)A 1964).[238] Upon the death of one's spouse or civil partner, the survivor[239] has a number of rights, either known as "prior rights"[240] or "legal rights".[241] Prior rights, which only operate when the deceased dies intestate,[242] include rights to the deceased's interest in the dwelling-house which the deceased and the surviving spouse or civil partner formerly shared,[243] and its furniture and plenishings.[244] If the deceased was the owner, the surviving spouse or civil partner is entitled to a right to the house itself, whilst if the deceased was a tenant, the survivor is entitled to take on the tenancy.[245] Furthermore, the surviving spouse or civil partner is also entitled to monetary provision.[246] The amount of such monetary provision is dependent on whether the deceased was also survived by issue. Where there are issue, the surviving spouse or civil partner is entitled to a sum of £35,000, and where there are none to £58,000.[247] This monetary right is borne by the heritable and moveable parts of the estate in proportion to their respective amounts after deduction of the dwelling-house and furniture.[248]

---

237 Despite the heavy criticism levied by the **Scottish** Law Commission, the S(S)A 1964 still forms the basis of inheritance law in **Scotland** and forms the basis of the amendments made by the CPA 2004. See SCOTTISH LAW COMMISSION (1990) §2.3-2.17. It is first of all important to note a distinction in **Scots** law between moveable and heritable property, see further EDWARDS/GRIFFITHS (1997) p. 297, §10.31; CLIVE (1992) p. 664.

238 Part 1, Sch. 28, CPA 2004.

239 In Scots law, the survivor is often referred to as the *relict*.

240 As the name suggests, these rights are distributed first, prior to legal rights, although after funeral expenses and taxes: EDWARDS/GRIFFITHS (1997) p. 296, §10.30; CLIVE (1992) p. 664.

241 Legal rights are similar to the claims made under the I(PFD)A 1975 and I(PFD)(NI)O 1979, and are thus dealt with in **Section VII.5.8.2.B**.

242 Sec. 36(1), S(S)A 1964. This includes the situation when a deceased person dies partially intestate.

243 Up to a value of £130,000: Sec. 8(1), S(S)A 1964, as amended by the PRSS(S)O 1999.

244 Up to the value of £22,000: Sec. 8(3), S(S)A 1964, as amended by the PRSS(S)O 1999.

245 This latter rule does not apply if the tenant was a protected or statutory tenant under Sec. 8(6)(d), R(S)A 1984. See further CLIVE (1992) p. 665.

246 Sec. 9, S(S)A 1964, as amended by §5, Sch. 28, CPA 2004.

247 Sec. 9(1), S(S)A 1964, as amended by the PRSS(S)O 1999 and §5(a), Sch. 28, CPA 2004. These sums are also subject to interest.

248 Sec. 9(3), S(S)A 1964, as amended by the PRSS(S)O 1999 and §5(b), Sch. 28, CPA 2004.

When the deceased leaves a will but fails to provide for the surviving spouse or civil partner, then the surviving spouse or civil partner is also entitled to legal rights.[249] These legal rights cannot be defeated by any testamentary disposition on the part of the deceased and apply whether the deceased dies testate or intestate.[250] Once again, the sum the surviving spouse or civil partner receives depends on whether there are children or remoter issue of the deceased, since the children are also entitled to legal rights. Where there are no children or issue, the surviving spouse or civil partner is entitled to half the moveable estate, but otherwise only to one third.[251] The remaining half or two thirds of the moveable estate, plus any remaining heritage, is left for the deceased's heirs to inherit.[252] If on the other hand, the deceased has made provision for the surviving spouse or civil partner is his or her last will and testament, the surviving spouse or civil partner can elect whether to take such provision or renounce such a right and claim his or her legal rights.[253]

VII.5.8.3 Inheritance Tax

Prior to the enactment of the CPA 2004, same-sex couples were liable to pay a 40% inheritance tax[254] on any property which one partner left to the other if it exceeded the threshold, which is currently set at £263,000.[255] In a similar fashion to the law relating to other forms of taxation, Sec. 103, Finance Act 2005 grants the Treasury the power to enact regulations to equalise the position of spouses and civil partners with respect to inheritance tax. As soon as these changes occur, civil partners, like spouses, will be exempt from paying any inheritance tax whatsoever.[256]

---

249 These rights are referred to in the Act as *jus relicti* (where the husband is the surviving spouse) and *jus relictae* (where the wife is the surviving spouse). But these rights are identical and often referred to together as the relict's rights.

250 CLIVE (1992) p. 669.

251 **Marriage:** Sec. 1, S(S)A 1964; **CP**: Sec. 131(1) and (2), CPA 2004.

252 Sec. 2, S(S)A 1964. The heirs are listed in preferential order as children, remoter issue, parents, collaterals and collateral descendants.

253 Sec. 13, S(S)A 1964, as amended by §2, Sch. 28, CPA 2004. See CLIVE (1992) p. 680.

254 Current Government plans would however introduce a band system whereby estates between £263,000 and £288,000 would be levied at 22%, those between £288,000 and £763,000 at 40% and those over £763,000 at 50%: *The Telegraph,* 22nd August 2004.

255 Sec. 8 and Sch. 1, ITA 1984, as amended by Art. 2, Inheritance Tax (Indexation) Order 2004, SI 2004/771.

256 Sec. 18(1), ITA 1984.

VII.5.9 CHILDREN

VII.5.9.1 Parentage

The birth mother will be the legal mother of the child whether the child is born in or out of wedlock.[257] In cases where artificial reproductive techniques are employed, this position has also received statutory weight by virtue of Sec. 27(1), Human Fertilisation and Embryology Act 1990 (HFEA 1990).[258] The situation with respect to fathers is, however, somewhat more complicated. At common law the general position was that the biological father was the legal father.[259] This presumption could be proved in a number of ways, the easiest of which being the existence of a marriage, indicating that **Scottish**, **English** and **Northern Irish** parentage law all adhere to the maxim *pater est quem nuptiae demonstrant.*[260] This presumption is, however, not extended to children born during a civil partnership.[261]

If, however, the parties are not married, then a number of other options exist in order to establish paternity. If the child was conceived naturally, then no presumption of paternity arises in **England & Wales** or **Northern Ireland**.[262] However, entry of the man's name as that of the father at the registration of the child's birth is *prima facie* evidence of paternity.[263] Since only a male may be registered as the father on the child's birth certificate, it is therefore impossible for a female civil partner to use this method to assert paternity over a child. However, resort may be made to DNA profiling or a

---

257 *The Ampthill Peerage Case* [1977] AC 547 at 577.

258 This Act extends to **Scotland** and **Northern Ireland**: Sec. 48, HFEA 1990. For a detailed overview of the exceptions to the rule see WILKINSON/NORRIE (1993) p. 123-125.

259 Regardless of how fertilisation took place: *Re B (Parentage)* [1996] 2 FLR 15 at 21 *per* BRACEWELL J.

260 **Eng and NI:** *The Amphtill Peerage Case* [1977] AC 547 at 577 *per* Lord SIMON, *Gardner v. Gardner* (1877) 2 App Cas 723 *per* Lord GIFFORD; **Scot:** Sec. 5(1)(a), LR(PC)(S)A 1986. This presumption has also received added support in cases of artificial reproduction where even if the sperm was not that of the birth mother's husband, he will still be regarded to be the legal father of the child if he consented to the treatment: Sec. 28(2), HFEA 1990. See further, **Eng:** LOWE/DOUGLAS (1998) p. 266; CRETNEY *et al.* (2003a) p. 524, §18-003; **Scot:** WILKINSON/NORRIE (1993) p. 136-140; **NI:** O'HALLORAN (1997) p. 68.

261 This obviously is restricted to the case of a female civil partnership, since a child cannot be born "to" a male civil partnership.

262 **Eng:** LOWE/DOUGLAS (1998) p. 274; **NI:** O'HALLORAN (1997) p. 50.

263 *Brierley v. Brierley* [1918] P 257. **Eng:** Sec. 34(2), BDRS 1953; **NI:** Art. 14(3), BDR(NI)O 1976.

judicial determination. Nonetheless, these procedures still regard paternity as a male, singular concept, which cannot thus be exercised either by a female or a second male.[264] In **Scotland**, a man who is not married to the mother of the child will be presumed to be the father of the child if both he and the mother of the child have acknowledged that he is the father of the child and he has been registered as such in the Register of Births.[265] However, once again no alteration to this statute has been made by the passage of the CPA 2004. Nevertheless, involvement in a civil partnership is no bar to a male civil partner becoming registered as the child's father in any of the three jurisdictions, as long as paternity has not been established with respect to another.

Further provisions in the HFEA 1990 also determine that where a man has donated sperm to be used for licensed treatment with his consent he will not be deemed to be the legal father of the child.[266] The same is also true where a man's sperm is used after his death.[267] The HFEA 1990 goes on to provide that where donated sperm is used for a woman in the course of licensed treatment services provided for her and a man together,[268] then this man will be deemed to be the legal father of the child.[269] Once again, no amendments to this provision have been made, thus prohibiting a female civil partner to become the "legal father" of the child via this procedure. In summary and in contrast to married couples, no presumption or method is available in any of the countries of the **United Kingdom** to allow for both civil partners to become the legal parents of the child.[270]

VII.5.9.2 Parental Responsibilities

In **England & Wales** and **Northern Ireland** the term "parental responsibility" is used to delineate the package of rights, responsibilities, duties and obligations inherent upon a parent of a child.[271] In **Scotland** the

264 CRETNEY *et al.* (2003a) p. 526-533, §18-004 to §18-009.

265 Sec. 5(1)(b), LR(PC)(S)A 1986, WILKINSON/NORRIE (1993) p. 133-136.

266 Sec. 28(6)(a), HFEA 1990.

267 Sec. 28(6)(b), HFEA 1990, as in the case of *R v. Human Fertilisation and Embryology Authority, ex parte Bland* [1997] 2 FLR 742.

268 The precise meaning of the phrase "treatment together" is unclear. See *Re Q (Parental Order)* [1996] 1 FLR 369 at 372 *per* JOHNSON J.

269 Sec. 28(3), HFEA 1990.

270 This is obviously subject to the provisions on adoption as outlined in **Section VII.5.9.3**.

271 LOWE, in: BOELE-WOELKI/BRAAT/CURRY-SUMNER (2005) p. 5-6.

term "parental rights and responsibilities" is used as an overarching term to describe both parental rights and parental responsibilities.[272]

A. By operation of law

In all three jurisdictions, statutory legislation provides that where the father and mother of the child were married to each other at the time of the child's birth,[273] they will have joint parental responsibility.[274] These provisions have not been amended to allow for the automatic acquisition of parental responsibility by civil partners. If the mother is not married, or involved in a civil partnership, at the time of the child's birth, then she and only she will be vested with parental responsibility.[275]

B. Upon request

Besides the automatic ways in which a person may be vested with parental responsibility, other possibilities are available.[276] The possibilities vary depending on the status of the applicant. Three categories are discernible: unmarried fathers, step-parents and other interested parties. Unmarried fathers have the greatest number of ways in which to acquire parental responsibility over the child of their partner. As a result of the CPA 2004, civil partners have been placed on a similar footing to step-parents, who in turn are offered fewer opportunities than unmarried fathers, but more opportunities than those offered to other interested parties.

Those options only available to unmarried fathers, and thus not open to civil partners, are: (i) subsequently marrying the mother,[277] or (ii) becoming registered[278] as the child's father.[279] Option (i) is only open to different-sex

272 Parental responsibilities defined in Sec. 1(1), C(S)A 1995 and parental rights defined in Sec. 1(2), C(S)A 1995. WILKINSON/NORRIE (1993) p. 163.

273 Also if the child was born as a result of artificial insemination: Sec. 29(1), HFEA 1990.

274 **Eng:** Sec. 2(1), CA 1989; **Scot:** Sec. 3(1)(b), C(S)A 1995 (for pre C(S)A 1995 see WILKINSON/NORRIE (1993) p. 167 and Sec. 2(1)(a), LR(PC)(S)A 1986; **NI:** Art. 5(1), C(NI)O 1995.

275 **Eng:** Sec. 2(2)(a), CA 1989; **Scot:** Sec. 3(1)(a), C(S)A 1995; **NI:** Art. 5(2)(a), C(NI)O 1995.

276 MASSON (2003) p. 581-583.

277 By subsequently marrying the mother, the father brings himself within the scope of Sec. 2(1), CA89, Sec. 3(1)(b), C(S)A 1995 or Art. 5(1), C(NI)O 1995: **Eng:** Sec. 1, FLRA 1987; **Scot:** Sec. 1(1) LR(PC)(S)A 1986; **NI:** Art. 32(2)(a), MFP(NI)O 1989.

278 Registered in terms of Sec. 10(1), BDRA 1953, Sec. 18, RBDM(S)A 1965 or Art. 14(3), BDR(NI)O 1976. The ACA 2002 implements this new scheme for acquisition of parental responsibility for unmarried fathers. Although distinctions still exist between parental

couples, whilst option (ii) assumes that the applicant is the biological father of the child, thus excluding the possibility that same-sex couples (and hence civil partners) can benefit from these provisions.[280]

Due to a number of recent legislative amendments, the position of step-parents has been radically improved. Step-parents and civil partners, and of course unmarried fathers, may now be vested with parental responsibility by: (i) obtaining a parental responsibility order,[281] or (ii) obtaining a residence order (in which case a separate parental responsibility order must be made).[282] As a result of the passing of the CPA 2004, these options have all been extended to civil partners.[283] In all three jurisdictions of the **United Kingdom**, the unmarried father is also entitled to make a parental responsibility agreement with the mother,[284] however only in **England & Wales**, is this ability extended to step-parents.[285] In summary, although a civil partner is not entitled to be vested with parental responsibility automatically, he or she is able be acquire parental responsibility over the child of his or her partner either by virtue of an agreement (in **England & Wales**), by a court order or by obtaining a residence order (both available throughout the entire **United Kingdom**).

---

responsibility acquired via this provision and that acquired by married fathers. Parental responsibility acquired by virtue of registration at the child's birth may be removed without an adoption order: MASSON (2003) p. 581; CRETNEY *et al.* (2003a) p. 557-558, §18-036.

279 **Eng:** Sec. 4(1)(a), CA 1989, as amended by ACA 2002; **Scot:** This possibility is not currently provided for in **Scotland**, but will become available by virtue of Sec. 17, FL(S)B 2005, which amends Sec. 3, C(S)A 1995; **NI:** Sec. 7(1)(a), C(NI)O 1995, as amended by FLA(NI) 2001.

280 A person may also be vested with parental responsibility upon taking office as a formally appointed guardian of the child. However such an appointment can only take effect after the mother's death. **Eng:** Sec. 5(1), CA 1989; **Scot:** Sec. 7(1), C(S)A 1995; **NI:** Art. 159, C(NI)O 1995.

281 **Eng:** Sec. 4(1)(b), CA 1989 (parents) and Sec. $4^A(1)$(b), CA 1989, as amended by ACA 2002 (stepparents); **Scot:** Sec. 11(2)(b), C(S)A 1995 (parents and stepparents); **NI:** Art. 7(1)(b), C(NI)O 1995 (parents) and Sec. $7(1^A)$, C(NI)O 1995 (stepparents).

282 **Eng:** Sec. 12(1), CA 1989; **Scot:** Sec. 11(2)(c), C(S)A 1995; **NI:** Art. 12(1), C(NI)O 1995.

283 **Eng:** Sec. $4^A(1)$, CA 1989, as inserted by the ACA 2002, and amended by Sec. 75(1), CPA 2004; **Scot:** No legislation was necessary in Scotland, since the C(S)A 1995 already provided for such situations; **NI:** Sec $7(1^C)$, C(NI)O 1995, as inserted by FLA(NI) 2001, and amended by Sec. 199(4), CPA 2004.

284 **Eng:** Sec. 4(1)(c), CA 1989; **Scot:** Sec. 4(1), C(S)A 1995; **NI:** Art. 7(1)(c), C(NI)O 1995.

285 Sec. $4^A(1)$(a), CA 1989, as amended by ACA 2002 (step-parents).

VII.5.9.3 Adoption

The recent enactment of the Adoption and Children Act 2002 (ACA 2002) has been the first major overhaul of **English** adoption law since the passing of the Adoption Act 1976 (AA 1976).[286] Although the House of Lords eventually passed the Bill,[287] the debate surrounding the passage of the legislation was fervent with one Cabinet Minister resigning over the use of the three-line whip.[288] The furore centred on widening of the scope of those entitled to adopt in **England & Wales**. Although these legislative amendments have made a fundamental impact to the landscape of adoption law in **England & Wales**, these changes have as yet not been replicated in **Northern Ireland** or **Scotland**.[289] However, the CPA 2004 has slightly amended **Northern Irish** legislation with respect to adoption.[290] The end result is thus a complicated patchwork of provisions.

As a result of these legislative amendment in **England & Wales**, it is now possible for married couples, civil partners and unmarried couples "living as partners in an enduring family relationship" to jointly adopt.[291] Furthermore adoption orders may be made on the application of one person who has attained the age of twenty-one and is not married nor in a civil partnership.[292] The amendments made to the adoption law of **England & Wales** by virtue of the ACA 2002 signalled a vast departure from the old law, which although it had been held that a homosexual should not be

---

286 This road to reform has however been a long one beginning in 1992 and eventually culminating in the 2002 Act. See further BRIDGE/SWINDELS (2003); CRETNEY *et al.* (2003a) p. 794-796, §23-004.

287 *British House of Lords*, Vol. 640, Cols. 567-634 (5th November 2002). 215 votes to 184. See also HERRING (2003) p. 587-592.

288 "Three-line whips" are imposed on important occasions, such as second readings of significant Bills and motions of no confidence. Failure by a Member of Parliament to attend a vote with a three-line whip is usually seen as a rebellion against the party and may eventually result in disciplinary action.

289 Sec. 149, ACA 2002. Only certain provisions are applicable in **Northern Ireland** and **Scotland**. Scottish adoption law is, however, currently under review with the second phase of the Adoption Policy Review having taken place: SCOTTISH EXECUTIVE (2003b) p. 94-98. A recent announcement by the **Scottish** Executive indicates the **Scottish** Parliament's intention to open adoption to same-sex couples: www.365gay.com.

290 By virtue of Sec. 203, CPA 2004.

291 Sec. 50(1), ACA 2002 in conjunction with Sec. 144(4), ACA 2002, as amended by Sec. 79(12), CPA 2004.

292 Sec. 51(1), ACA 2002, as amended by Sec. 79(4), CPA 2004. An exception to this rule is made by virtue of Sec. 51(3A), ACA 2002, as amended by Sec. 79(5), CPA 2004. HERRING (2003) p. 592-593.

prevented from adopting as an individual under Sec. 15(1), AA 1976,[293] had prevented same-sex couples from submitting a joint application.[294] Nonetheless, single-parent adoptions are not generally regarded as favourably as adoption by couple by adoption agencies, and tend only to be used to care for children with special needs who are otherwise difficult to place.[295]

In **Northern Ireland** and **Scotland**, civil partners are not equated to spouses. As a result, civil partners are not entitled to apply for a joint adoption order, which is restricted to married couples.[296] In **Scotland** persons involved in a civil partnership are nonetheless entitled to apply to adopt individually.[297] This is, however, prohibited in **Northern Ireland**.[298] As a result, although either party involved in an unregistered same-sex relationship is entitled to avail oneself of an individual adoption order application, those involved in a civil partnership are totally prevented from adopting in **Northern Ireland**. Although individual adoption orders are less favoured than joint adoption applications, the **British** courts have taken an increasingly progressive approach, emphasising the parenting commitment of the same-sex adopters, and has increasingly stressed the need to interpret adoption legislation in a non-discriminatory way.[299] In one noteworthy **Scottish** case, an adoption order was made in favour of a gay male living in a long-term relationship.[300] The judgment of the **Scottish** Court of Session was notable for its rejection of homophobic preconceptions and for taking judicial notice of the lack of evidence on negative aspects of the same-sex parenting, *i.e.* the lack of substantiation for assertions that children will be stigmatised by peers, that they are more likely themselves to be homosexual, or that same-sex families are intrinsically less stable or supportive than their heterosexual counterparts.

As a result of Sec. 246(1), CPA 2004, all references to term "step-parent" listed in Schs. 21 and 22, CPA 2004, include a person who is the civil

---

293 *Re W (A Minor) (Adoption: Homosexual Adopter)* [1998] 2 Fam 58.

294 Sec. 14(1A) AA 1976.

295 BAILEY-HARRIS (2001).

296 **Scot:** Sec. 14(1A), A(S)A 1978; **NI:** Art. 14, A(NI)O 1987.

297 Sec. 15, A(S)A 1978.

298 Art. 15, A(NI)O 1987, as amended by Sec. 203(4), CPA 2004.

299 *Re W (Adoption: Homosexual Adopter)* [1997] 2 FLR 406; *Re E (Adoption: Freezing Order)* [1995] 1 FLR 382.

300 *AMT (Known as AC)(Petitioner For Authority to Adopt SR)* [1997] Fam 225.

partner of a child's parent.[301] Despite having wide-ranging implications across a spectrum of **British** legislation, this amended interpretation does not apply to adoption orders.[302] Nonetheless, in **England & Wales**, the civil partner of a parent may apply to adopt his or her partner's child on the basis of Sec. 51(2), ACA 2002, as long as he or she has attained the age of 21.[303]

VII.5.9.4 Artificial Insemination

The regulation of and access to artificial insemination is a reserved matter and thus legislated by Westminster and not by the devolved Parliaments and Assemblies in **Scotland**, **Northern Ireland** and **Wales**. The passage of the CPA 2004 has however left the regulation of artificial insemination unaltered, with no consequential amendments being made to the HFEA 1990. Although attempts to explicitly prevent lesbians and single women having access to donor insemination services were defeated, the HFEA 1990 contains provision that clinics are not allowed to provide donor insemination services without taking into account 'the welfare of any child who may be born as a result, including the need of that child for a father'.[304] This provision obviously has a detrimental effect on an application by a lesbian couple. Since 1995, the Code of Practice of the Human Fertilisation and Embryology Authority has been liberalised in order to focus on the individual clinic's assessment of the particular case. Although this inevitably has improved the situation somewhat, there still remains a discrepancy in practice, as BAILEY-HARRIS states "a same-sex couple's access to reproductive technology services is permitted but not guaranteed".[305]

VII.6 DISSOLUTION

VII.6.1 GENERAL

The rules for dissolving civil partnerships are almost identical to the equivalent rules for marriage, thus enabling a direct comparison. Therefore,

---

301 By virtue of Sec. 247 and 248, CPA 2004.

302 Sch. 21 includes references to Acts of the Scottish Parliament (Sec. 247(9), CPA 2004). There has thus been no amendment to **Scot:** Sec. 15(1)(aa), A(S)A 1978; **NI:** Art. 15(4), A(NI)O 1987. In **Scotland**, stepparent adoption is also under review: SCOTTISH EXECUTIVE (2003b) p. 111-114.

303 Sec. 51(2), ACA 2002.

304 Sec. 13, HFEA 1990.

305 BAILEY-HARRIS (2001) p. 610.

resort should also be made, when one attempts to interpret this legislation, to the ample case law on divorce. This section will be divided into a number of sub-sections according to the type of dissolution requested. Despite the existence of only one ground for the dissolution of a marriage or a civil partnership in the entire **United Kingdom**, namely that the relationship has irretrievably broken down,[306] in order to prove that the relationship has irretrievably broken down the parties must prove one of a number of facts.[307] Some of these grounds do not require the consent of both parties, whilst others do. These facts will thus be analysed according to those that require the consent of both parties (**Sections VII.6.2**) and those that do not (**Sections VII.6.3**). In any case, neither a marriage nor a civil partnership can be ended in **Northern Ireland** before a period of two years has elapsed since the marriage was celebrated or the civil partnership was registered.[308] In **England & Wales** this period is only one year,[309] whilst in **Scotland** no such period exists at all.[310]

VII.6.2 JUDICIAL: JOINT PETITION

In all three jurisdictions of the **United Kingdom**, the applicant[311] may establish that the marriage or civil partnership has irretrievably broken down by showing that the spouses or civil partners have lived apart for a continuous period of at least two years immediately preceding the presentation of the petition and that the respondent[312] consents to the decree being made.[313] This application rests on the proof of two criteria: that the parties have lived apart for two years[314] and that the respondent

---

306 **Eng:** Sec. 1(1), MCA 1973 (marriage) and Sec. 44(1), CPA 2004 (CP); **Scot:** Sec. 1(1), D(S)A 1976 (marriage) and Sec. 117(2)(a), CPA 2004 (CP); **NI:** Art. 3(1), MC(NI)O 1978 (marriage) and Sec. 168(1), CPA 2004 (CP).

307 **Eng:** Sec. 1(2), MCA 1973 (marriage) and Sec. 44(5), CPA 2004 (CP); **Scot:** Sec. 1(2), D(S)A 1976 (marriage) and Sec. 117(3), CPA 2004 (CP); **NI:** Art. 3(2), MC(NI)O 1978 (marriage) and Sec. 168(5), CPA 2004 (CP).

308 **Marriage:** Art. 5(1), MC(NI)O 1978 as amended by MFP(NI)O 1989; **CP:** Sec. 165(1), CPA 2004.

309 **Marriage** Sec. 3(1), MCA 1973; **CP:** Sec. 41(1), CPA 2004.

310 LOWE, in: BOELE-WOELKI/BRAAT/SUMNER (2003a) p. 200 and 414.

311 In **Scots** law, the applicant (which in turn replaces petitioner) is known as a *pursuer.*

312 In **Scots** law, the respondent is known as the *defender.*

313 **Eng:** Sec. 1(2)(d), MCA 1973 (marriage) and Sec. 44(5)(b), CPA 2004 (CP); **Scot:** Sec. 1(2)(d), D(S)A 1976 (marriage) and Sec. 117(3)(c), CPA 2004 (CP); **NI:** Art. 3(2)(d), MC(NI)O 1978 (marriage) and Sec. 168(5)(b), CPA 2004 (CP).

314 This requires that the parties have maintained separate households and is thus not conditional on proving that the parties live separately: *Brown v. Brown* [1992] 2 BNIL 48.

consents to the application. Therefore, although the petition is in technical terms a unilateral petition, it must be accompanied by the consent of the other party.[315]

It is interesting to note that the wording of the **Scottish** as opposed to the **English** and **Northern Irish** legislation on this point is significantly different. In **England & Wales** and **Northern Ireland**, the legislation is so phrased to have required the courts to interpret that the parties must have decided or recognised that the relationship was at an end.[316] In **Scotland**, however, such a requirement is not imposed and the requirement that the parties have lived apart is merely construed as a question of fact.[317]

VII.6.3 JUDICIAL: UNILATERAL PETITION

Unlike marriage, where four alternative grounds exist for proving that a marriage has irretrievably broken down, for civil partnerships only three of these have been incorporated into the CPA 2004. Each of these grounds will be dealt with in turn.

VII.6.3.1 Adultery

Unlike marriage, which can be dissolved on the ground that one party has committed adultery,[318] a civil partnership may not be dissolved on this ground. The reason for the absence of this ground is simple to explain. The term "adultery" according to **English**, **Scots** and **Northern Irish** law means "voluntary sexual intercourse by a married person with a person of a different sex to the marriage partner".[319] It would therefore require statutory amendment to the common law notion of adultery for this ground to be extended to civil partners. Instead, the Government has expressly allowed for voluntary sexual intercourse by a person involved in a civil partnership with a person other than the civil partner to be subsumed under

---

315 If the Family Law (Scotland) Bill 2005 is successful this period will be reduced to two years for both spouses and civil partners: Sec. 10, FL(S)B 2005 and §8, Sch. 1, FL(S)B 2005 amending Sec. 117, CPA 2004.

316 *Santos v. Santos* [1972] Fam 247.

317 CLIVE (1992) p. 427.

318 **Eng:** Sec. 1(2)(a), MCA 1973; **Scot:** Sec. 1(2)(a), D(S)A 1976; **NI:** Art. 3(2)(a), MC(NI)O 1978.

319 **Eng:** LOWE/DOUGLAS (1998) p. 228; **Scot:** CLIVE (1992) p. 403; THOMSON (1996) p. 101; *MacLennan v. MacLennan* (1958) SC 105; **NI:** O'HALLORAN (1997) p. 176.

the ground of unreasonable behaviour.[320] In this way, the common law notion of adultery is preserved and infidelity is dealt with the same way for both sets of couples. This has been welcomed by many not only because of the significant number of divorce petitions submitted on this ground, but also because it sends out a message that infidelity in a civil partnership will also be penalised.[321]

VII.6.3.2 Unreasonableness and a respondent's behaviour

As with marriage,[322] a civil partnership may be dissolved on the basis that the respondent has behaved in such a way that the applicant cannot be reasonably expected to live with the respondent.[323] The behaviour is to be judged subjectively according to its effect on the particular sensitivities of the applicant, namely:

> Would any right-thinking person come to the conclusion that this husband has behaved in such a way that this wife cannot reasonably be expected to live with him, taking into account the whole of the circumstances and the characters and personalities of the parties?[324]

VII.6.3.3 Desertion

According to the initial proposals put forward by the various Government bodies across the **United Kingdom**, no reference was made to the ground for desertion.[325] However, the CPA 2004 as passed does include reference to a ground for desertion, as is also the case for marriage.[326] Four separate elements must be proven for a divorce or dissolution to be granted according to one of these sections: (a) that the spouses or registered partners

---

320 Women and Equality Unit (2003b) p. 36.

321 According to the most recent statistics (2003): **Eng:** 33,331 (21.8%); **Scot:** 401 (3.7%); **NI:** 112 (4.8%). If the FL(S)B 2005 is enacted this ground will be abolished in **Scotland.** See also Sumner (2004b)

322 **Eng:** Sec. 1(2)(b), MCA 1973; **Scot:** Sec. 1(2)(b), D(S)A 1976. If the FL(S)B 2005 is passed this period will be reduced to one year; **NI:** Art. 3(2)(b), MC(NI)O 1978.

323 **Eng:** Sec. 44(5)(a), CPA 2004; **Scot:** Sec. 117(3)(a), CPA 2004. If the FL(S)B 2005 is passed this period will be reduced to one year; **NI:** Sec. 168(5)(a), CPA 2004.

324 *Livingstone Stallard v. Livingstone Stallard* [1974] 2 All ER 766 *per* Dunn J; *Birch v. Birch* [1992] 1 FLR 564.

325 Women and Equality Unit (2003).

326 **Eng:** Sec. 1(2)(c), MCA 1973 (marriage) and Sec. 44(5)(d), CPA 2004 (CP); **Scot:** Sec. 1(2)(c), D(S)A 1976 (marriage) and Sec. 117(3)(b), CPA 2004 (CP); **NI:** Art. 3(2)(c), MC(NI)O 1978 (marriage) and Sec. 178(5)(d), CPA 2004 (CP).

are living apart, (b) that it is the respondent's intention to permanently continue to do so, (c) that this occurs without the applicant's consent and (d) that the respondent has no reasonable cause for doing so.[327] This ground is seldom used, and thus it can only be expected to be used as little or less for applications for the dissolution of civil partnerships.[328]

VII.6.3.4 Living apart for five years

Once again, in an identical manner to the law on divorce,[329] an applicant is entitled to a divorce if he or she is able to prove that they have lived apart for a continuous period of at least five years immediately preceding the presentation of the petition.[330] The only evidential burden placed on the applicant in this scenario is that of proving that a period of separation has taken place and that this period has lasted for five years. A petition on this ground may only be refused if the respondent can prove that the granting of a decree would result in grave financial or other hardship.[331] However, the defence is rarely, if ever, successful.[332]

VII.6.4 ADMINISTRATIVE: MUTUAL CONSENT

Neither marriage nor civil partnership may be dissolved administratively in any part of the **United Kingdom**.

VII.6.5 ADMINISTRATIVE: UNILATERAL DISSOLUTION

Netiher marriage nor civil partnership may be dissolved administratively in any part of the **United Kingdom**.

---

327 **Eng:** LOWE/DOUGLAS (1998) p. 229; **Scot:** CLIVE (1992) p. 413-426; **NI:** O'HALLORAN (1997) p. 180-182.

328 According to the most recent statistics (2003) this ground was the by far the least used in all three jurisdictions. **Eng:** 665 (0.4%); **Scot:** 23 (0.2%); **NI:** 9 (0.4%).

329 **Eng:** Sec. 1(2)(e), MCA 1973; **Scot:** Sec. 1(2)(e), D(S)A 1976; **NI:** Art. 3(2)(e), MC(NI)O 1978.

330 **Eng:** Sec. 44(5)(c), CPA 2004; **Scot:** Sec. 117(3)(d), CPA 2004; **NI:** Sec. 168(5)(c), CPA 2004.

331 **Eng:** Sec. 5(1), MCA 1973 (marriage) and Sec. 47(1), CPA 2004 (CP); **Scot:** Sec. 1(5), D(S)A 1976 (marriage) and Sec. 117(6), CPA 2004 (CP); **NI:** Art. 7, MC(NI)O 1978 (marriage) and Sec. 171(1), CPA 2004 (CP).

332 LOWE, in: BOELE-WOELKI/BRAAT/SUMNER (2003a) p. 264-265.

VII.6.6 ANNULMENT PROCEEDINGS

In **England & Wales** and **Northern Ireland**, a distinction is drawn between void and voidable marriages and civil partnerships, whereas in **Scotland** such a distinction is not evident.[333] It is therefore more appropriate to consider the laws of **England & Wales** and **Northern Ireland** together and that of **Scotland** separately.

In **England & Wales** and **Northern Ireland**, if either of the parties were not eligible to enter into a civil partnership or celebrate a marriage or did not comply with the formalities of the registration, their registered relationship will be void *ab initio*.[334] The grounds are identical with respect to civil partnerships and marriages. In terms of voidable civil partnerships and marriages, all the grounds available to civil partners in **England & Wales** and **Northern Ireland** are likewise open to spouses.[335] However, three further grounds open to spouses wishing to annul their marriage are not extended to civil partners, namely, non-consummation owing to incapacity,[336] non-consummation owing to the wilful refusal of one of the parties,[337] and that at the time of the marriage one of the parties was suffering from a venereal disease.[338]

In **Scotland**, the grounds for annulling a marriage or civil partnership are identical, save for one exception.[339] Sec. 5(4)(f), M(S)A 1977 states that a

333 In **Scotland**, impotency is retained as a ground for a marriage to be declared voidable. However, the consequences of a voidable marriage are identical to those of a void marriage: EDWARDS/GRIFFITHS (1997) p. 266, §9.31 Void marriages and civil partnerships are deemed never to have existed and since they are void *ab initio* require no decree to annul them. Voidable marriages and civil partnerships on the other hand are deemed to be valid relationships up until a court pronounces a decree absolute (Sec. 15, MCA 1973): Sec. 16, MCA 1973, LOWE/DOUGLAS (1998) p. 78-80; O'HALLORAN (1997) p. 11.

334 **Eng:** Sec. 11, MCA 1973 in conjunction with Sec. 49, MA 1949 (marriage) and Sec. 49, CPA 2004 (CP); **NI:** Art. 13(1), MC(NI)O 1978, in conjunction with M(NI)O 2003 (marriage) and Sec. 173, CPA 2004 (CP).

335 **Eng:** Sec. 12(c), (d), (f) and (g), MCA 1973, as amended by the GRA 2004 (marriage) and Sec. 50(1), CPA 2004 (CP); **NI:** Sec. 14(c), (d), (f) and (g), MC(NI)A 1978, as amended by the GRA 2004 (marriage) and Sec. 174(1), CPA 2004.

336 **Eng:** Sec. 12(a), MCA 1973; **NI:** Art. 14(a), MC(NI)O 1978. See further BRUNNER (2001).

337 **Eng:** Sec. 12(b), MCA 1973; **NI:** Art. 14(b), MC(NI)O 1978. See further BRUNNER (2001).

338 **Eng:** Sec. 12(d), MCA 1973; **NI:** Art. 14(d), MC(NI)O 1978. This point received debate during the debates in the Standing Committee, where it was noted that this provision should also be removed from the laws on marriage: *British House of Commons*, Standing Committee D, Cols. 159-163 (26th October 2004 [a.m.]).

339 **Marriage:** Sec. 5(4), M(S)A 1977; **CP:** Sec. 123, CPA 2004.

legal impediment to a marriage will exist if one or both of the parties is, or are, not domiciled in **Scotland** and, on a ground other than one mentioned in Secs. 5(4)(a) to (e), a marriage in **Scotland** between the parties would be void *ab initio* according to the law of the domicile of the party or parties as the case may be. This ground has not been extended to civil partnerships.[340] Furthermore, unlike marriage where impotency is a ground for a marriage to be declared voidable at common law, no such ground exists for civil partners.[341]

VII.6.7 DEATH AND PRESUMPTION OF DEATH

The death of either party *ipso facto* brings a marriage or civil partnership to an end.[342] In all three jurisdictions, the court may, on the application of a civil partner, and in an identical manner to an application from a spouse, make a presumption of death order if it is satisfied that reasonable grounds exist for supposing that the other civil partner is dead.[343] The inference can be drawn either from the circumstances or from the fact that the person who has disappeared has been absent for seven years.[344]

VII.6.8 ENTRY INTO MARRIAGE / CONVERSION

Due to the same-sex requirement imposed on civil partnerships and the different-sex requirement imposed on marriages, there is no possibility provided for the conversion of one institution into another. As already mentioned in **Section VII.4.3** detailed procedures are laid down for those transsexuals who undergo gender reassignment treatment whilst involved in a marriage or civil partnership. In all three countries, an expedited procedure is available once one relationship has been terminated for the parties to enter into another without having to wait for the required "waiting period".[345]

---

340 For further details see **Chapter X**.

341 EDWARDS/GRIFFITHS (1997) p. 266, §9.31.

342 For marriage and by analogy for civil partnerships: LOWE/DOUGLAS (1998) p. 867; CLIVE (1992) p. 602-603; O'HALLORAN (1997) p. 44.

343 **Eng:** Sec. 19(1), MCA 1973 (marriage) and Sec. 55(1), CPA 2004 (CP); **Scot:** Sec. 1(1), PD(S)A 1977 (marriage) and Sec. 1(3), PD(S)A 1977, as amended by §44, Sch. 28, CPA 2004 (CP); **NI:** Art. 21, MC(NI)O 1978 (marriage) and Sec. 178(1), CPA 2004 (CP).

344 CLIVE (1992) p. 650; O'HALLORAN (1997) p. 44; LOWE/DOUGLAS (1998) p. 867-868; CRETNEY *et al.* (2003a) p. 315-317, §13-001 to §13-003.

345 See **Section VII.4.8** for further details on the required waiting period.

VII.6.9 EFFECTS OF DISSOLUTION

In the **United Kingdom**, no distinction is drawn between the division of matrimonial property and the award of maintenance.[346] Nonetheless it is possible to draw a distinction between financial orders (**Section VII.6.9.1**) on the one hand, and those orders relating to a party's capital and property on the other (**Section VII.6.9.3**).[347] In their totality, the new provisions laid down in the CPA 2004 propel same-sex couples from the realm of property law norms into the world of family law.[348] It must also be noted that any "pre-nuptial" agreement reached by civil partners probably will not be enforceable in an analogous manner as the approach adopted with pre-nuptial agreements reached by spouses.[349]

VII.6.9.1 Maintenance

In all three jurisdictions, a court is allowed to make a number of financial provision orders upon the termination of either a marriage or a civil partnership; namely a periodical payments order[350] or a lump sum order.[351] A periodical payments order requires the payment of funds to a spouse or civil partner (and/or to or for the benefit of a child) on a regular basis to be determined by the court, *i.e.* weekly, fortnightly, monthly or quarterly. The aim of any such order is, however, to bring dependency to an end as quickly as possible and is subject to the enjoinder that such orders end on the

---

346 See further SVERDRUP (2005) p. 119. When making financial orders the court is able to issues orders affecting all the property belonging to the parties or either of them whether acquired before or during the marriage.

347 The same distinction is also upheld with respect to civil partnerships with financial provision orders being dealt with in Parts 1 and 2, Sch. 5, CPA 2004 (**Eng**), Part 2, Sch. 28, CPA 2004 (**Scot**), Parts 1 and 2, Sch. 15, CPA 2004 (**NI**).

348 BARLOW (2001) Chapters 10 and 11; BARLOW/JAMES (2004) p. 148.

349 BARTON (1998); LEADERCRAMER (2000) and (2001); See also *N v. N (Jurisdiction: Pre-nupital agreement)* [1989] 2 FLR 745.

350 **Eng:** Sec. 23(1)(a) and (b), MCA 1973 (marriage) and §2(1)(a) and (b), Sch. 5, CPA 2004 (CP); **Scot:** Sec. 8(1)(b), FL(S)A 198, as amended by §14, Sch. 28, CPA 2004; **NI:** Art. 25(1)(a) and (b), MC(NI)O 1978 (marriage) and §2(1)(a) and (b), Sch. 15, CPA 2004 (CP). In **England & Wales** and **Northern Ireland** a distinction is made between secured and unsecured periodical payments. In **Scotland**, this is known as a "periodical allowance order".

351 **Eng:** Sec. 23(1)(c), MCA 1973 (marriage) and §2(1)(c), Sch. 5, CPA 2004 (CP); **Scot:** Sec. 8(1)(a), FL(S)A 1985, as amended by §14, Sch. 28, CPA 2004; **NI:** Art. 25(1)(c), MC(NI)O 1978 (marriage) and §2(1)(c), Sch. 15, CPA 2004 (CP). In **Scotland**, this is known as a "payment of a capital sum order".

claimant's death, remarriage or formation of a civil partnership.[352] Nonetheless, before making any order, the court is obliged to consider the possibility of making a clean break order.[353] As a result of the approximate replication of the relevant provisions of the MCA 1973 and the MC(NI)O 1978 in the Schedules to the CPA 2004 and the amendment of the FL(S)A 1985, the procedural calculation and determination of financial provision between former civil partners and former spouses are approached in an identical fashion.[354] A similar parity of treatment is also achieved in the court's power to earmark or share pensions between civil partners and spouses upon the termination of their marriage or civil partnership.[355] It must be noted that the Government's intention and the final provisions of the CPA 2004 convincingly argue for the analogous application of the wealth of case law developed in the field of ancillary relief upon dissolution of a marriage. If apparent reasons had existed as to why civil partners were to be treated differently from their spousal counterparts, this would have undoubtedly have been reflected in the various statutory provisions. This is not the case, therefore supporting the argument that the case law developed on the basis of MCA 1973, FL(S)A 1985 and MC(NI)O 1978 should be applied analogously.

---

352 **Eng:** Sec. 28(1), MCA 1973 (marriage) and §47(2), Sch. 5, CPA 2004 (CP); **Scot:** Sec. 13(7)(b), FL(S)A 1985, as amended by §20(4), Sch. 28, CPA 2004; **NI:** Art. 30(1), MC(NI)O 1978 (marriage) and §42(2), Sch. 15, CPA 2004 (CP).

353 **Eng:** Sec. 25A(1), MCA 1973 (marriage) and §23(2), Sch. 5, CPA 2004 (CP); **Scot:** Sec. 9(1)(d), FL(S)A 1985 and EDWARDS/GRIFFITHS (1997) p. 368, §13.38; **NI:** Art. 27A(1), MC(NI)O 1978 (marriage) and §18(2), Sch. 15, CPA 2004 (CP).

354 For more information on the determination and calculation of maintenance see LOWE, in: BOELE-WOELKI/BRAAT/SUMNER (2003b), English and Scottish answers. The English and Scottish reports can also be downloaded in its entirety from the CEFL website: www2.law.uu.nl/priv/cefl. The court in determining a "fair outcome" will consider "all the circumstances of the case" with the welfare of any children being the first (but not the paramount) consideration. See CLIVE (1992) p. 473-496; EDWARDS/GRIFFITHS (1997) p. 343-366, §13.04-§13.36; O'HALLORAN (1997) p. 561-566; LOWE/DOUGLAS (1998) p. 829-844; CRETNEY *et al.* (2003a) p. 353-378, §14-042 to §14-065; HERRING (2003) p. 201-213.

355 **Eng:** *Marriage:* Sec. 25B(1), MCA 1973, as inserted by PA 1995 (earmarking) and Sec. 21A(1), MCA 1973 as inserted by FLA 1996 (sharing); *CP:* §24(1), Sch. 5, CPA 2004 (earmarking) and §15(1), Sch. 5, CPA 2004 (sharing); **Scot:** Sec. 10(5), FL(S)A 1985; EDWARDS/GRIFFITHS (1997) p. 350-353, §13.15-13.18; **NI:** *Marriage:* Art. 27A(1), MC(NI)O 1978, as inserted by P(NI)O 1995 (earmarking) and Art. 26A(1), MC(NI)O 1978, as inserted by WRP(NI)O 1999 (sharing); *CP:* §19(1), Sch. 15, CPA 2004 (earmarking) and §10(1), Sch. 15, CPA 2004 (sharing).

VII.6.9.2 Effects with respect to children

The general schemes of the various pieces of child legislation throughout the **United Kingdom** begin from the premise that the responsibility of parents should not be unnecessarily disturbed as a result of the breakdown of their relationship.[356] If either one or both of the civil partners have been vested with parental responsibility, such parental responsibility will not end by virtue of the termination of the civil partnership. However, this golden thread cannot be followed throughout all the legislation relating to children. Although under **English** and **Northern Irish** law no power exists to allow a court to divest a parent of parental responsibility should he or she have been vested with parental responsibility by virtue of a marriage, a court order or a parental responsibility agreement, the power does exist for a father who has acquired parental responsibility by virtue of registration as the child's father to be divested of his parental responsibility.[357] Under **Scots** law, a court possesses a general power to divest a parent of parental responsibility.[358] Nevertheless, this provision applies equally across the board and thus applies equally to civil partners and spouses alike.

VII.6.9.3 Effects with respect to property

A. England & Wales and Northern Ireland

As well as financial orders, a court is also entitled to direct one spouse to transfer, settle or sell property that he or she owns for the benefit of the other party. The most common transfer of property order is an order whereby one party transfers a share in the matrimonial home to the other. A transfer of property order could also be used to transfer ownership of other property such as a car or furniture. The order for sale of property is generally used as an ancillary to a lump sum order[359] and generally forces a

---

356 BAINHAM (1998) p. 116; LOWE, in: BOELE-WOELKI/BRAAT/CURRY-SUMNER (2005) p. 282.

357 MASSON (2003); LOWE, in: BOELE-WOELKI/BRAAT/CURRY-SUMNER (2005) p. 56-57.

358 Sec. 11(2)(a), C(S)A 1995. See further EDWARDS/GRIFFITHS (1997) p. 101, §4.50.

359 Although an order for the sale of property may seem appropriate this is not an independent possibility and may only be utilised in combination with a secured periodical payments order, a lump sum order or a property adjustment order. *Omielan v. Omielan* [1996] 2 FLR 306, *Harper v. O'Reilley v. Harper* [1997] 2 FLR 816, *Burton v. Burton* [1986] 2 FLR 419, *Thompson v. Thompson* [1986] Fam 38.

spouse who owns property outright to sell such property so that the proceeds can be divided.[360]

In both jurisdictions a stockpile of case law has developed on the basis of the settlement of property orders. A temporary solution to the problem of housing has thus been to defer the sale of the house until the children have left home so that the parent with whom they have been living can reasonably be expected to move into smaller accommodation. This was the case in *Mesher v. Mesher*.[361] Alternatively the court can set a date dependent on the possibility for the resident spouse to find alternative accommodation, as was the case in *Martin v. Martin*.[362] It is expected, since the legislative basis upon which these orders were made corresponds to the legislative basis upon which orders for civil partners can be made, that this abundant case law will equally apply to civil partners claiming financial relief on the basis of §14(2), Sch. 5, CPA 2004 (**England & Wales**) or §7(3), Sch. 15, CPA 2004 (**Northern Ireland**). Although an increasing impetus is provided for the parties to reach an agreement without resorting to the court,[363] the court retains the power to examine any agreement reached.[364]

In divorce, and thus, it is submitted, by analogy upon the termination of a civil partnership, the division of assets between spouses or civil partners must be measured against the yardstick of equality.[365] However, the landmark decision in *White v. White*[366] brought not only a torrent of academic writing,[367] but also a plethora of new cases. It is of interest to note a number of issues raised since the *White* decision and their possible impact

---

360 A third party's interests must be taken into account but do not necessarily prohibit the sale. Although this duty is not compulsory in **Northern Ireland**, the difference in the phraseology of the sections implies that this will be the case: O'HALLORAN (1997) p. 561. **Eng:** Sec. $24^{A}(6)$, MCA 1973 (marriage) and §14(2), Sch. 5, CPA 2004 (CP); **NI:** Art. 26(4), MC(NI)O 1978 (marriage) and §7(3), Sch. 15, CPA 2004 (CP).

361 [1980] 1 All ER 126.

362 *Martin v. Martin* [1978] Fam 12. For more detailed information on these orders see LOWE/DOUGLAS (1998) p. 844-848, O'HALLORAN (1997) p. 560.

363 As can be seen, for example, from the Family Proceedings Rules 1999.

364 In *Harris v. Manahan*, WARD LJ described this in saying "the court is no rubber stamp nor is it some kind of forensic ferret": [1997] 1 FLR 205.

365 *White v. White* [2000] 3 WLR 1571; [2000] 2 FLR 981 at 989 *per* Lord NICHOLLS.

366 As well as the lesser known case of *Piglowska v. Piglowski* [1989] 2 FLR 763.

367 DA COSTA (2001), DUCKWORTH/HUDSON (2001), HAYWARD SMITH (2001), ROSS (2001a) and (2001b), BRASSE (2001), CRETNEY (2001), BAILEY-HARRIS (2001a) and (2001b), EEKELAAR (2001), COOKE (2001).

on civil partners.[368] In *Cowan v. Cowan*,[369] the Court of Appeal noted that the husband's contribution was "stellar", providing reason enough to depart from the yardstick of equality. Yet THORPE LJ made it clear in *Lambert v. Lambert* that only in "exceptional cases" will the contribution of one of the parties be regarded as a sufficient reason for departing from equality.[370] It has also been difficult to apply the *White* principles to so-called small money cases where equality is simply impossible. In these cases, the familial pot does not contain sufficient funds to split the proceeds equally, raising claims that White only applies in big money cases. Whatever the exact position of the law in this field, it is submitted that courts should, and in fact must, apply the same principles to questions of financial relief between civil partners as they would do, and have done, in spousal cases. To do otherwise would be contrary to the aims of Parliament.

B. Scotland

Consequential amendments to the Family Law (Scotland) Act 1985 have resulted in total equality in the orders that a court is entitled to make at the dissolution of a relationship in relation to matrimonial property or partnership property.[371] With respect to property upon dissolution of either a marriage or a civil partnership, parties are allowed to apply for one of two orders: a transfer of property order or an incidental order.[372] An incidental order, however, covers a wide spectrum of orders including an order for the sale of property, an order for the valuation of property and an order for regulating the occupation of the matrimonial home or use of furniture and plenishinhgs therein.[373] As has already been stated, the underlying principle behind any order made with respect to property should be as far as possible be a "clean break" between the parties.[374]

---

368 *White v. White* [2000] 3 WLR 1571; [2000] 2 FLR 981.

369 *Cowan v. Cowan* [2001] 2 FLR 192; [2001] 3 WLR 684.

370 *Lambert v. Lambert* [2002] 3 FCR 673.

371 Part 2, Sch. 28, CPA 2004.

372 **Marriage:** Sec. 8(1)(aa), FL(S)A 1985 (transfer of property order) and Sec. 8(1)(b), FL(S)A 1985 (incidental order), as amended by §13, Sch. 28, CPA 2004.

373 Sec. 14(1), FL(S)A 1985.

374 EDWARDS/GRIFFITHS (1997) p. 341, §13.02.

CHAPTER VIII
COMPARISON AND EVALUATION

VIII.1 INTRODUCTION

On the basis of the research conducted into the substantive law regimes of seven representative European jurisdictions, this Chapter will address the similarities and differences between the different national forms of legislation. A number of models will be presented which, although based upon the research conducted in this book, could serve as templates for other non-marital registered relationship schemes across Europe and beyond. The existence of common functional bases will provide the springboard to the main part of this research, namely the search for the possibility of harmonised or possibly unified private international law rules.

This Chapter is divided into four sections along similar lines to the previous five chapters, dealing in turn with the issues relating to the establishment of (**Section VIII.2**), the dissolution of (**Section VIII.3**) and the legal effects attributed to forms of non-marital registered relationships (**Section VIII.4**).[1] The final section of this chapter (**Section VIII.5**) will be devoted to an overall evaluation of the comparisons in this field, providing an overview of the various models identified. Furthermore, attention will also be paid to the utility of such models for the field of private international law.

VIII.2 ESTABLISHMENT

Six specific eligibility criteria for the establishment of a non-marital registered relationship were examined in **Section 4** of **Chapters** III-VII: exclusivity, sex, age, residency, prohibited degrees of relationship and, competency and consent. However, before one can begin to compare the individual rules in each of these cases, one must first identify the question to which one is seeking answers. The answers which one receives to one's questions necessarily depend upon one's chosen phraseology. In turn, this phraseology depends upon the aim of the comparison. It is therefore

[1] Dissolution has been dealt with before the attributed legal effects for reasons that will become apparent later in **Sections VIII.3** and **VIII.4**.

imperative to distil the aim of the comparison in order to ensure that one poses the most pertinent questions. The main research question, as already outlined in **Chapter I.3**, is not whether it is possible to harmonise substantive family law in this field, but whether it is desirable, and if so feasible, to harmonise or even unify the relevant private international law rules.[2] It is therefore important to note that internal consistency between the rules on marriage and the rules on non-marital registered relationships is essentially the key, determining factor.[3]

As one is well aware, the substantive law rules for the celebration of a marriage are diverse,[4] yet the possibility for harmonisation and unification of the relevant private international law rules still exists. As long as one is able to identify a *tertium comparationis,* one is able to group these often very different institutions in the same legal category and thus solve problems using the same rules of private international law. It is, however, imperative that one first recognises the existence of two different types of comparison.[5] The first, *external comparison*, involves the comparison of legal rules relating to putative equivalent legal institutions in different countries, *e.g.* a comparison of the legal rules relating to the PACS in **France** with the rules relating to statutory cohabitation in **Belgium**. If the rules are identical this results in *external consistency*. The second type of comparison is *internal comparison*, whereby different legal institutions in the same jurisdiction are compared, *e.g.* a comparison of marriage and registered partnership in **The Netherlands**. If the rules are identical this results in *internal consistency*.[6]

External comparison (if identical leading to external consistency) →

Internal comparison (if identical leading to internal consistency) ↓	**Belgium**	**France**	**Netherlands**	**Switzerland**	**UK**
	Statutory Cohabitation	PACS	Registered partnership	Registered partnership	Civil partnership
	Marriage	Marriage	Marriage	Marriage	Marriage

2 For the distinction between harmonisation and unification see **Chapter I.3**.

3 A search for the possibility to unify substantive family law would be counter-productive to the search for unification in the field of private international law, since any search for unified substantive law rules would necessarily negate the need for private international law rules: T DE BOER (1994) and FAUVARQUE-COSSON (2000) and (2001).

4 See the individual country reports in Part 2 of each section in HAMILTON/PERRY (2002).

5 This is also highlighted by KOKKINI-IATRIDOU (1988) p. 3.

6 The reasons for researching substantive law in order to deal with the issues at private international law are explained in **Chapters I and II.**

Both of these forms of comparison are important in this research and will be employed throughout this Chapter. This section is accordingly divided into three sub-sections. The first sub-section identifies those areas in which total consistency of result has been achieved, both internally and externally (**Section VIII.2.1**). The second sub-section deals with those aspects of the registration process that although externally inconsistent achieve internal consistency with the respective rules on marriage (**Section VIII.2.2**). The third sub-section deals with those situations in which neither internal nor external consistency has been achieved (**Section VIII.2.3**).

VIII.2.1 INTERNAL AND EXTERNAL CONSISTENCY

Two criteria, namely exclusivity and competency/consent, can be isolated which provide for total consistency of result, both internally in a given legal system and externally across the seven jurisdictions studied. Each of these criteria will be examined in turn with the aim of explaining the precise ambit of this consistency.

As was explained in **Chapter III.4.2**, the principle of exclusivity consists of two discrete facets. Firstly, the relationship must only consist of two persons, and secondly the parties are not able to possess a status in combination with another status of the same type.[7] In dealing sequentially with both of these components one is able to discern total unanimity. All seven jurisdictions restrict these new forms of partnership regulation to two people, replicating the equivalent rules for marriage.[8] "Polygamous" non-marital registered relationships are thus prohibited in all the jurisdictions studied.[9] Furthermore, all seven jurisdictions also satisfy the second facet to the exclusivity requirement, not only with respect to non-marital registered relationships but also with respect to marriage. In other words, the existence of a marriage prohibits either of the parties from celebrating a non-marital registered relationship, whilst the existence of a non-marital registered relationship prevents either of the parties from celebrating a marriage.

---

7 That is to say that the parties cannot already be married or involved in a non-marital registered relationship. This will be further discussed in **Chapter IX.5**.

8 See **Chapters III.4.2**, **IV.4.2**, **V.4.2**, **VI.4.2** and **VII.4.2**.

9 The term "polygamous" has been inserted between inverted commas since etymologically speaking the word polygamous refers to marriages. Stemming from the Greek word *polugamos*: *polu* meaning much or often, and *gamos* meaning marrying. Although not a correct etymological use of the word, it clearly indicates the issue in question.

This last proposition must however be justified with regard to **Belgium** and **France**. As has already been outlined in **Chapters III.4.2** and **IV.4.2**, the existence of a non-marital registered relationship does not form a prohibition to celebrating a marriage. However, if a non-marital relationship has already been registered it will be automatically and immediately terminated upon the celebration of a marriage.[10] As a result, both institutions remain independent of each other. The fact that the parties cannot be involved simultaneously in a non-marital registered relationship or marriage signifies that these two institutions are independent, or perhaps better said, exclusive of each other. The key factor remains thus mutual exclusivity. Such a result, however, is not surprising if one considers the total absence of laws permitting polygamy in Europe. Although many legal systems around the world permit polygamous marriages,[11] European nations have tended to prevent such relationship forms.[12] It is therefore to be expected that such fundamental tenets of European society would be echoed in forms of non-marital registered relationships.

When one turns one's attention to the concepts of competency and consent, one is also able to discern a veritable unanimity of approach. Without exception, all those countries surveyed impose the requirement that both parties must validly consent to the registration and must be competent according to domestic substantive law.[13] This statement must, however, be tempered. Although superficially identical with respect to the basic requirement of valid consent and competency, the countries surveyed impose different requirements with respect to when such competency and consent will be deemed to be absent. It is, therefore, on this level impossible to speak of external consistency. In comparing the rules on consent one must also, therefore, take into account the respective laws on annulment.[14]

Only **The Netherlands** provides for total internal consistency in the laws on consent and annulment.[15] In the **United Kingdom** the grounds for annulling a civil partnership are more stringent than the equivalent rules for marriage. This difference is a logical result of the removal of all references to the

10 **Chapters III.6.8** and **IV.6.8**.

11 SUMNER (2002a) p. 30.

12 Polygamy, in either form of polygyny (a man with multiple wives) or polyandry (a woman with multiple husbands), has never been permitted by Christianity, nor by the Greek and Roman Empires. Early Mormonism provides a notable exception to picture.

13 See **Chapters III.4.7, IV.4.7, V.4.7, VI.4.7** and **VII.4.7.**

14 See **Chapters III.6.6**, **IV.6.6**, **V.6.6**, **VI.6.6** and **VII.6.6**.

15 See **Chapter V.6.6**.

sexual obligation imposed on parties to a civil partnership.[16] The heterosexual nature of the duty to consummate made it virtually impossible to extend such annulment grounds to civil partners in **England & Wales** and **Northern Ireland**. It was therefore thought better to simply avoid all reference to consummation. Instead, in **England & Wales** and **Northern Ireland** the inability to consummate or the wilful refusal to consummate may be taken into account in a dissolution based on the "unreasonable behaviour" of the partner.[17] Similar argumentation can also be used to explain the absence of impotency as a ground of voidability in **Scotland**.[18]

In **Belgium**, **France** and **Switzerland** the reverse is true, with the rules for annulling a marriage being more stringent than the equivalent rules for annulling a non-marital registered relationship. These differences are of a more intrinsic nature and stem from the compromises struck between various political parties during the legislative parliamentary process.[19] As a result, in all three jurisdictions, the annulment grounds mirror those applicable to normal contracts and not marriages, where the *favor matrimonii* principle tends to restrict the possibilities for annulment. Nonetheless, the requirement that the parties must have voluntarily registered the relationship while legally competent to do so, forms one of the most crucial and fundamental elements of the registration process in all those countries researched regarding both the celebration of a marriage and the registration of non-marital relationships.

VIII.2.2 EXTERNAL INCONSISTENCY BUT INTERNAL CONSISTENCY

Certain differences in the laws on non-marital registered relationships have their origins in the national differences in the respective laws on marriage. This is the case in relation to two of the six eligibility criteria studied, namely age requirements and prohibited degrees of relationship. Each of these criteria will thus be examined in turn.

Although all seven jurisdictions impose a minimum age requirement on those wishing to register a non-marital relationship, certain important differences are patent. The fact the relevant age for non-marital registered relationships is different in the seven jurisdictions studied reflects the corresponding disparity of marital age limits. Three approaches can be

---

16 See **Chapter VII.5.6.2**.

17 See **Chapter VII.6.3.1**.

18 See **Chapter VII.6.6**.

19 See **Chapters III.6.6**, **IV.6.6** and **VI.6.6**.

identified. Firstly, there are those countries where the minimum age is set at eighteen without exception both for couples wishing to marry as well as for those registering a non-marital relationship (**Switzerland** and **Scotland**).[20] Secondly, there are those countries where although the minimum age to marry or register a non-marital relationship is set at eighteen, those under the age of eighteen are permitted to either marry or register a relationship should certain other conditions be fulfilled (**England & Wales**, **Northern Ireland** and **The Netherlands**).[21] In both of these approaches internal consistency is achieved. In the third and final approach, although the minimum age is set at eighteen for both marriage and non-marital registered relationships,[22] the exceptions provided for those wishing to marry are not duly extended to those wishing to register their non-marital relationship (**Belgium** and **France**).[23] Once again this can be explained with reference to the political compromises struck in these two countries. The *favor matrimonii* principle has thus once again not found replication in either of these jurisdictions with respect to non-marital registered relationships.

In six of the seven jurisdictions studied, internal consistency has also been accomplished with respect to "exogamy".[24] In **France**, **The Netherlands**, **Switzerland**, **England & Wales**, **Scotland** and **Northern Ireland**, the prohibitions placed upon those wishing to register a non-marital relationship are identical to those imposed upon couples wishing to marry.[25] In **Belgium**, however, these marital prohibitions have not been impressed on those wishing to register their relationship. The opening of statutory cohabitation to couples within the prohibited degrees of relationship was nevertheless heavily criticised during the parliamentary debates[26] and a Bill currently before the **Belgian** Chamber of Representatives would, if passed,

---

20 **Switzerland** (**Chapter VI.4.4**) and **Scotland** (**Chapter VIII.4.4**).

21 In **England & Wales** and **Northern Ireland**, parental consent must be obtained for those parties between the ages of 16 and 18 (**Chapter VII.4.4**). In **The Netherlands**, permission must be sought from the Minister of Justice (**Chapter V.4.4**).

22 Although the current age at which women are allowed to marry in **France** is set at fifteen, persons under the age of eighteen require parental consent. It is therefore only once both parties have reached the age of eighteen that they are free to celebrate a marriage without first obtaining parental consent: See Art. 144, Fr. CC.

23 **Chapters III.4.4** and **IV.4.4**.

24 Exogamy is the word used to describe the custom of marrying outside a specified group of people to which one belongs. Once again, as explained in **footnote 14**, the term exogamy is etymologically speaking restricted to use with marriage (Stems from Greek *exo* meaning outside and *gamos* meaning marrying).

25 See **Chapters IV.4.6**, **V.4.6**, **VI.4.6** and **VII.4.6**.

26 *Belgian Chamber,* 1996-1997, No. 170/8, p. 18.

introduce equivalent exogamous prohibitions as those imposed on aspirant spouses.[27] The precise reasons for removing such prohibitions can be traced to the relatively weak legal effects attached to the institution.[28] As a result the legal and social distance established between marriage and statutory cohabitation is relatively large, therefore weakening the arguments for imposing such prohibitions; the more contractual an institution appears, the weaker the arguments for imposing "exogamous" restrictions. It is also to be noted that in **France**, **The Netherlands** and the **United Kingdom**, a similar debate also took place, yet in these countries, due to the relatively extensive legal effects attached to the registration,[29] it was thought that such a solution would have resulted in impractical and disadvantageous results.[30]

VIII.2.3 INTERNAL AND EXTERNAL INCONSISTENCY

With respect to the final two eligibility criteria, namely sex and residency, one is unable to identify either internal or external consistency. With respect to the parties' sex, two approaches can be distinguished. The first approach, evidenced by the legislation in **Switzerland** and the **United Kingdom**, permits only same-sex couples to register their non-marital registered relationship. The other approach, adopted by **Belgium**, **France** and **The Netherlands**, opens non-marital registered relationship schemes to both different-sex and same-sex couples. In **Belgium** and **The Netherlands** this step has subsequently been followed by the opening-up of civil marriage to couples of the same-sex.

In the **United Kingdom** and **Switzerland**, the aim of introducing non-marital registered relationship regulation was confined to the protection of intimate relationships between same-sex couples.[31] The discrimination faced by such couples formed the sole concern for the Government in introducing legislation.[32] Although in **Belgium**, **France** and **The Netherlands** this was one of the aims of the legislature, the Governments in these countries also

---

27 *Belgian Chamber*, 2002-2003, No. 110/1, p. 21.

28 See **Section VIII.4.1.2**.

29 Although the legal effects attributed to the PACS are not as extensive as those in **The Netherlands** or the **United Kingdom**, the fact that the PACS legislation is to be found in Book 1, Fr. CC, clearly indicates the innate connection between marriage and the PACS: see further **Chapters IV.5.2** and **IX.3.2**.

30 See **Chapters IV.3.2**, **V.3.2** and **VII.4.6**.

31 **Chapter VI.4.3** and **VII.4.3**.

32 Although it was noted in **United Kingdom** that others also face discrimination, it was felt that this piece of legislation was not the place to deal with such issues: see **Chapter VII.4.3**.

strived for the improvement in the situation of different-sex couples who choose not to get married.[33] One of the core or principle aims of all these jurisdictions is the same: the protection and recognition of intimate, exclusive same-sex relationships. The fact that the institutions in **Belgium**, **France** and **The Netherlands** are also open to couples of different-sex does not detract from the aforementioned common objective. This ancillary aim simply enlarges the extent or scope of the institution itself rather than changing its fundamental character.[34]

The second area of difference arises in relation to residency requirements. It is here that possibly the greatest diversity of solution is proffered. Nonetheless, two different approaches can be identified. In the first group of countries, namely **The Netherlands** and the **United Kingdom**, the residency requirements imposed on prospective registered partners are identical to those imposed on couples wishing to marry, with internal consistency accordingly having been achieved.[35] In **France**, **Belgium** and **Switzerland**, on the other hand, the residency requirements imposed on those wishing to register a non-marital relationship are less flexible than the equivalent rules for marriage.[36] However, the rules in these three countries cannot be analysed in isolation and the relevant choice of law rules with respect to the registration of a relationship must be taken into consideration when analysing this material.[37]

The differences in the rules in this field can thus be explained with reference to the relatively flexible residency requirements imposed on aspirant married couples, coupled with the *lex loci registrationis* principle adopted with respect to the choice of law rules regarding the establishment of a non-marital registered relationship.[38] It was believed that these two factors combined would have led to a so-called phenomenon of "registration tourism". Accordingly, the residency requirements imposed on those wishing to register their relationship are more stringent than the equivalent rules on marriage. The fear of opening Pandora's box was sufficient to prevent these countries from emulating the marital residency requirements for non-marital registered relationships. Moreover, and perhaps indicative

---

33 **Chapters III.3.3**, **III.4.3**, **IV.3.7** and **V.3.2**.

34 This is explained in greater detail in **Section VIII.2.4**.

35 **Chapters V.4.5** and **VII.4.5**.

36 See **Chapters III.4.5**, **IV.4.5** and **VI.4.5**.

37 See **Chapter X.2**.

38 For further explanation of this rule in relation to non-marital registered relationships see **Chapter X.2.2.2** and the associated evaluation in **Chapter X.2.2.3**.

of a future trend, whilst **The Netherlands** currently adheres to a principle of internal consistency with respect to residency requirements, this was not the case prior to 2001, when more stringent requirements were imposed on partnership registration than on marriage. Once again, a fear of "registration tourism" played an enormous role in the eventual adoption of such a solution.[39]

Although not strictly related to the eligibility conditions required of registered partners, the issue of formal validity also deserves attention here. No single jurisdiction has provided an identical registration system for marriage and non-marital registered relationships. Despite this diversity, in the majority of jurisdictions the authority competent to register such relationships is also competent to celebrate marriages.[40] In the **United Kingdom**, where religious marriages are legally enforceable, an exception has been made restricting registration of civil partnerships to non-religious premises.[41] In contrast, although religious marriages are prohibited in **The Netherlands** prior to the celebration of a civil marriage, no such prohibition exists for the celebration of religious registered partnerships. Nonetheless, a religious registered partnership has no legal effect.[42] The contractual nature of the **French** PACS and the political compromises made during the parliamentary discussions have resulted in a quasi-contractual formality procedure with regards the registration thereof. Although the original PACS proposal conferred competency on the *maire*, this was eventually amended and competency is now conferred on the district court clerk. **France** therefore breaks from the approach of the other six jurisdictions by conferring registration competency on a different authority than that competent to celebrate marriages.

It is also striking that despite the various differences in result, all seven jurisdictions have departed from the law on marriage in one important aspect. In all jurisdictions a marriage is celebrated upon the parties' exchange of vows. In contrast, a non-marital registered relationship is validly concluded upon the registration of the parties' intent.[43] This difference in form has important consequences not just symbolically and

39 *Dutch Second Chamber*, 1993-1994, 23761, No. 3, p. 4 and 5. See also **Chapter V.4.5**.

40 See **Chapters III.4.8**, **V.4.8**, **VI.4.8**, **VII.4.8.1**, **VII.4.8.2** and **VII.4.8.3**.

41 **Chapter VII.4.8**.

42 **Chapter V.4.8**.

43 This is not, however, the case in **Denmark**, **Norway**, **Sweden** and **Iceland** where the exchange of vows is also sufficient for the registration of a partnership: JÄNTERÄ-JAREBORG/SÖRGJERD (2005) p. 585-587.

linguistically,[44] but also legally. The registration of marriages, although necessary to verify the existence of a marriage, is not determinative in assessing the moment at which the marriage is concluded. This is perhaps the most indicative example of the discernible trend away from status and towards contract in the field of familial relationships.[45]

VIII.2.4 OVERALL COMPARISON AND EVALUATION

It is submitted that despite the superficial diversity of domestic forms of non-marital registered relationships, a common core is evident. A fundamentally similar approach has been adopted in all seven countries. Generally speaking, in four of the six eligibility criteria surveyed, jurisdictions have achieved internal consistency between those wishing to marry and those wishing to register their non-marital relationship. As has been shown, this is true of those requirements other than the parties' sex and their residency. Before each of these areas is addressed, a number of other points stemming from the four general, internally consistent eligibility criteria deserve special attention.

Firstly, the approach adopted in **Belgium** and **France** in relation to age requirements is disappointing and serves only to reveal the inconsistent manner with which these Governments have addressed the issue of relationship registration. The paternalistic manner with which both Governments have dealt with the issue has simply replaced one form of discrimination with another. There is, in this author's opinion, no defensible explanation for the continued inconsistency between the law on non-marital registered relationships and the law on marriage in this respect. The imposition of an age requirement indicates the Governments' intention that this form of relationship is to be undertaken seriously and with commitment by adults. Yet the absence of the exceptions offered in the case

44 One 'celebrates' (*célébrer/ voltrekken*) a marriage whereas one 'registers' (*enregistrer/ registeren*) a non-marital relationship. In **French** an entirely new verb has been created to cater for the entry into the national form of non-marital registered, namely *pacser*. It could perhaps be submitted that this distinction has an important socio-linguistic impact on the manner in which persons view non-marital relationship registration; if the legislature has seen a need to use different terminology then there must necessarily be a difference in function. This differences was also noted in the Parliamentary debates in the **United Kingdom**: *British House of Commons*, 2004-2005, Vol. 425, Col. 184 (12th October 2004): "The difference is made clear in the drafting of the Bill. Registration is given effect by the signing of the register rather than by the verbal affirmation".

45 See **Chapter IX.3.1** and **IX.3.2**.

of marriage contradicts the stated willingness to respect non-marital relationships[46] and reduce the incidence of homophobia.[47]

The absence of a uniform, sex-neutral minimum marital age serves to highlight the dominant and persistent sex discrimination and stereotypical attitudes pervasive in the field of **French** family law. The lack of convincing arguments to treat marriage and non-marital registered relationships differently is the best argument to treat them equally. The time is now ripe for the **French** legislature to closely examine the discrimination in this field and achieve a solution equal to all.[48] It is indefensible to maintain a discriminatory age at which one can marry based on one's sex. The removal of such discrimination must then be coupled with a review of the age restrictions imposed on those wishing to register a PACS.

Similar questions can also be asked of the **Belgian** legislature. If the **Belgian** legislature believes there to be instances where a minor may marry, why is the same option denied to those wishing to register their relationship? If it is the belief of both the **Belgian** and **French** Governments that marriages may be celebrated between couples under the age of eighteen, there is absolutely no reason to deny the same option to those couples opting to register a non-marital relationship under similar circumstances.[49]

Secondly, although the **Belgian** legislature apparently identified similarities between couples consisting of relatives and couples in intimate relationships,[50] it is submitted that such a result is to be avoided.[51] The close ties between forms of non-marital registered relationship and marriage negate the possibility for such "familial relationships" to be dealt with in this same manner. The societal repugnance associated with incestuous

---

46 *E.g. Belgian Chamber*, 1995-1996, No. 170/8, p. 3.

47 See **Chapter IX**.

48 Such an approach has also been favoured by the COMMITTEE ON THE ELIMINATION OF ALL FORMS OF DISCRIMINATION AGAINST WOMEN, *Report of the Committee on the Elimination of Discrimination against Women, Twenty-Eighth Session (13th-31st January 2003) and Twenty-Ninth Session (30th June – 18th July 2003)*, New York: United Nations, 2003, Report A/58/38, p. 120-121, §267-268. As the law currently stands, **French** law contravenes both Art. 1, United Nations Convention on the Rights of the Child (CRC) and Art. 16(2), United Nations Convention on the Elimination of All Forms of Discrimination Against Women (CEDAW).

49 In **Belgium** the majority of cases concern teenagers under the age of eighteen with a pregnant girl: SENAEVE (2003c) p. 33, §1517.

50 The phrase "intimate relationships" refers here to both marriages and non-marital registered relationships.

51 See, for example, *Belgian Chamber*, 1995-1996, No. 170/8, p. 18 (MEULDERS).

relationships is, in this author's opinion, a sufficient reason to restrict entry into such relationship-based institutions to those outside the relevant prohibited degrees of relationship.[52] Although the problems faced by such groups may be very similar, institutional relationship frameworks should be restricted to those outside of domestically determined exogamous groups.

Thirdly, if countries are sincere about respecting the rights of same-sex couples, removing the discrimination faced by such couples and attempting to reduce the incidence of homophobia, such laudable aims should be followed through in the field of annulment. Instead of basing the annulment laws on the principles of contractual obligations, one should respect the equivalent principle of *favor matrimonii*, namely *favor registrationis*,[53] and base such laws on the equivalent marital rules. If these laws are considered old-fashioned, inappropriate or unexploited,[54] then these rules should be amended instead of creating a two-tier system, which further institutionalises discrimination. It could be counter-argued that the non-marital registered relationships schemes established in **Belgium** and **France** are indeed aimed at creating a contractual relationship between the parties.[55] Nevertheless, the relationship itself cannot be forgotten; the emotional union between the parties to such a contract justifies the imposition of the *sui generis* contractual status afforded to marriage, and thus correspondingly the respective annulment laws applicable to marriage. After all, the very function of the contract relates to the protection of the relationship itself, thus forming an integral component of the contract, rather than fulfilling a mere incidental or ancillary role.

Finally, one must address the fundamental distinctions in the two areas (residency and sex) where neither external nor a common core of internal consistency was found. As has already been explained, the residency requirements imposed on aspirant registered partners and spouses cannot be analysed in isolation. One must take into account that more stringent residency requirements are a reactionary response to a private international law rule referring to the *lex loci registrationis* in matters of relationship

---

52 See, for example, the ample wealth of anthropological studies on this topic, including: L. DEMAUSE, "The universality of incest", (1991) *Journal of Psychohistory*, Vol. 19.2, p. 1. J.L. PEACOCK and A.T. KIRSCH, *The human direction: An evolutionary approach to social and cultural anthropology*, 1970, New York: Appleton-Century-Crofts, p. 100.

53 See further **Chapter X.2.2.3**.

54 In **England & Wales**, for example, only 197 decrees of nullity were granted in 2002 compared to 147,538 divorces in the same year (equivalent to approximately 0.1% of all judicial marriage dissolutions).

55 *E.g. Belgian Chamber*, 1995-1996, No. 170/8, p. 1 (MOUREAUX).

validity.[56] The avoidance of registration tourism has been used in four countries to justify the imposition of more stringent residency requirements.[57] This argument was not, however, used in the **United Kingdom**. In order to explain this peculiarity, one must address a number of issues. The **United Kingdom** was relatively late, by Western European standards, to introduce a form of non-marital registered relationship. The argument that couples might travel to the **United Kingdom** in order to register their relationship was therefore no longer credible. Furthermore, unlike the other countries studied in this research, **Scotland** and **Northern Ireland** impose absolutely no residency requirements on those wishing to marry.[58] Even in **England & Wales** where seven days residency is required,[59] this amounts to a mere formality. Accordingly, even with respect to marriage, the **United Kingdom** adopts a much more liberal attitude with respect to residency than that embraced by the other four jurisdictions. For these reasons, it was believed better to parallel the rules on marriage than to impose stricter residency rules on registered partners.

In moving to the restrictions imposed on the parties' sex, it is suggested that all of the non-marital registered relationship schemes studied in this book perform a similar function in providing two persons an institutional framework in which to register their intimate, personal, exclusive relationship, resulting in the attribution of a number of rights, duties, obligations and responsibilities.[60] The fact that this framework has, in some countries also been extended to different-sex couples who do not wish to marry,[61] whilst in others restricted to same-sex couples, does not detract from this commonality in function. Provided that the variety of institutions studied fulfil a common purpose and their function is comparable, such institutions should be clustered under the same heading. Such an approach is not novel in the field of family law, having already been employed in the field of adoption.[62]

---

56 Despite the absence of such a rule in **French** law, it would appear that such a rule has been applied in practice. See **Chapter X.2.2.3 (footnote 130)**.

57 **Belgium**, **France**, **The Netherlands** and **Switzerland**.

58 **Chapters VII.4.5.2** and **VII.4.5.3**.

59 **Chapter VII.4.5.1**.

60 See **Chapters III.3.3**, **IV.3.7**, **V.3.3**, **VI.3.5** and **VII.3.5**.

61 As well as in the case of **Belgium** to couples who cannot marry: See **Chapter III.4.6**.

62 This was in fact highlighted during the Belgian parliamentary discussions: *Belgian Chamber*, 1995-1996, No. 170/1, p. 1.

Although forms of adoption, namely *adrogatio*[63] and *adoptio*,[64] were available in Roman law,[65] adoption was unavailable under the common law and in many civil law systems until rather recently.[66] The scarcity of adoption has, however, been upturned, with adoption now an almost universally acknowledged concept.[67] However, universality in concept does not translate into universality in procedural form or effects.[68] Although access to adoption was restricted to married couples in many jurisdictions,[69] many countries have recently opened adoption procedures to different-sex cohabiting couples and individuals,[70] as well as, although to a lesser extent, same-sex couples.[71] The question therefore arises whether these alterations to the restrictions on who is allowed to adopt have fundamentally changed the functions which adoption seeks to perform. The answer is that they have not. One must distinguish between the purposes of adoption and the inherent restrictions imposed upon aspirant adopters.

---

63 *Gai institutiones* 1.99-107 and later *Digesta Iustiniani* 1.7.2 (preamble). This was originally the adoption of a *sui iuris* male. This form of adoption thus involved the termination of a Roman family; the ending of a *pater familias*. BORKOWSKI (1994) p. 136-137, KASER/DANNENBRING (1993) p. 310, §60.III.2(a).

64 *Codex Iustinianius* 8.47.10, *Institutiones Iustiniani* 1.11.2 and *Digesta Iustiniani* 1.7.37 (preamble). See further, BORKOWSKI (1994) p. 135-138, KASER/DANNENBRING (1993) p. 311-312, §60.III.3.

65 Under JUSTINIAN'S rule, the procedure in *adoptio* was simplified. Instead of the old *mancipatio* form, he required a declaration, entered on the records of the competent official. He also restricted the full effects of *adoptio* to adoption of a descendant, *adoptio plena* (full adoption). In all others cases, *adoptio minus plena* (less than full adoption), the effects were considerably weaker. *Codex Iustinianius* 8.47.10.1a-g. See further BORKOWSKI (1994) p. 138, KASER/DANNENBRING (1993) p. 312, §60.III.3(b). See further **Section VIII.4.3** and VON BÓNÉ (2005).

66 KRAUSE (1976) p. 12. The **Scandinavian** nations and **Russia** on the other hand, appear to have received this Roman tradition with open arms: PERMANENT BUREAU OF THE HAGUE CONFERENCE, *Proceedings of the Seventeenth Session of The Hague Conference. Volume II*, The Hague, 1994, p. 27, §31.

67 Note however the exception of Islamic countries who do not currently allow for adoption: PERMANENT BUREAU OF THE HAGUE CONFERENCE, *Proceedings of the Seventeenth Session of The Hague Conference. Volume II*, The Hague, 1994, p. 25-26.

68 The analogy to the diverse legal effects created as a result of adoption see **Section VIII.4.3**.

69 See, for example, **Belg.**: Art. 343(1), Belg. CC prior to the Act of 24th April 2003; **Fr.**: Art. 343, Fr. CC prior to Act of 22nd December 1976, No. 76-1179; **Neth.**: Art. 227(1), Neth. CC prior to Act of 24th December 1997, *Neth. Staatsblad* 1997, No. 772; **Swit.**: Art. 264a, Sw. CC prior to Act of 30th June 1972; **Eng. and N.Ire., UK**: Law prior to the Adoption Act 1976; **Scot., UK**: Law prior to the Adoption (Scotland) Act 1978.

70 PERMANENT BUREAU OF THE HAGUE CONFERENCE, *Proceedings of the Seventeenth Session of The Hague Conference. Volume II*, The Hague, 1994, p. 59, §99.

71 See **Chapters III.5.9.3**, **IV.5.9.3**, **V.5.9.3**, **VI.5.9.3** and **VII.5.9.3**.

In deliberating the function of adoption, one unearths perceptible differences in approach. Today, although adoption has come to be viewed as a device to place parentless children with parents and vice versa,[72] this has been achieved in remarkably varied ways. In some jurisdictions adoption is viewed as a contract between the parties,[73] whilst in other States adoption is regarded as a purely governmental act.[74] Although at first sight this conspicuous disparity appears crucial, these differences are less decisive than they first appear. As KRAUSE indicates, the practical difference is simply one of emphasis.[75] He notes that in those systems that regard adoption as a governmental act, such systems cannot avoid the fact that in order for an adoption to occur, the consent of all the parties is needed. In those systems, on the other hand, where adoption is treated as a contract, a court is usually involved in a supervisory capacity.[76] In a broad, non-legal sense adoption may thus be defined as,

> The institutionalised social practice through which a person, belonging by birth to one family or kinship group, acquires new family or kinship ties that are socially defined as equivalent to biological ties and which supersede the old ones, either wholly or in part.[77]

If an institution as varied as adoption can thus find common legislative answers in the form of international treaties based on assumed common functional bases,[78] can the same be accomplished in relation to non-marital registered relationships? Can a common function be attributed to or found to be evident in the various forms of non-marital registered relationship schemes studied? Although it is clear that two distinct approaches have been taken, the principle aim is similar. Variance in the precise ambit of this purpose necessarily dictates variety in the restrictions on who may register with whom. However, variance does not necessarily come at the cost of incompatibility.

In attempting to determine the existence of a common function, one must also address the differences between the motives behind opening

---

72 CRETNEY *et al.* (2003a) p. 792, §23-001.

73 PERMANENT BUREAU OF THE HAGUE CONFERENCE, *Proceedings of the Seventeenth Session of The Hague Conference. Volume II*, 1994, p. 57, §92. KRAUSE (1976) p. 75, §155

74 Regardless of whether this be an administrative or judicial act. KRAUSE (1976) p. 73, §148.

75 KRAUSE (1976) p. 73, §149.

76 KRAUSE (1976) p. 73, §149.

77 PERMANENT BUREAU OF THE HAGUE CONFERENCE, *Proceedings of the Seventeenth Session of the Hague Conference. Volume II*, The Hague, 1994, p. 23.

78 *E.g.* the 1993 Hague AC.

relationship registration to couples of a different sex in **Belgium**, **France** and **The Netherlands**. In comparing these jurisdictions, ANTOKOLSKAIA argues that the aims of these jurisdictions should not be confused.[79] In **France** and **Belgium** the reasons for opening relationship registration to different-sex couples were very different than those postulated in **The Netherlands**. The **Dutch** Government wished to avoid the discrimination that would be created if registered partnership were restricted to same-sex couples. It was believed that if registered partnerships were so restricted it would in effect create a second-class marriage.[80] By opening registration to different-sex couples, the Government would ensure that such arguments could be avoided. In **France** and **Belgium**, on the other hand, the main reasons for opening registration to different-sex couples stemmed from the political impasse that would have been created if the Governments were perceived to be promoting same-sex relationships. As a result, a political compromise was struck and registration was open to both groups of couples. ANTOKOLSKAIA argues that these two approaches cannot be assimilated;[81] the function of relationship registration in these three countries for different-sex couples is based on different ideals.

It is submitted that although the reasons given are perhaps different, the essential aim of all three legislatures was the same. In **France**, **Belgium** and **The Netherlands** the Governments recognised two issues that needed resolution: the legal invisibility of same-sex couples and the problem of those different-sex couples who chose not to marry. In all three jurisdictions it was decided that these two aims could best be dealt with in the same piece of legislation. The political reasons for making this decision are indeed to some extent different. In **The Netherlands** the position adopted was reached from the principle of neutrality, whereas in **France** and **Belgium** the position was realised as the result of a political compromise. Yet in all three jurisdictions, although these reasons are different, the intentions were the same. It was the aim of reaching a political compromise and thus ensuring that same-sex couple registration was enacted, that eventually resulted in the opening up of registration to different-sex couples. The political compromise reached in **France** and **Belgium** has, of course, had serious implications on the rights and duties attributed to the institution; however, this does not detract from the underlying fundamental principle that all three jurisdictions saw the need

---

79 ANTOKOLSKAIA (2005) Chapter 4.4.

80 *Dutch Second Chamber*, 1995-1996, 23761, No. 7, p. 10.

81 ANTOKOLSKAIA (2005) Chapter 4.4.

to reach a compromise or chance the peril of the legislation being defeated in its entirety.

Returning to the question of functional comparability, one is supported in proposing the existence of a *tertium comparationis* if one examines the substantive law disparity in the field of marriage. One can hardly speak of an institution exemplified by an inherent and cohesive worldwide definition. The rules relating to marriage differ markedly between jurisdictions and yet a wide variety of marital notions are accepted as falling under a single umbrella term due to the existence of a common functional basis. Why should that be any different for non-marital registered relationships? Has the opening up of marriage to same-sex couples in **The Netherlands**, for example, caused a fundamental paradigm shift in the function, aims and nature of marriage under **Dutch** law? Of course not.

A number of issues must be clearly identified and dealt with independently. The topics of function and eligibility should remain clearly distinct from one another, as should the issues of comparability and compatibility with domestic, substantive law. Comparability deals with assessment and evaluation of whether domestic national institutions may be compared, whilst compatibility involves an in-depth investigation into the questions surrounding the recognition of non-marital relationships registered abroad. This latter question is evidently intricately associated with the notion of public policy and will be dealt with later.[82]

As already stated above, in attempting to answer the issues raised by comparability, one must espouse a functional analysis.[83] In doing so one must ask a series of separate yet interrelated questions. Firstly, do same-sex non-marital relationships registered in different countries fulfil a similar function? The answer to this question is obviously yes. The registration schemes in all seven jurisdictions attempt to provide same-sex couples with protection of their intimate personal relationships. The apparent existence of a *tertium comparationis* is undeniable.

Secondly, turning one's attention to the three jurisdictions where different-sex couples are permitted to register their relationships, is a distinction drawn between the function of the registration for different-sex couples and the function of the registration for same-sex couples? The answer to this

82 See **Chapter X.5.1**.

83 SCHWENZER (2003) p. 146-148.

question must be answered negatively. No distinction is drawn in **Belgium**, **France** or **The Netherlands** in terms of the function of the registration scheme dependent upon the sex of the parties registering. The reasons for the action taken may well be different, but the function of the registration is the same: to afford protection to intimate, personal relationships. If one takes these two basic tenets, *i.e.* that various national forms of same-sex non-marital registered relationships perform similar functions and that no distinction is drawn in those systems that have opened such registration schemes to different-sex couples, it is therefore logical to draw the conclusion that these registration schemes all perform a similar function. The common functional framework upon which one can analyse such laws is thus, it is submitted, broadly speaking: "Non-marital registered relationships aim at providing legal protection to the intimate, personal, exclusive relationship between two persons and result in the State attribution of a collection of rights, duties, obligations and responsibilities."

It is submitted that the proposition put forward in **Chapters** I and II for a putative *tertium comparationis* in this field has indeed been found to be present. Nonetheless, regardless of the existence of a *tertium comparationis*, the issue of sex cannot be ignored altogether. It is undeniable that the sex of the parties has played an important role in the eligibility criteria adopted in such legislation. Hence, and in bearing in mind the aforementioned distinction between eligibility criteria and functionality, it is possible to distinguish between two different approaches to the issues raised. At this stage it is also perhaps important to note that one must dissociate the rights and duties incumbent upon the parties to the relationship from the purpose of the registration scheme itself. Although these two are inherently and intrinsically connected, it is not true that they must necessarily be compared concurrently.[84]

As a result of all the aforementioned comparisons, two models can be distinguished. On the one hand, there is the PLURALISTIC MODEL, whereby couples irrespective of their gender are offered two possibilities, namely marriage or non-marital registered relationship. On the other hand, some countries have preferred the DUALISTIC MODEL, where couples are only provided with one institutionalised relationship form dependent on their sex: different-sex couples are able to marry, whilst same-sex couples are entitled to register their non-marital relationship. It must furthermore be

---

84 See, for example, the distinction drawn by KRAUSE (1976) p. 89, §184 with respect to adoption and the effects of adoption.

noted that countries adhering to the PLURALISTIC MODEL tend to attain the end phase of this model by virtue of a two-stage process, thereby necessitating the division of the PLURALISTIC MODEL into two time-periods. The first time-period involves opening non-marital registration to both different and same-sex couples, whilst leaving marriage legislation entirely intact and unaltered. Once this has been achieved, the arguments for opening civil marriage to same-sex couples are strengthened,[85] since the discrimination originally faced by same-sex couples, in not being able to marry, is simply replaced with a new form of discrimination; although different-sex couples are offered a choice of relationship forms, same-sex couples are not.[86] It is irrefutable that the option for different-sex couples to register their relationship along identical lines to same-sex couples in **The Netherlands** and **Belgium** played an important role in the pressure placed on these Governments to amend the laws prohibiting same-sex civil marriage.[87] Both these models can be represented diagrammatically.

THE PLURALISTIC MODEL

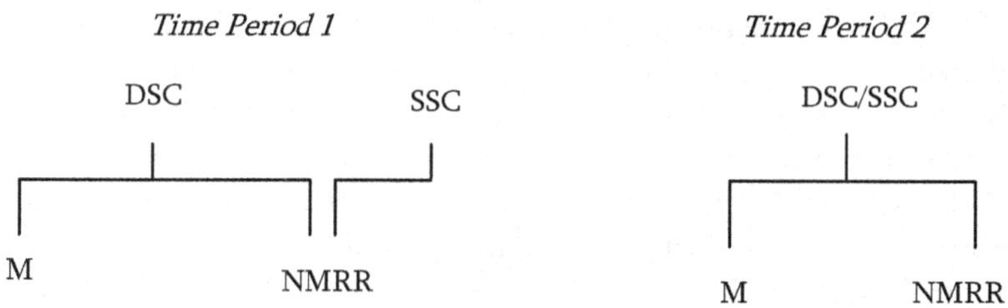

THE DUALISTIC MODEL

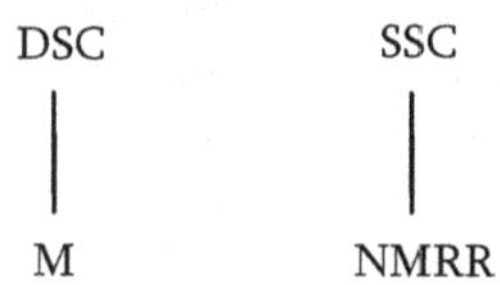

Key: **DSC**: *Different-Sex Couples*, **SSC**: *Same-Sex Couples*
M: *Marriage*, **NMRR**: *Non-Marital Registered Relationship*

---

85 See **Chapters III.3.5** and **V.3.3**.

86 See, for example, *Dutch Second Chamber*, 1995-1996, 23761, No. 7, p. 10.

87 It is, therefore, argued that over the course of time, **France** will gradually come to debate the issue of opening civil marriage to same-sex couples. This issue has in fact already been raised in the courts (See **Chapter IV.4.3**) as well as politically (MINISTRE DE LA JUSTICE (2004) p. 6).

In attempting to create a valued pluralistic system of family law[88] whereby couples are afforded choices dependent upon their needs rather than on the basis of their sex, one should support the eventual result achieved by the PLURALISTIC MODEL. By *time period 2* of this model, couples are offered two choices of institutionalised relationship forms regardless of their sex. The DUALISTIC MODEL, on the other hand, retains discrimination as its fundamental premise:[89] same-sex couples are entitled to register, whilst different-sex couples are entitled to marry. Although the legal effects incumbent upon the registration of a non-marital relationship and the celebration of a marriage may be negligible, one is reminded of the famous adage, "all animals are equal but some are more equal than others".[90] The symbolic significance of a distinction between two different institutions does, and always will, support a continued belief that the needs of same-sex and different-sex couples are fundamentally different and thus require different legislation. This proposition is already based on prejudicial fallacies. Legislatures should focus on the degree of commitment involved in the relationship, the function which institutionalised relationship legislation seeks to perform, as well as the presence of any children. On these bases, a functional pluralistic family law for the 21st century will gradually become a reality. Such a reality is in fact achieved by *time period 2* of the PLURALISTIC MODEL. The intrinsic discrimination faced by same-sex couples in the DUALISTIC MODEL is removed, and at the same time couples are offered a range of choices as to how to regulate their intimate, personal relationship. Discrimination could also be removed in the DUALISTIC MODEL by amalgamating the two institutions into one. This would lead to the creation of a third approach, the MONISTIC MODEL, whereby couples are offered one institutionalised relationship form (*i.e.* marriage) regardless of sex.[91] Although perhaps less favourable than the PLURALISTIC MODEL, in that couples are only provided with an all-or-nothing choice of institutionalised

---

88 During the twentieth century the term "valued pluralism" had almost become the buzz word in family law publications: see, for example, BAINHAM (1996); O'DONOVAN (2002); ESTIN (2004); SCHRAMA (2004) p. 572; SINCLAIR (2004).

89 Even if the differences are only to be found in the name given to the available institution.

90 GEORGE ORWELL, *Animal Farm,* Chapter X.

91 Outright adoption of the MONISTIC MODEL has, for example, been achieved in some common law States such as **Massachusetts, USA** and certain provinces in **Canada**. See **Appendix 4**.

relationship form,[92] it would remove the integral discriminatory basis upon which the DUALISTIC MODEL is based.[93]

THE MONISTIC MODEL

DSC/SSC

|

M

Key: **DSC**: *Different-Sex Couples*, **SSC**: *Same-Sex Couples*
M: *Marriage*, **NMRR**: *Non-Marital Registered Relationship*

The MONISTIC MODEL is also foreseeable in a country embracing the PLURALISTIC MODEL, if the options proffered are based on perceived choice rather than actual choice. In such a scenario, non-marital registered relationship would be abolished and couples would be left with only one choice of institutionalised relationship form (*i.e.* marriage). Although **The Netherlands** adheres to the PLURALISTIC MODEL, the choice offered to couples wishing to formally regulate, and thereby institutionalise, their relationship is in fact not a choice between different possibilities, but the same possibility with two different names.[94] Valued pluralism relates to the furnishing of genuine choices, not artificial alternatives. In this respect the distinction drawn in **Belgium** between a relatively weak form of non-marital registered relationship coupled with marriage open to both different-sex and same-sex couples, should be commended in its approach. Nonetheless, this does not detract from the numerous inadequacies inherent in the manner in which the **Belgian** legislation has been drafted. It is therefore clear that although all the seeds for a truly pluralistic, non-discriminatory model have been sown, there is, as yet, no single

---

92 Although in some jurisdictions this will not be an all-or-nothing choice, but instead an "all-or-not-quite-as-much" choice.

93 Such a shift from the dualistic model to the monistic model has already been signalled in **Sweden**, where calls for the abolition of registered partnership and the opening of marriage to same-sex couples have been heard: SWEDISH GOVERNMENTAL PRESS RELEASE, "Äktenskap eller partnerskap för homosexuella?", 27th January 2005, available at: http://www.regeringen.se/sb/d/5069/a/37931. See also SÖRGJERD (2005) p. 348. Such a shift has also been signalled in **Denmark**, LUND-ANDERSEN (2003) p. 23. For information on **Norway**, **Iceland** and **Finland** see JÄNTERÄ-JAREBORG/SÖRGJERD (2004) p. 587. As a result of the federal same-sex marriage legislation enacted in **Canada**, this result has been achieved in **Alberta**, **North Western Territories** and **Nunavut**. This is also true in 6 of the 17 regions in **Spain** and **Massachusetts, United States of America**. See further **Appendix 4**.

94 This has already been called for by SCHRAMA (2004) p. 566. See also **Section VIII.3.3**.

representative country able to claim to have reaped the full harvest of benefits.

VIII.3 DISSOLUTION

Obviously when creating new forms of registered relationships, the respective legislatures have also had to deal with issues relating to their possible dissolution. The information provided in **Section 6** of **Chapters III-VII** leads one to two conclusions. Firstly, it is questionable, but perhaps nonetheless arguable, that superficial external consistency exists in the dissolution procedures currently in operation (**Section VIII.3.1**). Secondly, two distinct dissolution models should be distinguished. On the one hand, there are those countries where, as far as possible, dissolution procedures available to registered partners mirror those available to spouses wishing to terminate their marriage. Although slightly modified, the general grounds and procedural provisions for dissolution are the same for both categories of couples: *internal consistency* is thus achieved. Such an approach has been adopted in **Switzerland** and the **United Kingdom** (**Section VII.3.2**).

On the other hand, there are those countries where, in light of registration being open to couples of a different sex, a distinction has been drawn between marriage and non-marital registered relationships: *internal inconsistency* is thus the result. A salient feature of such dissolution procedures lies in their relative informality, either in the form of an administrative or unilateral procedure. This approach is evident in **Belgium**, **France** and **The Netherlands** (**Section VII.3.3**).

VIII.3.1 EXTERNAL CONSISTENCY

Since the death of either or both partners automatically brings a non-marital registered relationship or marriage to an end in all seven jurisdictions, internal and external consistency has been achieved in this domain.[95] This is, however, not a particularly surprising result. Any alternative is almost impossible to imagine and would have broken with a time immemorial principle that death ends a relationship. Although such external consistency evaporates when one turns one's attention to the law on presumed death, internal consistency has nevertheless been achieved in all jurisdictions with respect to these rules.[96]

---

95 **Chapters III.6.7**, **IV.6.7**, **V.6.7**, **VI.6.7** and **VII.6.7**.

96 **Chapters III.6.7**, **IV.6.7**, **V.6.7**, **VI.6.7** and **VII.6.7**.

In searching for general overarching principles common to all jurisdictions in the field of relationship dissolution, it is important to note the recent publication by the CEFL presenting the first Principles of European Family Law.[97] Ten general principles have been formulated in the field of divorce based on a comparative survey of twenty-two European jurisdictions.[98] The first three principles provide a general framework. It is submitted that all three could, to a certain extent, be applied to the dissolution of non-marital registered relationships as well.

Principle 1:1 states that the law should permit divorce and that no duration of the marriage should be required.[99] In transposing these principles to the field at hand, one is clearly able to identify support for such statements. All countries provide for a method to terminate non-marital registered relationships.[100] This is sometimes judicial, sometimes administrative, sometimes based on mutual consent and other times not. Regardless, all systems that have enacted forms of non-marital registered relationships have also provided methods for their possible dissolution. This is, however, hardly a surprising result. The secular nature of non-marital registered relationships has inevitably avoided the religious pitfalls that have been a source of demise for many attempts to enact divorce legislation.

Unanimity of result is, however, absent in relation to any independent requirement that the relationship has lasted for a particular length of time. **England & Wales** and **Northern Ireland** both impose independent time-bars on the application for such a dissolution order.[101] Furthermore, all three jurisdictions in the **United Kingdom** also impose a minimum period of separation if the dissolution is based on mutual consent.[102] However, the CEFL exposed a similar state of affairs with respect to divorce. Although only two of the twenty-two jurisdictions surveyed for the CEFL Principles imposed an independent time-bar on divorce proceedings,[103] more than two-thirds of jurisdictions imposed a minimum separation period on divorce

---

97 BOELE-WOELKI *et al.* (2004). The CEFL has also formulated Principles in the field of maintenance between former spouses.

98 BOELE-WOELKI/BRAAT/SUMNER (2003a).

99 BOELE-WOELKI *et al.* (2004) p. 17.

100 **Chapters III.6**, **IV.6**, **V.6**, **VI.6** and **VII.6**.

101 See **Chapter VII.6.1**.

102 Namely two years: see **Chapter VII.6.2**.

103 **England & Wales** (BOELE-WOELKI/BRAAT/SUMNER (2003a) p. 197-198) and **Ireland** (BOELE-WOELKI/BRAAT/SUMNER (2003a) p. 198-199).

proceedings by mutual consent.[104] The absence of a common core has not, however, prevented the CEFL in reaching the conclusion laid down in Principle 1:1(2). The *dédramatisation* of the divorce procedure is highlighted as the foremost reason for removing all hindrances to obtaining a divorce.[105] It could be argued that such an aim should also be followed through in the field of non-marital registered relationship dissolution.

Turning one's attention to Principle 1:2, namely the divorce procedure and competent authority, one is also able to discern a veritably similar approach.[106] Although the dissolution of a non-marital registered relationship is regulated by law in all those countries surveyed,[107] in only three countries is a legal procedure the only means available.[108] Special mention must be made of the situation in **Belgium** and **France** where the celebration of a marriage also acts to dissolve any existing non-marital registered relationship.[109] In **France**, a legal procedure must, however, be followed before the marriage takes place. The party wishing to marry is obliged to send notice of his or her decision to the other by means of a bailiff's summons, a true copy of which must also be sent to the clerk of the district court who received the original PACS document.[110] The PACS is then deemed to have come to an immediate end by operation of law on the date on which the marriage was celebrated.[111] Nevertheless, failure to satisfy the legal procedure prior to celebrating the marriage does not effect the termination of the PACS. Such a legal procedure is, however, not necessary in **Belgium** and the celebration of a marriage is enough to bring a statutory cohabitation to an immediate and automatic end.[112]

It would therefore appear that in both these countries, it is not only a legal procedure that can terminate a non-marital registered relationship but also a legal act. Nevertheless, the wording of Principle 1:2(1) is such that this distinction can be accommodated.[113] Since Principle 1:2(1) emphasises the

---

104 Only **Finland**, **The Netherlands**, **Poland**, **Portugal**, **Russia**, **Sweden** and **Switzerland** do not impose any time periods in the case of divorce by mutual consent: see BOELE-WOELKI *et al.* (2004) p. 18.

105 BOELE-WOELKI *et al.* (2004) p. 19.

106 BOELE-WOELKI *et al.* (2004) p. 20.

107 **Chapters III.6**, **IV.6**, **V.6**, **VI.6** and **VII.6**.

108 **Chapters V.6**, **VI.6** and **VII.6**.

109 **Chapters III.6** and **IV.6**.

110 Art. 515(7)(3), Fr. CC.

111 Art. 515(7)(7)(3), Fr. CC.

112 Art. 1476(2)(1), Belg. CC.

113 Principle 1:2(1) is worded so as to cover both legal procedures and legal acts: "divorce procedure should be determined by law".

secular nature of the divorce procedure, which is indeed mirrored in procedures available to registered partners,[114] it is submitted that whether the dissolution occurs by means of a legal procedure or legal act is irrelevant.

In two jurisdictions, namely the **United Kingdom** and **Switzerland**, only judicial authorities are competent to proceed with dissolution procedures.[115] Although in **France** the declaration to terminate one's relationship must be registered with a judicial authority, the procedure itself is administrative in nature (*i.e.* lacking judicial scrutiny).[116] In **Belgium** competency rests with an administrative authority,[117] although there may indeed be no authority as such involved in the termination procedure (*i.e.* if the non-marital registered relationship is terminated by means of a subsequent marriage).[118] In contrast, in **The Netherlands** competent authority depends on the legal procedure used to terminate the relationship.[119] If the dissolution is jointly requested, the parties are obliged to terminate their registered partnership administratively (either by means of an administrative dissolution or conversion into a marriage), whilst judicial dissolution is only permitted via a unilateral dissolution request.

It is hence possible to conclude that from the comparative overview concerning the dissolution of non-marital registered relationships, the *ratione materiae* of Principle 1:2 could be extended to include non-marital registered relationships. Although the rationale exemplified by Principle 1:2(2) is reflected in the dissolution procedures available for these new institutional relationship forms, the phraseology is not entirely consistent with the manner in which non-marital registered relationships may be terminated.

With respect to Principle 1:3 one is also able to identify a perceptible common core of opinion.[120] All seven jurisdictions permit the dissolution of a non-marital registered relationship either on the basis of mutual consent or without the consent of one of the parties. The internal differences as to how this result is achieved necessitate at this juncture a departure from the

---

114 BOELE-WOELKI *et al.* (2004) p. 23.
115 **Chapters VI.6.2**, **VI.6.3**, **VII.6.2** and **VII.6.3**.
116 **Chapter IV.6.3** and **IV.6.4**.
117 **Chapter III.6.3** and **III.6.4**.
118 **Chapter III.6.8**.
119 **Chapter V.6.3**, **V.6.4** and **V.6.8**.
120 Principle 1:3 states that "the law should permit both divorce by mutual consent and divorce without the consent of one of the spouses": BOELE-WOELKI *et al.* (2004) p. 24.

structure of the Principles and a return to the structure espoused in **Section VIII.2**, namely between those countries having sought internal consistency and those who have not.

VIII.3.2 EXTERNAL INCONSISTENCY BUT INTERNAL CONSISTENCY

In both **Switzerland** and the **United Kingdom**, the legislature has decided to preserve the judicial mechanisms for dissolving non-marital registered relationships. Accordingly, no administrative form of dissolution is provided for in either country.[121] In retaining the judicial monopoly on relationship dissolution, both countries have, as far possible, attempted to create a corresponding procedure for non-marital registered relationship breakdown to that already applicable in cases of marital breakdown. Although a number of minor differences are apparent, this is often attributable to an attempt to achieve internal legislative consistency within the non-marital registered relationship legislation. For example, although adultery is not an explicit ground for the dissolution of a civil partnership in any of the three jurisdictions of the **United Kingdom**, as is the case for marriage, couples wishing to use adultery as a ground to dissolve their relationship will be able to file for dissolution of the relationship based on unreasonable behaviour.[122] The reason for the absence of such a ground can be traced to the Government's unwillingness to alter the common law definition of adultery, a position adopted throughout the CPA 2004.[123]

In **Switzerland**, despite the absence of a two-track joint dissolution petition procedure for registered partners,[124] the Sw. RPA does provide for both termination by mutual consent, as well as termination without the consent of one of the parties.[125] In justifying the absence of an equivalent distinction for registered partners as that made in Arts. 111 and 112, Sw. CC, the **Swiss** Ministry of Justice pointed to the simplification of the dissolution system due to the absence of children. Despite the characteristic of a two-track joint petition procedure for spouses, the absence of such a choice for registered partners is not of fundamental importance. The difference between the divorce procedures in Art. 111 and Art. 112, Sw. CC is

121 **Chapter VI.6.4**, **VI.6.5**, **VII.6.4** and **VII.6.5**.

122 See **Chapter VII.6.3.1**.

123 WOMEN AND EQUALITY UNIT (2003b) p. 36.

124 Unlike marriage were two possible grounds exist: Art. 111, Sw. CC (agreement as to all consequences) and Art. 112, Sw. CC (only partial agreement or lack of agreement as to consequences).

125 **Chapters VI.6.2** and **VI.6.3**.

restricted to procedural law. However, the absence of a reflection period for the termination of a registered partnership, as is provided for in Art. 111, Sw. CC indicates the haphazard manner in which the **Swiss** legislature has fused these two procedures into one.

All the same, the **Swiss** legislature has provided for a two-track system for relationship dissolution. On the one hand, a joint petition procedure is available if the parties are in agreement as to the need to terminate the relationship. On the other, a unilateral dissolution procedure is available if such a basic consensus is absent. Despite this superficial coherence, numerous minor differences are perceptible. For example, a unilateral request for divorce must be supplemented by proof that the parties have been separated for two years, whereas this separation period is fixed at one year for registered partners.[126] The reasons for these differences stem from the absence of constitutional protection afforded to the institution of registered partnership, the lack of children and the overriding desire to respect the will of the parties.[127] As a result, the dissolution procedure for registered partnership symbolises the political compromise achieved between adhering to the dissolution framework for marriage and the desire to achieve more procedural flexibility. The overall result is that of a dissolution system based entirely on that applicable to spouses with minor procedural alterations.[128] No new grounds for the dissolution of a non-marital registered relationship have been created and the same authorities competent to dissolve a marriage are also equally monopolistic in their competency to terminate non-marital registered relationships.

In both **Switzerland** and the **United Kingdom**, the legislature was thus very keen to ensure that parties embarked upon the registration of their relationship with commitment, sincerity and acknowledgment of the gravity of the undertaking. This was thus signalled, not only in the formalities that must be completed prior to registering a relationship, but also in relation to the procedures for terminating such relationships.

VIII.3.3 INTERNAL AND EXTERNAL INCONSISTENCY

This approach has not, however, been followed in **The Netherlands**, **Belgium** and **France**. In all these three countries, distinctive procedures have been created enabling couples to dissolve their non-marital registered

126 Art. 30, Sw. RPA.

127 FF 2003, p. 1192 at 1227-1228.

128 FF 2003, p. 1192 at 1228.

relationships on grounds not available to spouses wishing to divorce or via authorities not competent to grant a divorce. In opening registration to couples of a different sex, the Governments in all three jurisdictions have attempted to draw a clear line between marriage, on the one hand, and the less traditional form of registration on the other, and in so doing have contrived new dissolution procedures.

In contrast to the administrative methods available for terminating non-marital registered relationships in these three jurisdictions,[129] marriages can only be terminated on the basis of a judicial procedure.[130] This statement must, however, be read with caution with respect to **The Netherlands**, where a marriage may in fact be terminated administratively by means of the two step lightning divorce procedure.[131] Nevertheless, this procedure is extremely controversial and forms one of the focal points of two proposals currently before the Second Chamber of the **Dutch** Parliament. Both proposals aim to remove the possibility offered to married couples to convert their marriage into a registered partnership.[132] Furthermore, the LUCHTENVELD proposal aims to introduce a form of administrative divorce, whilst the DONNER proposal aspires to maintain the judicial monopoly on divorce proceedings. If the LUCHTENVELD proposal is indeed accepted, this would in effect remove any real distinction between the dissolution procedure open to spouses and registered partners.[133] This will, once again, no doubt raise questions as to the necessity and utility of maintaining the institution of registered partnership.[134]

Nonetheless, regardless of the current proposals in **The Netherlands**, registered partners wishing to terminate their registered partnership are provided with a judicial alternative. If the parties are unable to agree upon the need to terminate their partnership, **Dutch** law adopts a protective stance in providing resort to a judicial mechanism. Even if the parties opt for an administrative procedure, the weaker party is afforded protection by ensuring that the declaration to terminate their relationship is signed by one or more lawyers or notaries.[135] The involvement of a legal professional

---

129 See **Chapters III.6.4**, **III.6.5**, **III.6.8**, **IV.6.4**, **IV.6.5**, **IV.6.8**, **V.6.4** and **V.6.8**.

130 **Chapters III.6.1**, **IV.6.1** and **V.6.1**.

131 Art. 1:77a, in combination with 1:80c(c) and 1:80d, Neth. CC and further **Chapter V.6.8**.

132 *Dutch Second Chamber*, 2004-2005, 29676, No. 2, Art. I.B, p. 2 (LUCHTENVELD) and *Dutch Second Chamber*, 2004-2005, 30145, No. 2, Art. I.B, p. 1 (DONNER).

133 As a result internal consistency will have been achieved, although this will have been realised by amending the law on divorce.

134 See, for example, SCHRAMA (2004) p. 566.

135 See **Chapter V.6.4.2**.

attempts at ensuring the fairness of any agreements reached by the parties, whilst guaranteeing that respect is bestowed on the principle of party autonomy.

In **France** and **Belgium**, on the other hand, less protective measures have been adopted. The dissolution procedures available to couples involved in a non-marital registered relationship are totally devoid of judicial involvement. Instead the dissolution of a relationship takes place administratively, by means of a joint or unilateral declaration. If the parties disagree as to the need to terminate their relationship, either party may unilaterally and administratively terminate their relationship. In securing observance of the principle of party autonomy, both these jurisdictions have done so at the cost of the protection offered to the weaker party. This last method has been heavily criticised since it affords the weaker party absolutely no protection; formerly the traditional argument supporting the State's involvement in the divorce procedure. Hence, although **Belgium**, **France** and **The Netherlands** have all opted for a solution very different to that currently offered to married couples, these jurisdictions have not all approached such options in the same manner. Two different approaches must therefore be distinguished: protective dissolution (**The Netherlands**) and non-protective dissolution (**Belgium** and **France**).

The reason for this rudimentary distinction can be traced to the origins of the legislation. In enacting legislation creating a form of registered partnership, the **Dutch** Government initially believed that those different-sex couples opting for registered partnership would be childless, since the only differences between the legal effects of a registered partnership and marriage were in the field of child law.[136] The Government therefore argued that in the absence of any dependent children, a registered partnership should be able to be terminated at the will of the parties, as long as a number of specific points had been addressed and agreed upon.[137] In **France** and **Belgium**, on the other hand, the procedural differences were rooted in the contractual basis upon which the political compromises enacting the PACS and statutory cohabitation legislation were founded. In adhering to general principles of contractual freedom and party autonomy, the parties

---

136 *Dutch Second Chamber*, 1995-1996, 23761, No. 7, p. 10. See **Chapter V.5.9** and SCHERF (1998) p. 20 where it is shown that this conjecture has perhaps not evolved in practice. In SCHERF'S study 30% of the 151 interviewees were reported to have children whether from the relationship itself or a previous relationship.

137 These points are summarised in Art. 1:80d(1), Neth. CC. See further **Chapter V.6.4.1**.

to these registered relationship forms were provided with the opportunity to terminate their relationship at will.[138]

VIII.3.4 OVERALL COMPARISON AND EVALUATION

At first glance these results may appear surprising, yet it is submitted that the existence of two different approaches to dissolution is a logical consequence of the abovementioned differences concerning the establishment of non-marital registered relationships.[139] In both **Switzerland** and the **United Kingdom**, in creating a form of non-marital registered relationship restricted to same-sex couples, reference was made as far as possible to the institution of marriage, and thus accordingly the divorce procedure. The general position was that the rules should be the same, unless a reason existed for these rules to be different. With marriage as the foundation stone upon which to begin building, there appears to have been few reasons to depart from the existing divorce framework in creating a dissolution procedure for non-marital registered relationships. Whenever a difference is apparent between the two dissolution forms it appears to have been based either on principles of simplicity or inapplicability. Despite the almost contemporaneous review of divorce law in **Switzerland**, a dissolution procedure identical to divorce was not created. The Government's aim was to simplify the procedure based on the presumed absence of children. In the **United Kingdom**, the differences can be explained due to the heterosexual nature of some of the grounds for relationship dissolution.

It is, however, submitted that both of these reasons, although seemingly logical, are fundamentally flawed. Although this author is not in favour of adultery as a ground for the termination of a marriage, it is argued that if this ground is retained as a ground for divorce, then an equivalent ground should be created for the dissolution of a civil partnership. The absence of such a ground conveys an erroneous message to the general population. Sexual activity outside of the marital bond is not permitted, whereas such behaviour is ostensibly acceptable in a civil partnership. If the **British** Government believes that such behaviour can be subsumed under the ground "unreasonable behaviour" why has this not been done with respect to marriage? The singling out of adultery as a specific ground for divorce indicates the **British** Government's moral stance with respect to extra-marital sexual activity; a stance obviously not evident with respect to civil

[138] See **Chapters III.6.5** and **IV.6.5**.

[139] See **Chapter VIII.2.4**.

partnerships. It is submitted that the **British** Government should eradicate this discrepancy by removing adultery as a ground for divorce, thereby extending the ambit of the ground of unreasonable behaviour. Although perhaps technical in nature, the bearing on social norms and values is important.

In **Belgium**, **France** and **The Netherlands**, on the other hand, where these new forms of relationship recognition were opened to different-sex couples, the legislature attempted to draw a distinction between marriage and the new form of non-marital registered relationship. The inherent choice that this political compromise offered to different-sex couples had important and far-reaching effects vis-à-vis the dissolution of such a relationship. The legislature was confronted with a conundrum: if the legislation creates an identical dissolution procedure to divorce, the question will be readily posed: why open civil partnership to different-sex couples? The ultimate solutions to this thorny problem are as diverse as the justifications used to defend the differences.

In **The Netherlands**, the Government alleged that different-sex couples opting for registered partnership would typically be childless.[140] Furthermore, it was believed that the prohibition on same-sex adoption coupled with the impossibility of establishing parentage with both parties in a same-sex couple meant the children in such relationships would not constitute an element of dispute in any potential dissolution proceedings. The perceived absence of children in the case of registered partnership allowed the **Dutch** Government to provide for a simple, non-judicial procedure to terminate the relationship. Although this argument could possibly have been supported in 1998, this is certainly no longer the case in 2005.[141] Despite the absence of children, the **Dutch** Government still saw the need to protect the parties' respective interests and thus created a two-track dissolution procedure; a judicial track for unilateral requests and an administrative track for consensual requests. In this way, the **Dutch** Government has struck a good balance between respecting the principle of party autonomy and bestowing adequate protection on the weaker party.

In **France** and **Belgium** different arguments were used to justify the introduction of new procedures. It was argued in both jurisdictions that this new form of relationship was not to bring about a new stage in the parties'

140 *Dutch Second Chamber*, 1995-1996, No. 7, p. 10.

141 BOELE-WOELKI (2003b) p. 46.

lives.[142] Moreover, in balancing the principles of party autonomy and protection afforded to the weaker party, the Governments aimed to sustain the contractual nature of these forms of relationship. In so doing, and by removing the requirement of judicial scrutiny, the scales were balanced against the protection of the weaker party and in favour of broadening observance of the principle of party autonomy. Despite the obvious consistency in argumentation proffered by the **French** and **Belgian** legislatures, the waters are somewhat muddier than they first appear.

In allowing parties to marry whilst still involved in a non-marital registered relationship and providing a unilateral termination procedure, the **French** and **Belgian** legislatures have not entirely adhered to general principles of contract law with respect to indefinite contracts.[143] According to **French** and **Belgian** law, contracts for an indefinite period may be terminated unilaterally only after a period of reasonable notice.[144] Non-adherence to a reasonable period of notice can lead to a *rupture brusque* and constitutes an *abus de droit*.[145] This approach is moreover supported with reference to Art. 6:109, Principles of European Contract Law, where a contract for an indefinite period of time may only be terminated by one of the parties by giving notice of reasonable length.[146] It is thus clear that the ability of either party to the non-marital registered relationship to unilaterally terminate the relationship without notice of a reasonable length by celebrating a marriage, especially if this marriage is celebrated with a third person, not only provides for a non-protective dissolution procedure but also contravenes the basic tenets of contract law.[147] Although the unilateral

---

142 This was indicated in both jurisdictions by the refusal for such a relationship to affect the parties' civil status: **Chapters III.5.2** and **IV.5.2**.

143 for the contractual characterisation of these relationships see **Chapter IX.2.1.2**.

144 **Fr.:** BÉNABENT (1999) p. 212-214, §312-314; **Belg.:** VAN GERVEN/COVEMAKER (2001) p. 160-161 and CORNELIS (2000) p. 814-816, §629-631.

145 **Fr.:** Fr. Cass., Com. Ch., 5th December 1984, *Bull. Civ.* IV, No. 33; **Belg.:** Rb Antwerp, 13th April 1979, *RW* 1979-1980, p. 722, CORNELIS (2000) p. 815, §630.

146 According to 1:302, PECL reasonableness is to be "judged by what persons acting in good faith and in the same situation as the parties would consider to be reasonable. In particular, in assessing what is reasonable the nature and purpose of the contract, the circumstances of the case, and the usages and practices of the trades or professions involved should be taken into account." Comment C mentions factors such as the length of the contract, the efforts and investments that the other party has undertaken in the performance of the contract, the time it may take the other party to obtain another contract with another party and what is customary in the debtor's branch of business. See further LANDO/BEALE (2000) p. 316-317; SCHELHAAS *et al.* (2002) p. 279.

147 Furthermore, there is as far as this author is aware no other form of contract that is automatically terminated by the simple fact of a subsequent marriage celebration.

dissolution procedure in both countries is subject to a delay,[148] no reference is made to the concept of reasonableness. If one assumes that a non-marital registered relationship should be seen as a purely contractual matter than one must adhere to the normal rules applicable to contracts. This is not the case. Besides, is it reasonable that a non-marital registered relationship that has lasted one year should be subject to the same notice period as a relationship that has lasted twenty years?

As a result of the aforementioned comparisons, it is possible to expand upon the PLURALISTIC and DUALISTIC MODELS developed in **Section VIII.2.4**, to include the issue of relationship dissolution outlined in this section.

THE DUALISTIC MODEL

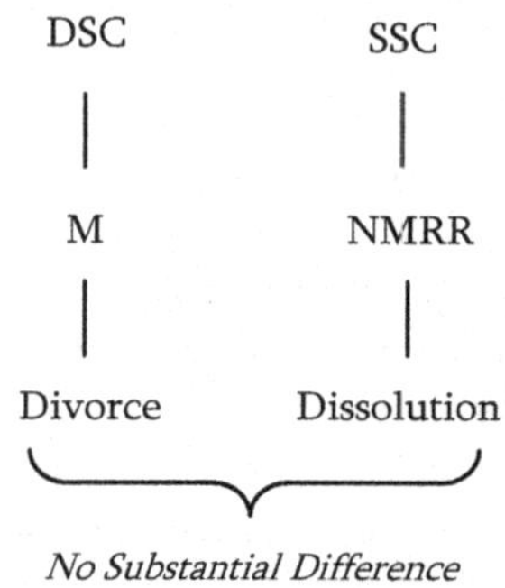

THE PLURALISTIC MODEL

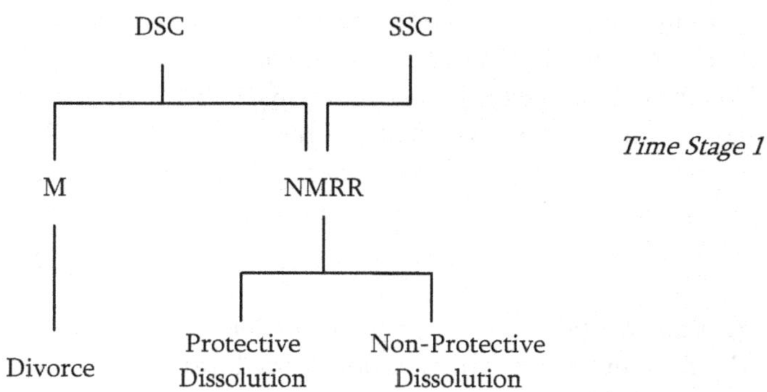

[148] 8 days in **Belgium** and 3 months in **France**. Art. 515-7(5), Fr. CC also provides that the notice of intent to marry must be sent at least two weeks prior to the marriage celebration: see **Chapter IV.6.8**.

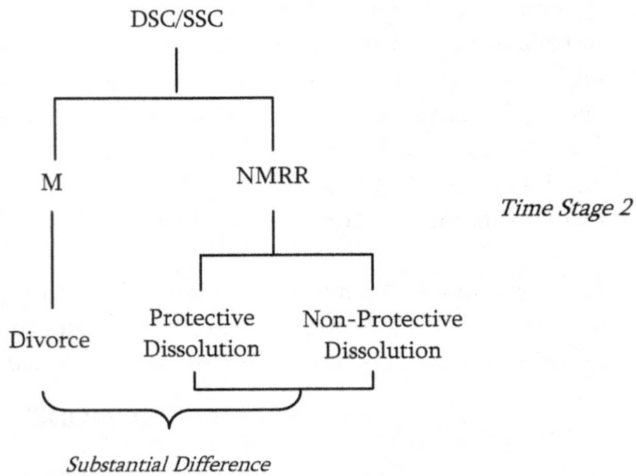

Key: **DSC**: *Different Sex Couples*, **SSC**: *Same-Sex Couples*
M: *Marriage*, **NMRR**: *Non-Marital Registered Relationship*

In evaluating these two models, it is clear that the same arguments could be forwarded here as those advanced with respect to the establishment of a non-marital registered relationship. In the PLURALISTIC MODEL, parties are offered a choice, at least theoretically, that is absent in the DUALISTIC MODEL. There are, however, serious problems associated with the enactment of non-protective dissolution procedures. The possibility to unilaterally dissolve a non-marital registered relationship without the provision of reasonable notice seriously undermines the protection that should be offered to the weaker party. Although one should not lose sight of the principle of party autonomy, this should not come at the cost of protection. For countries adopting a PLURALISTIC MODEL and striving for diversity in the dissolution procedures between marriage and non-marital registered relationships, the two-track system available in **The Netherlands** is, therefore, to be preferred, whereby the courts deal with contentious dissolutions and an administrative authority deals with non-contentious dissolutions.[149]

A fundamental difference must however be kept in mind when appraising the different types of dissolution procedures available. Unlike with respect to the establishment of the relationship, where the aspiration to create a valued pluralistic system triggers the desire to provide more options to

[149] It must, however, be noted that even in **The Netherlands**, the solutions are far from ideal, where the possibility to submit a joint petition to court is unavailable: see **Chapter V.6.3**.

couples wishing to institutionalise their relationship, the same is not true of dissolution procedures. If the parties disagree as to the need to terminate their relationship, the State is, and should be, involved in the termination procedure. In so doing, the State can ensure that both parties are protected and that the result is reasonable given the circumstances. Allowing this process to occur outside of court, without legal advice, denies the parties the protection they should be afforded. This State involvement should therefore transpire regardless of the relationship form. The necessity to protect not only the weaker party, but also any children involved should weigh heavier in the balance than the inclination to provide diversity.

It is therefore submitted that the approach adopted in the DUALISTIC MODEL is thus better suited to this aims. Couples, regardless of the form of their relationship, should be presented with equivalent options for terminating their relationship. Two procedures should be available, distinguishable on the basis of the consent of the parties.[150] On this basis, it would therefore seem that although the PLURALISTIC MODEL provides for the ideal solution in terms of the establishment of the relationship, the DUALISTIC MODEL provides for the preferred solution when one confines oneself to the dissolution of the relationship.

VIII.4 LEGAL EFFECTS

As has already been seen in **Section 5** of **Chapters** III-VII, the rights and duties extended to registered partners vary immensely from jurisdiction to jurisdiction. This section does not attempt to embark upon the immense task of comparing each and every individual legal right and duty conferred on registered partners. Instead, this section attempts to distinguish between general classifications of countries on the basis of the substantive law information provided, not only with respect to the purview of attributed legal effects (**Section VIII.4.1**), but also with respect to the method adopted in conferring these benefits (**Section VIII.4.2**).

VIII.4.1 EXTENT OF LEGAL EFFECTS

It is clear from the comparative overview that with respect to the legal effects attributed to the various forms of non-marital registered relationships, two distinct models can be discerned in relation to the

150 Whether these procedures should be administrative or judicial is ultimately a question for the State concerned and therefore falls outside the ambit of this research question.

jurisdictions studied: strong registration resulting in internal consistency (**Section VIII.4.1.1**) and weak registration resulting in internal inconsistency (**Section VIII.4.1.2**). Although these approaches are easy to distinguish, determining the dividing line between these two categories causes immeasurable difficulty. What are the criteria for determining whether a system has adopted a policy of strong or weak registration? Are certain legal effects essential for a jurisdiction to be deemed to have created "similar" rights to marriage? Is there a minimum benchmark that countries must attain in order to be eligible for acknowledgment as a non-marital registered relationship? These questions will, *inter alia*, be dealt with in the overall comparison and evaluation to this section (**Section VIII.4.3**).

VIII.4.1.1 Strong registration: Internal consistency

In the **United Kingdom**, **Switzerland** and **The Netherlands**, the vast majority of legal effects associated with marriage have been extended to partners involved in a non-marital registered relationship. Although these laws are externally inconsistent, internal consistency has been achieved in almost all fields. This section will attempt to highlight the similarities and differences in the various legal effects studied, as well as provide explanations for any differences uncovered.

All three jurisdictions concur that the registration of a non-marital relationship is to affect the parties' civil status in an identical fashion to marriage.[151] Although the notion of civil status *per se* is absent in the **United Kingdom**, it is intended that the registration of a civil partnership is to have the same impact on the parties' personal status as a marriage. Furthermore, in the **United Kingdom** and **The Netherlands**, internal equality has also been achieved with respect to registered partners and spouses in the fields of nationality and name law.[152] In **Switzerland**, although internal consistency has been achieved with respect to **Swiss** nationality,[153] this has not been followed through with respect to cantonal and communal nationality, or in the field of name law. The absence of consistency in relation to these issues stems from the existing sex discrimination in this field. The superior position afforded to the husband could not be translated into the registered partnership legislation without making a distinction between male registered partnerships and female registered partnerships. As a result, although internal consistency has not been achieved, alternative

151 **Chapters V.5.2**, **VI.5.2** and **VII.5.2**.

152 **Chapters V.5.3**, **V.5.4**, **VII.5.3** and **VII.5.4**.

153 **Chapter VI.5.3**.

solutions have been tendered, such as the possibility of using each other's *nom d'alliance*.[154]

In the field of fiscal law, total internal consistency has also been achieved in all three jurisdictions with the exception,[155] once again, of those areas in existing **Swiss** legislation where due to persistent gender discrimination a distinction is drawn on the basis of sex.[156] Finally, the field of inheritance law has also been equalised, with registered partners being placed in an identical position to a spouse with regards both testate and intestate succession.[157]

When one turns to the fields of property law and the personal obligations partners owe one another, one is confronted with an assortment of solutions. In **The Netherlands**, total consistency of result has been achieved. All the rights and duties applicable to spouses and relevant provisions on matrimonial property law have been declared *mutatis mutandis* applicable to registered partners.[158] In **Switzerland** and the **United Kingdom** the situation is more complicated. The rights and duties imposed on spouses in the **United Kingdom** are predominantly non-statutory, relying heavily on case law and precedent.[159] Consequently, one will have to wait and see whether judges will apply the common law rules on spousal rights to civil partners analogously or will adopt innovative solutions specific to this situation. It is, however, expected that a *mutatis mutandis* approach will be taken, especially since it is Parliament's obvious intent that marriage and civil partnership are to be regarded as equivalent institutions. The same is also expected to be the case with respect to the equivalent common law principles in the field of property law.[160]

In **Switzerland**, this field of law also reveals important differences in the rationale behind the institution of registered partnership. Instead of imposing the regime of *participation aux acquêts* as the default statutory property regime for registered partners, the **Swiss** legislature opted for a regime of *séparation des biens*. However, in doing so, they preserved the right for registered partners to opt-into the regime of *participation aux*

---

154 **Chapter VI.5.4.**

155 **Chapter V.5.5**, **VI.5.5** and **VII.5.5**.

156 FF 2003, p. 1192 at 1222. See further, **Chapter VI.5.5**.

157 **Chapters V.5.8**, **VI.5.8** and **VII.5.8**.

158 This is an example of the so-called exclusion method. See **Section VIII.4.2**.

159 See **Chapter VII.5.6**.

160 See **Chapter VII.5.7**.

acquêts. As a result, although the default situation differs for spouses and registered partners, the same choices are available to both groups. The same cannot, however, be said of the personal obligations that the parties owe to each other, in which **Switzerland's** legislation falters due to lack of clarity. This incertitude stems from the **Swiss** legislature's belief that registration of a partnership should not have any effect on children. As a result, any reference to the term *famille* or *logement de la famille* has been replaced by *communauté* and *logement commun* respectively. This replacement of terminology does, however, inevitably lead to speculation as to the precise ambit of such rights and duties. Nevertheless, it is submitted that despite these etymological difficulties, the personal obligations that registered partners owe to each other are the same as those incumbent upon spouses. It is only where these obligations are extended to the spouses' children where the parallel ceases to apply. This is perhaps no clearer than in the case of the duty to provide support and assistance.[161]

Although it is therefore true to say that the registration of a non-marital relationship has, wherever possible, been assimilated to a marital relationship in the vast majority of legal fields, this is far from universally true. Perhaps the most decisive area deals with issues relating to children: parentage, parental responsibilities, adoption and artificial insemination. Despite the variety in the solutions tendered, all three jurisdictions are in agreement in relation to one aspect. Although all three jurisdictions adhere to the maxim *mater certa semper est*, no country applies the maxim *pater is est quem nuptiae demonstrant* analogously to unmarried fathers or the female partner of the legal mother.[162] Different-sex non-marital registered partners in **The Netherlands** are, nevertheless, offered the same options as their spousal counterparts in attempting to establish parentage.[163] In **The Netherlands**, **Switzerland** and the **United Kingdom** same-sex couples[164] are excluded from all options open to different-sex couples wishing to establish parentage.[165] In **The Netherlands** and **England & Wales**, same-sex couples are, nonetheless, provided with the option to either adopt jointly or adopt their partner's child(ren).[166] In contrast, the inability for same-sex couples to

---

161 **Chapter VI.5.6.3**.

162 **Chapters V.5.9.1**, **VI.5.9.1** and **VII.5.9.1**.

163 Namely the possibility of recognition. See **Chapter V.5.9.1**.

164 Thus regardless of whether they are involved in a non-marital registered relationship, a marriage (in **The Netherlands**) or in a non-institutionalised relationship.

165 Recognition in **The Netherlands** and **Switzerland**, birth certificate registration in **England & Wales** and **Northern Ireland** and acknowledgement in **Scotland** is all restricted to couples of opposite-sex. See further **Chapters V.5.9.1**, **VI.5.9.1** and **VII.5.9.1**.

166 **Chapter V.5.9.3** and **VII.5.9.3**.

adopt in **Scotland**, **Northern Ireland** and **Switzerland** thwarts any possibility for same-sex couples to obtain joint parentage rights over the same child in these jurisdictions.[167]

In turning one's attention to parental responsibilities, one is also unable to discern a uniform approach. This is in part due to the restricted manner in which same-sex couples are able to establish legal parentage.[168] Although in **The Netherlands** legislation dealing with registered partners and married couples is dealt with in different provisions of the **Dutch** Civil Code, the eventual result is the same regardless; if a child is born during a marriage or registered partnership both parties are vested with joint parental authority[169] unless a third party has already established legal parentage over that child.[170] In the **United Kingdom**, civil partners can obtain parental responsibility, or parental rights and responsibilities (as it is known in **Scotland**) either by obtaining a parental responsibility order or a residence order.[171] Due to the fact that only legal parents in **Switzerland** are granted the possibility to be vested with parental responsibility, same-sex couples are denied the possibility to exercise joint parental responsibility.[172] Finally, only **Switzerland** restricts access to artificial insemination to different-sex couples.[173] Although theoretically possible in **The Netherlands** and the **United Kingdom**, practical access to artificial reproductive techniques is often restricted by hospital or clinic policy.[174]

---

167 **Chapter VI.5.9.3** and **VII.5.9.3**.

168 In the case of **Switzerland**, it is better to talk of a total prohibition.

169 Arts. 1:252 (marriage), 1:253aa (registered partnership two legal parents), 1:253sa (registered partnership legal parent with non-legal parent), Neth. CC.

170 The combination of the *mater semper certa est* rule and the prerequisite to the vesting of joint parental authority that there is no other legal parent means that a male couple can seldom rely on the provisions of Arts. 1:253aa and 1:253sa, Neth. CC directly. See, for example, *Dutch Second Chamber*, 1999-2000, 27047, No. 3, p. 3.

171 **Eng:** Sec. 4(1)(b), CA 1989 (parents) and Sec. $4^{A}(1)(b)$, CA 1989, as amended by ACA 2002 (stepparents); **Scot:** Sec. 11(2)(b), C(S)A 1995 (parents and stepparents); **NI:** Art. 7(1)(b), C(NI)O 1995 (parents) and Sec. $7(1^{A})$, C(NI)O 1995 (stepparents). See further **Chapter VII.5.9.2**. In **England & Wales** civil partners are also entitled to make a parental responsibility agreement with the mother: Sec. $4^{A}(1)(a)$, CA 1989, as amended by ACA 2002.

172 See further **Chapter VI.5.9.2**.

173 See **Chapter VI.5.9.4**.

174 See **Chapter V.5.9.4** and **VII.5.9.4**.

VIII.4.1.2 Weak registration: Internal inconsistency

Unlike the approach adopted in the **United Kingdom**, **Switzerland** and **The Netherlands**, the legislatures in **France** and **Belgium** have opted for a different tack. In both countries the "legal distance" between marriage and non-marital registered relationship has been maintained by ensuring that the package of legal effects attributed to the domestic form of non-marital registered relationship are dissimilar to those offered to spouses. In this respect a different starting point is taken than that espoused in **The Netherlands**, **Switzerland** and the **United Kingdom**. In **France** and **Belgium**, one begins with the assumption that the registration of a non-marital relationship should have no effects unless expressly agreed upon by the parties. In these jurisdictions, the Government was thus not constricted by the preconception that the rights and duties attendant on marriage must be extended to non-marital registered relationships. Instead, these Governments departed from the premise that the registration should be contractual in nature, with the principle of party autonomy playing a central role.[175]

With these principles underpinning the entire legislative framework for non-marital registered relationships, the **French** and **Belgian** legislatures have not seen the need to amend the law in the fields of civil status,[176] nationality law,[177] name law[178] child law,[179] or inheritance law,[180] due to the passage of the PACS or statutory cohabitation legislation. The benefits attributed to couples in these areas were believed to be inherent to the institution of marriage, and thus immune from extension to registered partners. Instead, the effects of both of these pieces of legislation are restricted to the fields of fiscal and tax law, property law and the rights and duties the parties owe to each other.

Although in both jurisdictions registered partners and spouses are treated identically with respect to tax law,[181] under **French** law this only occurs

[175] See for example the discussions surrounding the extension of Art. 221, Belg. CC to statutory cohabitants by means of Art. 1477(3), Belg. CC (**Chapter III.5.6.4**) and Art. 214, Fr. CC by virtue of Art. 515(4)(1), Fr. CC (**Chapter IV.5.6.4**).

[176] See **Chapters III.5.2** and **IV.5.2**.

[177] See **Chapters III.5.3** and **IV.5.3**.

[178] See **Chapters III.5.4** and **IV.5.4**.

[179] See **Chapters III.5.9** and **IV.5.9**.

[180] See **Chapters III.5.8** and **IV.5.8**.

[181] See **Chapters III.5.5** and **IV.5.5**.

once the parties have been registered for three years.[182] This equality is, however, currently restricted to the field of tax law, with the registration of a non-marital relationship having no effect on the parties' social security benefits or pensions.[183] With respect to the rights and duties that the partners owe each other, although at times somewhat vague[184] it would appear that in both jurisdictions the parties as subject to the duty to cohabit,[185] although not subject to a duty of fidelity or support and assistance.[186] It would also appear that the parties are treated identically to spouses with respect to the duty to contribute to the repayment of debts,[187] the duty to contribute to household expenses[188] and afforded similar protection with respect to the common home.[189] Although with respect to these fields it is perhaps possible to talk of a similar approach having been taken by these two jurisdictions, any such similarities dissipate when one broaches the topic of property law.

In principle, although spouses in **Belgium** are subject to a statutory community of property, statutory cohabitants are subject to the customary separation of property.[190] In **France**, on the other hand, along lines similar to the matrimonial community of property,[191] parties to a PACS are subject to a *régime de l'indivision*.[192] Although a distinction is drawn between *meubles meublants* and other goods, this distinction is in practice relatively insignificant. This difference would, however, be removed should the proposals made by the **French** Ministry of justice be accepted.[193] The group advising the **French** Ministry of Justice believed that the current application of Art. 515-5, Fr. CC is extremely rigid and complex, noting that this

---

182 Art. 6(1)(3), Fr. GTC inserted by virtue of Art. 4, Act of 15th November 1999, No. 99-944. Under current proposals this time period would be abolished: MINISTRE DE LA JUSTICE (2004) p. 17.

183 See **Chapters III.5.5** and **IV.5.5**. Under current proposals in **France** this would be difference in treatment would be abolished and registered partners would be treated in an identical manner to their spousal counterparts: MINISTRE DE LA JUSTICE (2004) p. 18-22.

184 This incertitude will hopefully be clarified with respect to **France** with the implementation of the proposals made by the Ministry of Justice: MINISTRE DE LA JUSTICE (2004) p. 14-15.

185 See **Chapters III.5.6.1** and **IV.5.6.1**.

186 See **Chapters III.5.6.2, III.5.6.3, IV.5.6.2** and **IV.5.6.3**.

187 See **Chapters III.5.6.4** and **IV.5.6.4**.

188 See **Chapters III.5.6.5** and **IV.5.6.5**.

189 See **Chapters III.5.6.6** and **IV.5.6.6**.

190 **Chapter III.5.7**.

191 **Chapter IV.5.7**.

192 **Chapter IV.5.7.1** and **IV.5.7.2**.

193 MINISTRE DE LA JUSTICE (2004) p. 15-16.

complexity has been virtually unanimously denounced.[194] It is not, however, entirely clear why the group did not examine the possibility of extending the matrimonial community of property regime to those involved in a PACS.

It is clear that the package of rights and duties to which registered partners benefit according to **French** and **Belgian** law is much more restricted than that which registered partners in **The Netherlands**, **Switzerland** and the **United Kingdom** enjoy. Nonetheless, the registration of a non-marital registered relationship in **Belgium** and **France** is not without consequence. Legal implications ensue not only as between the parties themselves but also with respect to the State. It is, nonetheless, important to note that the effects are restricted to the fields of fiscal and property law, as well as the personal obligations that the parties owe to one another.

VIII.4.2 METHOD OF EXTENDING LEGAL EFFECTS

As has been shown some countries have chosen to assimilate the domestic institution of non-marital registered relationship to marriage whilst others have not. Those countries to have opted for a weak form of non-marital registered relationship, *i.e.* **France** and **Belgium**, have thus explicitly enumerated all the rights and benefits that the couple enjoy. In those countries to have opted for strong registration, two distinct methods should be distinguished.[195] From the outset it should be emphasised that these methods are used interchangeably, dependent upon the field of law in question.

Some countries have chosen to catalogue all the legal effects that a registered couple enjoy. This approach results in masses of legislation and countless amendments to existing legislation. Wherever the words "spouse", "wife", "husband" and "marriage" occurrs, the words "registered partner", "partner" and "registered partnership" have been inserted. This is referred to as the *enumeration method.* The end result is a complex array of legislative amendments often running into hundreds of pages.[196] This approach,

---

194 MINISTRE DE LA JUSTICE (2004) p. 15.

195 These methods have also been identified by WINTEMUTE. However, he divides all non-marital registered relationship forms into two categories (enumeration and subtraction). It is however submitted that only those countries opting for strong registration will realistically make use of the subtraction method. See further WINTEMUTE (2001) p. 766.

196 In the **United Kingdom**, the CPA 2004 is approximately 400 pages long with over 200 Articles and 30 Schedules. In **The Netherlands**, the Registered Partnership Amendment Act explicitly detailed amendments to more than 300 individual statutes.

although capturing the precise range of the legislature's intent, can lead to oversights and mistakes.[197] This approach has been employed in **Switzerland** and the **United Kingdom**, as well as the majority of fields of law in **The Netherlands**.[198] Nevertheless, some areas of law have been spared such monumental amendment and one simple provision has sufficed.[199] In this latter method, a general provision is enacted which stipulates that the registration of a partnership is to have the same legal effects as the celebration of a marriage, subject to any exceptions listed.[200] This second method is referred to as the *exclusion method*.[201]

Although these methods have no direct overall impact on the extent of the rights and benefits extended to registered partners, this difference in approach is important to realise, due to the antipodean point of departure in these two methods. In those countries to have adhered to the *exclusion method*, spouses and registered partners are treated identically, unless otherwise stated. In those countries to have adhered to the *enumeration method*, the legal position of registered partners is unaltered, unless otherwise stated. Although the practical result will often be indistinguishable, the method will have obvious implications in more obscure areas of law that the legislature may have overlooked.

VIII.4.3 OVERALL COMPARISON AND EVALUATION

There exists an obvious enormous diversity vis-à-vis the legal effects attributed to non-marital registered relationships. In some countries, the legal effects attributed are similar, if not almost identical, to those attached to the institution of marriage. In other jurisdictions only minimal protection is offered to the parties. A distinction can nonetheless be made between "strong registration" and "weak registration". Strong registration involves the near assimilation of the legal effects attributed to registered partners and

---

197 WINTEMUTE (2001) p. 766.

198 See, for example, Titles 1-4, Book 1, Neth. CC. Although outside the ambit of this research, this approach has also been adopted in **Luxembourg**, regions in **Spain** and **Germany**.

199 See, for example, Art 1:80b and Art. 4:8, Neth. CC.

200 WINTEMUTE (2001) p. 766. WINTEMUTE calls this method the "subtraction method". The term "exclusion" has been used instead to more precisely convey the idea that everything is extended except those excluded rights. The word subtraction does not necessarily convey the idea that the package with which one begins is identical to the package of legal effects stemming from marriage.

201 Although outside the ambit of this research, this approach has been adopted in the **Nordic** countries, for example, §3(1), **Danish** Registered Partnership Act.

spouses. Although countries opting for this system often refrain, at least in the beginning, from amending the law relating to children (*i.e.* adoption, parentage and parental responsibility), all the legal effects affecting the partners themselves are generally equalised. In contrast, weak registration entails the enactment of only minimal protective measures. These forms of registration often have no impact on the parties' personal law, *e.g.* name law, nationality and civil status, or family and inheritance law, but are instead restricted to fiscal and property law issues, as well as the personal obligations that the parties have towards each other.

It would appear that the legal effects attributed to registered partners can be roughly divided into four categories:

- Property law and personal obligations;
- Fiscal law (tax, social security and pensions);
- Family and inheritance law; and
- Rights in relation to children.

It would appear that those countries adopting a system of weak registration confine the effects of such a registration to the first two categories. Hence, the effect of registering a statutory cohabitation or PACS is restricted to fiscal and property law. It is also clear from the comparison that it is not true to say that countries are gradually progressing along a spectrum towards granting the full package of marital rights to registered partners.[202] Although it is true to say that the legislatures in both **France** and **Belgium** have already or are in the process of granting more rights to registered partners, it is not true to talk of a steady progression towards total equality in the legal effects of marriage and non-marital registered relationships. Although similarity in function may well be discernible, it is clear that those countries that have limited themselves to the legal effects in the first two categories have done so with a different philosophy in mind than those countries that have broadened the range of rights to include effects in the latter two categories. Nevertheless, it is also clear that as one progresses from one category to the next, the relative level of associated political controversy increases accordingly.

The rights and duties associated with the first category are generally of a low politically sensitive nature. It is assumed that parties involved in an intimate relationship wish to commit to each other, and by imposing duties

202 This is, for example, proposed by ANTOKOLSKAIA (2005) Chapter 4.4, with reference to same-sex non-marital registered relationship schemes.

such as a duty to cohabit or contribute to the costs of the household, the State is merely indicating its moral stance at little financial burden to the State. Although opinions as to the best or proper matrimonial property regime differ markedly and have resulted in protracted political debates in many countries, the question of whether to enact rules determining the property law effects of registering a non-marital relationship is by and large uncontroversial. Moreover, in the majority of legal systems, parties are in any case able to draw up a contract regulating such issues themselves.[203] The State simply provides for a default system to operate in the absence of such an expression of the parties' will.[204] In addition, it appears that in any debate concerning the protection that should be offered to cohabitants, discussion centres on this field of law.[205] It is, therefore, not surprising that this field of law is one of the first to be legislated upon for non-marital registered relationships.

However, different approaches are often rooted in the inherent differences in the legal systems. The common law ancestry of the **British** legal system and the reluctance of the **British** legislature to intervene in the field of matrimonial law, has given rise to the absence of clear-cut rights and duties of civil partners to each other.[206] The peculiar Anglo-Saxon approach to the issues of matrimonial property has also been followed through with respect to civil partners, in that the registration of a civil partnership is devoid of effects on the property of the parties to the relationship.[207] In contrast, the abundant clarity of the approach adopted by the **Dutch** legislature denotes the legislature's intention that the registration of a partnership and the celebration of a marriage are to be viewed as equal institutions.[208]

Although rights and duties in the second category are generally of a less sensitive political nature than those in the third or fourth categories, the extension of fiscal benefits in the form of tax breaks, social security benefits and access to pension schemes, obviously comes at great financial cost to the

---

203 BOELE-WOELKI (2000b), p. 248. The absence of such a system in the **United Kingdom** can be explained by fear on the part of the common law system that spouses could be bound by a contract which they made many years before. The principle of reasonableness therefore outweighs the principle of legal certainty in this system.

204 This, of course, does not detract from any disparity in the property regime applicable to spouses and registered partners.

205 See, for example, SENAEVE (1992); BARLOW (2001); PINTENS/VAN DER MEERSCH/VANWINCKELEN (2002) and SCHRAMA (2004).

206 See further **Chapter VII.5.6**.

207 See **Chapter VII.5.7**.

208 Art. 1:80b, Neth. CC. See further **Chapter V.5.6** and **V.5.7**.

Government. The political will to remove fiscal discrimination is therefore often pitted against the available funds in the financial coffers.[209]

As one moves towards the third category of legal effects, one senses a shift in emphasis. If one accepts the extension of rights in this field it becomes difficult to make distinctions. Upon extending one right or duty, one must justify the almost unjustifiable in denying the extension of other rights in this category.[210] Rights and duties in this category also have a long-standing association with the law on marriage in many countries. On the continent the celebration of a marriage has an important impact on those personal law rights associated with one's civil status, name and nationality. This is to some extent also true of common law countries, where according to old authorities the celebration of a marriage for many purposes fuses the legal personalities of husband and wife into one.[211] As a result, the extension of such rights to those outside of the marital bond is a much more sensitive matter than the rights in the first two categories.

The final category, untouched in **France**, **Belgium**, **Switzerland**, **Northern Ireland** and **Scotland**, is possibly the most sensitive of all. This sensitivity stems from a multiplicity of dynamic factors: biology, tradition, third party rights and moral values. The law on parentage was originally based on the presumption of biology.[212] It was and still is simply presumed that the husband of a pregnant woman was the child's father, *pater is est quem nuptiae demonstrant*. The idea of extending such presumptions to same-sex

---

209 See, for example, the Annexes to the **English** proposal WOMEN AND EQUALITY UNIT (2003a) p. 75 (Tables 3 and 4, Annex A). In Table 3 it was estimated that introduction of the civil partnership schemes would cost the **British** Government £23-230 million per year by 2050 (for state pensions and bereavement benefits and public service pensions). In Table 4 it was estimated that the cost to private pension benefit schemes would be between £2.5-20 million. See also **Chapter VI.5.5** and the LOCHER report, LOCHER (1998).

210 The only justification which has been offered (in **Switzerland**) is that the rules in the field of marriage are discriminatory.

211 BLACKSTONE, *Commentaries*, *i*. 442.

212 **Neth.:** *Dutch Second Chamber*, 1999-2000, 27047, No. 5, p. 1-2 and VONK (2004) p. 103; **Swit.:** MINISTRY OF JUSTICE (1999) p. 26 and FF 2003, p. 1192 at 1223; **UK:** In the **UK** there was in fact no discussion on this point. This is due to the possibility for same-sex couples to adopt and the basic assumption that legal parentage is based on biology. See further, LOWE/DOUGLAS (1998) p. 261-262, BAINHAM (2005) p. 88. Despite the medical advancements made in recent decades, as yet a child's conception still necessitates the involvement of male sperm and female eggs (LOWE/DOUGLAS (1998) p. 262). This is also generally accepted, see, for example, HENSTRA (2002) p. 83, who in turn cites VAN MOURIK/NUYTINCK (1998) p. 141-142 "Hoe men het ook wendt of keert en ongeacht alle moderne voorplantingstechnieken, zoals bijvoorbeeld in-vitrofertilisatie, eiceldonatie en embryotransplantatie, een kind stamt altijd af van een man en een vrouw".

couples involves an enormous excursion from reality. Even if the husband of the legal mother is not the father of the child, there is a biological possibility that he could be, whereas such a biological possibility is completely absent in same-sex couples.[213] The controversy surrounding children raised in same-sex families has even prevented gay rights groups from asserting the need for equality in this field.[214]

The necessary absence of parentage rights for same-sex couples does not explain a total lack of attention to this field. However, one must also note the State's interest in the raising of children. The State imposes its moral values on the opportunity for same-sex couples to adopt or raise children. In the majority of European countries to have introduced forms of non-marital registered relationship schemes, it has almost universally been accepted that children need to be raised by a mother and a father and that it is therefore undesirable for children to be raised by same-sex couples.[215] If one joins this with the often prevailing presumption that the marital home is the best place for the child to be raised, then it is not surprising that the rights in this category are the last to be extended to registered partners. It is, in addition, generally noted that a fundamental difference between same-sex and different-sex couples lies in the necessity for third party involvement in the case of same-sex relationships, either by means of sperm, egg or embryo donation or surrogacy. The traditional view that a child should remain in contact, if not be raised by his or her biological parents, is therefore fundamentally besieged should one accept the proposition that same-sex couples are able to raise children. In avoiding the political quagmire associated with the venturing of an opinion in relation to these views, it is submitted that these reasons provide the explanation to the current absence of legislation with respect to children born or raised in non-marital registered relationships.

Although this division into rough categories of rights is merely illustrative and does not profess to be used for any higher purpose, it is perhaps effective in helping to identify the crucial difference between those countries adhering to a system of strong registration and those adopting a system of weak registration. Of course, any global classification on this superficial basis will be subject to exception and it is admitted that this model is merely an aid in any attempt to discern general uniform trends in

---

213 KORTMANN (1997) p. 5, §2.1.

214 See, for example, **Chapter VI.5.9**.

215 See, for example, the **Swiss** legislature's discussion regarding adoption and artificial reproductive techniques: FF 2003, p. 1192 at 1223.

this field. In **Switzerland,** for example, despite having adopted a relatively strong registration form, the continued unequal treatment of men and women in the field of family law has led to unequal treatment of spouses and registered partners. In the **United Kingdom**, the common law bases of property law have led to uncertainty as to the extent of such case law to civil partners.

At this stage it is perhaps constructive to return to the analogy of adoption, where one is also able to see clear differences in the legal effects attributed to adoption in different jurisdictions. As far back as Roman times, distinctions have been made between different types of adoption.[216] These forms of adoption remained even after JUSTINIAN'S reforms in AD 529. However, JUSTINIAN did fundamentally change the law of *adoptio*, drawing a distinction between *adoptio plena* (full or strong adoption) and *adoptio minus plena* (less than full or weak adoption).[217] *Adoptio plena* was subsequently limited to the case of adoption by a natural ascendant. For all other cases, he created the *adoptio minus plena*, which did not impair the rights of the natural family. As a result of JUSTINIAN'S alterations three different types of adoption could be brought under the umbrella term *adoptio*. Although the legal effects of each of these forms of adoption were different, the institutions were so similar in function and structure that they could be regarded as being different variants of the same classification.

These different forms of adoption are still perceptible in modern-day legal systems. In some jurisdictions weak adoption is the preferred form, whereas in others strong adoption is given the upper hand, whilst both forms exist side-by-side in others.[218] According to modern comparative studies, full adoption (*adoptio plena, volle adoptie, l'adoption plénière*) aims at integrating the child completely into the adoptive family; all systems providing for this type of adoption bestow the status of legitimate child of the adopters on the child. The current dominant view is that full integration

---

216 Under Roman law the adopter acquired *potestas* over the adopted person by way of both forms of adoption, *i.e. adrogatio* and *adoptio*. Furthermore, the adopted person changed families, *i.e.* became for all legal purposes a member of the family of the adopter, and ceased to be a member of his previous family. Although both forms of adoption were regulated in a similar manner, and fulfilled a similar function, different legal effects were attributed to the ultimate legal act. In *adoptio*, for example, only the adopted person passed into the *potestas* of the adopter, and not his entire family, as was the case with *adrogatio*. See also **Section VIII.2.4**.

217 BORKOWSKI (1994) p. 138.

218 PERMANENT BUREAU OF THE HAGUE CONFERENCE, *Proceedings of the Seventeenth Session of The Hague Conference. Volume II*, The Hague, 1994, p. 27-29, §31-33.

of the adoptee irrevocably terminates all ties with the biological family. In contrast, weak adoption (*adoptio minus plena*, *zwakke adoptie*, *l'adoption simple*) generally aims at providing the child with some form of social assistance, and for that purpose it is often neither necessary to fully integrate the child into the adoptive family, nor desirable to cut off those ties with the biological family, which do not interfere with this purpose.[219]

Such a distinction could also be drawn with respect to the various forms of non-marital registered relationship schemes currently available. There are some countries that have provided for a system of strong registration, ensuring that the couples are able to benefit from the provisions of family and inheritance law. In viewing non-marital registered relationships as an equivalent to marriage, the legal effects associated with the registration are strong and far-reaching. In contrast, there are other countries that have preferred to limit their legislation to the field of fiscal and property law. In viewing non-marital registered relationships as a contractual arrangement between the parties, the legal effects associated with the registration are relatively weak. It is submitted that this distinction in legal effects does not, however, necessarily correspond to either of the models outlines in **Sections VIII.2.4** and **VIII.3.4**.

With the exception of **The Netherlands**, those countries adhering to the PLURALISTIC MODEL have opted for a form of weak registration, whereas those countries adhering to the DUALISTIC MODEL have opted for strong registration. This is of course a natural consequence of the underlying principles behind the PLURALISTIC and DUALISTIC MODELS. Why did **The Netherlands** abide by the PLURALISTIC MODEL and yet elect for strong registration effects? Is it conceivable that a country pursuing registration based on the DUALISTIC MODEL would opt for a weak registration scheme?

The answer to the first question lies in the **Dutch** parliamentary discussions in 1995-1996. The initial aim of the legislation was to provide an alternative to marriage for those who could not marry (same-sex couples and those within the prohibited degrees of marriage).[220] However, as a result of an influential memorandum in 1995, the government decided that to do so would lead to calls of discrimination and therefore decided to open

---

219 PERMANENT BUREAU OF THE HAGUE CONFERENCE, *Proceedings of the Seventeenth Session of The Hague Conference. Volume II*, The Hague, 1994, p. 61, §103.

220 *Dutch Second Chamber*, 1993-1994, 23761, No. 1, p. 2 (Proposed Art. 1:80a); No. 3, p. 5.

registration to different-sex couples.[221] Nonetheless, in opening up registration to different-sex couples, the Government did not intend to lessen the effects of the registration, but instead merely offer different-sex couples an alternative to marriage. In so doing, the **Dutch** Government therefore combined the PLURALISTIC MODEL with strong registration. In answer to the second question, it is conceivable that a country would opt for the DUALISTIC MODEL, yet only provide for weak registration. Up until now, those European countries to have legislated in this field have done so as a result of national initiatives. However, as the number of countries in the European Union to have enacted legislation increases, the political and social pressure on the others to do so will equally increase. As soon as pressure begins to be exercised from outside the national order, it is conceivable that conservative Governments will attempt to provide for a rock bottom solution. The Government will do what it must to silence those calling for the Government to act, yet will do no more than an absolute bare minimum.[222]

With all this in mind it is perhaps difficult to combine the extent of legal effects into the division made between PLURALISTIC and DUALISTIC MODELS. The combination of the model of registration with the legal effects depends on a multitude of factors, including the influence of the church in State politics, the constitutional protection afforded to marriage and the general impact which marriage has upon the personal law of aspirant spouses. It is therefore possible to envisage four different scenarios, three of which are represented by countries studied in this book.

- PLURALISTIC MODEL with weak registration, *e.g.* **France**, **Belgium**
- PLURALISTIC MODEL with strong registration, *e.g.* **The Netherlands**
- DUALISTIC MODEL with weak registration, *e.g.* **Slovenia**
- DUALISTIC MODEL with strong registration, *e.g.* **UK**, **Switzerland**

221 It was felt that in not opening registration to opposite-sex couples, registered partnership would come to be seen as a "second class marriage": *Dutch Second Chamber*, 1994-1995, 22700, No. 5 (*Leefvormen*) and *Dutch Second Chamber*, 1995-1996, 23761, No. 7, p. 5.

222 On the 20th July 2005, the **Slovenian** Registered Partnership Act came into force. This form of non-marital registered relationship provides only weak legal effects and is restricted to same-sex couples, thus supporting the claims advanced here.

VIII.5 OVERALL EVALUATION

VIII.5.1 EXISTING CLASSIFICATIONS

In attempting to analyse and categorise the various forms of non-marital registered relationships throughout Europe and the rest of the world, a number of prominent legal authors have suggested various models, techniques and distinctions. FORDER, for example, distinguishes between six different types of protection offered to different and same-sex cohabitees: (1) cohabitation protection,[223] (2) optional cohabitation schemes,[224] (3) enrolled contract,[225] (4) registered partnership,[226] (5) marriage and (6) relationships not resembling marriage.[227] This is supported, although somewhat adapted, by ANTOKOLSKAIA who distinguishes between six different categories of legislative progression.[228]

COESTER identifies four different legislative responses to the problems faced by same-sex couples: (1) piecemeal regulation, (2) domestic partnership (cohabitation) legislation, (3) registered partnership and (4) same-sex marriage.[229] An alternative classification is sketched by WAALDIJK who distinguishes between forms of marriage, quasi-marital status and semi-marital status.[230] KESSLER, in his account of **French** private international law in relation to registered partnerships, distinguishes between *partenariats*

---

223 The main purpose of this type of provision is thus to offer financial protection. This protection occurs automatically based on the length of time the parties have lived together , the quality of the relationship (*i.e.* its resemblance to marriage) or the presence of a common child: FORDER (2000a) p. 375-383.

224 This category consists of the limited protection offered to cohabitants wishing to opt-into a registration scheme *e.g.* **Belgium** and regions of **Spain**: FORDER (2000A) p. 383-385.

225 FORDER thus presents the **French** PACS legislation with a separate category, distinguishing it from the **Belgian** statutory cohabitation legislation on the basis of the public law effects attached thereto: FORDER (2000) p. 386-389.

226 **Denmark**, **Norway**, **Sweden**, **Iceland**, **The Netherlands**, **Germany** all fall into this category according to FORDER (2000A) p. 390-430.

227 In this category, FORDER deals with all the other forms of relationship regulation which are not based on the traditional marital model. These can, in her opinion, also be subsumed in the first two categories: FORDER (2000a) p. 442-446.

228 Namely, (1) countries devoid of regulation, (2) countries which provided for ad hoc cohabitation regulation, (3) countries with specific legislation providing minimal *ipso facto* protection, (4) countries providing for a limited regulation between contract and status, (5) countries providing for registered cohabitation and (6) countries allowing same-sex marriage: ANTOKOLSKAIA (2005) Chapter 4.4, p. 6.

229 COESTER (2002) p. 752-758.

230 WAALDIJK (2004).

institutions and *partenariats contrats*,[231] a distinction mirroring that already made by FULCHIRON between *partenariats statuts* and *partenariats contrats*,[232] and DEVERS between *partenariats statuts* and *partenariats cadres*.[233] These **French** authors differentiate between two sorts of partnerships on the basis of the balance struck between contract and status.[234] In those cases where the status of the institution is more dominant, these authors classify these relationships as institutional or framework, whilst all other forms of registered relationship are deemed contractual. Finally, MCGLYNN, although not drawing a distinction based on national legislation, does suggest the existence of a hierarchy of families in Europe with heterosexual marriage at the pinnacle, followed by heterosexual cohabitation, transsexual partnerships and same-sex relationships.[235] On the basis of this hierarchy of family forms, jurisdictions could thus be classified according to their acceptance of different types of relationship.

Despite the palpable value of such distinctions and classifications, the majority do not address the fundamental differences in the function or structure of the non-marital registration schemes in Europe.[236] They focus predominantly on one or two aspects of the registration scheme, either the registration itself or the legal effects attributed thereto. Alternatively these two facets of the registration are not adequately distinguished from each other. Furthermore, a deficiency in the classifications of both FORDER and COESTER lies in their reference to the term "registered partnership". In attempting to form European-wide terminology, one must search for new and overarching phraseology that breaks lose from the shackles of domestic substantive law. Reference therefore to the term "registered partnership" should be avoided.[237]

WAALDIJK'S classification lacks clarity in defining categories on the basis of their similarity to marriage. What criteria can be used to distinguish between "quasi-marriage" and "semi-marriage"? How is one to determine when a country has attached *almost all* of the rights of marriage and when a

---

231 KESSLER does, however, explain his choice for different terminology: KESSLER (2004) p. 24, §32.

232 FULCHIRON (2000) p. 900.

233 DEVERS (2004) p. 132, §208.

234 A distinction which will be discussed at length in **Chapter IX**.

235 MCGLYNN (2003) p. 228-229. See also MCGLYNN (2000).

236 A notable exception is, however, DEVERS who addresses the nature and effects of the institutions of registered partnerships: DEVERS (2004) p. 33-41 and 51-70.

237 See **Chapter I.4.4** for more information on the choice of the term "non-marital registered relationships".

country has attached only *some*? Are there legal rights and duties that are essential in such a classification? The lack of definitional criteria makes it almost impossible to scientifically use WAALDIJK'S classification. Although on an elementary level COESTER'S overview provides a good guide to the state of European legislation in this field, it lacks sufficient analysis of the different forms of "registered partnership" available. It is moreover confined to same-sex relationships, whilst domestic legislation is not.

VIII.5.2 TOWARDS A NEW CLASSIFICATION

Accordingly, in attempting to compare and classify the legal institutions that have been studied in this book, a number of crucial factors have been taken into account. Firstly, one cannot base a classification solely on the basis of the legal effects attributed to the registration of the partnership. One must analyse and dissect the underlying *raison d'être* of these forms of non-marital registered relationships. In doing so one must also bear in mind the threefold distinction made throughout this book between the establishment of, the legal effects attributed to and the dissolution of a non-marital registered relationship. Secondly, in selecting terminology to identify and classify such institutions, one must attempt to denationalise one's choices. In using terms already utilised by nation States, one runs the risk that national attributes will be assumed to be present in other States. A registered partnership (*geregistreerd partnerschap*) in **The Netherlands** is not identical to a registered partnership (*partenariat enregistré*) in **Switzerland**, despite both being termed the same.[238] It is crucial to construct overarching terminology, which although avoiding reference to individual national legislation, adequately portrays the underlying similarities in the institutions covered. It is for this reason that the term non-marital registered relationships has been chosen.[239]

With this in mind, the jurisdictions studied in this book can be divided into two distinct models with respect to two of the three fields of study (*i.e.* establishment and dissolution): the DUALISTIC MODEL and the PLURALISTIC MODEL. Although the end result in each of these models is different, the underlying rationale and function is strikingly similar. In both models the legal invisibility of and disadvantages faced by same-sex couples provided the necessary fuel to ignite the legislative fire. Although this fuel was sufficient in the DUALISTIC MODEL to keep the fire alight, the risk of the fire

[238] KOKKINI-IATRIDOU (1988) p. 90-91.

[239] See further **Chapter I.4.4**.

being extinguished in the PLURALISTIC MODEL meant that further fuel was required. It was found in the form of the legal problems faced by different-sex cohabiting couples. Whether one is able to talk of comparable results depends on one's level of abstraction.

Although both fires burned, the chemical properties of these fires are different. If one compares them at micro-level (*i.e.* comparing the models at a national level) the fires are very different; having been fuelled by different elements, the chemical composition of the final product is different. However, if one compares the fires at a macro-level (*i.e.* comparing the models at an international level), then one observes that both fires were fed by a common fuel and resulted in combustion. It is important that one therefore fully appreciate the level of abstraction at which one is attempting to compare these models.

The differences at substantive law level are, at this point in time, too great to attempt harmonisation, let alone unification.[240] Yet this disparity in domestic solutions does not lead one to conclude that this field is not suitable for harmonisation at private international law level. In fact, the conclusions expounded here illustrate the opposite. The similarity of result in the systems studied is plainly evident. Although the systems studied can be classified into two general models, these models serve to highlight the underlying comparable aims and rationale of these systems.

In having distinguished between these two models, the question obviously arises why a country chooses a particular model. Is there any way in which one can predict whether a given country will opt for the PLURALISTIC MODEL or the DUALISTIC MODEL? The answer to this question is naturally politically weighted. However a number of general points can be made. Firstly, if constitutional protection is afforded to the institution of marriage, then the chances are greater that a country will opt for the DUALISTIC MODEL. In **Switzerland**, for example, the protection afforded to the institution of marriage on the basis of Art. 14, Sw. FC was seen as a prohibitive factor in opening registration to couples of a different sex. Providing an alternative to marriage for different-sex couples was thought to compete with the institution of marriage.[241] In passing the new **Swiss** Federal Constitution in 1999, the **Swiss** Federal Council confirmed the traditional interpretation of marriage as a monogamous union between parties of a different sex.[242] Any

240 See **Chapter XIII.1**.

241 FF 2003, p. 1192 at 1207-1208.

242 FF 1997, p. 1 at 155.

constitutional amendment can take many years to be enacted, and the urgency with which the Government wishes to pass such legislation forces the Government to accept such a compromise. Outside the jurisdictions studied, the constitutional protection offered to the institution of marriage has also been one of the main arguments raised for refusing to open non-marital registration to different-sex couples.[243]

Secondly, if a country allows for the legal celebration of religious marriages, the chances are also greater that a country will opt for the DUALISTIC MODEL of relationship registration. The involvement of the church in the celebration of marriages tends to increase reluctance on the part of the Government to introduce any form of institution that could be seen as competing with the "sacred institution of holy matrimony". For example, in the **United Kingdom**, where religious marriages do not need to be preceded by civil marriages, the parliamentary debates clearly indicate the important influence still exercised by the church on the celebration of marriages. Outside the jurisdictions studied in this book, this was also one of the main points of debate in all of the **Nordic** countries.[244] It is interesting to note that since 2000, when the Church of **Sweden** was officially separated from the State, there has been increased debate on the introduction of same-sex marriage and the consequential repeal of the registered partnership legislation.

Obviously these two criteria do not engender hard and fast rules, and there may well be places where the constitutional protection afforded to the institution of marriage is not seen as forming an impediment to allowing different-sex couples to register their relationships. However, these two issues have been crucial up until now in determining whether a debate is possible on opening registration to different-sex couples.

---

243 This has also played an important role in **Germany**: See SCHRAMA (2004) p. 287-300. See further the decision of the **German** Constitutional Court, 17th July 2002, (2002) *NJW* 2543. In **Spain**, although men and women have the right to marry according to Art. 32, **Spanish** Constitution, marriage itself as an institution is not constitutionally protected (**Spanish** Constitutional Court Decision, No. 184/1990. See further, ROCA (2001) p. 366). Art. 39, **Spanish** Constitution simply protects the "family": see GONZÁLEZ-BEILFUSS (2004) p. 44, ROCA (2001) p. 365-367. Following this trend it is expected that the current proposal in the **Republic of Ireland** (see **Appendix 1**) will not be accepted as it stands since it allows for the registration of opposite-sex couples, whilst Art. 41(3)(1), **Irish** Constitution affords the institution of marriage special protection. This has in fact already been outlined as the position adopted by the Government by MR. MCDOWELL, Minister for Justice, Equality and Law Reform: *Irish Seanad*, 2004-2005, Vol. 179, No. 8, p. 692 (16th February 2005). For further analysis of the Irish situation, see CURRY-SUMNER (2005b).

244 LUND-ANDERSEN (2003) p. 21-22 and JÄNTERÄ-JAREBORG/SÖRGJERD (2004) p. 585-587.

At this stage it is also important to summarise the evaluations made. In **Section VIII.2.4** it was noted that the PLURALISTIC MODEL best abides by the principles of a valued pluralistic family law, whilst in **Section VIII.3.4** it was noted that with respect to the dissolution procedure afforded, no distinction should be drawn between the relationship form, and therefore support was put forward for the DUALISTIC MODEL. In light of these evaluations, coupled with the scale of legal effects outlined in **Section VIII.4.3**, it is possible to propose a combination of these two models as the ideal solution to the issues at hand.

THE IDEAL MODEL

A COMBINATION OF PLURALISTIC/DUALISTIC MODELS

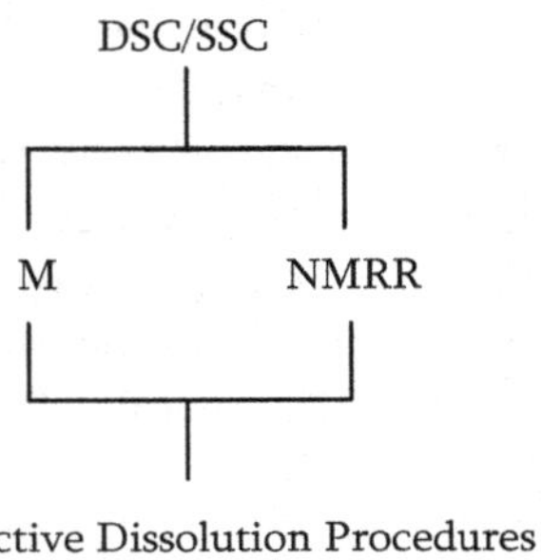

Key: **DSC**: *Different-Sex Couples*, **SSC**: *Same-Sex Couples*
M: *Marriage*, **NMRR**: *Non-Marital Registered Relationship*

Due to the existence of two different models of partnership registration outlined in this chapter, the question whether the rules of private international law in this field can be harmonised or even unified is of ever-greater significance. It is submitted that the fundamental approach and aims of the legislature are comparable in all seven jurisdictions. It is thus submitted that all seven legal systems have created: A State-regulated, legal registration scheme for two persons involved in an exclusive, intimate relationship. Opting into this system by means of registration of the relationship entails the attribution of rights and duties, and the assumption of obligations and responsibilities between the parties themselves, as well with third parties and the State.

Classification of living things is known as taxonomy. Scientists have classified all living organisms into five kingdoms along lines of commonality. Each kingdom is split into smaller groups called phyla. Each phylum is split into groups called classes, each class into orders, each order into families, each family into genera, and each genus into species. The same method of classification can be transposed into family law.[245] If one examines the topic at hand through the eyes of a scientist, one sees that marriage and non-marital registered relationships are merely different *genera* of the same *family*: close, intimate, personal relationships. The various different forms of non-marital registered relationships, as well as various sorts of marriages,[246] are simply different *species* derived from the same *genus*. Different varieties of the same grouping can thus, if possessing common functional properties, be bracketed together and thus assigned to the same private international law category. The question that now arises is: according to which private international law category should the various forms of substantive law legislation be assigned? Perhaps even more crucially: if a distinction between the PLURALISTIC, DUALISTIC and MONISTIC MODELS is evident at substantive law level, is such a distinction necessary at private international law? Does the distinction between different models of non-marital registered relationship legislation at substantive law level necessitate different rules in the field private international law? These questions form the springboard for the next part of this research: the search for harmonisation or unification possibilities in the field of cross-border non-marital registered relationships in Europe.

245 See, for example, SCHRAMA (2004) p. 569.

246 For example, polygamous marriages, child marriages, same-sex marriages, religious marriages *etc.*

PART III

PRIVATE INTERNATIONAL LAW

"I say to the noble Lord that there is a fundamental distinction between status and contract."

Lord Lester of Herne Hill, Grand Committee, House of Lords, 10th May 2004, Column GC9

CHAPTER IX
CHARACTERISATION REVISITED

IX.1 INTRODUCTION

The problem of characterisation surfaces persistently in all areas of law including the field of family law.[1] Today, private international law in the field of family law is once again confronted with a new characterisation dilemma: the phenomenon of non-marital registered relationships.[2] The increasing number of countries providing for some form of non-marital registered relationship poses problems in terms of characterisation: to which legal category should legal issues relating to non-marital registered relationships be assigned?

The theories with respect to characterisation have been summarised in **Chapter** II. However, the fundamental problem confronting an attempt to characterise legal issues is not a mere abstract, conjectural or theoretical exercise. In striving towards the ascertainment of an autonomous characterisation of the term non-marital registered relationship, it is necessary to embark on comparative research in order to fully appreciate the variety of solutions in domestic legislation.[3] However, even once one appreciates the differences and similarities between domestic rules,[4] one is still faced with the task of identifying the legal categories to which these institutions can be assigned.

---

1 The number of cases relating to family law matters is evidence of this statement *e.g.* parental consent, capacity to marriage, polygamous marriage. See **Chapter II**.

2 For a contrary viewpoint that characterisation of non-marital registered relationships is irrelevant, see RIGAUX (2000) p. 654. RIGAUX states, "The problem of characterisation as such is irrelevant. It concerns a contractual agreement set up by a special statue in the field of personal relationships and therefore it is not without analogy to family law affiliations or conjugal status." However, although this might be true, it is necessary to understand how to define non-marital registered relationships, especially for the purposes of recognition. In doing so, one must therefore attempt to find the essential criteria upon which one is able to characterise a legal issue as one stemming from a non-marital registered relationship instead of one raising purely contractual issues.

3 This has been done in **Chapters III** to **VII**.

4 See **Chapter VIII**.

When dealing with non-marital registered relationships the legal issue can be approached from two different perspectives. On the one hand, one can emphasise the contractual nature of the relationship. The parties to a non-marital registered relationship agree upon certain legal effects pursuant to a mutual agreement; the moment the relationship is registered the contract becomes enforceable.[5] Alternatively, one could place more emphasis on the effect on the parties' personal status. Upon registering the relationship, the parties acquire a status as registered partners, with certain rights and duties, capacities and incapacities attendant upon that status.[6] Accordingly, one is confronted with a choice between two traditional private international law legal categories: personal status and contract.[7]

Before one can ascribe legal categories to legal issues, one must first understand the substance of those categories. **Section IX.2** is devoted to an analysis of the theoretical background to this field. In enacting domestic legislation, the majority of jurisdictions studied have already adopted rules with respect to characterisation (**Section IX.3**). These characterisations will subsequently be compared and evaluated in **Section IX.4**. A number of criteria will be extrapolated, which will be applied in **Section IX.5** to all those jurisdictions around the world to have enacted registration schemes. Although this research is restricted to a comparison of seven countries, these countries will inevitably be confronted with forms of non-marital registered relationships from elsewhere around the world.

IX.2 THEORETICAL BACKGROUND

IX.2.1 CHARACTERISATION ACCORDING TO CONTRACT

IX.2.1.1 General Notion

If a contract purports to have ramifications related to a person's personal status, special considerations must be taken into account. Contracts of this nature are subject to certain overriding considerations of the *lex fori*. In fact

5 See **Chapters III.4.8**, **IV.4.8**, **V.4.8**, **VI.4.8** and **VII.4.8**, as well as **Chapter VIII.2.3**.

6 C. ALLEN (1930) p. 288. He comments on the fact that a status is the state of being from which a number of capacities and incapacities flow. A status is thus, according to him, "... the condition of belonging to a particular class of persons to whom the law assigns certain peculiar legal capacities or incapacities or both".

7 Some authors believe one should distinguish between the category of marriage and the category of contract: HENNERON (2003) p. 464-468 and KESSLER (2004) p. 69-76.

some authors argue that in such contracts the law plays so great a role and the agreement of the parties such a minor role, that it becomes doubtful whether such contracts can actually be classified as contractual at all.[8] The question whether a contractual relationship affects one's personal status must always be considered since any issue relating to a person's status is summarily excluded from the scope of Brussels I and the Rome Convention.[9] It is therefore important to attempt to delineate the moment at which the metaphorical pendulum swings away from the significance of the contract and towards the importance of the status gained as a result of the transaction. Take the following examples.[10]

Example 1 (Pure contract)
Annemarie offers to sell a car to Bente for €1,000. Bente accepts the offer and Annemarie agrees to deliver the car the following day. Annemarie delivers the car to Bente's house and Bente hands over €1,000.

Example 2 (Contract and relationship)
Carol and David have been in a close, personal relationship for six years and have lived together for the last year. The couple decide to buy a house together. Upon buying the house they also sign a cohabitation contract to regulate their rights and duties in relation to the house both during the relationship and should the relationship come to an end.

---

8 TREITEL (1999) p. 3. The same problem exists in the sphere of employee contracts that grant the status of an employee and employer respectively on the parties involved.

9 Art. 1(2)(a), Brussels I and Arts. 1(2)(a) and 1(2)(b), Rome Convention exclude matters relating to status or legal capacity of natural persons and contractual obligations related to wills and succession, rights in property arising out of a matrimonial relationship and rights and duties arising out of a family relationship, parentage, marriage or affinity, including maintenance obligations in respect of children, who are not legitimate. In the GIULIANO-LAGARDE Report, it is noted that these exemptions "intended (...) to exclude from the scope of the Convention all matters of family law".

10 These examples are meant as illustrations. They are not true of all situations in all legal systems. There are, for example, many systems that allow for common-law marriage and therefore do not require all marriages to be registered, *e.g.* **Alabama** (*Piel v. Brown*, 361 So.2d 90 (1978)), **Colorado** (*Deter v. Deter*, 484 P.2d 805 (App. 1971)), **Idaho** (§32-301, Idaho Code), **Iowa** (§595.11, Iowa Code Annotated), **Kansas** (§23-301, Kansas Statues Annotated), Montana (§26-1-602, §40-1-403/404, Montana Code Annotated), **Oklahoma** (§1, Title 43, Oklahoma Statues Annotated), **Pennsylvania** (§1-23, Title 48, Pennsylvania Statutes Annotated), **Rhode Island** (*Souza v. O'Hara*, 121 RI 88, 395 A.2a 1060 (1978)), **South Carolina** (§20-1-360, South Carolina Code Annotated), **Texas** (§1.91, Vernon's Texas Family Code Annotated) and the **District of Columbia** (*Johnson v. Young*, 372 A.2a 992 (DC App. 1977)).

Example 3 (Contract and registration)
Eveline and François have been married for a number of years when Eveline obtains a new job in a different city. The couple decide to move and buy a house. After finding a house and completing negotiations, a contract of sale is drawn up.

Example 4 (Contract, registration and relationship)
Gerry and Harriët have been in a relationship for two months and are planning to have children together. They intend to get married and so make an appointment with their local Registrar. Six months later they get married.

Each of the abovementioned examples consists of a contractual element: the sale of a car, a cohabitation contract, the sale of a house, the registration of a partnership or the contractual agreement to marry. However, the contractual element is of decreasing significance when one analyses *Examples 1* through *4* in ascending order. *Example 1* involves a pure contractual transaction: an offer, acceptance and performance of the contractual obligation. Despite the existence of a close, personal relationship in *Example 2*, the purpose of the contract is the regulation of mutual property rights and obligations.[11] The relationship is, *per se*, not enough to elevate the contract into the realm of status. This is not, however, the case in *Example 3* where one can argue that the significance of the parties' status is more important than the contract. At this stage it is essential that one distinguish between four major components of a typical land transfer: pre-contractual, contractual, conveyance and registration.[12]

---

11 Such contracts are not permitted in all countries since they are seen to be against public policy. They are however allowed in **The Netherlands.** The so-called *samenlevingscontract* is governed entirely by the law on contract and is not subject to registration. For further information see SCHRAMA (2004) p. 373-377, §4.2.2.1; LEKKERKERKER (1999). In **England & Wales** cohabitation contracts may be unenforceable. The validity of the contract may depend upon the contents as well as other factors. See BARLOW (2001) p. 14-21. This is however, not the case in all common law countries. In the **USA,** some seventeen States allow for enforceable cohabitation contracts, often being based on the *Marvin v. Marvin* [1976] 134 Cal. Rptr 815 as well as at least five provinces in **Canada**. In **Scotland,** the situation is the same as in **England & Wales**, although there have been calls by the **Scottish** Law Commission to the effect that "a contract between cohabitants or prospective cohabitants relating to property or financial matters should not be void or unenforceable solely because it was concluded between the parties in this type of relationships": SCOTTISH LAW COMMISSION, *Report on Family Law. Report No. 135*, Edinburgh: Scottish Law Commission, 1992, Clause 42. Such a cohabitation contract is also possible in **Germany** (SCHRAMA (2004) p. 377-380, §4.2.2.2), **Norway** (NOACK (2001) p. 112), **Belgium** (SENAEVE (2003a) p. 233-234, §2083-2085).

12 GARRO (2004) p. 56, §61. In some countries any number of these stages may be merged into one, *e.g.* the contractual and conveyancing stages in **England & Wales** have been merged since the 1925 reforms.

During the first phase negotiations take place. Upon the basis of these negotiations a contract is eventually drawn up detailing each party's rights and obligations.[13] Depending upon the country in which the land is to be found this contract may be embodied in a notarial deed.[14] The third component consists of the mode of transfer, whilst the fourth and final stage involves the registration of the act of conveyancing with the State registry. However, legal systems differ as to the operative stage at which ownership is deemed to be transferred.[15] Nevertheless, although it is common to draw lines between French-inspired, German-inspired and common-law inspired legal systems, or jurisdictions adhering to a system of registration of title or registration of deeds, as well as legal systems in which registration is constitutive or declarative, it appears that regardless of the role played by registration in the conveyancing process, most jurisdictions encourage the grantee to file the instrument of transfer for record, if the right is to be effective *erga omnes.*[16]

Such a registration requirement is imposed for a number of reasons. On the basis of an extensive comparison of legal systems around the world, GARRO concludes that the primary purpose of registration is to make the creation and transfer or conveyance of an interest in land simpler and more certain, and in so doing create an effective mechanism for the protection of third party interests. [17] MATTEI in his economic analysis of the basic principles of property law notes that mere physical control of immoveable property is not sufficient to obtain ownership.[18] Instead, a person must use a legal tool (*e.g.* registration) other than mere physical control in order to obtain ownership (*i.e.* the status of owner). However, this registration requirement is also present with respect to goods other than immoveable property, *e.g.* cars, boats and airplanes. While the value of these commodities is often the perceived reason for such a registration requirement, the rationale actually lies in the liability rules attached to these particular pieces of property. As MATTEI states,

---

13 The exact remedies available for breach of these obligations are not the purpose of this work. It must, however, be noted that legal systems around the world have addressed this question very differently. In civil law countries reference is often sought in the realm of compensatory damages, whereas in common law systems, one acquires a certain proprietal interest in the property that is equitably protected.

14 GARRO (2004) p. 51, §56.

15 GARRO (2004) p. 57, §62.

16 GARRO (2004) p. 57, §62.

17 GARRO (2004) p. 56, §61.

18 MATTEI (2000) p. 67.

> This kind of property creates externalities in the form of danger. Should the danger become outright harm, it becomes necessary to allocate it to a particular individual: the formalised, registered owner.[19]

If the element of registration distinguishes *Example 3* from *Examples 1* and *2*, the question thus rises whether there are further characteristics distinguishing *Examples 3* and *4*? The answer to this question is rooted at the heart of the contract. The close, intimate personal relationship between the parties, in *Example 4*, forms the basis for the creation of the contract. In *Example 3* the parties' relationship is not crucial to the contract itself. The contract concerns the sale of a house; the parties' relationship is merely a side issue. In elevating the importance of the close, intimate personal relationship between the parties in *Example 4*, one is able to justify the imposition of different principles at private international law to such contracts.[20] If one turns one's attention to the subject at hand, the question arises how such a non-marital registered relationship should be categorised. The answer to this question revolves around the importance of the relationship to the contract. The parties have opted for a formalised procedure to sanctify their relationship. In some countries, the contractual nature of the relationship has been emphasised.

IX.2.1.2 Contractual nature of non-marital registered relationships

Of the countries studied, only **France** and **Belgium** have made express reference to the contractual nature of these institutions.[21] According to Art. 515-1, Fr. CC "*le pacte civil de solidarité est un contrat*". According to

19 MATTEI (2000) p. 68.

20 A wealth of literature has been published on the contractual nature of marriage. See, for example, MAINE (1905) p. 139; GRAVESON (1953); LOWE/DOUGLAS (1998) p. 22-23; JESSURUN D'OLIVEIRA (2000a) p. 298; SCHWENZER (2001) p. 200; RIX (2002) p. 255; HUNTER-HENIN (2004) p. 254, §335, p. 260-271, §343-357; VRANKEN (2005) p. 95. Furthermore, numerous judicial decisions have dealt with this point, see, for example, *Bellinger v. Bellinger* [2001] 3 FCR 1, *per* Thorpe LJ "marriage is a contract for which the parties elect but which is regulated by the State, both in its formation and its termination by divorce, because it affects the status upon which depend a variety of entitlements, benefits and obligations".

21 See **Chapters III.5.1** and **IV.4.1**. In a recent parliamentary debate, the **Dutch** Minister of Justice also referred to the contractual nature of the **Dutch** registered partnership: "het idee om zonder rechterlijke tussenkomst een huwelijk te ontbinden het huwelijk in wezen gelijkstelt met wat in essentie het geregistreerd partnerschap is, namelijk een overeenkomst": *Dutch Second Chamber,* 17th December 2002, Parliamentary Discussion, 34-2576. This position is not supported in any **Dutch** literature: see **Chapter VI**. Also supported in relation to **Swiss** law: KREN KOSTKIEWICZ (2001) p. 104-107.

REVILLARD, this domestic definition of the PACS imposes a contractual characterisation on the institution.[22] She argues that evoking notions of personal status in relation to the PACS would be contrary to the aim of the legislature.[23] She is facilitated in her line of reasoning by a 1999 **French** Constitutional Court decision.[24] The Constitutional Court, asked to rule on the constitutionality of the PACS legislation,[25] discussed the issues relating to the juridical nature of the PACS.[26] The Court conceded that although the obligations imposed on those who register a PACS could inevitably lead to an internal characterisation in terms of status,[27] the Government's intention to create an institution fundamentally distinct from marriage could not be ignored. In doing so, it held that Arts. 1109 *et seq.*, Fr. CC with respect to contracts were correspondingly applicable with respect to a PACS.[28]

This approach has also been advocated by HUNTER-HENIN who advocates a reexamination of the term personal status in **French** law.[29] In dealing with the PACS, she states that,

> [L]e pacte civil de solidarité qui est institué n'est pas un statut indisponible mais un contrat, aux conditions de formation peu rigoureuses et à la force obligatoire douteuse, qui ne saurait donc prétendre relever en droit international privé de la catégorie statut personnel.[30]

If one characterises the PACS as a contract then what are the private international law consequences? According to REVILLARD and HAUSER,[31]

---

22 REVILLARD (2000) p. 340 and REVILLARD (2002) p. 588-590. This opinion is also supported by RAYMOND: "Si cette nouvelle création porte le nom de pacte, il ne peut s'agir d'un contrat relevant de la catégorie habituelle des contrats": RAYMOND (1999), p. 103.

23 Equally see: LEMOULAND (2000) p. 408; BEIGNIER (1999) p. 33; MICHEL/POULIQUEN (1999) p. 25; VIVIER (2001).

24 Conseil Const., 9th November 1999, Decision No. 99-149, *JO* 16th November 1999.

25 It must be noted that the court does not decide on the merits of the law referred it but only on its constitutionality.

26 For detailed commentary on this case see MOLFESSIS (2000).

27 The court made reference to Art. 515-4, Fr. CC: "Les partenaires liés par un pacte civil de solidarité s'apportent une aide mutuelle et matérielle", but not fidelity as in the case of marriage: Art. 212, Fr. CC.

28 Conseil Const., 9th November 1999, Decision No. 99-149, *JO* 16th November 1999, §28, §61: "le pacte civil de solidarité est une convention à durée indéterminée qui justifie qu'un partenaire puisse librement la résilier" and §67: "le pacte civil de solidarité est un contrat étranger au mariage".

29 HUNTER-HENIN (2004) p. 254-255, §336.

30 HUNTER-HENIN (2004) p. 254-255, §336.

31 REVILLARD (2000) p. 339; HAUSER (1999) p. 6.

this would result in choice of law questions, at least in European Union jurisdictions,[32] being adjudicated with reference to the Rome Convention.[33] In applying these provisions, neither author addresses the issue of the scope of this Convention.[34] Since the PACS is firmly situated in Book 1, Fr. CC, it would indeed be difficult to suggest that *even if* one adopts a contractual interpretation of the PACS that it should fall within the scope of the Rome Convention.[35]

If one instead insists upon the application of the Rome Convention, the basic principle of party autonomy would be applicable to non-marital registered relationships.[36] If this is the case, then which law have the parties to a PACS chosen? It is stated that the choice must be "express or demonstrated with reasonable certainty".[37] In fact the essence of Art. 3(1), Rome Convention is that the parties should have had the possibility to make a choice of law. If one analyses the provisions of the **French** Civil Code relating to the PACS, this opportunity is clearly absent. At no point in the conclusion of a PACS are the parties requested, or even advised, to elect the applicable law governing the PACS.[38]

Both REVILLARD and HAUSER fail to address the wide-ranging implications of the applicability of the Rome Convention, thus ignoring the possible consequences of *dépeçage* in relation to the application of the last sentence of Art. 3(1), as well as ignoring the possible application of Art. 4 and the search for the law of the country with which the PACS is most closely

---

32 In **Switzerland**, Arts. 116 and 117, Sw. CPIL are more-or-less identical to Arts. 3 and 4, Rome Convention. Therefore, when speaking of European Union countries, the law in Switzerland must be regarded in this sense as yielding an equivalent result.

33 Although not expressly stated, it can be assumed that these authors would also plead for the corresponding applicability of Brussels I, or the Lugano Convention.

34 See **footnote 9**.

35 Even if the 1980 Rome Convention is inapplicable, the consequence that the ordinary private international law rules with respect to contract would become operative would in effect cause little difference in the actual applicable law rule, since as stated in ECJ, *Commission v. CODEMI,* Case No. C-318/81 [1985] ECR 3693 at 3697 and 3712 *per* Lord SLYNN: "contractual provisions expressing the common interests of the parties must take precedence over any other criterion which might be used where the contract is silent on a particular point".

36 Art. 3(1), first sentence, Rome Convention.

37 Art. 3(1), second sentence, Rome Convention.

38 The parties would be seemingly free to choose the law of a wholly unrelated country to be applicable to their PACS. The only limitation here would be the idea of mandatory rules.

connected.[39] If, despite these problems, one attempts to characterise such relationships as contractual, one must also overcome the issue of functionality and the intrinsic differences between commercial contracts and the PACS. As outlined in **Chapter VIII.5**, a PACS, unlike a commercial contract, aims to provide social recognition to a couple's relationship.[40] Registration of a PACS extends beyond the purpose, function and scope of a pure business contract, in not only regulating the mutual relationship of the parties but also creating a *communauté de vie* that affects third parties, the State and the society in which the parties live. Furthermore, this approach is also supported by the decision of the **French** Constitutional Court having made the constitutionality of the PACS legislation dependent upon the requirement of a *vie commune*.[41] It is therefore clear that although the contractual elements of the PACS are plain to see, one cannot avoid reference to the special contractual nature of the PACS agreement.

Similar questions also emerge in relation to the **Belgian** institution of statutory cohabitation.[42] In order to fully accentuate Parliamentary intent that this law was not to cause the commencement of a new stage in the parties' lives,[43] as marriage entails, but instead only relate to the pragmatic rules with respect to property and financial matters, the new institution was inserted in Book III (property law) instead of Book I (family law) of the **Belgian** Civil Code.[44] It is therefore clear from the positioning of this law that the ambitions of this new institution are to some extent subordinate to those of the **French** PACS.

The contractual nature of the **Belgian** statutory cohabitation is further evidenced, as argued by some authors, by the absence of any effect on the parties' civil status.[45] At first sight, it would seem that the competence

---

39 The absurdity of a contractual characterisation emerges in attempting to apply Art. 4(2), for example, what is the characteristic performance and which party is to effect this characteristic performance?

40 KESSLER (2004) p. 75, §124.

41 Conseil Const., 9th November 1999, Decision No. 99-149, *JO* 16th November 1999, §§26 and 28. Reference was made to the Parliamentary debates where it was stated that a PACS should be seen as "une communauté de toit ... une communauté de lit" (*French National Assembly*, 30th March 1999, GUIGOU).

42 A literal translation of the **Dutch** term *wettelijke samenwoning* or the **French** *cohabitation légale. Loi du 23 novembre 1998 instaurant la cohabitation légale / De wet van 23 november 1998 tot invoering van de wettelijke samenwoning.*

43 See **Chapter III.4.1**.

44 See **Chapter III.5.1**.

45 See **Chapter III.5.2**.

afforded to the Registrar of Births, Deaths and Marriages would indeed constitute an event signifying a change in the parties' civil status.[46] As JESSURUN D'OLIVEIRA notes, intentions are however not sufficient and if the result is such to create a change in the parties' civil status then one must accept that such a change has taken place.[47] However, in order to effect a change in one's civil status according to **Belgian** law, the Registrar of Births, Deaths and Marriages must prepare a deed of civil status.[48] As a result the registration of a statutory cohabitation has no effect on a person's civil status. However it is essential that one unequivocally distinguish the notions of civil status and personal status.

IX.2.2 CHARACTERISATION ACCORDING TO PERSONAL STATUS

IX.2.2.1 General Notion

The legal, empirical and societal ordering of situations and rules, is also exemplified in the classification, for certain purposes, of persons within a legal system. Once ordered into predefined groups, these groups are assigned names and thus the seeds for the growth of a concept of status are planted. The predominant purpose behind this concept of status is therefore the ordering of society.[49] Yet, the *raison d'être* extends far further. Certain social relations and individual conditions are deemed to necessitate a society divided and classified into status groups. Where a personal condition or social relation exists which it is in the interest of the community to control or supervise, the law imposes a legal status on that person or persons.[50] Membership of a community or class thus prevents membership of certain other classes, *e.g.* belonging to the class infancy necessarily precludes membership of the class majority. When attempting to identify core facets of the legal category "personal status", one must ensure that one draw a fine line between the notion of *civil status,* on the one hand, and the broader term *personal status*, on the other. The concept of civil status is but a segment of a greater whole and cannot be said to embody the entire scope of the category personal status. Although any instrument duly and legally registered in the Civil Status Registry may act as *prima facie* evidence of a change in one's civil status, the absence of such an instrument does not

---

46 See further, FULCHIRON (2000) p. 899, footnote 43.

47 JESSURUN D'OLIVEIRA (2000a) p. 311.

48 See further **Chapter III.5.2**.

49 GRAVESON (1974) p. 227.

50 GRAVESON (1953).

preclude a change in one's personal status. Reference throughout this text will thus be made to the term *personal status*; a term broad enough to bring evident meaning to the seven chosen jurisdictions.

IX.2.2.2 With respect to non-marital registered relationships

In turning one's attention to the issue at hand, in **The Netherlands**, **Switzerland** and the **United Kingdom**, the legislature has avoided this entire debate by ensuring that registration of a non-marital relationship affects the parties' civil status.[51] In so doing the legislature has *a priori* solved the problem, since having an effect on the parties' civil status, the personal status of the parties is necessarily affected. This is, however, neither the case in **France** nor **Belgium**.[52] Therefore, the question that must be posed is whether the **French** PACS and **Belgian** statutory cohabitation can, despite the absence of an effect on the parties' civil status, still be regarded as affecting the parties' personal status.

Many commentators in **France** have vehemently disagreed with the contention that the PACS must be interpreted contractually.[53] Instead these authors put forward a number of arguments for a characterisation according to personal status. Firstly, the PACS legislation is to be found in Book 1, Fr. CC and not in the sections related to special contracts. Whilst admitting that this argument is highly formalistic, these authors vindicate its use by stating that since the PACS is placed squarely within the provisions related to persons, it seems self-evident that it should be regarded as affecting one's personal status.[54] Moreover, the **French** Ministry of Justice makes explicit use of this argument in their proposals for reform of the PACS regime, and the adoption of a provision explicitly providing for the PACS to be regarded as an institution falling within the ambit of the legal category of personal status.[55]

This formal argument is further supported by a more applied approach. If one examines those persons eligible to register a PACS, one is immediately

---

51 **Chapters V.5.2**, **VI.5.2** and **VII.5.2**.

52 **Chapters III.5.2** and **IV.5.2**.

53 CHANTELOUP (2000) p. 1716-1720; FULCHRION (2000) p. 900; AUDIT (2000) p. 173, §194 and p. 535, §623bis; MAYER/HEUZÉ (2001) p. 363-364, §547; DEVERS (2004) p. 40, §57; KESSLER (2004) p. 69-70, §113-114; LOUSSOUARN/BOUREL (2004) p. 389-391, §286.

54 CHANTELOUP (2000) p. 1718.

55 MINISTRE DE LA JUSTICE (2004) p. 28.

struck by the similarity to marital relationships.[56] FULCHIRON argues that even though it is stated that the PACS is based on contract, it is the fusion of the rules of personal status and contract which make the characterisation of the PACS as a pure contract difficult.[57] MIGNOT adds weight to a non-contractual analysis in his submission that the large number of inadaptable, non-negotiable legal prescriptions in the PACS make it difficult to adopt a contractual approach.[58]

These academic overtones have also found judicial resonance. On the 5th June 2002, the President of the *Tribunal de Grande Instance* in Lille issued a judgment in which he stated that in order for the obligation of support involved in a PACS to be performed faithfully, all forms of infidelity by the parties should be penalised.[59] Although not addressing the status/contract dichotomy directly, this case illustrates the manner in which the judiciary has begun to approach the problem, namely by analogy with the institution of marriage,[60] and thus as an issue related to one's personal status. In a similar fashion, the *Conseil d'État*, in a decision issued on the 23rd May 2003 and in excluding the jurisdiction of the administrative judge, referred to the nature of the PACS and the role of the court clerk in its registration.[61] Although holding that Arts. 1109 *et seq.*, Fr. CC are applicable *mutatis mutandis* to the PACS, even the *Conseil Constitutionnel* accentuated the constitutional importance of the *vie commune* underpinning the PACS legislation, as well as the many restrictions imposed on the registration of a PACS which "justifiés notamment par les mêmes motifs que ceux qui font obstacle au mariage".[62] Some authors have noted that these references support a characterisation according to the parties' personal status.[63]

It is submitted that a literal adherence to the text of Art. 515-1, Fr. CC does not assist an attempt to reach an autonomous characterisation. The object of the PACS legislation was to rectify the unsatisfactory legal position of those

56 TERRÉ (1999) and Art. 144, Fr. CC and further **Chapter IV.4.2**, **IV.4.4** and **IV.4.6**.

57 FULCHRION (2000) p. 899-900 and FULCHIRON (2004) p. 96-97.

58 MIGNOT (2001) p. 614.

59 TGI Lille, 5th July 2002 (2003) *D* 515, annotated LABBÉE (2003) p. 515. See also KESSLER (2004) p. 71, §115.

60 LABBÉE (2003) p. 518 as well as Conseil Const., 9th November 1999, Decision No. 99-149, *JO*, 16th November 1999.

61 Conseil d'État, 23rd May 2003, Appl. No. 248982. See also GOURDOU/LEMOULAND (2004) p. 296-297.

62 Conseil Const., 9th November 1999, Decision No. 99-419, *JO* 16th December 1999, §27.

63 HUET (2002) p. 543-544; KESSLER (2004) p. 71, §115.

couples who did not want to marry or who could not marry; Minister GUIGOU considered that the PACS would bring stability and security to non-married couples.[64] With these aims in mind, and having regard to the totality of the PACS legislation,[65] the express positioning of the PACS legislation in Book 1, Fr. CC, the similarities to the eligibility criteria of marriage and the mindful prohibitions on incest, the PACS can only properly be characterised as affecting the parties' personal status. After all it is the relationship and not the contract that forms the key element in the transaction.[66] A position that has recently been endorsed by the Ministry of Justice.[67]

But can this same approach be applied with respect to the **Belgian** statutory cohabitation? The arguments in favour of a contractual characterisation are probably weightier due to the placing of the legislation in Book III instead of Book I, Belg. CC. However, according to ERAUW and VERHELLEN intentions are not enough.[68] They argue that if a statutory cohabitation with one person precludes the celebration of a marriage[69] or registration of a statutory cohabitation with another person, then one's personal status is unavoidably affected.[70] The principle of exclusivity is adhered to and therefore registration of a statutory cohabitation has an impact on a person's personal status, regardless of whether this change is then registered in the civil status registers. Regardless of the academic debate surrounding the proper characterisation of the statutory cohabitation in **Belgium**, the recent codification of **Belgian** private international law has settled these doubts. It is now clear that regardless of whether a non-marital registered relationship is deemed to have an effect on the parties' personal status in the jurisdiction in which is was registered, if it can be characterised as a *relation de vie commune* according to Art. 58, Belg. CPIL then it will be judged according to the rules laid down in Chapter IV, Belg. CPIL. Chapter IV is, in turn,

---

64 Discussion with GUIGOU, *French National Assembly*, 3rd November 1998. Discussions can be found at: www.justice.gouv.fr/discours. See further **Chapter IV.3.8**.

65 Especially to the exclusivity restrictions, see **Chapters IV.4.2** and **VIII.2.1**.

66 See **Section IX.2.1**.

67 MINISTRE DE LA JUSTICE (2004) p. 28.

68 ERAUW/VERHELLEN (1999) p. 154, §17.

69 See **Chapters III.4.2**, **III.6.8** and **VIII.2.1**.

70 See also JESSURUN D'OLIVEIRA (2000a) p. 311.

placed squarely within the traditional boundaries of the realm of personal status.[71]

IX.2.3 CLASSIFICATION WITHIN THE CATEGORY OF STATUS

If one is to characterise these new forms of non-marital registered relationship as questions affecting the parties' personal status, a secondary question arises: how should one classify these non-marital registered relationships within the legal category of personal status?[72] Should one attempt to utilise an existing category, enlarging the ambit of these rules, and thereby determine legal questions according to these rules or should one create a new legal category designed to deal with issues relating to non-marital registered relationships?

The legal category of personal status is multifaceted and contains many different forms, *e.g.* marriage, infancy, majority, birth, death, illegitimacy, legitimacy and so forth. If one attempts to enlarge or broaden an existing class within the legal category of personal status, it is fairly self-evident that the most straightforward and appropriate class would be that of marriage (**Section IX.2.3.1**).[73] One could alternatively, however, choose to create new private international law rules with respect to such relationships (**Section IX.2.3.2**).

IX.2.3.1 Classification within the general category of marriage

This approach aims at enlarging the private international law category of marriage by simply referring questions related to non-marital registered relationships to the same private international law rules as marriage.[74] This approach has been adopted, for example, in **Switzerland**,[75] as well as having

71 Despite not hinging choice of law rules on the use of personal law factors, the choice of law rules applicable to such relationship are still characterised by a lack of party autonomy.

72 See, for example, FULCHIRON (2004) p. 97, who poses the same question. The word "classification" has been used here to accentuate the difference between this problem and that of "characterisation".

73 The term *non-marital* is intrinsically linked to marriage in being the negative sense of the former. See **Chapter I.4.4** for further explanation of the terminology selected.

74 MIGNOT (2001) p. 642.

75 Art. 65a, Sw. CPIL. This approach is also adopted in the **Nordic** countries, see **Denmark**: §3(2), Danish Registered Partnership Act; **Norway**: Sec. 3(2), Norwegian Registered Partnership Act; **Sweden**: JÄNTERÄ-JAREBORG (2003a) p. 143-145, JAKOB (2002) p. 27-32, BODGAN (2001a); **Iceland**: Art. 8, Icelandic Registered Partnership Act; **Finland**: Chapter

been advocated by CHANTELOUP in relation to the **French** PACS.[76] Those championing such an approach have done so on a number of bases. Firstly, there are those who have argued that non-marital registered relationships are inherently based upon the framework employed in the field of marriage law. The similarities between marriage and non-marital registered relationships at domestic substantive law level should be replicated in the rules of private international law.[77] MIGNOT, for example, argues that instead of reducing the foreign institution to something that it is not, one should instead adopt a *sui generis* definition of marriage.[78] Referring to **French** law, KESSLER indicates that such an approach adheres not only to the letter of the law, but also to the spirit of the law.[79]

This argument is closely connected to another oft forwarded argument, namely that when characterising foreign institutions one should adopt an enlightened *lex fori* approach. Such an approach is, however, not without its opponents. GULLIAUME, for example, argues that the classification of foreign institutions should reflect domestic principles and thus reflect a pure *lex fori* approach.[80]

> Une union homosexuelle ne pourrait être qualifiée de mariage en droit international privé suisse que si le droit matériel suisse admettait l'ouverture du mariage aux couples homosexuels. En absence d'une telle possibilité, la qualification mariage d'un partenariat homosexuel contracté à l'étranger devrait être exclue.[81]

Nonetheless, as was seen in **Chapter II.2.4** the enlightened *lex fori* approach has substantial authority in all seven countries studied. Building on this argument, other authors have analogised to the approach often taken with respect to the recognition of polygamous marriages.[82] This position has, however, been disparaged, most notably by DEVERS, who argues that unlike polygamous marriages, non-marital registered relationships may be

---

4, Finnish Registered Partnership Act. See also BODGAN (2004). Outside of Europe this approach has also been used in the **United States of America** in **Vermont** (§1204(b), Title 15, Vermont Statutes Annotated) and **Connecticut** (§13 and §15, An Act Concerning Civil Unions, Public Act No. 05-10).

76 CHANTELOUP (2000) p. 1719.

77 MIGNOT (2001) p. 651; FULCHIRON (2000) p. 900 and (2004) p. 93, KESSLER (2004) p. 69, §111.

78 MIGNOT (2001) p. 650.

79 KESSLER (2004) p. 69-70, §113-114.

80 GUILLUAME (2002) p. 180.

81 GUILLAUME (2002) p. 183.

82 MARTIN (1994) p. 419.

registered by persons of the same sex, thereby increasing the chances of a referral to public policy.[83] Others disagree arguing that no sustainable distinction can be drawn between the acceptability of polygamous marriages, on the one hand, and same-sex non-marital registered relationships, on the other.[84] According to BUCHER, the substantial number of jurisdictions across Europe and the rest of the world currently recognising non-marital registered relationships negates the need for the creation of a new legal category.[85] Yet this argument is extremely Euro-centric and fails to take into account the limited acceptance of non-marital registered relationship schemes outside of Europe, as well as the substantial number of non-European nationals living in Europe.[86]

KHAIRALLAH has suggested a different approach, dividing the forms of non-marital regulation into two categories under the umbrella term of "organised partnerships". On the one hand, those schemes corresponding to a new form of marriage such as in the **Nordic** countries and a category for the other weaker forms of regulation on the other.[87] Such a distinction is not supported by FULCHRION, who in his reflections on relationships outside marriage concludes that the crucial distinction is between cohabitating couples and registered couples.[88] Although noting that a distinction can be made at substantive law between *partenariats statuts* and *parternariats cadres,* he notes that such a distinction is not necessary at private international law.[89] As stated in the previous chapter, although one could endlessly categorise and subcategorise the multitude of regulated relationship forms available, the crucial question centres on the function of the institution.[90]

---

83 DEVERS (2004) p. 95-96, §146. Devers refers in turn to ECtHR decisions on this issue: ECtHR, *Rees v. United Kingdom,* Appl. No. 9532/81, 17th October 1986, §49; ECtHR, *Cossey v. United Kingdom,* Appl. No. 10843/84, 27th September 1990. Even in ECtHR, *Goodwin v. United Kingdom,* Appl. No. 28957/95, 11th July 2002, the ECtHR stressed the majority view that a marriage must be celebrated between two parties of a different-sex: see SUMNER (2002c)

84 MIGNOT (2001) p. 651; KHAIRALIAH (2000) p. 320.

85 BUCHER (2004b) p. 137.

86 **Appendices 1-3** and EUROSTAT, *Population Statistics: Data 1960 – 2003*, Brussels: Statistical Office of the European Communities, 2004.

87 KHAIRALIAH (2000) p. 320. This approach has also found legislative support in **Belgium**: **Section IX.3.1**.

88 FULCHRION (2000) p. 892.

89 FULCHIRON (2000) p. 901-902 and (2004) p. 92-99.

90 See **Chapter VIII.5**.

If one settles on distinguishing between different sorts of non-marital registered relationships one is able to examine how non-marital registered relationships are regulated in the place of origin. This leads one to the conclusion that in every State where registered forms of non-marital relationship have been adopted, a distinction has always been drawn between this new form of relationship and marriage.[91] Whether this distinction is in terms of gender, in terms of the legal rights and duties extended to such couples, or merely in nomenclature, a distinction is upheld. Whether this distinction is formal or practical is irrelevant at private international law level. Even if four countries have now accepted same-sex marriage,[92] these countries have retained forms of non-marital registered relationship, further highlighting the internal domestic distinction between marriage and non-marital registered relationships.[93] This very issue has also been addressed by the ECJ.[94] The negative response of the ECJ when asked to adjudicate whether a **Swedish** registered partner could be deemed to fall within the concept of spouse in the EC Staff Regulations has, however, been criticised by JESSURUN D'OLIVEIRA. He argues that according to domestic law, the two concepts of registered partnership and marriage are for all intents and purposes identical, and that the ECJ thus came to an incorrect interpretation of municipal **Swedish** law.[95] However it is the author's opinion, that one must view the two institutions as independent.[96] Although the legal effects and procedures of the **Swedish** registered partnership schemes may indeed be identical, the two institutions are still separated by the criteria of sex. Although this may not be reflected in differing rights and duties, the psychological dissociation

---

91 ECJ, *D and Sweden v. Council*, Case No. 122-125/99P, (2001) I ECR 4319. "It is equally true that since 1989, an increasing number of Member states have introduced, alongside marriage, statutory arrangements granting legal recognition to various forms of union between partners of the same-sex or of different sex and conferring on such unions certain effects which, both between the parties and as regards third parties, are the same as or comparable to those of marriage" (§35).

92 See **Appendix 4**.

93 BATIFFOL/LAGARDE (1983) p. 40, §415; GUILLAUME (2002) p. 183.

94 A point highlighted by the ECJ, *D and Sweden v. Council*, C122-125/99P, (2001) I ECR 4319. The Court insisted on the fact that "it is clear, that apart from their great diversity, such arrangements for registering relationships between couples not previously recognised in law are regarded in the Member States concerned as being distinct from marriage" (§36).

95 JESSURUN D'OLIVEIRIA (2000b) p. 527 and (2001b) p. 2039-2040. See also SCHRAMA, (1999b) p. 133.

96 In **Dutch** law, this distinction between the two institutions is seen more clearly in the differing dissolution procedures allowed for: See Chapter VII

of same-sex couples from the institution of marriage is nonetheless constitutive of a difference in treatment, albeit one merely of symbolism. If these two institutions were indeed identical then the **Swedish** Government would not have had to establish a Commission to examine the possibility to open marriages to same-sex couples.[97]

IX.2.3.2 Creation of a new category

If one is unable to subsume the various forms of non-marital registered relationships within the current legal category of marriage, then one must search for an alternative solution. Such a solution would be to create a distinct category for non-marital registered relationships within the legal category of personal status. This autonomous category would exist side-by-side the legal sub-category of marriage. Opponents who object to any form of recognition of these relationships on the basis of the perceived destabilisation of marriage would therefore be reassured that the two institutions would remain independent of each other both at substantive law and private international law level.[98] Proponents for the equalisation of legal rights for same-sex couples should gain solace from the fact that, although the institutions remain separate, in practice the private international law rules relating to such relationships would be largely based upon the rules applicable to marriage.[99] Such an approach has also gained academic credibility, and is seen as a seemingly more appropriate and somewhat more logical approach by many **French** authors.[100] These views have also been echoed in **The Netherlands** by BOELE-WOELKI.[101]

This approach has also received legislative support, perhaps not least due to its pragmatism.[102] In accepting the difficulties of, and acknowledging the shortcomings associated with, an enlargement of the legal category of marriage, one can better create a separate legal framework within the confines of the legal category of personal status specifically dealing with non-marital registered relationships. In this way not only can one compensate for the novelty and various permutations of these institutions

---

97 See **Chapter VIII.2.4** and SÖRGJERD (2005) p. 348.

98 BATIFFOL/LAGARDE (1983) p. 40, §415; DEVERS (2004) p. 96, §146

99 It is in no way suggested that the "separate but equal" argument should be used to defend the continued denial of marriage to same-sex couples, see SUMNER (2002c) p. 156.

100 FULCHRION (2000) p. 901; DEVERS (2004) p. 131-140, §207-221.

101 BOELE-WOELKI (1999c) p. 11 and BOELE-WOELKI (2000a) p. 1059.

102 See, for example, **Belgium** (**Section IX.3.1**), **The Netherlands** (**Section IX.3.3**) and the **United Kingdom** (**Section IX.3.5**).

but one can also provide for a pragmatic compromise acceptable to all sides. The crucial difference between marriage and non-marital registered relationships lies in the limited acceptance of such new relationship forms. This key difference translates into distinctions at private international law that in turn reduce the superficial simplicity offered by an analogous application of the private international law on marriage. This of course does not mean that inspiration and guidance cannot be drawn from an examination of the rules on marriage. On the contrary, these private international law rules should form the mould from which the private international law rules on non-marital registered relationships can be crafted. Where the rules on marriage are not suitable, then justifiable alternatives must be sought.

IX.3 COMPARATIVE OVERVIEW

IX.3.1 BELGIUM

Prior to the recent codification of **Belgian** private international law, uncertainty surrounded the way in which foreign non-marital registered relationships would be recognised in **Belgium.**[103] Although this ambiguity has recently been resolved, uncertainty is far from having been totally dispelled. According to the provisions of the Belg. CPIL, a distinction has been drawn between those registered relationships that create a bond akin to marriage and those that do not.[104] The first group of relationships are simply subsumed in the legal category of marriage, signalling the loosening of the traditional straitjacket encasing this legal category.[105] Nonetheless, it is also noted that there are many other forms of non-marital registered relationships that do not create such a bond. These relationships whether or not they affect *l'état de personne* are dealt with in a separate legal category, entitled "relationships of cohabitation".[106]

Although the codification is devoid of specific criteria for the assignment of relationships to this category, explicit reference was made during the Parliamentary debates to the **Belgian** statutory cohabitation and the **French**

103 ERAUW/VERHELLEN (1999) p. 160, §43-45; BARNICH (2000).

104 *Belgian Senate*, 2003-2004, No. 3-27/7, p. 128.

105 Chapter III, Belg. CPIL.

106 Chapter IV, Belg. CPIL.

pacte civil de solidarité.[107] According to Art. 58, Belg. CPIL a relationship of cohabitation is,

> visent une situation de vie commune donnant lieu à enregistrement par une autorité publique et ne créant pas entre les cohabitants de lien équivalent au mariage.

Although relationships of cohabitation need not necessarily have an effect on a party's personal status in order to be assigned to this legal category, the rules governing such relationships are intrinsically connected to the principles espoused in the legal category of personal status.[108] Furthermore, although reference is made in the circular of 28th September 2004 to a further circular that will provide more guidance as to the exact scope of this category no such information has yet been issued.[109] A similar vagueness is also evident if one turns one's attention to those non-marital registered relationships that are deemed to create a bond akin to marriage.

In the Parliamentary discussions, reference was made to the historical trend, beginning in **Scandinavia**, of introducing forms of registered partnership.[110] However, reference here was only made to a "same-sex union" which is created by means of a short Act of Parliament stating that the legal effects of marriage are *mutatis mutandis* applied to registered partners. Moreover, it was also stated that the legal category of marriage is to be understood as including different-sex marriage, same-sex marriage and the **Scandinavian**-style registered partnership.[111] It is thus still an open question how a **Belgian** judge will characterise a **Dutch** different-sex registered partnership. In referring only to the **Scandinavian**-style registered partnership, it could be interpreted that the **Belgian** legislature intented to exclude different-sex registered partnerships. One can also raise questions as to the proper positioning of institutions such as the **British** civil partnership or **Swiss** registered partnership, since both of these enactments use the ENUMERATION METHOD and not the EXCLUSION METHOD (in this author's terminology).[112]

---

107 *Belgian Senate*, 2003-2004, No. 3-27/7, p. 128.

108 *Belg. Staatsblad*, 28th September 2004, p. 69593-69610.

109 *Belg. Staatsblad*, 28th September 2004, p. 69606.

110 *Belgian Senate*, 2003-2004, No. 3-27/7, p. 94 (FALLON)

111 *Belgian Senate*, 2003-2004, No. 3-27/7, p. 96.

112 See **Chapter VIII.4.2**.

IX.3.2 FRANCE

In enacting the PACS legislation, the **French** legislature refrained from creating private international law rules. The failure to legislate has led to a proliferation in the discussion concerning the most appropriate legal category. As has already been seen, **French** commentators are profoundly divided on this question and it appears that no definitive answer is possible without legislative intervention.[113] The publication of a report by a group of experts commissioned to examine the need for reform of the PACS legislation indicates that legislative intervention is now on the horizon. The report, published in November 2004, as well as proposing substantial amendments to substantive law,[114] also proposed the introduction of a number of private international law rules. In finding that a contractual characterisation of the PACS raises many problems at private international law level, the group argued for a characterisation according to personal status.[115] In supporting their choice the group refers to the positioning of the PACS institution in Book 1, Fr. CC and the constituent elements of the PACS legislation that distinguish it from a simple contract.[116]

IX.3.3 THE NETHERLANDS

The starting point of both the **Dutch** Government and the **Dutch** Standing Committee on Private International Law is that the recognition rules on registered partnership should conform to the equivalent rules on marriage.[117] Art. 2(1), Neth. PIL(RP)A is thus a replica of Art. 5(1), Neth. PIL(M)A. Nevertheless, a substantial difference is evident in that Art. 2(5) provides for a list of criteria for the definition of a non-marital registered relationship.[118] Art. 2(5), in conjunction with Art. 2(4), ordains the following criteria:

---

113 See **Section IX.2.1** for those authors who advocate a contractual characterisation and **Section IX.2.2** for those who argue for a characterisation conform the effect on the parties' personal status.

114 MINISTRE DE LA JUSTICE (2004) p. 5-25.

115 MINISTRE DE LA JUSTICE (2004) p. 28.

116 The group refers specifically to the restrictions in terms of the prohibited degrees of relationship and the underlying *raison d'être* of the legislation to regulate the couple's *vie commun*: MINISTRE DE LA JUSTICE (2004) p. 28.

117 Art. 18 of the Standing Committee's proposed Act, STAATSCOMMISSIE (1998) p. 29 and *Dutch Second Chamber*, 2002-2003, 28924, No. 3, p. 10.

118 On the interaction of Art. 2(1) and 2(5), Neth. PIL(RP)A see SUMNER (2000b) p. 55-57.

- The registration was completed before a competent authority in the place where it was entered into;[119]
- The institution is exclusive, *i.e.* that a registered partnership cannot be concluded alongside another registered partnership or marriage;[120]
- The partnership must only be concluded between two persons;[121]
- The solemnisation of the registered partnership creates obligations between the partners that, in essence, correspond with those in connection to marriage;[122]
- The partnership must be based on a legally regulated form of cohabitation.[123]

The dearth of a characterisation provision in the original proposals by the **Dutch** Standing Committee on Private International Law and in the current work on the codification of **Dutch** private international law has not been followed in this field.[124] Nonetheless, although these criteria appear clear and workable, a certain degree of confusion surrounds the precise application of Art. 2(5)(c), Neth. PIL(RP)A. According to the wording of the Article, the obligations which the partners owe to each other should correspond with those in connection to marriage. However, in the explanatory notes to the Act it is stated,

> The proposed rules also lend themselves to application on legal institutions which do not have the name "registered partnership, but still possess the key characteristics thereof, even if this is not complete. Examples are the Belgian statutory cohabitation, the PACS in France and the statutory regulated cohabitation forms in Catalonia and Aragon.[125]

It is therefore not entirely clear how these criteria will be interpreted. Although the explanatory notes refer to the subsequent promulgation of information on these criteria, no such information has been released.

---

119 Art. 2(4) and 2(5)(a), Neth. PIL(RP)A.

120 Art. 2(5)(b), Neth. PIL(RP)A.

121 Art. 2(5)(b), Neth. PIL(RP)A.

122 Art. 2(5)(c), Neth. PIL(RP)A.

123 Art. 2(5), Neth. PIL(RP)A.

124 On the lack of a provision dealing with characterisation in the proposals for the codification of **Dutch** private international law, see JESSURUN D'OLIVEIRA (2003a) p. 1-4 and VLAS (2003) p. 443.

125 *Dutch Second Chamber*, 2002-2003, 28924, No. 3, p. 3.

IX.3.4 SWITZERLAND

The first proposal by the **Swiss** Ministry of Justice provided for a definition of registered partnership,

> Au sens de la présente loi, on entend par partenariat enregistré toute communauté de vie entre deux personnes du même sexe, enregistré auprès d'une autorité et entraînant des effets d'état civil, par laquelle elles se sont engagées à assumer une responsabilité l'une envers l'autre.[126]

The concept of registered partnership was thus restricted to two persons of the same-sex. In the reports leading up to this legislation it was noted that jurisdictions have tackled the topic of relationship registration in very different ways.[127] As a result of this diversity and in attempting to avoid unnecessary ambiguity, the **Swiss** legislature wished to define the notion of registered partnership so as to avoid the problems of characterisation.[128] Nonetheless, the eventual legislative enactment is notable for the absence of such a definition.[129] Only Art. 45(3), Sw. CPIL sheds some light on this issue, stating that same-sex marriages celebrated abroad will also be dealt with in accordance with the **Swiss** private international law rules on registered partnerships.

In the preparatory documents to the Sw. RPA, attention is paid to the question of which non-marital registered relationships fall within the ambit of Art. 45(1), Sw. CPIL.[130] It is stated that only those relationships that conform to the central facets of the **Swiss** registered partnership will be recognised in **Switzerland**. Since the registration of a **Swiss** registered partnership affects one's civil status and attaches rights and duties akin to marriage, these elements are regarded as essential prerequisites for the recognition of a non-marital relationship registered abroad. It is explicitly stated that certain regimes, such as the **French** PACS, do not satisfy these conditions and will therefore not be recognised in accordance with these provisions.[131] It is subsequently noted that this does not exclude the possibility for such forms of relationship to be recognised via other routes,

---

126 Proposed Art. 65a, Sw. CPIL in MINISTRY OF JUSTICE (2001) p. 63.

127 MINISTRY OF JUSTICE (1999) p. 6 *et seq*, (2000) p. 13 *et seq*, (2001) p. 5 *et seq*.

128 MINISTRY OF JUSTICE (2001) p. 40.

129 Arts. 65a to 65d, Sw. CPIL do not provide for a defintion: FF 2003, p. 1192 at 1258.

130 FF 2003, p. 1192 at 1260.

131 FF 2003, p. 1192 at 1260: "Ces conditions ne sont pas remplies par les liens de type contractuel instaurés par certains régimes juridiques étrangers, comme le PACS".

such as contract law or the law on associations.[132] It is submitted that the **Belgian** statutory cohabitation will thus likewise not be recognised, as would any other form of non-marital registered relationship that adopts a policy of WEAK REGISTRATION, whether adhering to the PLURALISTIC MODEL or the DUALISTIC MODEL.[133]

This approach has not, however, been unanimously supported. Although BUCHER, referring to the terminological distinctions drawn in **France** between *partenariats statuts* and *partenariats cadres*, notes that a similar distinction has been drawn in **Swiss** literature between partnerships involving a *changement de statut* and those which are *purement contractuel*,[134] he nonetheless does not believe that such a difference should be determinative in the field private international law.[135] Although aware of the problems that such an assimilation could cause in relation to the legal effects of such relationships, BUCHER believes that these differences can be solved with reference to the choice of law rules rather than in terms of the characterisation of the relationship.[136]

Discussion has also centred on the recognition of different-sex non-marital registered relationships. The absence of any reference to the recognition of different-sex non-marital registered relationships can be partly explained by the fact that the private international law rules are aimed at regulating equivalent relationships as provided for under domestic **Swiss** law.[137] If the domestic notion of the term "registered partnership" were to be adopted a situation would be created in which same-sex marriages,[138] same-sex non-marital registered relationships and different-sex marriages would be recognised in **Switzerland**, but different-sex non-marital registered relationships would be refused recognition. This distinction is, according to BUCHER, fundamentally objectionable.[139] He argues that the constitutional protection afforded to marriage as laid down in Art. 14, **Swiss** FC, despite thwarting attempts to open registered partnership to different-sex couples

---

132 FF 2003, p. 1192 at 1260.

133 See **Chapter VIII.4.1.2** and **VIII.4.3**.

134 DUTOIT (2005) p. 156-161, Art. 45, No. 5bis and 5ter.

135 BUCHER (2004a) p. 187, §521.

136 BUCHER (2004a) p. 187, §521. BUCHER notes that such a tendency has also been noted in **French** literature: HUET (2002) p. 544-549.

137 BUCHER (2004a) p. 185, §516.

138 As a result of the introduction of Art. 45(3), Sw. CPIL.

139 BUCHER (2004a) p. 186, §516.

in the domestic arena,[140] does not likewise prevent the recognition of different-sex non-marital relationships registered abroad.[141] BUCHER and BONOMI recommend that the solutions adopted in Chapter 3a, Sw. CPIL should serve as inspiration for solving questions relating to different-sex non-marital registered relationships.[142] Accordingly, the private international law rules on marriage should simply be applied analogously to different-sex non-marital registered relationships in an identical fashion to same-sex non-marital registered relationships by virtue of the Sw. RPA.[143] Furthermore, it would appear that **Swiss** commentators are, on the whole, in favour of such relationships being recognised in accordance with the rules on registered partnership.[144] Nevertheless, as yet, it is unclear exactly how the **Swiss** courts will deal with such relationships, since the explanatory notes to the Sw. RPA are silent on this issue and the only cases to have come before the **Swiss** Federal Supreme Court thus far have involved different-sex non-registered relationships or same-sex registered relationships.[145]

IX.3.5 UNITED KINGDOM

Aware of the issue of characterisation, the **United Kingdom** has opted for a rather novel approach. Chapter 2, Part 5, CPA 2004 deals with the characterisation of foreign overseas relationships. Sec. 212, CPA 2004 states:

> For the purposes of this Act an overseas relationships is a relationships which
> (a) is either a specified relationship or a relationship which meets the general conditions and

---

140 See MINISTRY OF JUSTICE (2000).

141 BUCHER (2004a) p. 186, §517.

142 BUCHER and BONOMI also argue that such rules should also apply for non-registered relationships (p. 193, §700e) but this question lies outside the scope of this research.

143 BUCHER/BONOMI (2004) p. 192-193, §700e.

144 SIEHR (2002) p. 79-80, §5.III; SCHWANDER (2001) p. 355, who argues that the recognition of different-sex non-marital registered relationships is not against Swiss public policy. Furthermore, no such distinction has been drawn in the provisions of Chapter 3a: GIRSBERGER/DROESE (2001) p. 98. BUCHER argues further that the absence of a clear exclusion in Chapter 3a, Sw. CPIL is decisive and supports the recognition of different-sex non-marital registered relationships: BUCHER (2004a) p. 186, §517. In support of these arguments, many authors refer to the commentary on Art. 17b, Ger. CCIL, WAGNER (2001) p. 292. MARKUS (2004) p. 150 also notes the need to refer initially to internal law before embarking upon the problem of characterisation. *Contra* see DUTOIT (2005) p. 222-223, Art. 65a, No. 1.

145 BUCHER (2004a) p. 210-211, §610-612 and Trib. Féd., 3rd March 1993 (1993) 119 II *ATF* 264.

(b) is registered (whether before or after the passing of the Act) with a responsible authority in a country or territory outside the United Kingdom, by two people –
  (i) who under the relevant law are of the same sex at the time when they do so, and
  (ii) neither of whom is already a civil partner or lawfully married.

Two types of relationships are therefore recognised in accordance with these provisions: specified relationships and those relationships meeting the general conditions. Specified relationships are listed in Schedule 20 to the Act and include statutory cohabitations (**Belgium**), domestic partnerships (**Nova Scotia, Canada**), civil unions (**Quebec**, **Canada** and **Vermont**, **USA**), registered partnerships (**Denmark**, **Finland**, **The Netherlands**, **Norway** and **Sweden**), PACS[s] (**France**), life partnerships (**Germany**), confirmed cohabitations (**Iceland**) and same-sex marriages (**Belgium** and **The Netherlands**). If one of these designated relationships is to be recognised, no further investigation is necessary. Furthermore, this list may be amended by statutory instrument by the Secretary of State by adding, amending the description of or omitting a relationship.[146]

If a foreign institution is not mentioned in this list, recognition may still be afforded if the relationship satisfies the general conditions in Sec. 214, CPA 2004, namely,

(a) the relationship may not be entered into if either of the parties is already a party to a relationship of that kind or lawfully married,
(b) the relationship is of indeterminate duration, and
(c) the effect of entering into it is that the parties are –
  (i) treated as a couple either generally or for specified purposes, or
  (ii) treated as married.

It is important to note that the recognition rules are restricted to same-sex couples only. Non-marital relationships registered between different-sex couples are thus not entitled to recognition according to the CPA 2004. That does not necessarily mean that different-sex non-marital registered relationships are denied recognition altogether. It could be argued that such relationships should be recognised in the **United Kingdom** by analogous application of the rules on marriage. According to the famous adage of Lord PENZANCE marriage is "the voluntary union of one man and one woman to

146 Sec. 213(2) and (4), CPA 2004. The power to amend simply removes doubt as to whether non-marital registered relationships from certain jurisdictions will be recognised.

the exclusion of all others."[147] Yet, all four components of Lord PENZANCE'S classic statement are satisfied by different-sex non-marital registered relationships.[148] Furthermore, **English** courts have upheld the principle that each legal system must be free to determine the attributes of the consensual union.[149] Furthermore, **English** judges are keen to espouse the functional approach to legislative interpretation, stressing the importance of interpreting legislation according to modern day standards.[150] If these assertions are placed side-by-side, it would appear that there is substantial weight to back the argument that non-marital registered relationships between different-sex couples should be recognised in accordance with the analogous application of the laws on marriage. The only possibility open to refuse recognition to such relationships rests in the notion of public policy.[151]

IX.4 COMPARISON AND EVALUATION

In **Chapters VIII.2.4**, **VIII.3.4** and **VIII.4.3**, conclusions were drawn as to the underlying function and structure of the non-marital registered relationship schemes introduced in the seven chosen jurisdictions. In **Chapter VIII.5** an attempt was made at outlining the common function underpinning these schemes. It was noted that non-marital registered relationships in the DUALISTIC and PLURALISTIC MODELS have the following commonality,

> A State-regulated registration scheme for two persons involved in an exclusive, intimate relationship. Opting into this system by means of registration of the relationship entails the attribution of rights and duties, and the assumption of obligations and responsibilities between the parties themselves, as well with third parties and the State.

In identifying a common function and having compared the institutions at substantive law, one is able to isolate a number of consistent characteristics essential for a private international law characterisation. However, from the outset it must be noted that only the **United Kingdom** and **The Netherlands**

---

147 *Hyde v. Hyde* (1866) LR 1 P&D 130 at 133.

148 Namely, "voluntary union" (**Chapters III.4.7**, **IV.4.7** and **V.4.7**), "for life" (**Chapters III.4.8**, **IV.4.8** and **IV.4.8**) "one man and one woman" (**Chapters III.4.3**, **IV.4.3** and **V.4.3**) and "to the exclusion of all others" (**Chapters III.4.2**, **IV.4.2** and **V.4.2**). See further, POULTER (1979).

149 NORTH/FAWCETT (1999) p. 704.

150 *Fitzpatrick v. Sterling Housing Association* [2001] 1 FLR 271.

151 See **Chapter X.5**.

have provided for explicit criteria and only the **United Kingdom** has provided for the explicit recognition of certain countries' institutions in the legislation itself.

Firstly, in all six jurisdictions to have enacted private international law rules, explicit recognition is given to the effect of such a registration on the parties' personal status by basing such rules on the private international law rules applicable to marriage. This is underscored by the requirement that the relationship adhere to both facets of the principle of exclusivity.[152] Secondly, despite the analogy approach adopted by **Switzerland** and the inclusion of marriage-like relationships in the legal category of marriage in **Belgium**, the creation of a separate framework for the solution of such problems appears to be the most popular approach.[153] Thirdly, similarities are also apparent in the condition that a competent authority must register the relationship; a notarised deed is thus not sufficient. Failure to be registered or registration by an incompetent authority renders the non-marital registered relationship incompatible with the characterisation criteria.

Fourthly, in all jurisdictions an attempt has been made, to varying degrees, to specify the rights and duties attendant upon the parties to such a relationship. In **Belgium**, if the rights and duties attributed to non-marital registered partners are such that they are deemed to be akin to marriage, the relationship will be re-characterised according to the legal category of marriage. In **The Netherlands**, on the other hand, a registration must create obligations between the parties corresponding to those affecting spouses. In **Switzerland** the registration must have an effect on the parties civil status and the parties must assume responsibility towards each other, whilst in the **United Kingdom** reference is only made to the parties being treated as a couple either generally or for specified purposes or being treated as married.

Hence, it is clear that the creation of characterisation criteria for non-marital registered relationships has drawn heavily on the key characteristics of such relationships at substantive law, *i.e.* close adherence to the *lex fori.* It striving for a harmonised or unified approach to this field of law, the

---

152 **Belg**: *Belgian Senate*, 2003-2004, No. 3-27/7, p. 128-140; **Neth.**: Art. 2(5)(b), Neth. PIL(RP)A; **Swit.**: FF 2003, p. 1192; **UK**: Sec. 212(b)(ii), CPA 2004. An approach also supported by the **French** Ministry of Justice: MINISTRE DE LA JUSTICE (2004) p. 28.

153 An approach that has also received widespread support in **French** literature, see **Section IX.2.3.2**.

function outlined in **Chapter VIII.5** should form the basis for the development of any characterisation criteria supplemented by a number of ancillary conditions. Firstly, the clear placement of such rules in the legal category of personal status is necessary in order to dispel any doubt as to the intentions and aims of such rules. Furthermore, it also appears necessary to specify that the registration must take place before a competent authority as designated by the State in which the relationship is registered. Nevertheless, despite these commonalities, two points of discussion remain unresolved, namely the eligibility restrictions imposed with regards the sex of the parties and the extent of the rights and duties imposed upon parties to the registration.

As has already been indicated in **Chapter II**, there are numerous instances when a foreign institution, decision or instrument will require recognition in a State where such an institution is unknown. This is true, for example, in all continental systems with respect to the common law trust.[154] An institution completely unknown to continental European jurisdictions has been able to be recognised by the majority of States. In **Belgium** and **Switzerland**, both countries having not signed or ratified the 1985 Hague Convention on the Law Applicable to Trusts and to their Recognition (1985 Hague TC), such recognition is afforded either by reference to the law on associations or contract.[155] Nonetheless, recognition is afforded to a foreign institution not recognised in one's own system. The problem has also been evident in **Anglo-American** legal systems with respect to the rules on matrimonial property. Despite the absence of such rules at substantive law, **English** private international law has had to recognise the existence of such rules in other legal systems, and has adapted accordingly.[156] VAN HECKE and LENAERTS abridge this principle exquisitely in their review of **Belgian** private international law.

> The permeability of legal systems in and of themselves also makes it possible for a legal system to recognise the legal consequences of or attach legal consequences to foreign institutions, which are unknown to the law of the forum.[157]

---

154 **France** and **The Netherlands** have both signed, although only **The Netherlands** has ratified, the 1985 Hague TC.

155 **Belg.:** VAN HECKE/LENAERTS (1989) p. 62, §97; **Swit.:** Trib. Féd., 29th January 1970 (1970) 96 II *ATF* 79 at 88-101.

156 NORTH/FAWCETT (1999) p. 1015-1029.

157 VAN HECKE/LENAERTS (1989) p. 61, §960 (author's own translation).

If one should thus accept the arguments proffered for a broad autonomous definition of the term non-marital registered relationships, one should allow for the recognition of different-sex registered relationships in those jurisdictions where such a registration is not possible.[158] After all, as has already been shown in **Chapter VIII.2.4** and **Chapter VIII.5**, the function of non-marital registered relationships is comparable regardless of the sex of the parties. Whether or not these relationships will eventually be recognised rests on the application of the relevant recognition rule and, of course, on whether recognition is regarded as in conformity with public policy.[159] If one does not submit to such an approach, one is left with the rather illogical solution that different-sex marriages, same-sex marriages and same-sex registered relationships are all afforded recognition, whilst different-sex registered relationships fall outside the recognition boat![160]

Turning one's attention to the rights and duties incumbent on the parties to a non-marital registered relationship, one is confronted with a vast array of different solutions, with respect to substantive law regulation and the respective private international law characterisation. Yet this diversity in substantive law rules is nothing new and occurs frequently in the field of family law. As was indicated in **Chapter VIII.4.1**, this is also the case in marriage and adoption; the extent to which a State imposes rights and duties upon a marriage or an adoption is irrelevant in determining whether or not a marriage or an adoption exists. The varying degree of these rights and duties is thus unimportant to the quest for characterisation criteria for non-marital registered relationships. Nonetheless, it is important that the registration of a non-marital registered relationship is not a mere symbolic act and does involve the attribution of some rights and duties. This is perhaps best evidenced by the registration of such relationship having an effect on the parties' personal status.

In summary, a common core of four individual yet cumulative characterisation criteria can be identified for a category of non-marital registered relationships, namely:

(1) The non-marital registered relationship is based on a State regulated institution;[161] and

158 In this sense see also JESSURUN D'OLIVEIRIA (2003a).

159 This will be dealt with in **Chapter X.5.5**.

160 See also BUCHER (2004a) p. 186, §516.

161 **Belg.:** Art. 58, Belg. CPIL (*autorité publique*); **Neth.:** Art. 2(5), Neth. PIL(RP)A; **Swit.:** FF 2003, p. 1192 at 1260, with reference to Art. 2(1), Sw. RPA; **UK:** Sec. 212(b), CPA 2004.

(2) The relationship is exclusive and has only been registered by two persons;[162] and
(3) The relationship must be registered by a competent authority as designated by the State in which in the relationship is registered;[163] and
(4) The registration of the relationship creates rights and duties between the parties and has a constitutive effect on their personal status.[164]

IX.5 APPLICATION OF THE CRITERIA

As illustrated in **Appendices 1-3**, there are many jurisdictions around the world besides the seven studied in this research that currently provide for non-marital registration schemes.[165] The jurisdictions surveyed will inevitably be confronted with couples having registered in other jurisdictions. It is therefore essential that these institutions be tested against these criteria.

IX.5.1 STATE REGULATED

In all seven jurisdictions studied, it is a State enacted, legislative instrument that has created a scheme for the registration of non-marital relationships.[166] Although this criterion may at first appear superfluous, it is important to note that there are certain registration schemes that would contravene such a criterion. Therefore, although in the majority of countries to have introduced forms of non-marital relationship registration this question will not pose significant problems, it is important to address.

---

162 **Belg.:** Art. 58, Belg. CPIL (*vie commune*); **Neth.:** Art. 2(5)(b)(ii), Neth. PIL(RP)A; **Swit.:** FF 2003, p. 1192 at 1260, with reference to Art. 2(1), Sw. RPA; **UK:** Sec. 212(b)(ii) and 214(a), CPA 2004.

163 **Belg.:** Art. 58, Belg. CPIL (*enregistrement*); **Neth.:** Art. 2(4) and 2(5)(a), Neth. PIL(RP)A; **Swit.:** FF 2003, p. 1192 at 1260, with reference to Art. 2(1), Sw. RPA; **UK:** Sec. 212(b), CPA 2004.

164 **Belg.:** *Belgian Senate*, 2003-2004, No. 3-27/7, p. 128; **Neth.:** Art. 2(5)(c), Neth. PIL(RP)A; **Swit.:** FF 2003, p. 1192 at 1260, with reference to Art. 2(1), Sw. RPA; **UK:** Sec. 214(c), CPA 2004.

165 See **Appendicies 1, 2 and 3**. At present 41 jurisdictions in 20 different countries.

166 **Chapters III.4.1**, **IV.4.1**, **V.4.1**, **VI.4.1** and **VII.4.1**. Although the positioning of this legislation differs between the jurisdictions (sometimes incorporated into the Civil Code and sometimes not).

Firstly, there are those schemes operated by private companies. In **Chapter VII.3.2** reference was made to the civil ceremonies performed in **Great Britain** by the Civil Ceremonies Ltd. Such registration schemes would therefore not fall under such a characterisation. Secondly, in those countries where religious marriage ceremonies prior to a civil ceremony are prohibited, any form of religious non-marital relationship registration would also be considered not to satisfy this criterion. Therefore any form of religious "registered partnership" in **The Netherlands**, although theoretically possible,[167] would not satisfy this criterion since it is not endorsed by the State. On the other hand, the constitutional governmental neutrality afforded religious bodies in the **United States of America** is reflected in the State recognition of marriages validly celebrated according to the rites and practices of a religious organisation.[168] This principle has been copied in the **Connecticut** legislation on civil unions.[169] As a result of this State recognition, such religious non-marital registrations will satisfy this criterion.

Thirdly, the criterion that the registration scheme be State regulated is also constructive in those countries where regional or territorial developments have transpired without legislative action having taken place at federal or national level.[170] The absence of a federal or devolved legislative system in **Andorra**, **Denmark**, **Finland**, **Iceland**, **Luxembourg**, **The Netherlands**, **New Zealand**, **Norway**, **Slovenia** and **Sweden** has prevented issues of this kind arising. Regions, territories, states, communities, provinces, or decentralised governmental entities have, however, been responsible for the enactment of forms of non-marital registered relationships in a number of countries. In

---

167 The non-applicability of Art. 1:67, Neth. CC to registered partnerships. See also **Chapter V.4.8** and LOONSTEIN (2005).

168 *E.g.*, §23-104a, Kansas Statutes Annotated; §307, California Family Code *etc.*

169 §4, An Act Concerning Civil Unions, Public Act No. 05-10.

170 From the outset distinctions must be drawn between confederations, federal states, decentralised states and devolved states. In decentralised states central powers of decision making are exercised by officials of the central government located in various regions. In devolved states, the unity of the nation is not affected nor is the power of the central government to repeal legislation creating devolvement. In federal states supremacy is divided between a federal legislature and regional legislatures. In a confederation, sovereign states together create a supreme body on the basis of a international law convention. Rules made at federal level only bind the Member States, whereas in a federal system, the citizens of the Member States are also bond by such enactments. See further H.F. MUNNEKE, C. RIEZEBOOS and G.F.M. VAN DER TANG, *Federalisme*, Zwolle: W.E.J.Tjeenk Willink, 1992, p. 2 *et seq.*

Argentina,[171] **Australia**,[172] **Canada**,[173] **Spain**,[174] **Switzerland**,[175] and the **United States of America**[176] regional legislation has developed in the absence of federal intervention. Without wishing to explore the intricate constitutional and legislative distribution of power within each of these nation-states,[177] it is important to note that as long as such legislation is enacted in accordance with the power granted to the regional government by the federal nation-state, such legislative enactments will satisfy the condition that they are State regulated. In other confederate, federal or

---

171 **Argentina** is a federal state consisting of twenty-three provinces (Buenos Aires Province, Catamarca, Chaco, Chubut, Córdoba, Corrientes, Entre Ríos, Formosa, Jujuy, La Pampa, La Rioja, Mendoza, Misiones, Neuquén, Río Negro, Salta, San Juan, San Luis, Santa Cruz, Santa Fe, Santiago del Estero, Tierra del Fuego and Tucumán) and one federal district (Buenos Aires).

172 **Australia** is a federal state consisting of six states (New South Wales, Victoria, Queensland, South Australia, Western Australia and Tasmania) and two territories (Australian Capital Territory and Northern Territory).

173 **Canada** is a federal state consisting of ten provinces (Alberta, British Columbia, Manitoba, New Brunswick, Newfoundland and Labrador, Nova Scotia, Ontario, Prince Edward Island, Quebec and Saskatchewan) and three territories (Northwestern Territories, Nunavut and Yukon).

174 Although **Spain** is not strictly a federal state it does have a highly decentralised form of government. The State is thus divided into seventeen autonomous communities (Andalucia, Aragon, Asturias, Balearic Islands, Basque Country, Canary Islands, Cantabria, Castilla-y-Leon, Castilla La Mancha, Catalonia, Extremadura, Galicia, La Rioja, Madrid, Murcia, Navarre and Valencia) each with differing competency, as well as two autonomous cities (Ceuta and Melilla). See EUROPEAN COMMISSION FOR DEMORACY THROUGH LAW, *Federal and regional states in the perspective of European integration*, Strasbourg: Council of Europe, 1999, p. 62-65.

175 **Switzerland** is a federal state consisting of twenty cantons (Argovia, Fribourg, Geneva, Grisons, Jura, Lucerne, Neuchâtel, Schaffhausen, Schwyz, Solothurn, St. Gall, Thurgovia, Ticino, Uri, Valais, Vaud, Zug and Zurich) and six half-cantons (Basel-City, Basel County, Appenzell Inner Rhodes, Appenzell Outer Rhodes, Nidwald and Obwald).

176 The **United States of America** consists of 50 States (Alabama, Alaska, Arkansas, Arizona, California, Colorado, Connecticut, Delaware, Florida, Georgia, Hawai'i, Idaho, Illinois, Indiana, Iowa, Louisiana, Kansas, Kentucky, Maine, Maryland, Massachusetts, Michigan, Minnesota, Mississippi, Missouri, Montana, Nebraska, Nevada, New Hampshire, New Jersey, New Mexico, New York, North Carolina, North Dakota, Ohio, Oklahoma, Oregon, Pennsylvania, Rhode Island, South Carolina, South Dakota, Tennessee, Texas, Utah, Vermont, Virginia, Washington, West Virginia, Wisconsin and Wyoming) which are all treated identically, as well as six territories (American Samoa, District of Columbia, Guam, Northern Mariana Islands, Puerto Rico and US Virgin Islands).

177 For example, the difference between administration of federal laws in **Germany** by the individual states and in the **United States of America** by the federal administrative authority: see EUROPEAN COMMISSION FOR DEMOCRACY THROUGH LAW, *Federal and regional states in the perspective of European integration*, Strasbourg: Council of Europe, 1999, p. 33.

devolved nation-states, for example **Belgium**,[178] **Germany**[179] and the **United Kingdom**,[180] legislation has been enacted on a national or federal level, thus causing no problem in relation to this criterion.

IX.5.2 EXCLUSIVITY

As already stated in **Chapter VIII.2.1**, the principle of exclusivity consists of two discrete facets.[181] Firstly, only two people should be allowed to register a non-marital relationship. In all the jurisdictions currently to have introduced forms of non-martial registered relationships this principle has been adhered to.[182] Secondly, the existence of a marriage or non-marital

---

178 **Belgium** is a federal state consisting of three levels of government. The country is divided into three *regions* (Brussels Capital Region, the Flemish Region {consisting of the provinces of Antwerp, East Flanders, Flemish Brabant, Limburg and West Flanders} and the Walloon Region {consisting of the provinces Hainault, Liege, Luxembourg, Namur and Walloon Brabant}), three *communities* (French community, Flemish community and German-speaking community) and four *linguistic regions* (French speaking region, Dutch speaking region, German speaking region and the Brussels Capital bilingual region). See further see EUROPEAN COMMISSION FOR DEMORACY THROUGH LAW, *Federal and regional states in the perspective of European integration*, Strasbourg: Council of Europe, 1999, p. 22-24.

179 **Germany** is a federal state consisting of sixteen states (Baden-Württemburg, Bavaria, Berlin (city), Brandenburg, Bremen (city), Hamburg (city), Hessen, Mecklenburg-West Pomerania, Lower Saxony, North-Rhine Westphalia, Rhineland Palatinate, Saarland, Saxony, Saxony-Anhalt, Schleswig Holstein, Thuringia, Lower Saxony).

180 The **United Kingdom** is a unitary nation-state consisting of four countries (England, Northern Ireland, Scotland and Wales) and a devolved parliamentary system operational in Northern Ireland, Scotland and Wales.

181 See **Chapter III.4.2, p. 46.**

182 **Andorra**: Art. 2(1), Llei 4/2005; **Buenos Aires:** Art. 1(a), Ley No. 1004; **Río Negro:** Art. 2, Ley No. 3736; **Tasmania**: Sec. 4(1), Relationships Act 2003; **Belgium**: Art. 1475(1), Belg. CC; **Manitoba**: Definition of "common-law relationship", Art. 1, Vital Statistics Act, as amended by The Common-Law Partners' Property and Related Amendments Act, SM 2002, c.48; **Nova Scotia**: Sec. 53(1), Vital Statistics Act, Chapter 494, Nova Scotia Revised Statutes; **Quebec**: Art. 521.1, Quebec Civil Code; **Denmark**: §1, Registered Partnership Act; **Finland**: Sec. 1, Registered Partnership Act; **France**: Art. 515-1, Fr. CC; **Germany**: §1 para. 1, Life Partnership Act; **Iceland**: Art. 1, Registered Partnerships Act; **Luxembourg**: Art. 2, Partnership Act; **The Netherlands**: Art. 1:80a(1) and (2), Neth. CC; **New Zealand**: Sec. 4(1), Civil Union Act 2004; **Norway**: Art. 1, Registered Partnership Act; **Sweden**: §1, Registered Partnership Act; **Andalucia**: Art. 1, Ley 5/2002; **Aragon**: Art. 1, Ley 6/1999; **Asturias**: Art. 1, Ley 4/2002; **Balearic Islands**: Art. 1(1), Ley 18/2001; **Basque Country**: Art. 1(2), Ley 2/2003; **Canary Islands**: Art. 1, Ley 5/2003; **Catalonia**: Art. 1(1), Ley 10/1998 (different-sex) and Art. 19, Ley 10.1998 (same-sex); **Extremadura**: Art. 2(1), Ley 5/2003; **Madrid**: Art. 1(1), Ley 11/2001; **Navarre**: Art. 1, Ley Foral 6/2000; **Valencia**: Art. 1(1), Ley 1/2001; **Switzerland**: Art. 2(1), Sw. RPA; **England & Wales**: Sec. 2(1), CPA 2004; **Northern Ireland**: Sec. 137(1), CPA 2004; **Scotland**: Sec. 85(1), CPA 2004; **California**: §297(1),

registered partnership forms an obstacle to the registration of a non-marital relationship. Once again, this principle has also been adhered to in all those jurisdictions examined,[183] save for **Manitoba**. According to the legislative amendments made by the Common-Law Partners' Property and Related Amendments Act aspirant parties to a registered common law relationship in **Manitoba** are not permitted to already be involved in a registered common law relationship nor already married.[184] However, no alteration of the equivalent prohibitions imposed on those wishing to marry has been made.[185] Therefore a registered common-law relationship does not form a prohibition to entry into a marriage and any subsequent marriage does not affect the legality of the pre-existing common-law relationship. Although the registration of a life partnership in **Germany** prior to 1st January 2005 did not prevent either of the parties from marrying a third party, this legal loophole has since been amended.[186]

Division 2.5, California Family Code; **Connecticut**: Sec. 1(1), Act Concerning Civil Unions; **Hawai'i**: §572C-1, Title 31, Division 3, Hawai'i Revised Statutes Annotated; **Maine**: §2710(2), Chapter 701, Part 6, Subtitle 2, Title 22, Maine Revised Statutes Annotated; **New Jersey**: PL 2003, Chapter 246, C.26:8A-4(a); **Vermont**: §1201(2), Chapter 23, Vermont Statutes Annotated.

183 **Andorra**: Art. 2(2), Llei 4/2005; **Buenos Aires**: Art. 5(3) and (f), Ley No. 1004; **Río Negro**: Art. 3(e), Ley No. 3736; **Tasmania**: Sec. 4(1)(b) in conjunction with Sec. 11(2)(a)(iii), Relationships Act 2003; **Belgium**: Art. 1475(2)(1), Belg. CC; **Nova Scotia**: Sec. 53(5) and (6), Nova Scotia Vital Statistics Act; **Quebec**: Art. 521.1(2), Quebec Civil Code; **Denmark**: §2(1), Registered Partnership Act; **Finland**: Sec. 2(1)(1), Registered Partnership Act; **France**: Art. 515-2(2) and (2)(3), Fr. CC; **Germany**: §1, para. 2(1), Life Partnerships Act; **Iceland**: Art. 2, Registered Partnership Act; **Luxembourg**: Art. 4(2), Partnership Act; **The Netherlands**: Art. 1:80a(1) and (2), Neth. CC; **New Zealand**: Sec. 4(1)(c), Civil Union Act 2004; **Norway**: Sec. 2, Registered Partnership Act; **Sweden**: §3(3), Registered Partnership Act; **Andalucia**: Art. 3(2)(b), Ley 5/2002; **Aragon**: Art. 4(a) and (d), Ley 6/1999; **Asturias**: Art. 3(1), Ley 4/2002; **Balearic Islands**: Art. 2(1)(a) and (d), Ley 18/2001; **Basque Country**: Art. 2(1), Ley 2/2003; **Canary Islands**: Art. 2(1)(b) and (c), Ley 5/2003; **Catalonia**: Arts. 1 and 12(1)(e), Ley 10/1998 (different-sex) and Art. 20, Ley 10.1998 (same-sex); **Extremadura**: Art. 3(1)(b) and (c), Ley 5/2003; **Madrid**: Art. 2(1)(b) and (c), Ley 11/2001; **Navarre**: Art. 2(1), Ley Foral 6/2000; **Valencia**: Art. 2(1)(b) and (c), Ley 1/2001; **Switzerland**: Art. 4(1), Sw. RPA; **England & Wales**: Sec. 3(1)(b), CPA 2004; **Scotland**: Sec. 86(1)(d), CPA 2004; **Northern Ireland**: Sec. 138(1)(b), CPA 2004; **California**: §297(b)(2), Division 2.5, California Family Code; **Connecticut**: Sec. 2(1), Act Concerning Civil Unions; **Hawai'i**: §572C-4(2), Title 31, Division 3, Hawai'i Revised Statutes Annotated; **Maine**: §2710(2)(C), Chapter 701, Part 6, Subtitle 2, Title 22, Maine Revised Statutes Annotated; **New Jersey**: C.26:8A-4a(3), Chapter 246, PL 2003; **Vermont**: §1202(1), Chapter 23, Vermont Statutes Annotated.

184 Sec. 13.1(2)(c), Vital Statistics Act, CCSM, c. V60.

185 See Marriage Act, CCSM, c. M50.

186 §1306, Ger. CC, as amended by *Gesetz zur Überarbeitung des Lebenspartnerschaftsrechts*, BGBl I 2004, 3396. This was regarded by many as an oversight on the part of the

Moreover, a number of further problems must also be addressed. In three of the autonomous regions in **Spain**, namely **Madrid**, the **Canary Islands** and **Extremadura**,[187] parties who are judicially separated but not yet divorced are entitled to enter into a domestic form of non-marital registered relationship. Couples who do so would therefore contravene the second facet of the principle of exclusivity and thus not fall within the scope of this characterisation. One must also be aware that a number of jurisdictions have followed the example of **Belgium**[188] and **France**[189] in allowing for a non-marital registered relationship to be terminated upon the subsequent marriage of one of the parties, either to each other or to a third party.[190]

IX.5.3 REGISTRATION BY COMPETENT AUTHORITY

One of the crucial elements in the acquisition of personal status, according to GRAVESON, is the element of public acknowledgement.[191] This public acknowledgment often goes hand-in-hand with a requirement of public scrutiny. In the field of marriage these two elements have been combined by means of a public celebration. In the field of non-marital registered relationships, this has become more formalistic and is evidenced in the form of a registration requirement. In all of the **Nordic** countries registration of

---

Government: DETHLOFF (2001) p. 234. Failure to adhere to this provision also forms a ground for nullity in accordance with §1314 I, Ger. CC. See further WELLENHOFER (2005) p. 709 and STÜBER (2005) p. 575.

187 **Canary Islands**: Art. 2(1)(b), Ley 5/2003; **Extremadura**: Art. 3(1)(b), Ley 5/2003; **Madrid**: Art. 2(1)(b), Ley 11/2001.

188 See **Chapter III.6.8.**

189 See **Chapter IV.6.8.**

190 **Andalucia, Spain**: Art. 12(1)(b), Ley 5/2002; **Aragon, Spain**: Art. 6(1)(e), Ley 6/1999; **Asturias, Spain**: Art. 4(1)(b), Ley 4/2002; **Balearic Islands, Spain**: Art. 8(1)(d), Ley 18/2001; **Basque Country, Spain**: Art. 18(d) and (e), Ley 2/2003; **Canary Islands, Spain**: Art. 9(1)(e), Ley 5/2003; **Catalonia, Spain**: Art. 12(1)(e), Ley 10/1998 (different-sex) and Art. 30(1)(e), Ley 10.1998 (same-sex); **Extremadura, Spain**: Art. 5(1)(b), Ley 5/2003; **Madrid, Spain**: Art. 6(1)(e) Ley 11/2001; **Navarre, Spain**: Art. 4(1)(b), Ley Foral 6/2000; **Valencia, Spain**: Art. 6(1)(e), Ley 1/2001; **Maine**: §2710.4, Chapter 701, Part 6, Subtitle 2, Title 22, Maine Revised Statutes Annotated; **Hawai'i**: §572C-7(c), Title 31, Division 3, Hawai 'i Revised Statutes Annotated; **Nova Scotia**: Sec. 55(1)(c), Vital Statistics Act, Chapter 494, Nova Scotia Revised Statutes; **Tasmania**: Sec. 15(1)(b), Relationships Act 2003; **Andorra**: Art. 17(1)(d), Llei 4/2005; **Luxembourg**: Art. 13(1), Luxembourg Partnership Act. In **Quebec** the partners are allowed to marry each other but no one else, Art. 521.12.2, Quebec Civil Code (as inserted by Law 23/2004 and in force since 10th November 2004), and in **New Zealand** the parties to a civil union are entitled to convert it into a marriage, but not vice versa, Sec. 18, Civil Union Act 2004. For **The Netherlands** see **Chapter V.6.8.**

191 GRAVESON (1953) and GRAVESON (1974) p. 227.

the partnership is an integral part of the legislation.[192] In these five jurisdictions, the ceremony of registration must comply with the same formalities of the marriage ceremony, making a public celebration and corresponding registration compulsory.[193] The registration requirement is also evident for the relationship schemes in **Germany**,[194] **The Netherlands**,[195] **England & Wales**,[196] **Scotland**,[197] **Northern Ireland**,[198] **Switzerland**,[199] **California**,[200] **Luxembourg**,[201] **Vermont**,[202] **Nova Scotia**,[203] **Quebec**,[204] **New Jersey**,[205] **Andorra**,[206] **Connecticut**,[207] **Hawai'i**[208] and **New Zealand**.[209] Even in **Belgium** were the contractual nature of the registration is stressed, the declaration of statutory cohabitation is to be registered in the same register as documents relating to births, deaths and marriages.[210] In **France**, the situation is somewhat different, since the PACS agreement must be deposited with the *tribunal d'instance* and not celebrated before the *mairie*

---

192 **Denmark**: §2(1) and 2(4), Registered Partnership Act; **Norway**: Sec. 2, Registered Partnership Act; **Sweden**: §6, Registered Partnership Act; **Iceland**: Arts. 3 and 4, Confirmed Cohabitation Act; **Finland**: Secs. 3 and 4, Registered Partnership Act.

193 **Denmark**: Secs. 12, 13(1) and 13(2)(1), Marriage (Formation and Dissolution) Act; **Norway**: Ch. 1 and 2, Marriage Act; **Sweden**: Ch. 3 and 15, Marriage Act; **Iceland**: Ch. III and Arts. 21-26, Marriage Act; **Finland**: Secs. 11-13, Marriage Act.

194 §1 I, Registered Partnership Act.

195 Art. 80a(6) Neth. CC, in conjunction with Arts. 44 to 49, Neth. CC.

196 Sec. 1(1)(a)(i), CPA 2004 and see further **Chapter VII.4.8.1**.

197 Sec. 1(1)(a)(ii), CPA 2004 and see further **Chapter VII.4.8.2**.

198 Sec. 1(1)(a)(iii), CPA 2004 and see further **Chapter VII.4.8.3**.

199 Art. 5(1), Sw. RPA. Art. 7(1), Sw. RPA expressly states that the registered partnership is a public act.

200 Secs. 298 and 298.5 in conjunction with Sec. 350, Californian Family Code require the deposition of a declaration of domestic partnership at the county clerk's office, as is the case for marriage.

201 Art. 3, Loi relative aux effets légaux de certains partenariats. The partnership is registered before the court clerk of the Justice of the Peace in the legal arrondissement of the parties' joint domicile.

202 §1202(3), Title 15 in conjunction §§5160 and 5161, Title 18, Vermont Statutes Annotated provide for identical procedures for the registration of marriages and civil unions.

203 Secs. 53(2) and 54(1), Vital Statistics Act provide for identical procedures as Sec. 2(5), Vital Statistics Act for marriage.

204 Sec. 121(3) Quebec Code Civil.

205 PL 2003, Chapter 246, C.26:8A-4(a).

206 Art. 4, Llei 4/2005.

207 Sec. 4(a), an Act Concerning Civil Unions, Public Act No. 05-10.

208 Sec. 572C-5(a), Title 3, Division 3, Hawai'i Revised Statutes Annotated.

209 Secs. 14(1), 15(1) and 16(1), New Zealand Civil Unions Act 2004

210 Art. 1475, Belg. CC and see further **Chapter III.4.8**.

as is the case with marriage.[211] However, the PACS agreement only becomes binding and legally effective upon the moment it is registered.[212]

The federal system in **Spain** has created numerous problems in relation to this criterion. According to Art. 149(1)(8), **Spanish** Constitution, only the federal State of **Spain** is competent to regulate public registers.[213] This has therefore induced the need to create administrative registers for the newly created forms of non-marital registered relationships.[214] However, not all of these autonomous regions have adopted the same policy. Although many of the laws refer to the registration of a non-marital relationship as a constitutive requirement, there are a number of exceptions to this general rule. In **Asturias**, couples will be regarded as involved in a *pareja estable* in three situations, namely having lived together as husband and wife for one year, or if they live together and have had children together, or if they have registered their relationship in the *Registro de Uniones de Hecho del Principado de Asturias.*[215] In the **Canary Islands**, registration is not compulsory at all and fulfils a mere declarative function. As long as the couple have lived together for one year, they are automatically entitled to the benefits granted to *parejas de hecho.*[216] Similarly in **Aragon**, although Art. 2, Ley 6/1999 establishes an administrative registry in which all *parejas estables* must be registered, this registration is purely declarative and does not in and of itself produce civil effects.[217]

In contrast, in **Navarre** no register has been established. Couples wishing to be regarded as having established a *pareja estable* simply need to prove that they have lived together for one year, or have had children together and are living together, or that they have declared their intention to be so regarded in a public deed. Although, a distinction is made in **Catalonia** between different-sex and same-sex couples, the fundamental elements of the registration scheme are very similar to those in **Navarre**. Different-sex

---

211 Art. 515-3, Fr. CC and see further **Chapter IV.4.8**.

212 BRAAT (2000) p. 75.

213 ROCA (2001) p. 371; MARTIN CASALS (2003) p. 65.

214 **Andalucia**: Art. 6, Ley 5/2002; **Aragon**: Art. 2, Ley 6/1999. Registry has been established by Decree 203/1999 of 2nd November 1999; **Asturias**: Art. 3(2), Ley 4/2002; **Balearic Islands**: Art. 1(2), Ley 18/2001; **Basque Country**: Arts. 3(1) and 4, Ley 2/2003; **Canary Islands**: Art. 3(1), Ley 5/2003; **Extremadura:** Art. 2(1), Ley 5/2003; **Madrid**: Art. 1(1), Ley 11/2001; **Valencia**: Art. 1(1), Ley 1/2001.

215 Art. 3(2), Ley 4/2002.

216 Art. 1(1) and 4(1), Ley 5/2003.

217 Arts. 2 and 3(1), Ley 6/1999. See also ROCA (2001) p. 373.

couples are provided with three methods to establish a *union estable de pareja*: by having lived together for a continuous period of two years, or by living together and having had children together, or having expressed their desire to be involved in such a union in a public deed.[218] A same-sex *union estable de pareja* can only be formed, on the other hand, by means of a public deed.[219] It is therefore clear that although many non-marital partnerships registered in **Spain** will be eligible for recognition according to these conditions this is certainly not true of all relationships.

Similarly in **Maine**,[220] **Manitoba** and **Tasmania** a registration scheme is established whereby couples are entitled, but not obliged, to register their relationship. In **Tasmania**, a *significant relationship* can be established either by virtue of the circumstances of the relationship,[221] or by registering their relationship.[222] The same distinction is also maintained with respect to *caring relationships*.[223] In **Manitoba** couples involved in a common-law relationship are entitled to register their relationship if they so desire.[224]

IX.5.4 RIGHTS AND DUTIES ATTRIBUTED

As already outlined in **Chapter VIII.4.3**, two different approaches can be identified with respect to the extent of rights and duties conferred on parties to a non-marital registered relationship: WEAK REGISTRATION and STRONG REGISTRATION, which have been achieved via two methods: EXCLUSION and ENUMERATION.

All those countries where registration is restricted to couples of the same-sex have, thus far, adopted STRONG REGISTRATION schemes, bar one.[225] Differences are, however, noticeable in the method adopted. In the **Nordic** countries use of the EXCLUSION METHOD has resulted in the simple *mutatis*

---

218 Arts. 1(1), 1(2) and 10, Ley 10/1998.

219 Arts. 19 and 21, Ley 10/1998.

220 §2710(2), Chapter 701, Part 6, Subtitle 2, Title 22, Maine Revised Statutes Annotated.

221 Sec. 4(3), Tasmania Relationships Act 2003. These circumstances include: (a) the duration of the relationship, (b) the nature and extent of common residence and (c) whether or not a sexual relationship exists.

222 Art. 4(2), Tasmania Relationships Act 2003. The registration must occur in accordance with Part II of the Act.

223 Sec. 5(4) and 5(5), Tasmania Relationships Act 2003. the registration mentioned in Sec. 5(4) must occur in accordance with Part II of the Act.

224 Sec. 13.1(1) and (4), Manitoba Vital Statistics Act.

225 See **Chapter VIII.4.3**.

mutandis application of all rules on marriage to registered partnerships.[226] Outside of Europe, such an approach is also evident in **Vermont**[227] and **Connecticut**.[228] In **Germany**,[229] the **United Kingdom**[230] and **Switzerland**[231] although opting for a strong registration system, use has instead been made of the ENUMERATION METHOD. Moreover, as was seen in **Chapter VIII.4.1.1**, a STRONG REGISTRATION scheme is not restricted to those countries where relationships registration is confined to same-sex couples. In **Quebec** a STRONG REGISTRATION scheme is achieved using the EXCLUSION METHOD.[232] In **New Zealand** and **Nova Scotia** the same result is achieved by means of the ENUMERATION METHOD,[233] whilst in **The Netherlands** use is made of both methods.[234]

In contrast, all those systems to have opted for a WEAK REGISTRATION scheme have not restricted registration to couples of the same-sex and have obviously utilised the ENUMERATION METHOD.[235] Nonetheless, regardless of these distinctions, it is important to note that all of these schemes attach rights and duties to the registration.

IX.5.5 AIMS OF LEGISLATION AND SOCIAL INTEREST

As has been pointed out in **Section 3** of **Chapters III-VII**, two distinct trends have led to the enactment of many of the schemes allowing for non-marital registered relationships. On the one hand, one is able to discern a noticeable increase in the tolerance shown towards homosexuality. On the other, there

---

226 **Denmark** and **Greenland**: §§3 and 4, Danish Registered Partnership Act; **Norway**: Secs. 3 and 4, Norwegian Registered Partnership Act; **Sweden**: Chapter 3, Swedish Registered Partnership Act; **Iceland**: Arts. 5 and 6, Icelandic Registered Partnership; **Finland**: Chapter 3, Finnish Registered Partnership Act.

227 §1204(b), Title 15, Vermont Statutes Annotated.

228 Sec. 15, An Act Concerning Civil Unions, Public Act No. 05-10.

229 §§2, 3, 9, 10 and 11, German Life Partnership Act. See further THORN (2003a) p. 90-94.

230 See **Chapter VII.5**.

231 See **Chapter VI.5**.

232 Art. 521-6.4, Quebec Civil Code.

233 Schedule 5, New Zealand Civil Unions Act 2004 and Sec. 54(2), Vital Statistics Act, Chapter 494, Nova Scotia Revised Statutes.

234 **Chapter V.5**.

235 **Tasmania**: Part 5, Relationships Act 2003; **Belgium**: See **Chapter III.5**; **Manitoba**: The Common-Law Partners' Property and Related Amendments Act, SM 2002, c. 48; **France**: See **Chapter IV.5**; **Luxembourg**: Chapter I.II, II and III, Luxembourg Partnership Act; **Hawai'i**: §572C-6, Title 31, Division 3, Hawai'i Revised Statutes Annotated; **Maine**: An Act to Promote the Financial Security of Maine's Families and Children Chapter 572; **New Jersey**: Domestic Partnership Act, Chapter 246, PL 2003.

is an increased legislative willingness to accept the social phenomenon of non-marital cohabitation. These two trends have, to differing extents, spurred the enactment of legislation.

Until rather recently, homosexuality was regarded as a criminal offence across a large portion of Europe. However, since 2003 homosexuality has thus been legal in all 45 States in the Council of Europe.[236] This increasing tolerance shown towards gays and lesbians is also evident in an associated equalisation in the age of consent in many countries.[237] Calls from the European Parliament,[238] the Council of Europe[239] and the European Court of

---

236 Homosexuality was decriminalised in the Council of Europe countries in: **Albania** (1995), **Andorra** (date unclear), **Armenia** (2003), **Austria** (1971), **Azerbaijan** (2000), **Belgium** (1792), **Bosnia-Herzegovina** (1998), **Bulgaria** (1968), **Croatia** (1977), **Cyprus** (1998), **Czech Republic** (1961), **Denmark** (1930), **England & Wales** (1967), **Estonia** (1992), **Finland** (1971), **France** (1791), **Germany** (1969), **Georgia** (1998), **Greece** (1950), **Hungary** (1961), **Iceland** (1930), **Ireland** (1993), **Italy** (1889), **Latvia** (1992), **Liechtenstein** (1989), **Lithuania** (1993), **Luxembourg** (1792), **Malta** (1973), **Moldova** (1995), **The Netherlands** (1811), **Northern Ireland** (1982), **Norway** (1972), **Poland** (1932), **Portugal** (1945), **Romania** (1996), **Russian Federation** (1993), **San Marino** (1997), **Scotland** (1980), **Serbia and Montenegro** (1994), **Slovakia** (1961), **Slovenia** (1977), **Spain** (1822), **Sweden** (1944), **Switzerland** (1942), **Former Yugoslav Republic of Macedonia** (1998), **Turkey** (1858), and **Ukraine** (1991). Homosexuality was also decriminalised in **Belarus** in 1994, which is not a member of the Council of Europe.

237 The age of consent is equal in the following countries at the age indicated in brackets: **Andorra** (16), **Armenia** (16), **Austria** (14), **Azerbaijan** (16), **Belgium** (16), **Bosnia-Herzegovina** (16), **Bulgaria** (14), **Croatia** (14), **Cyprus** (17), **Czech Republic** (15), **Denmark** (15), **England & Wales** (16), **Estonia** (14), **Finland** (16), **France** (15), **Germany** (14/16), **Georgia** (16), **Greece** (17), **Hungary** (14), **Iceland** (14), **Ireland** (17), **Italy** (14), **Latvia** (14), **Liechtenstein** (14), **Lithuania** (unequal), **Luxembourg** (16), **Malta** (12/18), **Moldova** (16), **The Netherlands** (12/16), **Northern Ireland** (17), **Norway** (16), **Poland** (15), **Portugal** (16), **Russian Federation** (14/16), **San Marino** (14/16), **Scotland** (16), **Serbia and Montenegro** (14), **Slovakia** (15), **Slovenia** (14), **Spain** (13), **Sweden** (15), **Switzerland** (16), **Turkey** (18), and **Ukraine** (16). The age of consent is also equalised in **Belarus** at 16. In the following countries the age of consent is higher for homosexuals than heterosexuals: **Albania** (14 heterosexuals, 18 for homosexuals), **Romania** (15 heterosexuals, 18 for homosexuals; although there are proposals for its removal). The age of consent is unclear in the **Former Yugoslav Republic of Macedonia**.

238 Report on respect for human rights in the European Union (1998-1999), A5-0050/2000, §56 published as non-legislative resolution T5-0111/2000, *OJ* C-377, 29th December 2000, p. 172-344E; Report on the situation as regards fundamental rights in the European Union (2000), A5-0223/2001, §78 published as non-legislative resolution T5-0400/2001, *OJ* C-65, 14th March 2003, p. 177-350E; Report on the human rights situation in the European Union (2001), A5-0451/2002, §81 published as non-legislative resolution T5-0012/2003, *OJ* C-38, 12th February 2004, p. 174-246E; Report on the situation as regards fundamental rights in the European Union (2002), A5-0281/2003, §83-84 published as non-legislative

Human Rights[240] for the age of consent to be equalised have added increasing political pressure on those countries that have yet to remove discriminatory provisions. Alongside these amendments to criminal legislation, the removal of discrimination in the field of employment and other areas of public service has been of growing concern. Yet until recently, the removal of discrimination was limited to respecting the rights of gays and lesbians as individuals.[241] Since the mid 1970s a number of countries have also begun to recognise the need to remove discrimination against same-sex couples.[242] WAALDIJK has referred to this trend as the "law of small change" and the "trend of standard sequences", noting that all countries (with minor exceptions) appear to be following similar patterns of development at differing speeds.[243]

This trend has occurred side-by-side a very different trend in social attitudes. Until recently marriage heralded the beginning of a first union for the majority of couples in Europe.[244] Since the late 1960s and the early 1970s marriage rates in most European countries have declined.[245] One of the reasons proffered for this decline is the rise in non-martial cohabitation.[246] As KIERNAN notes, prior to the 1970s cohabiting unions

---

resolution T5-0376/2003, *OJ* C-76, 25th March 2003, p. 245-412E; Report on the situation as regards fundamental rights in the European Union (2003), A5-0207/2004, §102.

239 Parliamentary Assembly of the Council of Europe, Recommendation 924/1981 on discrimination against homosexuals, §7(ii), adopted on 1st October 1981.

240 ECtHR, *Dudgeon v. United Kingdom*, Appl. No. 7525/76, 22nd October 1981; ECtHR, *Norris v. Republic of Ireland*, Appl. No. 10581/83, 26th October 1988; ECtHR, *Modinos v. Cyprus*, Appl. No. 15070/89, 22nd April 1993; ECmHR, *Sutherland v. United Kingdom*, Appl. No. 25186/94, 1st July 1997; ECtHR, *L and V v. Austria*, Appl. No. 39292/98 and 29829/98, 9th January 2003; ECtHR, *SL v. Austria*, Appl. No. 45330/99, 9th January 2003; ECtHR, *BB v. United Kingdom*, Appl. No. 53760/00, 10th February 2004.

241 In the European Union, this has for example led to the enactment of Directive 2000/78/EC of 27th November 2000 Establishing a General Framework for Equal Treatment in Employment and Occupation.

242 This trend has not yet been taken up by the ECtHR which insists that homosexuals cannot enjoy the protection of the provisions on family life: ECmHR, *S v. United Kingdom*, Appl. No. 11716/85, 14th May 1986 and ECtHR, *Keegan v. The Netherlands*, Appl. No. 15666/89, 19th May 1992. There is some evidence, however, to suggest that this position might be changing: ECtHR, *Salgueiro da Silva Mounta v. Portugal*, Appl. No. 33290/96, 1st December 1999. See also MCGLYNN (2003) p. 229.

243 WAALDIJK (2001) p. 636-638. A theory also supported by ANTOKOLSKAIA (2005).

244 DOUGLAS (2000b) p. 214.

245 EUROSTAT, *Population Statistics 2004*, Brussels: European Commission, 2004, Chapter G: Nuptiality, p. 115-128. The marriage rate (per 1000 of the population) in the EU has fallen from 8.0 in 1960 to 4.8 in 2002 (see table G-1, p. 117).

246 KIERNAN (1999) p. 25.

were largely invisible both statistically and socially.[247] Although a great deal of diversity is evident across Europe, in almost all Northern and Western European Union countries a large percentage of respondents identify themselves as being involved in non-cohabitating unions.[248]

European nations have thus progressed considerably since NAPOLEON declared that "*les concubins ignorent la loi et la loi ignore donc les concubins*"[249] and criminal sanctions could be imposed on those cohabiting outside of wedlock. The steady removal of such sanctions led European nations into an era of neutrality, when the law granted neither advantage nor disadvantage to those living outside the bonds of marriage. As time progresses and social attitudes develop, rights and obligations have gradually been granted to those couples living together outside of the bonds of marriage.

The delicate interplay of these two trends (increasing tolerance towards homosexuality and the increased incidence of non-martial cohabitation) coupled with other factors including the social diversity of the population, the legal standing of homosexual lobby groups, the existence of constitutional protection afforded to marriage and the involvement of the church in the celebration of legal marriages, have caused the great diversity of solutions seen today.[250] It is therefore important at this juncture to distinguish between those countries where registration is open to same-sex couples only, followed by a discussion of the aims of the legislative enactments in those countries where no such restriction exists.

IX.5.5.1 Same-sex couples only

The principal objective in enacting registered partnership legislation in each of the five Nordic countries was to equalise the social and legal status of same-sex couples with that of married couples. The parliamentary discussions in the five **Nordic** countries have been remarkably similar.

247 KIERNAN (2001) p. 1.

248 High levels of non-marital cohabitation are thus apparent in **Denmark**, **Sweden**, **Finland** and **France**, and mid-levels in **The Netherlands**, **Belgium**, **Luxembourg**, **Great Britain**, **Germany** and **Austria**. (see Figure 1, KIERNAN (2001) p. 5). In countries such as **Ireland**, **Spain**, **Portugal**, **Greece** and **Italy**, the incidence of non-marital cohabitation is still relatively low.

249 P. MALAURIE, "Mariage et concubinage en droit français contemporain", in: ARCHIVES DE PHILOSOPHIE DU DROIT, *Réformes du droit de la famille*, Paris: Sirey, 1975, p. 19.

250 See further analysis on these last two points in **Chapter VIII.5.2**.

Although the various ambitions were allocated varying degrees of importance, the main objectives of these legislative enactments can be summarised as follows:[251]

- To increase social acceptance and stimulate increased openness and awareness of homosexuality. Homosexuals were believed to be surrounded by prejudice and misunderstanding and such legislative enactments would go some way to decreasing this discrimination and acknowledging the equal value of homosexual relationships.
- An institutional framework was thought necessary to be able to achieve this desired escalation in social acceptance. The creation of such a framework for same-sex partners would improve their opportunities for regulating their lives in accordance with their own wishes and preferences.
- Formal recognition through express legislation would also improve the chances of long-lasting and stable relationships between persons of the same-sex. In **Denmark** reference was also made to the consequent reduction in the possible spread of AIDS.[252]
- A legal institution for two persons of the same sex who live in a permanent partnership was thought to be a precondition for securing the same legal rights as married couples, rights regarding such matters as housing, pensions, immigration and entitlement to work.
- The device of registration gives the partners the right to choose between formalisation and non-formalisation. Thus they have the same choice as heterosexual partners. This right of choice therefore brings with it the necessary equality before the law that the legislation attempted to achieve.

These broad, social and equality orientated objectives are also evident in those other jurisdictions were non-marital registered relationship schemes are restricted to couples of the same sex, for example as has already been seen in the **United Kingdom** and **Switzerland**.[253] In **Germany** the principal aim of the partnership legislation has been to create a legal framework for

---

251 For the aims of the individual legislative enactments see, **Denmark**: *Danish Folketing (Parliament)*, 26th May 1989 (1988-1989), *Bemaerkinger til lovforslaget*, No. 117; **Norway**: LØDRUP (1996) p. 388-392; **Sweden**: SOU, 1993:98; **Iceland**: FORDER (1999c); **Finland**: MERIN (2002) p. 107-110, SAVOLAINEN (2003) p. 26.

252 NIELSEN (1990) p. 298.

253 See **Chapters VI.3** and **VIII.3**. See also HARPER *et al.* (2005) p. 40

same-sex couples to enter into a legally recognised life partnership.[254] The new law allows same-sex couples to express their close bond through the acceptance of legal responsibility, thus adhering to the broad social interest of the **Nordic** model.[255] In **Vermont**, the original driving force to equalise the position of same-sex couples came not from the legislature but from the judiciary.[256] The bill was forwarded to the Senate, were following minor alterations was approved on the 19 April 2000. Identical reasoning also lay behind the decision by a court in the Brazilian province of **Río Grande do Sul** to force the legislature to create a civil union registry mirroring that already existing for marriage.[257] In **Connecticut** on the other hand, although it was the legislature who took the initiative to legislate for civil unions, the reasoning mirrors that advanced by the **Vermont** Supreme Court.[258]

IX.5.5.2 Same-sex and different-sex couples

In those countries were non-marital registered relationships are also open to couples of a different sex, the social and legal inequality faced by same-sex couples has only been half of the story. A number of different arguments have been proffered for opening new registration schemes to different-sex couples as well. These reasons can be roughly divided into three different categories: the principle of equality, a political compromise and vulnerable position of elderly couples.

As in **The Netherlands**, the driving force behind the introduction of legislation in **New Zealand**, **Manitoba**, **Nova Scotia** and **Quebec** came for the desire to improve the legal position of same-sex couples. Yet the pressure to ensure equality with different-sex unmarried couples also dominated the debate.[259] In **Spain**, the increasing number of different-sex couples who have chosen not to marry, coupled with the increasing acceptance of this alternative family form and the lack of legal protection afforded to them form the normal staple of arguments offered alongside the current

---

254 HOHLOCH/KJELLAND (2001) p. 224.

255 DETHLOFF (2001) p. 240.

256 Vermont Supreme Court, *Baker v. State of Vermont* (1999) 744 A.2d 864. The **Vermont** Supreme Court enjoined the state legislature to extend same-sex couples the benefits and protections associated with marriage, yet did not prescribe the methods to be used. After months of discussion, the **Vermont** House of Representatives passed the Civil Union Act in March 2000 bill by a vote of 89 to 76.

257 www.unionolove.com/tribalspeak/main/messages/1969.html.

258 Summary, OLR Bill, Analysis to Substituted Bill No. 963, available at www.cga.ct.gov.

259 *E.g.* An act instituting civil unions and establishing new rules of filiation, c.6 2002.

discrimination of those in same-sex relationships.[260] During the Parliamentary debates in **Luxembourg**, the fact that there are those who chose to live together simply because they cannot get married was explicitly acknowledged alongside the problems faced by same-sex couples.[261]

As already stated,[262] the main reasons for opening registration to same-sex couples in **France** and **Belgium** stemmed from the political impasse that would have been created if the Governments were perceived to be promoting same-sex relationships. As a result, a political compromise was struck and registration was opened to both groups of couples.[263] Yet it should be noted that, in a similar manner as **Denmark**, one of the original driving forces behind the **French** proposals was the aim of combating the injustices faced by those same-sex couples dealing with the AIDS virus.[264] In **Maine** a similar political compromise was struck. In ensuring that the most controversial exclusions of same-sex couples are specifically and legislatively dealt with (*i.e.* the ability to make decisions for a partner in hospital and inheritance rights), the State legislature has attempted to silence the calls from homosexual lobby groups, whilst appeasing the conservative groups wishing to ensure the stability of marriage and the family.[265]

In **New Jersey** and **California** a very different policy has been adopted. In both these States domestic partnership is open to same-sex couples as well as those different-sex couples over the age of sixty-two.[266] In both States it was noted that the potential loss of, or reduction in, retirement benefits for

260 **Andalucia**: Art. 1, Ley 5/2002; **Aragon**: Preamble, Ley 6/1999; **Asturias**: Art. 1, Ley 4/2002; **Balearic Islands**: Art. 1, Ley 18/2001; **Basque Country**: Art. 1, Ley 7/2003; **Canary Islands**: Preamble, Ley 5/2003; **Catalonia**: Preamble, Ley 10/1998; **Extremadura**: Explanation of Motives, Ley 5/2003; **Madrid**: Preamble, Ley 11/2001; **Navarre**: Explanation of Motives, Ley Foral 6/2000; **Valencia**: Preamble, Ley 1/2001.

261 *Luxembourg Chamber of Deputies*, 2001-2002, No. 4946/1, p. 23: "Si l'État doit respect ces choix, il ne peut toutefois ignorer les effects de ces choix." and *Luxembourg Chamber of Deputies*, 2003-2004, No. 4946/10, p. 4.

262 **Chapter VIII.2.4**.

263 See **Chapters III.3** and **IV.3**. See also RICHARDS (2002) p. 315.

264 BRAAT (2000) p. 75-81. See **Chapter IV.3.1**.

265 Marriage is defined as a union between one man and one woman: §701.5, Chapter 23, Title 19-A, Maine Revised Statutes Annotated.

266 **New Jersey**: C.26:8A-4b(5), Chapter 246, PL 2003; **California**: §297(b)(5)(B), Part 1, Division 2.5, California Family Code.

senior couples sometimes make them reticent to marry, despite being in a committed relationship.[267]

IX.6 SUMMARY OF CONCLUSIONS

The issue of characterisation is one of the most crucial in this field of law. An accurate and clear characterisation of the term "non-marital registered relationship" will lead to increased certainty and uniformity of solution, as well as a reduction in the incidence of limping relationships. However, the ultimate form, shape and boundaries of any characterisation will necessarily depend upon the level of international co-operation that can be achieved. In striving for such altruistic goals, it is clear that although the domestic forms of non-marital registered relationship are very different, similar common elements can be discerned.[268] These elements have been exceedingly influential in determining the respective characterisation criteria espoused in the different jurisdictions surveyed.[269] Two different approaches are, however, evident in those countries to have enacted private international law rules. Firstly, all countries have set about formulating so-called characterisation criteria; a standard against which foreign institutions can be measured. A domestic institution confronted with a relationship registered abroad must therefore use these characterisation criteria in order to determine whether or not the relationship is eligible for recognition in accordance with these rules. This approach is supplemented in the **United Kingdom** by a second approach, namely the enumeration of countries whose relationship schemes are, without further investigation, characterised as overseas relationships, and thus fall within the private international law scheme of the CPA 2004. This list can be amended by the Secretary of State as and when needed.

In searching for certainty and uniformity of result, and at the same time wishing to improve international co-operation in this field, the solution adopted by the **United Kingdom** is to be commended. Certainty is achieved with regards certain relationships by virtue of a list of specified relationships. In this way, doubt is removed with respect to a large number

---

267 **New Jersey**: C.26:8A-2(a), Chapter 246, PL 2003. In the original proposal and the first reprint of the law this possibility was not included: New Jersey Bill 2003, No. 3743, introduced 5th June 2003. For policy reasons see al;so C.26:8A-2e, Chapter 246, PL 2003; **California**: §297(b)(5)(B), Part 1, Division 2.5, California Family Code.

268 See **Chapter VIII.5**.

269 See **Chapter IX.4**.

of relationships. The recognising authority is thus not required to test the relationship according to certain conditions. If the relationship is on the list, it will be regarded as a "non-marital registered relationship". In not providing such a list, confusion and uncertainty reign. Take, for example, the situation of **The Netherlands**. A list of criteria is expounded in Art. 2(5), Neth. PIL(RP)A. According to the explanatory notes accompanying the original Bill, even if certain registration schemes do not satisfy these criteria they may still be eligible for recognition under the private international law rules laid down by the Act.[270] If this is the case, what purpose do these criteria serve if strict adherence to them is not necessary? On the basis of the aforementioned criteria and the analysis undertaken in **Section IX.5**, it would appear that the following non-marital registration schemes should be characterised as non-marital registered relationships in the seven countries studied in this research.

***Table 9:** Relationship schemes eligible for specified mention*

Jurisdiction	Name of relationship
Andorra	union estable
Argentina: Buenos Aires City	unión civil
Argentina: Río Negro Province	unión civil
Belgium	wettelijke samenwoning
Canada: Nova Scotia	domestic partnership
Canada: Quebec	civil union
Denmark	registreret partnerskab
Finland	rekisteröity parisuhde
France	pacte civil de solidarité
Germany	Lebenspartnerschaft
Iceland	staðfesta samvist
Luxembourg	partneariat
The Netherlands	geregistreerd partnerschap
New Zealand	civil union
Norway	registrert partnerskap
Sweden	registrerat partnerskap
Spain: Andalucia	parjea de hecho
Spain: Balearic Islands	parjea estable
Spain: Basque Country	parjea de hecho
Spain: Valencia	union de hecho
Switzerland	partenariat enregistré
UK (all 3 jurisdictions)	civil partnership

270 *Dutch Second Chamber*, 2002-2003, 28924, No. 3, p. 3.

USA: California	domestic partnership
USA: Connecticut	civil union
USA: Hawai'i	reciprocal benefits
USA: New Jersey	domestic partnership
USA: Vermont	civil union

The list is not, however, intended to function exclusively. If the jurisdiction from which the relationship emanates is listed, the relationship will be characterised as a non-marital registered relationships and thus eligible for recognition in accordance with the relevant private international law rules on non-marital registered relationships. If it is not listed, the recognising authority will have to test the relationship against the general conditions listed in **Section IX.4** in order to assess whether the relationship can be regarded as a non-marital registered relationship. In this way, this list of jurisdictions acts as a timesaver by having already undertaken the task of testing certain relationships against the characterisation criteria.

In dealing with relationships emanating from jurisdictions not listed above, a recognising authority would need to investigate whether the relationship satisfies the characterisation criteria. In this way, the application of the criteria is carried out on a case-by-case basis. Some relationships may fall foul of certain conditions, whilst others may not. For example, according to the legislation of **Tasmania**, **Aragon**, **Asturias**, the **Canary Islands** and **Maine**, a party entitled to the benefits of non-marital relationships may not necessarily have registered their relationship. In these cases, only those relationships which have been registered would be eligible for recognition. Furthermore, the legislation in **Manitoba**, the **Canary Islands**, **Extremadura** and **Madrid** provide for the possibility that a person may be involved in a non-marital registered relationship and a marriage at the same time. Therefore, if either of the parties involved in a registered relationship is also involved in a marriage, the registered relationship will not be characterised as a non-marital registered relationship.[271]

Finally, as far as this research has been able to determine, relationships emanating from **Catalonia** and **Navarre** should be completely excluded from the ambit of any proposed legislative framework. Although express reference is often made to the non-marital registered relationship provided

---

271 An alternative would be to characterise such relationships as non-marital registered relationships, yet subsequently deny recognition on the basis of public policy. See further **Chapter X.5.4.**

for in **Catalonia** as an example of a registration scheme which should be covered by emerging legislation, serious doubts must be raised in relation to such a characterisation. **Catalonia** provides merely for the signing of the public deed without the subsequent requirement of registration. The lack of registration thus challenges the very foundation upon which the legal category of non-marital *registered* relationships has been based.

Once one has established the bounds of any new category, one must proceed to the rules themselves. It is therefore necessary to examine the private international law rules developed in the jurisdictions surveyed with respect to the establishment, the dissolution and the legal effects attributed to non-marital registered relationships.

CHAPTER X
ESTABLISHMENT OF A NON-MARITAL REGISTERED RELATIONSHIP

X.1 INTRODUCTION

There are many different situations in which the existence of a non-marital registered relationship will form the central issue before a court. There are also other situations when the existence of such a relationship will need to be established as a preliminary to legal proceedings, *e.g.* when a person claims money due under an insurance policy as the surviving registered partner of the deceased. This chapter is devoted to answering questions related to the relevant choice of law rules for determining the validity of non-marital registered relationships, (**Section X.2**) as well as the recognition of such relationships registered abroad (**Section X.3**). The special situation of relationships registered before consular and diplomatic representations is dealt with in **Section X.4**, whilst **Section X.5** tackles the use of corrective measures in this field.

However, before one can begin to analyse the rules on non-marital registered relationships in this sphere, it is important to draw attention to the existence of two fundamentally divergent approaches to the topics dealt with in this book with respect to marriage.[1] Some countries have opted to apply a "choice of law test"[2] within their marital recognition rules.[3] This means that in order to be eligible for recognition, a foreign marriage will need to be valid according to the domestic choice of law rules, as well as according to the law of the place where it was celebrated. This choice of law

---

1 The extent to which these systems also apply to non-marital registered relationships will be discussed in **Section X.3.1**.

2 In Dutch this is succinctly known as the *conflictenrechtelijke toets*. See further BUCHER (2004a) p. 54, §128-129; STAATSCOMMISSIE (2004a). See also HR, 27th June 2003, NJ 2004, 615, §21 *et seq*: "De vraag naar het toepasselijk recht is een andere dan de vraag of een vreemd vonnis voor erkenning in aanmerking komt."

3 See, for example, Art. 27(1), Belg. CPIL which determines that any authentic instrument or deed obtained abroad will be recognised in **Belgium** if it satisfies the law of the place where it was obtained as well as the law determined applicable by **Belgian** choice of law rules. See ERAUW (2004) p. 124-125; VAN HECKE/LENAERTS (1989) p. 218, §455.

test is employed in the **United Kingdom, France** and **Belgium** (throughout this chapter referred to as the "Anglo-Franco-Belgian system").[4] This is, however, not the case in **The Netherlands** and **Switzerland**,[5] where the recognition rules are devoid of any choice of law test (throughout this chapter referred to as the "Dutch-Swiss system").[6] In the Dutch-Swiss system no choice of law test is subsequently imposed on the recognition of foreign marriages.[7] This distinction is important to bear in mind when one begins to analyse the relevant rules for non-marital registered relationships.

X.2 CHOICE OF LAW RULES

Six of the seven countries studied in this book have enacted private international law rules to regulate non-marital registered relationships.[8] **France** is the only country studied to have not yet enacted rules regulating such relationships.[9] In the absence of such rules, reference will be made to the array of current academic opinion, as well as the existing private international law rules with respect to marriage.[10] In referring to the rules on marriage, one is not only able to gain inspiration in attempting to craft equivalent rules for non-marital registered relationships, but one is also able to profit from a solid grounding in the fundamental principles of private international law in the field of personal status.[11]

---

4 Arts. 3(3) and 170, Fr. CC, have been interpreted by the **French** courts as being equally applicable to marriages celebrated inside and outside the jurisdiction, subject to a couple of exceptions. Although, in the **United Kingdom** no distinction is drawn between marriages celebrated inside or outside the jurisdiction, this is not the case with respect to non-marital registered relationships where a distinction is indeed drawn.

5 **Neth.:** The choice of law test has now been abolished in many Dutch recognition rules including, marriage (Neth. PIL(M)A) as well as divorce (Neth. PIL(D)A) and the recognition of foreign surnames (Neth. PIL(N)A). **Swit.:** BUCHER (2004a) p. 54, §128-129 and DUTOIT (2005) p. 154-155, Art. 45, No. 1-3. In general, this is also the position adopted by the Hague Conference in the 1978 Hague MC.

6 For the purposes of this chapter, foreign consular and diplomatic representations are to be regarded as a separate, distinct section and will accordingly be dealt with seperately in **Section X.4**.

7 *E.g.* HR, 27th June 2003, NJ 2004, 615, §21.

8 **Belg.:** Chapters III and IV, Belg. CPIL; **Neth.:** Neth. PIL(RP)A; **Swit.:** Chapter 3a, Sw. CPIL; **Eng**, **Scot** and **NI**, **UK:** Part V, CPA 2004. It must be noted that the private international law rules of **Northern Ireland** are identical to those of **England & Wales** unless otherwise stated. See **Chapter I**.

9 Proposals have, however, recently been published: MINISTRE DE LA JUSTICE (2004).

10 It must be noted that at present **Dutch**, **Belgian**, **Swiss** and **British** consulates in **France** advise nationals that non-marital registered relationships will not be recognised in **France**, although it will form an obstacle to the registration of a PACS in France. On the current obstacles to recognition of foreign relationships in **France** see KESSLER (2004) p. 201-242.

11 See FULCHIRON (2004) p. 92-95. See also **Chapter IX.5**.

In a similar vein to marriage, all the jurisdictions researched have drawn a distinction between questions relating to the formal validity and essential validity of non-marital registered relationships.[12] Each category is thus subject to an independent choice of law rule. A comparison of the rules determining the formal validity of non-marital registered relationships will be discussed first (**Section X.2.1**), followed by a comparison of the rules governing the essential validity of such relationships (**Section X.2.2**). Although this inevitably leads to the issue of characterisation, it is submitted that any such issues that arise in relation to the distinction between formal and essential validity will be solved in exactly the same manner as their counterparts in relation to marriage.[13] In fact, one of the most contentious areas with respect to this characterisation, namely the characterisation of religious marriages, will cause few, if any, problems with respect to non-marital registered relationships due to the express prohibition of such religious registrations.[14]

X.2.1 FORMAL VALIDITY

With respect to marriage there is no rule more firmly established in the private international law of all the countries researched than that which applies the maxim *locus regit actum* to the formalities of a marriage.[15] In turning one's attention to the respective rules on non-marital registered

---

12 In Dutch *formele vereisten/huwelijksvoltrekking* and *materiële vereisten/huwelijksbevoegdheid.* In French *conditions du form* and *conditions du fond.*

13 See, for example, **Belg.**: RIGAUX/FALLON (1993) p. 308-311, §977-980; VANDER ELST/WEBER (1983) p. 80-81, §15.1-15.2; **Fr.**: MAYER/HEUZÉ (2001) p. 365-373, §549-564; BATIFFOL/LAGARDE (1983) p. 59-61, §426-427; AUDIT (2000) p. 541-545, §629-636; **Neth.**: STRIKWERDA (2000) p. 93-95; **Swit.**: HEINI *et al.* (1999) Art. 44(1); **Eng, UK:** COLLINS (2000) p. 671-682, §17-054 to §17-086; NORTH/FAWCETT (1999) p. 708-709; CLARKSON/HILL (2002) p. 311-313; **Scot, UK:** CLIVE (1997) p. 122-135, §09.040-09.074; ANTON/BEAUMONT (1990) p. 439-444; CRAWFORD (1998) p. 149-150, §9.26.

14 See **Chapters III.4.8, IV.4.8, VI.4.8** and **VII.4.8.** Although religious registrations are not expressly prohibited in **The Netherlands**, they do not occur with any frequency: see **Chapter V.4.8.**

15 **Belg.**: Art. 47(1), Belg. CPIL; HEYVAERT (2002) p. 148, §325; **Fr.**: AUDIT (2000) p. 545, §637; MAYER/HEUZÉ (2001) p. 368-372, §554-561; Art. 170(1), Fr. CC (foreign marriages); **Neth.**: Art. 4, Neth. PIL(M)A; **Swit.**: Art. 44(3), Sw. CPIL; **Eng, UK:** *Scrimshire v. Scrimshire* (1752) 2 Hagg Con 395; *Dalrymple v. Dalrymple* (1811) 2 Hagg Con 54; *Warrender v. Warrender* (1835) 1 Cl & Fin 488; *Harvey v. Farnie* (1882) 8 App Cas 43; *Berthiaume v. Dastous* [1930] AC 79 (PC); *Kenward v. Kenward* [1951] P 124; *R v. Bham* [1966] 1 QB 159; *Re Xs Marriage* (1983) 65 FLR 132 and *McCabe v. McCabe* [1994] 1 FCR 257. **Scot, UK:** *Bliersbach v. McEwen* (1959) SLT 81; *Burke v. Burke* (1983) SLT 331; Sec. 3 M(S)A 1977; ANTON/BEAUMONT (1990) p. 421; CLIVE (1997) p. 122, §09.040; CRAWFORD (1998) p. 127, §9.02. This would gain statutory force according to Sec. 28(1), FL(S)B 2005.

relationships, one is clearly able to see a similar common core developing. However, differences are evident in the manner in which these countries have adopted their respective rules. Some countries have opted for the analogous application of the rules on marriage to all forms of non-marital registered relationships, subject to a few exceptions (**Section X.2.1.1**).[16] Some countries have opted for a division between those non-marital registered relationships akin to marriage and those which are not (**Section X.2.1.2**), whilst others have preferred the creation of a separate set of rules applying to all non-marital registered relationships (**Section X.2.1.3**).[17]

X.2.1.1 Analogous application of marriage law

Switzerland is the only country studied in this book to have applied the private international law rules on marriage *mutatis mutandis* to all non-marital registered relationships.[18] As a result, questions relating to the formal validity of non-marital relationships registered in **Switzerland** will be answered according to **Swiss** law.[19] Despite many commentators in **France** referring to the possibility of analogously applying the rules on marriage to non-marital registered relationships,[20] there is no author, as far as this author is aware, who suggests the analogous application of these rules to all non-marital registered relationships without first drawing a distinction between (at least) two different categories of relationships.[21]

16 This approach has also been adopted by **Sweden**, **Norway**, **Denmark** and **Iceland**. For information on the private international law rules of Nordic countries, see JÄNTERÄ-JAREBORG (2003a) p. 143-144; BOGDAN (2004) p. 65.

17 This approach has also been adopted by **Germany** (THORN (2003a) p. 160-166) and **Finland** (JÄNTERÄ-JAREBORG (2003a) p. 147-148).

18 Art. 65a, Sw. CPIL. A number of exceptions do however apply, which will be dealt with in turn in subsequent sections.

19 Art. 65a, combined with Art. 44(1), Sw. CPIL. See DUTOIT (2005) p. 221, Art. 65a, No. 4.

20 MIGNOT (2001) p. 626, CHANTELOUP (2000) p. 1720; FULCHIRON (2000) p. 904.

21 Although CHANTELOUP suggest that the category of marriage should be enlarged she then goes on to explain all the alterations that would need to be made to the private international law rules for non-marital registered relationships. It is therefore better to analyse her arguments in accordance with a separate category based on marriage. See CHANTELOUP (2000) p. 1719-1720. See further LOUSSOUARN/BOUREL (2004) p. 393, §291. KESSLER also draws a distinction between *partenariats institutions* and *partenariats contrats*, but subjects these categories to the same choice of law rules: KESSLER (2004) p. 25-50.

X.2.1.2 Two categories of non-marital registered relationships

As has already been noted in **Chapter IX**, some **French** commentators have proposed that a distinction be drawn between those forms of non-marital registered relationship that create a bond akin to marriage and those that do not.[22] Although MIGNOT distinguishes between those countries that have fashioned a virtual *mariage homosexuel* (*i.e.* the **Scandinavian** countries and **The Netherlands**) and those that have not, he argues that both forms of non-marital registered relationship should be subject to the analogous application of the private international law rules on marriage in relation to issues of formal validity.[23] However, with respect to those non-marital registered relationships that not create a bond akin to marriage, MIGNOT goes on to propose a further distinction between, on the one hand, questions relating to the formal validity of the instrument itself and, on the other, the formal validity of the registration.[24] For questions in the former category, he proposes that one should apply the maxim *locus regit actum*, whilst in dealing with issues in the latter category one should apply the maxim *auctor regit actum*.

The academic overtones sounded in **France** have found resonance in **Belgium**, where the creation of two categories has not only found favour amongst academics,[25] but also legislative force in the recent codification of private international law.[26] Those non-marital registered relationships akin to marriage are subsumed under the private international law category of marriage and the rules on marriage are, hence, applied analogously.[27] As a result, Art. 47(1), Belg. CPIL states that questions of formal validity will be determined according to the *lex loci celebrationis*. Those non-marital registered relationships that do not create a bond akin to marriage, yet are still regarded as non-marital registered relationships, are regulated in a separate chapter of the Belg. CPIL.[28] Nonetheless, despite the fact that **Belgian** law draws this distinction, questions of formal validity with respect to relationships falling into this second category, known as "relationships of

---

22 KHAIRALLAH (2000) p. 321; MIGNOT (2001) p. 650.

23 MIGNOT (2001) p. 626. This approach is also supported by KHAIRALLAH (2001).

24 MIGNOT (2001) p. 627-628. The former category deals with issues as to the formal validity of the instrument whereas the latter category deals with the international competence of the national authorities to proceed with the registration of the instrument (*i.e.* dealing with the competency of consular and diplomatic representations to register relationships).

25 BARNICH (2000) p. 1 *et seq.*

26 *Belgian Senate*, 2002-2003, No. 3-27/1, p. 91-92, and Chapters III and IV, Belg. CPIL.

27 Chapter III, Belg. CPIL. For an explanation of this distinction see **Chapter IX.6.**

28 Chapter IV, Belg. CPIL. For an explanation of this distinction see **Chapter IX.6.**

cohabitation" are also determined according to the law of the place of registration, *i.e* the *lex loci registrationis*.[29]

X.2.1.3 Separate rules but identical to marriage

Despite the obvious similarities in the result achieved, the approach adopted by the **United Kingdom** and **The Netherlands** is somewhat different. Instead of extending the purview of existing marriage legislation to cover non-marital registered relationships or creating a distinction between different categories of relationships, a separate legislative framework has been created in order to deal with these new forms of relationship. In accordance with the traditional orthodoxy in the **United Kingdom**,[30] in order for a person to be able to register a civil partnership in **England & Wales**, **Scotland** or **Northern Ireland** the formal conditions in the respective country must first be satisfied.[31] An identical result is also achieved in **The Netherlands**, with questions of formal validity being determined according to **Dutch** law.[32]

A number of **French** authors have also expressed support for such a solution. These authors all note the difficulties of referring to the *lex loci registrationis*. Their concerns arise due to the nature of the registration of the **French** PACS and the possibility of registering non-marital relationships before consular and diplomatic representations.[33] FULCHIRON distinguishes between two categories of unions, namely *unions libres* (free unions) and *unions légales* (legal unions). He suggests dividing the category of legal unions further into two separate categories, namely *partenariats cadres* (framework partnerships) and *partenariats statuts* (status partnerships).[34] However, despite recognising the existence of two different types of legal union, he argues that both groups should be subject to the same rules, and thus characterised according to the broader overarching term of legal unions.[35] He goes on to advocate that all issues relating to the formal validity

---

29 Art. 60(1), Belg. CPIL.

30 With respect to marriage, there is no rule more firmly established than that which applies the maxim *locus regit actum* to the formalities of a marriage (see **fn. 5, p. 388**).

31 **Eng, UK:** Sec. 1(1)(a)(i), CPA 2004; **Scot, UK:** Sec. 1(1)(a)(ii), CPA 2004; **NI, UK:** Sec. 1(1)(a)(iii), CPA 2004.

32 Art. 1(1), Neth. PIL(RP)A.

33 See **Chapter IV.4.8** for details on the formal registration procedure of a French PACS.

34 Examples of the first category are the Belgian statutory cohabitation (see **Chapter III**) and the French PACS (see **Chapter IV**), whilst an example of the second category is the Dutch registered partnership (see **Chapter V**). No doubt, FULCHIRON would also add the Swiss registered partnership (see **Chapter VI**) and the British civil partnership (see **Chapter VII**) to this latter category.

35 FULCHIRON (2000) p. 901-902.

of legal unions should be determined according to the *loi de l'institution*.[36] DEVERS, in supporting FULCHIRON, goes one step further than MIGNOT, stating that questions relating to the formal validity of all non-marital registered relationships should be governed by the principle *auctor regit actum*.[37] CHANTELOUP also notes the difficulties of referring to the *lex loci registrationis*, whilst using the private international law rules for marriage as a template for attempting to create rules with respect to non-marital registered relationships.[38] She argues that an exact replication of the choice of law rules for marriage would result in the application of the law of the place where the registration formalities take place.[39] Instead CHANTELOUP argues for the formal validity of non-marital registered relationships to be judged according to the law of the parties' common habitual residence.[40]

X.2.1.4 Evaluation

In those countries to have enacted legislation in this field, and despite the assorted techniques employed by the countries examined in this book, the eventual outcome is identical regardless. In solving problems relating to the formal validity of non-marital registered relationships, the law of the place where the relationship is registered is determinative. In other words, issues relating to the formal validity of a non-marital registered relationship are determined according to the *lex loci registrationis*. There appears to have been no reason to depart from the traditional orthodoxy educed in the private international law rules on marriage. Since non-marital registered relationships have been shown to affect the personal status of the parties involved,[41] the rules applicable to other institutions affecting the parties' personal status should, as far as possible, be embraced, unless there is a

---

36 FULCHIRON (2000) p. 908-910.

37 DEVERS (2003) p. 215; DEVERS (2004) p. 248, §330. Although DEVERS in turn cites the law of Quebec in relation to civil unions to support his claim, Art. 3090(1), Quebec Civil Code actually supports reference to the *lex loci registrationis* and not *la loi de l'institution*.

38 CHANTELOUP (2000) p. 1720. This difficulty arises due to the ambiguity of such a rule: "*la loi du lieu où sont accomplies les formalités d'enregistrement du Pacte ou bien est-elle la loi du lieu où le pacte est effectivement rédigé par les partenaires?*".

39 CHANTELOUP quotes the example of two persons domiciled in France, who conclude a PACS in France but register the agreement abroad. In this case, according to the analogous application of the choice of law rules on marriage, it would be the law of the place of registration that would be applicable. This author raises doubts as to the soundness of this argument, since there would appear to be no reason to treat this scenario any differently from the case when a PACS is registered entirely before a consular or diplomatic representation: see **Chapter IV.4.8.3**.

40 CHANTELOUP (2000) p. 1721.

41 See **Chapter IX**.

significant reason to depart therefrom.[42] In bearing in mind that one of the principle aims of any choice of law rule in this field is to promote, and as far as possible, facilitate the recognition of personal relationships as well as the legitimate expectations of the parties,[43] it is argued that there appears to be no reason to depart from this almost universal common core of opinion on this issue uncovered in the jurisdictions studied in this book. Nonetheless, it is crucial that one remember that the legal quandary appears not to be the result to be achieved, but instead how one is to achieve such an outcome.

In dealing with the arguments put forward by a number of **French** authors for avoiding the application of the *lex loci registrationis* and instead applying the law of the institution registering the relationship, it is submitted that altering the main rule in order to accommodate for those rare relationships registered before consular and diplomatic representations is unjustifiable. The general rule should, as far as possible, remain clear, unambiguous and subject to exception only in limited circumstances. The current rule as adopted by six of the seven jurisdictions studied, namely determining questions of formal validity with reference to the *lex loci registrationis*, operates in the preponderance of cases and satisfies these criteria. Consular and diplomatic registrations are best dealt with according to a strictly limited exception clause.[44]

Thus, despite the obvious soundness of the arguments of MIGNOT, KHAIRALLAH, DEVERS and FULCHIRON, it is submitted that it is best to deal with these exceptions separately. In doing so, and in attempting to harmonise the rules in this field, such a solution would permit those countries that do not allow for foreign consular and diplomatic representations to register relationships on their own soil, to simply choose not to apply the relevant exceptions.[45] As a result, any eventual rule developed with respect to the formal validity of non-marital registered relationships would be equally acceptable to those countries allowing for consular and diplomatic registrations and those that do not.[46]

---

42 See, for example, **UK:** *House of Commons*, Vol. 426, Col. 776 (9th November 2004) (SMITH); **Neth.:** *Dutch Second Chamber*, 2002-2003, 28924, No. 3, p. 3; **Swit.:** FF 2002, p. 1192 at 1258-1259.

43 See, for example, FULCHIRON (2000) p. 911.

44 See also **Section X.2.2.3**.

45 See **Section X.4** for further discussion of the exceptions for consular and diplomatic representation registrations.

46 Such an approach is not without support in **France**. See KESSLER (2004) p. 120-140.

It is for all the reasons expressed above that, in attempting to harmonise or unify this field of law, one should adopt a rule determining questions of the formal validity of non-marital registered relationships according to the *lex loci registrationis*.

X.2.2 ESSENTIAL VALIDITY

Before one embarks upon an analysis of the choice of law rules for determining questions of essential validity, it is important to delineate the rationale and policy-objectives behind such a rule. In doing so one is better able to fully justify any subsequent choices made with reference to selected criteria or laws favoured.[47] With respect to marriage, the legislature in all seven researched countries has aimed to expedite the validity of marriages by allowing for broad choice of law rules, thus supporting the *favor matrimonii* principle, and in turn respecting the reasonable expectations of the parties.[48] In attempting to broaden the ambit of the choice of law rule, one can opt for one of two different approaches. Firstly, one can adopt a choice of law ladder that provides for multiple choice of law rules. Each subsequent rung of the ladder becomes effective should the previous rung be inapplicable.[49] The second option is to utilise connecting factors that allow for the widest possible scope of application.[50] In doing so, not only are the reasonable expectations of the parties protected but one also increases the flexibility afforded to judges.[51]

With respect to relationships that affect the personal status of the parties involved, the most appropriate connecting factor is thought to be one that impacts upon the personal law of the parties.[52] With this in mind, and with the added restriction that any choice of law rule adopted should yield a result deemed appropriate in the given circumstances, a variety of connecting factors have been tendered, *e.g.* a person's domicile, nationality or habitual residence. It must nevertheless be remembered that one is

47 For an explanation of the necessity of such an approach see: ANTOKOLSKAIA (2003) p. 162; BOELE-WOELKI *et al.* (2004) p. 2.

48 HARTLEY (1972) p. 571-572; JOINT LAW COMMISSIONS (1985) §2.35(e); JOUSTRA (1989) p. 262 (on **The Netherlands**) and p. 264-265 (on **Switzerland**); REED (2000) p. 388; CRAWFORD (1998) p. 147, §9.23.

49 Such an approach has been adopted, for example, in Art. 3(2), Neth. PIL(A)A.

50 By for example choosing broader connecting factors such as "real and substantial connection" which can be interpreted broader than the "nationality of the parties".

51 P.M. NORTH, "Development of rules of private international", *HC*, 1980, Vol. 166, p. 43-45. This is, however, often at the expense of legal certainty and predictability.

52 See, for example, KESSLER (2004) p. 107-112.

confronted with an important difference when attempting to forge a choice of law rule for non-marital registered relationships as opposed to marriage; that being the limited acceptability of the new phenomenon of non-marital registered relationships. Whilst it is important to seek guidance from the rules on marriage, this inherent difference could have an important impact on any possible choice of law rule adopted.

Due to the multiplicity of the existing solutions in relation to marriage, **Section X.3.2.1** is devoted to a comparative exposé of these possibilities. It is important not only to seek guidance from the rules on marriage in order to identify some of the possibilities available in creating rules for non-marital registered relationships but also to sketch the pros and cons of each connecting factor. **Section X.3.2.2** will subsequently build upon this work, comparing the current rules with respect to non-marital registered relationships. On the basis of these two sections, it will be possible to analyse, evaluate and assess areas of similarity and difference, allowing for conclusions to be drawn as to whether the possibility for harmonisation or unification of these rules exists (**Section X.3.2.3**).

X.2.2.1 Rules with respect to marriage

Opinions differ significantly with respect to the most appropriate connecting factor for questions relating to the essential validity of a marriage, resulting in a plethora of solutions in the seven countries studied.[53] The following section outlines the main variety of solutions tendered in these jurisdictions, as well as any objections levied at such factors.

A. Place of celebration of the marriage

The Netherlands, having ratified and enacted the 1978 Hague Convention on the Celebration and Recognition of the Validity of Marriages (1978 Hague MC),[54] refers questions of essential validity to the *lex loci celebrationis*, on the condition that one of the future spouses possesses **Dutch** nationality or is habitually resident in **The Netherlands**.[55] In **England**

---

53 JOUSTRA only notes two options. However, due to the limited scope of this article (only covering **The Netherlands**, **Switzerland** and **Germany**) options favoured in common law jurisdictions were overlooked: JOUSTRA (1989) p. 266.

54 The 1978 Hague MC is based on the principle of *favor matrimonii*: *Dutch Second Chamber*, 1987-1988, 20504, No. 3, p. 12. See also JOUSTRA (1989) p. 262.

55 Art. 2(a), Neth. PIL(M)A. For an alternative to this rule see **Section X.3.2.1.B**.

& Wales, although this principle has gained some credence in case law, no direct precedent exists as to the validity of this principle.[56] In support of the position adopted by the 1978 Hague MC, reference is often made to the comments of Lord SIMON in *Vervaeke v. Smith* that issues of quintessential validity might be referred to the place of celebration of the marriage.[57] An added complicating factor in **England & Wales** stems from the decision in *Sottomayor v. De Barros (No. 2)*,[58] as subsequently applied in *Ogden v. Ogden*[59] and upheld by the Court of Appeal in *Vervaeke v. Smith*.[60] This case held that a marriage will be deemed to be valid if celebrated in **England & Wales** and one of the spouses is an **English** domiciliary, so long as the rules of **English** law are satisfied, regardless of whether the marriage would be invalid according to the other spouses' domicil. This approach has been heavily criticised by the Joint Law Commissions of **England & Wales** and **Scotland**, and it has encountered widespread disapproval by commentators on both sides of Hadrian's Wall.[61] The Scottish Law Commission has argued that the rule laid down in *Sottomayor v. De Barros (No. 2)* is not applicable in **Scotland** and has proposed that legislative steps be taken to ensure that this position profit from legislative force.[62] In contrast to the uncertainty and complexity in **England & Wales**, all issues relating to the essential validity of marriages celebrated in **Scotland** are subject to **Scots** law,[63] over and above any further requirements imposed as a result of any choice of law rule.[64]

---

56 See generally, COLLINS (2000) p. 684-685, §17-093 to 17-100. Support can however be inferred from the the **English** cases of *Pugh v. Pugh* [1951] P 482 at 491-492 and *Breen v. Breen* [1964] P 144 and the **Scottish** case of *Lendrum v. Chakravarti* (1929) SLT 96 at 103 *per* Lord MACKAY, *Starkowski v. Attorney General* [1954] AC 155 at 174 *per* Lord TUCKER and *Berthiaume v. Dastous* [1930] AC 79 at 83 *per* Lord DUNEDIN: "If the so-called marriage is no marriage in the place where it is celebrated, there is no marriage anywhere.". However, such a rule has also received judicial criticism in various British Commonwealth jurisdictions: *Reed v. Reed* (1969) 6 DLR (3d) 617 (**British Columbia, Canada**) and *In the Will of Swan* (1871) 2 VR (IP & M) 47 (**Australia**), although **Australia** has subsequently legislated on this point: COLLINS (2000) p. 684, §17-096.

57 *Vervaeke v. Smith* [1983] 1 AC 145 at 165-166.

58 *Sottomayor v. De Barros* (No. 2) (1879) 5 PD 94.

59 *Ogden v. Ogden* [1908] P 46 at 74-77.

60 *Vervaeke v. Smith* [1981] Fam 77 at 121.

61 See JOINT LAW COMMISSIONS (1987a) p. 13-14, §§3.21-3.23. Questions have actually been raised as to the actually accuracy of this decision, since the cases referred to by Lord SIMON pre-date the classic distinction made between formal and essential validity in *Brook v. Brook* (1861) 9 HL Cas 193. See also COLLINS (2000) p. 686, §17-101 to 17-104; NORTH/FAWCETT (1999) p. 730-731.

62 SCOTTISH LAW COMMISSION (1992) §14.14.

63 Although there is prior precedent to the contrary: *MacDougall v. Chitnavis* (1937) SC 390 at 403 and 407. This rule would gain statutory force by virtue of Sec. 28(3), FL(S)B 2005.

64 Secs. 1(2) and 2(1)(a), M(S)A 1977. See further **Section X.3.2.1.D**.

The place of celebration of the marriage is also determinate for marriages celebrated in **Switzerland**, where questions of essential validity will generally be determined according to **Swiss** law.[65] One is unable to ascertain whether there is any support, legislative or academic, for the adoption of such a rule in either **Belgium** or **France**.

B. Nationality

In **Belgium** and **France**, questions of essential validity are instead merely determined according to the law of the parties' nationality; the essential validity of each spouse being determined according to the law of his or her own nationality respectively.[66] Despite the absence of any exception to this rule in **French** law, **Belgian** law does provide for an exception should the marriage involve a couple of the same-sex.[67]

In **The Netherlands** and **Switzerland** nationality provides for a subsidiary or alternative connecting factor. According to **Dutch** law Art. 2(b), Neth. PIL(M)A provides an alternative to Art. 2(a), Neth. PIL(M)A stating that questions of essential validity will be determined according to the nationality of each of the future spouses.[68] Art. 2(b), Neth. PIL(M)A also provides for situations when a spouse possesses more than one nationality. In such cases, the law of the nationality with which the spouse has his or her closest connection will be deemed to be applicable.[69] The same is true in

65 Art. 44(1), Sw. CPIL. For the exception to this rule see **Section X.3.2.1.B**.

66 **Fr.:** Art 3(3), Fr. CC; **Belg.:** Art. 46(1), Belg. CPIL, which simply reiterates the previous law in **Belgium** which was to be found in Art. 170-*ter*, Belg. CC. It must however be noted that if the parties do not give evidence as to their national law, the public official will perform the marriage and inform the spouses that their marriage may not be valid according to their national law: SIEHR (1982) p. 48.

67 See **Section X.2.2.2**.

68 This is a reiteration of Art. 6, Act of 15th May 1829, *Neth. Staatsblad 1829*, No. 28. This rule subsequently resurfaced in the 1902 Hague MC.

69 HR, 9th December 1965, NJ 1966, 378. The case concerned a woman who possessed both Norwegian and **Dutch** nationality. The *Hoge Raad* applied **Norwegian** law since it was decided that she had more connections with Norway than with **The Netherlands**. However from the explanatory notes from the Neth. PIL(M)A it would appear that when a person has more than one nationality and one of those nationalities is **Dutch**, it is **Dutch** law that is applicable: *Dutch Second Chamber*, 1987-1988, 20507, No. 3, p. 5; STRIKWERDA (2002) p. 94. In coming to such a decision, all relevant circumstances must be taken into account: Hof The Hague, 5th July 2000 (2000) *NIPR* 266 and Hof Amsterdam, 21st September 2000 (2002) *NIPR* 83. For more information see STRIKWERDA (2002) p. 81-82. The current codification of **Dutch** private international law could present a slight problem in this field. The proposal by the **Dutch** Standing Committee elucidates a different way of establishing the effective nationality should a party possess more than one nationality

Switzerland, where, if the conditions of **Swiss** law are not satisfied, a marriage between non-**Swiss** nationals may still be performed if the conditions of the law of the State(s) of both parties' nationality(ies) allow(s) for such a marriage.[70] In the **United Kingdom** nationality has never played a role in determining questions relating to the essential validity of the marriage.[71]

The inherent stability and certainty offered by a person's nationality is often cited by proponents as one of the key factors supporting its usage, especially in **Belgium**, **France**, **The Netherlands** and **Switzerland**.[72] Opponents of nationality, on the other hand, regard this rigidity as dissuasive. Regardless of these viewpoints, the continued use of nationality as a connecting factor may well have to be re-examined in light of the *Garcia Avello* case and the pending ECJ decision in the *Grunkin* case.[73] The question that arose before the court in *Garcia Avello* was whether the **Belgian** authorities were authorised to register the children according to the laws of **Spain**.[74] The ECJ was required to analyse whether the two categories of persons (*i.e.* **Belgians** and multinational **Belgians**) were in an identical situation or whether their situations were different. If their situations were indeed different, the principle of non-discrimination would mean that multinational **Belgians** may assert their right to be treated in a manner different to that in which **Belgians** were treated, unless the treatment could be objectively justified. The ECJ in answering this question in the affirmative noted that the **Belgian** Government was unable to produce any valid justification for treating Belgians and multinational Belgians in an identical fashion.[75] Although no explicit reference was made to the discriminatory nature of the use of nationality as a connecting factor, the eventual holding in the case certainly

---

(Art. 4, Proposed Neth. CPIL). Here a preference is given to the law of the habitual residence if this law is the law of one of the nationalities involved. The question arises which rule will take precedence: see further JESSURUN D'OLIVEIRA (2003b) p. 455.

70 Art. 44(2), Sw. CPIL. See DUTOIT (2005) p. 150, Art. 44, No. 3-4.

71 For further explanation as to why see JOINT LAW COMMISSIONS (1987a) p. 10-11.

72 Many of the proponents of nationality cite the reduction in forum shopping as one of the crucial advantages in the legal category of personal status *e.g.* KHAIRALLAH (2000) p. 322.

73 ECJ, *Grunkin*, Case. No. 96/04, *case pending*. This case involves a prejudicial question from the *Amtsgericht* in Niebüll, Schleswig-Hollstein in **Germany**.

74 According to **Belgian** private international law such questions are referred to the nationality of the parties. However where a **Belgian** national has one or more other nationalities at the same time, the **Belgian** authorities will give precedence to the **Belgian** nationality: ECJ, *Garcia Avello*, Case No. 148/02, §8.

75 ECJ, *Garcia Avello*, Case No. 148/02, §41.

points in this direction. The question accordingly arises whether the use of nationality as a connecting factor violates European Union law.[76]

According to the ECJs holding, it seems almost impossible to conceive of nationality as a sole connecting factor withstanding further scrutiny in situations where EU law is concerned.[77] It is expected that the decision in the *Grunkin* case will resolve this uncertainty. This case involves two **German** nationals living in **Denmark** who wish to register their child's surname according to **Danish** law, despite the fact that **German** law refers to the law of the child's nationality.[78] The question, unlike *Garcia Avello*, raises the direct issue of whether a sole connecting factor of nationality is contrary to Art. 12, EC Treaty.[79] Some authors believe that the ECJ will answer this question in the affirmative and thus require choices to be afforded to European citizens who have exercised their EU rights in situations where nationality would deny them a right granted to those in their new EU domicile.[80] This case could well signal the end of nationality as a sole connecting factor in areas affecting EU law. This must thus be borne in mind in any attempt to harmonise or unify the rules with respect to non-marital registered relationships.[81]

C. Law of the intended matrimonial home

It is argued, most ardently by the late Professor CHESHIRE that,

> Whether the intermarriage of two persons should be prohibited for social, religious, eugenic or other like reasons is a question that pre-eminently, if not exclusively, affects the community in which the parties live together as man and wife.[82]

This has since been reiterated by numerous **English, Scottish** and **Commonwealth** judges including MOLESWORTH J.,[83] Lord CAMPBELL,[84] Lord

---

76 DE GROOT/RUTTEN (2004) p. 282.

77 See support for this statement: DE GROOT/RUTTEN (2004) p. 277 and 288.

78 According to Art. 10(3), Ger. CCIL, connection to a State other than the parties' nationality is only allowed if one of the parties possesses the nationality of that State.

79 A number of Scandinavian authors have already noted this problem with respect to registered partnerships: JÄNTERÄ-JAREBORG (2003a) p. 151-152, BOGDAN (2004) p. 64.

80 *E.g.* DE GROOT/RUTTEN (2004) p. 274-277, §4; JESSURUN D'OLIVEIRA (2003c) p. 2241-2243.

81 BOELE-WOELKI (2005a); LUIJENDIJK (2005) p. 309 and 323; OOSTEROM-STAPLES (2004) p. 60-61.

82 NORTH/FAWCETT (1999) p. 722, originally in the 7th Edition (1965) p. 278.

83 *In the Will of Swan* (1871) 2 VR (IE & M) 47 (**Australia**). Although, here a similar result would have been achieved with reference to the dual domicile test.

84 *Brook v. Brook* (1861) 9 HLC 193 at 207, 212, 213.

GREENE,[85] Lord DENNING,[86] Sir BAKER,[87] Lord SORN,[88] CUMMING-BRUCE J.,[89] and Sir CAIRNS.[90] In advocating such an approach, CHESHIRE goes on to argue that it is surely more logical to maintain that the place where the parties are intending to establish their home is the country with the most interest in their marriage. If the parties after their marriage intend to leave their respective domiciles and set up home elsewhere, then it is this law and no other that is most affected by the marriage. However, the objections to such a rule are, in this author's opinion, weighty. It is surely objectionable to adhere to a rule that renders it impossible to decide whether a marriage is valid or invalid at the time of celebration.[91] Although in some cases the questions raised by the applicable law to the marriage will occur after the marriage has been celebrated,[92] there are cases where such questions will be raised prior to the celebration of the marriage. Further reservations can also be raised with respect to the practical implications of such a rule: what happens if it is not clear where the parties intend to establish their matrimonial home? What happens if they intend to delay the decision for a year or more? What would be the result if the parties subsequently change their mind and do not establish their home in that jurisdiction? It can also be contended that it is somewhat paradoxical to determine pre-nuptial capacity according to a post-nuptial intention. This "crystal ball" type of choice of law rule should, in this author's opinion, be avoided at all costs, since it not only increases legal uncertainty but also increases the need to initiate costly litigious proceedings, not to mention failing to respect the parties' reasonable expectations. Choice of law rules, especially in the field of marriage, should be clear, concise, simple and easy to apply. A choice of law rule making reference to the intended matrimonial home contradicts such principles. In **Scotland** this rule is, fortunately, believed to be

---

85 *De Reneville v. De Reneville* [1948] P 100 at 114.

86 *Kenward v. Kenward* [1951] P 124 at 143. This judgment can be heavily criticised since it basically applies different rules to different forms of incapacity: "nothing in this judgment bears upon the capacity of minors, the law of affinity or the effect of bigamy upon capacity to enter into a monogamous marriage". This author is in agreement on this issue with NORTH AND FAWCETT who argue for the same rule being applied in all cases: NORTH/FAWCETT (1999) p. 734-35.

87 *Perrini v. Perrini* [1979] Fam 84.

88 *Bliersbach v. McEwan* (1959) SC 43 at 55.

89 *Radwan v. Radwan (No. 2)* [1973] Fam 35 at 54.

90 *Lawrence v. Lawrence* [1985] Fam 106 at 134.

91 Supported by dicta in *Lawrence v. Lawrence* [1985] Fam 106 at 127-128.

92 As a result of the choice of law test imposed on the recognition of foreign marriages.

erroneous in principle,[93] and in **Switzerland**, **The Netherlands**, **Belgium** and **France**, such a rule has never found any credence at all.

D. Dual domicil theory

In the **United Kingdom** this test has attracted the most support not only from the judiciary,[94] but also from academics and lawmakers alike.[95] The country of domicil, the theory states, is the country to which the future spouses "belong".[96] This theory conforms to the reasonable expectations of the parties, allows capacity to be determined definitively prior to the marriage and recognises that marriage is an issue affecting the personal status of the parties thus requiring resort to their personal law.[97] Furthermore, the theory respects the inherent value of both parties to the marriage by examining the law of the domicil of both parties.[98] Despite the objections of NORTH and FAWCETT,[99] the dual domicil theory offers at the very least *a priori* certainty to the celebration of the marriage in the **United Kingdom**. A situation that can, in this author's opinion, only be commended.[100] On the other hand, the cumulative nature of the test generally increases the likelihood of the marriage being prohibited or declared invalid than if a single law was determinate.[101] Such a result runs counter to the policy objectives of the choice of law rules as expounded earlier. Difficulties also arise due to the idiosyncratic nature of the **British**

---

93 See, for example, the ruling of Lord MACNAGHTEN in *Cooper v. Cooper's Trustees* (1888) 15 R(HL) 21 at 31. It is thought that the rule is too difficult to apply in practice to prospective spouses because such a decision is not always clear.

94 **Scot, UK**: *Lendrum v. Chakravarti* (1929) SLT 96 at 103; *MacDougall v. Chitnavis* (1937) SC 390 at 406. **Eng, UK**: *Re Paine* [1940] Ch 46; *Pugh v. Pugh* [1951] P 482; *R v. Brentwood Superintendent Registrar of Marriages, ex parte Arias* [1968] 2 QB 956; *Padolecchia v. Padolecchia* [1968] P 314; *Szechter v. Szechter* [1971] P 286; *Motala and Others v. Attorney General*, (1989) TLR 13th December 1989. According to the current Family Law (Scotland) Bill thuis rule would for the first time find statutory footing: Sec. 28(2), FL(S)B 2005, subject to Sec. 28(3), FL(S)B 2005.

95 COLLINS (2000) p. 622-623; JOINT LAW COMMISSIONS (1987a) p. 92-93. A number of statutory provisions also support such a claim: Sec. 1(3), Marriage (Enabling) Act 1960; Sec. 11(d), MCA 1973; Secs. 1(2), 2(1), 2(3) and 5(4)(f), M(S)A 1977.

96 HARTLEY (1972) p. 576.

97 ANTON/BEAUMONT (1990) p. 431.

98 Although, HARTLEY argues for a rule that determines questions of essential validity according to the law of the domicil of either one of the parties at the time of the marriage: HARTLEY (1972) p. 576.

99 NORTH/FAWCETT (1999) p. 724.

100 Supported by JOINT LAW COMMISSIONS (1987a) p. 4-5, §2.5-2.9.

101 HARTLEY (1972) p. 576.

rules on domicil.[102] However, the problem with such an outcome lies with the rules on domicil and not with the choice of law rules that utilise such a connecting factor. Once again, this connecting factor has not been the subject of support in any of the other countries studied in this book.

E. Real and substantial connection

This connecting factor derived from the proper law test in issues of contract,[103] and the **English** common law test for foreign divorce recognition established in *Indyka v. Indyka,*[104] designates the proper law of the marriage as the system of law that has the most real and substantial connection to the case. This will undoubtedly often correlate to the State where the parties intended to establish their matrimonial home, but need not necessarily be the case. The inherent flexibility of the test allows consideration of a multitude of relevant factors including residence, nationality, domicile, intention and the place of celebration of the marriage. The test, although first proposed by SYKES in 1955,[105] lay quiescent until Lord SIMON referred to the "real and substantial connection" for questions of "quintessential validity" in *Vervaeke v. Smith.*[106] This test has received support on the basis of its flexibility and the fact that its sound, policy-orientated solution ameliorates some of the problems encountered with the dual domicil or intended matrimonial home tests. Although this author expresses sympathy with the intentions of Lord SIMON in the *Vervaeke* case, it seems far-fetched to expect such an in-depth analysis to be undertaken every time such a choice of law rule needs to be applied. This is thus an inherently vague and unpredictable test, which introduces an unacceptable degree of uncertainty into the law. It was in fact for this very reason that such a connecting factor was removed from the recognition rules in terms of foreign divorces in **England & Wales** in 1971.[107] Once again, such a connecting factor is notably absent in all the other legal systems studied in this book.

---

102 For objections to the law of domicil see JOINT LAW COMMISSIONS (1987a) p. 8-13.

103 *E.g.* NORTH/FAWCETT (1999) p. 564-574 and see further Art. 4, Rome Convention.

104 *Indyka v. Indyka* [1969] 1 AC 33.

105 SYKES (1955) p. 165.

106 *Vervaeke v. Smith* [1983] 1 AC 145 at 165-166. Lord SIMON proposes in this passage two solutions to the essential validity in marriages. See above for his proposal (*i.e. lex loci celebrationis*). This is also supported in *Lawrence v. Lawrence* [1985] Fam 106.

107 The Recognition of Divorces and Legal Separations Act 1971 abolished the rule laid down in *Indyka v. Indyka* [1969] 1 AC 33. This Act has subsequently been replaced by Part II, FLA 1986 and further still by the Brussels II and IIa.

X.2.2.2 Rules with respect to non-marital registered relationships

In contrast to the considerable disagreement as to the most appropriate connecting factor with respect to questions relating to the essential validity of a marriage, there appears to be almost unanimous support, at least in those countries to have enacted legislation, that questions relating to the essential validity of non-marital registered relationships should be determined according to the law of the place where the relationship was registered, *i.e.* the *lex loci registrationis.*[108] Only **Belgium** provides a glitch to this uniformity. The anomaly arises due to the way in which **Belgium** has characterised non-marital registered relationships.[109] As stated earlier, those non-marital registered relationships akin to marriage are subject to the analogous application of the private international law rules on marriage.[110] As a result, questions of essential validity of such relationships are determined according to the law of each party's nationality.[111] However, an exception to this rule is provided for same-sex marriages, and thus, as the term "marriage" is to be understood in a broad sense, same-sex non-marital registered relationships akin to marriage as well.[112] The exception provides that if the law declared applicable by virtue of Art. 46(1), Belg. CPIL, prohibits a marriage between persons of the same sex, this law will be applied without reference to the provision prohibiting such marriages, provided one of the spouses possesses the nationality of a State that allows for such a marriage or has his or her habitual residence in such a State.[113] If one examines the cumulative effect of Art. 46(2), Belg. CPIL and the broad interpretation of the term marriage, one is able to discern three categories of non-marital registered relationships in **Belgium**, as outlined below.

---

108 **Belg.:** Art. 60(1), Belg. CPIL (non-marital registered relationships not akin to marriage); **Neth.:** Art. 1(2), Neth. PIL (RP) Act; **Swit.:** Art 65a, in conjunction with Art. 44(1), Sw. CPIL; **Eng, UK:** Sec. 1(1)(a)(i), Brit. CPA; **Scot, UK**: Sec. 1(1)(a)(ii), Brit. CPA; **NI, UK:** Sec. 1(1)(a)(iii), Brit. CPA.

109 See **Chapter IX.6.1** for further explanation.

110 ERAUW (2004) p. 126.

111 Art. 46(1), Belg. CPIL. See **Section X.2.2.1.B.**

112 This exception results in the repeal of certain paragraphs of the circular of the 23rd January 2004 which replaced the circular of the 8th May 2003 relating to same-sex marriages: *Belg. Staatsblad*, 28th September 2004, No. 349, p. 69604.

113 This Article was introduced by the Government on the 3rd February 2004 as an amendment to the original Art. 46, Belg. CPIL. *Belgian Chamber*, 2003-2004, No. 3-27/3, p. 12, Amendment 24. It was not in the original proposal since Belgium at that point in time prohibited same-sex marriages: ERAUW (2004) p. 126-127. As a result of this provision, as long as one of the parties has his or her habitual residence in **Belgium**, the parties, subject to the conditions on entry into marriage, will be permitted to marry in **Belgium**: *Belg. Staatsblad*, 28th September 2004, No. 349, p. 69604.

Table 10: *Essential validity of non-marital registered relationships in Belgium*

Group of relationships	Rule	Applicable Law
NMRR not akin to marriage	Art. 60(1), Belg. CPIL	Law of place of registration
NMRR akin to marriage where national law of both parties permits the registration	Art. 46(1), Belg. CPIL	Law of each party's nationality
Same-sex NMRR akin to marriage where national law of one or both parties forbids the registration of such a relationship	Art. 46(1) and 46(2), Belg. CPIL	Law of each party's nationality excluding reference to the rule prohibiting same-sex registrations if one of the parties possesses the nationality or habitual residence of a State that allows for such relationships

The complexity of these rules is certainly not supported by all. BARNICH, for example, writing prior to the enactment of the codification, has suggested that nationality should continue to be used as the connecting factor in the determination of questions of essential validity.[114] ERAUW and VERHELLEN, also writing prior to the introduction of the codification, argue for the avoidance of one-sided choice of law rules, especially those that provide for the application of the law of the place of registration.[115] In their opinion the almost "missionary-like" application of the law of the place of registration does not sufficiently guarantee the recognition of foreign law.[116] Fear that the application of a foreign law may create too many lacunas is not, in their mind, a sufficient reason for deviating from the application of foreign law and opting for a "pusillanimous solution".[117]

In turning one's attention to **France**, where there have been no legislative moves to regulate this topic, one must resort to extrapolation from existing choice of law rules, as well as a wealth of academic opinion. In doing so, one is immediately confronted with a similar diversity of opinion as that

---

114 BARNICH (2000).

115 ERAUW/VERHELLEN (1999) p. 154. Therefore, in effect, objecting to the solution adopted in Art. 60(1), Belg. CPIL.

116 On the contrary see KESSLER (2004) p. 142: "Le *registration shopping* devrait être un bon moyen pour les couples homosexuals de faire pression sur les États afin de les conduire à légiférer à leur tour." In this sense see also YTTERBERG (2001).

117 The phrase "pusillanimous solution" attempts to translate ERAUW and VERHELLEN'S criticism summed up in the phrase *verlegenheidsoplossing.* Although, ERAUW and VERHELLEN talk exclusively of the Belgian situation (p. 154), they do refer to the proposals that had been made at that time by the **Dutch** Standing Committee on Private International Law. As a result, it is not clear whether ERAUW and VERHELLEN are in favour of a distinction being drawn between those non-marital registered relationships akin to marriage and those not akin to marriage, as drawn in the Belg. CPIL.

posed with respect to questions related to formal validity. Some authors believe in the need for a distinction to be drawn between those non-marital registered relationships akin to marriage and those that are not. In support of this solution, MIGNOT and KHAIRALLAH both suggest that the rules on marriage should simply be applied *mutatis mutandis* to those non-marital registered relationships that create a virtual *mariage homosexuel*.[118] With regard to the latter category of non-marital registered relationships, these authors have suggested that such relationships should also be judged according to the standards of the choice of law rules on marriage.[119] Other **French** authors, principally DEVERS and FULCHIRON, advocate the creation of an autonomous category whereby all non-marital registered relationships should be dealt with according to the same rules.[120] DEVERS notes that the traditional hierarchy of connecting factors applicable to questions of essential validity of marriages is not suitable to non-marital registered relationships.[121] DEVERS argues, citing FULCHIRON as a *point d'appui*,[122] for the use of a connecting factor based on the national law of the authority that registered the non-marital relationship, *i.e. la loi de l'institution*.[123]

However not all authors are in agreement with these solutions. CHANTELOUP, in a similar fashion to MAYER and HEUZÉ,[124] argues that one must "*insérer le PACS dans la catégorie de rattachement qui est la plus proche: celle du mariage*".[125] In doing so, she argues that all non-marital registered relationships should be subject to the *mutatis mutandis* application of the rules on marriage, except in certain cases when new rules need to be developed. In respect of the essential validity of non-marital registered relationships, CHANTELOUP contends that a distinction should be made between those conditions of a unilateral nature, *e.g.* age, sex, consent and representation, and those conditions of a bilateral nature, *e.g.* prohibited degrees of relationship and exclusivity.[126] Despite such a distinction, CHANTELOUP argues that both categories should, in fact, be subject to the distributive application of the national law of the parties.[127]

---

118 KHAIRALLAH (2000) p. 321 and p. 328; MIGNOT (2001) p. 650-653.

119 KHAIRALLAH (2000) p. 323; MIGNOT (2001) p. 630-634.

120 FULCHIRON (2000) p. 909; DEVERS (2004) p. 216-247, §284-329.

121 DEVERS (2004) p. 249, §332.

122 DEVERS (2004) p. 249, §332.

123 DEVERS (2004) p. 250, §332.

124 MAYER/HEUZÉ (2001) p. 365-366, §549-550.

125 CHANTELOUP (2000) p. 1718.

126 CHANTELOUP (2000) p. 1719.

127 CHANTELOUP (2000) p. 1720. She refers to the statement of the French Minister of Justice, GUIGOU who stated "le pacte civil de solidarité est un contrat et les conditions de capacité

X.2.2.3 Evaluation

A number of States could be affected by the registration of a non-marital relationship and thus could be said to have an interest in regulating such a relationship. These are: firstly, the State in which the incidents of the enduring relationship are to be enjoyed, secondly, the State where the parties are domiciled or habitually resident, thirdly, the State where the relationship is registered or, finally, the State(s) of the parties' respective nationality(ies). It is clear from the above exposé that a common core of opinion is developing, and arguably, has already developed. This common core refers questions of essential validity to the *lex loci registrationis*. However, this approach is not universal, with authors in both **Belgium** and **France** imploring for alternative solutions to be adopted. Having found legislative force in the recent codification of private international law, these pleas have, at least in **Belgium**, not fallen on deaf ears. It is therefore crucial that one analyse the fundamental bases upon which such a common core is founded in order to substantiate one's argument for its universal adoption.[128] Unlike marriage,[129] factors that refer to the personal law of the parties do not provide an adequate solution to the problem posed and will inevitably lead to more couples being prevented from entering into such relationships. Reference to the parties' national law may lead to the parties being prevented from registering their relationship. In **France**, where no private international law rule currently exists, the adoption of a rule referring to the parties' personal law could, if applied retrospectively, run the risk of invalidating countless PACSs registered by multinational couples.[130] In those

---

applicables à ce type d'acte relevant en droit international privé de la loi nationale de la loi du pays don't il est le ressortissant": *French Senate*, 8th November 1999.

128 For a similar approach see the Principles of European Family Law developed by the Commission on European Family Law (CEFL). Although having found substantial evidence to suggest the existence of a common core of opinion in the countries studied, in recommending Principles of European Family Law, the CEFL substantiates such choices with reference to the underlying ideology upon which these rules are founded. In some cases this results in adoption of the common core approach, *e.g.* Principles 1:1(1) and 1:4(3), in other cases, this does not, *e.g.* Principles 1:1(2) and 1:5. See further, BOELE-WOELKI (2005a) p. 31-32.

129 Arguments of legal certainty, coherence in the legal category of personal status and a reduction in the problems associated with forum shopping are often cited as adequate reasons for the maintenance of a personal law connecting factor for marriage.

130 KESSLER (2004) p. 112-113. According to REVILLARD, PACSs have been concluded by as many as 22 different nationalities (*i.e.* Dutch, Russian, Belgian, American, German, Italian, English, Swiss, Ukrainian, Moroccan, Cuban, Australian, Tunisian, Burkinan (from Burkina-Faso), Thai, Luxembourger, Belorussian, French, Canadian, Swedish, Romanian and Algerian): REVILLARD (2002) p. 588.

countries to have legislated on this topic, similar arguments are easy to distil from the parliamentary discussions.

During the parliamentary discussions in **The Netherlands** on the abandonment of the parties' personal law as a connecting factor for determining questions of essential validity, the **Dutch** Government noted, sharing the view of the **Dutch** Standing Committee on Private International Law,[131] that it was totally acceptable to adopt such a standpoint. Parties who do not satisfy the entry requirements of **Dutch** substantive law will simply not be allowed to register a partnership in **The Netherlands**, even if according to the law of their nationality they would have been able to do so.[132] A similar discussion also took place in **Switzerland**, where the insertion of a Chapter 3a in the Sw. CPIL expressly excludes the analogous application of Art. 44(2), Sw. CPIL to registered partnerships. Accordingly, parties wishing to register their partnership in **Switzerland** are not provided with a second opportunity to satisfy the **Swiss** choice of law rules should the law of the parties' nationality allow for such a registered partnership to be celebrated.[133] In both countries, reference was also made to the fact that such a rule, coupled with strict residency requirements, will help in the fight against registration tourism.

Although eventually embracing the abandonment of a personal law connecting factor with respect to non-marital registered relationships not akin to marriage, the **Belgian** legislature was more taciturn in the abandonment of a personal law connecting factor with respect to non-marital registered relationships akin to marriage.[134] It was argued that such relationships bear all the hallmarks of a marriage and therefore require the *mutatis mutandis* application of the private international law rules on marriage. The limited acceptability of such institutions appears not to have convinced the **Belgian** legislature for the need to tweak the legislation. Finally, although the **United Kingdom** has also opted for private international law rules with respect to civil partnerships that deviate from the traditional rules applicable to marriage, no explanation for such a deviation has been provided.[135]

---

131 STAATSCOMMISSIE (1998) p. 19.

132 *Dutch Second Chamber*, 2002-2003, 28924, No. 3, p. 10.

133 FF 2002, p. 1192 at 1259-1260.

134 *Belgian Chamber*, 2002-2003, No. 3-27/1, p. 93-94.

135 The notable absence of an explanation to Clause 152 in §279 of the explanatory notes to Bill HL-53, available at www.parliament.uk.

All those countries to have legislated in this field of law refer to the need to promote the formal recognition of non-marital registered relationships, thus substituting the *favor matrimonii* principle with a principle of *favor registrationis*.[136] Although the rules for marriage are based on the principle of *favor matrimonii*, the *mutatis mutandis* application of such rules to non-marital registered relationships would lead to many couples being prohibited from registering their relationship and hence would depart from the *favor registrationis* principle.

Example 5: Nationality as a connecting factor
Two Italians living in France wish to register their partnership. They satisfy all the conditions in Art. 515, Fr. CC for entry into a PACS. However, if nationality was used as a connecting factor for determining questions of essential validity, they would not be entitled to register a PACS in France since their national law, namely Italian law, does not provide for this possibility.

Example 6: Domicil(e) or habitual residence as a connecting factor
An Austrian man and an Englishman live in Salzburg, Austria. The Austrian receives notification of a job opportunity in Belfast, Northern Ireland. They decide to move to Belfast. Upon arrival they wish to register a civil partnership. They satisfy all the conditions laid down in Part III, CPA 2004. However, they have moved to Northern Ireland three months ago and therefore have not yet obtained a Northern Irish domicile, domicil or habitual residence. If any one of these connecting factors were used to test issues of essential validity (imagine that Part V, CPA 2004 was not in force), they would be prevented from entering into a civil partnership due to the fact that neither their domicile nor habitual residence, namely Austria, provides for this possibility.[137]

In both of these examples use of the traditional personal law connecting factors would lead to both couples being prevented from entering into a non-marital registered relationship in the country in which they now lived. It is for these reasons that all those countries to have legislated on this issue have opted for a law that refers questions of essential validity to the country where the non-marital relationship is registered. Thus despite departing from the applicable rules on marriage, and thus one would assume the equivalent principle of *favor matrimonii*, the apparent trend is to create rules which cleave to the principle of *favor registrationis* by applying the *lex loci registrationis* to issues of essential validity.[138] In doing so one not only expedites the validity of such relationships but also ultimately respects

---

136 See **Chapter IX.4.2.**

137 It is assumed in this scenario that both of the parties had their domicil in Austria.

138 Such a solution is also not totally excluded from the marital rules in this field, having found some level of favour in at least five of the seven jurisdictions studied in this book: See **Section X.2.2.1.A.**

the reasonable expectations of the parties.[139] The parties, in choosing a country to register their relationship, and ensuring that they satisfy the domestic law of that country, would necessarily expect to be legally entitled to register their partnership. In adopting a rule referring questions of essential validity to the *lex loci registrationis* one therefore augments the legal security bestowed upon the couple by the country where the relationship is to be registered.

One of the most decisive arguments levied against the use of the *lex loci registrationis* in relation to questions of essential validity is, however, that this would allow parties to evade the restrictions imposed on them by their personal law, thus increasing the possibility of "forum shopping" or "registration tourism".[140] It is assumed that the country of the parties' personal law, as the country to which the parties belong, has a more enduring concern with the parties' personal status than the place where the relationship is registered. Although this argument is obviously a valid one with respect to marriage, with respect to non-marital registered relationships it must be counterbalanced with the argument that the vast majority of legal systems worldwide do not currently recognise forms of non-marital registered relationships.[141] Accordingly due to the sizeable number of countries that, up until now, do not recognise such relationships, alteration of the traditional rules on determining questions of essential validity is necessary. Although not true of all countries to have enacted

139 The "reasonable expectations of the parties" are to be understood as: "If a particular legal rule is applied to the parties in circumstances where they could not prudently have anticipated this, there are grounds for doubting the appropriateness of the outcome".

140 See, for example, ERAUW/VERHELLEN (1999) p. 154 who also oppose such a rule since it fails to recognise to the possible application of foreign law, thus failing to adhere to the principle of comity.

141 There are currently 191 Member States to the United Nations (only **Taiwan** and the **Vatican City** are not Member States). According to information available, and outlined in **Appendicies 1-3**, fewer than 20 countries, or regions of a country, currently provide for non-marital registered relationships. This figure represents approximately 10% of the nations of the world, as well as 10% of the world's population. Although this does not represent the total number of legal systems in the world, since this figure obviously does not include the various legal systems within federal states such as the **United States of America**, **Australia** or **Canada**, it does provide an indication of the scarcity of non-marital registered relationship regulations. These connecting factors do not, however, provide obstacles if the parties choose to register in the State of their nationality, domicil(e) or habitual residence, However, for a choice of law rule to be fully functional it should also look to those cases where parties do not register in the State of their nationality or domicil(e)/habitual residence.

legislation in this field,[142] many jurisdictions have imposed minor residency, domicile, habitual residence or nationality requirements on those wishing to register their relationship.[143] It is argued that such an approach is the best all-round solution. In creating simple, clear, easy to apply private international law rules with respect to questions of essential validity that do not refer to the personal law of the parties, one adheres to the criteria expounded at the beginning of this section. Not only does such a solution increase legal certainty it would be easy to apply in any given scenario. Furthermore, if such a rule were coupled with domestic substantive law residency requirements, the interaction of these two sets of rules would counter arguments raised against registration tourism and people avoiding the application of their personal law.[144]

Such an approach is supported from the research conducted in this book. As was seen in **Chapter V.4.5**, **The Netherlands** imposes a residency requirement on all those wishing to register their partnership. This residency requirement entails a necessary, yet reasonable hurdle on those wishing to enter into a registered partnership in **The Netherlands**.[145] In satisfying this requirement the parties would, in this author's opinion, have indicated an appropriate and sufficient connection to **The Netherlands** in order to justify benefiting from and being subject to the provisions of **Dutch** law. At the same time the hurdle does not violate principles of discrimination on the basis of nationality[146] nor impose a restriction that

---

142 Of the countries studied only **Scotland** and **Northern Ireland** do not impose some form of residency requirement: **Chapter VII.4.5.2** and **VII.4.5.3.** The rules enacted in **Germany** (THORN (2003b) p. 88) and **Vermont, USA** are also devoid of a residency requirement.

143 See for example **Chapters III.4.5, IV.4.5, V.4.5, VI.4.5** and **VII.4.5.1.** This is also the case in all of the **Nordic** countries (See JÄNTERÄ-JAREBORG (2003a) p. 139, 141, 142 and 147).

144 Not all authors are against the possibility of "registration tourism": see for example JESSURUN D'OLIVEIRA (1995) p. 1567. However, the important immigration rights often attached to forms of non-marital registered relationships have led many jurisdictions to enact legislation aimed at preventing registration tourism as well as sham registrations.

145 This residency requirement was originally stricter and was aimed at preventing "registration tourism". See further JESSURUN D'OLIVEIRA (1995) p. 1567.

146 According to Art. 12, EC Treaty discrimination on the basis of nationality is prohibited in the EU: "Within the scope of application of this Treaty, and without prejudice to any special provisions contained therein, any discrimination on grounds of nationality shall be prohibited". In the **Nordic** countries, the question had been raised whether the prohibition of a **Greek** citizen habitually resident in **Greece** from entering into a registered partnership in **Sweden** with his **Austrian** partner was contrary to this principle. This question was answered in the negative initially in **Sweden** due to the fact that the entry into a registered partnership was a pure family law matter and therefore fell outside the scope of EU law: *Swedish Riksdag (Parliament),* 1993-1994, Report of the Committee on Civil Law (LU), No. 28, p. 17-18. However, the entry into force of the Amsterdam

could be seen as an obstacle to the free movement of persons within the European Union.[147]

The Netherlands is, however, not alone in implementing such dovetailed legislation[148] with an analogous approach also being adopted in **Belgium** and **Switzerland**.[149] Whilst the laws in **England & Wales** do not provide an intimidating residency requirement upon an aspirant couple,[150] the aim of the legislature was still the same.[151] Furthermore, such a solution is not confined to the countries studied in this book. Support for such an approach can also be gleaned from the **Nordic** countries. When registered partnership was first introduced in **Denmark** in 1989,[152] strict entry requirements were imposed prohibiting those without **Danish** citizenship and habitual residence from registering their partnership.[153] With the opening of registered partnership in the other four **Nordic** nations, these rules have since been mitigated and proof of two-years habitual residence is now sufficient in order to register a partnership in any of the **Nordic** nations.[154]
The dovetailing solution provides for clear, certain and simple legislation, which would be suitable for straightforward application in practice. This pragmatic solution would be convenient for the parties since they have recourse during the registration procedure to those skilled professionals equipped to answer questions relating to the law of the place where the relationship is to be registered. Problems of characterisation would also

---

Treaty, which extended co-operation to cross-border family matters under Arts. 61c, 65 and 67, EC Treaty, has distorted this picture somewhat and requires clarification from the ECJ. For further discussion of the notion of EU discrimination see JÄNTERÄ-JAREBORG (2003a) p. 151-152.

147 See WAALDIJK (1996); JESSURUN D'OLIVEIRA (2000b) and (2001a).

148 Dovetailing in the sense of a simple private international law rule referring to the place of registration of the relationship should be supplemented with domestic substantive residency requirements.

149 See **Chapters III.4.5** and **VI.4.5**.

150 See **Chapter VII.4.5**.

151 A more stringent residency requirement was not possible without also altering the respective legislation with respect to marriage; a route that the **British** Government has avoided at all costs. The avoidance of amendments to marriage legislation is also the reason for the absence of residency requirements in **Scotland** and **Northern Ireland**.

152 See BOELE-WOELE/TANGE (1989), NIELSEN (1990) and LUND-ANDERSEN (1998).

153 Sec. 2, Danish Registered Partnership Act prior to amendments made in 1999.

154 **Denmark**: Sec. 2.2.2, Registered Partnership Act; **Sweden**: Chapter 1, Sec. 2.1, Registered Partnership Act; **Norway**: Sec. 2.3.2, Registered Partnership Act; **Iceland**: Sec. 2.2.b, Registered Partnership Act; **Finland**: Sec. 10.1.2, Registered Partnership Act. In **Denmark**, **Iceland** and **Finland** both parties must satisfy this requirement, whereas in **Sweden** and **Norway** this requirement need only be satisfied by one of the parties. See further BOGDAN (2004) p. 63-64.

disappear in view of the fact that both formal and essential validity would be tested according to the same law. All these factors would lead to the operation of a predictable set of rules. In adapting domestic substantive law residency requirements to prevent, or, at the very least, hinder the incidence of so-called "registration tourism", an all-round workable solution would thus be achieved.

It is submitted that reference to the *loi de l'institution* would create unnecessary complication.[155] DEVERS argues that questions of essential validity should be determined according to the *loi de l'institution*, in order to cater for registrations before consular and diplomatic representations. It is submitted, however, that the negligible number of relationships registered before consular and diplomatic representations does not constitute enough of a reason to justify the alteration of the current law in those countries to have already adopted legislation. However, the blanket application of the *lex loci registrationis* would lead to undesirable consequences.

In rejecting any reference to the parties' nationality, as suggested, for example, by CHANTLEOUP, one must take heed of the ECJ decision in *Garcia Avello v. Belgium* and the pending decision in the *Grunkin* case.[156] Although the full extent of the *Garcia Avello* decision is, as yet, not entirely clear and although the points raised in this case may not be decisive in and of themselves, the trend away from nationality as a sole connecting factor in the field of personal status adds further weight to the already convincing arguments furthered above.[157] Furthermore, the advantages of using nationality as a connecting factor are heavily outweighed by the numerous associated disadvantages. The very rigidity and legal certainty offered by a person's nationality counters the aims and principles upon which choice of law rules in this field should be based. The increased likelihood that couples will be prohibited from registering a relationship due to the absence of similar legislation in the country of their nationality, runs counter to the *favor registrationis* principle.[158]

---

155 See **Section X.2.4.1.**

156 See **Section X.2.2.1.B.**

157 This trend was noted in the recent private international law codification in **Belgium**. Traditionally **Belgium** adheres to nationality as a sole connecting factor in issues relating to the personal law of the parties. However, the increasing importance of habitual residence was noted and nationality has been toned down: See *Belgian Senate*, 2003-2004, 3/27-1, p. 5.

158 The *favor registrationis* principle should be preferred for the same reasons that the *favor matrimonii* principle is preferred in the field of marriage validity. See **Section X.2.2.**

It is therefore submitted that the most suitable approach is that which has been adopted in **The Netherlands**. The general rule (*i.e.* which applies the *lex loci registrationis* to questions of essential validity) should apply to all non-marital registered relationships, unless the relationship is registered at a consular or diplomatic representation, in which case alternative rules should apply. This solution not only retains the simplicity of the general rule, but also caters for those registrations registered at consular and diplomatic representations.[159] Although some commentators have pointed to the increase of territoriality in using the *lex loci registrationis* to determine questions of essential validity,[160] and the subsequent inconsistencies within the legal category of personal status, it must be noted that this is a natural consequence of the variety of substantive law solutions available coupled with the reticence with which legal systems approached the issue of recognition.[161] If countries had paid more attention to the international consequences when enacting domestic legislation, perhaps a common solution could have been found for marriage and non-marital registered relationships. Unfortunately, this is not the case, and a pragmatic solution must be found to solve the problems as they currently stand.

X.3 RECOGNITION RULES

As already indicated in **Section X.1**, there are two distinct structures expounded in the jurisdictions studied with respect to this field of law. On the one hand, the **Anglo-Franco-Belgian** system, which subjects the recognition of foreign marriages to a choice of law test. On the other hand, in the **Dutch-Swiss** system, in which no choice of law test is evident in the recognition rule. The distinction between these two systems has been maintained in this Section; the **Anglo-Franco-Belgian** system will be discussed in **Section X.3.1**, prior to deliberation of the **Dutch-Swiss** system in **Section X.3.2**.

Although rules governing the recognition of non-marital relationships registered abroad have been enacted in six of the countries studied in this book, this is not the case in **France**. As a result, it is to this date unclear how and indeed whether, non-marital relationships registered abroad will be recognised in **France**. KESSLER outlines two main reasons why a non-marital

159 See **Section X.4.**

160 ERAUW/VERHELLEN (1999) p. 154; JOSSELIN-GALL (2000) p. 493. See also KESSLER (2004) p. 141, §238.

161 A situation that, unfortunately, also prevails in Europe, with fifteen European Union jurisdictions up until now failing to legislate for non-marital registered relationships.

registered relationship may be refused recognition in **France**, namely on grounds of public policy and on grounds of the difficulty in inserting the relationship into the current framework of **French** private international law.[162] In relation to the issues of public policy, KESSLER makes a further distinction between using public policy on the basis of domestic conceptions and adopting a solution on the basis of proximity. The fact that a comparable regulation for registration of non-marital relationships exists in **France** negates, in KESSLER'S view,[163] the possibility for a **French** judge to refuse to recognise a foreign non-marital registered relationship on these grounds.[164] In dealing with the second path, KESSLER outlines the problems associated with *forum shopping* or as he describes it *registration shopping*.

KESSLER also notes that apart from the possibility of refusing recognition on the basis of public policy, a **French** judge may also find it difficult to classify foreign non-marital registered relationships in the **French** legal order, and thus resort to the wholesale refusal to recognise such relationships.[165] However, once again, KESSLER dismisses these claims and arrives at the conclusion that such relationships cannot be refused recognition in **France**. The vast majority of **French** authors in this field also support this point of view.[166] In light of the overwhelming support in **French** legal literature for the recognition of foreign non-marital registered relationships in **France**, such a view will be adopted throughout this and subsequent chapters.[167]

Although the *raison d'être* behind any recognition rule is identical to that previously explained with respect to the choice of law rules, one must not lose sight of the fundamental objective of supporting international uniformity in relation to an individual's personal status. Practical inconvenience and hardship can result for people who are treated as involved in a marriage or non-marital registered relationship in one State and not in another. This phenomenon is commonly known as the

---

162 KESSLER (2004) p. 201-242, §349-423.

163 KESSLER (2004) p. 218, §377.

164 This is, of course, tempered by the limits of tolerance in relation to the prohibited degrees of relationship, age, exclusivity and incapacity. See further **Section X.5.**

165 KESSLER (2004) p. 225-231, §389-402.

166 See **Section X.2.2.2.**

167 It must however be noted with caution that such a position is not yet supported legislatively in **France.** In fact, the French Ministry of Foreign Affairs has refused the Swedish consulate in Paris from registering partnerships since "*la conception de l'ordre public français ne permet pas de reconnaître une union matrimoniale de personnes de même sexe*": MÉRCAY (2000) p. 193.

prevention of "limping relationships".[168] Nonetheless, the prevention of limping relationships is not the supreme policy goal in the recognition of foreign relationships. There may indeed be situations where it would be unjust and inappropriate for the law of one country to be bound by a determination by the law of another country as to a person's personal status. A balance must thus be struck between the avoidance of limping relationships and the various other goals of the rules on recognition (**Section X.3.4**). This section will also deal with some specific problems that arise regarding the recognition of non-marital registered relationships irrespective of whether one embraces a choice of law test (**Section X.3.3**).

X.3.1 ANGLO-FRANCO-BELGIAN SYSTEM

Due to the fact that **Belgium**, **France** and the **United Kingdom** apply a choice of law test in order to establish whether a relationship registered outside of the jurisdiction is eligible for recognition,[169] the same distinction between formal and essential validity is upheld.

X.3.1.1 Formal validity

As is the case in marriage and as has already been outlined in **Section X.2.1.2**,[170] the formal validity of a non-marital registered relationship in **Belgium** and the **United Kingdom** will be determined according to the law of the State in which the relationship was registered.[171] The vast majority of **French** authors also believe the formal validity of relationships registered

168 In Dutch as *hinkende relaties* and in French as *relations boiteux*.

169 See, for example, Art. 27(1), Belg. CPIL which determines that any authentic instrument or deed obtained abroad will be recognised in Belgium if it satisfies the law of the place where it was obtained as well as the law determined applicable by **Belgian** choice of law rules. See also VAN HECKE/LENAERTS (1989) p. 218, §455; ERAUW (2004) p. 124-125.

170 **Belg.:** Art. 47(1), Belg. CPIL; **UK:** The **British** case of *McCabe v. McCabe* [1994] 1 FCR 257, illustrates this rule exquisitely. In *McCabe*, a marriage ceremony was performed in Ghana. The respective parties, Irish and Ghanaian domiciliaries, were absent from the ceremony but the putative husband sent £100 and a bottle of gin to those family members in Ghana who were to attend the ceremony. The relatives for both sides of the union were present and toasted the health of the absent spouses, and distributed the dowry amongst themselves. The marriage in compliance with African custom and valid according to the laws of Ghana was upheld. See further MURPHY (1996) p. 35-46.

171 **Belgium:** Art. 47(1), Belg. CPIL (non-marital registered relationships akin to marriages) and Art. 60(1), Belg. CPIL (non-marital registered relationships not akin to marriage); **United Kingdom:** Sec. 207(1)(b), CPA 2004.

abroad should be tested, as is the case with marriages,[172] according to the law of the institution which registers the non-marital relationship. In the overwhelming majority of cases this will correspond to the law of the place where the non-marital relationship is registered.[173]

However, in **England & Wales** a number of small anomalies exist with respect to the recognition of foreign marriages.[174] Firstly, a marriage celebrated abroad will be recognised as formally valid if it complies with the formal requirements of **English common law** and the circumstances are such that compliance with the law of the place of celebration is impossible or extremely difficult.[175] This exception is also extended to some marriages in countries under belligerent occupation, at least where one of the parties is a member of, or directly associated with, the occupying forces.[176] The second situation arises where the parties, though not subject to the common law in the foreign place of celebration have, without regard to the local formalities, taken each other as husband and wife during a ceremony performed by an Episcopally ordained priest. In such a case the marriage will be recognised if compliance with the local formalities had been prevented by some insuperable difficulty.[177] Although these exceptions are well established with respect to the law on marriage, they have not been duly replicated in the CPA 2004.[178]

---

172 Art. 170(1), Fr. CC (at least one French national) and AUDIT (2000) p. 546, §638, LOUSSOUARN/BOUREL (2004) p. 393-395, §293 (extended by analogy to marriages between foreigners).

173 See for further discussion of **French** authors' opinions with respect to non-marital registered relationships see **Sections X.2.1.2** and **X.2.1.3**. Also KESSLER (2004) p. 245, §424.

174 The extent to which these exceptions also apply to **Northern Ireland** is not known. The exact rules applicable in **Scotland** are also unclear, although it is probable that the *lex loci celebrationis* would not be applied in cases where of impossibility of extreme difficulty: CLIVE (1997) p. 124-125, §09.045; ANTON/BEAUMONT (1990) p. 428; JOINT LAW COMMISSIONS (1987a) p. 3, §2.2.

175 *Wolfenden v. Wolfenden* [1946] P 61; *Issac Penhas v. Tan Soo Eng* [1953] AC 304. See also NORTH/FAWCETT (1999) p. 714-715; COLLINS (2000) p. 652-661, §17-004 to §17-025; LEVY/KASHI (2000) p. 192.

176 *Taczanowska v. Taczanowska* [1957] P 301; *Preston v. Preston* [1963] P 411. See also NORTH/FAWCETT (1999) p. 716; COLLINS (2000) p. 661-663, §17-026 to §17-028.

177 *Kent v. Burgess* (1840) 11 Sim 361; *Ruding v. Smith* (1821) 2 Hag Con 371. See also NORTH/FAWCETT (1999) p. 715; COLLINS (2000) p. 658, §17-020.

178 This can be explained for two reasons. Firstly, all these exceptions have been established by common law and therefore do not have statutory force. The CPA 2004 in constructing a civil partnership scheme modelled this on the legislative equivalent for marriage. Secondly, these exceptions have their history either in the Second World War or with respect to religious services, both of which have little relevance for civil partnerships.

X.3.1.2 Essential validity

Unlike the choice of law rules on the essential validity of marriages celebrated abroad,[179] questions relating to the essential validity of foreign relationships to be recognised in the **United Kingdom** are determined according to the *lex loci registrationis*, subject to one exception.[180] If either one of the parties to a non-marital registered relationship is domiciled in a part of the **United Kingdom**, their non-marital registered relationship will not be recognised if it falls foul of the relevant section of Art. 217, CPA 2004.[181] In summary, these provisions prevent the recognition of a non-marital registered relationship in the **United Kingdom** if either one of the parties is domiciled in a part of the **United Kingdom** and is either under the age of sixteen or related within the prohibited degrees of relationship.[182] Although at first glance it would appear that such a rule has no equivalent in the **British** private international law rules on marriage, this is not the case. According to the **British** choice of law rules, questions of essential validity are determined according to the law of the parties' domicil. As a result, should either of the parties be domiciled in a part of the **United Kingdom**, **English**, **Scots** or **Northern Irish** law will apply respectively, thus preventing the recognition of a marriage between persons under the legal marriageable age or related within the prohibited degrees of relationship. As a result of the adapted choice of law rule in determining questions of essential validity of non-marital registered relationships, **British** domiciliaries would have been able to avoid the law of the **United Kingdom** by registering their relationship abroad. Accordingly, although there appears to be a significant difference between the private international law applicable to marriages and the rules applicable to non-marital registered relationships, this is simply a direct consequence of the alteration of the choice of law rule for determining questions of essential validity. As a result **United Kingdom** domiciliaries are treated in an identical fashion with respect to marriages and non-marital registered relationships.[183]

---

179 See **Section X.2.2.1**.

180 Sec. 207(1)(a), CPA.

181 The "relevant section" refers thus to: **Eng:** Art. 217(2), CPA 2004 and one of the parties was domiciled in **England & Wales**; **Scot:** Art. 217(4), CPA 2004 and one of the parties was domiciled in **Scotland**; **NI:** Art. 217(6), CPA 2004 and one of the parties was domiciled in **Northern Ireland.**

182 In **Scotland** one must also be capable of understanding the nature of the relationship or validly consenting to its formation: Sec. 86(1)(e), CPA 2004.

183 As is the case for foreign marriages celebrated abroad between two non-British domiciliaries, age requirements and relationships within the prohibited degrees of relationships are dealt with with leniency, with British public policy seldom being

In contrast, in **Belgium** a distinction is drawn between two categories of non-marital registered relationships on the basis of whether these relationships are akin to marriage or not. Although non-marital registered relationships not akin to marriage are judged according to the *lex loci registrationis*,[184] non-marital registered relationships akin to marriage are in contrast subject to the respective *lex patriae*,[185] subject to the exception provided for in Art. 46(2), Belg. CPIL.[186] For further discussion of these issues see **Table 9** in **Section X.2.2.2.**

The situation is even more complicated in **France** where, in the absence of a legislative or judicial framework, reference must instead be made to the wealth of academic opinion on this topic. As has already been stated,[187] opinion is divided as to whether questions relating to the essential validity of non-marital registered relationships should be subject to the *lex loci registrationis* (KESSLER), the national law of the authority registering the relationship (MIGNOT, DEVERS and FULCHIRON) or, as is the case in marriage,[188] the *lex patriae* (CHANTELOUP and MAYER & HEUZÉ).

X.3.2 DUTCH-SWISS SYSTEM

In both **The Netherlands** and **Switzerland**, as is also the case for marriage,[189] a simple rule has been developed for the recognition of non-marital relationships registered abroad. A foreign non-marital registered relationship will be recognised if it conforms to the *lex loci registrationis*.[190] In **Switzerland**, this rule is however, like the rules applicable to the

---

invoked. See, for example *Cheni v. Cheni* [1965] P 85 (uncle and niece marriage recognised) and *Mohamed v. Knott* [1969] 1 QB 1 (marriage to a 13 year-old girl recognised). See ANTON/BEAUMONT (1990) p. 439 and NORTH/FAWCETT (1999) p. 733-734. In *Cheni*, Sir SIMON stated that in recognising a marriage between an uncle and niece, that: "I believe the true test whether the marriage is so offensive to the conscience of the English court that it should refuse to recognise and give effect to the proper foreign law. In deciding that question the court will seek to exercise common sense, good manners and a reasonable tolerance. In my view it would be altogether too queasy a judicial conscience which would recoil from a marriage acceptable to many peoples of deep religious convictions, lofty ethical standards and high civilisation." (p. 99).

184 Art. 60(1), Belg. CPIL.

185 Art. 47(1), Belg. CPIL.

186 See **Section X.2.2.2.**

187 See **Section X.2.2.2.**

188 See **Section X.2.2.1.B.**

189 **Neth.:** Art. 5, PIL(M)A. See further FROHN (2001) and REINHARTZ (2002b); **Swit.:** Art. 45(1), Sw. CPIL. See also Trib. Féd., 22nd January 1988 (1988) 114 II *ATF* 1, §5 and §6.

190 **Neth.:** Art. 2(1), PIL(RP)A; **Swit.:** Art. 65a, in conjunction with Art. 45(1), Sw. CPIL.

recognition of foreign marriages,[191] subject to one exception in addition to the public policy exception, namely that if the relationship registered abroad was entered into with the aim of avoiding the rules of **Swiss** law, the relationship will not be recognised.[192]

Such an approach is, moreover, also supported by KESSLER in relation to **French** law.[193] In arguing for all issues of non-marital registered relationships to be governed, subject to certain exceptions, by the *lex loci registrationis*,[194] KESSLER thus argues for the abolition of a choice of law test in relation to the recognition of foreign non-marital registered relationships in **France**.[195]

X.3.3 SPECIFIC PROBLEMS

X.3.3.1 Multiple registrations

Due to the rapidly increasing number of jurisdictions introducing legislation in this field[196] and the often foetal state of private international law rules with respect to the recognition of foreign forms of non-marital registered relationships, multiple registrations can (and arguably do) occur.[197] This phenomenon arises when the parties have registered their relationship in one jurisdiction and subsequently re-register their relationship in another jurisdiction.

Example 7: Multiple registration
Katrina and Portia, two Irish nationals, habitually resident and domiciled in Belgium decide in 2000 to enter into a statutory cohabitation. However, a week later, due to Katrina's work the couple move to Strasbourg, where they decide to register a PACS

191 PATOCCHI/GEISINGER (1995) p. 197-198, Art. 45(2), SW. CPIL and DUTOIT (2005) p. 161-162, Art. 45, No. 6-9.

192 Art. 65a, in conjunction with Art. 45(2), Sw. CPIL. BUCHER (2004a) p. 190, §533 and DUTOIT (2005) p. 161-162, Art. 45, No. 6.

193 KESSLER (2004).

194 Although KESSLER refers to *la loi de l'enregistrement*, he refers to the *favor validitatis* instead of the *favor registrationis*.

195 KESSLER (2004) p. 245, §424.

196 See **Chapter IX** and **Appendices I-III** for an overview.

197 This author knows personally of at least two such cases. This section is thus confined to the issue of multiple registrations between the same parties. Multiple registrations by persons with third persons will be dealt with separately in **Section X.5.1**.

in 2001.[198] After having lived a year in France, Katrina's work takes the pair to Uppsala, Sweden where in 2005 they decide to register their partnership again.[199]

The reason for the subsequent registrations may be that the parties wish to alter the law applicable to their relationship.[200] Alternatively, such a situation could also occur, where the jurisdiction in which the second relationship is registered does not recognise the first registration,[201] thus forcing the parties to re-register their relationship without having to terminate the previous one. However, only one of the countries studied in this book has provided an explicit, legislative answer to this question.[202] In the recent codification of **Belgian** private international law, Art. 60(1) states, "a relationship of cohabitation will be regulated by the law of the State on whose territory it was first registered".[203] No such equivalent has however been enacted with respect to non-marital registered relationships akin to marriage, which must thus be dealt with along identical lines to the current law on marriage. Accordingly, despite the lack of legislative enactments, an attempt can nevertheless be made to answer this question either by extrapolation from general private international law principles or the parliamentary discussions on the introduction of rules governing non-marital registered relationships.

It is perhaps true to say that until now the law has not readily been confronted with such problems. A couple married in one jurisdiction will not readily attempt to remarry with one another in a different jurisdiction. This stems from the recognition afforded to such marriages in foreign legal systems. The same is not, however, true of non-marital registered relationships. Registered partners may have to reregister their relationship

---

198 In this case the couple would require a *certificat de coutume* from their respective national countries, *i.e.* the Republic of Ireland. Since the Republic of Ireland does not, as yet, recognise such relationships, such a certificate will not be provided.

199 In Sweden only relationships specifically mentioned in the Swedish Registered Partnership Act are eligible for recognition. As yet, the French PACS and the Belgian statutory cohabitation are not listed, therefore the parties will be considered "unmarried and unregistered according to Swedish law".

200 THORN (2003a) p. 165. This might be for example to benefit from different rights and duties or profit from less stringent termination procedures.

201 KESSLER (2004) p. 316-317, §547.

202 **Germany** has also made express reference to this situation. Art. 17b(3), Ger. CCIL provides that only the last registration will be recognised: *Bestehen zwischen denselben Personen eingetragene Lebenspartnerschaften in verschiedenen Staaten, so ist die zuletzt begründete Lebenspartnerschaft vom Zeitpunkt ihrer Begründung an für die in Absatz 1 umschriebenen Wirkungen und Folgen maßgebend.* See further THORN (2003a) p. 165.

203 See further Govt. Circular, *Belg. Staatsblad*, 28th September 2004, p. 69607, *Parl. Doc., Belgian Senate*, 2002-2003, No. 3/27-4, p. 9-10, Amendment No. 58.

in order to benefit from the legal rights and duties afforded to registered partners in that jurisdiction. The lack of a suitable comparator invokes the need for one to search for comparable situations. The phenomenon of multiple registrations raises similar questions as that raised by the issue of polygamous marriages. In dealing with a polygamous marriage a judge will thus be required to assess the validity to two (or more) putatively valid legal acts; a marriage valid according to one jurisdiction and another marriage valid according to the same jurisdiction or indeed a third jurisdiction. This methodological analysis pertaining to this situation could thus be applied analogously to multiple registrations, despite the fundamental distinction that multiple registrations involve the same two persons. In both situations the judge is confronted with multiple legal acts, on the one hand, with the same person (multiple registration)[204] and on the other, with a third person (polygamous relationships).[205]

In **The Netherlands**, although not entirely identical, one can contend that only the first registration will be recognised since the same would also be true of marriages. Polygamous marriages are not recognised in **The Netherlands**; only the first marriage in time is eligible for recognition according to the Neth. PIL(M)A.[206] Any subsequent marriages by one of the parties will not be recognised as it is contrary to **Dutch** public policy.[207] If one follows this line of argument, only the first non-marital relationship registered is eligible for recognition in **The Netherlands**.[208] Any subsequent relationship will be deemed contrary to **Dutch** public policy and thus not recognised. However, this reasoning is not entirely airtight. Firstly, a fundamental difference exists between these two scenarios. With respect to polygamous marriages the parties are different, whereas the parties to a multiple registration are the same. Secondly, although it is clear why the recognition of polygamous marriages is deemed contrary to **Dutch** public policy, it is less clear why the recognition of successive non-marital

---

204 This will be dealt with here.

205 This will be dealt with in **Chapter X.5.4**.

206 This is subject to the proviso that the first marriage is still in existence. If the first marriage is terminated before the case comes to court, then the second marriage (although polygamous at the time of its celebration) will be recognised. See Hof Amsterdam, 12th November 1998 (1999) *NIPR* 137, on appeal from Rb Amsterdam, 19th October 1997, Case. No. 97.3425F. See also annotation RUTTEN (2001) *NIPR* 44-52. This principle only applies if the first marriage is legally dissolved before the case comes to court. The general rule thus remains unaffected.

207 STRIKWERDA (2002) p. 96.

208 The provisions of the Neth. PIL(RP)A are based entirely on the Neth. PIL(M)A and therefore will adopt a similar approach: see also Rb Roermond, 29th March 2001 (2001) *NIPR* 188.

registered relationships would be held to be contrary to **Dutch** public policy. In contrast, one could argue that the last registration should be the one that is recognised since this is the most recent expression of the parties' will. Although unanswered as yet, there appears to be little evidence to suggest that the approach to multiple registrations would be any different than that adopted with respect to polygamous marriages, *i.e.* recognition only being granted to the first registration in time.

In **France**,[209] a similar prognostication is possible, although the argumentation is more complex. The issue of polygamous marriages has raised interesting, and to some extent related, questions in **France**.[210] It has been increasingly concluded that the effects of a subsequent polygamous marriage will be recognised in **France**, thus allowing, for example, a second wife to claim maintenance from her husband.[211] By analogy, it would at first sight, seem possible to recognise more than one non-marital registered relationship. Although as with the problem posed by polygamous marriages, the question raised by multiple registrations normally revolves around whether a particular right or duty is applicable, a distinction between polygamous marriages and multiple registrations lies grounded in the fact that multiple registrations involve the same parties. Accordingly, the legal issue at stake is different. If according to one registration a right is granted and according to the other not, eventually a choice will have to be made as to which registration takes precedence. As a result only one non-marital registered relationship may be recognised. From this point of view it would seem more plausible that a **French** court would analogously apply the decisions in which polygamous marriages were declared contrary to **French** public policy. In these cases only the first marriage was recognised, which would in turn lead to the recognition of the first non-marital relationship registered.[212] There appears to be no case law to suggest that in polygamous marriage cases the latter marriage should be recognised above and beyond the first marriage. However, not all commentators agree with such a solution. Although admitting the inherent danger involved in recognising the last registered relationship, KESSLER argues that

---

209 KESSLER (2004) p. 316-317, §542-547.

210 For example, TGI Versailles, 31st March 1965 (1966) *JDI* 97, annotated PONSARD (first spouse not obliged to live with the second); TGI Seine, 12th November 1965 (1966) *Rev. crit. DIP* 624, annotated DECROUX; TGI Lyon, 20th November 1975 (1976) *Rev. crit. DIP* 477, annotated LAGARDE. See also OTHENIN-GIRARD (1999a) p. 397-405, §630-644.

211 LOUSSOUARN/BOUREL (2004) p. 407-408, §306; AUDIT (2000) p. 281, §313.

212 There appears to be no authority in which only the latter marriage was recognised.

en présence d'enregistrement de partenariats par les mêmes individus dans des pays différents, le partenariat enregistré en dernier lieu est déterminant si la loi qui régit le précédent l'autorise et si les statuts concernés sont de même nature.[213]

As already stated, despite express legislative provision dealing with multiple non-marital registered relationships not akin to marriage, the codification of private international law in **Belgium** does not provide any answers to the issues raised by multiple non-marital registered relationships akin to marriage, *i.e.* those covered by the *mutatis mutandis* application of the rules on marriage. The issue of polygamous marriages has raised somewhat related questions in **Belgium**. It has been increasingly concluded that the effects of a subsequent polygamous marriage will be recognised in **Belgium**.[214] As has been explained with reference to the **French** situation, although the problem of polygamous marriages is intrinsically different to that of multiple registrations, logical analysis also leads one here to the conclusion that only the first non-marital registered relationship can be recognised.[215]

Although absent in the legislative text, the **Swiss** Federal Council has explicitly dealt with the situation of multiple registrations, arguing that according to general principle,[216] only the first registration, in such a situation as outlined in *Example 3*, will be deemed valid.[217] However, the Federal Council also noted the possibility that it may be better to leave this issue to the parties themselves and thus could, and possibly should, be decided on a case-by-case basis.[218] In the **United Kingdom**, the question is of less importance although not entirely irrelevant.[219] WOELKE argues that a strict interpretation of **British** legislation leads one to the conclusion that only the first registration will be recognised.[220] It is argued here that such an

213 KESSLER (2004) p. 316-317, §547.

214 VANDER ELST/WEBER (1983) p. 338, §81.1; HEYVAERT (2002) p. 15-16, §37; RIGAUX (1987) p. 353, §518 who mentions the **French** case if Fr. Cass.,1 Civ. Ch., 28th January 1958 (1958) *Rev. crit. DIP* 110; Cour d'Appel Liege, 23rd April 1970 (1971) *Rev. crit. jur. belge.* 5.

215 Rb Brussels, 20th November 1990 (1991) *JT* 283; Rb Antwerp, 14th September 1998, No. 98/3431/A (unpublished). In both these cases the second marriage was not recognised. These cases involved a man whose national law permitted polygamy, whilst his first marriage (which had been celebrated in Belgium) was with a woman whose national law did not permit polygamy.

216 As can be deduced from Art. 27(2)(c), Sw. CPIL.

217 FF 2002, p. 1192 at 1260.

218 FF 2002, p. 1192 at 1260.

219 The question is nonetheless slightly different in the **United Kingdom** because the question raises more of a general issue of recognition instead of multiple registrations, due to the fact that all overseas relationships are recognised as **British** civil partnerships.

220 WOELKE (2004) p. 113.

interpretation is indeed correct but requires explanation. According to Sec. 212, CPA 2004, two groups of relationships are eligible for recognition as an "overseas relationship": specified relationships and relationships that meet the general conditions laid out in Sec. 214, CPA 2004.[221] If a relationship is deemed to have satisfied the conditions of either of these categories, it will be treated as a civil partnership.[222] Therefore, as long as the parties are deemed to have entered into an "overseas relationship", they will be treated, for the purposes of **British** law, as though they had registered a **British** civil partnership.[223] In such a case, a judge will no doubt begin with the first putative registration in time and proceed forwards until he or she reaches a registration that is eligible for recognition. Once this has been done, any further registration will not be recognised.[224] Determining the first recognisable registration in the **United Kingdom** may be important in areas such as tax and property settlement, where the length of the relationship can have an impact.

X.3.3.2 Recognition according to forum or place of registration

Once it is clear that a relationship is eligible for recognition, it must be determined according to which law this relationship will be regulated. It is here that the answer to the previous question becomes particularly important. This issue will be dealt with extensively in **Chapter XII.4** since the most important effect of recognising a non-marital registered relationship according to the *lex fori* or the *lex loci registrationis* is that it can have important effects upon the rights and duties that one is able to enjoy as a result. However it is important here to note the relevance of the question of recognition and the scope of such recognition.[225]

> ***Example 8: Applicable Law***
> Hans and Jan, two Belgians enter into a statutory cohabitation in Brussels, Belgium. As a result they are able to obtain all the rights and duties inherent upon statutory cohabitants according to Belgian law. They subsequently move to Manchester, England, UK. Without their knowledge their statutory cohabitation will be recognised in England as an English civil partnership with all the incumbent rights

---

221 A similar approach is also adopted with respect to adoptions: see NORTH/FAWCETT (1999) p. 907-913 and Part IV, AA 1976. For further details on the characterisation of non-marital registered relationships in the **United Kingdom** see **Chapter IX.3.5**.

222 Subject to the condition that it satisfies the law of the place where it was registered: Sec. 215(1), CPA 2004.

223 See further **Section X.3.3.2** and **Chapter XII.3.4.2**.

224 Sec. 212(1)(b)(ii), CPA 2004 states that the parties may not already be involved in a civil partnership or married.

225 See for example WOELKE (2004) p. 112.

and duties being imposed upon them. This therefore means that should one of them wish to terminate their relationship in England, English law would be applied to the termination procedure and the possibility for unilateral termination would no longer apply.

X.3.3.3 The meaning of "law"

When a recognition rule refers to a particular country to determine the validity of a foreign instrument or decision, a question arises as to the scope of such a referral. When the law of the forum refers to the law of the place of registration in order to determine whether a non-marital registered relationship is eligible for recognition, the question arises whether this referral denotes the law of the place of registration in its entirety (*Gesamtverweisung*) or only to its substantive domestic law rules (*Sachnormverweisung*). This issue is thus inherently and closely related to the issue of *renvoi*.[226]

When a choice of law rule refers to the law of a particular country, a question arises whether such a referral includes the private international law of that country.[227] The question, termed *renvoi*, arises where the choice of law rules of the forum refer an issue to the courts of another country which, under its choice of law rules in turn refers the issue back to the law of the forum (*renvoi au premier degré/Rückverweisung/terugverwijzing*) or to the law of a third country (*renvoi au second degré/Weiterverweisung/verderverwijzing*). However when dealing with recognition, the issue at stake is not whether the jurisdiction selected by the recognition rule has correctly applied its own rules of private international law but instead whether the relationship is valid according to the law stipulated by virtue of the recognition rule. Take the following sketches:

---

226 STRIKWERDA (2002) p. 97; NIEUWENHUIS (2004) p. 1637, Art. 5(3), Neth. PIL(M)A; BUCHER/BONOMI (2004) p. 174, §632-634. In contrast with respect to the recognition of foreign marriages, see AUDIT (2000) p. 553, §646.

227 See generally: **Belg:** RIGAUX (1987) p. 265-279, §391-408; VANDER ELST/WEBER (1983) p. 320-329, §76 **Fr.:** AUDIT (2000) p. 185-194, §208-220; BATIFFOL/LAGARDE (1993) p. 492-509, §300-311; MAYER/HEUZÉ (2001) p. 146-154, §216-231; LOUSSOUARN/BOUREL (2004) p. 252-282, §198-221; **Neth.:** STRIKWERDA (2002) p. 61-66, §69-75; **Swit.:** PATOCCHI/GEISINGER (1995) p. 110-111, Art. 14, Sw. CPIL; BUCHER/BONOMI (2004) p. 111-117, §413-440; KNOEPFLER *et al.* (2005) p. 205-212, §407-425; **Eng, UK:** NORTH/FAWCETT (1999) p. 51-66; COLLINS (2000) p. 65-80, §4-002 to §4-036; **Scot, UK:** ANTON/BEAUMONT (1990) p. 75-84. And generally, SAUVEPLANNE (1990).

Example 9: Sachnormverweisung

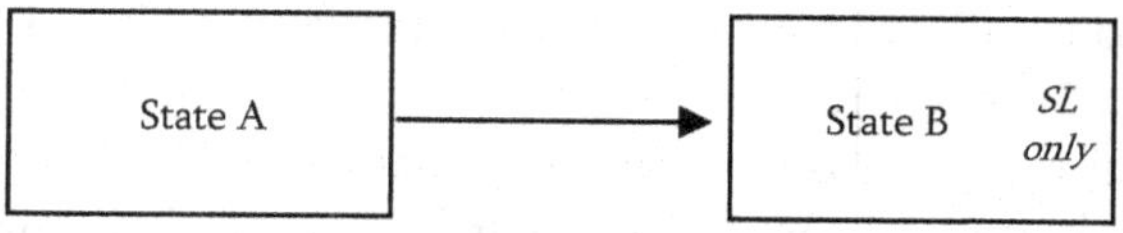

Example 10: Gesamtverweisung - Rückverweisung

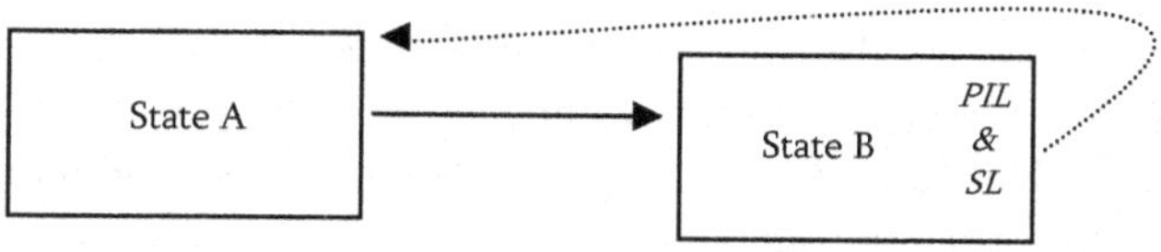

Example 11: Gesamtverweisung - Weiterverweisung

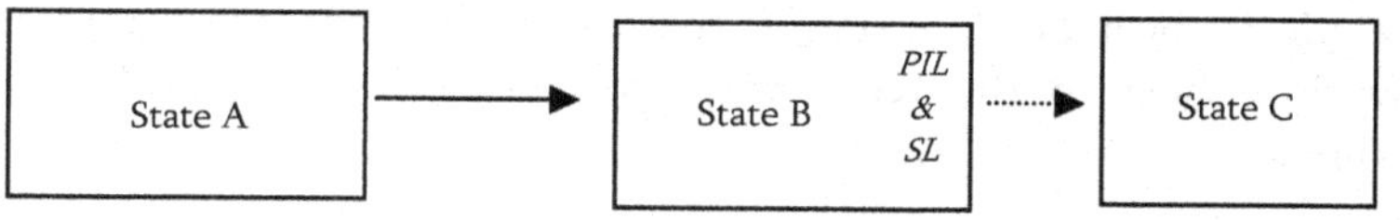

Abbreviations: **PIL**: Private International Law; **SL**: Substantive Law

In dealing with the issue at hand, namely the recognition of non-marital registered relationships, in *Example 9* the recognition rule refers only to those relationships validly recognised in accordance with the substantive law of State B (*Sachnormverweisung*). If the relationship is not valid according to this law then it will not be recognised by State A. In *Examples 10* and *11*, the recognition rule also allows for the relationship to be valid according to the private international law rules of State B (*Gesamtverweisung*). This necessarily increases the possibilities for validity, thus adhering to the principle of *favor registrationis*. In *Example 10*, the private international law rules of State B refer either back to State A or internally to State B, whilst in *Example 11* this referral leads in turn to State C. The issue at stake here is how one interprets the term "law" in the recognition rule: is this referral a *Sachnormverweisung* or a *Gesamtverweisung*?[228]

In **Switzerland**, this issue is neatly avoided due to the wording of the relevant recognition rule. Art. 45(1), Sw. CPIL, applicable to both marriages

[228] Confusion between the issue of *renvoi* and the meaning of the term "law" in a recognition rule can occur if a country applies a choice of law test to the recognition of foreign relationships, as is the case with foreign marriage recognition in **Belgium**, **France** and the **United Kingdom**. Nevertheless, these two issues must be distinguished.

and registered partnerships by virtue of Art. 65a, Sw. CPIL, states that a marriage (and thus a non-marital registered relationship by analogy) validly celebrated abroad will be recognised in **Switzerland**.[229] This formulation thus allows for a **Swiss** court to refer not only to the substantive law of the foreign State, but also to its private international law rules. The same result has also been achieved in **The Netherlands** and the **United Kingdom**, by virtue of explicit provisions.[230]

A similar situation is also discernible in **France.** In the *Zagha* case,[231] a couple was validly married abroad, where according to private international law the parties had capacity to marry according to their common national law. In deciding that the marriage was valid, the **French** Supreme Court accepted that in referring to the law of the place of celebration, this included that country's private international law. There is no indication, academic or judicial, to suggest that a different approach would be adopted with respect to the recognition of non-marital relationships registered abroad.

In **Belgium**, on the other hand, a different approach has been adopted. As has already been stated, **Belgium** maintains a choice of law test in its recognition rules,[232] therefore the blanket ban on applying *renvoi* in the field of choice of law, equally applies in terms of the recognition of foreign marriages or non-marital registered relationships.[233] In this case, a referral by **Belgium** to the law of the place where the non-marital relationship was registered only refers to that country's substantive law provisions.[234]

X.3.4 EVALUATION

In defending the difference between the rules relating to non-marital registered relationships and those relating to marriage, the national

---

229 BUCHER (2004a) p. 56, §136; BUCHER/BONOMI (2004) p. 174, §633; Trib. Féd., 22nd January 1988 (1988) 114 II *ATF* 1 at §5-9; HONSELL/VOGT/SCHNYDER (1996) Art. 45, No. 9 (SIEHR); HEINI *et al.* (1993) Art. 45, No. 9-14. See also OTHENIN-GIRARD (1999a) p. 368, §575 and DUTOIT (2005) p. 154-155, Art. 45, No. 1-2.

230 **Neth.:** Art. 2(3), Neth. PIL(RP)A. This is contrary to the general approach adopted with respect to *renvoi* in the choice of law, see FROHN (2003) p. 464 and Art. 6, Proposed Neth. CPIL; **UK:** Sec. 212(2), CPA 2004.

231 Fr. Cass., 15th June 1982 (1983) *D* 431, annotated AGOSTINI, (1983) *JDI* 595, annotated LEHMAN, (1983) *Rev. Crit. DIP* 300, annotated BISCHOFF.

232 See **Section X.1** and VAN HECKE/LENAERTS (1989) p. 218, §455.

233 Art. 16, Belg. CPIL.

234 This is substantially different from the situation prior to the codification, see, for example, Hof Brussels, *JLMB,* 18th October 1988.

legislatures in all countries studied have referred to the problem that these new forms of relationship regulation are not, as yet, widely accepted and therefore reference to one of the personal law connecting factors as espoused for marriage could increase the number of limping relationships, and thus depart from the principle of *favor registrationis*. Although at first sight it would appear that the laws of the six countries to have enacted legislation in this field differ vastly on this point, on closer inspection the rules are surprisingly similar.

In all six jurisdictions to have enacted legislation in this field (**Belgium**, **The Netherlands**, **Switzerland**, **England & Wales**, **Scotland** and **Northern Ireland**), and despite the intrinsic differences in both the structure of the private international law rules in these countries as well as the differences in the substantive law solutions espoused, it is generally the law of the place where the non-marital relationship was registered that will always be determinative. However, this general principle is subject to a number of exceptions.

Firstly, in the **United Kingdom**, if one of the parties to a non-marital registered relationship is a **British** domiciliary and the eligibility criteria are not met, then the non-marital registered relationship will not be recognised. As has already been explained, this rule is a natural consequence of the alteration in the choice of law rules. However, this rule is almost indistinguishable from a case decided upon grounds of public policy; recognition will not be afforded to child registrations or registrations between persons within the prohibited degrees of relationship since they would be contrary to the public policy of the **United Kingdom**, should one of the parties have a domicile in a part of the **United Kingdom**. It would thus appear that the provisions laid down in Sec. 217, CPA 2004 cover situations that are also enveloped in the public policy exception (discussed in **Section X.5**). It is therefore submitted that such a rule does not add anything new to the recognition rules in the **United Kingdom** but merely serves to elevate one particular case where the public policy exception may be used. Accordingly the absence of such an explicit rule in the other jurisdictions studied should not be seen as a sign of non-uniformity of result, since a similar result is achieved using different means.

Secondly, an exception is provided for in **Swiss** law in cases where it is felt that the parties have registered abroad in order to evade the provisions of **Swiss** law. Here, once again, such a rule could clearly be brought within a general public policy exception. And finally, in relation to **Belgian** law, one must remember that due to the method of characterising non-marital registered relationships, certain non-marital registered relationships will not be subject to this general principle and will thus instead be subject to a choice of law test, with questions of essential validity being determined according to the *lex patriae*, subject to the exception provided for in Art. 46(2), Belg. CPIL.[235]

In **France**, opinion is divided along similar lines to that in relation to the choice of rules laws, with the majority of authors choosing to refer to the *loi de l'institution*. However, for the same reasons as expressed with respect to issues of essential validity, and bearing in mind the similarity in the rationale behind the recognition rules and the choice of law rules with respect to essential validity, a recognition rule referring to the *lex loci registrationis* is preferable. This approach is, furthermore, not without express support in **France**.[236]

It must be noted that with respect to the specific issue of multiple registrations, the entire problem arises due to the restrictive manner in which certain countries have responded to issues of the recognition of foreign non-marital registered relationships, coupled with the inconsequential manner in which such rules are developed. In *Example 3* above, the crux of the problem arises due to the non-recognition in **France** of the **Belgian** statutory cohabitation and the subsequent non-recognition of both the **French** PACS and **Belgian** statutory cohabitation in **Sweden**. It is submitted that instead of attempting to solve these issues with complicated rules determining which and to what extent a relationship will be recognised, attention should instead be focused on broadening the rules of recognition so as to avoid such questions in the first place. Nonetheless, pragmatically speaking, unless worldwide consensus is achieved on these issues (which is highly unlikely), the phenomenon of multiple registrations will continue and thus interim rules will need to be crafted.[237] From the material presented in **Section X.3.3.1**, it is clear that the balance tips in favour of recognising the relationship first registered.[238]

---

235 Art. 47(1), Belg. CPIL, subject to the exception provided for in Art. 47(2), Belg. CPIL with respect to same-sex marriages and non-marital registered relationships.

236 KESSLER (2004) p. 311-321, §537-§555.

237 Although it is acknowledged that this problem is a rare one, this does not detract from the necessity to deal with such problems before they arise.

238 However, this approach is not supported by all. See, contra, Art. 7(1) of the June 2004 proposal of the European Group of Private International Law. See **Chapter XIII.4.5**.

Furthermore, in attempting to adhere to the principles of *favor matrimonii* and *favor registrationis*, the term "law" in any recognition rule at private international law level should include the private international law of that country. In this way one increases the chances of recognising the relevant relationship whilst at the same time respecting the parties' reasonable expectations, but also simultaneously seriously limits the possibility of limping relationships. The path chosen by the **Belgian** legislature is thus, in this respect, disappointing.

In summary, it is submitted that this area of law, despite the pitfalls and minefields, is an area where a common approach is clear. Recognition should be afforded to foreign non-marital registered relationships if they are valid according to the law of the place where they were first registered. These rules should apply whether the issue arises in the context of a principal issue or incidental question and should refer to the law of the place of registration, including that country's private international law rules.[239]

X.4 CONSULAR AND DIPLOMATIC REGISTRATIONS

Non-marital registered relationships may, under certain circumstances and often in a similar manner to marriages, be registered before consular or diplomatic representations.[240] For example, the **Belgian** consulate in **The Netherlands** may register a statutory cohabitation according to **Belgian** law provided certain conditions are satisfied. Likewise, the **Dutch** consulate in **Belgium** may register a registered partnership according to **Dutch** law provided certain conditions are satisfied. An important distinction must however be drawn between those non-marital registered relationships registered before consular and diplomatic representations in the forum (**Section X.3.4.1**) and those registered abroad (**Section X.3.4.2**).[241]

---

239 Issues relating to different-sex non-marital registered relationships are best dealt with under the heading of characterisation.

240 This field of law is extremely complex, and this book only scratches the surface of the intricacies of this area. The rules outlined in this section form the minimum basis upon which countries negotiate international or bilateral treaties. When a Treaty has been concluded between two States, this Treaty can determine within which margins these rules are entitled to be applied. It is therefore important to note that although these rules are laid down in domestic legislation, they often require further bilateral Treaties in order to be able to be implemented. The capacities of consular offices must also be analysed with reference to the 1963 Vienna Convention on Consular Relations.

241 For instance, if one were studying **Belgian** law, a non-marital registered relationship registered in **Belgium** before a consular or diplomatic representation would fall into the

X.4.1 RELATIONSHIPS REGISTERED IN THE FORUM

Apart from **Switzerland** and **France**,[242] all of the countries studied in this book permit non-marital registered relationships to be performed at consular and diplomatic representations within their own territory.[243] In **Switzerland**, due to the analogous application of the private international law rules on marriage to non-marital registered relationships, and despite the prohibition on registering a partnership or celebrating a marriage before a consular or diplomatic representation, if a marriage or non-marital registered relationship is performed before a diplomatic or consular representation in **Switzerland**, the marriage or non-marital registered relationship will be treated as though it were celebrated in the State of the "spouses'" or "registered partners'" nationality.[244] The case will thus be analysed according to the rules on the recognition of foreign marriages or non-marital registered relationships.[245]

In those countries in which registrations before consular or diplomatic representations are permitted, a number of conditions must first be satisfied before such a registration may take place. In **The Netherlands**, in an analogous fashion to marriage,[246] a consular or diplomatic representation is not permitted to register a non-marital relationship if either of the partners possesses **Dutch** nationality either exclusively or in combination with the nationality of another country.[247] This rule is also applicable to such marriages in **Belgium**, although it is not expressly extended to non-marital

---

first category whilst a non-marital registered relationship registered abroad before a **Belgian** consular or diplomatic representation would fall in the second category.

242 **Swit.:** BUCHER (2004a) p. 48, §111 and DUTOIT (2005) p. 146, Art. 43, No. 8; **Fr.:** The **French** Ministry of Foreign Affairs has refused the **Swedish** consulate in Paris from registering relationships since "la conception de l'ordre public français ne permet pas de reconnaître une union matrimoniale de personnes de même sexe": MÉRCAY (2000) p. 193.

243 **Belg.:** HEYVAERT (2002) p. 148, §325, VAN HECKE/LENAERTS (1989) p. 223, No. 468; **Neth.:** Art. 4, Neth. PIL(M)A (marriages) and Art. 1(3), Neth. PIL(RP)A (registered partnerships); **UK:** NORTH/FAWCETT (1999) p. 709-710 and 711-712; FMA 1892, FMA 1949 and FM(A)A1988.

244 BUCHER (2004a) p. 48, §111. The words "spouse" and "registered partner" have been set between inverted commas in order to highlight the fact that these marriages and registered partnerships may not necessarily be recognised.

245 See **Section X.3**.

246 **Belg.:** HEYVAERT (2002) p. 148, §325; Hof Liege, 16th November 1993 (1994) *TBBR* 503, annotated BARNICH; **Neth.:** *Neth. Staatsblad* 1999, No. 1 (15th January 1999), overturning HR, 13th December 1996, NJ 1997, 469. For comment see RUTTEN (1999).

247 **Marriage:** Art. 4, Neth. PIL(M)A; **Registered Partnership:** Art. 1(3), Neth. PIL(RP)A.

registered relationships.[248] Furthermore, **Belgium** only recognises marriages celebrated before consular and diplomatic representations if both of the parties are nationals of the State represented,[249] whilst in **The Netherlands** the provisions are understood as stipulating that one of the parties must possess the nationality of the State represented.[250] However, this condition has not been expressly extended to the registration of non-marital relationships before consular or diplomatic representations in either **Belgium** or **The Netherlands**. However, there appears to be no obvious reason, either logically or in legal literature, to indicate that this rule will be dealt with any differently for non-marital registered relationships.[251] If these conditions are satisfied, the marriage or non-marital registered relationship will be recognised if it conforms with the law of the State represented.[252]

In **France**, the situation is more complicated by virtue of an announcement by the **French** Ministry of Foreign Affairs, which refused to allow the **Swedish** consulate to perform a registered partnership on consulate grounds according to **Swedish** law. Whether such a ban applies to all consulates is unclear and it is dubious whether such a ban could withstand judicial scrutiny.[253] If one assumes that such a prohibition does not create a blanket ban on all registrations, and although not regulated in the PACS legislation expressly, it is conceivable that **French** authorities might allow foreign consular and diplomatic representations to register non-marital registered relationships in **France** under strict conditions.[254] With respect to marriages, AUDIT argues that if **France** recognises marriages validly celebrated abroad, it must also recognise marriages celebrated under the same conditions before consular and diplomatic representations in **France** between nationals of the represented State.[255] One can take this argument a step further and argue that since **France** recognises certain foreign non-marital registered relationships, the same rules should apply to non-marital registered relationships concluded before consular or diplomatic representations in

---

248 Hof Liege, 16th November 1993 (1994) *TBBR* 503, annotated BARNICH; VAN HECKE/LENAERTS (1989) p. 223, §468.

249 Rb Brussels, 24th February 1987 (1989) *TBBR* 165. Also known as the "sending State".

250 RUTTEN (1999) p. 115; *Dutch Second Chamber*, 1987-1988, 20507, No. 3, p. 7; NIEUWENHUIS (2004) p. 1633-34, Art. 4, Neth. PIL(M)A.

251 As is the case with the vast majority of the provisions in the Neth. PIL(RP)A, interpretation of the provisions will be done on the basis of the relevant provisions in the relevant private international law provisions related to marriage.

252 **Belg.**: HEYVAERT (2002) p. 148, §325; **Neth.**: STRIKWERDA (2002) p. 95.

253 KESSLER (2004) p. 220, §381.

254 DEVERS (2004) p. 265, §353. *Cf.* AUDIT (2000) p. 551, §644; KESSLER (2004) p. 210, §381.

255 AUDIT (2000) p. 551, §644.

France. If this argument is accepted, then the same rules would apply as in **Belgium**, in that both parties must possess the nationality of the represented State,[256] neither of the parties must be in possession of **French** nationality, and the registration must conform with the law of the State represented.[257]

The situation in the **United Kingdom** is likewise also far from ideal. The CPA 2004 provides no guidelines on the possibility for consular and diplomatic representations to register forms of non-marital relationships in the **United Kingdom**. According to a small number of cases, there is authority to believe that marriages celebrated before foreign consular or diplomatic representations in the **United Kingdom** will be regarded as valid if both parties are nationals of the State represented and the marriage is celebrated in accordance with the law of that State.[258] However, the leading case on the question of marriages in foreign consulates and embassies, namely *Radwan v. Radwan*, would appear to contradict this reasoning.[259] According to *Radwan*, such a marriage must instead comply with the domestic rules of the State where the consular or diplomatic representation is situated.[260] This is also the logical result of the decision of *Radwan v. Radwan (No. 2)*.[261] However, in the last sentence of CUMMING-BRUCE J.s decision in *Radwan*, he states that this holding applies to the divorce of an **English** domiciliary at a foreign embassy in London. He furthermore acknowledges that this decision is limited to this scenario. If this is the case, it would add weight to the suggestion that if neither of the parties to the non-marital registered relationship is domiciled in a part of the **United Kingdom**, there is no precedent to object to this non-marital registered relationship being registered according to the law of the State that the consular or diplomatic representation represents. If, on the other hand, one of the parties is a **British** domiciliary, then the parties must comply with the law according to the relevant part of the **United Kingdom**.

---

256 BATIFFOL/LAGARDE (1983) p. 56, §424 and especially fn. 5; See for example TGI Paris, 24th February 1975 (1975) *D* 379, annotated PAIRE. On the analogous application of Art. 170, Fr. CC.

257 TGI Reims, 16th January 1976, (1976) *JDI* 916, annotated FADLALLAH; LOUSSOURAN/BOUREL (2004) p. 399-400, §298; MAYER/HÉUZE (2001) p. 370-372, §559-561.

258 *Bailet v. Bailet* (1901) 17 TLR 317. See also *Khan v. Khan* (1959) 21 DLR (2d) 171 at §11 (Supreme Court of **British Columbia**, **Canada**). Although this case has since been reversed in *Savelieff v. Glouchkoff* (1963) 41 DLR (2d) 767 (Supreme Court of **British Columbia**, **Canada**), the comments made by MANSON J. in *Khan* were only *obiter dicta*.

259 *Radwan v. Radwan* [1973] Fam 24.

260 In that case **French** law since the **Egyptian** consulate was situated in **France**. See also NORTH/FAWCETT (1999) p. 710.

261 *Radwan v. Radwan* [1973] Fam 24.

X.4.2 RELATIONSHIPS REGISTERED ABROAD

In six of the seven countries studied in this book provision is made for non-marital relationships to be registered abroad before consular and diplomatic representations.[262] However, in the case of the **United Kingdom**, a distinction is made between those cases where the relationship is registered before a **British** consular or diplomatic representation abroad (**Section X.4.2.1**) and those cases where the relationship is registered before a foreign consular or diplomatic representation abroad (**Section X.4.2.2**). Since, none of the other countries in this book make such a distinction, the rules of these jurisdictions will only be dealt with in **Section X.4.2.1**.

X.4.2.1 Forum consular or diplomatic representations

In **The Netherlands**, a non-marital relationship registered before a consulate or diplomatic representation abroad will be recognised only if the State in which the registration took place (*i.e.* the State in which the consular or diplomatic representation is to be found, also known as the Receiving State) permits such a registration.[263] If the State permits such registrations to take place, the non-marital registered relationship will be recognised if it complies with **Dutch** law. In a similar fashion to marriages celebrated before **British** consular and diplomatic representations abroad,[264] **British** consular

[262] **Belg.:** Act of 12th July 1931, *Belg. Staatsblad*, 31st July 1931. As a result the heads of Belgian diplomatic and consular representations are by operation of law granted the status of Registrar and thus all the capacities of that status, including the registration of statutory cohabitations abroad: See ERAUW, Chapter 3: *De huwelijkssluting*, §3, p. 3, available at www.ipr.be; **UK:** Sec. 210, CPA 2004; **Neth.:** Art. 2(2), Neth. PIL(RP)A; **Fr.:** Art. 515-3(8), Fr. CC. **Swit.:** The authority must first be granted to consular and diplomatic representations before they are permitted to act as a Registrar. This has at present not been done. *Cf.* DUTOIT (2005) p. 146, Art. 43, No. 8.

[263] Art. 2(2), Neth. PIL(RP)A.

[264] Regulated by FMA 1892, as amended by the FMA 1947 and FM(A)A 1988, and FMO 1970. Marriages before consular or diplomatic representations must however be celebrated before "foreign consular or diplomatic representations" thus excluding representations in countries belonging to the Commonwealth, *i.e.* Antigua and Barbuda, Australia, Bangladesh, Barbados, Belize, Botswana, Brunei, Cameroon, Canada, Cyprus, Dominica, Fiji, Ghana, Grenada, Guyana, India, Jamaica, Kenya, Kiribati, Lesotho, Malawi, Malaysia, Maldives, Malta, Mauritius, Mozambique, Namibia, Nauru, New Zealand, Nigeria, Pakistan, Papua New Guinea, Samoa, Seychelles, Sierra Leone, Singapore, Solomon Islands, South Africa, Sri Lanka, St. Kitts and Nevis, St. Lucia, St. Vincent and the Grenadines, Swaziland, The Bahamas, The Gambia, Tonga, Trinidad and Tobago, Tuvalu, Uganda, United Republic of Tanzania, Vanuatu, Zambia and Zimbabwe. Such an provision does not however apply to civil partnerships.

and diplomatic representations abroad are entitled to register civil partnerships if a number of conditions are satisfied,[265] namely that:

(a) one of the parties to the non-marital registered relationship is British,[266]
(b) the proposed civil partners would have been eligible to register as civil partners of each other in such part of the United Kingdom as it determined in accordance with the Order;
(c) the authorities of the country or territory in which it is proposed that they register as civil partners will not object to the registration;[267] and
(d) insufficient facilities exist for them to enter into an overseas relationship under the law of that country or territory.

Furthermore, **French** law specifically allows for a PACS to be concluded at a **French** consular or diplomatic representation abroad,[268] provided that this is permitted by the State in which the consular or diplomatic representation is to be found.[269] In this case, and in a similar manner to marriages, a **French** consular and diplomatic representation may only register a PACS agreement if one of the parties possesses **French** nationality.[270] According to MIGNOT since **French** law is applicable to two foreigners wishing to enter into a PACS in **France**, there is no reason to regulate otherwise for PACS[s] registered in **French** consulates abroad.[271]

According to Art. 44(2), Sw. CC, **Swiss** consular and diplomatic representations abroad are allowed to perform marriages if they have the

265 Regulated by Sec. 210, CPA 2004 and the power to regulate by Order in Council.

266 Sec. 210(2)(a), CPA 2004. A national is namely (a) a British citizen, a British Dependent Territories citizen, a British Overseas citizen or a British National (Overseas), (b) a British subject under the BNA 1981, or (c) a British protected person, within the meaning of that Act: Sec. 1(2), FMA 1892 as inserted by Sec. 1(2) of the FM(M)A 1988. For more information on British Dependent Territories see **Chapter VII.5.3.**

267 **Marriage:** FMO 1970; **Civil Partnership:** Sec. 210(2)(c), CPA 2004.

268 Art. 515(3)(8), Fr. CC.

269 DEVERS (2004) p. 265, §353.

270 Prior to 1901 both parties had to have French nationality: see the Fr. SC decision on the interpretation of Art. 48, Fr. CC, Fr. Cass., 1 Civ. Ch., 10th August 1819 (see BATIFFOL/LAGARDE (1983) p. 54, §423. However as a result of Act of the 29th November 1901, this is now possible should only one of the parties possess French nationality. Moreover, this amendment also stated that in order to celebrate such a marriage the consulate office must be granted permission. At present only the representations in Afghanistan, Cambodia, China, Egypt, Iraq, Iran, Japan, Laos, Lebanon, Morocco, Oman, Saudi Arabia, Syria, Thailand and Yemen. In contrast see MIGNOT (2001) p. 630 who argues that neither of the parties need possess the French nationality, so long as the parties have an intent to create legal relations with France.

271 MIGNOT (2001) p. 630.

required permission to do so.[272] In that case, Arts. 43 and 44, Sw. CPIL are applied analogously with the result that **Swiss** law will be applicable to questions of both formal and essential validity.[273] Moreover, Art. 63(2), Sw. OCS states that if the future spouses live abroad they will be entitled to present their marriage notice to the competent **Swiss** representation. According to Art. 73(2)(a), Sw. OCS, the notice of intent to marry must also be accompanied by a declaration that the marriage will be recognised by the State of the parties' domicile. At present **Swiss** consular and diplomatic representations abroad have not been provided with the required authorisation to perform registered partnerships.

Prior to the introduction of the Belg. CPIL, the ability for **Belgian** consular and diplomatic representations abroad to celebrate marriages was governed by Art. 170 *et seq.*, Belg. CC.[274] These rules resulted in the fact that marriages celebrated before a **Belgian** consular or diplomatic representation would be recognised as valid in **Belgium** if they satisfied **Belgian** law and involved at least one **Belgian** national.[275] Furthermore, the Receiving State must also accept such a registration.[276] At present, there is no clear guidance on the position of **Belgian** consular or diplomatic representations abroad with respect to the registration of statutory cohabitations.

X.4.2.2 Foreign consular or diplomatic representations

Only the **United Kingdom** appears to apply separate rules to non-marital registered relationships registered before foreign consular and diplomatic representations abroad. Nonetheless, the current law with regard to marriages celebrated in consulates and embassies is in a state of uncertainty and flux. The law was considered in *Radwan v. Radwan (No. 2).*

Radwan v. Radwan (No. 2)
In 1951, the husband, domiciled in Egypt married his wife, I, in Egypt in polygamous form. In 1952, he married his second wife, M, a woman domiciled in England, in the Egyptian Consulate General in Paris, in polygamous form and established their matrimonial home in Egypt. In 1953, the husband divorced his first wife, I, by *talak.*

---

272 At present that thus includes the representations in Cairo (Egypt), Baghdad (Iraq), Tehran (for Afghanistan), Damascus (Syria) and Beirut (Lebanon).

273 BUCHER (2004a) p. 38 and DUTOIT (2005) p. 146, Art. 43, No. 8.

274 As amended by the Act of 13th February 2003 opening marriage to couples of the same sex, *Belg. Staatsblad,* 28th February 2003. See also VAN HECKE/LENAERTS (1989) p. 222-223, §466-467.

275 ERAUW (2003) Ch 3: *De huwelijkssluiting,* §3, p. 3.

276 Art. 5f, 1963 Vienna Convention on Consular Relations; VAN HECKE/LENAERTS (1989) p. 222, §467.

In 1956, he and M came to live in England and acquired a domicil there. In 1970, the husband obtained a *talak* divorce from M in the Consulate General of the United Arab Emirates in London. M petitioned the English courts for divorce.[277]

CUMMING-BRUCE J. held that according to the **English** choice of law rules, although M did not have capacity to enter into a marriage according to **English** law, she did have capacity according to her intended matrimonial home, *i.e.* **Egyptian** law.[278] However, because the **Egyptian** Consulate was on **French** soil, it was **French** law that applied to the formal validity of the marriage, *i.e.* the *lex loci celebrationis*. As a result, the marriage was not valid. It would therefore appear that if the **United Kingdom** were to recognise non-marital relationships registered before foreign consular or diplomatic representations abroad, it would only do so if the relationship was valid according to the law of the place where the consular or diplomatic representation was situated (and thus not the law of the country which the consular or diplomatic representation represents).

X.4.3 EVALUATION

Consular or diplomatic representations are generally competent for all matters that are usually dealt with by the administration of the State represented. As well as providing general assistance to nationals abroad and foreigners wishing to receive information on their nation, consuls and diplomats are, under certain conditions and in certain circumstances, permitted to act as Registrars and thus celebrate marriages. Despite this authority the number of marriages celebrated before consular and diplomatic representations remains negligible. Nonetheless, rules have been developed to regulate such situations and allow for consular and diplomatic representations to also register non-marital relationships.

It would appear that those countries that allow for relationships to be registered on their own territory stipulate a number of general conditions, which in turn appear to provide a common core in this field. In order for a non-marital relationship registered at a consular or diplomatic representation to be recognised in the Receiving State, it must, in general, satisfy the following conditions:

---

277 *Radwan v. Radwan (No 2)* [1973] Fam 35.

278 [1973] Fam 35 at 53-54.

- Both of the parties must possess the nationality of the sending State;[279]
- The registration performed must be in accordance with the law of the sending State; and
- Neither party is a national, or a domiciliary in the case of the **United Kingdom**, of the State in which the consular or diplomatic representation is located.

In turning one's attention to the recognition of non-marital relationships registered before consular and diplomatic representations abroad, a similar common core is evident. It is true to say that the authority of the consular or diplomatic representation to celebrate marriages and act generally as a Registrar is based on notions of reciprocity and comity. It is therefore reasonable to expect that similar conditions be imposed on such relationships as those imposed above. Accordingly one is able to establish the following common principles:

- One of the parties must be a national of the State represented (although such a requirement is not applicable in **The Netherlands**);
- The relationship must be registered in accordance with the law of the State represented (subject to an element of doubt in the **United Kingdom**); and
- The State in which the representation is located must permit the registration.

It would therefore seem that although a common core of opinion is to be found, national variations still litter this field of law. For example, above and beyond these conditions, the **United Kingdom** also imposes the requirement that "insufficient facilities exist for [the parties] to enter into an overseas relationship". It is clear that this area is fraught with tension and poses a veritable political minefield. If the number of marriages celebrated before consular and diplomatic representations is negligible in comparison to the total number of marriages celebrated, the number of non-marital registered relationships will be even less. This difficulty does not however detract from the need to develop rules regulating such situations. However, with an eye on the difficulties posed and the intrinsic public law aspect of these rules, it is best to leave the particular conditions for registration to national law. These conditions need to form part of a

279 In **The Netherlands** this rule is less stringent requiring only one of the parties to possess the nationality of the sending State.

greater whole and although some uniformity of result can be extrapolated, such rules must be consistent with other domestic rules pertaining to consular and diplomatic representations.

X.5 PUBLIC POLICY EXCEPTION

It is clear that three distinct approaches can be identified in the seven jurisdictions studied in relation to public policy exceptions. Firstly, in those countries to have enacted codifications of private international law (**Belgium** and **Switzerland**), the public policy exception is contained in the general provisions of the codification.[280] No separate public policy exception is required, since these conditions have general working throughout the entire text of the Code. Secondly, in those countries without private international law codifications where separate legislation has been passed to deal with the issues raised by non-marital registered relationships (**The Netherlands** and the **United Kingdom**), a public policy exception is included in this legislation.[281] This highlights the existence of a public policy exception in relation to the recognition of foreign relationships and removes any doubt as to whether general public policy concepts apply. A third and final approach is also noticeable in the absence of either a general private international law codification or specific legislation in this field (**France**), where authors tend to rely on general principles of private international law to read a public policy exception into any recognition afforded to foreign non-marital registered relationships.[282]

Despite these structural differences, all three approaches make use of a public policy exception. In order to articulate the scope of such an exception, reference is often made, either directly or indirectly, to the equivalent public policy exception in the field of marriage. This section will not attempt to inventory all possible scenarios where the public policy exception may be used. In order to illustrate the possible use of this corrective measure, a number of particular situations have been selected on the basis of the differences in national legislation highlighted in **Chapter VIII**. Five situations will thus be discussed: firstly, non-marital registered relationships where one of the parties is a minor (**Section X.5.1.1**), secondly,

[280] **Bel.:** Art. 21, Belg. CPIL; **Swit.:** Arts. 17 and 18, Sw. CPIL. See further DUTOIT (2005) p. 67-75, Arts. 17 and 18.

[281] **Neth.:** Art. 3, Neth. PIL(RP)A. This is equivalent to Art. 6, PIL(M)A, which is referred to in order to assess the extent of this provision; **UK:** Sec. 218, CPA 2004.

[282] BATIFFOL/LAGARDE (1993) p. 567-594, §354-369; AUDIT (2000) p. 267-285, §300-316; LOUSSOUARN/BOUREL (2004) p. 333-361, §248-263.

non-marital registered relationships where the parties are related within the prohibited degrees of relationships proscribed by the law of the forum (**Section X.5.1.2**), thirdly, forced non-marital registered relationships (**Section X.5.1.3**), and finally, "polygamous"[283] non-marital registered relationships (**Section X.5.1.4**).

X.5.1 AGE REQUIREMENTS

As has been seen, all those countries studied in this book impose age requirements upon the registration of a non-marital relationship.[284] Although, these age requirements are, in themselves, not identical, a general common core is perceptible.[285] Age restrictions are accordingly imposed in the region of sixteen to eighteen years of age. In those cases where parties below the age of eighteen are permitted to enter into such relationships,[286] safeguards of parent consent or administrative permission are generally imposed. It would therefore be safe to say that non-marital relationships registered between parties above the age of sixteen in conformity with the law of the place of registration should be eligible for recognition. Those non-marital relationships registered whereby one of the parties is below this age may, however, for the same reasons espoused in relation to child marriages fall foul of the public policy exception.[287]

X.5.2 PROHIBITED DEGREES OF RELATIONSHIP

As has been seen, six of the seven jurisdictions studied in this book impose identical or almost identical prohibitions with respect to the degrees of relationships forbidden to register their relationship as those imposed on aspirant spouses.[288] However, as was seen in **Chapter III.4.6**, this is not the

---

283 The term "polygamous" has been inserted between inverted commas since etymologically speaking the word polygamous refers to marriages. Stemming from the Greek word *polugamos*: *polu* meaning much or often, and *gamos* meaning marrying. Although not a correct etymological use of the word, it clearly indicates the issue in question.

284 **Chapters III.4.4**, **IV.4.4**, **V.4.4**, **VI.4.4** and **VII.4.4.**

285 See **Chapter VIII.2.1**.

286 See in particular **The Netherlands** (**Chapter V.4.4**) and **England & Wales** and **Northern Ireland** (**Chapter VII.4.4**).

287 **Belg.**: *Belgian Senate*, 2003-2004, No. 3-27/7, p. 54; **Fr.**: AUDIT (2000) p. 542-3, §631; **Neth.**: Art. 3(1)(a), Neth. PIL(M)A (under the age of 15); **Swit.**: OTHENIN-GIRARD (1999a) p. 372-374, §582; **UK**: *Mohamed v. Knott* [1969] 1 QB 1, a marriage with a 13-year old girl was held to be valid. This rule holds true as long as neither of the parties as domiciled in a part of the **United Kingdom** and such relationships are accepted according to the *lex loci registrationis.*

288 **Chapters IV.4.6**, **V.4.6**, **VI.4.6** and **VII.4.6.**

case in **Belgium**. Thus although such relationships are permitted in **Belgium**, it is more than likely that many of the other six jurisdictions will refuse to recognise such relationships, whether between couples of the same or different-sex. The situation is, however, not as simple as it may at first seem.

In the **United Kingdom**, a distinction must be drawn between those relationships registered by **United Kingdom** domiciliaries and those not. It is provided that should a foreign non-marital relationship be registered between parties who are forbidden from doing so by the law of the part of the **United Kingdom** in which they are domiciled, such a relationship will not be recognised.[289] Nevertheless, should neither of the parties be domiciled in a part of the **United Kingdom**, it is submitted that their relationship may well be recognised if accepted in the place where it is registered.[290] In **France**, **Switzerland** and **The Netherlands**, on the other hand, these relationships will not be recognised.[291]

X.5.3 CONSENT REQUIREMENTS

As has been seen in **Chapter VIII.2**, all jurisdictions impose a condition of valid consent and competency on those wishing to register a non-marital relationship. Non-adherence to such a condition is sanctionable in all seven jurisdictions by annulment proceedings.[292] It is, therefore, to be predicted that a jurisdiction would utilise the public policy exception if consent was absent. This is, furthermore, supported with reference to the use of the public policy exception in the field of marriage.[293]

X.5.4 EXCLUSIVITY REQUIREMENTS

As has also been seen in **Chapter VIII.2**, one of the most fundamental conditions imposed on those wishing to register a non-marital relationship

---

289 Sec. 216, CPA 2004. See further **Section X.3.1.2**.

290 By analogy from *Cheni v. Cheni* [1965] P 85.

291 **Fr.:** Along similar lines to marriage: AUDIT (2000) p. 544, §634 and KESSLER (2004) p. 215, §373; **Neth.:** Art. 3, Neth. PIL(RP)A corresponds directly to Art. 6, Neth. PIL(M)A which implements 1978 Hague MC. Although Art. 11, 1978 Hague MC is not transposed, the **Dutch** Government saw that Art. 6, Neth. PIL(M)A was broad enough to cover such situations as was intended. Art. 11, 1978 Hague MC thus refers to marriages between relatives as a possible ground for a refusal to recognise; **Swit.:** OTHENIN-GIRARD (1999a) p. 371-2, §579.

292 See **Chapters III.6.6**, **IV.6.6**, **V.6.6**, **VI.6.6** and **VII.6.6**.

293 **Belg.:** reference; **Fr.:** AUDIT (2000) p. 543, §632; **Neth.:** Art. 3(1)(b), Neth. PIL(M)A; **Swit.:** HEINI *et al.* (1993) Art. 45, No. 4 (VOLKEN); OTHENIN-GIRARD (1999a) p. 372, §580; **UK:** NORTH/FAWCETT (1999) p. 733-734.

is that of exclusivity. "Polygamous" relationships are prohibited, whether the parties are already married or already involved in a non-marital registered relationship. However, despite these prohibitions, it is conceivable that in the future a country may enact legislation permitting polygamous non-marital registered relationships.[294] If such a situation where to arise, would resort be made to the public policy exception? It is suggested that countries would, and arguably should, adopt an identical approach to that taken in relation to polygamous marriages. Therefore, although prohibited in domestic law, the **United Kingdom**, **Belgium**, **France** and **Switzerland** would probably afford some degree of recognition to such relationships.[295] It must however be noted that for the foreseeable future this problem would be limited to the situation described in **Section X.3.3.1**.

X.5.5 DIFFERENT-SEX RELATIONSHIPS

Marriage, at least in those countries where different-sex non-marital registered relationships are prohibited, is only permitted between couples of different-sex. Granting recognition to foreign non-marital registered relationships between couples of different-sex could therefore be seen to undermine the institution of marriage, and hence be contrary to the strong public policy of the forum jurisdiction.[296] However, this argument is fundamentally flawed.[297] Recognition of a foreign institution does not necessarily mean that such a position need be adopted in domestic substantive rules. Take for instance the issue of polygamous marriages. In **Switzerland** and the **United Kingdom**, as has already been indicated, polygamous marriages, in certain cases will be recognised as valid marriages.[298] Despite the prohibition of celebrating polygamous marriages at substantive law, recognition of foreign polygamous marriages has not led to an undermining *per se* of the institution of marriage. It is further tantamount to ludicrous to argue that the recognition of different-sex relationships is contrary to domestic public policy.[299]

---

294 Although this possibility is highly unlikely when one considers that the majority of countries permitting polygamous marriages are Islamic States. The tolerance afforded to same-sex couples by these States is negligible. See **Chapter I.8**.

295 In **The Netherlands** such relationships would be refused recognition on similar grounds to those expounded in Art. 3(1)(e), Neth. PIL(M)A.

296 In **Switzerland** it could even be said to be unconstitutional: Art. 14, Sw. FC.

297 See **Chapters VIII.2.4 and IX.3.4, IX.3.5, IX.4** and **IX.5.5**.

298 **Swit.:** OTHENIN-GIRARD (1999a) p. 425, §683; **UK:** NORTH/FAWCETT (1999) p. 755-760.

299 See, for example, the conclusions drawn by OTHENIN-GIRARD on this point with respect to **Switzerland**: OTHENIN-GIRARD (1999a).

It would, after all, be difficult for a judge to argue that the recognition of a committed, intimate relationship between one man and one woman to the exclusion of all others registered abroad in accordance with the law is contrary to public policy. If the domestic concept of public policy is to be understood as narrower in private international law than in internal law, it is unjustifiable, even in the light of the constitutional protection afforded to marriage, to deny recognition to such relationships.[300] By imposing residency requirements on those wishing to register a non-marital relationship, one ensures that the parties have a connection to the jurisdiction in which they register their relationship. In combining this restriction with a provision refusing to recognise those relationships registered abroad on fraudulent purposes, different-sex relationship validly registered abroad pose absolutely no threat to the domestic institution of marriage, and cannot therefore be said to be contrary to public policy.

However, even if these relationships are to be recognised, the question remains exactly how such recognition would take place. Serious practical problems may be encountered by Registrars and courts in trying to find a suitable equivalent status. In those countries were domestic registration is restricted to same-sex couples new official forms will need to be created. Therefore, although different-sex relationships may not directly be deemed contrary to public policy, such relationships could lead to such serious practical problems which could in turn endanger their recognition. It is, therefore, crucial that when different-sex couples register their relationships they are adequately advised of the risks that their relationship may not be recognised beyond national borders.

X.5.6 EVALUATION

This section has not attempted to inventory all those cases in which public policy may or may not be used. The aim of this section has been simply to identify whether such possibilities exist, when they might apply and to which fields of private international law. The public policy exception should be used sparingly and the cases illustrated here indicate the limited boundaries of such an exception.

However, it is important to note that public policy is not the only exception mechanism in the field of private international law. Exceptions to any choice of law rules developed in relation to non-marital registered

---

300 *Vervaeke v. Smith* [1983] 1 AC 145 at 164 (*per* Lord SIMON).

relationships exist and thus could lead to a different law being applied than the one designated by virtue of such rules. It is also important to note that in a statutory system of private international law a balance between legal certainty and flexibility must be struck and can best be achieved by including pressure valves such a general exception clause. The need for such a corrective mechanism is evident when, under the rules of private international law, it would be inappropriate to apply the law designated. Although the arguments against the inclusion of such an exception clause in the rules of private international law cannot be ignored (*i.e.* of the inherent uncertainty which such a clause introduces),[301] the arguments in favour of such a principle are convincing and are on the whole supported, in one form or another, in all the jurisdictions studied in this book. Nevertheless, it is submitted that such a rule remains the domain of the general provisions of private international law and should not be supplemented with a specific clause with respect to non-marital registered relationships.[302]

X.6 SUMMARY OF CONCLUSIONS

The novelty of non-marital registered relationship forms poses one of the greatest challenges to the field of private international law. How can one sustain reference to the traditional connecting factors in the field of family law and personal status in light of the frequent denial by many countries to recognise such institutions? The answer is clear. References to the parties' nationality, domicile or habitual residence should, for the time being, be put to one side and replaced with reference to the place where the relationship was registered. In this way, a simple, easy-to-apply choice of law can be developed referring both questions of essential validity and formal validity to the *lex loci registrationis.*

In mirroring this approach with respect to non-marital relationships registered abroad, a similar recognition rule should be developed. In this way, non-marital relationships validly registered in a foreign jurisdiction should be deemed valid everywhere, subject to a public policy exception and general exception clauses. Although opponents to such a liberal recognition scheme point to problems of forum shopping, these issues can be readily solved if countries introduce national residency requirements before parties are allowed to register their relationship, thus ensuring a suitable link with the country in which the relationship is registered.

---

301 See, for example, GUTZWILLER, mentioned in MEYER (1994) p. 301.

302 See, for example, KOKKINI-IATRIDOU (1994).

Moreover, one must not forget the particular problems in the field of non-marital registered relationships especially with respect to multiple registrations nor the more general topics of private international law, such as the meaning of "law" in the field of recognition and the approach to be taken with respect to the incidental question.

Furthermore, in adopting such simple, straightforward choice of law and recognition rules, one must take into consideration that certain relationships may be registered at consular or diplomatic representations, in which case special rules would need to be created, which in turn should need to conform with the rules laid down in the 1963 Vienna Convention on Consular Relations promulgated by the United Nations.

CHAPTER XI
DISSOLUTION OF A NON-MARITAL REGISTERED RELATIONSHIP

XI.1 INTRODUCTION

Although one should never underestimate the importance of the schemes regulating non-marital registered relationships, it is not true to say that they are the panacea to the problems of unmarried same-sex or different-sex couples. Once registered, couples do not necessarily live "happily ever after". If these relationships do break down, questions may arise with respect to international jurisdiction (**Section XI.2**), the applicable law (**Section XI.3**) or the recognition and enforcement of a dissolution order obtained abroad (**Section XI.4**). Although it is important to note that ancillary proceedings often form the crux issue in many cases, these matters will be dealt with, *inter alia*, in **Chapter XII**. **Section XI.5** is devoted to the corrective measures available in this field.

XI.2 INTERNATIONAL JURISDICTION

XI.2.1 BRUSSELS IIBIS REGULATION

On the 1st March 2001, a new European Union Regulation, the so-called Brussels II Regulation (hereinafter Brussels II), entered into force, affecting the practice of every family lawyer in every Member State of the European Union (except Denmark).[1] The Regulation was, however, the subject of widespread criticism and has subsequently been amended and extended.[2] As

1 Council Regulation (EC) No. 1347/2000 of 29th May 2000 on jurisdiction and the recognition and enforcement of judgments in matrimonial matters and in matters of parental responsibility for children of both spouses. **Denmark** is excluded from the applicability of the Regulation by virtue of Art. 1(3). Obviously **Switzerland** also falls outside the territorial scope of the Brussels II. The **Swiss** jurisdictional rules will be dealt with in **Section XI.2.2.4**. Brussels II replaces the 1998 Brussels II Convention, which never came into force. See further COLLINS (2004) p. 217 and JÄNTERÄ-JAREBORG (1999).

2 Within two months of publication, requests were already submitted for the repeal and/or amendment of the Brussels II Regulation: Initiative of the French Republic with a view to adopting a Council Regulation on the mutual enforcement of judgments in rights of access

of the 1st March 2005, Brussels II has been replaced by a new Regulation (hereinafter Brussels IIbis), which, although substantially amending the rules relating to parental responsibility,[3] has left the jurisdictional and recognition rules on marriage dissolution virtually intact. The scope of Brussels IIbis will be discussed first (**Section XI.2.1.1**),[4] before providing a brief sketch of the jurisdictional rules themselves (**Section XI.2.1.2**).

XI.2.1.1 Scope of Brussels IIbis

Since Brussels IIbis only covers proceedings relating to the termination of the marital bond,[5] it would seem that this Regulation does not affect the new institutions dealt with in this book.[6] This point of view is reinforced with reference to the ECJ decision in *D and Kingdom of Sweden v. Council*.[7] In this case the ECJ stated that the definition of "marriage" as generally accepted in the Member States referred to a union between two persons of a different sex.[8] Although noting the increasing number of countries to introduce registration schemes allowing for same-sex couples to register their relationships, such schemes, it was felt, were different from marriage. In such circumstances, the ECJ did not feel that the two situations could be treated identically and thus rejected the appeal.[9] Accordingly, if the registration of a non-marital relationship cannot be accorded the same

---

to children, 15th August 2000, *OJ*, C-234, p. 7; Proposal for a Council Regulation concerning jurisdiction and the recognition and enforcement of judgements in matrimonial matters and in matters of parental responsibility repealing Regulation (EC) No. 1347/2000 and amending Regulation (EC) No. 44/2001 in matters relating to maintenance, 17th May 2002, COM (2002) 222. For criticism of the process through which Brussels II was adopted, see BOELE-WOELKI (1998).

3 See **Chapter XII.3.1**.

4 Although many problems have been noted as regards the interplay between Regs. 6 and 7, Brussels IIbis, this will not be addressed here. For further information see T. DE BOER (2002) p. 320-323 and references.

5 BORRÁS REPORT, *Explanatory report on the Convention, drawn up on the basis of Article K.3 of the Treaty on European Union, on Jurisdiction and the Recognition and Enforcement of Judgments in Matrimonial Matters*, 16th July 1998, *OJ*, 98/C-221/04, §22.

6 Throughout this section reference made to marriage dissolution should be understood to include divorce, judicial separation and declarations of annulment. Before a divorce can be decreed, it must first be proven that there has been a valid marriage (more often than not this is simply a formality). For further information on this issue see **Chapter X.3**.

7 ECJ, *D and Sweden v. Council*, Case No. 122/99 and 125/99P [2001] I ECR 4319. Art 1(2), Annex VII, EC Staff Regulations stipulated that a household allowance shall be granted to, *inter alia*, a "married official". Unmarried officials are also able to claim an allowance if they can prove that they have assumed familial responsibility. The applicant refused, however, to claim on this basis.

8 ECJ, *D and Sweden v. Council*, Case No. 122/99 and 125/99P [2001] I ECR 4319, §34.

9 For further analysis, see BODGAN (2001a) p. 171-175.

treatment as the celebration of a marriage, neither can the dissolution of such a relationship and a divorce. Accordingly, the dissolution of a non-marital registered relationship does not fall within the material scope of Brussels IIbis.[10] Nonetheless, Brussels IIbis could serve as a possible template for the creation of similar rules. It is hence necessary to examine the relevant jurisdictional rules laid down by Brussels IIbis.

XI.2.1.2 Jurisdictional Rules

The criteria for determining jurisdiction are listed in Art. 3, Brussels IIbis. In supporting the arguments forwarded by DE BOER and MOSTERMANS,[11] it is more logical and more systematic to outline these jurisdictional grounds according to the following four criteria:

1. The respondent is habitually resident in the forum state.[12]
2. The petitioner is habitually resident in the forum state, *and*
    a. both spouses had their last habitual residence there,[13] *or*
    b. the petitioner resided there for at least one year,[14] *or*
    c. the petitioner resided there for at least six months and is a national of that state.[15]
3. In the case of a joint petition, either spouse is habitually resident in the forum state.[16]
4. Both spouses are nationals of the forum State or domiciled there.[17]

XI.2.2 DOMESTIC JURISDICTIONAL RULES FOR MARRIAGE DISSOLUTION[18]

If, however, the forum court has no jurisdiction according to Brussels IIbis and there is no other Member State that would have jurisdiction under

---

10 This opinion is shared by FULCHIRON (2000) p. 901; JESSURUN D'OLIVEIRA (2000b) p. 531-533 and (2001a) p. 207-208; HUET (2002) p. 551; DEVERS (2004) p. 307-312, §507-509; REINHARTZ (2004) p.495. See also *Dutch Second Chamber*, 2002-2003, 28924, No. 3, p. 8. For a detailed discussion of the similarity in the field of legal effects see **Chapter VIII.4.1**.

11 T. DE BOER (2002) p. 316; MOSTERMANS (2003) p. 12-14.

12 Art. 3(1)(a)(1) and (3), Brussels IIbis.

13 Art. 3(1)(a)(2), Brussels IIbis.

14 Art. 3(1)(a)(5), Brussels IIbis.

15 Art. 3(1)(a)(6), Brussels IIbis.

16 Art. 3(1)(a)(4), Brussels IIbis.

17 Art. 3(1)(b), Brussels IIbis. The term domicile is applied in the case of the UK and Ireland.

18 The term "domestic" is used in this chapter to refer to those cases falling outside the scope of Brussels IIbis.

Brussels IIbis,[19] a Member State must refer to its traditional rules of jurisdiction.[20] In attempting to craft similar jurisdictional rules for the dissolution of non-marital registered relationships, it is important to also analyse these domestic jurisdictional rules. The complexity of the rules in this field and the associated difficulties in attempting a simultaneous comparison necessitate a country-by-country analysis.

XI.2.2.1 Belgium

Since 1st October 2004,[21] the exorbitant jurisdictional ground based on the respondent's **Belgian** nationality has been removed.[22] Although in **Belgium** the rules of Brussels IIbis are not *mutatis mutandis* applicable to cases falling outside of its scope, a similar array of jurisdictional bases is created by virtue of Arts. 5 and 42, Belg. CPIL.[23] An interesting dichotomy is hereby created with the traditional jurisdictional rules being both broader[24] and narrower at the same time.[25] Nonetheless, the similarities between the traditional jurisdictional rules in **Belgian** law and the grounds available under Brussels IIbis should not be underestimated.[26]

---

19 Art. 17, Brussels IIbis. If another Member State does have jurisdiction under the Regulation, the court seized should declare on its own motion that it does not have jurisdiction.

20 Art. 7(1), Brussels IIbis.

21 ERAUW (2004) p. 126.

22 Art. 15, Belg. CC. See further VANDER ELST/WEBER (1985) p. 416-417, §113.1.2; VAN HECKE/LENAERTS (1989) p. 35, §86 and HEYVAERT (2002) p. 85, §199. Art. 14, Belg. CC (jurisdiction on the basis of the applicant's **Belgian** nationality) was abolished in 1949, although was still in operation in the field of personal status and capacity by virtue of Art. 3(3), Belg. CC. See further RIGAUX/FALLON (1993) p. 200-201, §818.

23 Art. 42, Belg. CPIL must be read in conjunction with Arts. 2 and 5, Belg. CPIL. Art. 2, Belg. CPIL provides for the superiority of European and international instruments while Art. 5, Belg. CPIL provides for the general grounds of jurisdiction based on the respondent's residence or habitual residence.

24 Art. 5, Belg. CPIL refers for example to the "residence" of the respondent and not merely his or her habitual residence.

25 There is, for example, no equivalent to the limited *forum actoris* grounds provided for in Arts. 3(1)(a)(2) and 3(1)(a)(6), Brussels IIbis. Art. 42(2), Belg. CPIL provides a similar ground to that in Art. 3(1)(a)(2), Brussels IIbis, although this is nonetheless more restrictive. According to Art. 42(2), Belg. CPIL the Belgian courts are competent if the last HR of the parties was in Belgium, no more than twelve months prior to the commencement of proceedings. No such time restraint is evident in Art. 3(1)(a)(2).

26 This was indeed one of the aims of the codification, to ensure that national legislation mirrored as far as possible discernible trends in European and international private international law instruments: ERAUW (2004) p. 124 .

XI.2.2.2 France

International jurisdiction is determined in accordance with a number of different procedural provisions. According to Art. 1070, Fr. NCCP a jurisdictional ladder is created by which jurisdiction is allocated on a hierarchical basis.[27] Although at first sight it would appear only to apply to the assignment of internal jurisdiction, this provision has also been held to apply bilaterally and assign international jurisdiction to a **French** judge.[28] Competency is thus allocated to the court of the familial residence, or if the parties have separated, to the court of the place where the spouse with custody of the children lives, or in all other cases the court of the residence (*résidence*) of the respondent spouse.[29] This residual category corresponds closely to the jurisdictional ground laid down in Art. 42, Fr. NCCP, which grants jurisdiction to the courts of the respondent's abode (*demeure*).[30] Furthermore, in cases of a joint petition, the parties are entitled to file for marriage dissolution in either spouse's residence.[31] Nonetheless, even if a **French** court is not competent on any of these bases, Arts. 14 and 15, Fr. CC provide for exorbitant jurisdictional grounds on the basis of the applicant's or respondent's **French** nationality.[32]

XI.2.2.3 The Netherlands

In **The Netherlands** the international jurisdictional rules of Brussels IIbis have been extended analogously to all divorce cases.[33] Accordingly, despite the difference in legal source, one set of international jurisdictional grounds

---

27 See further LOUSSOUARN/BOUREL (2004) p. 606-607 and AUDIT (2000) p. 306-307, §340.

28 See Fr. Cass., 1 Civ. Ch., 13th January 1981 (*De Bendern*) (1981) *Rev. crit. DIP* 331, annotated GAUDEMET-TALLON (critical) and (1981) *JDI* 360, annotated HUET (supportive).

29 The same rules are also applicable to judicial separations (Art. 1139, Fr. NCCP) and the conversion of a legal separation into a divorce (Art. 1141, Fr. NCCP).

30 The term residence is defined with reference to Art. 43, Fr. NCCP, namely in relation to a physical person, the place where he or she is domiciled or in the absence thereof the place where he or she resides.

31 Art. 1070(2), Fr. NCCP.

32 See, for example, Fr. Cass., 1 Civ. Ch., 9th July 1991 (1992) *D* 334, annotated MASSIP, (1992) II *JCP Éd. G.* 21818, annotated MUIR-WATT and Fr. Cass., 1 Civ. Ch., 6th December 1988 (1989) *D* 257, annotated AUDIT, (1989) II *JCP Éd. G.* 21270, annotated CADIET, (1989) 2 *Gaz. Pal.* 264, annotated MASSIP. See further AUDIT (2000) p. 315 *et seq*, §350 *et seq*.

33 On the 1st January 2002, Art. 4(1), Neth. CCP was enacted and replaced Art. 814, Neth. CCP. See MOSTERMANNS (2003) p. 2, §5. Although this Article provides for the direct application of Arts. 2, 5 and 6, Brussels II in all cases, as of the 1st March 2005 this must be read as meaning Arts. 3, 4 and 5, Brussels IIbis. These changes will be implemented soon: *Dutch Second Chamber*, 2004-2005, 29980, No. 2, proposed Art. 28.

has been created applicable in all cases.[34] Although there have been calls to introduce the possibility to recognise a forum choice by the parties for **The Netherlands**, this has as yet not been followed up with legislative action.[35]

XI.2.2.4 Switzerland

According to Art. 59(a), Sw. CPIL, a **Swiss** court is competent to hear a divorce or legal separation if the respondent has his or her domicile in **Switzerland**.[36] Furthermore, a **Swiss** court will also be competent if an applicant has his or her domicile in **Switzerland** and has either lived in **Switzerland** for at least one year or is a **Swiss** national.[37] In reading these provisions in conjunction with Art. 20(2), Sw. CPIL, one can also replace the notion of domicile with that of habitual residence, if a party is deemed not to have a domicile anywhere.[38] Moreover, as a result of the recent revision of divorce legislation, it is now possible to commence a divorce procedure by means of joint petition.[39] BUCHER, among others, has called for Art. 59, Sw. CPIL to be interpreted to allow for the **Swiss** domicile of either spouse to be sufficient for establishing jurisdiction in these cases.[40]

If the spouses are not domiciled or habitually resident in **Switzerland** but one of the spouses is a **Swiss** national,[41] Art. 60, Sw. CPIL grants jurisdiction to the courts of the place of origin of the **Swiss** spouse,[42] so long as the parties are confronted with the *impossibilité ou grande difficulté d'accéder à la justice* in the State of the parties' domicile.[43] It would appear that the **Swiss** authorities must also take into account whether a divorce decree

34 Although these grounds may be the same, the difference in legal source is important in terms of the exclusive nature of Brussels IIbis, as well as the interpretation power granted to the ECJ by virtue of Brussels IIbis.

35 T. DE BOER (1996) p. 67-88 and MOSTERMANS (2001) p. 303.

36 PATOCCHI/GEISINGER (1995) Art. 59, p. 213; SIEHR (2002) p. 50-51; BUCHER (2004a) p. 105; BUCHER/BONOMI (2004) p. 184-185, §671-674; DUTOIT (2005) p. 194 *et seq*, Art. 59, No. 1.

37 Art. 59(b), Sw. CPIL.

38 Art. 59(b), Sw. CPIL in conjunction with Art. 20(2), Sw. CPIL (marriage). See further BONOMI (2002) p. 251 and DUTOIT (2005) p. 86, Art. 20, No. 10.

39 See **Chapter VII.6.2**.

40 BUCHER (2001) p. 26; BONOMI (2002) p. 252; DUTOIT (2005) p. 197, Art. 59, No. 8bis.

41 In the case of double nationality, possession of **Swiss** nationality is sufficient (Art. 23(1), Sw. CPIL). See DUTOIT (2005) p. 91, Art. 23, No. 1.

42 See further BUCHER/BONOMI (2004) p. 156, §157 and BUCHER (2004a) p. 115, §327.

43 BONOMI (2002) p. 253; SIEHR (2002) p. 50-51; BUCHER (2004a) p. 110, §293; BUCHER/BONOMI (2004) p. 184-185, §671-674; DUTOIT (2005) p. 198-199, Art. 60, No. 1-3. This option is also open to the foreign spouse of a **Swiss** national: BUCHER (2004a) p. 109, §290. The exact boundaries of the notion of "impossibility" and "unreasonable effects" is dealt with extensively by BUCHER (2004a) p. 110-111, §293-299.

granted in **Switzerland** would in fact be recognised in the place of domicile of the parties.[44] Furthermore, **Swiss** law also provides for a *forum necessitatis* by virtue of Art. 3, Sw. CPIL.[45] In this way, even if the **Swiss** courts are not granted competency on the basis of Arts. 59 and 60, Sw. CPIL, a **Swiss** court may still declare itself competent if a procedure abroad is impossible or it cannot be reasonably required of the parties to proceed abroad. This provision must, however, be interpreted extremely restrictively and should only be used in limited circumstances.[46]

Unlike for divorce, the **Swiss** Code of Private International Law does not provide for jurisdictional rules governing the annulment of a marriage. As a result, the rules applicable to divorces are generally applied analogously.[47]

XI.2.2.5 United Kingdom

In the **United Kingdom** different jurisdictional rules apply depending upon the means by which the marriage is terminated. Three categories of jurisdictional rules can thus be distinguished: (1) divorce and legal separation, (2) nullity and (3) presumption of death. In dealing with divorce and legal separation first, in non-Brussels IIbis cases,[48] a **British** court[49] is only competent if either of the parties to the marriage is domicilied in a part of the **United Kingdom** on the date when the proceedings are begun.[50]

---

44 SIEHR (2002) p. 51.

45 BUCHER (2004a) p. 109, §291; DUTOIT (2005) p. 8-9, Art. 3.

46 PATOCCHI/GEIZINGER (1995) p. 78-80, Art. 3; BUCHER (2004a) p. 109, §291 and DUTOIT (2005) p. 8-9, Art. 3, No. 5. For a case in which this ground was rejected see Tribunal Zurich, 27th August 1990 (1990) *BIZR* 139, No. 65.

47 BUCHER (2004a) p. 69, §164; DUTOIT (2005) p. 144-145, Art. 43, No. 2 and references.

48 These Regulations have been implemented in the **UK** by virtue of: *Brussels II* - European Communities (Matrimonial Jurisdiction and Judgments) Regulations 2001, SI 2001, No. 310; European Communities (Matrimonial Jurisdiction and Judgments)(Scotland) Regulations 2001, SSI 2001, No. 36; European Communities (Matrimonial Jurisdiction and Judgments)(Northern Ireland) Regulations 2001, SI 2001, No. 660; and *Brussels IIbis* - European Communities (Jurisdiction and Judgments in Matrimonial and Parental Responsibility Matters) Regulations 2005, SI 2005, No. 265 and The European Communities (Jurisdiction and Judgments in Matrimonial and Parental Responsibility Matters)(Scotland) Regulations 2005, SSI 2005, No. 42.

49 Sch. 1 (**England & Wales**) and Sch. 3 (**Scotland**), DMPA 1973 also provides for the situation when a court within the **United Kingdom** is already seized. In **England & Wales** the matrimonial proceedings are stayed, whereas in **Scotland** the consistorial proceedings are sisted. For **Northern Ireland** see Schedule 1, MC(NI)O 1978.

50 **Eng.**: Sec. 5(2), DMPA 1973; **NI.**: Art. 49(2)(b), MC(NI)O 1978; **Scot.**: Sec. 7(3), DMPA 1973 (Court of Session) and Sec. 8(2), DMPA 1973 (Sherrifs court). In the sherrifs court either party must also have been (i) a resident in the sheriffdom for a period of forty days ending with that date, or (ii) had been resident in the sheriffdom for a period of not less

Domicil also forms the keystone to jurisdiction with respect to nullity. A court in the **United Kingdom** will thus be competent to hear a case if either of the parties to the marriage is domiciled in the relevant part of the **United Kingdom** or died before the action was commenced and either was domiciled in the relevant part of the **United Kingdom** at the date of death, or had been habitually resident there for at least one year prior to the date of death.[51] A similar jurisdictional structure is also crafted with respect to proceedings for the presumption of death, namely that the court shall have jurisdiction if the petitioner is domiciled in the relevant part of the **United Kingdom** on the date when the proceedings are begun, or was habitually resident in the relevant part of the **United Kingdom** throughout the period of one year ending with that date.[52]

XI.2.3 DOMESTIC JURISDICTIONAL RULES FOR DISSOLUTION OF NON-MARITAL REGISTERED RELATIONSHIPS

In some countries specific jurisdictional rules have been enacted dealing with the dissolution of non-marital registered relationships, whereas this is not the case in others. Once again due to the complexity of this field of law and the subtle differences in national legislation, this section has been dealt with on a country-by-country basis.

XI.2.3.1 Belgium

Due to the initial characterisation of non-marital registered relationships in **Belgium** between those akin to marriage and those not akin to marriage,[53] two sets of jurisdictional regimes are established. Those non-marital registered relationships akin to marriage are characterised as marriages. The same jurisdictional rules are thus applied to the dissolution of non-marital registered relationships as are applied to marriage dissolutions.[54] Non-marital registered relationships not akin to marriage are, however, subject to a further distinction depending on whether the relationship was registered in **Belgium**. As a result the following structure can be discerned:

than forty days ending not more than forty days before the said date, and has no known residence in **Scotland** at that date.

51 **Eng.**: Sec. 5(3)(b), DMPA 1973; **NI.**: Art. 49(3)(b), MC(NI)O 1978; **Scot.**: Sec. 7(3A), DMPA 1973 (Court of Session only).

52 **Eng.**: Sec. 5(4), DMPA 1973; **NI.**: Art. 49(4), MC(NI)O 1978; **Scot.**: Sec. 1(3), PD(S)A 1977.

53 See **Chapter IX.3.1**.

54 See **Section XI.2.2.1**.

As a result, only dissolutions of non-marital registered relationships not akin to marriage and registered in **Belgium**, *i.e.* the dissolution of statutory cohabitations, are subject to different jurisdictional rules. In these cases,[55] the **Belgian** administrative authorities are always competent.[56] As a result of this distinction, and despite the fact that a **Belgian** court is not competent to dissolve a **Belgian** statutory cohabitation,[57] the court is declared exclusively competent to dissolve non-marital relationships not akin to marriage that have been registered abroad.[58] In practice this means that should a couple having entered into a **French** PACS wish to dissolve their relationship in **Belgium** they must go to the **Belgian** courts and not to the administrative authorities competent to dissolve a **Belgian** statutory cohabitation.

XI.2.3.2 France

As was already illustrated in **Chapter IV.6.2** and **IV.6.3**, according to **French** law non-marital registered relationships cannot be dissolved judicially. However, although not competent to dissolve relationships registered domestically, the question arises whether a French court is competent to dissolve a relationship registered abroad? One option is for the **French** court to declare itself *forum non conveniens* to pronounce the dissolution of a non-marital relationship registered abroad.[59] Alternatively, the court, once seized, could simply apply **French** law. The problem here would be that the **French** court would then need to perform a procedure that according to **French** law falls outside the court's competency.[60] Regardless of these problems, it would appear that the majority of French authors believe that the courts should, in principle, be competent to dissolve such relationships.

Although a recent proposal has been published by the Ministry of Justice aimed at reforming the law surrounding the PACS legislation, both at substantive and private international law level, no reference to the rules of international jurisdiction in cases of relationship dissolution were

---

55 *I.e.* the dissolution of a statutory cohabitation.

56 Art. 59(3), Belg. CPIL.

57 On the absence of judicial procedures to dissolve the statutory cohabitation, see **Chapter III.6.2** and **III.6.3**.

58 *Belg. Staatsblad,* 28th September 2004, p. 69606, §M.2. Obviously subject to the applicable choice of law rules and public policy discussed in **Section XI.3** and **XI.5**.

59 KESSLER (2004) p. 353-354, §618.

60 It could be argued, as KESSLER does, that in doing so the court would apply a similar procedure to that available in divorce cases, although this is in effect giving indirect recognition to same-sex marriages: KESSLER (2004) p. 355, §619.

included.[61] In the absence of explicit rules, it is therefore necessary to delve into current academic opinion on the matter. Firstly, it is explicitly stated that Art. 1070, Fr. NCCP is only applicable to divorces and thus these jurisdictional grounds are not applicable to the dissolution of non-marital registered relationships.[62] Nonetheless, some authors have pleaded for a widening of the scope of this Article not only to non-marital registered relationships but also to non-registered cohabiting relationships.[63]

Regardless of whether Art. 1070, Fr. NCCP is applicable, the majority of academic opinion supports the idea that Art. 42, Fr. NCCP is applicable in such cases, providing a party with recourse to the **French** courts if the respondent has his or her abode (*demeure*) in **France**.[64] Although some authors suggest the use of Art. 46, Fr. NCCP,[65] this provision deals exclusively with issues of contract and tort and hence as a result of the proposed characterisation would not be suitable for determining these issues.[66] In the absence of any other jurisdictional grounds the court can resort to Arts. 14 and 15, Fr. CC, providing the French courts with jurisdiction if either of the parties is a **French** national.[67]

XI.2.3.3 The Netherlands

The Netherlands is perhaps the best example of a country that has strived for simplicity in the field of international jurisdiction. By virtue of Art. 4(4), Neth. CCP, the rules of Brussels IIbis are *mutatis mutandis* applicable to all questions of international jurisdiction with respect to the dissolution of non-marital registered relationships. In this way, **The Netherlands** endorses one set of jurisdictional rules applicable in all situations; the same grounds apply whether inside or outside the scope of Brussels IIbis and whether dealing with marriage or non-marital registered relationships. Alongside these rules, **Dutch** law also provides for the residuary jurisdiction of **Dutch**

61 MINISTRE DE LA JUSTICE (2004).

62 HUET (2002) p. 551-552 and DEVERS (2004) p. 317, §517. This can also be derived from the explicit application of Art. 1070, Fr. NCCP to judicial separations (Art. 1139, Fr. NCCP) and the conversion of judicial separations into divorces (Art. 1141, Fr. NCCP)

63 DEVERS (2004) p. 319, §522 and references.

64 KHAIRALLAH (2001) p. 328, §21; HUET (2002) p. 552; DEVERS (2004) p. 316, §516.

65 LEMOULAND (2000) p. 408; REVILLARD (2000) p. 337 *et seq*; HAUSER (2001) p. 673 *et seq.*

66 See further **Chapter IX.2.**

67 DEVERS (2004) p. 318, §518.

courts if the relationship was registered in **The Netherlands**.[68] In this way, **Dutch** law recognises the need for a *forum necessitatis*.[69]

Furthermore, as a result of the passing of the Neth. PIL(RP)A, Art. 1:80c, Neth. CC has also been amended so as to provide a general rule of competency for the **Dutch** Registrar of Births, Deaths, Marriages and Registered Partnerships with respect to the administrative dissolution of non-marital registered relationships.[70] Art. 1:80c(2), Neth. CC now provides that the **Dutch** Registrar is competent on identical grounds to those laid down in Brussels IIbis,[71] thus furthering the simplicity in jurisdictional grounds for relationship breakdown in **The Netherlands**.

XI.2.3.4 Switzerland

The general analogous application of the private international law rules on marriage to non-marital registered relationships is also adopted with respect to issues of international jurisdiction in cases involving the dissolution of the relationship.[72] Although the rules are in fact identical, it is to be expected that in relation to the dissolution of non-marital registered relationships, more frequent resort will be made to Art. 60, Sw. CPIL due to the limited acceptability of such relationships abroad.[73] Nonetheless, the **Swiss** legislature has recognised the possibility that persons having registered their relationship in **Switzerland** may end up without recourse to a forum to dissolve their relationship, and has thus created a restricted *forum necessitatis*.[74] If neither of the partners are **Swiss**, nor domiciled in **Switzerland**, but the non-marital relationship was registered in **Switzerland**, then the **Swiss** courts will be competent to hear a case for dissolution, if such a petition is not possible before a court of either parties' domicile or such a procedure cannot be reasonably expected of the parties.[75]

---

68 Last sentence, Art. 4(4), Neth. CCP.

69 *Dutch Second Chamber*, 1999-2000, 26855, No. 3, p. 33 and thus following the advice of the **Dutch** Standing Committee on Private International Law, see STAATSCOMMISSIE (1998) p. 35. Such a solution has also found academic support, *e.g.* JOPPE (2000b) p. 393-394 and MOSTERMANS (2001) p. 304.

70 For this procedure see **Chapter V.6.4**.

71 Art. 1:80c(2), Neth CC refers to Art. 4(4), Neth. CCP, which in turn refers to Art. 4(1), Neth. CCP and thus to the application of the jurisdictional grounds stated in Brussels IIbis.

72 Art. 65a, Sw. CPIL.

73 GIRSBERGER/DROESE (2001) p. 96.

74 Art. 65b, Sw. CPIL. See also DUTOIT (2005) p. 223-224, Art. 65b, No. 3.

75 FF 2003, p. 1192 at 1260. See further BUCHER (2004a) p. 582-583, §582-585. The similarities between this Article and Art. 60, Sw. CPIL are marked, but Art. 65b, Sw. CPIL deals with those cases in which neither party is a **Swiss** national.

Due to the absence of jurisdictional rules for the annulment of a marriage, the analogous reference to Chapter 3, Sw. CPIL provided by Art. 65a, Sw. CPIL yields no direct results with respect to the jurisdictional rules applicable for the annulment of a registered partnership. According to the mainstay of **Swiss** academic opinion, it is assumed that the same rules will apply to the annulment of a registered partnership as to the annulment of a marriage.[76]

XI.2.3.5 United Kingdom

By virtue of Sec. 219, CPA 2004, the Lord Chancellor and the Scottish Ministers are granted the power to make provision by means of regulations as to the jurisdiction of **United Kingdom** courts in proceedings for the dissolution or annulment of a civil partnership.[77] At present, no such power has been exercised and thus the only grounds of jurisdiction are those expounded in Chapter 3, Part 5, CPA 2004. The CPA 2004 has sought to achieve total harmony between the jurisdictional rules applicable to civil partners and those in marriage. As a result the traditional jurisdictional rules applicable to non-marital registered relationships in the **United Kingdom** are identical to those described in **Section XI.2.2.5**. Nonetheless, the possibility that persons who have registered a civil partnership in a part of the **United Kingdom** may find themselves without a forum to dissolve their relationship has been addressed. As a result, a restricted *forum necessitatis* has been created in each of the various grounds for dissolution of a civil partnership.[78] However, this may only be used should the judge feel that it would be in the interests of justice to exercise this discretion.

XI.2.4 EVALUATION

Those advocating the harmonisation of the jurisdictional rules with respect to marriage dissolution have done so on a number of bases. Although

---

[76] BUCHER (2004a) p. 204, §585; DUTOIT (2005) p. 222, Art. 65a, No. 7.

[77] These regulations may in particular parallel those laid down in Brussels IIbis (emphasis added): Sec. 219(3), CPA 2004. It is expected that such regulations will indeed duplicate the relevant regulations of Brussels IIbis. For criticism of this approach see WOELKE (2004) p. 113-114.

[78] **Eng.:** Sec. 221(1)(c)(iii), CPA 2004 (dissolution), Sec. 221(2)(c)(iii), CPA 2004 (nullity) and Sec. 222(c), CPA 2004 (presumption of death); **Scot.:** Sec. 225(1)(c)(iii), CPA 2004 (dissolution), Sec. 225(3)(c)(iii), CPA 2004 (nullity) and Sec. 1(3)(c), PD(S)A 1977 as amended by §44, Sch. 28, CPA 2004 (presumption of death); **NI.:** Sec. 229(1)(c)(iii), CPA 2004 (dissolution), Sec. 229(2)(c)(iii), CPA 2004 (nullity) and Sec. 230(c), CPA 2004 (presumption of death).

European integration was initially restricted to economic affairs, that situation has fundamentally changed.[79] The European Community has set the objective of creating an area of freedom, security and justice in which the free movement of persons is ensured.[80] In order to achieve such a goal the Community must adopt measures in the field of judicial co-operation in civil matters. The Tampere European Council endorsed the principle of mutual recognition of judicial decisions as the cornerstone for the creation of a genuine judicial area.[81] On this basis, the desire to introduce uniform standards for jurisdiction in matrimonial matters, the need to introduce modern rules for the recognition and enforcement of judgments on annulment, divorce and separation between Member States and the avoidance of *lis pendens* proceedings were able to be realised. The end result was the Brussels II Regulation, which sowed the seeds for the Brussels IIbis Regulation.

In following this line of reasoning, there would appear to be no reason to hesitate in attempting to harmonise the jurisdictional rules relating to the dissolution of non-marital registered relationships. The same problems faced at private international law level when a marital bond is terminated are also faced, if not to an even greater extent, when a non-marital registered relationship is dissolved. In striving towards the goals of simplicity, uniformity and certainty of result in the field of civil matters, it is undoubtedly desirable to endeavour to harmonise, if not unify, the jurisdictional rules applicable to the dissolution of non-marital registered relationships.[82] If this is indeed desirable, the question rises how such a result can feasibly be achieved. There are four possible solutions to this question.

1. Broaden the material scope of Brussels IIbis so as to include non-marital registered relationships (only applicable in EU countries)
2. Adopt a new instrument with identical rules to those laid down in Brussels IIbis with respect to marriage dissolution.
3. Create a new instrument based on Brussels IIbis, although amended where necessary.

---

79 BORRÁS REPORT, 16th July 1998, *OJ*, 98/C-221/04, §1. See also JÄNTERÄ-JAREBORG (1999).

80 Recital 1, Brussels IIbis and Vienna Action Plan, *OJ*, 99/C-19/01, p. 10.

81 Recital 2, Brussels IIbis and Tampere European Council Conclusions, §33, as confirmed in the Laeken European Council Conclusions, §45. See for further details: europa.eu.int/european council/conclusions/index en.htm. See also the Tampere Mandate, Brussels, 18th October 2001, 12735/01, JUSTCIV 124, §11-27.

82 For further arguments as to why it is desirable see **Chapter XIII.3.1**.

4. Do not use the rules laid down in Brussels IIbis at all, and create a completely new jurisdictional framework.

In noting the current approach adopted by the institutions of the EU towards non-marital registered relationships, it is highly unlikely that the material scope of Brussels IIbis will be extended to encompass the dissolution of non-marital registered relationships (Solution 1).[83] Even in an area as technically complicated as the one at hand, the political sensitivity of removing a distinction between marriage and non-marital registered relationships may be too great to achieve such a result.

Nonetheless, it would appear that all those legislatures to have enacted private international law provisions have adopted a similar approach. In creating jurisdictional rules applicable to the dissolution of non-marital registered relationships, inspiration has been sought from the existing rules with respect to marriage dissolution. In the European Union this has meant that the Brussels IIbis jurisdictional scheme has, as far as possible, been copied with respect to the dissolution of non-marital registered relationships. In **The Netherlands** this has been achieved by virtue of one provision analogously applying the Brussels IIbis jurisdictional scheme to the dissolution of non-marital registered relationships.[84] In the **United Kingdom** the Lord Chancellor and Scottish Ministers have been granted the power to enact Regulations mirroring those in Brussels IIbis.[85] Although no reference to Brussels IIbis has been made in the traditional rules of jurisdiction in **Belgium**, the jurisdictional rules applicable to the dissolution of non-marital registered relationships are almost identical to those applicable to marriage dissolution, which in turn correspond closely to the scheme established by Brussels IIbis.[86] Although there are no specific

83 The ECJ has ensured that the word "spouse" not be broadened to cover non-marital registered relationships: ECJ, *D and Sweden v. Council*, Case No. 122/99 and 125/99P [2001] I ECR 4319. Since this case the relevant Staff Regulations have been amended so as to refer to "an official who is registered as a stable non-marital partner" (Council Regulation No. 723/2004 of 22nd March 2004 amending the Staff Regulations of the European Communities, *OJ*, 2004, L-124/1, §97(a)(ii)). This approach is also followed in two recent European directives in the field of cross-border relationships: Council Directive 2003/86/EC of 22nd September 2003 on the right to family reunification, *OJ* L-251/12 and European Parliament and Council Directive 2004/38/EC of 29th April 2004 on the right of citizens of the Union and their family member to move and freely reside within the territory of the Member states, *OJ* L-158/77. The term "registered partnership" is used here to reflect the choice in terminology made by the European Union.

84 Art. 4(4), Neth. CCP.

85 Sec. 219, CPA 2004.

86 See **Table 10**, in **Section XI.2.3.1**.

jurisdictional rules dealing with such issues in **France**, a number of **French** authors are in favour of ensuring one uniform set of jurisdictional rules applicable in all cases of relationship breakdown. All in all, the arguments for the European Commission to propose a new Regulation along similar lines to Brussels IIbis dealing specifically with the jurisdictional issues surrounding the dissolution of non-marital registered relationships are formidable.[87] Perhaps the most formidable obstacle in achieving such a solution is that many EU Member states have not yet legislated for non-marital registered relationships. The exact method by which the EU could proceed will be discussed in **Chapter XIII.4**. It is submitted that the most appropriate route along which to proceed is that exemplified in solution 3. In non-EU countries, a similar approach should be followed and the international jurisdiction rules with respect to marriage dissolution should be applied *mutatis mutandis* to the dissolution of non-marital registered relationships.

One should not, however, lose sight of a number of important differences between the dissolution of a non-marital registered relationship and divorce. As already stated, non-marital registered relationship forms do not attract the same universal acceptance that marriage enjoys.[88] Consequently, parties who have registered a non-marital relationship and subsequently cross international borders may find themselves without recourse to a forum to formally dissolve their relationship. Take the following example,

> ***Example 12 (Forum necessitatis)***
> Yolanda, a Belgian national, and Burak, a Turkish national, enter into a statutory cohabitation in Belgium. Two years later they decide to move to the Austria. Once there, they realise that their relationship has hit rocky ground and wish to dissolve their relationship. Their relationship not being recognised in the Austria would mean that they would be without recourse to a forum dissolve their relationship.

In order to avoid such a situation, all those jurisdictions to have legislated on this point have included a provision in the form of a so-called *forum necessitatis*. In so doing, all the surveyed jurisdictions have acknowledged the fact that parties who have registered a relationship should have the possibility to revert to the courts of that jurisdiction to have their

87 This obviously does not apply to any harmonisation of the rules with respect to **Switzerland**. However, if any future agreement is concluded with **Switzerland** as to a sort of Lugano II, then this could be dealt with in the same discussions. Such an approach is also supported by BONOMI (2002) p. 262.

88 See **Chapter X.2.2.3**.

relationship dissolved. In the absence of legislation in **France**, commentators have also acknowledged the need for such a forum. HUET notes,

> s'il apparaissait qu'aucun tribunal étranger n'accepterait de statuer sur la séparation de concubins unis par un PACS français – ce qui n'est pas invraisemblable si ces concubins demeurent dans un pays qui ne reconnaît pas le concubinage – les tribunaux français pourraient recouvrer les compétence sur las base du "for de nécessité" ou du "risque de déni de justice".[89]

A *forum necessitatis* would allow Yolanda and Burak in the abovementioned example to dissolve their statutory cohabitation in **Belgium**, despite there being no other ground upon which the **Belgian** authorities could seize jurisdiction. Although in **Belgium** and **The Netherlands** such a provision is provided unconditionally, in **Switzerland** and the **United Kingdom**, this freedom is restricted.[90] In the **United Kingdom** the court must determine that it be "in the interests of justice to assume jurisdiction in the case",[91] whilst the **Swiss** courts will only have jurisdiction if it is impossible or it cannot be reasonably required of the parties that proceedings be commenced in the domicile of either partner.[92] The question must therefore be posed whether a *forum necessitatis* should be provided unconditionally or should be subject to some conditional factor. In order to answer this question it is first necessary to analyse the rationale behind providing a *forum necessitatis*.

According to general principles of private international law, such grounds of jurisdiction should only be used in exceptional cases.[93] In **Belgium**, **Switzerland** and **The Netherlands**, statutory provisions provide that a *forum necessitatis* is normally only allowed in cases if the possibility of proceeding abroad is restricted.[94] A similar approach is also apparent from a line of **French** case law, in which the **French** courts have appeared increasingly acquiescent in allowing claimants to proceed in **France** on the basis of a

---

89 HUET (2002) p. 553. In a similar light see also DEVERS (2004) p. 321-322, §924 and KESSLER (2004) p. 180, §321,

90 It is the latter approach which has also been preferred in **France**: see previous footnote.

91 **Swit.**: Art. 65b, Sw. CPIL; **UK**: See **footnote 77**.

92 Art. 65b, Sw. CPIL.

93 **Belg.**: *Belgian Senate*, 2002-2003, No. 3-27/7, p. 31, 66 and 261; **Neth.**: STRIKWERDA (2002) p. 236, §228. A *forum necessitatis* has been recognised in cases of natural disaster and war, *e.g.* HR, 20th January 1984, NJ 1984, 751; HR, 13th February 1987 NJ 1987, 1014 and Hof The Hague, 18th July 1997 (1997) *NIPR* No. 303; **Swit.**: KNOEPFLER *et al.* (2005) p. 351, §615a-616a.

94 **Belg.**: Art. 11, Belg. CPIL; **Neth.**: Art. 9(b) and 9(c), Neth. CCP; **Swit.**: Art. 3, Sw. CPIL. On the use of Art. 3, Sw. CPIL see also OTHENIN-GIRARD (1999b).

denial of justice elsewhere.[95] AUDIT notes, however, that this option is restricted to those cases where the claimant can prove that no other jurisdiction is available, either by virtue of impossibility of fact or of law, and that they have a sufficient connection with **France.**[96] In the **United Kingdom**, on the other hand, a slightly different approach is adopted. A court must first have jurisdiction either according to general common law principle[97] or on the basis of statutory "service out of the jurisdiction".[98] In determining whether it has jurisdiction, the court will have to determine whether it is *forum conveniens* and in this sense no *forum necessitatis* exists.[99] Nonetheless, in determining whether it is *forum conveniens*, the court may consider that even though it is not the natural forum, it may still grant leave if it can be established that substantial justice will not be served abroad.[100]

Turning to the question at hand, the issue boils down to whether a *forum necessitatis* should be provided unconditionally or only in narrow circumstances. When the **Dutch** Standing Committee of Private International Law published its proposals in 1998, there were in fact only four countries besides **The Netherlands** that had introduced equivalent legislation. It was thus deemed suitable to provide an unconditional forum to all those couples who had registered their partnership in **The Netherlands**. In contrast, **Belgium** has only recently introduced legislation dealing with the private international law issues surrounding non-marital registered relationships, and it too has opted for an unconditional *forum necessitatis.* Although the exact reasoning for this choice is absent in the parliamentary debates and explanatory notes, it is clear that the administrative nature of the dissolution procedure provided for in **Belgian**

95 BATIFFOL/LAGARDE (1983) p. 463, §674-1 (especially at footnote 9); AUDIT (2000) p. 314-315, §348; LOUSSOUARN/BOUREL (2004) p. 609, §451.

96 AUDIT (2000) p. 314-315, §348.

97 NORTH/FAWCETT (1999) p. 285-296.

98 **Eng.**: Part 6, Civil Procedure Rules; **NI.**: Rules of the Supreme Court (Northern Ireland) Order 1980; **Scot.**: Schedule 8, Civil Jurisdiction and Judgments Act 1982.

99 See, for example, NORTH/FAWCETT (1999) p. 323-324; COLLINS (2000) p. 308-309, §11-124-§11-125.

100 *The Spiliada Maritime Corporation v. Cansulex Ltd* [1987] AC 460 at 480, per Lord GOFF, where he stated that the fundamental principle was "to identify the forum in which the cases can be suitable tried for the interests of all the parties and for the ends of justice". See further, *e.g.*, *Mohammend v. Bank of Kuwait & Middle East KSC* [1996] 1 WLR 1483; *Oppenheimer v. Louis Rosenthal* [1937] 1 All ER 23; *The Vishva Ajay* [1989] 2 LLR 558; *Amin Rasheed v. Kuwait Insurance* [1984] AC 50 at 72; *Banco Atlantico v. British Bank of Middle East* [1990] 2 LLR 504; *Connelly v. RTZ* [1997] 3 WLR 373.

law played a large role in this choice.[101] By the time **Switzerland** and the **United Kingdom** legislated on these issues, the number of jurisdictions providing for domestic forms of registration had risen dramatically, reducing the need to provide for such an unconditional jurisdictional ground. In attempting to create a set of unified rules of jurisdiction applicable across all of these countries, the arguments for allowing an unconditional *forum necessitatis* are weak.

One must strike a balance between, on the one hand, the relative rarity of non-marital registered relationship forms with, on the other, the ever-increasing number of jurisdictions providing for such legislation. Limping relationships should be prevented and the parties' expectations should be reflected in any eventual rule, but this should not come at the cost of general private international law principle. Resort to exorbitant grounds of jurisdiction should be restricted. With this in mind, the **Anglo-Swiss** approach, namely the provision of a *forum necessitatis* in all those cases where substantial justice would otherwise be denied, goes furthest in ensuring that a sound balance is struck.[102]

A second difference between the dissolution of a non-marital registered relationship and a divorce relates to the administrative methods available to dissolve the relationship.[103]

> ***Example 13 (Dissolution requested in place of registration)***
> Michelle and Nick are both living in Strasbourg, France where they decide to enter into a PACS. Six months later, Michelle is offered a job in a French shoe company in London, England. They move to London where they have lived since 2000. They now wish to dissolve their PACS.

---

101 *Belgian Senate*, 2003-2004, No. 3-27/4, p. 8-9, Amendment 57; *Belgian Senate*, 2003-2004, No. 3-27/6, p. 23, Amendment No. 97; *Belgian Senate*, 2003-2004, No. 3-27/7, p. 332-333.

102 In a circular on the application of the **Danish** Registered Partnership, reference is made to the decreasing need to exploit exorbitant grounds of jurisdiction. Instead the jurisdictional grounds for marriage dissolution will now be applied analogously (namely in §448, Danish Civil Procedural Act). A *forum necessitatis* will be granted to those couples who are unable to dissolve their partnership elsewhere if they registered their partnership in **Demark**: §3, Cirkulæreskrivelse om ændring af reglerne om indgåelse og opløsning af registreret partnerskab og ægteskab, Bekendtgørelse No. 930 af 14 september 2004, CIS No. 9669, af 28 september 2004.

103 Although administrative divorce is also possible in some countries (see COENRAAD (2005) p. 259), resort to a judicial authority is still available in cases of dispute: BOELE-WOELKI/BRAAT/SUMNER (2003a) p. 117-129.

In this scenario and assuming that an identical set of jurisdictional rules as laid down by Brussels IIbis would be applied to the dissolution of non-marital registered relationships, both the courts in **England** and **France** would be competent to dissolve the relationship.[104] If the couple decided to proceed in **France**, the **French** court would thus be competent to dissolve a **French** PACS. This would be a rather bizarre result, since if the couple had remained in **France**, the court would not have been granted such jurisdiction.[105] It would thus appear necessary and desirable to create a provision specifically dealing with the allocation of jurisdiction in cases where a non-marital relationship was registered in the forum. As such, it is necessary to ensure that should the parties wish to dissolve their relationship in the country in which it was registered, that the relevant competent authority is determined according to the law of that country.

However, in advocating the use of the jurisdictional rules of Brussels IIbis as the springboard for the creation of equivalent jurisdiction rules for the dissolution of non-marital registered relationships in the EU, one must take into account the current criticism levied at such rules. Brussels IIbis has been criticised for the way in which it can lead to a race to court, thus reducing or even eliminating any attempt to achieve conciliation or reconciliation.[106] However, as has already been noted by the European Commission, this problem is, in part, a result of the diversity of substantive divorce law in Europe,[107] as well as the respective choice of law rules.[108] It is, therefore, impossible to anticipate the problem of forum shopping and a race to the courts without first having addressed the issues surrounding the relevant choice of law rules in the jurisdictions studied. Although, as JÄNTERÄ-JAREBORG has noted, the possibility for harmonising the choice of law rules in the field of divorce is unlikely,[109] it should not be surmised that such difficulty will also be evident with respect to the choice of law rules applicable to the dissolution of non-marital registered relationships.

---

104 **England** would be competent by virtue of their habitual residence (Art. 3(1)(a)(4), Brussels IIbis) and **France** by virtue of their common nationality (Art. 3(1)(b), Brussels IIbis).

105 See **Chapter IV.6.4** and **IV.6.5**.

106 PIRRUNG (1999) p. 844; MOSTYN (2000) p. 165-166 and (2001) p. 363-365; TRUEX (2001) p. 8; MOSTERMANS (2001) p. 304; JÄNTERÄ-JAREBORG (2002) p. 70-72.

107 For an overview of substantive divorce law in 22 legal systems in Europe, see BOELE-WOELKI/BRAAT/SUMNER (2003a).

108 COM (2005) 82, p. 3.

109 JÄNTERÄ-JAREBORG (1999) p. 7-10, (2002) p. 70-72 and (2003b) p. 207-208.

XI.3 CHOICE OF LAW RULES

The 1902 Hague Convention relating to the Settlement of the Conflict of Laws and Jurisdictions as regards to Divorce and Separation (1902 Hague DC) was the first international instrument that recognised the decreasing value of the wholesale application of the *lex fori* in determining the applicable law to questions of marriage dissolution.[110] The strict and wholesale application of the *lex fori* often resulted in divorces being granted which would not be recognised elsewhere, since many jurisdictions would, as a preliminary to recognition, verify the validity of such divorces according to the parties' personal law.[111] Instead, the 1902 Hague DC introduced a choice of law rule based on the personal law of the parties. However, the deficiencies inherent in the 1902 Hague DC led to its limited adoption, and ultimately to its demise. In the absence of a workable international convention in this field, the number of different solutions to choice of law problems has continued to burgeon.

It is, therefore, essential that before one begins to examine the choice of law rules applicable to the dissolution of a non-marital registered relationship, one understand the underlying rationale behind such choice of law rules. With respect to relationships that affect the personal status of the parties involved, the most appropriate connecting factors are thought to be those that refer to the personal law of the parties. With this in mind, and with the added restriction that any choice of law rule adopted should yield a result deemed appropriate in the given circumstances, a variety of connecting factors have been tendered in determining questions related to the dissolution of a marriage or non-marital registered relationship.

Moreover, the choice of law rule is often not impartial to the substantive outcome of the dispute. In the field of international divorce, this has been translated into the *favor divortii* principle.[112] In those countries where

---

110 The following countries signed the Convention (dates in brackets indicate the date of entry into force and date of repudiation): **Belgium** (1904/1919), **France** (1904/1913), **Germany** (1904/1933), **Hungary** (1911/1973), Italy (1905/1990), **Luxembourg** (1904/1974), **The Netherlands** (1904/1968), **Poland** (1929/1969), **Portugal** (1907), **Romania** (1904), **Sweden** (1904/1933) and **Switzerland** (1905/1928). Although the Convention became inoperative, the principles have continued to be used in many European jurisdictions.

111 See, for example, the **English** case of *Tursi v. Tursi* [1958] P. 54 at 60.

112 This is more pertinent in some countries than others and often reflects the internal, domestic attitude towards divorce. See further SIEHR (1982) p. 50 and VAN EECKHOUT (2004) p. 57. In **The Netherlands**, for example, divorce is generally quite easy with the length of the marriage irrelevant as to when a divorce will be granted and the parties

divorce is characterised by a supple, relatively easy procedure, the most common device to facilitate a divorce and adhere to the *favor divortii* principle is to designate the *lex fori* as the sole or subsidiary applicable law or allow a wide degree of party autonomy.[113] However, these methods must be counterbalanced by the need to limit the possibilities for forum shopping and preventing limping relationships.[114] In those countries espousing the *favor divortii* principle, with respect to marriage dissolution also often adopt a similar stance with respect to the dissolution of non-marital registered relationships. In those countries where such an attempt has been made, reference has been made to the *favor dissolutionis* principle.

As was stated with respect to the choice of law rules in questions of essential validity,[115] it must be remembered that one is confronted with an important difference between marriage and non-marital registered relationships when attempting to forge a choice of law rule for such new forms of relationships; that being the limited acceptability of the new phenomenon of non-marital registered relationships, and the associated difficulty in having such relationships dissolved.[116]
Due to the multiplicity of the existing solutions in relation to marriage dissolution, **Section XI.3.1** is devoted to an explanation of these solutions. It is important to seek guidance from the rules on marriage dissolution not

---

agreement being allowed without a period of separation: SHANNON and PATTI/CARLEO/BELLISARIO, in: BOELE-WOELKI/BRAAT/SUMNER (2003a) p. 199 and 203. In contrast, domestic divorce legislation in **Italy** or the **Republic of Ireland** imposes strict requirements regarding the granting of a divorce decree: see further SHANNON (**Ireland**) and PATTI/CARLEO/BELLISARIO (**Italy**), in: BOELE-WOELKI/BRAAT/SUMNER (2003a).

113 SIEHR (1982) p. 50. The *favour divortii* principle is furthermore supported if one examines the jurisdictional grounds under Brussels IIbis: T. DE BOER (1996); VAN EECKHOUT (2004) p. 58 and BOELE-WOELKI/JOUSTRA/STEENHOFF (1998) p. 218-220 and 223.

114 Forum shopping is presumed to be undesirable since it favours one of the litigants, namely the applicant, providing him or her with a significant advantage. It also can lead to an increase in costs if the court chosen is not the nearest or most suitable for the case.

115 See **Chapter X.2.2**.

116 It is interesting to note that the problem of dissolving non-marital registered relationships has become of increasing importance in the **United States of America**. A judge in **Texas** granted a "divorce" to a male same-sex couple who had registered their civil union in **Vermont**. After the story hit the press, the **Texas** Attorney General intervened in the case and the judge reversed his judgment and set the order aside. See, for example, EDITOR, "Judge dismisses divorce filed by gay Texas couple", *AP Newswires*, 2nd April 2003; F.A. BERNSTEIN, "Same-sex union hard to dissolve; Vermont offers divorces, but only for residents", *South Florida Sun-Sentinel*, 14th April 2003. Such a situation also arose in *Rosengarten v. Downes* 802 A.2d 170 (Conn Ct. App. 2002). A **Connecticut** Court of Appeals held that because it did not recognise civil unions, it had no jurisdiction to dissolve the civil union relationship. Whilst the case was pending appeal, Mr. ROSENGARTEN died and the appeal was dismissed.

only in order to identify some of the possibilities in creating rules for non-marital registered relationships but also to sketch some of the pros and cons of each connecting factor. **Section XI.3.2** is devoted to examining the current rules with respect to the dissolution of non-marital registered relationships. On the basis of these two sections, it will be possible to analyse and assess areas of similarity and difference, allowing for conclusions to be drawn as to whether the possibility for harmonisation, or possibly unification, of the choice of law rules in relation to non-marital registered relationships exists (**Section XI.3.3**).

XI.3.1 RULES WITH RESPECT TO MARRIAGE DISSOLUTION

Despite the existence of unified rules in the European Union with respect to international jurisdiction in divorce cases, no unified set of choice of law rules has yet been enacted in the field of marriage dissolution.[117] Initial studies have, however, been conducted into the practical problems resulting from the absence of harmonised rules.[118] Further activity in this field is also to be expected with the recent publication of a European Commission Green Paper on the applicable law and jurisdiction in divorce matters.[119] It is nonetheless striking that in these initial studies, the four EU countries studied in this research were all unsupportive of the need to harmonise this field of law.[120] **Belgium** and **The Netherlands** both believed that such a task should be conducted worldwide and not restricted to the European Union.[121] The **United Kingdom**, assuming that the rules would depart from the current **British** wholesale application of the *lex fori,* believed that such an instrument would lead to increased litigation costs since foreign law would need to be proven.[122] Finally, **France**, believing there to be numerous problems associated with any harmonisation attempt, felt that any proposed instrument should not be accorded a high priority.[123] Despite this increased activity, Europe is still a number of years away from a "Rome III

---

117 SEC (2005) 331, p. 9, §3.5.

118 Council of the EU, Document No. 8838/00, JUSTCIV 66, 31st May 2000 and No. 8839/00, JUSTCIV 67, 5th June 2000, as well EU Commission, *Practical problems resulting from the non-harmonisation of choice of law rules in divorce matters,* The Hague: TMC Asser Institute, Document No. JAI/A3/2001/04.

119 COM (2005) 82, published on the 14th March 2005. This came as a result of the invitation by the European Council to the Commission, "The Hague Programme: strengthening freedom, security and justice in the European Union", adopted by the European Council, 4th – 5th November 2004.

120 Council of the EU, Document No. 8838/00, JUSTCIV 66, 31st May 2000, p. 19.

121 Council of the EU, Document No. 8839/00, JUSTCIV 67, 5th June 2000, p. 87 and 88.

122 Council of the EU, Document No. 8839/00, JUSTCIV 67, 5th June 2000, p. 91-92.

123 Council of the EU, Document No. 8839/00, JUSTCIV 67, 5th June 2000, p. 87-88.

Regulation".[124] Until such an instrument is agreed upon and enacted, countries will continue to apply their national choice of law rules with respect to divorce.

XI.3.1.1 Choice of the parties

In **Belgium** and **The Netherlands** parties requesting the dissolution of their marriage are granted a limited possibility to choose the applicable law. In both countries, the parties are limited in their choice by the requirement that the law selected must correspond either to the *lex fori* or the law of their common nationality.[125] In choosing the law of their common nationality, unlike in those cases where the law of the common nationality is applied by operation of law,[126] it is irrelevant under **Dutch** law that the parties have no societal connection with the country of their nationality.[127] Such an authenticity test is also absent in the **Belgian** provisions. Both countries also provide for rules in determining the application of nationality in those cases where a person possesses more than one.[128] However, unlike in **The Netherlands**,[129] **Belgian** nationality is afforded priority, such that this will be deemed determinative in cases of multinationals.[130]

If the proposals of the **Dutch** Standing Committee on Private International Law are accepted and adopted in any future codification, this field of **Dutch** law will undergo revision. It is proposed to only allow the parties to choose the law of their common nationality. The choice must be made jointly or by one party without being contested by the other.[131] The removal of a choice for the *lex fori* is avoided by ensuring that **Dutch** law applies in all cases,

---

124 EU COMMISSION, *Practical problems resulting from the non-harmonisation of choice of law rules in divorce matters*, The Hague: TMC Asser Institute, Document No. JAI/A3/2001/04, p. 59-60.

125 **Belg.:** Art. 55(2), Belg. CPIL; **Neth.:** Art. 1(2), last sentence and 1(4), Neth. PIL(D)A.

126 See **Section XI.3.1.2.**

127 Art. 1(2), Neth. PIL(D)A. For the reasoning behind this choice see STRIKWERDA (2002) p. 100, §115 and *Dutch Second Chamber*, 1979-1980, 16004, No. 3, p. 15.

128 Art. 3, Belg. CPIL. This solution is thus in conformity with the position adopted in the Convention drawn up on the 12th April 1930 in The Hague. See further *Belgian Senate*, 2003-2004, No. 3-27/1, p. 27.

129 MOSTERMANS (2003) p. 53, §140.

130 This is subject to the exclusion clause in Art. 19, Belg. CPIL, which states that a **Belgian** judge may apply another law if in the circumstances of the case only a weak bond is established with **Belgian** law. This was discussed extensively as a result of Amendment No. 25 (NYSSENS), see further, *Belgian Senate*, 2003-2004, No. 3-27/7, p. 258. This provision actually more-or-less replicates the pre-2004 law, to be found in Art. 2, Act of 27th June 1960.

131 STAATSCOMMISSIE (1995) p. 7.

except those in which the parties choose the law of their common nationality. The choice of law rules in **France,**[132] **Switzerland** and the **United Kingdom** provide no possibility for the parties to choose the law applicable to their divorce.

XI.3.1.2 Nationality

In **The Netherlands, Belgium** and **Switzerland**, the possibility exists for a court to apply the law of the parties' common nationality to the dissolution of a marriage. Despite the apparent commonality of this approach, each country applies this law under different circumstances.

In **The Netherlands**, the parties' common nationality is applied should the parties have made no choice of law as explained above. In determining whether the parties possess a common nationality, the parties' nationality is subject to an authenticity test (*realiteitstoets*),[133] or an effectivity test (*effectiviteitstoets*).[134] With respect to the authenticity test,[135] Art. 1(2), Neth. PIL(D)A states that no common nationality will be deemed to exist if either of the parties manifestly lacks a "real societal connection" with the country of their nationality.[136] This concept, discussed at length in **Dutch** literature and case law,[137] implies that all the circumstances of the given case will be taken into account, including the connections that tie a person to

---

132 This is also true of the pre-Art. 310, Fr. CC, position stemming from the decisions in Fr. Cass., 1 Civ. Ch., 17th April 1953 (1953) 42 *Rev. Crit. DIP* 412, annotated BATIFFOL (*Rivière v. Rivière*), Fr. Cass., 1 Civ. Ch, 15th March 1955 (1955) 44 *Rev. Crit. DIP* 320, annotated BATIFFOL (*Lewandowski v. Lewandowski*) and Fr. Cass., 1 Civ. Ch., 15th May 1961 (1961) 50 *Rev. Crit. DIP* 547, annotated BATIFFOL (*Tarwid v. Wirtensohn*). See further CARBONNEAU (1978) p. 449-452.

133 In cases of single nationality. See MOSTERMANS (2003) p. 46-47, §121-122

134 In cases of double nationality. See MOSTERMANS (2003) p. 53-56, §139-145. According to the *Hof* in Amsterdam, in determining whether a choice for the parties' common nationality is valid, one must first apply the effectivity test if either or both of the parties possess a double nationality, Hof Amsterdam, 20th July 2000 (2002) *NIPR* 82. However, this point of view is heavily debated, with others believing that parties are entitled to choose the "non-effective" common nationality: STAATSCOMMISSIE (1995) P.5, §16; MOSTERMANS (2001) p. 56, §145 and Rb The Hague, 15th November 1988 (1989) *NIPR* 209 and Rb The Hague, 10th April 1996 (1996) *NIPR* 215a.

135 The authenticity and effectivity tests are in practice based on identical criteria: MOSTERMANS (2003) p. 54, §141.

136 The absence of a societal connection with the country of the party's nationality may not be accepted lightly: Rb The Hague, 26th January 2001 (2001) *NIPR* 100.

137 For a critical analysis of the authenticity test, see T. DE BOER (1991).

another country.[138] If a real societal connection with the country of a person's nationality is absent, then this law will not be applied, unless the parties have expressly chosen this law, or a choice by one of the parties remains uncontested.[139] The proposals of the **Dutch** Standing Committee on Private International Law would bring about certain changes to this situation. Firstly, instead of acting as the primary choice of law rule in the field of marriage dissolution, the parties' common nationality would only operate should the parties jointly choose such a law, or should a choice of one of the parties remain uncontested.[140] As a result of these changes, the court would possess no *ex officio* authority to apply the law of the parties' common nationality.[141]

In contrast to the law prior to the enactment of the **Belgian** Code on Private International Law,[142] nationality is only used as a connecting factor when the parties chose this law or if the parties have neither chosen **Belgian** law nor have a common habitual residence.[143] Although **Swiss** law is normally applied in divorce proceedings, when the spouses possess a common foreign nationality and one of them is domiciled in **Switzerland**, the law of their common nationality will be applied.[144] Nonetheless, a *favor divortii* twist in Art. 61(3), Sw. CPIL states that if the foreign national law designated by means of Art. 61(2), Sw. CPIL does not permit divorce or makes it subject to extraordinarily strict conditions, **Swiss** law will apply, provided that one of the spouses is **Swiss** or has resided in **Switzerland** for at least two years.[145]

---

138 HR, 9th June 1995, NJ 1995, 617. In this case both parties possessed **Turkish** nationality but had lived in **The Netherlands** for 20 and 22 years respectively. The *rechtbank* in The Hague had applied **Turkish** law due to their common nationality, whilst the *Hof* in The Hague applied **Dutch** law since it felt that the link with **Turkey** had been broken due to the links established with **The Netherlands**. The *Hoge Raad* upheld the latter position.

139 Hof 's-Hertogenbosch, 1st July 1994 (1994) *NIPR* 366, §4.3.1.

140 STAATSCOMMISSIE (2001a) p. 7. In support see also T. DE BOER (1991) p. 260.

141 STAATSCOMMISSIE (2001a) p. 3-5.

142 Act of 27th June 1960, *Belg. Staatsblad*, 9th July 1960. See for commentary VAN HECKE/LENAERTS (1989) p. 231-234, §495-500; RIGAUX/FALLON (1993) p. 332-349, §1014-1037; VANDER ELST (1983) p. 88-96, §17.

143 Art. 55(1)(3), Belg. CPIL. The relevant date is that when the proceedings were commenced.

144 Art. 61(2), Sw. CPIL. See further PATOCCHI/GEISINGER (1995) Art. 61, p. 217-219; BUCHER (2004a) p. 114-118, §309-325 and p. 204-207, §586-597; BUCHER/BONOMI (2004) p. 185-186, §675-679. In cases of double nationality, the effective nationality is determined in accordance with Art. 23(2), Sw. CPIL (subject to Art. 15, Sw. CPIL. See further DUTOIT (2005) p. 201, Art. 61, No. 6).

145 Art. 61(3), Sw. CPIL. DUTOIT (2005) p. 202-203, Art. 61, No. 8 and KNOEPFLER *et al.* (2005) p. 131, §249.

In **France**, nationality has always played an important role in determining the applicable law in the field of divorce.[146] As a result of the legislative changes brought about by the introduction of Art. 310, Fr. CC, this situation was merely given legislative force.[147] However, Art. 310, Fr. CC only provides for unilateral choice of law rules.[148] Although reciprocal effect has been granted to other unilateral choice of law rules,[149] Art. 310, Fr. CC has not been granted such a privilege.[150] As a result, this Article only determines when **French** law is applicable. Accordingly, if both of the parties possess **French** nationality, **French** law will be applied to their divorce.[151] Nationality has, in contrast, never played a role in the choice of law rules in any of the jurisdictions of the **United Kingdom**.

XI.3.1.3 Habitual residence or domicile

Although habitual residence forms an important connecting factor in both **Belgium** and **The Netherlands,** the rules are structured in a slightly different fashion. Whereas habitual residence is the primary connecting factor in **Belgium**, it provides a secondary connection in **The Netherlands** in the absence of a common nationality.[152] Furthermore, two separate grounds relating to the habitual residence of the parties are provided for in **Belgium**, whereas in **The Netherlands** only one such ground exists. Accordingly, in both countries, if the parties are habitually resident in the same State, then the law of this State will be applied (although in **The Netherlands** this will only be done in the absence of a common nationality). In **Belgium**, if the parties are no longer habitually resident in the same State, yet one of the parties still resides in the parties' last common habitual residence, then the

---

146 In *Rivière v. Rivière* (Fr. Cass., 1 Civ. Ch., 17th April 1953 (1953) 42 *Rev. Crit. DIP* 412, annotated BATIFFOL), it was held indirectly that if a common nationality exists, this law of this nationality should be applied.

147 Art. 310, Fr. CC was introduced as a result of Act of 11th July 1975, No. 75-617.

148 This approach has, however, been heavily criticised: FOYER, "Tourant et retour aux sources en droit international privé?", *JCP Éd. N,* 1976, No. 2762; SIMON-DEPITRE, "Le nouveau article 310 du Code civil", *JDI,* 1976, p. 823; FRANCESCAKIS, "Le surprenant article 310 nouveau du Code civil sur le divorce international", *Rev. Crit. DIP,* 1975, p. 553 at p. 554; CARBONNEAU (1978) p. 459-460.

149 For example, Art. 3, Fr. CC.

150 TGI Paris, 1 Civ. Ch., 20th January 1977 (1977) 66 *Rev. Crit. DIP* 335, annotated GAUDEMET-TALLON (*Lofiego v. Lofiego*).

151 Art. 310(a), Fr. CC. See further AUDIT (2000) p. 564, §659.

152 **Belg.**: Art. 55(1)(2), Belg. CPIL and **Neth.**: Art. 1(1)(b), Neth. PIL(D)A.

law of this State will be applied;[153] a provision not mirrored in **The Netherlands**.

However, if the proposed codification of **Dutch** private international law is successful, all references to the parties' habitual residence will be removed from the choice of law rules in the field of divorce.[154] It is argued that if both parties are habitually resident outside **The Netherlands**, a **Dutch** court will only be seized according to **Dutch** jurisdictional rules if both parties possess **Dutch** nationality. The arguments for applying **Dutch** law in this case are convincing, since **Dutch** law would not only be the *lex fori* but also the *lex patriae*. The **Dutch** Standing Committee on Private International Law believed there to be insufficient grounds to grant parties the possibility to choose the law of their common habitual residence at the cost of a complicated choice of law rule.

Although **France** also maintains a choice of law rule based on a geographical connection to the **French** State, a number of differences are apparent. Firstly, instead of referring to the spouses' common habitual residence, **French** law refers to the parties' common domicile.[155] Secondly, **French** law, in having adopted unilateral choice of law rules, only refers to the situation whereby the parties have their common domicile in **France,** in which case **French** law will apply. This choice of law rule is silent on situations in which the parties have their domicile abroad. Thirdly, as with the situation in **The Netherlands** and unlike the position adopted in **Belgium**, this choice of law rule is only applied should neither of the parties possess **French** nationality.

Although **British** courts encounter little difficulty in the application of foreign law in divorce cases,[156] this is not the case in nullity suits. A nullity decree is concerned with the validity of the creation of a marriage and differs substantially from divorce, which dissolves a marriage that is

---

153 Art. 55(1)(2), Belg. CPIL. This change came as a result of Senator DE T' SERCLAES' remarks during the debate in the Senate. Senator DE T' SERCLAES was concerned that a husband would leave the jurisdiction so as to ensure that the parties no longer possessed a common habitual residence: *Belgian Senate*, 2003-2004, No. 3-27/3, p. 23-24, Amendment No. 40.

154 Art. 2.2.4.2, Proposed Neth. CPIL. See further STAATSCOMMISSIE (2001a) p. 10. It is, however, to be noted that any such changes will only be introduced alongside a general codification of **Dutch** private international law. For the original proposals see STAATSCOMMISSIE (1995) p. 7.

155 Art. 310(b), Fr. CC.

156 See **Section XI.3.1.4.**

admittedly validly created.[157] In these cases the court must first engage in a characterisation of the relevant defect before it can ascertain which law to apply.[158] In so doing, the court will apply the same choice of law rules as those expounded in **Chapter X.2.2.1**. Although this area of law is still unsettled, the **English** Law Commission in tackling the issue of the law to be applied to matters of consent thought it would be "contrary to principle and inconvenient in practice to fragment the question of essential validity".[159] This has led to the conclusion, as adopted in *Szechter v. Szechter*,[160] that the *lex domicili* should be applied in nullity cases to defects affecting the essential validity of the marriage.[161] The application of foreign law in nullity cases is also supported with reference to Sec. 14(1), MCA 1973. Although this area is without clear rules, it is plain that here the courts are more amenable to the application of foreign law.

XI.3.1.4 Lex fori

In **Belgium** and **The Netherlands**, the *lex fori* is applied where the abovementioned rules do not lead to a determination of an applicable law, and thus acts as a default rule. In **The Netherlands**, further support for the *lex fori* theory has been provided by the proposals of the **Dutch** Standing Committee on Private International Law. If this proposal is adopted,[162] the *lex fori* will be applied in all cases, unless the parties have chosen for the application of the law of their common nationality.[163] In **Switzerland**, reference to the *lex fori* is standard unless the parties have a common nationality and one of them is domiciled in **Switzerland**.[164]

In the **United Kingdom**, the *lex fori* is applied in all divorce cases without exception. This rule was, however, created in an era where little distinction

---

157 NORTH/FAWCETT (1999) p. 776.

158 *i.e.* a characterisation of whether the defect affects the formal or essential validity of the relationship. Due to the distinction made in **English** law, this also therefore includes the characterisation of a particular defect as void or voidable: NORTH/FAWCETT (1999) p. 787.

159 ENGLISH LAW COMMISSION, *Working Paper No. 89*, (1985), §5.6-5.24.

160 *Szechter v. Szechter* [1971] P 286, [1970] 3 All ER 905. Also supported with reference to *Vervaeke v. Smith* [1981] Fam 77 at 121.

161 This is also the approach followed in **Scotland**, ANTON/BEAUMONT (1990) p. 452 and CRAWFORD (1998) p. 186. One must not, however, lose sight of the fact that the court can refuse to apply this law if it would be contrary to public policy. See, for example, *Prawdzic-Lazarska v. Prawdzic-Lazarski* (1954) SC 98 at 102.

162 As is expected to be the case as soon as the Neth. CPIL is enacted.

163 Art. 2.2.4.2, Proposed Neth. CPIL. See further STAATSCOMMISSIE (2001a) p. 10-11.

164 PATOCCHI/GEISINGER (1995) Art. 61, p. 218 and DUTOIT (2005) p. 200-201, Art. 61, No. 1-2. See also Trib. Féd, 15th May 2000 (2000) 126 III *ATF* 298 at 302, §2a/bb and Trib. Féd, 27th January 1992 (1992) 118 II *ATF* 79 at 80-81, §2.

was made between questions of jurisdiction and questions of choice of law. At that time, jurisdiction in divorce could only be established on the basis of the husband's domicil.[165] However, this rule could, and often did, produce unnecessary hardship for the wife who wished to pursue matrimonial remedies in a distant jurisdiction. After a number of cases[166] and recommendations from the **English** and **Scottish** Law Commissions,[167] the Domicile and Matrimonial Proceedings Act 1973 (DMPA 1973) was passed to clarify and improve the situation.[168] The jurisdictional rules have thus been substantially revised and are no longer solely based on the parties' domicil. Although as a result of these changes, the need for choice of law rules arose,[169] the DMPA 1973 did not provide for any such rules, and thus gave no more than tacit support for the continued wholesale application of the *lex fori*. Hence, the *lex loci celebrationis*,[170] the *lex domicilii*,[171] the *lex patriae* and the law of the place where the facts took place are all irrelevant in determining the applicable law.[172] Although there have been calls for this rule to be replaced, both the **Scottish** and **English** Law Commissions rejected such recommendations, instead calling for the retention of the application of the *lex fori* in all cases.[173] The arguments put forward by the Law Commissions stated that the risks of forum shopping were outweighed by other factors, including the costs incurred in attempting to ascertain the personal law of the parties (or the proper law of the marriage should that be

165 The domicil of the wife followed that of the husband's, thus in that sense was irrelevant. For more information on the law of domicil, see JOINT LAW COMMISSIONS (1987b).

166 The previous law had been stated in *Le Mesurier v. Le Mesurier* [1895] AC 517, where domicil provided the only ground for jurisdiction in **England & Wales**. *Indyka v. Indyka* [1969] 1 AC 33 is the most important in a long list of cases which highlights the problems of using domicil as a sole jurisdictional ground.

167 SCOTTISH LAW COMMISSION, *Consultation Memorandum No. 13* (1970) and ENGLISH LAW COMMISSION, *Working Paper No. 28* (1970). Reported in SCOTTISH LAW COMMISSION, *Report No. 25: Family Law: Report on Jurisdiction and Consistorial Causes Affecting Matrimonial Status* (1972) and ENGLISH LAW COMMISSION, *Report No. 48: Family Law: Report on Jurisdiction in Matrimonial Causes* (1972).

168 These rules have now also been in part replaced by Brussels IIbis.

169 *Zanelli v. Zanelli* (1948) 64 TLR 556. Here, **English** law was uniformly applied, despite the fact that **Italian** law (the law of the domicil of the husband) did not permit divorce at that time. PÅLSSON (1978) p. 126-129; ANTON/BEAUMONT (1990) p. 465-466; CLIVE (1992) p. 619; NORTH/FAWCETT (1999) p. 775-776.

170 *Holland v. Holland* (1973) SA 897 (T).

171 *Grummett v. Grummett* (1965) 7 FLR 415.

172 *Czepek v. Czepek* [1962] 3 All ER 990.

173 SCOTTISH LAW COMMISSION, *Report No. 25: Family Law: Report on Jurisdiction and Consistorial Causes Affecting Matrimonial Status* (1972) p. 10-13; ENGLISH LAW COMMISSION, *Report No. 48: Family Law: Report on Jurisdiction in Matrimonial Causes* (1972) p. 38-39.

used as a connecting factor), and the payment of expert witnesses on that law.

In **France**, prior to the legislative changes in 1975, if the spouses lacked a common nationality or common domicile, a seized **French** court would simply apply the *lex fori*.[174] Since 1975, reference to the *lex fori* is sought in all those cases where no foreign law considers itself applicable and the **French** courts are seized of jurisdiction.[175] The application of this rule has resulted in many practical problems. Before this rule can be applied, the **French** judge must first assess whether any foreign law could be applicable in the case.[176] However, it seems excessive to expect the **French** judge to examine all the jurisdictions of the world in order to assess whether a foreign law regards itself as applicable. There are, after all, many possible connecting factors that could be used to determine this question.[177] This determination has, however, been held by the **French** Supreme Court to involve an assessment whether the laws alleged to be applicable by the parties are indeed competent.[178] Furthermore, Art. 310, Fr. CC does not provide for possible conflict situations. If the law of only one country is deemed applicable, then the law of that country will be applied.[179] If no country's law is deemed applicable, then **French** law will be applied. If two or more laws are deemed applicable, then there is no other option than to refer to the case law prior to the enactment of the Act of 11th July 1975.[180]

XI.3.2 RULES WITH RESPECT TO DISSOLUTION OF NON-MARITAL REGISTERED RELATIONSHIPS

Unlike in the field of essential validity of the relationship where a certain unanimity of opinion was to be found,[181] the choice of law rules in relation to the dissolution of the relationship are less cohesive. Three main

---

174 Fr. Cass., 1 Civ. Ch., 10th July 1975 (*Tarwid*) (1980) *JDI* 310, annotated AUDIT. See further, AUDIT (2000) p. 568, §663; MAYER/HEUZÉ (2001) p. 382-385, §578-581; LOUSSOUARN/BOUREL (2004) p. 420-422, §319.

175 Art. 310(c), Fr. CC. This case could thus arise on the basis of the residence of the respondent, the familial residence if this is different from their domicile, or either of the parties possesses **French** nationality.

176 AUDIT (2000) p. 565, §661.

177 AUDIT mentions fifteen such connecting factors: AUDIT (2000) p. 567, §662.

178 Fr. Cass., 1 Civ. Ch., 1st June 1994 (1995) *Rev. crit. DIP* 117, annotated GAUDEMET-TALLON.

179 Fr. Cass., 1 Civ. Ch., 1st April 1981 (1981) *JDI* 812, annotated ALEXANDRE; TGI Paris, 23rd February 1978 (1979) *Rev. crit. DIP* 598, annotated POISSON-DROCOURT.

180 MAYER/HEUZÉ (2001) p. 384, §579.

181 See **Chapter X.2.2.2**.

approaches can be identified. Firstly, there are those systems that advocate the predominant application of the *lex fori* (**Section XI.3.2.1**). Secondly, there are those systems that determine such questions primarily on the basis of the *lex loci registrationis* (**Section XI.3.2.2**), and finally, there are those jurisdictions where reference is still made to the personal law of the parties (**Section XI.3.2.3**).

XI.3.2.1 Predominance of lex fori

According to Art. 61(1), Sw. CPIL, analogously applicable to the dissolution of a registered partnership by virtue of Art. 65a, Sw. CPIL, the dissolution of a registered partnership is governed by **Swiss** law. The only exception to this rule applies if the parties possess the same foreign nationality.[182]

Following the attitude adopted in the **United Kingdom** with respect to marriage dissolution,[183] there are no specific rules governing the choice of law in cases involving the dissolution of a civil partnership (or overseas relationship subsequently recognised as a civil partnership). It can therefore only be assumed that the same approach will thus be applied, namely that the *lex fori* will apply in all cases.[184] With respect to the annulment of such relationships, the question is presently open-ended. The uncertainty which shrouds the choice of law rules with respect to marriage annulment in the **United Kingdom** seemingly leaves the courts a wide margin of appreciation in order to determine the best possible approach.[185] In the absence of choice of law rules for the annulment of civil partnerships in the **United Kingdom**, it is suggested that reference will thus be made to the current law in the field of marriage nullity, namely reference to the *lex domicilii*.

Despite the apparent complexity of the **Dutch** choice of law rules laid down in the Neth. PIL(RP)A, the ultimate scheme is based on a simple distinction. It is assumed that **Dutch** law will apply in all cases unless certain conditions are present.[186] As a result, three categories must be distinguished, namely,

- non-marital registered relationships registered in **The Netherlands**;
- non-marital registered relationships registered abroad where dissolution is sought on grounds of mutual consent and,

---

182 Art. 61(2), Sw. CPIL, applicable by virtue of Art. 65a, Sw. CPIL. See **Section XI.3.2.3**.

183 See **Section XI.3.1.4**.

184 This is also true for interregional conflict cases if **English** parties begin proceedings in either **Scotland** or **Northern Ireland**.

185 See **Section XI.3.1.3**.

186 JOPPE (2000b) p. 393; FROHN (2004) p. 293; REINHARTZ (2004) p. 495-496.

- non-marital registered relationships registered abroad where dissolution is sought on grounds of a sole petition.

In the first category, **Dutch** law, as both *lex fori* and *lex loci registrationis*, will be applied in all cases.[187] In the second category, **Dutch** law will be applied,[188] unless the parties have made a choice for the *lex loci registrationis*.[189] In the third category, **Dutch** law will also be applied,[190] unless either the parties have jointly chosen for the *lex loci registrationis* or this choice has been made by one party and is not contested by the other,[191] or one party has made a choice of law for the place where the relationship was registered and both parties have close ties with that country.[192] The choice is, however, restricted to the substantive requirements of the dissolution; the form and manner in which the dissolution takes place will be determined according to **Dutch** law.[193] This approach is therefore based on the choice of law rules in the field of divorce as proposed by the **Dutch** Standing Committee on Private International Law, save for the replacement of the choice for the *lex patriae* with the *lex loci registrationis*.

XI.3.2.2 Predominance of lex loci registrationis

Belgium makes a clear distinction between those non-marital registered relationships akin to marriage and those which are not. Those akin to marriage are characterised as marriages, and hence the choice of law rules with respect to their dissolution are determined according to the same rules as those applicable to divorces.[194] All other non-martial registered relationships are dealt with according to Chapter IV, Belg. CPIL.

Art. 60(1), in conjunction with Art. 60(2), Belg. CPIL states that the dissolution of a non-marital registered relationship is to be regulated by the *lex loci registrationis*. Despite the simplicity of the rule eventually adopted, a fierce debate was played out in the **Belgian** Senate during the enactment of the Belg. CPIL. In the original proposal a distinction was drawn between the dissolution of a relationship registered in **Belgium** and a relationship registered abroad. According to Art. 60(3)(1) of the original proposal, relationships registered in **Belgium** would be governed by **Belgian** law,

187 Art. 22, Neth. PIL(RP)A.
188 Art. 23(1), Neth. PIL(RP)A.
189 Art. 23(2), Net. PIL(RP)A.
190 Art. 23(1), Neth. PIL(RP)A.
191 Art. 23(3), first sentence, Neth. PIL(RP)A.
192 Art. 23(3), second sentence, Neth. PIL(RP)A.
193 Art. 23(4), Neth. PIL(RP)A.
194 See **Section XI.3.1**.

whilst those registered abroad would be governed in accordance with the choice of law rules on marriage.[195] It was felt that applying the choice of law rules on the dissolution of a marriage to the dissolution of a non-marital registered relationship would lead to too many problems with regards those countries that do not recognise such relationship forms.

Many **French** authors also support the wholesale application of the *lex loci registrationis* to all forms of non-marital registered relationships.[196] Although DEVERS and FULCHIRON admittedly prefer the term *loi de l'institution*, this will correspond, in the majority of cases, to the *lex loci registrationis*.[197] Furthermore, this result has received support from the MINISTRY OF JUSTICE in a recently published report.[198]

XI.3.2.3 Reference to personal law of the parties

A number of commentators in **France** have argued that if non-marital registered relationships are to be classified as having an affect upon the personal status of the parties concerned, then this stance should be sustained when dealing with issues of choice of law. Accordingly, many **French** authors argue for a choice of law ladder referring first to the parties' common nationality, thereafter to their common domicile, and in the absence thereof to the *lex fori*.[199] Nonetheless, even these authors prefer to avoid the analogous application of the choice of law rules on divorce, due to the unilateral nature of such rules.

Switzerland is the only country of those researched to refer to the personal law of the parties. According to Art. 61(2), Sw. CPIL, if the parties have a common foreign nationality, that law will be applied to the dissolution of their non-marital registered relationship. If this law does not recognise the form of non-marital registered relationship, then the court must find "*dispositions applicables*".[200] In so doing the court must look to the country in which the non-marital relationship was registered. If this country

---

195 *Belgian Senate*, 2003-2004, N° 3-27/1, p. 172.

196 FULCHIRON (2000) p. 908 and (2001b) p. 13-14; DEVERS (2004) p. 333, §550.

197 See **Chapter X.2.2.2** for further details and **Chapter X.2.3** for further discussion.

198 MINISTRE DE LA JUSTICE (2004) p. 28-29.

199 JOSSELIN-GALL (2000) p. 494-495; KHAILRALLAH (2000) p. 323-329, NO. 16-22; MIGNOT (2001) p. 639; HUET (2002) p. 549. CHANTELOUP (2000) p. 14. Although CHANTELOUP, as a default CHANTELOUP refers to the last common residence of the parties. She therefore fails to cater for those situations where the couple have never lived together. Although impossible in **France**, this is possible elsewhere: see **Chapter VII.5.6.1** and **V.5.6.1**.

200 Art. 65c(1), Sw. CPIL.

imposes requirements on the dissolution of a non-marital registered relationship similar to those imposed on a divorce, then the relevant divorce law (as *dispositions applicables*) of the law of the parties' common nationality will be applied.[201] If, however, the parties have registered their non-marital relationship in a country in which a specific dissolution scheme has been established, **Swiss** law will, by virtue of Art. 65c(1), Sw. CPIL, be applied. To clarify:

Table 11*: Swiss choice of law rules in dissolution cases*

Situation	**Provisions**	**Applicable Law**
No joint nationality	Arts. 65a and 61(1)	Swiss law
Joint nationality and this law recognises a registered partnership institution	Arts. 65a and 61(2)	Lex patriae
Joint nationality and this law does not recognise a registered partnership institution, but partnership registered in a country in which dissolution of registered partnership is almost identical to divorce.	Arts. 65a, 61(2) and 65c(1)	Divorce law of common nationality
Joint nationality, and this law does not recognise a registered partnership institution; and partnership registered in a country in which dissolution of registered partnership is different to divorce.	Arts. 65a, 61(2) and 65c(1)	Swiss law

XI.3.3 EVALUATION

Unlike many of the areas examined thus far, there appears to be no common core in the approach taken in the countries researched in relation to the choice of law rules in the field of relationship dissolution. It is not possible to discern one definite trend, nor is it possible to distinguish a trend towards one single solution. In this case, any search for harmonised or unified private international law rules will be based on a better law approach.[202] Of the countries researched, only **Switzerland** has referred to the personal law of the parties. However, this solution can only be reviled for its unnecessarily convoluted approach.[203] The artificial manner in which the parties' national law is applied despite the relationship not being recognised in accordance with that law is undesirable and the result only serves to bring disdain to the aims of private international law. Applying the divorce

201 BUCHER (2004a) p. 205, §588; DUTOIT (2005) p. 224, Art. 65c, No. 1.

202 See **Chapter I.4.2, p. 8.**

203 Other countries have recognised the problems associated with such references: *Belgian Senate*, 2003-2004, No. 3-27/7, p. 128-139 and *Dutch Second Chamber*, 2002-2003, 28924, No. 3, p. 16-17.

law of the parties' national law despite the fact that this law does not recognise the relationship only serves to increase the possibility that the dissolution will not recognised either in the State where the relationship was registered or in the State of the parties' nationality, thus leading to limping relationships. For these and the many other reasons forwarded in **Chapter X.2.2.3**, references to the personal law of the parties in the field of non-marital registered relationships should presently be avoided.

Nonetheless, two predominant schools of thought can be identified, both of which are amenable to approbation, namely the *lex fori* approach and the *lex loci registrationis* approach. However, choice of law rules cannot be analysed in isolation from the jurisdictional rules examined in **Section XI.3.2**. As has already been stated, the search for harmonised choice of law rules would assist in alleviating many of the criticisms levied at a harmonised jurisdictional scheme, such as that created by Brussels IIbis. Therefore, on this basis and despite the highly sensitive and problem-enveloped nature of this field of law, it is necessary to attempt to identify whether any possibility exists for harmonisation or unification of the choice of law rules.

Whichever route one selects one will be confronted with difficulties. The question arises whether there is a way in which the application of the *lex fori* and the application of the *lex loci registrationis* can be combined so as to ensure that these aims are satisfied. This problem can, and arguably should, be seen from two different perspectives. On the one hand, one could analyse the situation from a purely academic point of view, placing both solutions side-by-side comparing the advantages and disadvantages of each. On the other hand, one could examine the issue from a political standpoint, proffering a solution which is politically attractive. However, often an academically sound conclusion is simply politically unfeasible, and *vice versa*. Add to this melting pot the national differences in the degree to which a given solution will be deemed to be politically feasible, and one quickly grasps the formidable task faced by proponents of harmonisation in this field.

Nonetheless, before conceding defeat, it is important to note the arguments used for the application of both the *lex fori* and the *lex loci registrationis*. In those countries where the *lex fori* is applied in all divorce cases, it is difficult to envisage a situation where the courts would begin to apply foreign law in dissolution cases on a regular basis.[204] In support of the blanket application of the *lex fori* in cases of relationship dissolution, it is often argued that the dissolution of a relationship is a part of the public law of the forum and should therefore be seen as constituting part of the country's mandatory laws (*voorrangsregels/règles d'application immediate*).[205] However, it is difficult to justify the use of this argument at a time when jurisdiction is no longer based solely on the husband's domicil.[206] If the ever-increasing flexibility injected into the rules of jurisdiction is not followed through in the field of choice of law, one runs the risk of unsynchronised principles in these fields leading to an increase in the possibility of forum shopping.

Another argument used by those defending the wholesale application of the *lex fori* is that the manner in which foreign law is proved can lead to increased litigation costs.[207] In the **United Kingdom**, for example, foreign law is treated as a fact and must be proved, generally by expert evidence.[208] Although this obviously substantially increases litigation costs, if foreign law is not pleaded, or not pleaded adequately, the relevant law of the **United Kingdom** will be applied instead.[209] However, if the parties voluntarily choose for the application of foreign law,[210] fully aware of the increased procedural costs, the argument that expenses will be higher cannot be used. This argument is, in effect, only valid if parties are forced to

---

204 In a recent briefing paper, the **Scottish** Executive noted: "to apply the law of a foreign jurisdiction in the UK would involve considerable practical difficulties. Judges would need to be able to apply laws of foreign jurisdictions, which would cause delays and increase costs, because it would be necessary to call expert evidence as to the law in other jurisdictions ... It is also Government policy that the costs to parties in family cases should be reasonable": p. 8, SPICe briefing, 26th May 2005, "EU Family Law: an introduction to the Green Paper on 'international divorces'". Available at www.scottish.parliament.uk.

205 VON SAVIGNY (1880) p. 298. In a famous **Dutch** case (HR, 13th December 1907, W 8636, *Boon-Schimdt*), the **Dutch** *Hoge Raad* held that divorce proceedings concerned "de openbare orde en de goede zeden" (public policy and good morals), and therefore applied **Dutch** law in all cases. As a result of increasing opposition from lower courts and academics, this situation changed and the *Hoge Raad* allowed for the application of foreign law (Hof Arnhem, 1st February 1972, NJ 1972, 188; Hof Amsterdam, 18th October 1972, NJ 1973, 340; HR, 23 February 1973, NJ 1973, 366; HR, 27 May 1977, NJ 1977, 600; HR, 9th February 1979, NJ 1979, 546). See further BOELE-WOELKI/JOUSTRA/STEENHOFF (1998) p. 223, footnote 59.

206 VON SAVIGNY (1880) p. 299 and WOLFF (1950) p. 372-375, §351-354 both point to the jurisdictional justification for applying the *lex fori.* This counter-argument is supported by NORTH/FAWCETT (1999) p. 773-776; COLLIER (2001) P. 320.

207 EU COMMISSION (2002) p. 18.

208 FENTIMAN (1998) p. 3 and p. 173-202.

209 *Bumper Development Corp. v. Commissioner of Police* [1991] 1 WLR 1362 at 1368 (CA).

210 FENTIMAN (1998) p. 64-66.

plead foreign law and thus forced to foot the bill for increased litigation costs.

With all these arguments in mind, namely (a) the increasing flexibility afforded to the court in the field of jurisdiction, (b) the acceptance of increased litigation costs in cases where the parties agree to the application of foreign law, (c) the general principles of comity in private international law, (d) the prevention of limping relationships and (e) the coherence of the choice of law rules in the field of establishment and dissolution of non-marital registered relationships, it is submitted that one should strive for a combination of the *lex fori* and the *lex loci registrationis*. In doing so, the general application of the *lex fori*, with the possibility for the parties to choose the *lex loci registrationis*, would appear to strike a justifiable balance between political practicality and academic acceptability. In applying the *lex fori* to issues of choice of law in dissolution cases and arguing for the identical rules to be drafted as those laid down in Brussels IIbis, one would ensure that law eventually applied would also have a close relationship to the parties, being either the habitual residence of at least one of them or the State of the parties' nationality.[211]

Obviously, integrated into this debate are the necessary implications of such jurisdictional and choice of law rules on the recognition and enforcement of such decisions. Will decisions rendered abroad on the basis of such rules be recognised in the country where the relationship was registered, or alternatively where the parties are habitually resident?

XI.4 RECOGNITION AND ENFORCEMENT

XI.4.1 BRUSSELS IIBIS REGULATION

XI.4.1.1 Material scope

According to Brussels IIbis, "judgment" refers to a "divorce, legal separation or marriage annulment ... pronounced by a court of a Member State, whatever the judgment may be called, including a decree, order or decision".[212] The term "court" in turn covers "all the authorities in the Member States with jurisdiction in the matters falling within the scope of

---

211 In those cases where jurisdiction was founded on forum necessitates grounds, the applicable law would be both the *lex fori* and the *lex loci registrationis*.

212 Art. 2(4), Brussels IIbis.

this Regulation pursuant to Article 1".[213] However, as has already been mentioned, it is clear that the dissolution of a non-marital registered relationship does not fall within the material scope of the Regulation and therefore a judgment pronounced abroad relating to the dissolution of such a relationship is also prevented from benefiting from these provisions.[214] It is, nonetheless, important to sketch the relevant recognition provisions, if Brussels IIbis is to form the foundation stone for any future harmonisation of the rules relating to non-marital registered relationships.

XI.4.1.2 Recognition rule and non-recognition grounds

According to Art. 21, Brussels IIbis, a judgment issued in a Member State shall be recognised in the other Member States without any special procedure being required.[215] A judgment can only be refused recognition if it satisfies one of the grounds listed in Art. 22, Brussels IIbis.[216] A judgment must, thus, be refused if it is proved that: (1) it is manifestly contrary to the public policy of the Member State in which recognition is sought,[217] (2) where it was given in default of appearance, the respondent was not served with the document which instituted the proceedings,[218] (3) it is irreconcilable with a judgment given in earlier proceedings between the same parties in the Member State in which recognition is sought or (4) it is irreconcilable with an earlier judgment in another Member State or non-Member State between the same parties provided that that judgment satisfies the conditions necessary for recognition in the Member State in which recognition is sought.[219]

---

213 Art. 2(1), Brussels IIbis.

214 For confirmation of this approach see *Dutch Second Chamber*, 2002-2003, 28924, No. 3, p. 4 and 17; Rb Roermond, 29th March 2001, (2001) *NIPR* 188; MOSTERMANS (2002) p. 267; VLAS (2001) p. 444; JOPPE (2001b) p. 393.

215 This replaces the old Art. 14, Brussels II rule. The removal of an exequatur procedure forms one of the general principles of the legislation. See STORME (2005) p. 64, §27.

216 Previously Art. 15, Brussels II.

217 BORRÁS REPORT, 16th July 1998, *OJ*, 98/C-221/04, §69; GAUDEMET-TALLON (2001) p. 411, §74; MOSTERMANS (2002) p. 269-270; VAN DER VELDEN (2000) p. 758; MOSTERMANS (2003) p. 79-82, §212-219; COLLINS (2004) p. 223, §18R-125(a).

218 BORRÁS REPORT, 16th July 1998, *OJ*, 98/C-221/04, §70; GAUDEMET-TALLON (2001) p. 411, §75; MOSTERMANS (2002) p. 271-272; VAN DER VELDEN (2000) p. 758; MOSTERMANS (2003) p. 83-85, §224-227; COLLINS (2004) p. 223, §18R-125(b).

219 BORRÁS REPORT, 16th July 1998, *OJ*, 98/C-221/04, §71; GAUDEMET-TALLON (2001) p. 411-412, §76; MOSTERMANS (2002) p. 272; VAN DER VELDEN (2000) p. 758; MOSTERMANS (2003) p. 85-86, §228-232; COLLINS (2004) p. 223, §18R-125(c) and (d).

With regard to the public policy exception, although no definition is provided, a number of areas are specifically excluded from the scope of this exception.[220] The jurisdiction of a Member State cannot be reviewed,[221] nor can a refusal to recognise be based on the law applied by the foreign authority.[222] These two restrictions are extremely important, since, as will be seen, many countries impose some form of jurisdictional or choice of law test to the recognition of foreign relationship dissolutions. The *favor divortii* principle has, therefore, also found manifestation in the recognition rules.

XI.4.2 DOMESTIC RULES ON THE RECOGNITION OF FOREIGN DIVORCES AND DISSOLUTIONS OF NON-MARITAL REGISTERED RELATIONSHIPS[223]

It is with respect to the rules on the recognition of foreign dissolutions of non-marital registered relationships that one is most clearly able to see the tendency to replicate the applicable rules in the field of the recognition of foreign divorces. By virtue of the facsimile nature of these two sets of rules, these rules have been dealt with simultaneously in this section. Nonetheless, recourse has still been made to a sequential, country-by-country analysis for reasons of overall clarity.

XI.4.2.1 Belgium

No special rules have been created for the recognition of foreign divorces or dissolutions of non-marital registered relationships (other than for one-sided repudiations by the man).[224] As a result, the normal recognition rules apply, and a distinction is accordingly drawn between the recognition of judicial foreign decisions and the recognition of foreign authentic

220 Regardless of the absence of a definition, it is clear that the use of the word "manifest" has been used to highlight the idea that this ground is to be used sparingly. See, for example, the ECJ's interpretation of the public policy exception in Art. 27, Brussels I: *Krombach v. Bamberski*, 28th March 2000, Case No. 7/98 and ECJ, *Renault v. Maxicar*, 11th May 2000, Case No. 38/98. See further LOUSSOUARN/BOUREL (2004) p. 765-766, §507-1

221 Art. 17, Brussels IIbis. See further MOSTERMANS (2002) p. 270. Although there are a few exceptions to this rule, they are significant enough to deserve attention here.

222 Art. 18, Brussels IIbis. See further MOSTERMANS (2002) p. 269 and BORRÁS REPORT, 16th July 1998, *OJ*, 98/C-221/04, §76

223 Again the term "domestic" has been used here to refer to those situations falling outside the material scope of Brussels IIbis.

224 ERAUW (2005) p. 14. One-sided repudiations by the man are dealt with according to Art. 57, Belg. CPIL. See further *Belg. Staatsblad*, 28th September 2004, p. 69605.

instruments.[225] Although these rules apply only in the absence of international treaties or bilateral conventions,[226] **Belgium** has currently not signed any bilateral treaties with respect to the recognition of a foreign dissolution of a non-marital registered relationship.

With respect to those relationships dissolved by means of a judicial decree, Art. 22(2), Belg. CPIL states that such a decision will be recognised in **Belgium** without any special enforcement procedure.[227] Nonetheless, such a decision will be refused recognition if it is contrary to any of the grounds listed in Art. 25, Belg. CPIL, including the fact that it is contrary to **Belgian** public policy,[228] the foreign proceedings were begun after proceedings had already been commenced in **Belgium** and are still pending between the same parties on the same issue,[229] or that the decision has only been acquired so as to avoid the choice of law rules laid down in the Belg. CPIL.[230] Furthermore, although the **Belgian** court will not subject recognition of a foreign judicial decision to a jurisdictional test, an examination will be made to ensure that the **Belgian** judge was not exclusively competent and that the foreign court has not based its jurisdiction on an exorbitant criterion.[231] As a result of these provisions, a simple and effective set of rules has been created so as to deal even more efficiently with the recognition of foreign judicial decisions. It is clear that the same rules apply to the recognition of foreign divorces by judicial decree as to foreign dissolutions of non-marital registered relationships by judicial decree.[232]

As has been seen, some jurisdictions provide for an administrative procedure to dissolve a non-marital registered relationship.[233] As long as the

---

225 *Belg. Staatsblad*, 28th September 2004, p. 69607, §M.4. Arts. 22-26 deal with judicial decisions and Arts. 27-28 deal with authentic instruments. ERAUW (2004) p. 124.

226 Art. 2, Belg. CPIL. In the field of divorce recognition **Belgium** has concluded bilateral conventions with **France** (8th July 1899), **The Netherlands** (28th March 1925), **Germany** (30th June 1958) and **Switzerland** (29th April 1959). Since the enactment of Brussels IIbis, the conventions with EU countries have only limited application.

227 ERAUW (2004) p. 124. This rule is no different to the law prior to 1st October 2004: *Belg. Staatsblad*, 28th September 2004, p. 69600, §G.5 and 69599, §G2.

228 Art. 25(1), Belg. CPIL.

229 Art. 25(6), Belg. CPIL.

230 Art. 25(3), Belg. CPIL.

231 Art. 27(7) and (8), Belg. CPIL.

232 ERAUW (2004) p. 124.

233 **Chapters III.6.4, III.6.5, IV.6.4, IV.6.5** and **V.6.4**.

authentic instrument satisfies the conditions listed in Art. 27, Belg. CPIL[234] and the relevant documents listed in Art. 24, Belg. CPIL are handed over, the authentic instrument will be recognised in **Belgium**. For those documents which are deemed to affect the personal status or capacity of the parties involved, Art. 31, Belg. CPIL provides for further details as to how these matters should be dealt with. Whether a particular non-marital registered relationship is deemed to have an impact on the parties' civil status is determined according to the *lex loci registrationis*.[235]

XI.4.2.2 France

The absence of legislation in **France** dealing with the private international law aspects of non-marital registered relationships casts doubt on the actual state of the law in this field. This section will thus focus on the current rules applicable to the recognition of foreign divorces, before examining the current academic opinion as to the most appropriate solution with respect to the recognition of foreign dissolutions of non-marital registered relationships.

A marriage dissolution[236] obtained abroad will be recognised in **France** without a special procedure.[237] Control will only be exercised if such recognition is contested (*action en opposabilité*) or enforcement of a particular right is sought.[238] If a court must exercise this controlling function, it must ensure that (a) the decision was issued by a competent authority, (b) that the law applied to the dissolution was acceptable according to **French** law, (c) that the decision is not contrary to public policy and (d) that the decision was not obtained fraudulently.[239]

---

234 Art. 27, Belg. CPIL subjects the recognition of all foreign authentic instruments to a choice of law test, in that the law applied to such instruments must satisfy the law that would have been applied in **Belgium**.

235 *Belg. Staatsblad*, 28th September 2004, p. 69607, §M.5 and **Chapter XII.3.4**.

236 The term "dissolution" is also to be understand broadly and includes administrative decisions: Fr. Cass., 1 Civ. Ch., 17th April 1953 (1953) *Rev. crit. DIP* 412 (*Rivière*), annotated BATIFFOL. See also LOUSSOUARN/BOUREL (2004) p. 705, §492-5.

237 Fr. Cass., Civ., 9th May 1900 (1900) *JDI* 613 (*De Wrède*) and Fr. Cass, Civ., 3rd March 1930 (1930) *JDI* 981 (*Hainard*).

238 Although the *action en opposabilité* (an action for a declaration that a judgment should not be recognised) is similar to enforceability proceedings, a number of differences are apparent. However, these differences are not crucial to this research. On this point see LOUSSOUARN/BOUREL (2004) p. 751 -752, §502-5.

239 Fr. Cass., 1 Civ. Ch., 7th January 1964 (1964) *Rev. crit. DIP* 344, annotated BATIFFOL; (1964) *JDI* 302 annotated GOLDMAN (*Munzer*).

In determining whether the decision was issued by a competent court, the **French** courts must ensure not only that the relevant court assumed jurisdiction correctly,[240] but also that the **French** courts are not exclusively competent by virtue of a provision of **French** law.[241] With respect to divorce, it has been held that although Art. 1070, Fr. NCCP does not provide a ground of exclusive competence,[242] Arts. 14 and 15, Fr. CC do provide such grounds.[243] Furthermore, a **French** court must also determine whether the case has been decided in conformity with the **French** choice of law rules laid down in Art. 310, Fr. CC.[244] Although one is able to unearth an abundance of case law on the precise meaning of this criterion, the *raison d'être* for the imposition of a choice of law test is sadly lacking.[245] The final two criteria, namely that the decision be neither contrary to **French** public policy nor have been obtained fraudulently, will both be dealt with in **Section XI.5**.

Turning one's attention to academic opinion surrounding non-marital registered relationships, many **French** authors have noted the obstacles that the imposition of such criteria would cause for the recognition of foreign non-marital registered relationship dissolutions.[246] If the jurisdictional and choice of law tests imposed prior to enforcing a dissolution order are applied to the dissolution of non-marital registered relationships, the probability

---

240 Fr. Cass., 1 Civ. Ch., 4th February 1958 (1958) *Rev. crit. DIP* 389, annotated BATIFFOL (*Lundwall*).

241 Fr. Cass, 1 Civ. Ch., 6th February 1985 (1985) *Rev. crit. DIP* 369, (1985) *JDI* 460, annotated HUET, (1985) *D* 469, annotated MASSIP (*Simitch*).

242 Unless otherwise determined: Fr. Cass., 1 Ch. Civ., 17th February 2004, Case No. 02-17.479, where according to Art. 1(a), *Convention relative à l'exequatur et à l'extradition*, 27th August 1964, the **Algerian** court must also have been competent according to **French** jurisdictional grounds (thus including Art. 1070, Fr. NCCP).

243 This has, however, been heavily criticized in **French** literature: BATIFFOL/LAGARDE (1983) p. 562-566, §718; AUDIT (2000) p. 399-400, §460; MAYER/HEUZÉ (2001) p. 253-254, §376. Although this is repeatedly referred to by the courts, this is now susceptible to a degree of renunciation: see further MAYER/HEUZÉ (2001) p. 196-197, §296-298.

244 This is, however, subject to a number of tempering factors. Firstly, that renvoi is permitted: Tribunal civil de la Seine, 22nd October 1956 (1958) *Rev. crit. DIP* 117, annotated BATIFFOL. Secondly, if the parties possess two or more nationalities, the **French** nationality will not eclipse the others: Fr. Cass., 1 Civ. Ch., 22nd July 1987 (1988) *Rev. crit. DIP* 85 (*Dujaque*).

245 See. for example, DEVERS (2004) p. 351, §582.

246 The status of relationships registered in **Andorra** under the *Llei 4/2005 del 21 de febrer*, is unclear since decisions emanating from **Andorra** are not considered as foreign, and are thus treated as though they were **French** decisions: Fr. Cass., 1 Civ. Ch., 6th January 1971 (1971) *D* 338, annotated SACOTTE.

quickly multiplies that the dissolution will not be enforced in **France**.[247] In order to avoid this problem, two different approaches have been proposed. HUET suggests that the recognition of a foreign dissolution order should be subject to a choice of law test according to the personal law of the parties.[248] In contrast, the other authors plead for a choice of law test based on the application of the *lex loci registrationis*.[249] DEVERS, in noting the problems associated with such an approach[250] argues that such problems could be ameliorated by applying the theory of equivalence, whereby formal and substantive equivalence could be sought between the law applied and the law designated by the **French** choice of law rule.[251] All authors go on to state that if the dissolution is valid according to the relevant law then it should be recognised in **France**, subject of course to the public policy and fraud exceptions, but without a jurisdictional competency test.

XI.4.2.3 The Netherlands

The recognition of divorces obtained abroad is dealt with in accordance with a number of international treaties and bilateral agreements.[252] Besides

---

247 FULCHIRON (2000) p. 900; HUET (2002) p. 553-554; DEVERS (2004) p. 351, §582; KESSLER (2004) p. 361-362, §630;.

248 HUET (2002) p. 554, see also **Section XI.3.2.3.**

249 FULCHIRON (2000) p. 900; DEVERS (2004) p. 351, §582; KESSLER (2004) p. 365, §635.

250 Problems would arise in those situations where a non-marital registered relationship is dissolved in a country other than where it was registered. In testing the validity of a dissolution against the *lex loci registrationis*, the chances are high that such a dissolution would not be enforced: DEVERS (2004) p. 351-352, §582.

251 DEVERS (2004) p. 352-353, §584-585. In effect, this approach ignores the fact that the law designated by **French** law is not applied, if the end result is "equivalent" to that which would have been reached by a **French** court. This approach has also be used in relation to the recognition of foreign marriage dissolutions: Fr. Cass., 1. Civ. Ch, 29th July 1929 (1931) Rev. crit. DIP, 334, (*Drichemont*); Fr. Cass., 1 Civ. Ch., 22nd April 1986 (1989) *Rev. crit. DIP* 89 (*Lemaire*). See further MAYER/HEUZÉ (2001) p. 728-729, §496-3; AUDIT (2000) p. 403-404, §464.

252 The Hague Convention of 1st June 1970 on the Recognition of Divorces and Legal Separations (1970 Hague DC) (As of the 1st July 2005, this Convention is in force in **Australia**, **Cyprus**, **Czech Republic**, **Denmark**, **Egypt**, **Estonia**, **Finland**, **Hong Kong**, **Italy**, **Luxembourg**, **The Netherlands**, **Norway**, **Poland**, **Portugal**, **Slovakia**, **Sweden**, **Switzerland** and the **United Kingdom**) and ICCS Convention No. 11 on the Recognition of Decisions relating to the Matrimonial Bond signed in Luxembourg on 8th September 1967 (As of the 1st July 2005, this Convention is in force between **The Netherlands**, **Austria** and **Turkey**, and as been signed but not yet ratified by **Belgium**, **France**, **Germany** and **Greece**). Furthermore, **The Netherlands** has two bilateral treaties, namely with **Belgium** (*Neth. Staatsblad* 1929, No. 405) and with **Italy** (*Neth. Tractatenblad* 1959, No. 137). Both of these treaties are only of importance for divorces issued before Brussels II, and subsequently Brussels IIbis, came into force.

these treaties, which will not be discussed here since they are not applicable to the dissolution of non-marital registered relationships and have relatively little impact on the recognition of divorces in **The Netherlands**, specific rules on the recognition of foreign divorces have been in force since 1981.[253] In drafting equivalent rules for the recognition of foreign dissolutions of non-marital registered relationships, both the **Dutch** Standing Committee on Private International Law and the **Dutch** Government saw little reason to diverge from the existing rules laid down in Neth. PIL(D)A. Accordingly the principles in Art. 24, Neth. PIL(RP)A are identical to those laid down in Art. 2, Neth. PIL(D)A.[254]

Although a distinction has been drawn between relationships terminated by mutual consent and those relationships dissolved upon the request of one of the parties, the principles are the same.[255] Four minimum conditions must thus be satisfied.

1. A foreign relationship dissolution (whether of a marriage or a non-marital registered relationship) must have been obtained by a competent authority.[256] Whether the authority was competent is to be judged according to "international standards" and not the jurisdictional rules of the issuing country or **Dutch** law.[257] However, if the **Dutch** authorities would have been competent on identical grounds, then it would appear somewhat hypocritical to refuse recognition on the basis that jurisdiction was assumed on grounds

253 This Act is known as the Private International Law (Divorces) Act (the Neth. PIL(D)A). For the recognition of decisions within the Kingdom of The Netherlands, *i.e.* from Aruba or the Netherlands Antilles, reference will be made to Art. 40, Act of the Kingdom of The Netherlands (*Neth. Staatsblad* 1954, No. 503). See further MOSTERMANS (2003) p. 113, §331.

254 STAATSCOMMISSIE (1998) p. 38; *Dutch Second Chamber,* 2002-2003, 28924, No. 3, p. 17-18; MOSTERMANS (2003) p. 109-111.

255 **Mutual Consent:** Art. 24(1), Neth. PIL(RP)A; **Unilateral Petition:** Art. 24(2), Neth. PIL(RP)A.

256 With respect to divorces, no definitive answer has yet been given as to whether administrative divorces fall within the scope of Art. 2, Neth. PIL(D)A. In Rb Amsterdam, 6th June 1984 (1985) *NIPR* 111, the *rechtbank* decided that an administrative decision granted by a **Thai** Registrar fell within the scope of Art. 2, Neth. PIL(D)A. With respect to registered partnerships, administrative decisions have been expressly included: MOSTERMANS (2003) p. 112-113, §328-329. It has been suggested that such an approach should also be adapted with respect to administrative divorces, see K. BOELE-WOELKI, "Internationaal Privaatrecht. Katern 77", *AA*, 2000, p. 3971-3973; HR, 13th July 2001, NJ 2002, 223, annotated T. DE BOER, §9; MOSTERMANS (2003) p. 96, §271. *Contra* Hof The Hague, 3rd May 2000 (2000) *NIPR* 175, which regarded such divorces as falling under Art. 3, Neth. PIL(D)A.

257 STRIKWERDA (2002) p. 278, §270; MOSTERMANS (2003) p. 99-100, §279-282.

not in accordance with international standards. This could thus be important in cases where a foreign judge assumes jurisdiction on the basis of an unconditional *forum necessitatis*.[258]

2. If the dissolution was obtained as a result of a unilateral petition, it will only be recognised if it was obtained as the result of a proper legal process (*behoorlijke rechtspleging*).[259] Nonetheless, even if either of these first two criteria are not met then the dissolution may still be recognised if the other party either expressly or implicitly consented to the procedure.[260]
3. A foreign decision may also not be contrary to **Dutch** public policy. This will be discussed further in **Section XI.5**.
4. Finally, a decision will not be recognised, even if it complies with the aforementioned criteria if it is not in conformity with a previous decision.[261]

XI.4.2.4 Switzerland

Although the 1970 Hague DC is applicable to the recognition of foreign divorces in **Switzerland**,[262] it is not applicable to the recognition of foreign dissolutions of non-marital registered relationships.[263] Nevertheless, by virtue of Art. 65a, Sw. CPIL all domestic provisions applicable to the recognition of foreign marriage dissolutions are *mutatis mutandis* applicable to the recognition of the dissolution of non-marital registered relationships.[264] As a result, Art. 65, Sw. CPIL is applicable to the recognition of foreign dissolutions of non-marital registered relationships. Art. 65, Sw. CPIL states that foreign divorces and judicial separations will be recognised in **Switzerland** if they have been rendered in the State of the domicile, habitual residence or nationality of either spouse, or if they are

---

258 An unconditional *forum necessitatis* is not an internationally recognised standard of jurisdiction and would thus, under normal circumstances not be recognised. However, such a ground is also recognised in **Dutch** internal procedural law, and it would therefore be rather hypocritical to refuse to grant recognition to a foreign dissolution on this basis, if a **Dutch** court would be able to grant a dissolution having declared itself competent on identical grounds. For more on this ground of jurisdiction, see **Section XI.2.3.3** and the evaluation of such criteria in **Section XI.2.4**.

259 Art. 24(2), Neth. PIL(RP)A, corresponds to Art. 2(1), Neth. PIL(D)A. MOSTERMANS (2003) p. 97-98, §275-278; STRIKWERDA (2002) p. 278-9, §270.

260 Art. 2(2), Neth. PIL(D)A and Art. 24(2), Neth. PIL(RP)A. This is another example of the *favor divortii* and *favor dissolutionis* principles explained in **Section XI.3**.

261 MOSTERMANS (2003) p. 102-103, §289-293.

262 BUCHER (2004a) p. 155-157, §441-448; DUTOIT (2005) p. 219-220, Art. 65, No.7.

263 BUCHER (2004a) p. 207-208, §600.

264 BUCHER (2004a) p. 207, §598; DUTOIT (2005) p. 222, Art. 65a, No. 7.

recognised in one of these States.[265] The broad nature of these rules allow for any procedure, administrative or religious, to be recognised in **Switzerland** as long as it is a *procédure officielle*.[266] Nonetheless, unilateral repudiations, such as the *talaq*, will not be recognised as these are deemed to be against **Swiss** public policy.[267]

In noting that the parties may have made use of the *forum necessitatis* and dissolved their non-marital registered relationship in the country in which it was registered, Art. 65d, Sw. CPIL provides that decisions and measures rendered in the State in which the relationship was registered will be recognised in **Switzerland**,[268] if the action could not have been brought or could not have been reasonably required of the parties in a foreign State whose competence was recognised in **Switzerland**.[269]

XI.4.2.5 United Kingdom

The recognition of foreign divorces, legal separations and annulments has been virtually codified as a result of Part II, Family Law Act 1986 (FLA 1986).[270] These provisions are nigh on identical to those found in Secs. 233-238, CPA 2004. Both pieces of legislation thus draw a distinction between marriage dissolutions granted in other jurisdictions within the **British Isles**[271] and those obtained elsewhere.[272]

A. Obtained in another part of the United Kingdom/British Isles

---

265 Subject to also meeting the conditions laid down in Arts. 25 and 26: BUCHER (2004) p. 147-157, §416-448; DUTOIT (2005) p. 214-220, Art. 65. See further PATOCCHI/GEISINGER (1995) p. 147-157, Arts. 25 and 26.

266 BUCHER (2004a) p. 147, §416 and references. See also Trib. Féd., 3rd September 1996 (1996) 122 III *ATF* 344, (1996) *REC* 400 and (1998) *RSDIE* 262.

267 Tribunal St-Gall, 14 September 1995 (1997) *RSJ* 464, No. 4 and (1998) *RSDIE* 270, where the cantonal court did not recognise the *talaq*. The court said that this would be against **Swiss** public policy because the wife opposed the divorce. See further DUTOIT (2005) p. 215-216, Art. 65, No. 3. For further information on impact of this rule for non-marital registered partnerships see **Section XI.5.2**.

268 This thus includes those dissolutions obtained through administrative proceedings.

269 See further BUCHER (2004a) p. 207, §599; DUTOIT (2005) p. 225, Art. 65d.

270 This is subject to very few exceptions, for which refer to NORTH/FAWCETT (1999) p. 798, 795 and 812.

271 Sch. 1, Interpretation Act 1978: the **UK**, the **Channel Islands** and the **Isle of Man**.

272 Part II, FLA 1986 creates one scheme applicable in all three jurisdictions of the **United Kingdom**. This same principle is copied in the CPA 2004.

If a relationship is terminated in another part of the **United Kingdom** (or **British Isles** for the purposes of marriages) by a court of civil jurisdiction,[273] it will be recognised throughout the **United Kingdom.**[274] A dissolution may only be refused if (a) the dissolution was obtained at a time when it was irreconcilable with a decision determining the question of the subsistence of the non-marital registered relationship,[275] or (b) if at the time the dissolution was obtained there was no subsisting relationship.[276]

B. Obtained outside of the United Kingdom/British Isles

When dealing with dissolutions obtained outside of the **United Kingdom**, a distinction is drawn between those dissolutions obtained "by means of proceedings" and those obtained "without proceedings".[277] The provisions of the CPA 2004 dealing with this topic are identical to those in the FLA 1986, and it is expected that the courts will apply the case law surrounding the FLA 1986 analogously as far as possible.

(a) *With proceedings:* The dissolution will be recognised if,[278]

> (a) the divorce [dissolution], annulment of legal separation is effective under the law of the country in which it was obtained;
> (b) at the relevant date[279] either party to the marriage [civil partner]:
> (i) was habitually resident in the country in which the divorce, annulment or legal separation was obtained; or
> (ii) was domiciled[280] in that country; or

---

273 Sec. 44(1), FLA 1986 and Sec. 233(1), CPA 2004.

274 Sec. 44(1), FLA 1986 and Sec. 233(2), CPA 2004.

275 Sec. 51(1)(a), FLA 1986 and Sec. 233(3), CPA 2004.

276 Sec. 51(2)(a), FLA 1986 and Sec. 233(4), CPA 2004.

277 No distinction is thus drawn between judicial and non-judicial proceedings.

278 The text in square brackets represents the wording used in the CPA 2004

279 *I.e.* the date when the proceedings began: Sec. 46(3)(2), FLA 1986 and Sec. 235(3)(a), CPA 2004. There are two exceptions to this rule: in cases of annulment, the date is the date of death (Sec. 46(4), FLA 1986 and Sec. 235(4), CPA 2004) and in cases of cross-proceedings, the date is the time of proceedings or cross-proceedings (Sec. 47(1)(a), FLA 1986).

280 According to both the FLA 1986 and the CPA 2004, a person is to be treated as "domiciled" in a country if he has was domiciled there either in accordance with the law of the relevant part of the **United Kingdom** or the law of that country: Sec. 46(5), FLA 1986 and Sec. 237(1), CPA 2004. With respect to divorces this thus allows the so-called **Nevada**-style divorce [NRS 125.020.1(e)]: *Messina v. Smith* [1971] P 322 *per* ORMROD J. at 326; *Lawrence v. Lawrence* [1985] Fam. 106 at 121. In other states in the **USA** the residency requirements are also relatively low: 30 days (**Alaska** [AS 25.24.900]), 6 weeks (**Idaho** [IC §32.701]), 60 days (**Arkansas** [AC Sec. 9-12-307(a)(1)(A)], **Kansas** [KSA §60-1603(a)], **Wyoming** [WS 20-2-107(a)]) or 90 days (**Arizona** [ARS Sec. 25-312(1)], **Colorado**

(iii) was a national of that country.[281]

(b) *Without proceedings:* Such a dissolution will be recognised if,

(a) the divorce [dissolution], annulment or legal separation is effective under the law of the country in which it was obtained,
(b) at the relevant date –
(i) each party to the marriage [civil partner] was domiciled in that country, or
(ii) either party to the marriage [civil partner] was domiciled in that country and the other was domiciled in a country under whose law the divorce [dissolution: CPA 2004], annulment or legal separation is recognised as valid, and
(c) neither party to the marriage [civil partner] was habitually resident in the United Kingdom throughout the period of 1 year immediately preceding that date.[282]

(c) *Definition of "proceedings":* The distinction between dissolutions obtained "by proceedings" and those "without proceedings" is especially important with respect to non-marital registered relationships, where it has been shown that dissolution procedures are often declared administratively without a formal "hearing".[283] In *Quazi v. Quazi*,[284] Lord SCARMAN held that a *talaq* which subsequently involved the procedures of the Pakistan Muslim Family Laws Ordinance 1961 was obtained by proceedings, whereas OLIVER LJ held in *Chaudhary v. Chaudhary*[285] that a *bare talaq* (*talaq biddat, i.e.* one in which a thrice repudiation is in and of itself sufficient), was not obtained by proceedings. The term proceedings thus imparts "a degree of formality and at least the involvement of some agency, whether lay or religious, or recognised by the State having a function that is more than simply probative".[286]

The question arises whether the administrative forms of dissolution available in **Belgium**, **France** and **The Netherlands** constitute proceedings according to this definition.[287] In examining the **Dutch** administrative dissolution procedure, it is submitted that the two-stage process to dissolve the relationship will suffice to ensure that this form of dissolution

[CS Sec. 14-10-106(1)(a)(I)], **Illinois** [Chapter 750 ILCS 5/401(a)], **Missouri** [RSMo Sec. 452.300.5(1)], **Montana** [MCA 40-4-104(1)(b)(i)], **Utah** [UC 30-3-1(2)]).

281 Sec. 46(1), FLA 1986 and 235(1), CPA 2004.

282 Sec. 46(2), FLA 1986 and Sec. 235(2), CPA 2004.

283 **Chapters III.6.4**, **III.6.5**, **IV.6.4**, **IV.6.5**, **V.6.4** and **VIII.3**.

284 *Quazi v. Quazi* [1980] AC 744, [1979] 3 All ER 897.

285 *Chaudhary v. Chaudhary* [1985] Fam 19.

286 *Chaudhary v. Chaudhary* [1985] Fam 19 at 41, per OLIVER LJ.

287 See further **Chapters III.6.4, III.6.5, IV.6.4, IV.6.5 and V.6.4.**

procedure is regarded as having been obtained by "proceedings".[288] In turning one's attention to the forms of dissolution provided for in **France** and **Belgium**, it is likely that the administrative forms of dissolution on the basis of the parties' consent will also be regarded as having been obtained by "proceedings", whereas those unilateral decisions or declarations will more-than-likely be regarded as having been obtained without proceedings, due to the lack of anything more than a mere probative formality.[289] This therefore imposes a serious restriction on the recognition of such dissolutions, since dissolutions obtained other than by proceedings will only be recognised if the dissolution is recognised in the parties' domicil.

(d) *Refusal of recognition*: Nonetheless, a dissolution may be refused recognition if,[290] (i) the dissolution was obtained at a time when it was irreconcilable with a decision determining the question of the subsistence of the non-marital registered relationship,[291] or (ii) if at the time the dissolution was obtained there was no subsisting relationship.[292] Furthermore, if the dissolution was obtained by means of proceedings it may also be refused recognition if it was obtained without such steps having been taken for giving notice of the proceedings to the other party or if the other party was not given such an opportunity to take part in the proceedings.[293] On the other hand, if the dissolution was obtained other than by means of proceedings, the dissolution will not be recognised unless there is an official document certifying that the dissolution is effective under the law of the country where it was obtained or, if either party was domiciled in another country at the relevant date,[294] unless there is an official document certifying that the dissolution was recognised as valid under the law of the country of domicile.[295]

288 The decisive moment is when this declaration is registered: see the distinction drawn between the agreement to terminate (**Chapter V.6.4.1**) and the declaration to terminate (**Chapter V.6.4.2**). See also SUMNER (2004a) p. 235-237.

289 See also **Section XI.5**.

290 These provisions provide for a discretionary power: *Duhur-Johnson v. Duhur-Johnson*, 18th May 2005, The Times, Judgment pronounced on 3rd May 2005.

291 Sec. 51(1)(b), FLA 1986 and Sec. 236(1)(a), CPA 2004. See NORTH/FAWCETT (1999) p. 811.

292 Sec. 51(2)(b), FLA 1986 and Sec. 236(1)(b), CPA 2004. See NORTH/FAWCETT (1999) p. 812.

293 Sec. 51(3)(a), FLA 1986 and Sec. 236(3)(a), CPA 2004.

294 As determined in accordance with Sec. 46, FLA 1986 or Sec. 235, CPA 2004.

295 Sec. 51(3)(b), FLA 1986 and Sec 236(3), CPA 2004.

XI.4.4 EVALUATION

If an identical jurisdictional scheme to that laid down in Brussels IIbis would be made created for the dissolution of non-marital registered relationships,[296] there is no reason why the same cannot also be achieved with respect to the Brussels IIbis recognition regime. However, unlike in relation to the jurisdictional rules laid down in Brussels IIbis, there are no areas with respect to the recognition of foreign dissolutions that require different rules than the *favour recognitionis* framework established by Brussels IIbis. If one accepts that the recognition rules should be the same for the two forms of relationship dissolution, there is no obstacle, other than political will, for the creation of a Brussels IIbis type recognition scheme for non-marital registered relationship dissolutions obtained abroad.

Others are, however, not so convinced. MOSTERMANS, in agreeing with the conclusions of JESSURUN D'OLIVEIRA,[297] notes that "*differentiatie is onvermijdelijk*" and that only those new relationship forms similar to marriage should be granted equivalence under the Brussels IIbis regime.[298] However, as has been shown in both **Chapters VIII** and **IX**, the arguments for distinguishing between various types of domestic substantive regulations, although perhaps academically justifiable at substantive law level, are difficult to rationalise and thus mimic at private international law level. What specific characteristics of the **French** PACS or the **Belgian** statutory cohabitation cause them to be so irreconcilable with the analogous application of rules laid down in Brussels IIbis? If one adopts the characterisation proposed in **Chapter IX.4**, it is virtually impossible to justify inconsistent treatment of these relationships.

Nonetheless, if the European Union is wanting of the political will to embark upon such a task, other alternatives should be sought.[299] If the Hague Conference were to begin with such issues, close attention should be paid to the 1970 Hague DC. This Convention, having been ratified by eighteen nations (many of which also recognise a form of non-marital registered relationship) is a good starting point from which to discuss further possibilities for harmonisation or unification instruments. Nonetheless, if a jurisdictional test is to be included, as was the case in the

---

296 **Section XI.2.4.**

297 JESSURUN D'OLIVEIRA (2001b) p. 2040.

298 MOSTERMANS (2002) p. 267, "differentiation is unavoidable" (author's translation).

299 For the various institutions which could develop such rules, see **Chapter XIII.4**.

1970 Hague DC,[300] provisions should also be made for the case where a court is seized of a dissolution on the basis of a *forum necessitatis*. Whichever international institution takes upon itself to embark upon drafting rules in this field,[301] it is crucial that in attempting to create a set of rules which reflect the parties' expectations, prevent limping relationships and increase international co-operation in the field of international recognition, any rules eventually adopted resemble those applicable to the recognition of divorces as closely as possible.

Since Brussels IIbis is currently not applicable to the recognition of non-marital registered relationship dissolutions, all jurisdictions will need to resort to domestic private international law rules. All six jurisdictions to have enacted private international law legislation dealing with the recognition of foreign dissolutions of non-marital registered relationships have sought to duplicate the existing rules on the recognition of foreign divorces. Even in **France** where legislation is currently absent, authors agree on the corresponding application of the rules on the recognition of foreign dissolutions to non-marital registered relationships. Nonetheless, two issues must be addressed, namely the imposition of a choice of law test and/or a jurisdictional test.

In dealing with those countries that have imposed a jurisdictional test prior to the recognition of a foreign dissolution, only **Switzerland** has openly addressed the issue of those dissolutions obtained in the State where the relationship was registered on grounds of a *forum necessitatis*.[302] No express reference is made to such situations in **The Netherlands** or **Belgium**.[303] Although the **United Kingdom** expressly provides for a *forum necessitatis*, it has failed to provide for an equivalent ground with respect to the recognition of foreign dissolutions which have been rendered by a court that has assumed jurisdiction on this basis. Imagine the following situation,

Example 14 (Recognition and forum necessitatis)
Mel, a Malaysian citizen, and Barbara, an Italian citizen, are habitually resident in The Netherlands and both work for a multinational corporation. They enter into a registered partnership in Rotterdam. Two years later Mel receives a posting in Tokyo,

---

300 Art. 2, 1970 Hague DC.

301 See **Chapter XIII.4** with respect to the institution best suited to deal with these issues.

302 Art. 65d, Sw. CPIL.

303 Neither Art. 27, Belg. CPIL nor Art. 24, Neth. PIL(RP)A addresses the issue directly. Both Articles would appear to allow for the recognition of a dissolution order granted in the State where the relationship was registered. In **Belgium** this would be subject to the **Belgian** courts not be exclusively competent: Art. 27(7), Belg. CPIL.

Japan and the couple move. Whilst in Tokyo they decide to terminate their registered partnership. The only forum in which this is possible is The Netherlands, on the grounds of the *forum necessitatis.* The Registrar grants the dissolution on grounds of their mutual consent, in accordance with Art. 1:80d, Neth. CC. Mel, is subsequently posted to the London office and seeks recognition of the dissolution.

According to the law as it currently stands in the **United Kingdom**, this dissolution would not be recognised because it was not obtained in a country where the parties were nationals, habitually resident or domiciled. This is a loophole that should be filled. A dissolution should be recognised if it is obtained in the country in which the relationship was registered.

Turning one's attention to the imposition of a choice of law test, only **France** and **Belgium** impose such a condition. In **Belgium**, although the recognition of a foreign judicial decision is not subject to a choice of law test,[304] the recognition of a foreign authentic instrument is. The recent enactment of the **Belgian** codification of private international law provided the legislature with an opportunity to re-examine the choice of law rules in the field of relationship dissolution. Since it is normally non-marital registered relationships not akin to marriage which can be dissolved administratively,[305] the recognition of these dissolutions will be subject to the condition that they are valid according to the place where the relationship was originally registered.[306] In **France**, due to the fact that the choice of law rules in the field of divorce have been the subject matter of intense criticism and if applied to the dissolution of non-marital registered relationships would often lead to their non-recognition, the majority of authors have suggested alternatives.[307]

However, in light of the desire to increase international co-operation in the field of civil matters coupled with an aspiration to prevent limping relationships, the recognition of non-marital registered relationship dissolutions should not be subject to a choice of law test at all. A jurisdiction which uses such a choice of law test has less confidence in foreign jurisdictions than in its own. One should instead create rules which adhere

---

304 Art. 27(3), Belg. CPIL does impose the condition that the judicial decision will not be recognised if the sole reason for obtaining the decision was to avoid the application of **Belgian** law.

305 See **Chapter VIII.3.4** and **IX.3.1**.

306 Recognition of authentic instrument governed by Art. 27, Belg. CPIL; choice of law test imposed by Art. 27(1), Belg. CPIL; relationship characterised in accordance with Art. 58, Belg. CPIL, and choice of law rule applied by Art. 60(2), Belg. CPIL.

307 See **Section XI.4.2.2**.

to the *favor recognitionis* principle.[308] In doing so, one should perhaps seek inspiration from the recognition rules laid down in Brussels IIbis, where neither a jurisdictional nor a choice of law test is imposed.

In conclusion and in bearing in mind one of the overriding goals of this research, namely to ensure the increased co-operation in the field of the recognition of foreign decisions with respect to non-marital registered relationships,[309] one should strive for a recognition framework that gives effect to dissolutions obtained abroad. In having already created such a scheme for the recognition of foreign marriage dissolutions, and there being no reason to diverge from this scheme, an identical set of recognition rules as those laid down in Brussels IIbis should be created with respect to the recognition of non-marital registered relationship dissolutions.

XI.5 PUBLIC POLICY

In advocating the *mutatis mutandis* application of the existing recognition rules on marriage dissolution to the dissolution of non-marital registered relationships, one must not lose sight of the role of public policy. Although it is clear that the public policy exception should be used sparingly in international and European instruments,[310] as well as national legislation, it may still nonetheless be called upon in extreme cases. Although the public policy exception may be invoked at any stage of the proceedings, this section will only deal with three particular problematic types of dissolution.

XI.5.1 ADMINISTRATIVE DISSOLUTIONS

In some countries, a divorce can be obtained by means of an administrative procedure.[311] Such administrative procedures have raised questions with respect to their international recognition, with some countries refusing to recognise such divorces on grounds of public policy.[312] In those countries

---

308 See, for example, SIEHR (2002) p. 57.

309 See **Chapter I.3**.

310 See **footnote 222, page 489**.

311 For an overview of those European jurisdictions see BOELE-WOELKI *et al.* (2004) p. 21-22 and COENRAAD (2005) p. 259.

312 In 2003, the **Dutch** Government conducted a survey of 19 countries of which 9 replied (**Cyprus**, **Czech Republic**, **Finland**, **France**, **Latvia**, **Romania**, **Slovakia**, **Switzerland** and **Turkey**) that administrative divorces will not be recognised since they are contrary to public policy. 5 other countries (**Austria**, **Germany**, **Greece**, **Slovenia** and **Sweden**) doubted whether administrative divorces would be recognized. It must, however, be noted that the accuracy of this survey is doubtful since according to case law in both

where administrative divorces are refused recognition, the question can be asked whether similar administrative dissolutions of non-marital registered relationships will also fall afoul of such rules. In those countries where administrative divorces are recognised, one does not anticipate any problems with regards the recognition of administrative dissolutions of non-marital registered relationships.

Although administrative divorce procedures are not permitted in any of the seven jurisdictions surveyed in this research,[313] divorces obtained elsewhere by means of administrative procedures are recognised, subject to varying conditions. It is therefore unlikely that the recognition of foreign administrative dissolutions of non-marital registered relationships will raise substantial problems in the countries studied. This is even less likely in **Belgium**, **France** and **The Netherlands**, where domestic substantive law allows for an administrative procedure to terminate non-marital registered relationships.[314]

XI.5.2 UNILATERAL DISSOLUTIONS

In the field of divorce recognition, problems have occurred with regard to the recognition of extra-judicial divorces obtained without proceedings. This type of marriage dissolution is best illustrated by the Islamic religious divorce in the form of the *talaq*.[315] Under Shari'a law, a husband has the right to divorce his wife by *talaq* provided that he has reached the age of majority, is sane, and is acting on his own free will.[316] Although of a very different nature, some countries allow for non-marital registered

---

France and **Switzerland**, administrative divorces will be recognised if they satisfy certain conditions. **Fr.**: See, Fr. Cass., 1 Civ. Ch., 17th April 1953 (1953) *Rev. crit. DIP* 412, annotated BATIFFOL; (1953) *JDI* 860, annotated PLAISANT (*Rivière*). See further LOUSSOUARN/BOUREL (2004) p. 708, §492-5, footnote 7. **Swit.**: Trib. Féd., 3rd September 1996 (1996) 122 III *ATF* 344 and **Section XI.4.2.4**.

313 Although **The Netherlands** does not allow for an administrative divorce procedure, administrative dissolution of a marriage is possible: see **Chapter V.6.4** and **V.6.8**. See also **Chapter VIII.3.3** with respect to the LUCHTENVELD proposal to introduce a form of administrative divorce.

314 See **Chapter III.6.4**, **III.6.5**, **IV.6.4** and **IV.6.5**. In **Belgium** this power is restricted to those non-marital relationships registered in **Belgium**: see further **Section XI.2.3.1**.

315 The *talaq*, either in the form of a bare *talaq* or self-repudiation (*talaq at-tafwid*). The Jewish *ghet* and the Islamic *khula* are both forms of consensual, albeit highly minimalistic divorce.

316 See further, F.J.A. VAN DER VELDEN, *Talaq in de rechtszaal?*, Deventer: Kluwer, Ars Notariatus CXVIII, 2003, p. 4-11. Little problem is caused by the judicial form of divorce (*tafriq*) permitted according to Islamic law.

relationships to be dissolved upon the unilateral declaration of one of the parties; in effect a kind of repudiation. Of the countries surveyed, only **France** and **Belgium** have procedures which could be seen as equivalent to such forms of repudiations, and therefore may create problems in relation to public policy.

Although both **French** and **Belgian** law provide for the dissolution of a non-marital registered relationship upon the unilateral declaration of one of the parties, both countries also impose the condition that any declaration be subsequently registered by a competent authority.[317] The question therefore arises whether these registered, unilateral declarations terminating a non-marital registered relationship will be regarded as against the public policy of **The Netherlands**, **Switzerland** and the **United Kingdom**. In answering this question it must be noted that the reason for refusing to recognise a *talaq* is rooted in the discriminatory nature of the repudiation.[318] Only the man is afforded the right to repudiate the relationship. This is not, however, the case in non-marital registered relationships were this right is afforded to both parties on an equal footing.

The second problem lies in the fact that the party to whom the repudiation is addressed is not able to contest the declaration. This is, however, also the case with regards non-marital registered relationships. In **Belgium** and **France**, the repudiated party is simply informed of the dissolution. The dissolution procedure is characterised by a non-contradictory and unilateral act. It is submitted that the problems created at private international law level by such unilateral dissolutions are better solved at domestic substantive law level. As has already been stated, these dissolution forms should simply not be permitted, since they provide the weaker party with absolutely no protection against the whim of their partner, and contradict not only the principles of family law but also those of contract law.[319]

XI.5.3 DISSOLUTION BY VIRTUE OF MARRIAGE

As has been seen, both **France** and **Belgium** allow for a non-marital registered relationship to be dissolved upon the subsequent marriage of one

---

317 In **Belgium** this is the Registrar (**Chapter III.6.5**) and in the **France** the court clerk (**Chapter IV.6.5**).

318 See for example DEVERS (2004) p. 355, §590.

319 See **Chapter VIII.3.4**.

of the parties.[320] Although this author disagrees with the possibility to dissolve a non-marital registered relationship on such a ground,[321] these procedures are currently available and may therefore raise issues of public policy. However, if one examines the situation carefully one realises that this issues is actually a non-conflict case.

> ***Example 15 (Public policy and dissolution by subsequent marriage)***
> Jill and Jack are both habitually resident in France and decide to register a PACS. They subsequently both move to Utopia, where Jill falls in love with Humpty and subsequently decides to marry him. According to French law Jill's marriage to Humpty terminates her PACS with Jack.

If the law of Utopia (as is the case in **The Netherlands**, **Switzerland** and the **United Kingdom**) deemed the existence of a non-marital registered relationship to form a prohibition to entering into marriage, then Jill and Humpty would not be allowed to marry. If, however, the law of Utopia (as is the case in **Belgium** and **France**) did not prevent the celebration of a marriage despite the parties being involved in non-marital registered relationship, then it would seem unlikely that resort would be made to the public policy exception. In this scenario,[322] it would seem that the subsequent celebration of the marriage would conform to the parties' expectations, conform to the public policy of the country where the relationship was registered and conform to the public policy of the country where either party wished to marry. In this situation, the *lex fori* should be applied in order to determine exactly how and when the subsequent marriage terminates the original non-marital registered relationship.[323]

XI.5.4 EVALUATION

From these three examples it is clear that the role of public policy in this field is likely to be negligible. In accepting that the recognition rules laid down in Brussels IIbis are equally suitable to be applied in the case of non-marital registered relationship dissolution, public policy should be seen as being an escape clause for extreme situations. Nonetheless, one should not overlook the fact that unilateral dissolutions, such as those provided for in **France** and **Belgium**, will raise serious questions in the field of public policy.

---

320 See **Chapter III.6.8** and **IV.6.8.** This is also possible in other jurisdictions: see for a summary **footnote 250** in **Chapter IX**.

321 See **Chapter VIII.3.4.**

322 Say for example instead of moving to Utopia Lieke and Gert-Jan moved to **Belgium**.

323 This, therefore, also ensures continuity with the choice of law rules applicable to the dissolution of non-marital registered relationships.

Yet the underlying principles of private international law should not be undermined in attempting to prevent limping relationships at all costs. If **France** and **Belgium** are unwilling to change their law accordingly, parties opting for such dissolutions in these countries should be warned of the international implications of these actions.

XI.6 SUMMARY OF CONCLUSIONS

It has been stated that with respect to the field of divorce law, the unification of private international law alone is unable to remove the obstacles experienced by European citizens moving from jurisdiction to jurisdiction.[324] Although the only solution in the field of divorce is thus to search for possible harmonised or unified rules of substantive law, the veritable Gordian knot of any attempt to harmonise or unify substantive law in the field of non-marital registered relationships, necessitates a temporary solution in the form of harmonised or unified private international law rules.

The unified framework already established in the field of jurisdiction and recognition and enforcement of judgments by Brussels IIbis with regards divorce should serve as the basis for equivalent rules with respect to non-marital registered relationships. However, in order to deal with the possibility that couples will be left without a forum in which to dissolve their relationship, a restricted *forum necessitatis* in the State in which the relationship was registered is needed.

Furthermore, it is also clear that issues of jurisdiction and choice of law are inextricably interwoven and one cannot be solved without reference to the other. In providing for a very similar jurisdictional scheme as that laid down by Brussels IIbis, one must attempt to curb any ensuing race to court. Moreover, unlike the diversity to be found in the choice of law rules in the field of divorce, only three approaches are evident with respect to non-marital registered relationships. Only two of these approaches serve to promote the aims of uniformity and certainty in the field of private international law and actively prevent the creation of limping relationships, namely the application of the *lex loci registrationis* or the *lex fori*. In conformance with the more modern codifications of choice of law rules in the field of divorce, and at the same time ensuring adherence to the need to avert forum shopping and provide flexibility, the wholesale application of

[324] BOELE-WOELKI (2002b) p. 171-189 at 174.

the *lex fori* should be mitigated in allowing the parties to choose the application of the *lex loci registrationis*. Furthermore, domestic substantive law should apply in order to determine the competent authority to dissolve the relationship, if the relationship was registered in the forum. In cases involving the dissolution of a relationship registered abroad, the courts should be exclusively competent.

With respect to the recognition of foreign dissolutions, it is also feasible that a similar framework could be created as already in force in the field of marriage dissolution recognition. All in all, it would appear that this field of law, as with the establishment of the relationship is suitable to harmonised or unified private international law rules, should the necessary political will exist to enact them.

CHAPTER XII
LEGAL EFFECTS OF A NON-MARITAL REGISTERED RELATIONSHIP

XII.1 INTRODUCTION

Once it has been determined that a non-marital registered relationship has been validly created, a number of rights will be granted and duties imposed on the parties. Their status as "registered partners" will affect not only their social standing, but will also have important and often far-reaching legal effects in both their personal and economic lives. As was shown in **Section 5** of **Chapters III-VII**, the effect of registering a non-marital relationship differs enormously depending upon the country in which it is registered. These differences in national attitude raise complicated issues when cases demonstrate an international element. Nonetheless, it is not proposed to analyse each and every right individually in terms of jurisdiction, choice of law and the recognition and enforcement of foreign judgments.

Instead, this chapter is divided into two main sections: legal effects in the public law sphere (**Section XII.2**) and legal effects in the private law sphere (**Section XII.3**). Although a public/private law distinction is perhaps most suited to continental European jurisdictions, it serves a convenient expositional purpose that is also acknowledged in the **United Kingdom**.[1] Moreover, although any classification will inevitably lead to questions of characterisation,[2] the aim of this chapter is simply to highlight the shear diversity of problems and outline some of the different approaches proffered for their solution.

---

1 See, for example, the classification used by P. Shears and G. Stephenson, *James' Introduction to English Law*, London: Butterworths, 1996, 13th Edition, p. 5.

2 See **Chapter II**.

XII.2 LEGAL EFFECTS IN THE PUBLIC LAW SPHERE

SAVIGNY'S model of private international law, which is still highly influential across continental Europe,[3] is restricted to the private law field.[4] The same distinction is equally endorsed in the **United Kingdom**.[5] As a result, public law is, generally and traditionally speaking,[6] never applied beyond its territorial boundaries. Although this has led to an extensive discussion of the extraterritorial nature of certain public law fields, this will not form the focus of this section. Furthermore, although the research conducted in this book is focused on the desirability and feasibility of harmonising or unifying private international law rules with respect to non-marital registered relationships in Europe, it is important to note the corollary effect of any such rules in the field of public law.

It is, however, not easy to define the scope of public law. Although pure public law rights and duties are not difficult to identify, *e.g.* tax law, procedural law, social security benefits, public pensions, immigration, criminal law, *etc.*,[7] problems arise with respect to semi-public law rights, such as those in the field of employment law and tenancy law. Instead of attempting to determine whether private international law rules apply to such legal effects, a category apart has been created known as mandatory rules (*règles d'application immediate* or *voorrangsregels*).[8]

---

3 AUDIT (2000) p. 81, §98; STRIKWERDA (2002) p. 21; BUCHER/BONOMI (2004) p. 99, §374. Although the basis of the common law is not logic but experience, and thus not entirely in conformity with SAVIGNY'S model, the method adopted in practice in **English** law corresponds generally with that suggested by SAVIGNY: NORTH/FAWCETT (1992) p. 23.

4 See, for example, STRIKWERDA (2002) p. 66-67, §77-79.

5 **English** lawyers, employing the words of Lord DENNING, impose a three-fold classification of foreign law that are not enforced by **English** courts, namely revenue laws, penal laws and other public laws: NORTH/FAWCETT (1999) p. 106-132, ANTON/BEAUMONT (1990) p. 105-106 and *Attorney General of New Zealand v. Otiz* [1984] AC 1 at 20 *et seq.* This classification has furthermore been endorsed by the Court of Appeal on numerous occasions, *e.g. United States of America v. Inkley* [1989] QB 255 at 265 and *Camdex International Ltd v. Bank of Zambia (No. 2)* (1997) The Times, 28th January 1997 (CA).

6 It is not intended here to begin to embark upon a discussion of the extraterritorial effect of public law. For a discussion of such issues in the field of criminal law see J. HIRST, *Jurisdiction and the ambit of criminal law*, Oxford: Oxford University Press, 2003.

7 It is also noteworthy that for the purposes of this distinction the law on the acquisition or loss of nationality would also be regarded as public law.

8 NORTH/FAWCETT (1999) p. 132; STRIKWERDA (2002) p. 66-72, §77-83; BUCHER/BONOMI (2004) p. 121, §453. These rules have been defined by the English Law Commission as "so important that as a matter of construction or policy they must apply in action before a court of the forum even where the issues are in principle governed by a foreign law

Nevertheless, regardless of these definitional problems, it is submitted that the approach adopted is independent of the relationship to which the right or duty is attached. Whether a particular right in, for example, the field of employment law is regarded as a mandatory rule is independent from the question, whether it is granted to those involved in a marriage or non-marital registered relationship. Hence, this definitional debate falls outside the ambit of this research.[9]

As has already been shown in **Section 5** of **Chapters III-VII**, the existence of a non-marital registered relationship may engender significant consequences in certain public law fields. In order to determine whether someone is permitted to benefit from a public law entitlement by virtue of their "status", reference will be made to the rules of private international law.[10] Referring incidental questions in the field of public law to the rules of private international law is a natural consequence of attempting to ensure uniformity of status within the same legal order. Although marriage and non-marital registered relationships are private law institutions, they have extensive public law consequences. As a result, reference is made in the field of public law to the private international law rules in order to determine the validity of such relationships. Take the following example:

> ***Example 16 (Effect of private international law in public law)***
> Chris and Janine enter into a registered partnership in Vleuterweide, The Netherlands. According to Dutch law they must file joint tax returns from the date their registered partnership is valid (*fiscale partnerschap*). One year later they move to France and seek recognition of their non-marital registered relationship. According to French law, registered partners (*i.e.* those involved in a PACS) are only entitled to file joint tax returns (*l'imposition commune*) once three years have elapsed since the registration of their relationship.[11] Furthermore, two friends of Chris and Janine, Chloe and Edgar, entered into a PACS in Paris, France. They subsequently move to The Netherlands.

If one accepts that the term "non-marital registered relationship" should be interpreted as broadly as possible[12] so as to prevent the possibility of limping relationships, one must be aware of the impact that such a characterisation will have outside of the field of private international law. A broad definition

---

selected by a choice of law rule": ENGLISH LAW COMMISSION, *Choice of Law in Tort and Delict. Working Paper No. 87*, London: HMSO, 1984.

9 For a similar argument in relation to the distinction between formal and essential validity see **Chapter X.2, page 393**.

10 DETHLOFF (2003) p. 46, footnote 47.

11 See **Chapters V.5.5** and **IV.5.5** respectively.

12 As has been advocated in **Chapter IX.4** and **IX.6**.

will lead to more foreign relationships being treated in an identical fashion to those relationships registered domestically. In some situations this will mean that the parties will benefit from a more favourable situation. In the aforementioned example, Chloe and Edgar, upon moving to **The Netherlands**, will be able to file joint tax returns and could thus benefit financially. In other situations, the parties will be worse off. In the aforementioned example, Janine and Chris, upon moving to **France**, would no longer be able to file joint tax returns and could thus be worse off financially. Although the same can also be said of spouses who travel from one country to another, the marked diversity between jurisdictions is not as great as is the case with regards non-marital registered relationships.

Another solution, as has been employed in **Belgium**,[13] is to make a distinction between non-marital registered relationships akin to marriage (characterised as marriages) and non-marital registered relationships not akin to marriage (characterised as cohabitating relationships). Although this approach offers a solution to the above mentioned problems in the field of public law, other problems are created as a consequence. Accordingly, it is submitted that the negative public law effects of accepting a broad characterisation must be weighed against the prevailing aims of ensuring the uniformity of personal status and preventing limping relationships. Instead of seeking answers in the field of private international law, more pressure should be exerted on national governments to treat spouses and registered partners alike. However, as was outlined in **Chapter VIII.4**, those countries having reached stage 2 of the PLURALISTIC MODEL have often attempted to draw a distinction between non-marital registered relationships and marriages. Such distinctions can be drawn in the field of public law, for example, by restricting financial benefits in the field of tax and social security law to spouses. Even so, the adverse consequences of this broad characterisation are not enough to detract from the greater aim of preventing limping relationships and ensuring uniformity of status in a politically feasible manner.

XII.3 LEGAL EFFECTS IN THE PRIVATE LAW SPHERE

The celebration of a marriage or the registration of a non-marital relationship can also have sweeping consequences in the field of private law. However, for the purposes of this research, these rights and duties have been divided into four general categories: matters relating to children

13 See **Chapter IX.3.1**.

(**Section XII.3.1**), matters relating to inheritance (**Section XII.3.2**), pecuniary matters (**Section XII.3.3**) and non-pecuniary matters (**Section XII.3.4**).

The legal effects with regards children and inheritance have been dealt with separately for a specific reason. In both these fields the focus of the private international law rules is not the parties' relationship itself. The rules are instead "triggered" by other events, *e.g.* the birth or adoption of a child or a person's death. In this way, the existence of a marriage or non-marital registered relationship is not the crucial factor in determining the guiding principle or rationale behind these rules; these rules are focused on individuals and not on an individual's relationship. For this reason, these two areas of law should be, and have been, dealt with separately.

In contrast, the private international law rules with respect to pecuniary and non-pecuniary rights and duties are triggered by the registration of a non-marital relationship or the celebration of a marriage, *e.g.* a right to maintenance, the right to change one's surname, a change in one's property rights *etc.*[14] With regards these rights and duties the private international law rules attach primarily to the existence of such a relationship. For ease of analysis these rights have been grouped together into two categories (pecuniary and non-pecuniary matters), in accordance with VON BAR'S classifications in his comparisons in the field of the personal effects of marriage.[15]

XII.3.1 MATTERS RELATING TO CHILDREN

As has already been stated, many private international law rules should be analysed within the broader context of their fields of operation, instead of being dealt with independently in relation to non-marital registered relationships. Many private international law rules with respect to children do not focus solely on the parent's relationship. Instead the primary concern in the fields of parentage, parental responsibilities or adoption is normally the protection of children and the aspiration that decisions are taken in their best interests. In this way, both the jurisdiction and choice of law rules

---

14 These rights are often collectively referred to as the "personal effects" of a marriage or non-marital registered relationship: VON BAR (1986) p. 3, §1 and p. 5, §3. For example, the term is used in the **Dutch** Private International Law (Legal Marital Relations) Act (*Wet Conflictenrecht Huwelijksbetrekkingen*) in Art. 1(1), "*persoonlijke rechtsbetrekkingen tussen de echtgenoten*". However, although the term "personal effects" is used extensively, it is seldom defined and thus leads to confusion. For this reason, the term has been avoided throughout this section.

15 VON BAR (1986) p. 30 *et seq.*

often reflect a greater degree of physical proximity than is perhaps evident in other areas of private international law.[16] The physical presence of the child is often determinative for jurisdiction, *i.e.* the child's habitual residence, and the *lex fori* is usually applied automatically by virtue of child law being rooted in a country's public policy.[17] These aims are no different if the child is born in or brought to a non-marital registered relationship. Therefore, non-marital registered relationships should simply be taken into account in the cornucopia of instruments already dealing with issues relating to children.

This approach is clearly evident in **Belgium**, **The Netherlands**, **Switzerland**, the **United Kingdom** and the proposals by the **French** Ministry of Justice. None of the private international law schemes created in these countries provide for special rules in the field of child law. This approach has also been embraced by the European Union. The original jurisdictional rules laid down in Art. 3(1), Brussels II only applied to those children born of both spouses. Children in other relationships fell outside the scope of the Regulation ensuring the creation of a two-track system. On the one hand, a unified European fast-track for children born in marriages and, on the other, a domestic national track for children born outside of wedlock. This differential treatment was, however, the subject of general criticism and led to a **French** amendment submitted on the 3rd July 2000.[18] As a result, Brussels II was repealed and replaced by Brussels IIbis which ensures equal treatment for all children, regardless of whether the matrimonial dissolution proceedings are covered by Brussels IIbis.[19] The same approach is also taken in the 1996 Hague Convention on jurisdiction, applicable law, recognition, enforcement and co-operation in respect of parental responsibility and measures for the protection of children (1996 Hague CC).[20]

---

16 See, for example, Recital 12, Brussels IIbis. This is furthermore underlined in allowing a *forum non conveniens* exception with respect to parental responsibility proceedings (Art. 15, Brussels IIbis) and not in the field of divorce.

17 See, for example, the decision of *Johnstone v. Beattie* (1843) 10 Cl. & Fin 42 at 120, where Lord Copley, Lord Chancellor stated that, "The Lord Chancellor, representing the Sovereign as *parens patriae*, has a clear right to interpose the authority of the court for the protection of the person and property of all infants resident in England ..." and later, at p. 122: "the benefit of the infant, which is the foundation of the jurisdiction, must be the test of its right exercise."

18 15th August 2000, *OJ*, 2000/C-234/01, p. 7.

19 Recital 5, Brussels IIbis.

20 Art. 2 refers to all "children from the moment of their birth until they reach the age of eighteen years".

Although this trend is becoming more and more widespread, this is not the case in all fields of child law. According to Art. 1a of the 1993 Hague Convention on protection of children and co-operation in respect of intercountry adoption (1993 Hague AC), one of the objects of this Convention is to establish safeguards that intercountry adoptions take place in the best interests of the child and with respect for his or her fundamental rights as recognised in international law.[21] However, the majority of countries from which children are adopted belong to the group of countries which still regard homosexuality as a criminal offence.[22] As a result, these countries saw it necessary to ensure that the 1993 Hague AC was restricted to adoptions by "spouses and individuals".[23]

---

21 Nonetheless, this object is to be seen as a paramount consideration and does not therefore operate to the exclusion of the other persons involved in the adoption: G. PARRA-ARANGUREN, *Explanatory Report on the Convention on protection of children and co-operation in respect of intercountry adoption. Volume II*, The Hague, 1993, 13, §63.

22 In the following countries sentences of *maximum seven years* can be imposed: **Botswana**: Sec. 164 Penal Code; **Cook Islands**: Sec. 155 Penal Code (14 years if with a female); **Kuwait**: Sec. 193 Penal Code; **Western Samoa**: Secs. 58b-58j Penal Code. In the following countries sentences of *maximum ten years* can be imposed: **Bahrain**: Art. 377 Penal Code; **Brunei**: Secs. 292, 294, 377 Penal Code; **Burma**: Secs. 1882-88 Penal Code; **Jamaica**: Secs. 76-79 Penal Code (as well as hard labour); **Marshall Islands**: Sec. 53 Penal Code; **Niue (New Zealand Dependency)**: Sec. 170 Penal Code; **Qatar**: Art. 201 Penal Code; **Sri Lanka**: Sec. 365a Penal Code; **Tokelau (New Zealand Dependency)**: Sec. 170 Penal Code; **Tonga**: Sec. 136 Penal Code; **Trinidad and Tobago**: Secs. 13 and 16, Sexual Offences Act 1986. In the following countries sentences *exceeding fourteen years* can be imposed: **Fiji**: Sec. 175 Penal Code (with or without corporal punishment); **Gambia**: Art. 144 Criminal Code; **Kiribati**: Sec. 153 Penal Code; **Kenya**: Secs. 162-165 Penal Code; **Malaysia**: Arts. 377A and 377B, Penal Code (20 years); **Papua New Guinea**: Sec. 210 Penal Code; **Puerto Rico**: Art. 103 Penal Code (20 years); **Solomon Islands**: Sec. 153 Penal Code; **Tanzania**: Secs. 154-157 Penal Code; **Tuvalu**: Sec. 153 Penal Code; **Zambia**: Sec. 155 Penal Code. In the following countries *life imprisonment* is or can be imposed: **Bhutan**: Sec. 377 Indian Penal Code; **Guyana**: Sec. 353 Penal Code; **India**: Sec. 377 Indian Penal Code; **Maldives**: Sec. 377 Indian Penal Code; **Nepal**: Sec. 377 Indian Penal Code; **Singapore**: Sec. 377 Penal Code; **Uganda**: Sec. 140 Penal Code. In at least a further thirty-six countries same-sex sexual relations are still penalised with financial penalties, limited custodial sentences or corporal punishment. In four **US** States sentences more severe than seven years were possible in four States (**Mississippi:** Art. 27-29-59 Mississippi Statutes (7 years); **Michigan**: Art. 750-158 Michigan Statutes (15 years)); **Oklahoma**: Art. 21-886 Oklahoma Statutes (20 years); **Idaho:** Art. 18-6605 Idaho Statutes (life in prison)). However, since the US Supreme Court decision in *Lawerence v. Texas*, 539 US 558 (2003), these provisions are no longer enforceable. In **Afghanistan**, **Chechnya**, **Iran**, **Mauritania**, **Nigeria**, **Pakistan**, **Saudi Arabia**, **Sudan**, **United Arab Emirates** and **Yemen**, same-sex sexual activity is punishable by execution. The majority of these countries refer to Shari'a law (Islamic law), which allows for a punishment of law.

23 Art. 2, 1993 Hague AC. Even the phrase "spouse" is probably to be interpreted, in light of the *travaux préperatioires* of the 1993 Hague AC, as limited to spouses of different sex: STAATSCOMMISSIE (2001b) p. 31.

Moreover, although the 1996 Hague CC does not generally make a distinction based upon the parent's relationship, an exception is made if this would benefit the paramount concerns of child protection and ensure that the best interests of the child were safeguarded. Bearing this in mind, Art. 8(2)(c), 1996 Hague CC states that a court seized by virtue of Arts. 5 or 6, 1996 Hague CC may suspend proceedings if it is felt that the State whose authorities are seized of an application for the dissolution of a marriage would be better placed to hear proceedings in relation to the child.[24] This possibility is not, however, extended to dissolution proceedings involving a non-marital registered relationship.

Nonetheless, despite these problems it is strongly recommended to sustain an inclusive approach whereby the position of those involved in non-marital registered relationships is dealt with within the context of existing private international law rules in the field of child law. Creating separate private international law rules specifically aimed at registered partners with children will only serve to fragment and further complicate the existing framework of rules, which in turn only increases the possibility that the underlying rationale behind such rules will be lost.

XII.3.2 MATTERS RELATING TO INHERITANCE

A rationale similar to that applied in the field of child law is also pertinent in the field of inheritance law.[25] The private international law rules with respect to inheritance only become operational upon a person's death. The existence of a non-marital registered relationship or marriage only plays a subsidiary or incidental role in determining the overall form of such private international law rules. Consequently, any private international law rules relating to registered partners and their inheritance rights should be incorporated within the range of current and future inheritance law rules. Although any such rules must also be in conformity with the principles laid down with respect to the private international law aspects of non-marital registered relationships,[26] it is crucially important to ensure constancy of principle within the field of inheritance law.

This inclusive approach has already received passive support from the European Commission in a recently published Green Paper on the possibilities for harmonisation of the private international law rules in the

---

24 The same principle is also provided for in Art. 15, Brussels IIbis.

25 See, for example, BUCHER (2004a) p. 201, §573.

26 *I.e.* in conformity with the rules espoused in **Chapters IX**, **X** and **XI**.

field of succession and wills.[27] Noting the growing mobility of people in an area without internal frontiers and the increasing frequency of unions between nationals of different Member States often involving the acquisition of property in the territory of several Union countries, the European Commission has felt it necessary to open a broad-based consultation on the private international law rules in testate and intestate succession.[28] Observing that the validity of a marriage or a non-marital registered relationship can often surface as an incidental question, the European Commission asked which law should be used to determine the law applicable to such preliminary questions.[29] In dealing with both marriages and non-marital registered relationships at the same time the European Commission has wholeheartedly embraced an inclusive approach and should be commended for endorsing for this technique.

Of all the countries to have addressed the private international law problems raised by non-marital registered relationships, only **Belgium** and **Switzerland** have specifically addressed the issues raised when the *lex successionis* points to a legal system that does not recognise non-marital registered relationships. In **Switzerland**, reference is first made to the transposition method, whereby "*dispositions applicables*" are sought before ultimately applying the *lex fori*.[30] **Belgium**, on the other hand, has opted for the designated law to be substituted by the *lex loci registrationis*.[31] This approach has, however, attracted some criticism from **French** authors, who feel that such a solution disregards the basic principles of private international law.[32] Instead, French authors appear to support the more practical approach eventually taken in **The Netherlands**. It was felt that when the law designated by the choice of law rule refers to a jurisdiction that does not recognise non-marital registered relationships, there is very little chance that a registered partner will be able to claim part of the deceased's estate on the basis of his or her status as registered partner.[33] As a result, instead of tampering with the existing private international law rules in inheritance, the **Dutch** Government has committed itself to investing

27 COM (2005) 65 and SEC (2005) 270.

28 COM (2005) 65, p. 3 and SEC (2005) 270, p. 4-5.

29 COM (2005) 65, p. 7 and SEC (2005) 270, p. 24. From the comparative overview it appears that all countries in the European Union support the view that the choice of law rules of the forum should apply to both main and incidental questions (an independent approach).

30 Art. 65c(1), Sw. CPIL. For more explanation see **Chapter XI.3.2.3** and **Table 12**.

31 Art. 60(3), second sentence, Belg. CPIL. A solution borrowed from **Germany**: Art. 17a(1), Ger. CCIL. See further, THORN (2003a) p. 163-164, HOHLOCH/KJELLAND (2001) p. 232.

32 DEVERS (2004) p. 376, §630; KESSLER (2004) p. 346, §601.

33 STAATSCOMMISSIE (1998) p. 9-12.

more time and money in advising aspirant registered partners of the complications that may arise as a result of not drawing up a will.[34] In the **United Kingdom** the issue has not been raised at all, despite the private international law rules in the field of inheritance law often leading to the application of foreign law.[35]

Although certain problems are encountered when the *lex loci registrationis* grants the parties a right which is not granted in accordance with the *lex successionis* (or *vice versa*), or the *lex successionis* grants the parties inheritance rights which are not available according to the *lex fori*, these issues are best dealt with in realm of inheritance law. Fracturing the applicable instruments depending upon the personal status of the deceased will only lead to confusion and arbitrary treatment. It is perhaps opportune at the moment of registration to ensure that parties are advised of the necessity to draw up a will regulating their affairs in the case of either party's death in order to minimise future problems. Although this will not necessarily prevent the use of a public policy exception, drafting a will will inevitably generate more certainty and security, going some way to avoiding the application of complicated choice of law rules.[36]

XII.3.3 PECUNIARY MATTERS

XII.3.3.1 Maintenance between former partners

The issue of maintenance, unlike child and inheritance law, is more closely related to the relationship itself, since it is the relationship that causes the rules on maintenance to become operational, in turn activating any necessary private international law rules. Although not all countries allow for a maintenance claim by a former registered partner,[37] those countries that do allow for such a claim do so on the same grounds as maintenance claims between former spouses.[38] If the substantive rules on maintenance

---

34 *Dutch Second Chamber*, 2002-2003, 28924, No. 3, p. 7.

35 The **English** choice of law rules with respect to intestate succession are relatively clear. For movables they point to the application of the law of the deceased's domicile at the time of his or her death: *Pipon v. Pipon* (1744) Amb 25. See further NORTH/FAWCETT (1999) p. 985 and COLLINS (2000) p. 1026, §27R-010, whilst for immovables they point to the application of the *lex siate*: *Nelson v. Lord Bridport* (1846) 8 Beav. 547.

36 Such a conclusion is also shared by STAATSCOMMISSIE (1998) p, 12; *Dutch Second Chamber*, 2002-2003, 28924, No. 3, p. 6; KESSLER (2004) p. 346, §601.

37 See **Chapters III.6.9.1** (**Belgium**) and **IV.6.9.1** (**France**).

38 See **Section 6.9.1** in **Chapters V-VII**. See BOELE-WOELKI *et al.* (2004) p. 69-70, for some of the reasons why maintenance is imposed between former spouses. These same reasons are

between former registered partners are based on the same underlying principles as maintenance claims between former spouses, there is consequently little reason to deviate from the existing private international law rules in the field of maintenance between former spouses in attempting to create similar rules for maintenance claims between registered partners. This section will address the issues of jurisdiction (**Section A**), choice of law (**Section B**) and the recognition and enforcement of foreign judgments (**Section C**).

A. Jurisdiction

In the European Union, jurisdiction issues relating to maintenance claims nominally fall under the scope of Brussels I. Accordingly, the courts of the Member State where the creditor is domiciled or habitually resident (Art. 5(2), Brussels I) or where the debtor is domiciled (Art. 2, Brussels I) are competent to proceed in "matters relating to maintenance". Furthermore, if the matter is ancillary to proceedings concerning the status of a person, the maintenance creditor is also entitled to proceed in the jurisdiction which, according to its own law, has jurisdiction to entertain those proceedings.[39] Identical jurisdictional grounds are also provided for in Arts. 2 and 5(2), Lugano Convention in relation to jurisdiction in **Switzerland**.[40]

The term "matters relating to maintenance" is not defined in the 1968 Brussels Convention, the 1982 Lugano Convention or in Brussels I.[41] Since Art. 5(2), Brussels I makes no reference to the marital bond and no such restriction has been imposed by the ECJ, it is submitted that Art. 5(2) should be read so as to include registered partners. This broad interpretation of the term is further supported by the fact that maintenance claims by children are covered by the provision; the provision is thus not exclusive to maintenance claims between former spouses.[42] Furthermore, the ECJ has

---

to be found in the field of non-marital registered relationships in those countries where maintenance claims are allowed.

[39] Art. 5(2), last sentence, Brussels I.

[40] BUCHER (2004a) p. 74-75, §179.

[41] SCHLOSSER REPORT, *Report on the convention on the association of the Kingdom of Denmark, Ireland and the United Kingdom of Great Britain and Northern Ireland to the convention on the jurisdiction and the enforcement of judgments in civil and commercial matters*, 9th October 1978, *OJ*, 79/C-59/71 at p. 101-105.

[42] Recital 11, Brussels IIa, COM (2004) 254, p. 14 and JENARD REPORT, *Report on the Convention on jurisdiction and the enforcement of judgments in civil and commercial matters*, *OJ*, 79/C-59/01, p. 10-11, "[t]he EEC Convention ... applies to maintenance even where the obligation stems from the status of the persons and irrespective of whether rights and duties between spouses or between parents and children are involved." And at

been called upon to clarify the extent to which different sorts of maintenance claims fall within the scope of the 1968 Brussels Convention (and thus Brussels I).[43] In all of these cases the ECJ has clarified that the term "maintenance creditor" must be interpreted autonomously and broadly.[44]

Moreover, in the recent Green Paper published by the European Commission proposing uniform private international law rules in the field of maintenance obligations, the question was asked whether any future instrument should include maintenance obligations between former registered partners.[45] In nearly all the responses received during the consultation process an affirmative answer has been provided.[46] Nonetheless, it is submitted that such a definition would only serve to further clarify the existing situation; namely that maintenance claims between former registered partners fall within the scope of Brussels I.

Furthermore, no real problem arises with regards the application of these grounds of jurisdiction. In combining the last sentence of Art. 5(2), Brussels I with the conditional *forum necessitatis* jurisdictional ground proposed in **Chapter XI.2.4**, even in those situations where neither the State of the habitual residence of the creditor nor of the debtor recognise a form of non-marital registered relationship, the maintenance creditor will always be able to bring a maintenance claim in the State where the relationship was

p. 24-25, "[s]ince it [EEC convention] ensures the recognition and enforcement of judgments granting maintenance to creditors other than children."

43 ECJ, *De Cavel v. De Cavel*, 6th March 1980, Case No. 120/79 (1980) ECR 731; ECJ, *van den Boogaard v. Laumen*, 27th February 1997, Case No. 220/95 (1997) ECR-I 1147; ECJ, *Jackie Farrell v. James Long*, 20th March 1997, Case No. 295/95 (1997) ECR-I 1683; ECJ, *Freistaat Bayern v. Jan Blijdenstein*, 15th January 2004, Case No. 433/01.

44 In *De Cavel* it was confirmed that maintenance in the form of periodical payments is covered by the Convention (now Regulation); in *van den Boogaard* it was confirmed that lump sum payments aimed at ensuring the spouse's maintenance are also covered; in *Farrell v. Long* it was confirmed that maintenance claims by a person bringing a claim for the first time are covered, whilst in *Blijdenstein* it was confirmed that reimbursement for education grants paid by a public body are not covered by the provision. Furthermore, the **Austrian** *Oberster Gerichtshof* has held that "... daβ die Regeln über den Ausstattungsanspruch der Kinder ... nicht Ehegüterrecht enthalten, sondern Familienansprüche, die als endgültige Unterhaltsansprüche aufgefaβt werden ...;": Oberster Gerichtshof, 28th August 1997, *JBl* 1998, 184. See also *ZfRv* 1998, p. 39-41.

45 COM (2004) 254, p. 11.

46 For example, by the English Bar Association, Associaçaõ Portuguese Para o Service Social Internacional, Parliament of the Czech Republic, French Ministry of Justice, Dutch Ministry of Justice, Irish Ministry of Justice and the Law Society of England & Wales. See for more details: europa.eu.int/comm/justice_home/ejn/index_en.htm.

registered. Accordingly, a maintenance creditor will always have recourse to a court in relation to his or her claim for maintenance.

Outside of the scope of Brussels I, domestic jurisdictional rules adopt one of either two approaches. Maintenance claims are either dealt with in accordance with the general rules on jurisdiction, as is the case in **The Netherlands**[47] and **Switzerland**,[48] or are subject to special grounds of jurisdiction, as is in the case in **Belgium**,[49] **France**,[50] **England & Wales**,[51] **Scotland**,[52] and **Northern Ireland**.[53] All seven jurisdictions also provide for a jurisdictional ground in ancillary relief claims if the judge has jurisdiction over the dissolution of the relationship.[54] Nonetheless, regardless of the approach taken, it is clear that all seven jurisdictions make no distinction between maintenance claims between former spouses and maintenance claims between former registered partners.

In summary, this area of law requires little alteration or attention. It would nevertheless be advisable for the ECJ (in any future decision) or the European Commission (in any future legislative instrument) to expressly

---

47 Art. 3, Neth. CCP. Although no separate jurisdictional criteria are provided for maintenance claims, this is not needed due to the manner in which Art. 3, Neth. CCP is worded, *i.e.* that the **Dutch** courts are competent if either the claimant or defendant is habitually resident or domiciled in **The Netherlands**.

48 Arts. 46 and 47, Sw. CPIL. Although these provisions are not specifically aimed at maintenance obligations, these grounds of jurisdiction are particular to the effects of the marriage (thus including maintenance). See further BUCHER (2004a) p. 192, §542-543.

49 Art. 73, Belg. CPIL.

50 Art. 46, last paragraph, Fr. NCCP. See further AUDIT (2000) p. 305, §337.

51 A number of different legislative instruments regulate this field: Maintenance Orders (Facilities for Enforcement) Act 1920 (This Act only applies to Commonwealth countries to which it has been extended by an Order in Council) and the Maintenance Orders (Reciprocal Enforcement) Act 1972 (This Act applies to all countries with whom reciprocal agreements have been reached, including **Scotland**). For divorces obtained outside the **United Kingdom** jurisdiction in maintenance claims may only be based on Sec. 15, MFPA 1984. If financial relief is claimed during the course of the relationship then jurisdiction is founded either upon Sec. 27, MCA 1973 or Sec. 1, DPMCA 1978.

52 Sec. 2(3), first sentence, Schedule 8, CJJA 1982 (divorce obtained in **Scotland**) and Sec. 28, MFPA 1984 (divorce obtained outside **Scotland**).

53 Sec. 19, MFP(NI)O 1989.

54 **Belg.**: Art. 73(2), Belg. CPIL; **Fr.**: Art. 1072, Fr. NCCP; **Neth.**: Art. 4(2) and 4(4), Neth. CCP; **Swit.**: Art. 46 and 47, Sw. CPIL (the jurisdictional grounds are identical to those applicable in the field of marriage dissolution); **Eng.**: *Cammell v. Cammell* [1965] P 467, [1964] 3 All ER 255 and COLLINS (2000) p. 769, §18R-157; **Scot.**: Sec. 2(e), second sentence, Schedule 8, CJJA 1982 (divorce) and Sec. 227(3), CPA 2004 (dissolution); **NI.**: O'HALLORAN (1997) p. 550-551.

include maintenance obligations between former registered partners in the scope of Art. 5(2), Brussels I.

B. Applicable law

Although the Rome Convention specifically excludes maintenance agreements from the scope of the Convention,[55] the 1973 Hague Convention on the law applicable to maintenance obligations (1973 Hague LAMO) has broached the subject. This Convention has been ratified by, *inter alia*, **France**, **The Netherlands** and **Switzerland**, and has furthermore been signed by **Belgium**.[56] Although **Belgium** has not gone so far as to ratify the Convention, Art. 74, Belg. CPIL provides for identical choice of law rules.[57]

A general choice of law ladder is created by virtue of Arts. 4 to 6, 1973 Hague LAMO. Those obligations falling within the ambit of the Convention are governed primarily by the internal law of the habitual residence of the maintenance creditor.[58] If this law does not entitle the maintenance creditor to claim, then the law of the parties' common nationality will apply.[59] If a claim is still impossible then reference will eventually be made to the *lex fori*.[60] According to the majority of academic opinion, the 1973 Hague LAMO applies to maintenance obligations between registered partners, since the phrase "family relationships" used in Art. 1, 1973 Hague LAMO is broad enough to include such relationships.[61] In order to avoid any possible

---

55 Art. 1(2)(b), Rome Convention. No change in the scope of the Convention is envisaged with the conversion into a Regulation: COM (2002) 654, p. 13-16.

56 In **Belgium** (signed 1976 but the Convention is not in force), **France** (1st October 1977), **The Netherlands** (1st March 1981), **Switzerland** (1st October 1977). The Convention has also been signed by **Estonia**, **Germany**, **Greece**, **Italy**, **Japan**, **Lithuania**, **Luxembourg**, **Poland**, **Portugal**, **Spain** and **Turkey**.

57 Art. 74(1)(2), Belg. CPIL provides for the extra possibility to apply the *lex patriae* instead of the law of the habitual residence of the maintenance creditor, if both parties have the same nationality and the maintenance debtor lives in that country. For the reasoning on the introduction of this rule see *Belgian Senate*, 2003-2004, No. 3-27/7, p. 153. This possibility is provided for in the 1973 Hague LAMO by virtue of a reservation in Art. 15.

58 Art. 3(1), 1973 Hague LAMO. If the habitual residence of the creditor changes, the internal law of the maintenance creditor's new habitual residence will apply: Art. 3(2), 1973 Hague LAMO.

59 Art. 4, 1973 Hague LAMO.

60 Art. 5, 1973 Hague LAMO.

61 JESSURUN D'OLIVEIRA (2000a) p. 301; JOPPE (2000b) p. 394; BUCHER (2004a) p. 200, §568; DEVERS (2004) p. 339-340, §561; REINHARTZ (2004) p. 496. *Contra* SCHWANDER (2001) p. 356.

confusion, **The Netherlands** has declared these provisions *mutatis mutandis* applicable to maintenance obligations between former registered partners.[62]

However, regardless of the abovementioned choice of law ladder, in cases of maintenance obligations stemming from a divorce, the law applicable to such maintenance obligations is the same law as that applied to the divorce.[63] A distinction is therefore drawn between the law applied to maintenance obligations in divorce cases and the law applied to maintenance obligations in all other cases. This special provision applicable in divorce cases should also apply to maintenance claims between former registered partners.[64] Although specific attention was paid to this distinction in **The Netherlands**,[65] no explicit provision has been enacted to guarantee this position.[66] This is unfortunate, since according to a literal interpretation of Art. 8, 1973 Hague LAMO maintenance obligations between former registered partners are not covered by this provision but instead subject to the general choice of law ladder in Arts. 4 to 6, 1973 Hague LAMO.[67]

Turning one's attention to the **United Kingdom**, which has not signed the 1973 Hague LAMO, one must remember that no distinction is drawn between maintenance and matrimonial property.[68] Despite this fact, and irrespective of the jurisdictional changes made by the enactment of the DMPA 1973, it is without doubt that an **English**, **Scottish** or **Northern Irish** court will only apply the *lex fori* in financial relief cases.[69] This therefore never leads to the application of a law that does not recognise non-marital registered relationships. However, consistency of result is presently

---

62 Art. 25, Neth. PIL(RP)A. An approach also taken by **Germany**: Art. 18(1)(1), Ger. CCIL.

63 Art. 8, 1973 Hague LAMO. This section will not discuss the question whether the spouses can, despite this Article, still choose to apply a different law. See, for example, HR, 21st February 1997, NJ 1998, 416. See further STRIKWERDA (2002) p. 124-125.

64 Contra BUCHER (2004a) p. 200, §569, who assumes that the general choice of law ladder created by Arts. 4 and 6, 1973 Hague LAMO is applicable to non-marital registered relationships, since the Convention could designate a law which does not recognise a form of non-marital registered relationship. This could not happen in the case of applying Art. 8, 1973 Hague LAMO.

65 STAATSCOMMISSIE (1998) p. 34; *Dutch Second Chamber*, 2002-2003, 28924, No. 3, p. 18.

66 Despite the absence of a direct provision, any **Dutch** judge would simply apply Art. 8, 1973 Hague LAMO by analogy. See JOPPE (2000b) p. 394.

67 This option has also been suggested by DEVERS, who argues for an amendment to the 1973 Hague LAMO itself: DEVERS (2004) p. 342, §562. With regards the countries that have ratified this convention such an amendment is unlikely and is better enacted via national private international laws.

68 See **Chapter VII.6.9**.

69 *Sealey v. Callan* [1953] P 135, [1953] 1 All ER 942, NORTH/FAWCETT (1999) p. 849; ANTON/BEAUMONT (1990) p. 544.

achieved by virtue of the wholesale application of the *lex fori* in both divorce proceedings and ancillary maintenance claims. If, however, the **United Kingdom** where to adopt the choice of law rules proposed in **Chapter XI.3.3** to the dissolution of non-marital registered relationships (*i.e.* allowing the parties to choose the application of the *lex loci registrationis*), this consistency would be disturbed. It is therefore submitted that should the **United Kingdom** opt for a choice of law rule in the field of divorce along the lines of that proposed in **Chapter XI.3.3**, this decision should be reflected in the choice of law rules in the field of maintenance. A similar provision to that of Art. 8, 1973 Hague LAMO should therefore be adopted. As a result, the applicable law in maintenance claims between former registered partners in all seven countries studied would always be the same as that applied to the dissolution proceedings.

C. Recognition and enforcement of obligations

There exist a number of international instruments with regards the recognition of maintenance obligations. Within the European Union, Brussels I and the Lugano Convention regulate the recognition and enforcement of maintenance decisions issued within an EU or EFTA Member State.[70] Moreover, the recently enacted European Union Regulation creating a European Enforcement Order for uncontested claims also applies to uncontested maintenance claims, irrespective of whether the claim is between former spouses or former registered partners.[71]

Furthermore, all the countries researched in this book have signed the 1973 Hague Convention on the recognition and enforcement of decisions relating to maintenance obligations (1973 Hague REMO).[72] However, despite having signed the Convention on the 9th November 1976, **Belgium** has yet to ratify. For the same reasons as explained above in relation to the 1973 Hague LAMO, the 1973 Hague REMO also applies to maintenance obligations between former registered partners as a result of the reference to "family

70 Art. 38(1), Brussels I and Art. 31, Lugano Convention. According to Art. 38(2), Brussels I and Art. 31(2), Lugano Convention, a judgment needs to be registered first in the **United Kingdom** before it can be enforced there.

71 Regulation (EC) No. 805/2004 of the European Parliament and of the Council of 21st April 2004 creating a European Enforcement Order for uncontested claims, 20th April 2004, *OJ*, L143/15.

72 **Belgium** (signed on 9th November 1976), **France** (in force since 1st October 1977), **The Netherlands** (in force since 1st March 1981), **Switzerland** (in force since 1st August 1976) and the **United Kingdom** (in force since 1st March 1980).

relationship" in Art. 1.[73] In addition, the 1956 New York Convention on the Recovery Abroad of Maintenance,[74] which has also been ratified by all seven countries studied,[75] also refrains from defining the term maintenance, and would thus appear to cover a wide range of maintenance claims. Finally, all domestic legislation which regulates the reciprocal enforcement of maintenance orders makes no distinction in terms of marital and non-marital relationships.[76]

In summary, it would appear that the array of international, European and national instruments regulating the recognition and enforcement of maintenance obligations are applicable to maintenance obligations between registered partners.

XII.3.3.2 Familial property regimes

Disputes relating to familial property can arise in a number of different ways, namely through divorce proceedings, maintenance orders during the relationship, financial relief after a divorce and succession to property. Jurisdiction is normally determined according to the rules of one of these fields. Since all these individual aspects have already been dealt with elsewhere in this research,[77] jurisdictional issues will not be covered again here. Instead this section is devoted to the specific choice of law problems that arise with respect to issues of familial property law.

---

73 JESSURUN D'OLIVEIRA (2000a) p. 301.

74 See further the *Vienna Action Plan*, 23rd January 1999, *OJ*, 99/C-19/01, p. 10, §41(c).

75 **Belgium** (acceded on the 1st July 1966), **France** (ratified on the 24th June 1960), **The Netherlands** (ratified on the 31st July 1962), **Switzerland** (acceded on the 5th October 1977) and the **United Kingdom** (acceded on the 13th March 1975).

76 *E.g.* **Belg.**: Section 6, Chapter II, Belg. CPIL; **Neth.**: PELLIS (1996) p. 84-87; **Swit.**: Art. 50, Sw. CPIL, applicable to registered partnerships by virtue of Art. 65a, Sw. CPIL; **UK:** Maintenance Orders (Facilities for Enforcement) Act 1920 (recognition within the Commonwealth), Maintenance Orders Act 1950 (recognition within the United Kingdom) and Maintenance Orders (Reciprocal Enforcement) Act 1972 (recognition of maintenance orders from Anguilla, Australia, Barbados, Bermuda, Brunei, Canada (except Prince Edward Island, Quebec and Yukon Territory), Falkland Islands, Fiji, Ghana, Gibraltar, Hong Kong, India, Isle of Man, Kenya, Malta, Nauru, New Zealand, Norfolk Island, Papua New Guinea, St. Helena, Singapore, South Africa, Tanzania, Turks and Caicos Islands and Zimbabwe. List last amended SI 2002, No. 788) and the Reciprocal Enforcement of Maintenance Orders (Republic of Ireland) Order 1974.

77 Divorce proceedings (**Chapter XI.2**), maintenance during relationship and after breakdown (**Section XII.3.3.1.A**) and succession (**Section XII.3.2**)

As a direct result of the conclusions reached during the Tampere Council in 1999,[78] the European Union launched an investigation into the current legal situation in the Member States with regards substantive and private international law in the field of matrimonial property law and the property law of unmarried couples.[79] A comparative study was subsequently published based on a detailed analysis of the sixteen national reports.[80] On the basis of this comparison, the authors of the report were able to draw attention to a number of points of convergence and divergence and thus make conclusions as to any envisaged harmonisation in this field of law. Although far too early to predict the possible results of such discussions, the report points to two distinct approaches in the private international law rules with respect to familial property regimes in those countries to have enacted domestic forms of non-marital registered relationships schemes.[81] Taking into account the lack of further progress in terms of the harmonisation of the rules of private international law since the publication of this comparative report, these national private international law rules in the field of property law will remain, for the time being, the main source of law in this field, and thus form the focal point of this section.

Although a new set of private international law rules applicable to the property law aspects of registered partners has been created in **The Netherlands**, these rules are based entirely on those rules laid down in the 1978 Hague Convention on the law applicable to matrimonial property regimes (1978 Hague MPR).[82] Although, as with spouses,[83] parties to a non-marital registered relationship have the freedom to choose the law applicable to their property regime regardless of where the relationship was registered,[84] a substantial difference in approach is apparent. Spouses are restricted in their choice of legal systems to the national law of the parties, the law of the habitual residence of the parties, the law of the first

78 EUROPEAN UNION, "Action Plan of the council and the Commission on how best to implement the provisions of the Treaty of Amsterdam on an Area of Freedom, Security and Justice", *OJ*, 23rd January 1999, C-19/1, p. 10, §41(c).

79 CLARKSON (2002). As a result of this initiative, a study on the substantive and private international law rules in these fields has been conducted: JAI/A3/2001/03, Available at europa.eu.int/comm/justice_home/doc_centre/civil/studies/doc_civil_studies_en.htm.

80 T.M.C. ASSER INSTITUTE, *Étude sur les régimes matrimoniaux des couples mariés et sur le patrimoine des couples non mariés dans le droit international privé et le droit interne des états membres de l'union européenne. Effectuée à la demande de la Commission Européenne*, The Hague: T.M.C. Asser Institute, December 2002.

81 *Ibid*, p. 222, Deuxième partie, Section II, §2.1.3.

82 JOPPE (2000b) p. 392-393; FROHN (2004) p. 292-293.

83 Art. 3, 1978 Hague MPR.

84 Art. 6(1), Neth. PIL(RP)A. See further JOPPE (2000b) p. 392.

matrimonial habitual residence or the law of the place where immovable property is situated, for as far as this choice affects such immovable property.[85]

Registered partners, on the other hand, are totally free to choose any legal system to govern their property issues, as long as the chosen system recognises a form of non-marital registered relationship in the sense of the Neth. PIL(RP)A.[86] The parties need not have any connection with the chosen jurisdiction at all. However, it was probably not the intention of the **Dutch** legislature to grant registered partners such a wide freedom to choose their applicable law. When the **Dutch** Standing Committee on Private International Law published its proposals outlining a set of private international law rules for registered partnerships,[87] the freedom to choose any country was enormously restricted by the need to choose a country which recognised a form of non-marital registered relationship.[88] By the time the proposals were eventually enacted, this freedom had grown substantially and should thus have been restricted in a similar manner to the restriction imposed on spouses.

For those non-marital registered relationships akin to marriage,[89] **Belgian** law applies the private international law rules in the field of matrimonial property law analogously.[90] Those non-marital registered relationships not akin to marriage are instead subject to a choice of law rule which states that all questions regarding the property law of the parties will be determined according to the *lex loci registrationis.*[91] Although the 1978 Hague MPR is also in force in **France**, and thus one could have expected a similar approach

---

85 Art. 3, 1978 Hague MPR. Prior to 1978, spouses were entitled to a total freedom in their choice of jurisdiction. HR, 10th December 1976, NJ 1977, 275 (*Chelouche-Van Leer*). See further STRIKWERDA (2002) p. 131-134, §142-143.

86 Art. 6(2), Neth. PIL(RP)A. See further STEENHOFF (2005) p. 9.

87 STAATSCOMMISSIE (1998) p. 21.

88 At that time, there were only four other countries with similar schemes (**Denmark**, **Norway**, **Iceland** and **Sweden**. See **Appendix 1** for more details). STEENHOFF (2005) p. 10.

89 See **Chapter IX.3.1** for an explanation of this characterisation.

90 Accordingly, the parties are able to choose between the law of the parties' common habitual residence, the habitual residence of either one of them, and the law of either of their nationalities (Art. 49, Belg. CPIL). In the absence of a choice, the property will be dealt with in accordance with the law of the parties' common habitual residence after the celebration of the marriage/non-marital registered relationship akin to marriage; in the absence thereof, their common nationality, and ultimately the place where the marriage was celebrated or non-marital relationship registered (Art. 51, Belg. CPIL).

91 Art. 60(2), Belg. CPIL. Nonetheless, certain rights of third parties are protected by virtue of Art. 60(3), Belg. CPIL, by referring to Art,. 54, Belg. CPIL.

to that adopted in **The Netherlands**, it would appear that the **French** legislature prefers to follow in the footsteps of **Belgium** and apply the *lex loci registrationis.*[92] DEVERS, noting that any choice made by the parties must be limited to those countries which recognise a domestic form of non-marital registered relationship, comments that a similar solution is also adopted in Art. 6(2), 1985 Hague TC, where it is stated that "when the law chosen does not provide for trusts or the category of trust involved, the choice shall not be effective".[93]

In the **United Kingdom**, the private international law rules in the field of matrimonial property law are still largely governed by common law precedent. It is, therefore, as yet unclear as to how far these principles will be analogously applied to the property law relationship of civil partners.[94] It is nevertheless submitted that the same approach should, and probably will, be taken as that adopted at substantive law level, namely that any common law principle in the field of marriage will be analogously applied to civil partners, unless there is a strong reason not to do so. With this in mind, in determining the applicable law to the familial property regime, a distinction is drawn between those cases in which a pre-nuptial or ante-nuptial[95] contract has been drawn up and those were no such contract exists.[96] Furthermore, different rules are applicable with respect to movable and immovable property.[97] Nevertheless, no specific rules for the private

92 MINISTRE DE LA JUSTICE (2004) p. 28-29. A solution supported by the majority of **French** authors, *e.g.* FULCHIRON (2000) p. 908 *et seq.*; DEVERS (2004), p. 264, §431-432 and p. 276, §449; KESSLER (2004) p. 336-338, §584-586. DEVERS in turn refers to the **German** solution embodied in Art. 17a(1), Ger. CCIL. See further THORN (2003) p. 163.

93 DEVERS (2004) p. 264, §432.

94 See for further discussion of this problem **Chapter VII.5.6.**

95 Although reference has been made to the term "nuptial" and thus indirectly to the institution of marriage (nuptial stems from the Latin word *nupitae* meaning wedding), this term should be interpreted as including contracts made before and after the registration of a non-marital relationship.

96 In those cases where a pre-nuptial or post-nuptial contract has been drawn up, the contract will be governed by the ordinary common law rules on contract, *e.g. De Nicols v. Cartier* [1900] AC 21 (no distinction drawn between express and tacit contracts). Formal validity will be governed by the *lex loci contractus* or the proper law of the contract: *Re Bankes* [1902] 2 Ch. 333. Essential validity is governed by the proper law of the contract: *Chiwell v. Carlyon* (1897) 14 SC 61, *Brown v. Brown* (1913) 2 SLT 314. See further ANTON/BEAUMONT (1990) p. 588, NORTH/FACWETT (1999) p. 1023-1024.

97 Where no contract exists, movable property rights are determined according to the law of the husband's domicil: *Re Martin* [1900] P 211 at 233. However, since the coming into force of Sec. 1, DMPA 1973, a wife can also acquire a domicil independent of her husband and thus opinion tends to suggest that reference will now be made to the matrimonial domicil: CRAWFORD (1998) §9.27, NORTH/FAWCETT (1999) p. 1018, ANTON/BEAUMONT (1990)p. 586. With respect to immovable property, rights are determined according to the

international law aspects for the property law issues raised by civil partnerships have been created. As a result, it is as yet uncertain which law will apply in cases where the choice of law rule designates the law of a country which does not recognise a form of non-marital registered relationship. However, it should be noted that in cases where a contract has been drawn up, the place where the relationship was registered will be extremely influential in determining the "proper law of the contract".

Although **Swiss** law has generally attempted to ensure the same private international law rules apply to both marriage and registered partnership, in the field of property law a number of differences are apparent. Firstly, spouses and registered partners are entitled to choose the law applicable to their property regime. Spouses may, however, only choose between the law of either of their domiciles, the law of their post-marital domicile or the law of one of their nationalities.[98] Registered partners, on the other hand, as well as having these choices are also offered the possibility to choose the *lex loci registrationis*.[99] If the parties have not made a choice of law, then the basic choice of law ladder laid down in matrimonial property law cases will apply.[100] However, should these choice of law rules designate a law which does not recognise non-marital registered relationships, the principle of transposition will apply.[101] If the designated law does not recognise a form of non-marital registered relationship, or should the law designated treat non-marital registered relationships and marriages identically, then no "*dispositions applicables*" will be available, and **Swiss** law will be applied instead.[102]

In concurring with the conclusions reached by the T.M.C. ASSER INSTITUTE,[103] it would appear that this field of law displays anything but uniformity of approach. Although each country has sought an analogy to the current private international law rules in the field of matrimonial property law, all those countries to have legislated on these issues have acknowledged the limits of any such analogy. The limited acceptance of forms of non-marital registered relationships has an important impact upon the respective private international law rules. This acknowledgement has,

---

lex sitae: *Welch v. Tennent* [1891] AC 639 at 644. See also NORTH/FAWCETT (1999) p. 1016-1022, ANTON/BEAUMONT (1990) p. 587.

98 Art. 52(2), Sw. CPIL.

99 Arts. 52(5), 65a and 65c(2), Sw. CPIL.

100 Art. 54(1), Sw. CPIL.

101 See for further explanation **Chapter XI.3.2.3** and **Table 12**.

102 Art. 65c(1), Sw. CPIL. See further BUCHER (2004a) p. 198, §563.

103 The main authors of the report are M.J. DE ROOIJ and M. VERWILGHEN.

however, come in various forms and guises. The absence of any common core solution portends that any attempt at harmonisation or unification in this field of law will need to engage in a debate as to the "better law".[104]

Whatever the outcome, it is clear that this topic needs to be the subject of further extensive research. In this respect, the European Commission should be commended in embracing an inclusive approach and dealing with the private international law issues surrounding non-marital registered relationships at the same time as dealing with those issues relating to matrimonial property law. Although it is clear that the solutions should, as far as possible, mirror each other, certain additional considerations will need be taken into account when dealing with non-marital registered relationships.

All those countries studied allow both spouses and registered partners to designate the law applicable to their property. However, this choice is not without restriction, with some connection between the chosen law and the parties themselves needing to be demonstrated. These restrictions are imposed on registered partners for the same reasons as they are imposed spouses, *e.g.* to assist in the international recognition of such choices and ensure a restriction in the possibilities for forum shopping. However, since the alternatives open to registered partners may lead to the application of a law which does not recognise a form of non-marital registered relationship, the parties should also be given the opportunity to select the *lex loci registrationis*. In this way, one ensures as far as possible that the rules for both sets of institutions are identical, yet at the same time recognises that leeway must be granted to registered partners due to the limited recognition of these familial institutions. This solution has, in fact, been embraced by **Switzerland**. Such a solution would result in a restriction in the options open to registered partners in **The Netherlands** and broaden the options open to couples in **Belgium**. Nonetheless, this solution provides the parties with a reasonable selection of systems from which to chose, whilst ensuring that any choice made is within the accepted bounds of private international law in the field of familial property law, *i.e.* that there is a reasonable connection between the choice of law made and the parties themselves.

A similar approach can also be applied in those cases where no such choice of law has been made by the parties. The same choice of law ladder can be applied to registered partners as is applied to spouses. Should any of the

---

104 See **Chapter I.3.**

applicable laws not recognise a form of non-marital registered relationship, one should proceed to the subsequent rung on the choice of law ladder.[105] This method is preferable to that proposed in **Switzerland** whereby "applicable provisions" are sought, leading to a denaturalisation of the private international law rules. Nonetheless, a similar provision should also be included above and beyond any choice of law ladder, ensuring that the *lex loci registrationis* will be applied should no other law be designated. This solution is explicitly provided for in **Belgium** with respect to those relationships akin to marriage. This solution would also be preferable than the one opted for in **The Netherlands**. Should registered partners have made no choice for an applicable law, their familial property regime will be determined according to the *lex loci registrationis*.[106] This differs substantially from the rules applicable to matrimonial property law, where reference is first made to the parties' first common habitual residence,[107] and in the absence thereof to their common nationality,[108] and only in the absence thereof to the law of the State with the closest connection to the case.[109] Only this last rule would result in a similar result to that achieved in relation to registered partners.

Nonetheless, any proposed rules advocating the eventual harmonisation or unification of the private international law rules in this field should be adopted within the framework of the current debate on the harmonisation and unification of private international law rules in the field of matrimonial property law. Although, it is clear that additional criteria will also need to be considered in developing rules with respect to non-marital registered relationships, these criteria can, and ultimately should, be subordinate to the overarching guiding principles with respect to familial property law.

XII.3.4 NON-PECUNIARY MATTERS

Three different approaches to this topic can be identified in the countries surveyed. Firstly, non-marital registered relationships can be recognised as such and the relationship can be administered, as far as possible, in accordance with the law of the place where it was registered, a so-called *lex*

105 For the arguments against the application of the transposition method see **Chapter XI.3.2.3**.
106 Art. 7(1), Neth. PIL(RP)A (partnerships registered in The Netherlands) and Art. 7(2), Neth. PIL(RP)A (non-marital relationships registered abroad).
107 Art. 4(1), 1978 Hague MPR.
108 Art. 4(2), 1978 Hague MPR.
109 Art. 4(3), 1978 Hague MPR.

loci registrationis approach (**Section XII.3.3.1**). Secondly, one could aim to naturalise the relationship and accordingly treat the parties as though they had registered their relationship domestically, a so-called *lex fori* approach (**Section XII.3.3.2**). Finally, one could refer to the same rules as those applied in the field of marriage, a so-called *lex domicilii/lex patriae* approach (**Section XII.3.3.3**).

From the outset, however, it must be noted that this section has no bearing upon the effect that registering a non-marital relationship has upon the parties' civil status. As was seen in **Section 5.2** of **Chapters III-VI**, registration of a non-marital relationship has an effect on the parties' civil status in some jurisdictions but not others. In order to prevent limping relationships, "bigamous" and multiple registrations, whilst guaranteeing the uniformity of personal status, it is crucial that if the relationship affects the parties' civil status **either** according to the *lex loci registrationis* **or** the *lex fori*, this effect should be recognised. In this way, problems such as those discussed in **Chapters X.3.3.1, X.5.4** and **XI.5.3** will be reduced.

XII.3.4.1 Lex loci registrationis approach

The *lex loci registrationis* approach refers all non-pecuniary matters to the law of the place where the relationship was registered. Many of the proponents of a contractual analysis of non-marital registered relationships support this approach.[110] Upon registering a non-marital relationship, the parties assume rights and responsibilities with respect to each other and third parties. The extent of these rights and duties is determined according to the law of the place where the relationship is registered. Since the parties are assumed to be aware of the legal consequences of their actions,[111] they are also assumed to have fully consented to the rights and duties imposed on them as a result of registering their relationship. In having fully consented to the rights and duties laid down by the law of the place where the relationship is registered, those asserting a contractual analysis argue that these rights and duties can be compared to contractual standard terms and conditions and do not therefore change upon crossing a border.[112]

---

110 See further **Chapter IX.2.1** for information on characterisation according to contract.

111 This is basically an extension of the legal principle *ignorantia juris non excusat*. As a citizen, one is assumed to know the law in force, otherwise one could simply use ignorance as an excuse for its non-application. This is translated in **Dutch** as *iedere burger wordt geacht de wet te kennen* and in **French** as *nul n'est censé ignorer la loi.*

112 See **Chapter IX.2.1.2**.

Alternative justifications have, however, also been advanced by those asserting a more status orientated approach. Advocates argue that applying the *lex loci registrationis* underscores the uniformity of status across national borders, whilst achieving certainty of result and ensuring that the parties' expectations are respected.[113] Nonetheless, if one supports the *lex loci registrationis* approach,[114] the associated danger of forum shopping increases. Parties wanting the "best deal" can acquire an habitual residence in a particular country with the sole aim of registering a relationship there. Upon their return, their home State would be forced to recognise the non-pecuniary effects of the parties' relationship according to the *lex loci registrationis*, which may go further than those effects that would have been granted had the parties registered their relationship domestically. Such scenarios could, however, be avoided by ensuring that relationships registered abroad for fraudulent purposes would never be eligible for recognition.[115] Although such a proposition defies the aim of preventing limping relationships, this principle should be displaced by the policy of preventing fraud.

Nonetheless, although perhaps academically attractive, application of the *lex loci registrationis* approach is fraught with practical complications. Administrative lists would need to be drawn up and constantly updated to ensure that Registrars and courts are aware of the non-pecuniary rights and duties inherent in each and every type of non-marital registered relationship. Are parties registered in **Vermont** subject to an enforceable duty of fidelity? Are parties in **Tasmania** under a duty to cohabit? Are parties in **Luxembourg** under a duty to provide mutual support and assistance during the course of the relationship?

Furthermore, this approach could lead to a judge having to grant rights or enforce duties which go beyond those granted according to domestic, substantive law.[116] Although this result is common in the field of private

---

113 STAATSCOMMISSIE (1998) p. 7 and KESSLER (2004) p. 297, §512.

114 This has been labelled the "traditional approach" by KESSLER (2004) p. 293-297, §502-512.

115 This is often called the refusal to recognize evasive relationships, namely parties who register their relationship in one country so as to "evade" the law of their home state. This approach has been adopted in **Switzerland** (Art. 45(2), Sw. CPIL in conjunction with Art. 65a, Sw. CPIL) and **Belgium** (Art. 25(1)(3), Belg. CPIL). Probably if such a case did arise in **The Netherlands** or **France**, resort would be made to the public policy exception. Due to the application of the *lex fori* to all such matters in the **United Kingdom**, the parties can never avoid the application of the relevant law of the **United Kingdom**. See further **Section XII.3.4.2**.

116 KESSLER (2004) p. 293-295, §503-508.

international law and thus ideologically compelling, it is likely that judges may, in such cases, resort to the public policy exception.[117] One possible way in which this solution can be ameliorated is to introduce a ceiling beyond which rights will not be recognised.[118] In this way, the non-pecuniary effects of a non-marital registered relationship cannot exceed those rights and duties granted domestically. In fixing such a ceiling, one embeds a public policy clause into any choice of law rule. This restricted form of the *lex loci registrationis* approach would perhaps be most attractive to those countries where the non-pecuniary effects attached to non-marital registered relationships are not as extensive as in other countries. In countries where registered partners are granted comprehensive non-pecuniary rights and duties, this limitation would seldom cause problems.

The application of the *lex loci registrationis* has been embraced in **Belgium** and **The Netherlands** (in its unrestricted form),[119] as well as being advocated by many authors in **France** (in its restricted form).[120] In **The Netherlands**, where this choice breaks with the traditional choice of law rule ladder applicable to spouses,[121] both the Government and the **Dutch** Standing Committee on Private International Law have pointed to the limited recognition afforded to non-marital registered relationships.[122] Nonetheless, this choice of law rule does not extend as far as name law, which is governed by the ordinary private international law rules on names.[123] In

117 KESSLER notes that this method is perhaps more suitable to a time when such institutions are regarded as "normal": KESSLER (2004) p. 297, §512.

118 KESSLER (2004) p. 297-301. Kessler refers to this approach as the restrictive approach, citing Germany as an example: Art. 17b(4), Ger. CCIL. See further THORN (2003a) p. 165.

119 **Belg.**: Art. 60(2), Belg. CPIL, but only with respect to non-marital registered relationships not akin to marriage. Non-marital registered relationships akin to marriage are dealt with in accordance with the ordinary private international law rules in the field of marriage (See **Section XII.3.4.3**). Therefore, although **Belgium** has embraced an unrestricted application of the *lex loci registrationis*, a restriction is already embedded in the characterisation; **Neth.:** Art. 5(1), Neth PIL(RP)A (with respect to partnerships registered in **The Netherlands**) and Art. 5(2), Neth. PIL(RP)A (with respect to non-marital relationships registered abroad). This also follows from the interpretation of Art. 2(1), since non-marital registered relationships are recognised "*als zodanig*" (as such). See further JESSURUN D'OLIVEIRA (2003a) p. 12.

120 DEVERS (2004) p. 245, §399 (rights and duties of the partners to each other) and p. 248-249, §404 (name law); KESSLER (2004) p. 336, §583.

121 Art. 1, PIL(LPR)A refers to the common national law of the parties, the common habitual residence in default thereof and to the place where the parties have the closest connection, should neither the previous two conditions be met.

122 *Dutch Second Chamber*, 2002-2003, 28924, No. 3, p. 11-12.

123 Art. 5a(1), Neth. PIL(N)A (*Wet conflictenrecht namen*), which refers to the recognition of surnames changed abroad as a consequence of a change in the personal status of the parties, and not to the celebration of a marriage.

Belgium similar reasons were also espoused for the application of the *lex loci registrationis* to the non-pecuniary legal effects of non-marital registered relationships not akin to marriage.[124] Although Art. 60(2), Belg. CPIL does not refer to a change of the parties' surname, this question is probably illusory since those relationships registered in countries where parties are entitled to adopt each others' surnames will be characterised as non-marital registered relationships akin to marriage and thus subject to the same private international law rules as spouses wishing to change their surnames.[125] The application of the *lex loci registrationis* has also found favour with many commentators in **France** and the **French** Ministry of Justice.[126] However, once again, it has been suggested that the issue of name law should be left to the general realm of private international law on surnames.[127]

In the original **Swiss** Ministry of Justice proposal for private international law rules, **Swiss** law was deemed to apply in all cases, unless the parties had a common domicile in the State where the relationship was registered, in which case the law of that country would apply.[128] According to the explanatory notes, reference to the law of the parties domicile would only result in complex analogies to be made by the court.[129] Accordingly, a compromise solution was adopted so as to ameliorate the wholesale application of the *lex fori* by applying the *lex loci registrationis* if the parties had their common domicile in that country. Nevertheless, the eventual private international law rules adopted by the Swiss legislature diverge from this position and apply the *lex domicilii*.[130]

XII.3.4.2 Lex fori approach

It is clear that a general and unlimited application of the *lex fori* to the non-pecuniary effects of a non-marital registered relationship, irrespective of the foreign elements in a particular case, would eliminate all choice of law issues in this field.[131] It would, however, also detract from the ideal of

124 *Belgian Senate*, 2003-2004, No. 3-27/7, p. 329.

125 Art. 38(2), Belg, CPIL.

126 MINISTRE DE LA JUSTICE (2004) p. 28-29.

127 KESSLER (2004) p. 322, §559.

128 MINISTRY OF JUSTICE (2001) Art. 65f, p. 64.

129 MINISTRY OF JUSTICE (2001) p. 41.

130 See further **Section XII.3.4.3**.

131 This adheres closer to the Anglo-Saxon approach to private international law, whereby solutions are more readily sought in the field of jurisdictional rules than in intricate choice of law rules.

attaining uniformity of judgment in different jurisdictions, thus opening the door to forum shopping. Nevertheless, such an approach is common in other areas of family law. In many countries, for example, foreign adoptions are "naturalised" and deemed to create the same effects as adoptions according to domestic law.[132] The reason for this naturalisation derives from the problems that would arise if numerous different forms of adoption were present in the same legal order.[133]

With respect to non-marital registered relationships, this approach has received support in common law countries where the wholesale application of the *lex fori* is customary. Sec. 215, CPA 2004 states that an overseas relationship will be recognised as a civil partnership, thus generating the exact same legal rights and duties as a civil partnership registered according to the relevant law of the **United Kingdom**. However this approach is problematic since it can often lead to arbitrary results. Persons on an extended holiday or study-leave would thus be subject to the same rules as those having registered their relationship domestically. Persons involved in a non-marital registered relationship would, therefore, need to be informed of the new rights and duties applicable to their relationship upon crossing national boundaries. Hence, if such a solution were to be adopted, the State would need to be burdened with an information duty.[134] This information could be promulgated when the parties register at the local municipality or, as is the case in **United Kingdom**, upon receiving a (provisional) national insurance number.[135] A similar information duty is also imposed in other areas of European Union law.[136]

Nonetheless, this does not solve the problem entirely since many persons would "slip through the net". The lack of a municipality registration scheme in the **United Kingdom**, means that short-term students, holidaymakers and travellers not required to register with the local municipality or apply for a

---

132 This approach is adopted, for example, in **France** (Art. 370-5, Fr. CC) and **England & Wales** (Sec. 38 and 39, AA 1976). It is also possible under the 1993 Hague AC, under certain circumstances, to recognise weak adoptions as strong adoptions.

133 See reference made by KESSLER (2004) p. 299, §518.

134 Already mentioned by **Dutch** Standing Committee on Private International Law: STAATSCOMMISSIE (1998) p.14.

135 Persons entering or moving to the UK from other EU countries do not need to register upon arrival in the **United Kingdom**. Their first compulsory confrontation with the **English** authorities is thus upon request for a provisional National Insurance Number.

136 See, for example, EUROPEAN COMMISSION, *Code of Conduct approved by the group of coordinators for the general system of recognition of diplomas*, written pursuant to Directives 89/48/EEC and 92/51/EEC on the recognition of diplomas. Available europa.eu.int/comm/internal_market/qualifications/docs/codeconduct/code_en.pdf.

national insurance number, would be subject to a different set of rights and duties without being aware of it. Although this is often the case with respect to spouses too, the question is whether this rule really reflects the parties' legitimate expectations.

XII.3.4.3 Lex domicilii/lex patriae approach

Taking into account ever-increasing international mobility, there may well be no real connection between the parties and jurisdiction where the relationship was registered. Some authors argue that it is, therefore, perhaps preferable to draw a distinction between the law applicable to the structure of the relationship (*i.e.* establishment and dissolution) and the law applicable to the effects of the relationship (*i.e.* the legal effects). The establishment and dissolution of the relationship should be regulated in accordance with the *lex loci registrationis* but the legal effects should be regulated in accordance with the *lex domicilii* or the *lex patriae* depending on the predominant opinion in a particular country.[137]

Switzerland is the only country to have opted for such a choice of law rule. According to Art. 48(1), Sw. CPIL,[138] the non-pecuniary effects of a non-martial registered relationship are governed by the *lex domicilii*. Since **Swiss** jurisdiction is founded primarily on the basis of the parties' domicile, this will generally lead to the applicable of **Swiss** law (*i.e.* coinciding with the *lex fori*).[139] If the parties are not domiciled in the same State, then law of the party's domicile with which the claim is most closely connected will apply.[140] The problem with this approach is that it can lead to the application of a law that does not provide for a non-marital registered relationship institution. For this scenario, **Switzerland** has created a system of "transposition".[141] Although this solution is perhaps ideologically sound, it is too soon to attempt such utopian ideals.[142]

---

137 This solution is supported by the status-orientated approach advocated in **Chapter X.2.2**.

138 Applicable to non-marital registered relationship by virtue of Art. 65a, Sw. CPIL,

139 BUCHER (2004a) p. 193-193, §546. Furthermore, Swiss law will be applied if the authorities of the place of origin of the parties are competent: Art. 48(3), Sw. CPIL.

140 Art. 48(2), Sw. CPIL.

141 BUCHER (2004a) p. 193, §544 and FF 2003 p. 1260. For further explanation of this method see **Chapter XI.3.2.3**.

142 See **Chapter XI.3.3** and **XI.3.2.3** for criticism of such an approach.

XII.3.4.4 Evaluation

From this survey it would appear that there is no uniform approach to this question. In the absence of a common core, any search for harmonised or unified rules will thus need to rely on the better law approach. In searching for this solution, it is important to understand the advantages and disadvantages of each method, taking into account the restrictions imposed by EU law. Nonetheless, for the same reasons as have been espoused throughout this research, reference to the *lex domicilii* or the *lex patriae* only serve to proliferate existing problems, instead of serving to improve the current situation. Accordingly, a choice must be made between the *lex fori* approach and the *lex loci registrationis* approach, whether in a restricted or unrestricted form.

Non-pecuniary rights and duties are similar to a suitcase. When parties register their relationship they acquire a suitcase; a suitcase full of rights, duties, responsibilities and obligations. If one supports the unrestricted *lex loci registrationis* approach, one accepts that the parties, upon acquiring their suitcase, should be entitled to take it with them wherever they go, without restriction. In this way, a country confronted with a non-marital relationship registered abroad will need to examine the contents of the suitcase in order to determine the rights and duties attributed to the parties. If one supports the application of a restricted *lex loci registrationis* approach, one accepts in principle that one may carry one's suitcase wherever one goes, so long as the contents of the suitcase conform to national domestic standards. As a result, certain rights and duties in the suitcase may need to be restricted. Finally, in supporting the *lex fori* approach, one espouses the replacement of all foreign suitcases for domestic suitcases regardless of the contents; as a result everyone in the same country has an identical suitcase. Although this comparison paints a somewhat oversimplified picture of the situation under discussion, it goes some way to clarify the implications of each approach.

The possible consequences at the EU level should, however, not be overlooked. All three approaches could have far-reaching implications, and could possibly be held to be contrary to EU law. Two separate questions must therefore be posed. Firstly, whether the rule adopted falls afoul of the rules of non-discrimination, and secondly whether the relevant rule imposes a restriction to free movement. In answering the first question, one must take into account three separate considerations. Firstly, one needs to assess whether the parties are in similar situations (*i.e.* couples registered domestically and couples registered abroad), secondly whether the parties are treated differently and thirdly whether this difference in treatment is justifiable.

Since any harmonisation in this field is based upon the principle of treating all those having registered a non-marital relationship identically, it would be difficult to argue that two couples registered in different countries are not in a similar situation. Since the *lex fori* approach treats all registered partners in the same country in the same way, this approach could not be regarded as discriminatory. However, the opposite is true of the *lex loci registrationis* approach which treats each couple differently depending upon where they have registered their relationship. This difference in treatment would therefore require justification. In attempting to find a connecting factor which adequately reflects the status-orientated approach, yet at the same time recognises the limited acceptability of such relationships, reference to the *lex loci registrationis* can be justified. Moreover, such a system serves to reflect the parties' legitimate expectations and secures an element of consistency and decisional harmony.

In answering the second question, it must be noted that the freedom of movement guaranteed by the EC Treaty is more than a simple prohibition of discrimination. The ECJ has held on numerous occasions that the right to the free movement of persons establishes a general prohibition on the imposition of restraints of any kind.[143] By assimilating foreign non-marital registered relationships and domestic non-marital registered relationships, one could argue that an obstacle to free movement would be realised. This would be especially true should a couple move from a country where the rights and duties attributed to non-marital registered relationships are greater than in the country to which they move. Regardless of the fact that substantive family law falls outside the scope of EU law, the ECJ has already held that status-law provisions can fall within the scope of the basic freedoms granted by the Treaties.[144] It is therefore plausible that the *lex fori* approach could be seen as imposing an unnecessary restraint on the free movement of persons.[145] In a similar vein and for the same reasons, it could also be said that a restricted application of the *lex loci registrationis*

143 ECJ, *Bosman*, 15th December 1995, Case No. 415/93 [1995] ECR I-4921, §94 *et seq.*

144 ECJ, *Konstantinidis*, 30th March 1993, Case No. 168/91 [1993] ECR I-1191.

145 In a similar vein to the decision in *Garcia Avello* (See **Chapter X.2.2.1.B** and **X.2.3**), even though the subject matter is not within the competency of the EU, the restraint causes a restriction to one's free movement, and thus falls within the competency of the EU.

principle would also act as a hindrance to the free movement of persons, and thus also be contrary to EU law.

In summary, although it would seem that all solutions are fraught with problems, the application of the *lex loci registrationis* to the non-pecuniary effects of a non-marital registered relationship appears to provide the greatest possible opportunity for success.[146] Whether or not this is subject to a ceiling restriction will ultimately depend on political compromise. In an era of increasing international co-operation and mutual trust, it is hoped that one can strive for the unfettered application of the *lex loci registrationis*.

XII.4 SUMMARY OF CONCLUSIONS

Relationships, whether registered or not, have an important impact on the social, economic and emotional ties that exist between the couple themselves, as well as between the couple and the society in which they live. However, different effects affect the relationship in different ways. Care should be taken when dealing with such rights and duties to ensure that harmony within the legal order from which the particular rights emanate is not marred. Those rules in which the existence of a non-marital registered relationship only plays an incidental role should be excluded from the scope of any future instrument dealing with non-marital registered relationships.

In those areas where the private international law rules are primarily based on an individual's relationship, any rules should attempt to mirror the equivalent rules on marriage as closely as possible. In some areas, such as maintenance, it would appear that little needs to be done in order to achieve this aim. In others, such as familial property law and non-pecuniary effects, it would seem that a lot of work still needs to be done. Solutions are possible that not only respect the parties' legitimate expectations but also maintain some semblance of uniformity in the rationale behind these private international law rules. Whether such results will also receive the endorsement of European legislatures is simply a question of political willpower and willingness to compromise. The EU should therefore be commended on the approach it has taken with respect to maintenance, inheritance and familial property law, where non-marital registered relationships have been included in future plans.

146 Apart from in the field of name law where the ordinary rules should apply.

CHAPTER XIII
TOWARDS A UNIFIED SYSTEM OF LAW?

XIII.1 INTRODUCTION

In 1989 a new institution, registered partnership, was born. During its infancy registered partnership developed slowly; its personality nurtured by those in the vicinity. Even during its early days registered partnership remained relatively unaffected by outside influence. Yet, with the onset of adolescence things began to change and a period of progress dawned. New and exciting external influences demanded that registered partnership change and adapt. Confronted with new ideas and perspectives, registered partnership had to fight for its territory and determine where its boundaries lay. Yet as adolescence drew to a close, registered partnership began to mature, find its own path and recognise its core value system. Although its upbringing and roots had left indelible marks on its personality and character, registered partnership had, after painstaking development, managed to mould itself and become an individual. With a turbulent time behind it and the tests of maturity and old age yet to come, it seems clear that registered partnership has managed to carve a little piece of the world for itself.

Although the story appears to end happily with non-marital registered relationships woven into the fabric of family law in Europe, it is not true to say that all's well that ends registered. Although more than forty jurisdictions worldwide have created non-marital registered relationship schemes, a couple registered in one country can still face problems of recognition as soon as they cross the border and leave the territory where their relationship was registered. The question arises how one can best solve this and many other private international law problems.

One could begin with the harmonisation or unification of substantive family law in this field.[1] Although the battle lines have been drawn

[1] See T. DE BOER (1994) and FAUVARQUE-COSSON (2000) and (2001) on the interaction between substantive law and private international law. Despite having many things in

between those who believe in the desirability of harmonising or unifying substantive family law and those who believe otherwise,[2] this debate has been circumvented in this research. It has been presupposed that irrespective of whether the harmonisation or unification of family law in this field is desirable, it is evidently not feasible. The conclusions reached as a result of the comparisons realised in **Chapter VIII** support this statement. As is the case with matrimonial property law,[3] it is possible to differentiate a number of models of relationship registration. Although one may prefer one model above and beyond the others, the eventual choice may simply be no more than an amalgamation of socio-political and legal-structural factors. At this time it is therefore fully justifiable to assume that any attempt to harmonise or unify the substantive law rules in this field would be destined to fail.

Bearing this in mind, the search for answers to the aforementioned problems turns to the domain of private international law.[4] Questions of jurisdiction, choice of law and the recognition and enforcement of judgments will inevitably arise with respect to non-marital registered relationships. With more than six million European citizens migrating yearly, coupled with the one and half million third country nationals moving to the EU each year, the number of cross-border familial relationships is only set to rise.[5] This rise leads in turn to an increase in the number of cases with an international element, and thus an increase in the resort made to private international law. As long as private international law rules remain national, application of these rules could lead to decisional discord and limping relationships. As a result one could strive for the harmonisation or unification of private international law rules with respect to non-marital registered relationships.

However, before embarking upon any such pursuit one must ask oneself whether it is desirable, and if so feasible, to harmonise or even unify the

---

common, the unification of substantive law threatens to eradicate the need for private international law.

2 For publications in the harmonisation and unification of substantive family law in Europe see www.law.uu.nl/priv/cefl.

3 BOELE-WOELKI (2005b) p. 19.

4 This approach is also suggested by the English Law Society in relation to family law in general: ENGLISH LAW SOCIETY, *European Commission Communication: Assessment of the Tampere programme and future orientations. Response of the Law Society of England & Wales*, London: Law Society, 2004, p. 13, §43.

5 See **Chapter I.2**.

private international law rules with regards such relationships.[6] This question can be broken down into four separate, yet interrelated facets: desirability, feasibility, harmonisation and unification. Although throughout this research a distinction has been drawn between the terms harmonisation and unification,[7] this distinction will ultimately not be made in this chapter. After all, the aim to which one aspires necessarily depends upon the institution which tackles the task. The European Union, for example, is more suited to unification than the International Commission on Civil Status, simply by virtue of the legislative mandate granted to it by the respective Member States. Furthermore, any decision will also inevitably depend upon the political will of the countries concerned. As has already been noted, unification often involves a greater sacrifice on the part of national law than harmonisation.[8] Although it has already been shown in **Chapters IX-XII** that harmonised or unified rules are possible to achieve (these conclusions will be briefly summarised in **Section XIII.2**), the question remains whether this goal is worth striving for (**Section XIII.3**) and whether it is ultimately attainable (**Section XIII.4**).

XIII.2 SUMMARY OF CONCLUSIONS

In **Chapters IX-XII** a number of conclusions were drawn as to the most appropriate private international law rules in the field of non-marital registered relationships. These conclusions are summarised briefly in this section. Firstly, it is crucial that should a private international law instrument be drafted, that a number of characterisation criteria are included; namely, that (a) the non-marital registered relationship is based on a State regulated institution, (b) the institution is exclusive and can only be registered by two persons, (c) the relationship must be registered by a competent authority as designated by the state in which the relationship is registered and (d) the registration of the relationship creates rights and duties between the parties and has a constitutive effect on their personal status.[9]

In turning to the rules themselves, it is submitted that both the formal and essential validity of non-marital registered relationships should be tested according to the law of the place where the relationship was (or is to be)

---

6 See T. DE BOER (1994) p. 57.

7 See **Chapter I.3** for this distinction.

8 See **Chapter I.4.4**.

9 See **Chapter IX.4**. These criteria reflect the conclusions drawn from the substantive law research conducted in **Chapters III-VIII**.

registered, *i.e.* the *lex loci registrationis.*[10] With respect to the recognition of those relationships registered abroad, recognition should be afforded to foreign non-marital registered relationships if they are valid according to the law of the place where they are first registered. These rules should apply whether the issue arises in the context of a principal issue or incidental question and should refer to the law of the place of registration, including that country's private international law.[11] However, special choice of law and recognition rules should also be created for those relationships registered before consular or diplomatic representations.[12]

In terms of the dissolution of non-marital registered relationships, an identical jurisdictional and recognition scheme to that created by Brussels IIbis should be conceived for EU countries.[13] Other countries should endeavour to apply the same rules to the dissolution of non-marital registered relationships as they apply to divorces. Minor amendments to the jurisdictional rules will, however, be necessary to ensure that the authority competent to dissolve a relationship registered in the forum jurisdiction is always determined according to domestic, substantive law, and that a conditional *forum necessitatis* should be provided for enabling those couples without recourse to a court are able to proceed in the courts of the State where the relationship was registered.[14] The choice of law rules with respect to the dissolution of a non-marital registered relationship should attempt to combine the application of the *lex fori* and the *lex loci registrationis.* In ensuring the predominance of the *lex fori,* and allowing the parties to opt for the application of the *lex loci registrationis,* one retains for an element of flexibility, whilst ensuring that any increase in litigation costs would only be at the parties' own behest.[15]

Turning one's attention to the legal effects of the dissolution of a non-marital registered relationship, a distinction must be drawn between legal effects in the public law and private law spheres. With respect to those public law effects, it must be noted that the *lex fori* will always be applied to determine a party's entitlement to a particular benefit.[16] Those rights and duties created by virtue of the registration of a non-marital relationship in

---

10 See **Chapter X.2.1.4** (formal validity) and **X.2.2.3** (essential validity).

11 See **Chapter X.3.4.**

12 See **Chapter X.4.3.**

13 See **Chapter XI.2.4** (jurisdiction) and **XI.4.4** (recognition).

14 See **Chapter XI.2.4**, especially examples 12 and 13.

15 See **Chapter XI.3.3.**

16 See **Chapter XII.2.**

the field of child law, inheritance law and familial property law should be dealt with within these fields of law, instead of specific private international law rules being created for registered partners.[17] In the field of maintenance, it would appear that the jurisdictional, choice of law and recognition rules already cater for non-marital registered relationships.[18] And finally, with respect to those non-pecuniary matters, a choice will need to be made between the application of the *lex loci registrationis* and the *lex fori*.[19] Although both solutions are fraught with problems, the application of the *lex loci registrationis* to the non-pecuniary effects appears to provide the greatest possible opportunity for success. Whether or not this is subject to a ceiling restriction will ultimately depend upon on political compromise.[20]

XIII.3 DESIRABILITY

Bearing in mind the evaluation criteria of attempting to prevent limping relationships, increase the international flow of decisions and respect the parties' legitimate expectations, whilst adhering to the general principles of private international law, it is necessary to briefly examine the possible advantages and disadvantages of harmonising or unifying the private international law rules with respect to non-marital registered relationships.

XIII.3.1 ADVANTAGES OF HARMONISATION/UNIFICATION

One of the quixotic premises upon which private international law is based is the abiding search for decisional harmony. Since this can only be achieved if all States involved are in agreement as to the assignment of a legal issue to a particular legal category, the rules of jurisdiction and applicable law, the desirability of harmonising private international law in this field is strong. It would, therefore, almost seem to go without saying that the quest for harmonised rules of private international law is inherently desirable. With decisional harmony comes certainty and added simplicity.[21] If all countries applied the same private international law rules, divergent solutions as to matters of jurisdiction and the law to be applied in

---

17 See **Chapter XII.3.1** (children), **XII.3.2** (inheritance law) and **XII.3.3.2** (familial property law).

18 See **Chapter XII.3.3.1**.

19 See **Chapter XII.3.4.1** (*lex fori*) and **XII.3.4.2** (*lex loci registrationis*).

20 See **Chapter XII.3.4.4**.

21 T. DE BOER (1994) p. 54. For example, the unification of the choice of law rules in the field of contract has been completed in approximately twenty articles (Rome Convention, shortly to be converted into Rome I Regulation), whilst the harmonisation of European Contract Law has been much more difficult and protracted.

a particular case would be minimalised as far as possible.[22] Furthermore, the harmonisation or unification of private international law in this field is of a relatively "low impact", since it only affects those cases involving cross-border family ties; purely domestic situations remain within the exclusive domain of domestic substantive law. With private international law already viewed as a peculiarly technical and abstract field, the political sensitivity of harmonised or unified private international law rules is thus of a lesser degree than should one attempt the unification or harmonisation of the respective substantive law rules.

Nevertheless, perhaps the greatest possible advantage to harmonising or unifying private international law in this field is the prevention of limping relationships. The general interest to ensure the continuity of legal status is perhaps greatest in the field of family law. People live in reliance of the continued existence of the familial relationships which they enter into.[23] The loss of such a legal position upon crossing borders can ultimately lead to a loss in confidence in the legal system; a situation which will undoubtedly hinder the free movement of persons.[24]

XIII.3.2 DISADVANTAGES OF HARMONISATION/UNIFICATION

Yet the harmonisation and unification of private international law is not without its difficulties. Jurisdictional rules, however framed, normally leave the claimant with a number of different fora in which to proceed.[25] Even uniform jurisdictional rules may thus not provide the parties with any assurance as to where a case will be brought. In providing the claimant with multiple jurisdictions in which to proceed, one ultimately favours the financially stronger party since they are more likely to be able forum shop and thus possibly obtain a better solution. This is even more probable when one combines the multiple jurisdictional possibilities with the differences in the field of choice of law rules.[26] All in all, these factors do nothing to limit the dangers of forum shopping.[27]

---

22 They are obviously not removed altogether, since even harmonised or unified rules require interpretation which can differ.

23 Dethloff (2003) p. 50.

24 It is perhaps on this basis that future EU instruments could be based. See **Section XIII.3.4**.

25 *E.g.* the multiple jurisdictions created by Brussels IIbis: **Chapter XI.2.1.2**.

26 Dethloff (2003) p. 40-41.

27 See the problems created by Brussels IIbis in the race to court: **Chapter XI.2.4**.

Moreover, should a choice of law rule point to the application of a foreign law, problems can also arise in the ascertainment and application of this law.[28] As has already been stated,[29] the common law approach that prevails in the whole of the **United Kingdom** ensures that foreign law is treated as a fact, and must be pleaded and proved.[30] The converse is true in **Belgium** and **The Netherlands** where foreign law is regarded as a legal issue and the court always has a duty to apply foreign law even if its application has not been pleaded by the parties (the principle of *iura novit curia*).[31] These two extremes are subject to exception and concession in both **Switzerland** and **France**.

In **Switzerland**, the principle rule is that the court must determine the content of foreign law *ex officio,* subject to two exceptions.[32] Firstly, in patrimonial matters the court may be relieved of its duty and instead the parties are charged with proving the application of foreign law.[33] Secondly, where the relevant choice of law allows the parties to choose the governing law, the parties are entitled to enter into an agreement that this law will not be applied. In both cases, the *lex fori* is substituted as a result.[34] The situation in **France** is slightly more complicated. This field is based almost entirely upon judicial decisions and has undergone a number of U-turns by the **French** Supreme Court. The original position seemed to be that a court was under no *ex officio* duty to apply foreign law, although if the parties did not plead it the court did possess a discretionary *ex officio* power to apply foreign law on its own motion.[35] However, in two more recent cases, the **French** Supreme Court appears to have made a drastic volte-face and stated that "*[l]e juge droit trancher le litige conformément aux règles de droit qui*

---

28 See for a detailed and clear overview, HARTLEY (1996) and MOSTERMANS (1996).

29 See **Chapter XI.3.1 (footnote 122) and XI.3.1.4.**

30 ANTON/BEAUMONT (1990) p. 773-780, HARTLEY (1996) p. 282-289 and NORTH/FAWCETT (1999) p. 99-101. Hartley notes, however, that a when a court is asked to provide a declaration/decree of status, it could be argued that the court is obliged *ex officio* to apply the relevant choice of law rules: HARTLEY (1996) p. 286-287.

31 **Belg.**: Art. 15(1), Belg. CPIL and see *Belgian Senate*, 2003-2004, No. 3-27/7, p. 38; **Neth.**: HR, 4th June 1915, NJ 1915, 865 (*Ehlers & Loewenthal v. Van Leeuwen*) and MOSTERMANS (1996) p. 34-40.

32 Art. 16, Sw. CPIL. See further PATOCCHI/GEISINGER (1995) p. 115-118, Art. 16 and BUCHER/BONOMI (2004) p. 122-124, §454-469.

33 Art. 16(2), Sw. CPIL. See further BUCHER (1995) §375-379.

34 HARTLEY (1996) p. 277.

35 As was adopted in Fr. Cass., 12th May 1959 (1960) *JDI* 810, annotated SIALELLI (*Bisbal*); Fr. Cass., 2nd March 1960 (1961) *JDI* 408, annotated GOLDMANN (*Chemouny*).

lui sont applicables."[36] The end result appears to be that if the parties do not request the application of foreign law, the judgment cannot be attacked on the ground that the court applied the *lex fori*.[37]

Finally, regardless of the degree of uniformity in private international law rules, questions will always persist with regards the underlying latent structural differences, namely with respect to issues such as characterisation, *renvoi* and incidental questions.

XIII.3.3 EVALUATION

Bearing in mind the difficulties already delineated with respect to the harmonisation or unification of substantive law in this field, one must set ones sights on the harmonisation or unification of private international law.[38] Although perhaps not the ideal answer to the problems encountered in this field,[39] this approach would go some way to ensuring that limping relationships are averted as much as possible. The benefits of harmonising or unifying the private international law rules in this field, even if only a temporary solution,[40] far outweigh the disadvantages of any such endeavour. With the harmonisation or unification of substantive family law many years away, cross-border familial relationships need security now, which can partly be achieved by uniform (or at least harmonised) private international law rules. Although this will never solve the problem of differences in the legal effects attributed to such relationships,[41] it will go some way to ensuring that the parties' reliance on the existence of a valid legal relationship is adequately guaranteed. Nonetheless, although this pragmatic approach may well be academically acceptable, the question remains whether it is politically palatable.

---

36 Fr. Cass., 1 Civ. Ch., 11th and 18th October 1988 (respectively) (1989) II *JCP* 21327, annotated COUBRE (*Rebouh* and *Schule*); Fr. Cass., 1 Civ. Ch., 18th November 1992 (1993) *JDI* 309, annotated LEQUETTE (*Makhlouf*).

37 Fr. Cass., 1 Civ. Ch., 4th December 1990 (1991) *JDI* 371, annotated BUREAU, (1991) *Rev. crit. DIP* 558, annotated NIBOYET-HOEGY (*Coveco*).

38 T. DE BOER (1994) p. 57-58 who argues that even if uniform substantive law can be achieved there will always be gaps, for which purpose one must resort to private international law.

39 *E.g.* BOELE-WOELKI (2002b), JÄNTERÄ-JAREBORG (2003b) and DETHLOFF (2003) p. 50-54.

40 VAN ERP (2002) §4, BOELE-WOELKI (2005a) and T. DE BOER (1994) p. 53.

41 DETHLOFF (2003) p. 53.

XIII.4 FEASIBILITY

Ensuring that a couple registered in one country will be regarded as registered elsewhere is a commendable goal that appropriately corresponds with the goals of respecting the parties' expectations and aiming to ensure increased co-operation in the field of mutual recognition in civil matters. In having established that the harmonisation or unification of private international law is desirable, the question which rises is whether it is also feasible to propose such legislation. In answering this question one must address the corollary matter of which institution/organisation is best suited to deal with these issues. This section will thus focus on the current and future activity undertaken by five supranational institutions and organisations.

XIII.4.1 EUROPEAN GROUP FOR PRIVATE INTERNATIONAL LAW

The European Group for Private International Law was established in 1991 and consists primarily of members of universities of EU Member States or international organisations. As such, documents adopted by the group have no direct legislative force and are instead aimed to encourage the dissemination of information. The topic of non-marital registered relationships has been discussed at every annual meeting since 2000.[42] During the 2004 meeting, a proposal was submitted dealing with the issue of non-marital registered relationships. Disagreement as to the terminology to be used,[43] the scope of the proposed rules and many other issues[44] led the group to postpone the discussion until 2005. One of the greatest obstacles facing the European Group lay in trying to reach a consensus acceptable to all the representatives, regardless of whether they have enacted domestic substantive legislation creating a non-marital relationship registration scheme. Moreover, although such attempts should be welcomed, any result achieved by the Group will ultimately need to be implemented by a legislative body and thus the question remains as to which institution is most suited to the task.

---

42 At the 10th meeting in Rome (15th to 17th September 2000), the 11th meeting in Lund (21st to 23rd September 2001), 12th meeting in Paris (20th to 22nd September 2002), the 13th meeting in Vienna (19th to 21st September 2003) and the 14th meeting in Tenerife (17th to 19th September 2004). See for further details: www.drt.ucl.ac.be/gedip/default.html.

43 The proposal only refers to the term "partnerships" which was felt by some to be too board. Furthermore some objected to reference to the term "recognition"; feeling more at ease with the term "validly registered in".

44 The original proposal also referred same-sex marriages to the same rules.

XIII.4.2 INTERNATIONAL COMMISSION ON CIVIL STATUS (ICCS)

There are currently sixteen Member States to the ICCS and six States with observer status.[45] The Madrid General Assembly approved the proposal that the ICCS should examine the question of registered partnerships. It decided to set up a working party to conduct a general review of the subject, notably as regards the recognition of such relationships. To prepare for the working party's meeting in February 2004, a note summarising the provisions in force in the various Member States was prepared, together with a questionnaire designed to gather additional details.[46] Discussions were pursued during the Strasbourg and Edinburgh General Assemblies in March and September 2004 respectively, where outline drafts of a convention were reviewed. It was ultimately decided that work should continue with an eye to the preparation of a convention on the recognition of the civil status effects of all non-marital registered relationships.[47] Although not publicly accessible, a draft Convention was issued in December 2004.[48]

Although it is clear that the ICCS has acknowledged the need to develop international rules in this field, it is perhaps not the most suited forum for dealing with all the issues raised by non-marital registered relationships.[49] As has been seen in **Chapters III.4.2** and **IV.4.2**, the forms of non-marital registered relationship in **Belgium** and **France** do not have an impact upon the parties' civil status. This express exclusion would therefore make it difficult for any agreement drafted by the ICCS to be ratified by **France** or **Belgium**. Furthermore, none of the **Nordic** countries are privy to the restricted Membership of the ICCS. It is vital that any system of harmonised rules covers the widest possible number of European (and global) jurisdictions in order to fully attain the goals sought. Furthermore, although the draft convention deals with the recognition of non-marital registered relationships and the dissolution thereof, it is restricted in its scope to legal

---

45 Members: **Belgium** (1949), **France** (1949), **Luxembourg** (1949), **The Netherlands** (1949), **Switzerland** (1949), **Turkey** (1953), **Germany** (1956), **Italy** (1958), **Greece** (1959), **Austria** (1961), **Portugal** (1973), **Spain** (1974), the **United Kingdom** (1996), **Poland** (1998), **Croatia** (1999) and **Hungary** (1999). Observers: **Cyprus** (1999), **the Holy See** (1992), **Lithuania** (1994), **Russia** (1993), **Slovenia** (1996) and **Sweden** (1993).

46 *Partenariat enregistre. Réponses au questionnaire*, Strasbourg: ICCS, 13th April 2004.

47 For more information see www.ciec1.org.

48 *Convention sur la reconnaissance des partenariats enregistrés*, Documents diffusés par LC 8/2004, Strasbourg: ICCS, 15th December 2004.

49 This deficit has, for example, been recognised by the ICCS representative to the Hague Conference: PERMANENT BUREAU, *Preliminary document No. 32A of May 2005 for the attention of the Twentieth Session*, The Hague: Hague Conference, 2005, p. 28.

effects in the field of civil status, as a result of the ICCSs mandate. Therefore, although progress in this field is laudable, the absence of jurisdiction and choice of law rules is an unfortunate consequence. Whatever the outcome of these discussions, further harmonising or unifying measures will be required.

XIII.4.3 COUNCIL OF EUROPE

Legislative instruments in the field of family law are not new to the Council of Europe.[50] The Parliamentary Assembly of the Council of Europe has adopted no less than fifteen Recommendations on topics as wide ranging as the rights of the child, family policy and international adoption. The Committee of Ministers has also seen its fair share of activity with eight Conventions, five Resolutions and nineteen Recommendations in the field of family law alone.[51] However, even within the more specific field of cross-border familial relationships, the Council of Europe has been effective in drafting a number of important documents.[52] Furthermore, the fifth European conference on family law, held in The Hague on the 15th and 16th March 1999, focused on the civil law aspects of the emerging forms of registered partnerships.[53] It is therefore clear that, as well as being active in the broader issues of cross-border familial relationships, the Council of Europe has already addressed the specific issues raised by non-marital registered relationships. If one assumes that the Council of Europe is willing to address the private international law issues surrounding non-marital registered relationships, the question remains exactly how such an instrument would be drafted and what force any resulting text would have.

Under the authority of the European Committee on Legal Co-operation (CDCJ), the Committee of Experts on Family Law (CJFA) has been instructed to promote an area of common legal standards in the field of family law in Europe. It would, therefore, be possible for the CJFA to

---

50 For a general overview of the harmonisation capabilities of the council of Europe, see COUNCIL OF EUROPE SECRETARIAT, *Manual of the Council of Europe*, London: Stevens & Sons, 1970, p. 20-49; KOKKINI-IATRIDOU (1988) p. 75-77; J. POLAKIEWICZ, *Treaty-making in the Council of Europe*, Strasbourg: Council of Europe Publishing, 1999, p. 19-28.

51 For a detailed list see COUNCIL OF EUROPE, *Council of Europe Achievements in the field of law. Family law and the protection of children*, Strasbourg: September 2002, DIR/JUR (2002) 9. This document is available at www.coe.int.

52 See especially, the Recommendations No. R (95) 6 and No. R (99) 7 on the application of the European Convention on recognition and enforcement of decisions concerning custody of children and on restoration of custody of children.

53 SCHRAMA (1999b).

propose for action to be taken in this field. However, although a simple majority is sufficient for the Consultative Assembly to adopt a resolution, reply or opinion, a two-thirds majority is necessary for the adoption of a recommendation. Although instruments emanating from the Council of Europe are not seen "like an incoming tide [which] flows into the estuaries and up the rivers", in a highly technical and politically sensitive field such as the one under discussion it seems unlikely that anything less than a recommendation would be constructive.[54] Yet even if all those countries which have enacted or are in the process of enacting legislation in the field of non-marital registered relationships were in favour of adopting a resolution, reply or opinion, only a simple majority would be achieved.[55]

A further disadvantage of instruments from the Council of Europe is that they lack direct legislative effect, first requiring ratification and sometimes even subsequent transposition into domestic law before they are effective and enforceable. In summary, although the Council of Europe appears to be in a position to commence work in this field, the sensitivity of the topic and the highly technical nature of the rules that need to be discussed do not fit squarely with the either legislative instruments at the Council's disposal or the methods by which such instruments are adopted.

XIII.4.4 EUROPEAN UNION

It has become abundantly clear in recent years that the European Union has, and is willing to exercise, its competency in the field of cross-border familial relationships. Despite not having competency in issues of substantive family law,[56] the EU does have competency on grounds of Art. 61(c), EC Treaty to progressively establish an area of freedom, security and justice, by introducing measures in the field of judicial co-operation in civil matters as provided for in Art. 65, EC Treaty. In turn, Art. 65, EC Treaty refers to civil matters having "cross-border implications" and the implementation of measures "insofar as necessary for the proper functioning of the internal market". With the EU having already embraced the developments taking place with respect to non-marital registered

---

54 Paraphrasing Lord DENNING'S comments on the impact of European Union law in *H.P. Bulmer Ltd v. J. Bollinger SA* (1974) Ch. 401 at 418.

55 See **Appendices 1** and **2** for a list of Council of Europe Members States with legislation or proposals in this field.

56 PINTENS (2003) p. 22, footnote 96. Although acknowledging the EUs lack of competency in the field of substantive family law, BOELE-WOELKI has argued that the absence of a time condition in Art. 65, EC Treaty could be read so as to grant the EU competency to act in all situations involving an international legal relationship: BOELE-WOELKI (2005a).

relationships in two recently enacted Directives,[57] and having amended the EC Staff Regulations in light of the ECJ decision in *D and Sweden v. Council*,[58] the question is not whether the EU is competent to act in this field, but whether it is willing to, and if so, by what means.

Assuming that such political will is present, the European Union disposes of a complex array of legislative arsenal.[59] If the European Union were to enact a regulation in this field, the Member States would be prohibited from adopting any method of implementation that would jeopardise its application and that would result in different or discriminatory treatment of European Union citizens according to national criteria. Whilst a regulation aims at unifying the law of the Member States in any given field, a directive calls upon the Member States to exercise their own legislative powers, either for the purpose of adapting their laws to common standards laid down by the European institutions, or for the purpose of carrying out the obligations arising from the Treaties. While regulations are of general application to all Member States, directives are primarily intended to create legal relationships between the European Community and the Member State(s) to which it is addressed. A directive is binding upon such States, but only as to the result achieved, while leaving to the national authorities the choice of form and method.

The other forms of secondary legislation at the EUs disposal are decisions, recommendations and opinions. These relatively weak forms of secondary legislation, although carrying considerable political and moral weight, are less useful in the highly technical field of private international law. Furthermore, the European Union also possesses the power to draft conventions, which was used in the field of private international law prior to the Treaty of Amsterdam (*i.e.* Brussels and Lugano Conventions).

---

57 Directive of the European Parliament and of the Council of 29th April 2004 on the right of citizens of the Union and their family members to move and reside freely within the territory of the Member States, *Directive 2004/38/EC, L-158/77* and Council Directive of 22nd September 2003 on the right to family reunification, *Directive 2003/86/EC, L-251/12.*

58 The ECJ has ensured that the word "spouse" not be broadened to cover non-marital registered relationships: ECJ, *D and Sweden v. Council*, Case No. 122/99 and 125/99P [2001] I ECR 4319. Since this case, the relevant Staff Regulations have been amended so as to refer to "an official who is registered as a stable non-marital partner" (Council Regulation No. 723/2004 of 22nd March 2004 amending the Staff Regulations of the European Communities, *OJ*, 2004, L-124/1, §97(a)(ii)).

59 Art. 249, EC Treaty: regulations, directives, decisions, recommendations and opinions.

The European Union, therefore, not only has the necessary legislative tools at its disposal, but also possesses the political weight to introduce comprehensive instruments regulating the private international law aspects of non-marital registered relationships. Yet progress should be made with caution and under the caveat that the EU selects its approach carefully. Perhaps the best option is to now proceed down the road of a convention with limited territorial scope and universal application.[60] Although this would perhaps go against the current trend in unifying private international law by means of regulations,[61] this can be explained by virtue of the unique nature of non-marital registered relationships. Unlike divorce,[62] which, barring **Malta**, is recognised in some form or another across the EU, non-marital registered relationships do not benefit from such widespread acknowledgement. This limited recognition would therefore make it onerous to achieve agreement on any sort of regulation.

Opting for a convention thus goes some way to acknowledging the fact that although some countries are ready for unified rules in the field of non-marital registered relationships, not all countries are. Furthermore, the same "sense of urgency" manifest during the discussions leading to the conclusion of the Rome Convention,[63] is also perceptible in this field. The upshot could be a sort of Schengen area for non-marital registered relationships, with relationships guaranteed recognition within the territory of the Contracting States according to the private international law rules agreed upon.[64] Such

---

60 This way the rules of those ratifying countries would be harmonised in a similar manner to the choice of law rules in the field of contract law by those Contracting States to the Rome Convention.

61 See, for example, Van Houtte/Pertegás Sender (2001), especially the contributions from Van Houtte (p. 1-10) and Van Den Eeckhout (p. 69-102). Regulations have the advantage that they do need to depend upon ratification for their legal effect, and are not subject to exasperating parliamentary discussions, as is the case with a convention.

62 Divorce being the subject matter for the first Regulation in the field of cross-border familial relationships, namely in the form of Brussels II (and subsequently Brussels IIbis).

63 It was felt that unified rules had to be introduced quickly, considering the reforms likely to take place in some countries: Giuliano Report, *Council report on the Convention on the law applicable o contractual obligations*, 31st October 1980, C282/1, p. 4, §1.

64 The Schengen Convention put into practice the terms of the Schengen Agreement drawn up on the 14th June 1985. Due to the highly sensitive nature of immigration controls, adopting a convention allowed those countries not yet ready for such moves (*e.g.* the **United Kingdom** and **Ireland** have still not signed up to the Treaty in its entirety) to remain outside of its terms, whilst ensuring those countries ready for such a move were able to progress unimpeded. The Convention was initially signed by **Belgium**, **The Netherlands**, **Luxembourg**, **Germany**, **France** (22nd September 2000, OJ, L239, p. 19-62), and later by **Italy** (27th November 1990), **Portugal** and **Spain** (25th June 1992), **Greece** (6th November 1992), **Austria** (28th April 1995), **Denmark**, **Finland**, **Iceland**, **Norway** and

an approach would also allow for countries outside of the EU to sign up to the convention and thus ensure a more uniform approach across the European continent. Although such a convention would technically be independent of the European Union, such developments could be incorporated into the community legislative framework at a later stage.[65]

An alternative option, perhaps more in keeping with current trends, would be for those interested EU Member States to make use of the enhanced co-operation possibilities created by the Treaty of Amsterdam and amended by the Treaty of Nice. Arts. 43 to 45, EU Treaty allow for a minimum of eight Member States to establish enhanced co-operation between themselves and thus avail themselves of the institutions, procedures and mechanisms laid down by the EU and EC Treaties.[66] Although such provisions can only be used as a last resort,[67] any subsequent agreement reached is open to all other Member States; the Commission is placed under an active responsibility to ensure that Member States are encouraged to participate.[68] This power is further explained with respect to the fields of competency covered by the EC Treaty in Arts. 11 and 11A, EC Treaty. Any group of Member States which intends to use the enhanced co-operation possibility must therefore submit a request to the Commission,[69] which submits a request to the Council. Permission is then granted by a qualified majority vote of the Council after consultation with the European Parliament.[70]

This procedure would thus allow a select group of Member States to avail themselves of the benefits of regulations, whilst at the same time avoiding the adverse consequences of having to ensure that any proposal is also acceptable to those countries without national forms of non-marital registered relationship. With these rules never having been used before, perhaps the time has come for the waters to be tested.

Sweden (19th December 1996), **Cyprus**, **Czech Republic**, **Estonia**, **Hungary**, **Latvia**, **Lithuania**, **Malta**, **Poland**, **Slovakia** and **Slovenia** (signed on the 1st May 2005 but not yet implemented) and **Switzerland** (16th October 2004, and ratified by referendum on the 5th June 2005; not yet implemented).

65 *E.g.*, this has already taken place with the Brussels Convention (now Brussels I) and is expected to take place with the Rome Convention (which will become Rome I).

66 Art. 43, EU Treaty.

67 Art. 43A, EU Treaty.

68 Art. 43B, EU Treaty.

69 The Commission also has the right to veto the proposal if it considers that the substantive conditions laid down in Art. 43, EU Treaty and Art. 11, EC Treaty are not met.

70 Art. 11, EC Treaty. Art. 11a, EC Treaty explains the subsequent participation procedure for other Member States.

XIII.4.5 HAGUE CONFERENCE

The Hague Conference on Private International Law was founded in 1898 and currently boosts sixty-five Member States and more than thirty-five conventions in various fields of private international law. The Hague Conference first dealt with the issues surrounding unmarried couples in 1987. The Permanent Bureau, although having acknowledged that the issues raised were important, did not suggest urgent consideration and the matter was adopted for further study.[71] Although a second note in April 1992 led to a comparative study, once again no direct results were achieved.[72] The matter was raised again three years later, and although some experts considered that the issue of homosexual couples should be included, others worried that this would be too controversial.[73] At the Eighteenth Session, it was once again decided to keep the issue on the agenda, although without priority.[74] This position was reiterated in 2005.[75]

In light of this background, it is clear that one of the main problems for the Hague Conference lies in the controversy surrounding the topic under debate.[76] However, some hope can be gleaned from the statement in the preliminary document from 2000, where it is stated that a "possibility which might be considered would be the establishment of a Working Group, comprising experts from interested States, with a mandate to review current developments and to formulate a possible strategy for developing a uniform approach to the issues of private international law."[77] A similar approach has also been adopted with respect to an optional Convention on

---

71 PERMANENT BUREAU, *Proceedings of the sixteenth session. Miscellaneous matters*, The Hague: Hague Conference, 1988, Tome I, p. 253 *et seq.*

72 PERMANENT BUREAU, *Preliminary document No. 5 of April 1992 for the attention of the Special Commission of June 1992 on General Affairs and Policy of the Conference*, The Hague: Hague Conference, 1992.

73 PERMANENT BUREAU, *Preliminary document No. 9 of December 1995. Conclusions of the Special Commission of June 1995 on General Affairs and Policy of the Conference*, The Hague: Hague Conference, 1996.

74 PERMANENT BUREAU, *Final Act of the Eighteenth Session of the Hague Conference on Private International Law*, 19th October 1996, under Part B.4.c.

75 PERMANENT BUREAU, *Preliminary document No. 32A of May 2005 for the attention of the Twentieth Session*, The Hague: Hague Conference, 2005, p. 28-29.

76 The **United States of America** is one of the clearest opponents of any work untaken by the Hague Conference on this issue, see p.28, *ibid.*

77 PERMANENT BUREAU, *Preliminary document No. 9 of May 2000 for the attention of the Special Commission of May 2000 on general affairs and policy of the conference*, The Hague: Hague Conference, 2000, §15.

the applicable law in any future convention in the field of maintenance.[78] Even so, no further progress has been made on this issue since 2000. Noting the reluctance of some experts of the Special Commission on maintenance obligations to include same-sex couples within the definition of those entitled to claim under any future convention, it seems unlikely that a plenary session would lead to substantial results.

XIII.4.6 EVALUATION

Whilst the role of private international law in an emerging European unification may well be transitory, its importance should neither be overlooked nor undermined. If private international law can be said to distribute international jurisdiction and "allocate international controversy to the most appropriate legal system", this will inevitably go some way to ensuring the achievement of the goals laid forth at the beginning of this research. In striving to achieve these goals, it is clear that although numerous organisations both at European and international level have recognised the need to address these issues, no single organisation has really tackled the topic directly.

Whilst the matter at issue is controversial in many countries around the world, it is important that steps are taken by those countries where developments have occurred in order to ensure that these couples having registered their relationship are offered the security of knowing that their relationship will be recognised, even if only in a limited number of jurisdictions. The restricted scope of the ICCSs mandate, the limited possibilities of reaching a workable solution in the Council of Europe and the lack of legislative force of the European Group for Private International Law, lead one to conclude that only the European Union or the Hague Conference are really suited to dealing with the issues raised.

In focusing on the possibilities at the disposal of these organisations, one must bear in mind the current lack of unanimity on the need to address the issues surrounding non-marital registered relationships. The fact that not all of the participating countries in the EU or the Hague Conference would be prepared to ratify or accept a proposal in this field of law, will have ramifications for the form of any eventual proposals. Progress at EU level could best therefore be realised either by means of a convention or via the

---

78 Permanent Bureau, *Preliminary document No. 12 of 12th September 2004 for the attention of the Special Commission on the international recovery of child support and other forms of family maintenance*, The Hague: Hague Conference, 2004, p. 3.

enhanced co-operation procedure. If a worldwide convention is, however, to be drawn up, it would seem logical and most appropriate that such discussions took place in the forum of the Hague Conference. As long as the Hague Conference remains ambivalent towards these issues, the EU should step forwards and take action. However, since overlap of international instruments should be avoided, if the Hague Conference was to commence work, those interested EU Member States would be best advised to take an active role in such discussions, ensuring the creation of a worldwide instrument.[79]

XIII.5 THE FUTURE

The tragedy embodied in Romeo and Juliet stems from the failure of the society surrounding them to recognise their relationship. Although today's society has begun to address the issues surrounding non-marital relationships, domestic solutions are not enough to ensure respect. In an ever globalising world where political borders, at least within the European Union, are of increasingly less importance, it is imperative that we harmonise or unify the private international law rules in this field. It has been proven that this is not only desirable and feasible, but also possible. Responsibility now rests with the politicians and legislatures. With more than fifteen European countries having introduced domestic forms of non-marital registered relationships and more set to do so, the time has come for legislatures to tackle these issues and provide certainty to thousands of registered partners. After all let us not forget,

> "it is easy to dodge our responsibilities, but we cannot dodge the consequences of dodging our responsibilities".[80]

---

79 For a critical comment on the relationship between the Hague Conference and the EU see JÄNTERÄ-JAREBORG (2003b) p. 199-201.

80 JOSIAH CHARLES STAMP (1880-1941).

PART IV

APPENDICES

"'We were not the first, but I am sure we will not be the last.
After us will come many other countries,
driven, ladies and gentlemen, by two unstoppable forces:
freedom and equality."

Jose Luis Rodriguez Zapatero, Prime Minister of Spain
30th June 2005, after the Spanish Parliament voted
to pass legislation allowing for same-sex marriage.

APPENDIX 1
NON-MARITAL REGISTERED RELATIONSHIP LEGISLATION IN THE EUROPEAN UNION

AUSTRIA
No legislation and no legislative proposals.[1]

BELGIUM (2000)
Loi instaurant la cohabitation légale, 23 novembre 1999 / Wet van 23 november 1999 tot invoering van de wettelijke samenwoning.

CYPRUS
No legislation and no legislative proposals.

CZECH REPUBLIC
No legislation, but four proposals have gone before Parliament.[2]

DENMARK AND GREENLAND (1989)
Lov nr. 372 af 07-06-1989 amended by Lov nr. 821 af 19-12-1989, Lov nr. 360 af 02-06-1999 (and Ministerial Orders nr. 929/2001 and nr. 198/2002). Since 26th April 1996, Instrument of Enforcement N°. 320, Anordning om inkrafttraeden for Grøenland af lov om registreret partnerskab.

ESTONIA
No legislation and no legislative proposals.

FINLAND (2001)
Laki rekisteröidystä parisuhteesta (N°. 950/2001) amended by Laki rekisteröidystä parisuhteesta annetun lain 13 ja 14 §:n muuttamisesta (N°. 1229/2001).

---

1 At the December 2004 Austrian Social Democratic Party biannual convention, the party took a sensational move and announced it would, if elected, immediately introduce same-sex registered partnership.

2 The 1997 bill was rejected at first reading. The 1999 Bill was rejected at second reading. The 2000 Bill was rejected at first reading. In 2004, the Bill was not approved by the Government and so was submitted by a group of Members of Parliament. Although passing first reading (18th June 2004) and second reading (22nd September 2004) but was failed to achieve a majority by one vote at third reading (11th February 2005). For more information see http://gay.iniciativa.cz/www/index.php/index.php/index.php?page=clanek?id=74.

FRANCE (1999)
Loi N°. 99-944 du 15 novembre 1999 relative au pacte civil de solidarité.

GERMANY (2001)
Gesetz zur Beendigung der Diskriminierung gleichgeschlechticher Gemeinschaften: Lebenspartnerschaften, BGBl I 2001, 266, as amended by Gesetz zur Überarbeitung des Lebenspartnerschaftsrechts, BGBl I 2004, 3396.

GREECE
No legislation and no legislative proposals.[3]

HUNGARY
No legislation but the Government has announced legislative proposals.[4]

IRELAND
No legislation, but proposal has been submitted to Parliament in 2004.[5]

ITALY
No legislation and no legislative proposals.[6]

---

3 On the 25th February 2005, the Greek National Commission for Human Rights issued a report instructing the Government to create a civil unions registry for same-sex couples.

4 In 1996, the Hungarian Supreme Court did extend the concept of "common law marriage" to same-sex couples and subsequently enacted §578/G, Hungarian Civil Code. On the 3rd March 2005, the Hungarian Government announced plans to create a domestic partnership registry for same-sex couples. The Bill is expected to be published before the end of 2005, debate in 2006 and enacted in 2007.

5 See FINE GAEL, *Civil partnership*, Dublin: Fine Gael, 2003 NATIONAL ECONOMIC AND SOCIAL FORUM, *Equality Policies for Lesbian, Gay and Bisexual People: Implementation Issues. Forum Report No. 27*, Dublin: National Economic and Social Forum, 2003; EQUALITY AUTHORITY, *Implementing equality for lesbians, gays and bisexuals*, Dublin: Equality Authority, 2002; EQUALITY AUTHORITY, *Partnership rights of same-sex couples*, Dublin: Equality Authority, 2000. A proposal has been submitted to the Seanad Éireann in 2005: Civil Partnerships Bill 2004 (In Irish: Bille dá ngairtear Acht do dhéanamh socrú maidir le, agus i dtaca le, páirtíocht shibhialta). The Bill was debated at second reading on the 16th February 2005.

6 Many members of the Italian Parliament (both *Camera dei Deputati* and *Senato*) have presented proposals. The first was submitted in December 1993 (CIONI [PDS], TARADASH [Partito Radicale] and VENDOLA [Rifonazione Comunista]) and a second in 1994 (VENDOLA, CIONI and MANCONI [Green Party]). In the 13th Session two bills were submitted to the chamber of Deputies (VENDOLA and BUFFO [PDS]) and one to the Senate (MANCONI). However none of these bills have even been discussed.

LATVIA
No legislation but Parliament rejected a proposal in 1999.[7]

LITHUANIA
Articles 229-235, Chapter XV, Part VI, Book 3, Lithuanian Civil Code.[8]

LUXEMBOURG (2004)
Loi N°. 4946 relative aux effets légaux de certains partenariats.

MALTA
No legislation and no legislative proposals.

THE NETHERLANDS (1998)
Wet van 5 juli 1997, Staatsblad N°. 324, tot wijziging van Boek 1 van het Burgerlijk Wetboek en van het wetboek rechtsvordering in verband met opneming daarin van bepalingen voor het geregistreerd partnerschap.

POLAND
No legislation, but proposal has been submitted to Parliament in 2004.[9]

PORTUGAL
No legislation but proposals have gone before Parliament in 2001.[10]

SLOVAKIA
No legislation and no proposals.

SLOVENIA
Zakon o registraciji istospolne partnerske skupnosti (ZRIPS).[11]

---

7 The draft bill was submitted to the Parliamentary Committee on Human Rights and Public Affairs on the 5th October 1999. On the 30th November 1999, the Parliament Commission of the Saeima (Latvian Parliament) rejected the bill. See further, www.igla.info/Information/legal survey/europe/latvia.html.

8 This legislation is, however, not yet in force.

9 This passed through the Senate on the 3rd December 2004 and it due to be debated by the lower chamber of Parliament (*Sejm*) in 2005. The bill is however only supported by two political parties (SLD-UP and SdPL). Since all other parties are either against the Bill or indifferent, it would appear that the Bill has little chance of success).

10 Portugal has enacted legislation to allow for the recognition of non-marital unregistered relationships regardless of sex: Lei N°. 7/2001 de 11-5-2001, adopta medidas de protecção das uniões de facto. At the time when this law was enacted, there were different projects, some of which would have allowed for the introduction of non-marital registered relationships: propostas de alteração da lei N°. 135/99 de 28 Agosto e de outras que afectam as uniões de facto.

SPAIN: ANDALUCIA (2002)
Ley 5/2002 de 16 de diciembre de parejas de hecho de Andalucía.

SPAIN: ARÁGON (1999)
Ley 6/1999 de 26 de marzo relativa a parejas estables no casadas.

SPAIN: ASTURIAS (2002)
Ley 4/2002 de 23 de mayo de parejas estables del Principado de Astruias.

SPAIN: BALEARIC ISLANDS (2001)
Ley 18/2001 de 19 de diciembre de parejas estables.

SPAIN: BASQUE COUNTRY (2003)
Ley 2/2003 de 7 de mayo reguladora de las parejas de hecho.

SPAIN: CANARY ISLANDS (2003)
Ley 5/2003 de 6 de marzo para la regulación de las parejas de hecho de la Comunidad Autónoma de Canarias.

SPAIN: CANTABRIA
No legislation and no proposals.

SPAIN: CASTILLA-LA MANCHA
No legislation and no proposals.

SPAIN: CASTILLA Y LEON
No legislation but two proposals submitted in 2002.[12]

SPAIN: CATALONIA (1998)
Ley 10/1998 de 15 de julio de uniones estables de pareja.

---

11 Original 2003 proposal: Predloga zakona o partnerski skupnosti (available at www.ljudmila.org/lesbo/lesbo_1920_zakon.htm). The 2003 proposal after changes by the right-wing Slovenian People's Party: Predloga zakona o istospolni partnerski zvezi (http://www2.gov.si:8000/zak/Pre_Zak.nsf/zak_po_UNID/4C6AF192DF5B27AEC1256E84003437A6?OpenDocument). On the 24th February 2005, a Governmental Committee quashed an opposition bill on same-sex unions, which was subsequently supported by Parliament (44 votes to 27). The Government published its own bill was subsequently passed 44 votes to 3 on the 22nd June 2005.

12 PPL CcyL/13/5/2002, Proposición de ley para la igualdad juridical de parejas estables (Grupo Parlamentario Socialista) and PPL CcyL/5/11/2002, Proposición de ley para la igualdad juridical de las parejas estables de Castilla y León (Grupo Parlamentario Mixto)

SPAIN: EXTREMADURA (2003)
Ley 5/2003 de 20 de marzo de parejas de hecho de la Comunidad Autónoma de Extremadura.

SPAIN: GALICIA
No legislation and no proposals.

SPAIN: LA RIOJA
No legislation but a proposal was submitted in 2002.[13]

SPAIN: MADRID (2001)
Ley 11/2001 de 19 de diciembre de uniones de hecho de la Comunidad de Madrid.

SPAIN: MURCIA
No legislation and no proposals.

SPAIN: NAVARRE (2000)
Ley Foral 6/2000 de 3 de julio para la igualdad jurídica de las parejas estables.

SPAIN: VALENCIA (2001)
Ley 1/2001 de 6 de abril por la que se regulan las uniones de hecho.

SWEDEN (1995)
Lag (1994:1117) amended by Ändring (1995:1245), Ändring (2000:374) and Ändring (2002:603).

UNITED KINGDOM (2005)
Civil Partnerships Act 2004.

[13] Proposición de ley sobre la igualdad juridical de las parejas estables de La Rioja.

APPENDIX 2
NON-MARITAL REGISTERED RELATIONSHIP LEGISLATION IN THE OTHER COUNCIL OF EUROPE MEMBER STATES

ALBANIA
No legislation and no proposals.

ANDORRA
Llei 4/2005 del 21 de febrer qualificada de les unions estables de parella, BOPA N°. 25, any 17, 2005, p., 1022-1025.

ARMENIA
No legislation and no proposals.

AZERBAIJAN
No legislation and no proposals.

BOSNIA-HERZEGOVINA
No legislation and no proposals.

BULGARIA
No legislation and no proposals.

CROATIA
No legislation, but proposals.[1]

GEORGIA
No legislation and no proposals.

ICELAND (1996)
Act on Registered Partnership N°. 87, 12-06-1996 amended by Act N°. 52/2000.

---

[1] In 2003, the Croatian Parliament enacted legislation to allow for the non-marital unregistered same-sex civil unions: Law N°. 01-081-03/2597/2, 14th July 2003 (www.iglhrc.org/site/iglhrc/content.php?type=1&id=73&print=1)

LIECHTENSTEIN
No legislation, but a proposal was submitted to Parliament in 2003.[2]

MOLDOVA
No legislation and no proposals.

NORWAY (1993)
Lov nr. 40 af 30-04-1993 amended by Lov nr. 104 af 21-12-2000 and Lov nr. 36 af 15-06-2001.

ROMANIA
No legislation and no proposals.[3]

RUSSIAN FEDERATION
No legislation and no proposals.

SAN MARINO
No legislation and no proposals.

SERBIA AND MONTENEGRO
No legislation and no proposals.

SWITZERLAND (2007)
Loi fédérale sur le partenariat enregistré entre personnes du même sexe.

THE FORMER YUGOSLAV REPUBLIC OF MACEDONIA
No legislation and no proposals.

TURKEY
No legislation and no proposals.

UKRAINE
No legislation and no proposals.

---

2 REGIERUNG DES FÜRSTENTUMS LIECHTENSTEIN, Stellungnahme der reigerung an den Landtag des Füyrstentums Liechtenstein zur formulierten initiativen vom 19 voember 2001 über die registrierte Partnerschaft und zur Abänderung des Ehegesetzes, N°. 26/2003.

3 Traian Băsescu was elected President of Romania on the 12th December 2004. As part of his presidential election campaign he pledged to legalise same-sex marriages.

APPENDIX 3
NON-MARITAL REGISTERED RELATIONSHIP LEGISLATION AND CASE-LAW OUTSIDE EUROPE

ARGENTINA: BUENOS AIRES CITY (2003)
Ley de Unión Civil de la Ciudad Autónoma de Buenos Aires N° 1004/2.002 Y Decreto Reglamentario N° 556/2.003, published in BOCBA N°. 1617 on 27th January 2003.

ARGENTINA: SANTE FE (2005 PROPOSAL)
Le para uniones estables de pareja, N°. 0392/01.

ARGENTINA: RÍO NEGRO PROVINCE (2003)
Ley de Uniones Civiles de la Provincia de Río Negro, B.O. N° 100/2002.

AUSTRALIA: TASMANIA (2004)
Relationships Act 2003.

BRAZIL (1995 PROPOSAL)
Proyecto de Ley N°. 1.151 de 1.995 and Substitutivo adoptado pela Comissão Especial ao Projecto de Lei N°. 1.151 de 1.995.[1]

BRAZIL : RIO GRANDE DO SOL (2004)
Civil Unions declared legal by a judicial decision in March 2004.

CANADA: MANITOBA (2002)
The Common-Law Partners' Property and Related Amendments Act, SM 2002, c. 48.

CANADA: NOVA SCOTIA (2003)
Secs. 52-55, Vital Statistics Act.

CANADA: QUEBEC (2002)
Art. 521, Quebec Civil Code.

---

1 This bill has subsequently been dropped.

NEW ZEALAND (2005)
Civil Union Act 2004.

USA: CALIFORNIA (2003/2005)
Division 2.5, Domestic Partner Registration, California Family Code.

USA: CONNECTICUT (2005)
An Act Concerning Civil Unions, Public Act N°. 05-10, Substitute Senate Bill N°. 963.

USA: HAWAI'I (2002)
Chapter 572C: Reciprocal Benefits, Division 3: Property and Family; Title 31: Family, Hawai'i Revised Statutes Annotated.

USA: MAINE (2004)
An Act to promote the financial security of Maine's Families and Children. Enacted and changes Probate Code (Title 18-A, Maine Revised Statutes Annotated) and Health and Welfare statutes (Title 22, Maine Revised Statutes Annotated).

USA: MARYLAND (2005 PROPOSAL)
House Bill 1021, Medical Decision Making Act of 2005.[2]

USA: NEW JERSEY (2004)
Act establishing the rights and responsibilities of domestic partners, and revising parts of the statutory law, Chapter 246, New Jersey Statutes.

USA: VERMONT (1999)
Act relating to Civil Unions, §1201-1207, Title 15: Domestic Relations; Chapter 23: Civil Unions, Vermont Statutes Annotated.

2 The Bill passed through both houses, but was subsequently vetoed by the Governor.

APPENDIX 4
LEGISLATION / CASE-LAW ON SAME-SEX MARRIAGE AROUND THE WORLD

THE NETHERLANDS (2001)
Wet van 21 december 2000 tot wijziging van Boek 1 van het Burgerlijk Wetboek in verband met de openstelling van het huwelijk door personen van hetzelfde geslacht, *Staatsblad* 2001, N°. 9.

BELGIUM (2003)
Wet van 13 februari 2003 tot openstelling van het huwelijk voor personen van hetzelfde geslacht en tot wijziging van een aantal bepalingen van het Burgerlijk Wetboek, *Belgisch Staatsblad* 2003, 20th February 2003.

USA: MASSACHUSETTS (2004)
Goodridge v. Department of Public Health, 18th November 2003, 440 Mass 309, 798 N.E.2d. 941.

CANADA: FEDERAL LEGISLATION (2005)
Bill C-38: An Act respecting certain aspects of legal capacity for marriage for civil purposes, 2005, c.33.

CANADA: BRITISH COLUMBIA (2003)
Barbeau v. British Columbia (1st May 2003), 2003 BCCA 251 http://www.canlii.org/bc/cas/bcca/2003/2003bcca251.html

CANADA: MANITOBA (2004)
Vogel v. Canada [2004] MJ N°. 418 (QL)

CANADA: NEW BRUNSWICK (2005)
Harrison et al v. AG of Canada (23rd June 2005)
http://www.canlii.org/nb/cas/nbqb/2005/2005nbqb232.html

CANADA: NEWFOUNDLAND (2004)
Pottle and French v. Canada (21st December 2004)

CANADA: NOVA SCOTIA (2004)
Boutilier v. Nova Scotia (AG), [2004] NSJ N°. 357 (QL)

CANADA: ONTARIO (2002)
Halpern et. al. v. Canada (12th July 2002 (Divisional Court) and 10th June 2003 (Court of Appeal)), (2003) 65 OR (3d) 161.
http://www.canlii.org/on/cas/onca/2003/2003onca10314.html

CANADA: QUEBEC (2002)
Hendricks and Leboeuf v. Quebec (6th September 2002 (Superior Court) and 19th March 2003 (Court of Appeal)), [2002] RJQ N°. 2506
http://www.canlii.org/qc/jug/qccs/2002/2002qccs14544.html

CANADA: SASKATCHEWAN (2004)
NW and JR et al v. AG of Canada [2004] SJ N°. 669 (QL)
http://www.canlii.org/sk/cas/skqb/2004/2004skqb434.html

CANADA: YUKON TERRITORY (2004)
Dunbar & Edge v. Government of Yukon (AG), [2004] YJ N°. 61 (QL)
http://canlii.org/yk/cas/yksc/2004/2004yksc54.html

SOUTH AFRICA (2004)
Supreme Court of Appeal
Fourie and Another v. Minister of Home Affairs et al, 30th November 2004, Case No. 232/2003, [2004] JOL 13275 (SCA).

High Court of Bloemfontein
Satchwell v. President of Republic of South Africa, 2002 (9) BCLR 986 (CC), 2002 (6) SA 1(CC) *per* Madala J.

SPAIN (2005)
Ley 13/2005 de 1 julio 2005 por la que se modifica el Código Civil en materia de derecho a contraer matrimonio, BOE No. 153.

BIBLIOGRAPHY

ACHERMANN/CARONI (2001): A. ACHERMANN & M. CARONI, "Homosexuelle und heterosexuelle Konkubinatspaare im schweizerischen Ausländerrecht", *RSDIE*, 2001, p. 125-141.

ADAMS (1996): W.A. ADAMS, "Same-sex relationships and Anglo-Canadian choice of law: an argument for universal validity", *CYIL*, 1996, p. 103-136.

ADVIESBUREAU (2003): ADVIESBUREAU, "Met elkaar gehuwde vrouwen en naamskeuze (1) en (2)", *Burgerzaken en Recht*, 2003, p. 390.

AGNOSTI (2004): E. AGNOSTI, "Le mariage homosexuel? "Peut-être jamais, peut-être demain: mais pas aujourd'hui, c'est certain!" *Carmen, Acte I, scène III*", *D*, 2004, p. 2392-2395.

ALLEAUME (2000): C. ALLEAUME, "Solidarité contre solidarité. Étude comparative des avantages respectifs du mariage et du PACS au regard du droit du crédit", *D*, 2000, p. 450-454.

ALLEN, B. (1996): B.A. ALLEN, "A conflict of laws analysis for Oregon", *Will. LR*, 1996, p. 619-675.

ALLEN, C. (1930): C.K. ALLEN, "Status and capacity", *LQR*, 1930, Vol. 46, p. 277-310.

ALT-MAES (2000): F. ALT-MAES, "Le PACS à l'épreuve du droit pénal", *JCP Éd G*, 2000, p. 2171-2178.

ANCEL (1977): B. ANCEL, *Les conflict de qualifications à l'épreuve de la donation entre époux*, Paris: Dalloz, 1977.

ANCEL (1980): B. ANCEL, "L'objet de la qualification", *JDI*, 1980, p. 227.

ANCEL/LEQUETTE (2001): B. ANCEL & Y. LEQUETTE, *Les grands arrêts de la jurisprudence française de droit international privé*, Paris: Dalloz, 2001.

ANDERSEN (1997): L. ANDERSEN, "Registered personal relationships", *Fam. Law*, 1997, p. 174-177.

ANTOKOLSKAIA (2002a): M. ANTOKOLSKAIA, "Recent developments in Dutch filiation, adoption and joint custody law", *Familia*, 2002, p. 781-804.

ANTOKOLSKAIA (2002b): M. ANTOKOLSKAIA, "Would the harmonisation of family law in Europe enlarge the gap between the law in the books and the law in action?" *FamPra.ch*, 2002, p. 261-292.

ANTOKOLSKAIA (2002c): M. ANTOKOLSKAIA, "Enkele gedachten over de harmonisatie van het familierecht in Europa", *FJR*, 2002, p. 4-10.

ANTOKOLSKAIA (2003a): M. ANTOKOLSKAIA, "The harmonisation of family law: Old and new dilemmas", *ERPL*, 2003, p. 28-49.

ANTOKOLSKAIA (2003b): M. ANTOKOLSKAIA, "The 'better law' approach and the harmonisation of family law', in: K. BOELE-WOELKI (ed.), *EFL Series: Volume 4. Perspectives for the unification and harmonisation of family law in Europe*, Antwerp: Intersentia, 2003, p. 159-182.

ANTOKOLSKAIA (2005): M. ANTOKOLSKAIA, *Harmonisation of family law in Europe – An historical perspective*, Antwerp: Intersentia, 2006 (to be published).

ANTOKOLSKAIA/DE HONDT/STEENHOFF (1999): M. ANTOKOLSKAIA, W.A. DE HONDT & G.J.W. STEENHOFF, *Een zoektocht naar Europees Familierecht. Preadvies voor de Nederlandse Vereniging voor Rechtsvergelijking*, Deventer: Kluwer, 1999.

ANTON/BEAUMONT (1990): A.E. ANTON and P.R. BEAUMONT, *Private international law. A treatise from the standpoint of Scots Law*, Edinburgh: W. Green, 1990, 2nd Edition.

ARMINJON (1923): P. ARMINJON, "Les qualifications légales en droit international privé", *Rev. int. dr. com.*, 1923, p. 272.

ASUNCIION ASIN CABRERA (2004): M. ASUNCION ASIN CABRERA, "Le partenariat en droit espagnol: quel avenir pour une réglementation en droit international privé", in: A. BONOMI and B. COTTIER (eds.), *Aspects de droit international privé des partenariats enregistrés en Europe*, Zurich: Schulthess, 2004, Volume N°. 49, p. 71-84.

AUDIT (2000): B. AUDIT, *Droit international privé*, Paris: Economica, 2000, 3rd Edition.

AUDIT (2004): M. AUDIT, "L'interprétation autonome du droit international privé communautaire", *JDI*, 2004, p. 789-808.

AUGUST VON SACHSEN GESSAPHE (2004): K. AUGUST VON SACHSEN GESSAPHE, "Le partenariat enregistré en droit international privé allemand", in: A. BONOMI and B. COTTIER (eds.), *Aspects de droit international privé des partenariats enregistrés en Europe*, Zurich: Schulthess, 2004, Volume N°. 49, p. 9-28.

BAILEY (1998): M. BAILEY, "How will Canada respond to same-sex marriages?", *Creighton LR*, 1998, p. 105-119.

BAILEY-HARRIS (1999): R. BAILEY-HARRIS, "Third Stonewall Lecture – Lesbian and gay family values and the law", *Fam. Law*, 1999, p. 560-570.

BAILEY-HARRIS (2000): R. BAILEY-HARRIS, "New families for a new society?", in S. CRETNEY (ed.), *Family law essays for the new millenium*, Bristol: Jordan Publishing, 2000, p. 67-77.

BAILEY-HARRIS (2001): R. BAILEY-HARRIS, "Same-sex partnerships in English family law", in: R. Wintemute and M. Andenæs (eds.), *Legal recognition of same-sex partnerships*, Oxford: Hart Publishing, 2001, p. 605-619.

BAINHAM (1996): A. BAINHAM, "Family law in a pluralistic society: a view from England and Wales

BAINHAM (1998): A. BAINHAM, "Gay survivors and lesbian parents: Sexual orientation in family law", *CLJ*, 1998, p. 42-45.

BAINHAM (2000a): A. BAINHAM, "Homosexuality and the Lords: Shifting definitions of marriage and the family", *CLJ*, 2000, p. 39-42.

BAINHAM (2000b): A. BAINHAM, "Family rights in the next millennium", *CLP*, p. 471-503.

BAINHAM (2005): A. BAINHAM, *Children: The modern law*, Bristol: Jordans, 2005, 3rd Edition.

BARLOW (1999): A. BARLOW, *Advising gay and lesbian clients*, London: Butterworths, 1999.

BARLOW (2001): A. BARLOW, *Cohabitants and the law*, London: Butterworths, 2001, 3rd Edition.

BARLOW/BISSET JOHNSON (2003): A. BARLOW and A. BISSET-JOHNSON, "Cohabitation and the reform of Scots law", *JR*, 2003, p.105-128.

BARLOW/JAMES (2004): A. BARLOW and G. JAMES, "Regulating marriage and cohabitation in 21st century Britain", *MLR*, 2004, p. 143-176.

BARLOW/PROBERT (1999a): A. BARLOW and R. PROBERT, "Addressing the legal status of cohabitation in Britain and France: Plus ça change ...?", *Web JCLI*, 1999, http://webjcli.ncl.ac.uk/1999/issue3/barlow3.html.

BARLOW/PROBERT (1999b): A. BARLOW and R. PROBERT, "Reforming the rights of cohabitants – lessons from across the channel", *Fam*, 1999, p. 477-479.

BARNICH (2000): L. BARNICH, "Union libre et cohabitation légale, questions de droit international privé", in: D. STERCKX and J-L. LEDOUX (ed.), *Mélanges offertés à R. De Valkeneer*, Brussels: Bruylant, 2000, p. 1.

BARTIN (1897a): E. BARTIN, "De l'impossibilité d'arriver à la suppression définitive des conflits de lois", *JDI*, 1897, p. 225-255.

BARTIN (1897b): E. BARTIN, "De l'impossibilité d'arriver à la suppression définitive des conflits de lois", *JDI*, 1897, p. 466-495.

BARTIN (1897c): E. BARTIN, "De l'impossibilité d'arriver à la suppression définitive des conflits de lois", *JDI*, 1897, p. 720-738.

BARTON (1992): C. BARTON, "Pre-nuptial and cohabitation contracts: in at the birth?", *Fam Law*, 1992, p. 47-49.

BARTON (1996): C. BARTON, "The homosexual in the family", *Fam. Law*, 1996, p. 626-630.

BARTON (1998): C. BARTON, "Pre-marital contracts and equal shres on divorce", *Fam. Law*, 1998, p. 423-424.

BATES (1999): F. BATES, "Same-sex marriages, conflict of laws and public policy. A modern commentary", *LLR*, 1999, p. 49-76.

BATIFFOL/LAGARDE (1983): H. BATIFFOL and P. LAGARDE, *Traité de droit international privé. Tome II*, Paris: Librairie Générale de Droit et de Jurisprudence, 1983, 7th Edition.

BATIFFOL/LAGARDE (1993): H. BATIFFOL and P. LAGARDE, *Traité de droit international privé. Tome I*, Paris: Librairie Générale de Droit et de Jurisprudence, 1993, 8th Edition.

BATTEUR (2000): A. BATTEUR, "L'interdit de l'inceste, principe fondateur du droit de la famille", *Rev. trim. dr. civ.*, 2000, p. 759.

BAUR (2001): F.E. BAUR, "At the end of the fairy tale, will Heidi stay single? Same-sex partnerships in Switzerland", in: R. WINTEMUTE and M. ANDENÆS (eds.), *Legal recognition of same-sex partnerships*, Oxford: Hart, 2001.

BAURAIN (1998): P. BAURAIN, "La cohabitation légale: miracle ou mirage législatif?", *Rev. not. Bel*, 1998, p. 618-627.

BECKETT (1934): W.E. BECKETT, "The question of classification (qualification) in private international law", *BYIL*, 1934, Vol. 15, p. 46.

BEIGNIER (1999a): B. BEIGNIER, "Une nouvelle proposition de loi relative au contrat d'union sociale. Copie à revoir", *Hors série. Droit de la famille. Décembre 1999*, 1999, Vol. 4.

BEIGNIER (1999b): B. BEIGNIER, "Aspects civils", *Hors série. Droit de la famille. Décembre 1999*, 1999, p. 33.

BEIGNIER (2000): B. BEIGNIER, "Pacte civil de solidarité: Problème quant à l'acte authentique", *Rép. Not.*, 2000, Vol. 4, p. 211-213.

BEIGNIER (2001): B. BEIGNIER, "Pacte civil de solidarité. Nécessité du double original", *Rép. Not.*, 2001, p. 232-236.

BEIGNIER (1998): B. BEIGNIER, "A propos du concubinage homosexuel", *D*, 1998, p. 215-217.

BELL (2002): M. BELL, "We are family? Same-sex partners and EU migration law", *MJ*, 2002, p. 335-355.

BENABENT (1999): A. BENABENT, *Droit civil. Les obligations*, Paris: Montchrestien, 1999, 7th Edition.

BENABENT (2001): A. BENABENT, *Droit de la famille*, Paris: Litec, 2001, 10th Edition.

BERNIGAUD (2002): S. BERNIGAUD, "PACS et filiation", in: J. RUBELLIN-DEVICHI and L. BALESTRA (eds.), *Des concubinages. Droit interne, droit international et droit comparé. Études offertes à J. Rubellin-Devichi*, Paris: Litec, 2002, p. 183-191.

BJÖRGVINSSON (1997): D.T. BJÖRGVINSSON, "General principles and recent developments in Icelandic family law", in: A. BAINHAM (ed.), *International survey of family law*, Dordrecht: Nijhoff, 1997, p. 215-236.

BLAND (1957): A.J. BLAND, "Classification reclassified", *ICLQ*, 1957, Vol. 6, p. 10.

BOELE-WOELKI (1997a): K. BOELE-WOELKI, "The road towards a European family law", *EJCL*, 1997, Vol. 1.1.

BOELE-WOELKI (1997b): K. BOELE-WOELKI, "De weg naar een Europees familierecht?", *FJR*, 1997, p. 2-9.

BOELE-WOELKI (1998): K. BOELE-WOELKI, "Waarom Brussel II?", *FJR*, 1998, p. 152.

BOELE-WOELKI (1999a): K. BOELE-WOELKI, "Le partenariat enregistré: législation des Pays-Bas", (26th March 1999, Paris, Questions d'actualité en droit des personnes dans les Etats de la CIEC, Commission de l'Etat Civil).

BOELE-WOELKI (1999b): K. BOELE-WOELKI, "De prijs van het homohuwelijk", *FJR*, 1999, p. 113.

BOELE-WOELKI (1999c): K. BOELE-WOELKI, "De wenselijkheid van een IPR-verdrag inzake samenleving buiten huwelijk", *FJR*, 1999, p. 11-13.

BOELE-WOELKI (2000a): K. BOELE-WOELKI, "Private international law aspects of registered partnerships and other forms of non-marital cohabitation in Europe", *Louisiana LR*, 2000, p. 1053-1059.

BOELE-WOELKI (2000b): K. BOELE-WOELKI (ed.), *Huwelijksvermogensrecht in rechtsvergelijkend perspectief*, Deventer: Kluwer, 2000.

BOELE-WOELKI (2001a): K. BOELE-WOELKI, "Brüssel II: Die Verordnung über die Zuständigkeit und die Anerkennung von Entscheidungen in Ehesachen", *ZfRv*, 2001, Vol. 42, p. 121-130.

BOELE-WOELKI (2002a): K. BOELE-WOELKI, "Divorce in Europe: Unification of private international law and harmonisation of substantive law", in: H.F.G. LEMARIE and P. VLAS (eds.), *Met recht verkregen. Bundel opstellen aangeboden aan mr. Ingrid S. Joppe*, Deventer: Kluwer, 2002, p. 17-28.

BOELE-WOELKI (2002b): K. BOELE-WOELKI, "Comparative research-based drafting of principles of European family law", in: M. FAURE *et al.* (eds.), *Towards a European Ius Commune in legal education and research*, Antwerp: Intersentia, 2002, p. 171-189.

BOELE-WOELKI (2003a): K. BOELE-WOELKI, "De administratieve echtscheiding is een feit!", *FJR*, 2003, p. 121.

BOELE-WOELKI (2003b): K. BOELE-WOELKI, "Registered partnership and same-sex marriage in The Netherlands", in: K. BOELE-WOELKI and A. FUCHS (eds.), *EFL Series: Volume 1. Legal Recognition of Same-Sex Couples in Europe*, Antwerp: Intersentia, 2003, p. 49-52.

BOELE-WOELKI (2003c): K. BOELE-WOELKI, "B(l)oeiend vergelijkend familierecht: de Commission on European Family Law (CEFL)", in: K. BOELE-WOELKI, C.H. BRANTS and G.J. STEENHOFF (eds.), *Het plezier van de rechtsvergelijking. Opstellen over unificatie en harmonisatie van het recht in Europa, aangeboden aan prof. mr. E.H. Hondius bij gelegenheid van zijn afscheid als voorzitter en bestuurslid van de Nederlandse Vereniging voor Rechtsvergelijking*, Deventer: Kluwer, 2003, p. 141-159.

BOELE-WOELKI (2005a): K. BOELE-WOELKI, "De competentie van de Europese Unie in familiezaken", *FJR*, 2005, p. 1.

BOELE-WOELKI (2005b): K. BOELE-WOELKI, "The working method of the Commission on European Family Law", in: K. BOELE-WOELKI (ed.), *EFL Series: Volume 10. Common core and better law in European Family Law*, Antwerp: Intersentia, 2005, p. 15-38.

BOELE-WOELKI *et al.* (2004): K. BOELE-WOELKI, F. FERRAND, C. GONZÁLEZ BEILFUSS, M. JÄNTERÄ-JAREBORG, N. LOWE, D. MARTINY and W. PINTENS, *EFL Series: Volume 7. Principles of European family law regarding divorce and maintenance between former spouses*, Antwerp: Intersentia, 2004

BOELE-WOELKI/BRAAT/CURRY-SUMNER (2005): K. BOELE-WOELKI, B. BRAAT and I. CURRY-SUMNER (eds.), *EFL Series: Volume 9. European family law in action. Volume III: Parental responsibilities*, Antwerp: Intersentia, 2005.

BOELE-WOELKI/BRAAT/SUMNER (2003a): K. BOELE-WOELKI, B. BRAAT and I. SUMNER (eds.), *EFL Series: Volume 2. European family law in action. Volume I: Grounds for divorce*, Antwerp: Intersentia, 2003.

BOELE-WOELKI/BRAAT/SUMNER (2003b): K. BOELE-WOELKI, B. BRAAT and I. SUMNER (eds.), *EFL Series: Volume 3. European family law in action. Volume II: Maintenance between former spouses*, Antwerp: Intersentia, 2003.

BOELE-WOELKI/JOUSTRA/STEENHOFF (1998): K. BOELE-WOELKI, C. JOUSTRA and G. STEENHOFF, "Dutch private international law at the end of the 20th century: Pluralism of methods", in: E.H. HONDIUS (ed.), *Netherlands reports to the 15th International Congress of Comparative Law*, Bristol: Intersentia, 1998, p. 203-227.

BOELE-WOELKI/TANGE (1989): K. BOELE-WOELKI and P.C. TANGE, "De Deense Wet inzake het geregistreerd partnerschap: een voorbeeld voor Nederland?" *NJB*, p. 1537-1543.

BOELE-WOELKI/VAN OOIK (2002): K. BOELE-WOELKI and R. VAN OOIK "De ingrijpende communautarisering van het internationaal privaatrecht", *SEW*, 2002, p. 394-407.

DE BOER, J. (2002): J. DE BOER, *Mr. C Asser's handleiding tot de beoefening van het Nederlands burgerlijk recht. Personen- en familierecht*, Deventer: Kluwer, 2002, 16th Edition.

DE BOER, T. (1991): TH.M. DE BOER, "Internationale echtscheiding: het kennelijk ontbreken van een maatschappelijke band", *AA*, 1991, p. 252-260.

DE BOER, T. (1994): T.M. DE BOER, "The relation between uniform substantive law and private international law", in: A.S. HARTKAMP *et al.* (eds.), *Towards a European Civil Code*, Nijmegen: Ars Aequi Libri, 1994, p. 51-63.

DE BOER, T. (1996): T.M. DE BOER, "Favor divortii en rechtsmacht, Commentaar op artikel 2 van het voorstel voor een bevoegdheids- en executieverdrag in zaken familie- en erfrecht", in: S.C.J.J. KORTMANN *et al.* (eds.), *Op recht. Bundel opstellen aangeboden aan prof. mr. Struycken ter gelegenheid van zijn zilveren ambtsjubileum aan de Katholieke Universiteit Nijmegen*, Zwolle: W.E.J. Tjeenk Willink, 1996, p. 19-31.

DE BOER, T. (1999a): T.M. DE BOER, "Brussel II: een eerste stap naar een communautair IPR", *FJR*, 1999, p. 244-250.

DE BOER, T. (1999b): T.M. DE BOER, "Internationaal privaatrecht en rechtsvergelijking: een dubieuze relatie", in: E. HONDIUS (ed.), *De meerwaarde van de rechtsvergelijking. Opstellen aangeboden aan prof. mr. H.U. Jessurun D'Oliveira*, Deventer: Kluwer, 1999, p. 1-18.

DE BOER, T. (2002): T.M. DE BOER, "Jurisdiction and enforcement in international family law: a labyrinth of European and international legislation", *NILR*, 2002, p. 307-345.

BOGDAN (2001a): M. BOGDAN, "Registered partnerships and EC law", in: K. BOELE-WOELKI and A. FUCHS (eds.), *Legal recognition of same-sex couples in Europe*, Antwerp: Intersentia, 2001, p. 171-177.

BOGDAN (2001b): M. BODGAN, "Amendment of Swedish private international law regarding registered partnerships", *Praxis des Internationalen Privat- und Verfahrensrechts*, 2001, Vol. 4, p. 353.

Bogdan (2004): M. Bogdan, "Private international law of registered partnerships in the Nordic countries", in: A. Bonomi and B. Cottier (eds.), *Aspects de droit international privé des partenariats enregistrés en Europe*, Zurich: Schulthess, 2004, Volume N°. 49, p. 61-69.

Bogdan/Ryrstedt (1995): M. Bogdan and E. Ryrstedt, "Marriage in Swedish family law and Swedish conflicts of law", *FLQ*, 1995, p. 675-684.

Bonomi (2002): A. Bonomi, "Le nouveau règlement européen de divorce et de responsabilité parentale et ses implications pour la Suisse?: prélude à une Convention de "Lugano II"?", *PJA*, 2002, p. 248-262.

Boon (1988): L.J. Boon, "Those damned sodomites: Public images of sodomy in the Eighteenth Century Netherlands", *Journal of Homosexuality*, 1988, Vol. 16, p. 237-248.

Borghs (1998): P. Borghs, *Juridische aspecten van homoseksueel ouderschap. Het recht om lief te hebben*, Ghent: Mys & Breesch, 1998.

Borghs (2004a): P. Borghs, "Homoseksualiteit en ouderschap: Actuele stand van zaken", *NJT*, 2004, p. 290-302.

Borghs (2004b): P. Borghs, "Homoseksualiteit en ouderschap: Situatie in het buitenland en toekomstperspectief", *NJT*, 2004, p. 326-336.

Borkowski (1994): A. Borkowski, *Textbook on Roman law*, London: Blackstone, 1994, 2nd Edition.

Borrillo (2001a): D. Borrillo, "The Pacte Civil de Solidarité in France" in: R. Wintemute and M. Andenæs (eds.), *Legal recognition of same-sex partnerships*, Oxford: Hart Publishers, 2001, p. 475.

Borrillo (2001b): D. Borrillo, "Le pacte civil de solidarité: une reconnaissance timide des unions de même sexe", *PJA*, 2001, Vol. 3, p. 299-306.

Borrillo/Fassin/Iacub (1999): D. Borrillo, E. Fassin and M. Iacub, *Au-delà du PACS*, Paris: Presses Universitaires de France, 1999.

Bosse-Platiere (2002): H. Bosse-Platiere, "PACS et autorité parentale", in: J. Rubellin-Devichi and L. Balestra (eds.), *Des concubinages. Droit interne, droit international et droit compare. Études offertes à J. Rubellin-Devichi*, Paris: Litec, 2002, p. 193-211.

Braat (2000): B. Braat, "Nieuw Frans relatierecht: de PACS", *FJR*, 2000, p. 75.

Braat (2004): B. Braat, *EFL Series: Volume 6. Indépendance et interdépendance patrimoniales des époux dans le régime matrimonial légal des droits français, néerlandais et suisse*, Antwerp: Stämpfli, 2004.

Bradley (1998): D. Bradley, "Politics, culture and family law in Finland: Comparative approaches to the institutions of marriage", *IJLPF*, 1998, p. 288-306.

Bradley (1999): D. Bradley, "Convergence in family law: Mirrors, transplants and political economy", *MJ*, 1999, p. 22-50.

Bradley (2001): D. Bradley, "Regulation of unmarried cohabitation in West-European jurisdictions – determinants of legal policy", *IJLPF*, 2001, p. 22-50.

Bradley (2003): D. Bradley, "A family law for Europe?", in: K. Boele-Woelki (ed.), *EFL Series: Volume 4. Perspectives for the unification and harmonisation of family law in Europe*, 2003, Antwerp: Intersentia, p. 65- 104.

Bräm/Hasenböhler (1998): V. Bräm and F. Hasenböhler, *Das Familienrecht. Teilband II 1c. Die Wirkungen der Ehe im allgemeinen. Arts. 159-180. Zürich Kommentar*, Zurich: Schulthess Polygraphischer Verlag, 1998.

Brat (1998): S. Brat, "Le nouveau régime de la cohabitation légale: modèle revu et corrigé", *Divorce*, 1998, p. 121-125.

BRIDGE/SWINDELS (2003): C. BRIDGE and H. SWINDELS, *Adoption. The modern law*, Bristol: Jordans, 2003.

BROBERG (1996): M. BROBERG, "Registered partnership for same-sex couples in Denmark", *CFLQ*, 1996, p. 149-155.

BROEKHUIJSEN-MOLENAAR (1999): A. BROEKHUIJSEN-MOLENAAR, "Geoorloofdheid van draagmoederschap naar Nederlands (wenselijk) recht" in: K. BOELE-WOELKI and M. ODERKERK (eds.), *(On)geoorloofdheid van het draagmoederschap in rechtsvergelijkend perspectief*, Intersentia: Antwerp, 1999, p. 33-45.

BUCHER (1994): A. BUCHER, "Jurisprudence suisse en matière de droit international privé des personnes et de la famille", *RSDIE*, 1994, p. 279-282.

BUCHER (2001): A. BUCHER, "Jurisprudence suisse en matière de droit international privé des personnes et de la famille", *RSDIE*, 2001, p. 205-250.

BUCHER (2004a): A. BUCHER, *Le couple en droit international privé*, Basel: Helbing & Lichtenhahn, 2004.

BUCHER (2004b): A. BUCHER, "Le regard du législateur suisse sur les conflicts de lois en matière de partenariat enregistré", in: A. BONOMI and B. COTTIER (eds.), *Aspects de droit international privé des partenariats enregistrés en Europe*, Zurich: Schulthess, 2004, Volume N°. 49, p. 137-147.

BUCHER/BONOMI (2004): A. BUCHER and A. BONOMI, *Droit international privé*, Basel: Helbing & Lchtenhahn, 2004, 2nd Edition.

BUCKLEY/RIBSTEIN (2001): F.H. BUCKLEY and L.E. RIBSTEIN, "Calling a truce in the marriage wars", *University of Illinois Law Review*, 2001, p. 561-608.

VAN DER BUNT (2004): E. VAN DER BUNT, "Homohuwelijk en Artikel 40 Statuut revisited", *NJB*, 2004, p. 1216.

VAN DER BURG (1997): W. VAN DER BURG, "Het huwelijk – een omstreden instituut", *NJB*, 1997, p. 1321-1325.

VAN DER BURGHT/DOEK (2002): G. VAN DER BURGHT and J.E. DOEK, *Pitlo. Deel 1. Personen- en Familierecht*, Deventer: Kluwer, 2002.

BURROWS (2002): N. BURROWS, "This is Scotland's Parliament; let Scotland's Parliament legislate", *JR*, 2002, p. 213-236.

BUZZATTI (1899): G.C. BUZZATTI, "Di una neuva categoria di conflitti de leggi – I conflitti di qualificazione", in: *Studi giuridici varii pel cinquantesimo anno dínsegnamento di E. Pessina*, Naples, 1899, Volume III, p. 16.

CABRILLAC (1999): R. CABRILLAC, "Libres propos sur le PACS", *D*, 1999, p. 71-74.

CABRILLAC (2004): R. CABRILLAC, *Droit civil. Les régimes matrimoniaux*, Paris: Montchrestien, 2004, 5th Edition.

CALAIS-AULOY (1998): M-T. CALAIS-AULOY, "Faut-il craindre le contrat d'union civile et sociale?", *Les Petites Affiches,*, 1998, Vol. 37, p. 6-7.

CANOR (2000): I. CANOR, "Equality for lesbians and gay men in the European legal order – "they shall be male and female?", *MJ*, 2000, p. 273-299.

CARBONNEAU (1978): T.E. CARBONNEAU, "The new Article 310 of the French Civil Code for international divorce cases", *AJCL*, 1978, Vol. 26, p. 446-460.

CARBONNIER (1981): J. CARBONNIER, "La sécularisation du droit civil" in: *Christianisme, sécularisation et droit moderne*, Milan, 1981, p. 1007.

Carbonnier (2000): J. Carbonnier, *Droit civil. Tome III. Les biens,* Paris: Presses Universitaires de France, 2000, 19th Edition.

Carbonnier (2002): J. Carbonnier, *Droit civil. Tome II. La famille, l'enfant, le couple*, Paris: Presses Universitaires de France, 2002, 21st Edition.

Champenois (2002): G. Champenois, "Les présomptions d'indivision dans le PACS", in: J. Rubellin-Devichi and L. Balestra (eds.), *Des concubinages. Droit interne, droit international et droit compare. Études offertes à J. Rubellin-Devichi*, Paris: Litec, 2002, p. 83-95.

Chanteloup (2000): H. Chanteloup, "Menus propos autour du pacte civil de solidarité en droit international privé", *Gaz. Pal.*, 2000, p. 4

Clarkson (2002): C.M.V. Clarkson, "Brussel III – Matrimonial property European style", *Fam Law*, 2002, p. 683-686.

Clarkson/Hill (2002): C.M.V. Clarkson and J. Hill, *Jaffey on conflict of laws*, London: Butterworths/LexisNexis, 2002, 2nd Edition.

Clive (1992): E.M. Clive, *The law of husband and wife in Scotland*, Edinburgh: W. Green, 1997, 3rd Edition.

Coene (1998): E. Coene, "Wetsontwerp aangaande de wettelijke samenwoning", *EJ*, 1998, p. 67-68.

Coenraad (2005) L. Coenraad, "Mediation und die Scheidungsproblematik in den Niederlanden", *FamPra.ch*, 2005, p. 250-261.

Coester (2002): M. Coester, "Same-sex relationships: a comparative assessment of legal dveelopments across Europe", *FamPra.ch*, 2002, p. 748-764.

Coipel (1993): N. Coipel, "Réflexions sur la loi applicable aux effets du mariage", *Rev. trim. dr. fam.*, 1993, p. 141-179.

Collier (2001): J. Collier, *Conflict of laws*, Cambridge: Cambridge University Press, 2001, 3rd Edition.

Collins (2000): L. Collins, *Dicey and Morris on the conflict of laws*, London: Sweet and Maxwell, 2000, 13th Edition.

Collins (2004): L. Collins, *Dicey and Morris on the conflict of laws. Fourth supplement to the thirteenth edition*, London: Sweet and Maxwell, 2004, 13th Edition.

Combret (1999): J. Combret, "Point de vue d'un notaire", *Hors série. Droit de la famille. Décembre 1999*, 1999, p. 54-57.

Comm. Pers.: *Personen- en Familierecht. Artikelsgewijze Commentaar met Overzicht van Rechtspraak en Rechtsleer*, Mechelen: Kluwer, 1984, looseleaf.

Conway (2004): H.L. Conway, "The Gender Recognition Bill", *Fam*, 2004, p. 140-141.

Cook (1924): W.W. Cook, "Logical and legal bases of the conflict of laws", *Yale LJ*, 1924, Vol. 33, p. 457.

Cornelis (2000): L. Cornelis, *Algemene theorie van de verbintenis*, Antwerp: Intersentia, 2001.

Cornu (1997): G. Cornu, *Les régimes matrimoniaux*, Paris: Presses Universitaires de France, 1997, 9th Edition.

Cornu (2003): G. Cornu, *Droit civil. La famille*, Paris: Montchrestien, 2003, 8th Edition.

Cottier (2005): M. Cottier, "Registered partnerships for same-sex couples in Switzerland: constructing a new model of family relationships", in: M. MacClean (ed.), *Family law and family values,* Oxford: Hart Publishing, 2005, p.181-200.

COWARD (1980): D.A. COWARD, "Attitudes towards homosexuality in eighteenth century France", *JES*, 1980, Vol. 10, p. 231-255.

CRAWFORD (1998): E.B. CRAWFORD, *International private law in Scotland*, Edinburgh: W. Green, 1998.

CRETNEY (2003b): S. CRETNEY, *Family law in the twentieth century*, Oxford: Oxford University Press, 2003.

CRETNEY (2003c): S. CRETNEY, "The family and the law – status or contract?", *CFLQ*, 2003, p. 403-416.

CRETNEY *et al.* (2003a): S. CRETNEY, J. MASSON and R. BAILEY-HARRIS, *Principles of family law*, London: Butterworths, 2003.

CROSS/HARRIS (1991): R. CROSS and J.W. HARRIS, *Precedent in English law*, Oxford: Clarendon Law Series, 1991.

CURRIE/KAY/KRAMER (2001): D.P. CURRIE, H.H. KAY and L. KRAMER, *Conflict of laws. Cases-Comments-Questions*, St. Paul, Minnesota: West Group, 2001, 6th Edition.

CURRY-SUMNER (2005a): I. CURRY-SUMNER, "Uniform patterns regarding same-sex relationships", *ILF*, 2005, p. 9-14.

CURRY-SUMNER (2005b): I. CURRY-SUMNER, "General patterns in registration schemes for unmarried couples and the implications for Ireland", *IJFL*, 2005, p. 187-195.

DAMSLET (1993): O. DAMSLET, "Same-sex marriage", *NYLSJHR*, 1993, p. 555-593.

DE BUSSCHERE (1999): C. DE BUSSCHERE, "Het wettelijke samenwonen", *Notaris*, 1999, p. 18-25.

DE KEZEL (1999): E. DE KEZEL, "De wet tot invoering van de wettelijke samenwoning: Een maat voor niets?", *AJT*, 1999-2000, p. 129.

DE OLIVEIRA (2000): G. DE OLIVEIRA, "Een Europees familierecht? (Play it again, and again .. Europe!)", *FJR*, 2000, p. 272-277.

DEBUSSCHER (1999): E. DEBUSSCHER, "De wet van 23 november 1998 tot invoering van de wettelijke samenwoning en zijn belang voor de notariële praktijk", *WA*, 1999, p. 165-170.

DEECH (1980): R. DEECH, "The case against legal recognition of cohabitation", in: J. EEKELAAR and S. KATZ (eds.), *Marriage and cohabitation in contemporary society. areas of legal, social and ethical change*, Toronto: Butterworths, 1980.

DEKEUWER-DEFOSSEZ (2001): F. DEKEUWER-DEFOSSEZ, "PACS et famille. Retour sur l'analyse juridique d'un contrat controversé", *Rev. trim. dr. civ.*, 2001, Vol. 3, p. 529-546.

DEKEUWER-DEFOSSEZ/DECOUX (2002): F. DEKEUWER-DEFOSSEZ and A. DECOUX (eds.), *Droit des personnes et de la famille*, Paris: Collection Lamy Droit Civil, 2002.

DESCHENAUX *et al.* (2000): H. DESCHENAUX, P-H. STEINAUER, and M. BADDELEY, *Les effets du mariage*, Bern: Stämpfli, 2000.

DESPAGNET (1898): F. DESPAGNET, "Des conflits de lois relatifs à la qualification des rapports juridiques", *JDI*, 1898, p. 253.

DESSEMONTET/ANSAY (2004): F. DESSEMONTET and T. ANSAY (eds.), *Introduction to Swiss law*, The Hague: Kluwer, 2004, 3rd Edition.

DETHLOFF (2001): N. DETHLOFF, "Reform of German family law – a battle against discrimination", *EJLR*, 2001, p. 221-241.

DETHLOFF (2003): N. DETHLOFF, "Arguments for and against unification and harmonisation of family law in Europe", in K. BOELE-WOELKI (ed.), *EFL Series: Volume 4. Perspectives for the unification and harmonisation of family law in Europe*, 2003, Antwerp: Intersentia, p. 37-64.

DEVERS (2004): A. DEVERS, *Le concubinage en droit international privé*, Paris: LGDJ, 2004.

DEWAR/PARKER (2000): J. DEWAR and S. PARKER, "English family law since World War II: From status to chaos", in: S.N. KATZ, J. EEKELAAR and M. MACLEAN (eds.), *Cross currents*, Oxford: OUP, 2000, p. 123-140.

DIBOS-LACROUX (2001): S. DIBOS-LACROUX, *PACS: Le guide pratique. Pour qui? Pourquoi? Comment?*, Paris: PART, 2001, 2nd Edition.

DICKSON (2001): B. DICKSON (2001), *The legal system of Northern Ireland*, Belfast: SLS Legal Publishers, 2001, 4th Edition.

DOEK (2000): J.E. DOEK. "Het gezag over minderjarigen, iets over een doolhof en het zoeken van (rode?) draden", *FJR*, 2000, p. 217-226.

DOEK (2004): J.E. DOEK, "Rechten van kinderen: some concluding observations and recommendations. Afscheidsrede", Amsterdam: Vrije Universiteit, Afscheidsrede, 2004.

DOUGLAS (2000a): G. DOUGLAS, "Supporting families", in: A. BAINHAM (ed.), *International survey of family law*, Britsol: Jordans, 2000.

DOUGLAS (2000b): G. DOUGLAS, "Marriage, cohabitation and parenthood – from contract to status?", in: S.N. KATZ, J. EEKELAAR and M. MACLEAN (eds.), *Cross currents*, Oxford: OUP, 2000, p. 211-233.

DUTOIT (2005): B. DUTOIT, *Droit international privé suisse. Commentaire de la loi fédérale du 18 décembre 1987*, Basel: Stämpfli Verlag, 2005, 4th Edition.

EDWARDS/GRIFFITHS (1997): L. EDWARDS and A. GRIFFITHS, *Family Law*, Edinburgh: W. Green, 1997.

EEKELAAR (1994): J. EEKELAAR, "Parenthood, social engineering and rights", in: D. MORGAN and G. DOUGLAS (eds.), *Constituting families: A study in governance*, Stuttgart: Franz Steiner, 1994.

EEKELAAR (1998): J. EEKELAAR, "Registered same-sex partnerships and marriages – a statistical comparison", *Fam Law*, 1998, p. 561.

ELHOUEISS (2005): J.-L. ELHOUEISS, "Retour sur la qualifcation *leges causae* en droit international privé", *JDI*, 2005, p. 281-313.

ERAUW (1978): J. ERAUW, "De collisierechtelijke aanknoping van het patrimoniale basisstatuut (primari stauut) van het huwelijk", *RW*, 1978-1979, p. 882-896.

ERAUW (1985): J. ERAUW, *Beginselen van international privaatrecht*, Ghent: Story-Scientia, 1985.

ERAUW (2001a): J. ERAUW, "De codificatie van het Belgisch internationaal privaatrecht met het ontwerp van Wetboek IPR", *RW*, 2001-2002, p. 1557-1566.

ERAUW (2001b): J. ERAUW, "Een terugblik naat het IPR bij de uitgang van de twintigste Eeuw", *TPR*, 2001, p. 55-67.

ERAUW (2002): J. ERAUW, "Brief description of the draft Belgian code of private international law", in: P. SARCEVIC and P. VOLKEN (eds.), *Volume 4. Yearbook of private international law*, The Hague: Kluwer, 2002.

ERAUW (2002): J. ERAUW, "Het voorstel van Belgische wetboek internationaal privaatrecht en zijn algemene beplaingen", *WPNR*, Vol. 6537, p. 481-490.

ERAUW (2004): J. ERAUW, "Het vernieuwde internationaal privaatrecht van België wordt van kracht", *RW*, 2004, p. 121-132.

ERAUW (2005): J. ERAUW, "Het aankomende Wetboek IPR en de nieuwe minister en de senaat", Ghent: ipr.be, 2005, available on website: www.ipr.be.

ERAUW/VERHELLEN (1999): J. ERAUW & J. VERHELLEN, "Het conflictenrecht van de wettelijke samenwoning internationaal aspecten van de niet-huwelijkse samenwoningsvorm", *EJ*, 1999, p. 150-161.

VAN ERP (2005): S. VAN ERP, "European Private International Law as a Transition Stage?", *EJCL*, 2002, Vol 6.1.

ESTIN (2004): A. LAQUER ESTIN, "Human rights, pluralism and family law", in: P. LØDRUP and E. MODVAR (eds.), *Family life and human rights*, Oslo: Gyldendal, 2004, p. 210-228.

ETTELBRICK (2001): P.L. ETTELBRICK, "Domestic partnership, civil unions or marriage. One size does not fit all", *ALR*, 2001, p. 905-911.

EVERALL/NICHOLLS (2002): M. EVERALL and M. NICHOLLS, "Brussels I and II – the impact on family law", *Fam Law*, 2002, p. 675-682.

FALCONBRIDGE (1954): J.D. FALCONBRIDGE, *Essays on the conflict of laws*, Toronto: Canada Law Books Company, 1954.

FAUVARQUE-COSSON (2000): B. FAUVARQUE-COSSON, "Droit comparé et droit international privé: la confrontation de deux logiques à travers l'exemple des droits fondamentaux", *Rev. int. dr. com.*, 2000, p. 797-818.

FAUVARQUE-COSSON (2001): B. FAUVARQUE-COSSON, "Comparative law and conflict of laws: allies or enemies? New perspectives on an old couple", *AJCL*, 2001, p. 407-427.

FAWCETT (2000): J. FAWCETT, "Cross-fertilisation in private international law", *CLP*, 2000, p. 303-331.

FENTIMAN (1985): R. FENTIMAN, "The validity of marriage and the proper law", *CLJ*, 1985, p. 256-279.

FENTIMAN (1998): R. FENTIMAN, *Foreign law in the English courts. Pleading, proof and foreign law*, Oxford: Oxford University Press, 1998.

FESTY (2001): P. FESTY, "PACS l'impossible bilan", *Population et Sociétés*, 2001.

FLOUR (1999): Y. FLOUR, "Breves remarques sur l'indivision entre partenaires d'un pacte civil de solidarité", *Gaz. Pal.*, 1999, p. 284.

FORDER (1997): C. FORDER, "Re-thinking marriage, parenthood and adoption", in: A. BAINHAM (eds.), *International survey of family law 1995*, Dordrecht: Nijhoff, 1997, p. 359-382.

FORDER (1999a): C. FORDER, "National report on The Netherlands", The Hague: Council of Europe, Fifth European Conference on Family Law, 15th March 1999,

FORDER (1999b): C. FORDER, "Spieghel matrimoniael", *NJB*, 1999, Vol. 32, p. 1559-1560.

FORDER (1999c): C. FORDER, "National report on Iceland", The Hague: Council of Europe, Fifth European Conference on Family Law, 15th-16th March 1999.

FORDER (2000a): C. FORDER, "Opening up marriage to same sex partners and providing for adoption by same sex couples, managing information on sperm donors and lots of private international law", in: A. BAINHAM (eds.), *International survey of family law 2000 Edition*, Britsol: Jordans, 2000, p. 239-277.

FORDER (2000b): C. FORDER, "European models of domestic partnership laws: the field of choice", *CJFL*, 2000, p. 371-454.

FORDER (2001): C. FORDER, "To marry or not to marry: that is the question", in: A. BAINHAM (ed.), *International survey of family law. 2001 Edition*, Bristol: Family Law, 2001, p. 301-320.

FORSYTH (1996): C. FORSYTH, *Private international law. The modern Roman-Dutch law including the jurisdiction of the Supreme Court*, Cape Town: Juta & Co., 1996.

Forsyth (1998): C. Forsyth, "Characterisation revisited: An essay in the theory and practice of the English conflict of laws", *LQR*, 1998, Vol. 114, p. 141.

Frank (2001): R. Frank, "Civil marriages without legal consequences", in: A. Bainham (ed.), *International survey of family law,* Bristol: Jordans, 2001.

Freeman (2002): M. Freeman, "Some reflections on gay marriages at the beginning of the twenty-first century", in: J. Rubellin-Devichi and L. Balestra (eds.), *Des concubinages, droit intern, droit international et droit compare. Études offertés à J. Rubellin-Devichi*, Paris: Litec, 2002, p. 357-373.

Freiburghaus (2001): D. Freiburghaus, "Schweiz: Aktueller Stand der Diskussion über eine Gesetzgebung für gleichgeschlechtliche Paare", *AJT*, 2001, Vol. 3, p. 243-251.

Frensel (2001): F. Frensel, "L'intérêt de la qualification de l'acte dans le cadre d'une mesure de protection juridique", *Rev. jur. per. fam.*, 2001, p. 6.

Frohn (2001): E.N. Frohn, "Sprookjeshuwelijk of spookhuwelijk?", *FJR*, 2001, p. 166-170.

Frohn (2003): E.N. Frohn, "Artikel 3 (voorvraag) en artikel 6 (renvoi)", *WPNR*, 2004, Vol. 6537, p. 461-465.

Frohn (2004): E.N. Frohn, "De Wet conflictenrecht geregistreerd partnerschap", *FJR*, p. 290-294.

Frye/Meiselman (2001): P.R. Frye and A.D. Meiselman, "Same-sex marriages have existed legally in the United States for a long time now", *ALR*, 2001, p. 1031-1068.

Fulchiron (2000): H. Fulchiron, "Réflexions sur les unions hors mariage en droit international privé", *JDI*, 2000, p. 889.

Fulchiron (2001a): H. Fulchiron, "Les presumptions d'indivision et de communauté dans le couple", *Rép. Not.*, 2001, N°. 17, p. 949-969.

Fulchiron (2001b): H. Fulchiron, "La séparation du couple en droit international privé", *PA*, 28th March 2001, N°. 62, p. 4.

Fulchiron (2002): H. Fulchiron, "Couples, mariages et différence des sexes: une question de discrimination", in: J. Rubellin-Devichi and L. Balestra (eds.), *Des concubinages. Droit interne, droit international et droit compare. Études offertés à J. Rubellin-Devichi*, Paris: Litec, 2002, p. 29-52.

Fulchiron (2004): H. Fulchiron, "Pacs et partenariats enregistrés en DIP français", in: A. Bonomi and B. Cottier (eds.), *Aspects de droit international privé des partenariats enregistrés en Europe*, Zurich: Schulthess, 2004, Volume N°. 49, p. 85-84.

Garcia Cantero (1996): G. Garcia Cantero, "Marriage before the mayor and other matters" in: A. Bainham, *International survey of family law 1994*, Dordrecht: Nijhoff, 1996

Gardner (1993): S. Gardner, "Rethinking family property law", *LQR*, 1993, p. 263-300.

Garro (2004): A.M. Garro, "Chapter 8: Recordation of interests in land", in: A.N. Yiannopoulos (ed.), *International Encyclopaedia of Comparative Law. Volume VI: Property Law*, Tübingen: Mohr Siebeck, 2004.

Gaudemet-Tallon (2001): H. Gaudemet-Tallon, "Le Règlement N°. 1347/2000 du Conseil du 29 mai 2000: Compétence, reconnaissance et exécution des décisions en matière matrimoniale et en matière de reponsabilité parentale des enfants communs", *JDI*, 2001, p. 381-430.

Gaudu (1998): F. Gaudu, "A propos du contrat d'union civile: critique d'un profane", *D*, 1998, p. 19-24.

Gemma (1899): S. Gemma, *Propedeutica al diritto internazionale private*, Bologna, 1899.

Gijbels (2003): L.J.H. Gijbels, "Reparatie van de flitsscheiding", *EB*, 2003, p. 127-130.

GIJBELS/KAMERLING (2003): L.J.H. GIJBELS and J.A. KAMERLING, "De flitsscheiding; een snelle route maar niet zonder haken en ogen!", *JBN*, 2003, Vol. 16, p. 3-4.

GIRSBERGER/DROESE (2001): D. GIRSBERGER and L. DROESE, "Registrierte Partnerschaften – schweizerisches IPR de lege ferenda", *RSDIE*, 2001, p. 73-100.

GLENN (1977): H.P. GLENN, "Conflict of laws. The 1978 Hague Conventions on marriage and matrimonial property regimes", *CBR*, 1977, p. 586-605.

GLENNON (2000): L. GLENNON, "*Fitzpatrick v. Sterling Housing Association Ltd* – An endorsement of the functional family?", *IJLPF*, 2000, p. 226-255.

GONZÁLEZ BEILFUSS (2004): C. GONZÁLEZ BEILFUSS, *Parejas de hecho y matrimonios del mismo sexo en la unión europea*, Madrid: Marcial Pons, 2004.

GOONESEKERE (2000): S. GOONESEKERE, "Human rights as the foundation for family law reform", *IJCR*, 2000, p. 83-99.

GOOSSENS (1984): B. GOOSSENS, "Recht in kort bestek. De homosexueel en zijn relatie tot een partner in het kader van artikel 8 §1 van het Europees Verdrag voor de Rechten van de Mens", *JF*, 1984-1985, p. 527-541.

GORANSSON (1998): L. GORANSSON, "International trends in same-sex marriage" in: R.P. CABAJ and D.W. PURCELL (eds.), *On the road to same-sex marriage*, San Francisco: Jossey-Bass Publishers, 1998, p. 165.

GOURDOU/LEMOULAND (2004): J. GOURDOU and J-J. LEMOULAND, "Contentieux à l'occasion de la déclaration d'un PACS: les juridictions administratives ne sont pas compétentes", *D*, 2004, p. 295-299.

DE GRAAF (2003): J.H. DE GRAAF, "De modernisering van het ouderlijk gezag, de afgelopen twee decennia", *Advocatenblad*, 2003, Vol. 18, p. 792-794.

GRAHAM-SIEGENTHALER (1995): B. GRAHAM-SIEGENTHALER, "International marriage and divorce regulation and recognition in Switzerland", *FLQ*, 1995, p. 685-700.

GRANET (2002): F. GRANET, "Concubinages, partenariats enregistrés et mariages entre homosexuals en Europe", in: J. RUBELLIN-DEVICHI and L. BALESTRA (eds.), *Des concubinages. Droit interne, droit international et droit compare. Études offertés à J. Rubellin-Devichi*, Paris: Litec, 2002, p. 375-392.

GRANET/LECUYER (1999/2001): F. GRANET and H. LECUYER, *Juris-Classeur Droit Civil, V° Pacte Civil de Solidarité*, Fasc. 10, Supplement 11.

GRAVESON (1953): R.H. GRAVESON, *Status in the common law*, London: Althone Press, 1953

GRAVESON (1974): R.H. GRAVESON, *Conflict of laws. Private international law*, London: Sweet and Maxwell, 1974, 7th Edition.

GREMPER (2004): P. GREMPER, "Vermögensrechtliche Wirkungen der eingetragenen Partnerschaft", *FamPra.ch*, 2004, p. 475-506.

GRILLET-PONTON (2002): D. GRILLET-PONTON, "Quasi-conjugalité, pluri et post-conjugalité: Libres propos sur quelques situations atypiques", *JCP Éd. G*, 2002, Vol. 5, p. 229-234.

GRIMALDI (2001): M. GRIMALDI (ed.), *Droit patrimonial de la famille. 2001-2002*, Paris: Dalloz, 2001.

GRILLET-PONTON (2002): D. GRILLET-PONTON, "La fiscalité du PACS", in: J. RUBELLIN-DEVICHI and L. BALESTRA (eds.), *Des concubinages. Droit interne, droit international et droit compare. Études offertés à J. Rubellin-Devichi*, Paris: Litec, 2002, p. 271-284.

DE GROOT (1995): G.R DE GROOT, "Op weg naar een Europees personen- en familierecht", *AA*, 1995, p. 29-33.

DE GROOT (2002): G.R DE GROOT, *Personen- en familierecht*, Dordrecht: Kluwer, 2002, looseleaf.

DE GROOT (2004): G.R DE GROOT, "Towards a European Nationality law", *EJCL*, 2004, Vol. 8.3.

DE GROOT/RUTTEN (2004): R. DE GROOT and S. RUTTEN, "Op weg naar een Europese IPR op het gebied van het personen- en familierecht", *NIPR*, 2004, p. 273-282.

GROSSEN/ GUILLOD (1989): J-M. GROSSEN and O. GUILLOD, "Le concubinage en droit Suisse", in: J. RUBELLIN-DEVICHI (ed.), *Les concubinages en Europe*, Paris: Centre National de la Recherche, 1989, p. 269-299.

GRÜTTER/SUMMERMATTER (2004): M. GRÜTTER and D. SUMMERMATTER, "Das Partnerschaftsgesetz", *FamPra.ch*, 2004, p. 449-474.

GUIHO (1993): P. GUIHO, *Droit civil. 3: La famille*, Paris: L'Hermes, 1993, 4th Edition.

GUILLAUME (2002): F. GUILLAUME, "Une proposition de réglementation du partenariat insérable dans la LDIP" in : F. GUILLAUME and R. ARN (eds.), *Cohabitation non maritale. Evolution récente en droit suisse et étranger*, Geneva: Libraire Droz, 2002,Volume N°. 68, p. 180-199.

GUILLOD (1997): O. GUILLOD, "Choosing its own way or following others?", in: A. BAINHAM (ed.), *International survey of family law 1995*, Dordrecht: Nijhoff, 1997, p. 487-502.

HALE (2004): B. HALE, "Homosexual rights", *CFLQ*, 2004, p. 125-134.

HAMILTON/PERRY (2002): C. HAMILTON and A. PERRY (eds.), *Family law in Europe*, London: Butterworths, 2002, 2nd Edition.

HANGARTNER (2001): Y. HANGARTNER, "Verfassungrechtliche Grundlagen einer registrierten Partnerschaft für gleichgeschlechtliche Paare", *AJT*, 2001, Vol. 3, p. 252-263.

HARPER *et al.* (2005): M. HARPER, M. DOWNS, K. LANDELLS and G. WILSON, *Civil Partnership. The New Law*, Bristol: Family Law, 2005.

HARTLEY (1972): T.C. HARTLEY, "The policy basis of the English conflict of laws in marriage", *MLR*, 1972, p. 571.

HARTLEY (1996): T.C. HARTLEY, "Pleading and proof of foreign law: the major European systems compared", *ICLQ*, 1996, p. 271-292.

HAUSER (1998): J. HAUSER, *Comité de réflexion sur les conséquences financières de la séparation des couples. Le projet de pacte d'intérêt commun*, Paris: Ministry of Justice, April 1998.

HAUSER (1999): J. HAUSER: "Aujourd'hui et demain, le Pacs", *Droit de la famille*, 1999, Vol. 8/9, p. 6.

HAUSER (2000): J. HAUSER, "Statut civil des partenaires", *JCP Éd N*, 2000, p. 411-415.

HAUSER (2001): J. HAUSER, "Le pacte civil de solidarité est-il un contrat consensual ou un contrat solennel", *Rép. Not.*, 2001, Vol. 11, p. 673-679.

HAUSHEER (1999): H. HAUSHEER, "Die wesenlichen Neuerungen des neuen Scheidungsrechts", *Zeitschrift des Bernischen Juristenvereins*, 1999, Vol. 135, p. 1-35.

HAUSHEER/REUSSER/GEISER (1999): H. HAUSHEER, R. REUSSER and T. GEISER, *Berner Kommentar zum schweizerischen Privatrecht, Die Wirkungen der Ehe im allgemeinen*, Bern: Stämpfli, 1999.

HEGNAUER (1984): C. HEGNAUER, *Berner Kommentar. Volume II. Die Verwandtschaft. Teilband 1. Die Entstehung des Kindesverhältnisses*, Bern: Verlag Stämpfli AG, 1984.

HEGNAUER/BREITSCHMID (2000): C. HEGNAUER and C. BREITSCHMID, *Grundriss des Eherechts*, Bern: Stämpfli, 2000, 4th Edition.

HEIDA (2000): A. HEIDA, *Gids geregistreerd partnerschap*, Deventer: Kluwer, 2000.

HEIDA (2002): A. HEIDA, "Vaderschapsprocedures en DNA-onderzoek", *FJR*, 2002, p. 122-129.

HEIDA (2003): A. HEIDA, "Problemen bij flitsscheiding, een inventarisatie", *EB*, 2003, p. 112.

HEINI *et al.* (1993): A. HEINI *et al,, Kommentar zum Bundesgesetz über das Internationale Privatrecht (IPRG) vom 1. Januar 1989*, Zurich: publisher, 1993.

HELIN (1999): M. HELIN, "Enforcement of custody, access and residence orders, intercountry adoptions and registration of same-sex couples", in: A. BAINHAM (ed.), *International survey of family law 1997*, Dordrecht: Nijhoff, 1999.

HENNERON (2003): S. HENNERON, "New forms of cohabitation: private international law aspects of registered partnerships" in: K. BOELE-WOELKI (ed.), *EFL Series: Volume 4, Perspectives for the harmonisation and unification of family law in Europe*, Antwerp: Intersentia, 2003, p. 462-470.

HENSON (1993): D.M. HENSON, "A comparative analysis of same-sex partnership protections: recommendations for American reform", *IJLF*, 1993, p. 181-189.

HENSTRA (1998): A. HENSTRA, "Kroniek van het personen- en familierecht", *Nemesis*, 1998, Vol. 6, p. 181-189.

HENSTRA (2002): A. HENSTRA, *Van afstamming naar ouderschapsrecht*, Amsterdam: Boom Juridische Uitgevers, 2002.

HERNÁNDEZ-BRETON (2004): E. HERNÁNDEZ-BRETON, "An attempt to regulate the problem of 'characterisation' in private international law" in: H.-P. MANSEL *et al.* (eds.), *Festschrift für Erik Jayme. Band I*, Munich: Sellier, European Law Publishers, 2004, p. 331-338.

HERRING (2003): J. HERRING, *Family law*, Harlow, England: Pearson Publishing, 2003.

HEYVAERT (2002): A. HEYVAERT, *Belgisch internationaal privaatrecht, een inleiding*, Mechelen: Kluwer, 2002, 4th Edition.

HITCHINGS (2003): E., HITCHINGS, "*Mendoza v. Ghaidan* – Two steps forward, one step back", *CFLQ*, 2003, p. 313-325.

HOEVENAARS (1997): P.P.M. HOEVENAARS, "Het wetsvoorstel partnerschapregistratie", 1997, *WPNR*, Vol. 6264, p. 226-232.

HOHLOCH/KJELLAND (2001): G. HOHLOCH and C. KJELLAND, "The new German conflicts rules for registered partnerships", in: P. SARCEVIC and P. VOLKEN (eds.), *Volume 3. Yearbook of private international law*, 2001, p. 223-235.

HOME OFFICE (2000): HOME OFFICE, *Setting the boundaries: Reforming the law on sex offences*, Home Office: London, 2000.

HONSELL/VOGT/GEISER (2002): H. HONSELL, P. VOGT and T. GEISER (eds.), *Kommentar zum Schweizerischen Privatrecht. Zivilgesetzbuch I*, Basel: Helbing & Lichtenhahn, 2002.

HONSELL/VOGT/SCHNYDER (1996): H. HONSELL, P. VOGT and A. SCHYNDER (eds.), *Kommentar zum Schweizerischen Privatrecht. Internationales Privatrecht*, Basel: Helbing & Lichtenhahn, 2002.

HÖRSTER (2001): H.E. HÖRSTER, "Does Portugal need to legislate on *de facto* unions?", *IJLPF*, 2001, p. 274-279.

HOUBOLT (2001): K. HOUBOLT, "Wettelijke samenlevingsvormen in België, Frankrijk en Nederland", *FJR*, 2001, Vol. 4, p. 108-110.

HOUSERAND/HUET-WEILLER (1993): J. HOUSERAND and D. HUET-WEILLER, *Traité de droit de la famille. Part I: Foundation et vie de la famille*, Paris: Librarie Général de Droit et de Jurisprudence, 1993.

VAN HOUTTE (2000): H. VAN HOUTTE, "De internationalisatie van de openbare orde", in: H. COUSY *et al.*, *Liber Amicorum Walter van Gerven*, Deventer: Kluwer, 2000.

VAN HOUTTE/PERTEGÁS SENDER (2001): H. VAN HOUTTE and M. PERTEGÁS SENDER, *Het nieuwe Europese IPR: van verdrag naar verordening*, Antwerp: Intersentia, 2001.

HUET (2002): A. HUET, "Le séparation des concubins en droit international privé", in: J. RUBELLIN-DEVICHI and L. BALESTRA (eds.), *Des concubinages. Droit interne, droit international et droit compare. Études offertés à J. Rubellin-Devichi*, Paris: Litec, 2002, p. 539-554.

HUNTER-HENIN (2004): M. HUNTER-HENIN, *Pour une redéfinition du statut personnel*, Marseille: Presses Universitaires d'Aix-Marseille, 2004.

HUSA (2004): J. HUSA, "Classification of legal families today. Is is time for a memorial hymn?", *Rev. int. dr. com.*, 2004, p. 11-38.

HUUSSEN (1988): A.H. HUUSSEN, "Prosecution of sodomy in eighteenth century Frisia, Netherlands", *JH*, 1988, Vol. 16, p. 249-262.

INGLIS (2001a): A. INGLIS, "We are family? The uneasy engagement between gay men, lesbians and family law", *Fam. Law*, 2001, p. 830-834.

INGLIS (2001b): A. INGLIS, "We are family (after all) – inclusive family law", *Fam. Law*, 2001, p. 895-899.

JAFFEY (1978): A.J.E. JAFFEY, "The essential validity of marriage in the English conflict of laws", *MLR*, 1978, p. 38.

JAKOB (2002): D. JAKOB, *Die eingetragene Lebenspartnerschaft im Internationalen Privatrecht*, Cologne: Verlag Dr. Otto Scmidt, Schriften der Deutschen Notarrechtlichen Vereinigung: Band 13, 2002.

JANSEGERS (2002): K. JANSEGERS, "Problemen bij de erkenning in België van de Nederlandse 'flitsscheiding'", *Ipr.be*, 2002, p. 61-75.

JÄNTERÄ-JAREBORG (1999): M. JÄNTERÄ-JAREBORG, "Marriage dissolution in an integrated Europe: The 1998 European Union Convention on Jurisdiction and the Recognition and Enforcement of Judgments in Matrimonial Matters (Brussels II Convention)", in P. SARCEVIC and P. VOLKEN (eds.), *Volume 1. Yearbook of private international law*, The Hague: Kluwer, 1999.

JÄNTERÄ-JAREBORG (2002): M. JÄNTERÄ-JAREBORG, "European family law for cross-border situations – some reflections concerning the Brussels II regulation and its planned amendments", in: P. SARCEVIC and P. VOLKEN (eds.), *Volume 4. Yearbook of private international law*, The Hague: Kluwer, 2002.

JÄNTERÄ-JAREBORG (2003a): M. JÄNTERÄ-JAREBORG, "Registered partnerships in private international law: Scandinavian approach" in: K. BOELE-WOELKI and A. FUCHS (eds.), *EFL Series: Volume 1. Legal recognition of same-sex couples in Europe*, Antwerp: Intersentia, 2003, p. 137-158.

JÄNTERÄ-JAREBORG (2003b): M. JÄNTERÄ-JAREBORG, "Unification of international family law in Europe – a critical perspective", in: K. BOELE-WOELKI (ed.), *EFL Series: Volume 4. Perspectives for the harmonisation and unification of family law in Europe*, Antwerp: Intersentia, 2003, p. 194-216.

JÄNTERÄ-JAREBORG/SÖRGJERD (2004): M. JÄNTERÄ-JAREBORG and C. SÖRGJERD, "The experiences with registered partnership in Scandinavia", *FamPra.ch*, 2004, p. 577-597.

JESSURUN D'OLIVEIRA (1995): H.U. JESSURUN D'OLIVEIRA, "Geregistreerd partnerschap en de Europese Unie", *NJB*, 1995, p. 1566-1570.

JESSURUN D'OLIVEIRA (1996): H.U. JESSURUN D'OLIVEIRA, "Het raadselachtige buitenland, de partnerschapregistratie en het burgerlijk huwelijk voor homo's en lesbo's", *NJB*, 1996, p. 755-756.

JESSURUN D'OLIVEIRA (2000a): H.U. JESSURUN D'OLIVEIRA, "Registered partnerships, PACSs and private international law", *RDIPP*, 2000, p. 293.

JESSURUN D'OLIVEIRA (2000b): H.U. JESSURUN D'OLIVEIRA, "Freedom of movement and registered partners in the European Union", in: J. BASEDOW (ed.), *Liber Amicorum Kurt Siehr*, The Hague: T.M.C Asser, 2000.

JESSURUN D'OLIVEIRA (2000c): H.U. JESSURUN D'OLIVEIRA, "Het pacte civil de solidarité, het geregistreerd partnerschap en het Nederlandse internationaal privaatrecht", *NJB*, 2000, p. 884-886.

JESSURUN D'OLIVEIRA (2001a): H.U. JESSURUN D'OLIVEIRA, "Vrijheid van verkeer voor geregistreerde partners in de Europese Unie", *NJB*, 2001, p. 205-210.

JESSURUN D'OLIVEIRA (2001b): H.U. JESSURUN D'OLIVEIRA,"De Europese Commissie erkent het Nederlands huwelijk", *NJB*, p. 2035-2040.

JESSURUN D'OLIVEIRA (2002): H.U. JESSURUN D'OLIVEIRA, "Het homohuwelijk en de Europese Unie", *NJB*, 2002, p. 973.

JESSURUN D'OLIVEIRA (2003a): H.U. JESSURUN D'OLIVEIRA, "Autonome kwalificatie in het internationaal privaatrecht: geregistreerde niet-huwelijkse relaties", in: K. BOELE-WOELKI, C.H. BRANTS, and G.J.W. STEENHOFF (eds.), *Het plezier van de rechtsvergelijking. Opstellen over unificatie en harmonisatie van het recht in Europa, aangeboden aan prof. mr. E.H. Hondius bij gelegenheid van zijn afscheid als voorzitter en bestuurslid van de Nederlandse Vereniging voor Rechtsvergelijking*, Deventer: Kluwer, 2003, p. 141-154.

JESSURUN D'OLIVIEIRA (2003b): H.U. JESSURUN D'OLIVEIRA, "De artikelen 4, 5, 7 en 17 van het Ontwerp", *WPNR*, 2003, p. 454-460.

JESSURUN D'OLIVEIRA (2003c): H.U. JESSURUN D'OLIVEIRA, "Het Europese Hof activeert het Europese burgerschap", *NJB*, 2004, p. 2238-2243.

JESSURUN D'OLIVEIRA (2004): H.U. JESSURUN D'OLIVEIRA, "Een plan voor het Nederlandse voorzitterschap van de EU: erkenning van geregistreerde niet-huwelijkse relaties", *NJB*, 2004, p. 1170-1171.

JESTAZ/GODE (1982): P. JESTAZ and P. GODE, "Législation française et communautaire", *Rev. trim. dr. civ.*, 1982, Vol. 2, p. 793-801.

JOINT LAW COMMISSIONS (1970): JOINT ENGLISH AND SCOTTISH LAW COMMISSIONS, *Report No. 34/16. Hague Convention on recognition of divorces and legal separations*, London: HMSO, 1970.

JOINT LAW COMMISSIONS (1984): JOINT ENGLISH AND SCOTTISH LAW COMMISSIONS, *Report No. 137/88. Private international law. Report on the recognition of foreign nullity decrees and related matters*, London: HMSO, 1984.

JOINT LAW COMMISSIONS (1985): JOINT ENGLISH AND SCOTTISH LAW COMMISSIONS, *Report No. 146/96. Private international law. Report on capacity to contract a polygamous marriage and related issues*, London: HMSO, 1985.

JOINT LAW COMMISSIONS (1987a): JOINT ENGLISH AND SCOTTISH LAW COMMISSIONS, *Report No. 165/105. Private international law. Choice of law rules in marriage*, London: HMSO, 1987.

JOINT LAW COMMISSIONS (1987b): JOINT ENGLISH AND SCOTTISH LAW COMMISSIONS, *Report No. 168/107. Private international law. The law of domicile*, London: HMSO, 1987.

JOPPE (2000a): I.S. JOPPE, "Het geregistreerd partnerschap in het Nederlandse IPR (I)", *WPNR*, 2000, p. 371-375.

JOPPE (2000b): I.S. JOPPE, "Het geregistreerd partnerschap in het Nederlandse IPR (II)", *WPNR*, 2000, p. 391-395.

JOPPE (2003): I.S. JOPPE, *Huwelijksvermogensrecht*, Deventer: Kluwer, 2003, 2nd Edition.

JOSSELIN-GALL (2000): M. JOSSELIN-GALL, "Pacte civil de solidarité. Quelques éléments de droit international privé", *JCP Éd. N.*, 2000, p. 489.

JOUSTRA (1989): C. JOUSTRA, "Het Haags Huwelijksverdrag van 1978 in Nederland", *AA*, 1989, p. 261-269.

JUENGER (1993): F.K. JUENGER, *Choice of law and multistate justice*, Dordrecht: Martinus Nijhoff, 1993.

KADDOUS (2001): C. KADDOUS, "La situation des partenaires de même sexe en droit communautaire et dans le cadre de l'Accord sectoriel sur la libre circulation des personnes entre la Suisse et l'Union européenne", *RSDIE*, 2001, Vol. 1, p. 143-172.

KADDOUS (2004): C. KADDOUS, "Le droit communautaire et les partenaires de même sexe", *FamPra.ch*, 2004, p. 598-621.

KAHN (1891): F. KAHN, *Abhandlungen zum internationalen Privatrecht*, Munich: Duncker & Humbolt, 1891, p. 92-123.

KAHN-FREUD (1980): O. KAHN-FREUD, *General problems of private international law*, Alphen aan den Rijn: Sijthoff & Noordhoff, 1980.

KASER/DANNENBRING (1993): M. KASER (translated by R. DANNENBRING), *Roman private law*, Pretoria: South Africa, 1993, 4th Edition.

KATZ (1999): S. KATZ, "Domestic partnership laws", in: A. BAINHAM (ed.), *International survey of family law 1997*, Dordrecht: Nijhoff, 1999.

KEMPER (2005): R. KEMPER, "Der zweite Schritt. Die Lebenspartnerschaft auf dem Weg vom eheähnlichen zum ehegleichen Rechtsinstitut", *Forum Familien- und Erbrecht*, 2005, Vol. 3, p. 88-96.

KESSLER (2004): G. KESSLER, *Les partenariats enregistrés en droit international privé*, Paris: LGDJ, 2004.

KHAIRALLAH (2000): G. KHAIRALLAH, "Les "partenariats organisés" en droit international privé (propos autour de la loi du 15 novembre 1999 sur le pacte civil de solidarité)", *Rev crit. DIP*, 2000, p. 317-330.

KIERNAN (1999): K. KIERNAN, "Cohabitation in Western Europe", *Population Trends*, 1999, p. 25-32.

KIERNAN (2001): K. KIERNAN, "The rise of cohabitation and childbearing outside marriage in Western Europe", *IJLPF*, 2001, p. 1-21.

KNOEPFLER *et al.* (2005): F. KNOEPFLER, P. SCHWEIZER and S. OTHENIN-GIRARD, *Précis de droit international privé Suisse*, Bern: Stämpfli, 2005, 3rd Edition.

KOENS (2001): M.J.C. KOENS, *Personen- en familierecht. Supplement 152. Titel 12. Adoptie*, Deventer: Kluwer, 2001.

KOKKINI-IATRIDOU (1986): D. KOKKINI-IATRIDOU, "Some methodological aspects of comparative law", *NILR*, 1986, p. 143-194.

KOKKINI-IATRIDOU (1988): D. KOKKINI-IATRIDOU, *Een inleiding tot het rechtsvergelijkende onderzoek*, Deventer: Kluwer, 1988.

Kokkini-Iatridou (1994): D. Kokkini-Iatridou, *Exception clauses in conflicts of laws and conflicts of jurisdictions – or the principle of proximity*, Dordrecht: Martinus Nijhoff Publishers, 1994.

Kokkini-Iatridou/Frohn (1987a): D. Kokkini-Iatridou and E.N. Frohn, "De voorvraag in het Nederlandse IPR (I)", *WPNR*, 1987, Vol. 5835, p. 371-375.

Kokkini-Iatridou/Frohn (1987b): D. Kokkini-Iatridou and E.N. Frohn, "De voorvraag in het Nederlandse IPR (II)", *WPNR*, 1987, Vol. 5836, p. 387-390.

Kokkini-Iatridou/Frohn (1987c): D. Kokkini-Iatridou and E.N. Frohn, "De voorvraag in het Nederlandse IPR (III, slot)", *WPNR*, 1987, Vol. 5837, p. 413-415.

Koolhoven (2005): R. Koolhoven, "Het Nederlandse opengestelde huwelijk in het Duitse IPR. De eerste rechterlijke uitspraak is daar!", *NIPR*, 2005, p. 138-142.

Koppen/Lekkerkerker (1992a): P.A. Koppen and J.G.C. Lekkerkerker, "Geregistreerd samenwonen, verbintenis en lotsverbondenheid (I)", *WPNR*, 1992, Vol. 6067, p. 772-775.

Koppen/Lekkerkerker (1992b): P.A. Koppen and J.G.C. Lekkerkerker, "Geregistreerd samenwonen, verbintenis en lotsverbondenheid (II)", *WPNR*, 1992, Vol. 6068, p. 794-797.

Kortmann (1997): Kortmann Commissie, *Commissie inzake openstelling van het burgerlijk huwelijk voor personen van hetzelfde geslacht*, The Hague: Ministry of Justice, 1997.

Kosters (1962): J. Kosters, *Algemeen deel van het Nederlandse internationaal privaatrecht*, Haarlem: De Erven F. Bohn, 1962.

Kostkiewicz (2001): J.K. Kostkiewicz, "Registrierte Partnerschaften gleichgeschlechtlicher Personen aus der Sicht des IPR (de lege lata)", *RSDIE*, 2001, p. 101-107.

Kotterman-Van De Vosse (2001): I. Kotterman-Van De Vosse, "Krijgt het homohuwelijk een wettige status?", *FJR*, 2001, p. 108-111.

Kraan (1997): C.A. Kraan, "Het geregistreerd partnerschap", *EB*, 1997, Vol. 10, p. 4.

Kraan (2003): C.A. Kraan, *Het huwelijksvermogensrecht*, The Hague: Boom Legal Publishers, 2003, 4th Edition.

Kramer (1997): L. Kramer, "Same-sex marriage, conflict of laws and the unconstitutional public policy exception", *Yale LJ*, 1997, p. 1965-2008.

Krause (1976): H.D. Krause, *Creation of relationships of kinship. Volume III.6: International Encyclopaedia of Comparative Law*, 1976, Mouton: The Hague.

Krause (2000): H.D. Krause, "Marriage, the new millennium: Heterosexual, same-sex or not at all?", *FLQ*, 2000, p. 271-300.

Kren Kostkiewicz (2001): J. Kren Kostkiewicz, "Registrierte Partnerschaften gleichgeschlechtlicher Personen aus der Sicht des IPR (de lege lata)", *RSDIE*, 2001, p. 101-107.

Labbee (2003): X. Labbee, "PACS Hominibus ... ou l'infidélité entre homosexuels", *D*, 2003, p. 515.

Labbee (2004): X. Labbee, "Le faux PACS et les vrais papiers", *D*, 2004, p. 587-589.

Lando (1976): O. Lando, "Chapter 24: Contracts", in: K. Lipstein, *International Encyclopaedia of Comparative Law. Volume III: Private International Law*, Mouton: The Hague, 1976.

Lando/Beale (2000): O. Lando and H. Beale (eds.), *Principle of European contrcat law. Parts I and II (combined and revised)*, The Hague: Kluwer, 2000.

Law Commission (1971): English Law Commission, *Report No. 42. Family law report on polygamous marriages*, London: HMSO, 1971

Law Commission (1988): English Law Commission, *Report No. 172. Review of child law, guardianship and custody*, London: HMSO, 1988.

LAW COMMISSION (2002): ENGLISH LAW COMMISSION, *Report No. 278. Sharing homes: A discussion paper*, London: HMSO, 2002.

LE GUIDEC (2002): R. LE GUIDEC, "Le PACS et la transmission des biens entre concubins", in: J. RUBELLIN-DEVICHI and L. BALESTRA (eds.), *Des concubinages. Droit interne, droit international et droit comparé. Études offertés à J. Rubellin-Devichi*, Paris: Litec, 2002, p. 133-142.

LEADERCRAMER (2000): D. LEADERCRAMER, "Prenuptial agreements – an idea whose time has come?", *Fam. Law*, 2000, p. 359-360.

LEADERCRAMER (2001): D. LEADERCRAMER, "Prenuptial contracts – new safeguards, new problems?", *Fam. Law*, 2001, p. 295-296.

LEDERMAN (1951): W.R. LEDERMAN, "Classification in private international law", *Canadian Bar Review*, 1951, Vol. 29, p. 168.

LEDUC (2003): J. LEDUC, P. MAHOUX, M. VANDEBERGHE and N. DE TSERCALES, "Voorontwerp van het houdende wetboek van international privaatrecht", Ghent: Ipr.be, 2003, available on website: www.ipr.be.

LEKKERKERKER (1999): G.J.C. LEKKERKERKER, "Het samenlevingscontract; zijn ordenende functie in privaatrechtelijke zin", *WPNR*, 1999, Vol. 6364, p. 529-534.

LELEU (1998): Y.H. LELEU, "Examen de jurisprudence (1982-1996). Régimes matrimoniaux", *Rev. crit. jur. belge*, 1998.

LELEU (1999): Y.H. LELEU, "De vermogensrechtelijke gevolgen van de wettelijke samenwoning. Commentaar bij de virtuele wet van 23 november 1998", *Notarieel en Fiscaal Maandblad*, 1999, Vol. 6, p. 123-134.

LELEU (2001): Y.H. LELEU, "Erfrechtelijke discriminatie van buitenhuwelijkse kinderen", *TPR*, 2001, p. 1353-1383.

LEMOULAND (1997): J-J. LEMOULAND, "Le pluralisme et le droit de la famille, post modernité ou pré-déclin?", *D*, 1997, Vol. 18, p. 133-137.

LEMOULAND (1999): J-J. LEMOULAND, "Présentation de la loi N°. 99-944 du 15 novembre 1999 relative au pacte civil de solidarité", *D*, 1999, N°. 43, p.483-487.

LEMOULAND (2000): J-J. LEMOULAND, "Pacte civil de solidarité. Formation et la dissolution du pacte civil de solidarité", *JCP Éd N*, 2000, p. 406.

LEMOULAND (2004): J-J. LEMOULAND, "La loi du 26 mai 2004 relative au divorce", *D*, 2004, p. 1825-1837.

LEVENEUR (1997): L. LEVENEUR, "Les dangers du contrat d'union civile ou sociale", *JCP Éd G*, 1997, Vol. 50, p. 513-515.

LEVONTIN (1976): A.V. LEVONTIN, *Choice of law and conflict of laws*, Leiden: A.W. Sijthoff, 1976.

LEVY/KASHI (2000): D. LEVY and T. KASHI, "Getting married abroad", *Fam Law*, 2000, p. 191-198.

LIJPHART (1968): A.J. LIJPHART, *The politics of accommodation: Pluralism and democracy in The Netherlands*, Berkley/Los Angeles: University of California Press, 1968.

LIPSTEIN (1981): K. LIPSTEIN, *Principles of conflict of laws, national and international*, The Hague: Martinus Nijhoff, 1981.

LIPSTEIN (1999): K. LIPSTEIN, "Chapter 5: Characterization", in: K. LIPSTEIN (ed.), *International Encyclopaedia of Comparative Law. Volume III: Private International Law*, Tübingen: Mohr Siebeck, 1999.

LOCHER (1998): P. LOCHER, *Rapport de la commission d'experts chargée d'examiner le système suisse d'imposition de la famille (Commission Imposition de la Famille)*, Bern: Federal Department of Finances, 1998.

LØDRUP (1996): P. LØDRUP, "Registered partnership in Norway", in: A. BAINHAM (ed.), *International survey of family law 1994*, Dordrecht: Nijhoff, 1996.

LOENEN (1995): T. LOENEN, "Echte of onechte ouders", *Nemesis*, 1995, Vol. 4, p. 93.

LOONSTEIN (2005): H. LOONSTEIN, "Geregistreerd partnerschap en het kerkelijk huwelijk", *FJR*, 2005, p. 126-128.

LORENZEN (1918): E.G. LORENZEN, "Recognition of 'Massachusetts Rights' by New York courts", *Yale LJ*, 1918, Vol. 27, p. 67 at 69.

LORENZEN (1920): E.G. LORENZEN, "The theory of qualifications and the conflict of laws", *Columbian Law Review*, 1920, Vol. 20, p. 247.

LOUSSOURAN/BOUREL (2004): Y. LOUSSOURAN and P. BOUREL, *Droit international Privé*, Paris: Dalloz, 2004, 8th Edition.

LOWE/DOUGLAS (1998): N. LOWE and G. DOUGLAS (eds.), *Bromley's Family Law*, London: Butterworths, 1998, 9th Edition.

LUIJENDIJK (2005): H. LUIJENDIJK, *Nederlandse gemeenten en het Europese personenverkeer*, Deventer: Kluwer, 2005.

LUND-ANDERSEN (1998): I. LUND-ANDERSEN, "Cohabitation and registered partnership in Scandinavia: The legal position of homosexuals", in: J. EEKELAAR and T. NHALPO (eds.), *The changing family*, Oxford: Hart, 1998, p. 397-404.

LUND-ANDERSEN (2003): I. LUND-ANDERSEN, "The Danish Registered Partnership Act", in: K. BOELE-WOELKI and A. FUCHS (eds.), *EFL Series: Volume 1. Legal recognition of same-sex couples in Europe*, Antwerp: Intersentia, 2003, p. 13-23.

MAHINGA (2004): J-G. MAHINGA, "L'interdiction de se marier deux fois avec la même personne: la fausse bigamie de l'article 147 du code civil", *D*, 2004, p. 3171-3174.

MAINE (1905): H.S. MAINE, *Ancient law*, London: Routledge, 1905.

MALAURIE (1997a): P. MALAURIE, "Les dangers du contrat d'union civile et sociale", *D*, 1997, N°. 35.

MALAURIE (1997b): P. MALAURIE, "Le mariage et les homosexuals", *D*, 1997, N°. 35.

MALAURIE (1998): P. MALAURIE, *Droit civil. Famille*, Paris: Cujas, 1998, 6th Edition.

MARCEL DORWLING-CARTER (1990): M. MARCEL DORWLING-CARTER, *Gaz. Pal.*, 1990, p. 216-228.

MARKUS (2001): A. MARKUS, "Registrierte Partnerschaften – Handlungsbedarf und Handlungsmöglichkeiten im IPR", *RSDIE*, 2001, p. 109-123.

MARKUS (2004): A. MARKUS, "Le droit international privé suisse du partenariat enregistré", in: A. BONOMI and B. COTTIER (eds.), *Aspects de droit international privé des partenariats enregistrés en Europe*, Zurich: Schulthess, 2004, Volume No. 49, p. 149-152.

MARTIN (1994): J. MARTIN, "English polygamy law and the Danish registered partnership act: a case for the consistent treatment of foreign polgaymous marriages and Danish same-sex marriages in England", *Cornell ILJ*, 1994, p. 419-446.

MARTIN CASALS (2003): M. MARTIN CASALS, "Same-sex partnerships in the legislation of Spanish aunomous communities", in: K. BOELE-WOELKI and A. FUCHS (eds.), *EFL Series: Volume 1. Legal recognition of same-sex couples in Europe*, Antwerp: Intersentia, 2003, p. 54-67.

MARTIN/THÉRY (2001): C. MARTIN and I. THÉRY, "The PACS and marriage and cohabitation in France", *IJLPF*, 2001, p. 135-158.

MARTINY (2002): D. MARTINY, "The harmonisation of family law in the European Community. Pro and contra", in: M. FAURE *et al.* (eds.), *Towards a European ius commune in legal education and research*, Antwerp: Intersentia, 2002.

MASSIP (1999): J. MASSIP, "Registered partnerships and civil status", 15th March 1999, The Hague, Fifth European Conference on Family Law.

MASSON (2003): J. MASSON, "The impact of the Adoption and Children Act 2002. Part I – Parental responsibility", *Fam Law*, 2003, p. 580-585.

MATTEI (2000): U. MATTEI, *Basic principles of property law. A comparative legal and economic introduction*, Connecticut: Greenwood Press, 2000.

MAXWELL (1999): N.G. MAXWELL *et al.*, "Legal protection for all the children: Dutch-American comparison of lesbian and gay parent adoptions", *EJCL*, 1999, Vol 3.1 (http://law.kub.nl/ejcl/31/art31-2.html).

MAXWELL (2001): N.G. MAXWELL, "Opening civil marriage to same-gender couples: A Netherlands-United States comparison", *Arizona JICL*, 2001, Vol. 18, 141-207.

MAYER/HEUZÉ (2001): P. MAYER and V. HEUZÉ, *Droit international privé*, Paris: Montchrestien, 2001, 7th Edition.

MCCAFFERTY (2002): C. MCCAFFERTY, "Gays, transsexuals and the right to marry", *Fam Law*, 2002, p. 362-366.

MCCLEAN (2000): D. MCCLEAN, *Morris: The conflict of laws*, London: Sweet and Maxwell, 2000, 5th Edition.

MCELEAVY (2002): P. MCELEAVY, "The Brussels II Regulation: How the European Community has moved into family law", *ICLQ*, 2002, p. 883-908.

MCELEAVY (2003): P. MCELEAVY, "Current developments. Private international law", *ICLQ*, 2003, p. 1039-1058.

MCGLYNN (2000): C. MCGLYNN, "The Europeanisation of family law", *CFLQ*, 2000, p. 35-49.

MCGLYNN (2003): C. MCGLYNN, "Challenging the European harmonisation of family law: Perspectives on "the family", in: K. BOELE-WOELKI (ed.), *EFL Series: Volume 4. Perspectives for the unification and harmonisation of family law in Europe*, Antwerp: Intersentia, 2003, p. 219-238.

MEAD (1995): H. MEAD (ed.), *Change of Name*, London: Law & Tax, 1995, 15th Edition.

VAN DER MEER (1988): T. VAN DER MEER, "The persecutions of sodomites in Eighteenth Century Amsterdam: Changing perceptions of sodonmy", *Journal of Homosexuality*, 1988, Vol. 16, p. 263-307.

VAN DER MEER (1997): T. VAN DER MEER, "Sodom's seed in The Netherlands: The emergence of homosexuality in the early modern period", *Journal of Homosexuality*, 1997, Vol. 34, p. 1-16.

VAN DER MEER (2001): T. VAN DER MEER, "Ernstige moraliteits-toestanden in de residentie. Een whodunnit over het Haagse zedenschandaal van 1920", *Pro Memorie*, 2001, Vol. 3, p. 372-404.

MELLEMA-KRANENBURG (1997): T.J. MELLEMA-KRANENBURG, "Gehuwd, ongehuwd of ... geregistreerd partner", *Nauta Dutilh Informatie,* 1997, Vol. 35, p. 2.

MÉRCAY (2000): C. MÉRCAY, "Droit et homosexualité", *D*, 2000, p. 193.

MERIN (2002): Y. MERIN, *Equality for same-sex couples*, Chicago: University of Chicago Press, 2002.

MEULDERS-KLEIN (2003): M.T. MEULDERS-KLEIN, "Towards a European Civil Code on Family Law?", in: K. BOELE-WOELKI (ed.), *EFL Series: Volume 4. Perspectives for the unification and harmonisation of family law in Europe*, 2003, Antwerp: Intersentia, p. 105-117.

MEYER (1994): R. MEYER, "Les clauses d'exception en matière de conflits de lois et de conflits de jurisdictions – Suisse", in: D. KOKKINI-IATRIDOU (ed.), *Exception clauses in conflicts of laws and conflicts of jurisdictions – or the principle of proximity*, Dordrecht: Martinus Nijhoff, 1994, p. 299-332.

MICHEL/POULIQUEN (1999): J-P. MICHEL and J-P. POULIQUEN, "L'élu, l'expert, le citoyen et le Conseil constitutionel", *Hors série. Droit de la famille.* Décembre 1999, 1999, p. 25.

MIGNOT (2001): M. MIGNOT, "Le partentariat enregistré en droit international privé", *Rev. int. dr. com.* 2001, p. 601.

MINISTRE DE LA JUSTICE (2004): MINISTRE DE LA JUSTICE, *Le pacte civil de solidarité. Réflexions et propositions de réforme. Rapport remis à Monsieur Dominique Perben*, Paris: Ministry of Justice, 2004.

MINISTRY OF JUSTICE (1999): MINISTRY OF JUSTICE, *La situation juridique des couples homosexuels en droit Suisse*, Bern: Ministry of Justice, 1999.

MINISTRY OF JUSTICE (2000): MINISTRY OF JUSTICE, *Résultats de la procedure de consultation. Rapport relative à la situation juridique des couples homosexuals en droit Suisse*, Bern: Ministry of Justice, August 2000.

MINISTRY OF JUSTICE (2001): MINISTRY OF JUSTICE, *Loi fédérale sur le partenariat enregistré entre personnes du même sexe*, Bern: Ministry of Justice, 14th November 2001.

MINISTRY OF JUSTICE (2002): MINISTRY OF JUSTICE, *Résultats de la procedure de consultation. Loi fédérale sur le partenariat enregistré entre personnes du même sexe*, Bern: Ministry of Justice, 28th February 2002.

MOLFESSIS (2000): N. MOLFESSIS, "Le réécriture de la loi relative du PACS par le conseil constitutionnel", *JCP Éd G*, 2000, Vol. 10, p. 399-407.

MOSSELMANS (2000): S. MOSSELMANS, "De wet van 23 november 1998 tot invoering van de wettelijke samenwoning en het gelijksbeginsel", *RW*, 2000, p. 1041-1048.

MOSTERMANS (1996): P.M.M. MOSTERMANS, *De processuele behandeling van het conflictenrecht*, Zwolle: W.E.J. Tjeenk Willink, 1996.

MOSTERMANS (2001): P.M.M. MOSTERMANS, "Nieuw Europese scheidingsprocesrecht onder de loep: de rechtsmacht bij echtscheiding", *NIPR*, 2001, p. 293-305.

MOSTERMANS (2002): P.M.M. MOSTERMANS, "De wederzijdse erkenning van echtscheidingen binnen de Europese Unie", *NIPR*, 2002, p. 263-273.

MOSTERMANS (2003): P.M.M. MOSTERMANS, *Echtscheiding. Praktijkreeks IPR. Deel 5*, Deventer: Kluwer, 2003, 2nd Edition.

MOSTYN (2000): N. MOSTYN, "Brussels II Regulation: Impact on forum disputes in relation to the main suit and ancillary relief proceedings", *IFL*, 2000, p. 162-166.

MOSTYN (2001): N. MOSTYN, "Burssels II – The impact on forum disputes", *Fam Law*, 2001, p. 359-367.

VAN MOURIK (1997): M.J.A. VAN MOURIK, "Geregistreerd Partnerschap!", *WPNR*, 1997, Vol. 6264, p. 225-226. mirror

VAN MOURIK/NUYTINCK (1998): M.J.A. VAN MOURIK and A.J.M. NUYTINCK, *Personen- en Familierecht, huwelijksvermogensrecht*, Deventer: Kluwer, 1998.

MOUTOUH (1998): H. MOUTOUH, "La question de la reconnaissance du couple homosexual: entre dogmatisme et empirisme", *D*, 1998, p. 369-372.

Mulder (1947): A.C.J. Mulder, *Inleiding tot het Nederlandsch international privaatrecht*, Arnhem: S. Gouda Quint, 1947, 2nd Edition.

Murphy (1996): J. Murphy, "The recognition of overseas marriages and divorces in the United Kingdom", *NILQ*, 1996, Vol. 47, p. 35-49.

Murphy (2000): J. Murphy, "Rationality and cultural pluralism in the non-recognition of foreign marriages", *ICLQ*, 2000, p. 643-659.

Murphy (2002): J. Murphy, "The recognition of same-sex families in Britain: the role of private international law", *IJLPF*, 2002, p. 181-201.

Murphy (2004): J. Murphy, "Same-sex marriages in England: a role for human rights?", *CFLQ*, 2004, p. 245-259.

Murray (2004): C. Murray, "Same-sex families and outcomes for children and parents", *Fam Law*, 2004, p. 136-139.

Nadelmann/von Mehren/Hazard (1961): K.H. Nadelmann, A.T. von Mehren and J.N. Hazard (eds.), *XXth century comparative and conflict of laws*, Leiden: A.W.Sijthoff, 1961.

Näf-Hofmann/Näf-Hofmann (1998): M. Näf-Hofmann and H. Näf-Hofmann, *Schweizerisches Ehe- und Erbrecht*, Zurich: Schulthess Verlag, 1998.

Neels (1989): J.C. Neels, "Current legal developments: Lesotho", *Comparative and International Law Journal of South Africa*, 1989, Vol. 22, p. 248.

Niboyet (1928): J.P. Niboyet, *Traité de droit international privé*, Paris: Sirey, 1928.

Nicol (2004): D. Nicol, "Gender reassignment and the transformation of the Human Rights Act", *LQR*, 2004, p. 194-198.

Niederer (1940): W. Niederer, *Die Frage der Qualifikation als Grundproblem des internationalen Privatrechts*, Zürich: Effingerhof A.G.Brugg, 1940.

Nielsen (1990): L. Nielsen, "Family rights and the 'registered partnership' in Denmark", *IJLPF*, 1990, p. 297-307.

Nielsen/Kronborg (1998): L. Nielsen and A. Kronborg, "Legislation on assisted reproduction, reports on adoption, the family principle and the individual principle and blessing registered partnerships", in: A. Bainham (ed.), *International survey of family law 1996*, Dordrecht: Nijhoff, 1998.

Nieuwenhuis (2004): J.H. Nieuwenhuis *et al.*, *Personen- en Familierecht. Tekst en Commentaar*, Deventer: Kluwer, 2004, 3rd Edition.

Noack (2001): T. Noack, "Cohabitation in Norway: An accepted and gradually more regulated way of living", *IJLPF*, 2001, p. 102-107.

Noordam (1988): D.J. Noordam, "Sodomy in the Dutch Republic, 1600-1725", *JH*, 1988, Vol. 16, p. 207-228.

Norrie (1994): K.McK. Norrie, "Reproductive technology, transsexualism and homosexuality: New problems for international private law", *ICLQ*, 1994, p. 757-775.

Norrie (2002): K.McK. Norrie, "Marriage is for heterosexuals – may the rets of us be saved from it", *CFLQ*, 2000, p. 363-369.

Norrie (2003a): K.McK. Norrie, "Sewel motions, devolution and family law", *Family Law Update*, 2003, Vol. 10.

Norrie (2003b): K.McK. Norrie, "Would Scots law recognise a Dutch same-sex marriage?", *Edin. LR*, 2003, Vol. 7, p. 147-173

North (1993): P.M. North, "Marriage", in: P.M. North (ed.), *Private international law problems in common law jurisdictions*, Dordrecht: Martinus Nijhoff, 1993, p. 23-56.

NORTH (2001): P.M. NORTH, "Private international law: change or decay?", *ICLQ*, 2001, p. 477-508.

NORTH (2002): P.M. NORTH, "Rethinking jurisdiction and recognition of judgments", *CLP*, 2002, p. 395-426.

NORTH/FAWCETT (1992): P.M. NORTH and J.J. FAWCETT, *Cheshire and North's private international law*, Londo: Butterworths, 1992, 12th Edition.

NORTH/FAWCETT (1999): P.M. NORTH and J.J. FAWCETT, *Cheshire and North's private international law*, Londo: Butterworths, 1999, 13th Edition.

NORTHERN IRELAND OFFICE OF LAW REFORM (2004a): NORTHERN IRELAND OFFICE OF LAW REFORM, "Civil Partnership: A Legal status for committed same-sex couples in Northern Ireland", Belfast: Northern Ireland Department of Finance and Personnel, 2004.

NORTHERN IRELAND OFFICE OF LAW REFORM (2004b): NORTHERN IRELAND OFFICE OF LAW REFORM, "Civil Partnership: A Legal status for committed same-sex couples in Northern Ireland. Analysis of Responses", Belfast: Northern Ireland Department of Finance and Personnel, 2004.

NUYTINCK (1996): A.J.M. NUYTINCK, "Het hete hangijzer van het homohuwelijk", *FJR*, 1996, p. 125

NUYTINCK (1999): A.J.M. NUYTINCK, "De wet openstelling huwelijk en de wet adoptie door personen van hetzelfde geslacht", in: M.J. VAN MOURIK (ed.), *Liber Amicorum Van Mourik*, The Hague: T.M.C. Asser, 1999.

NUYTINCK (2002): A. NUYTINCK, "De complexiteit van de gezagsregeling", *FJR*, 2002, p. 190-191.

NUYTINCK (2004): A.J.M. NUYTINCK, "Nietigverklaard partnerschap en gezag", *FJR*, 2004, p. 81

O'DONOVAN (2002): K. O'DONOVAN (2002), "Unmarried partners and 'traditional marriage' in English law", in: J. RUBELLIN-DEVICHI and L. BALESTRA (eds.), *Des concubinages, droit interne, droit international et droit compare. Études offertés à J. Rubellin-Devichi*, Paris: Litec, 2002, p. 455-471.

O'HALLORAN (1997): K. O'HALLORAN, *Family law in Northern Ireland*, Dublin: Gill & Macmillan, 1997.

ODERKERK (2004): A.E. ODERKERK, "Kwalificatie in het Internationaal Privaatrecht", in: R. KOTTING, J.A. PONTIER and L. STRIKWERDA (eds.), *Voorkeur voor de lex fori. symposium ter gelegenheid van het afscheid van Prof. Mr. Th. M. de Boer*, Deventer: Kluwer, 2004, p. 59-79.

OFFICE FOR NATIONAL STATISTICS (2002): OFFICE FOR NATIONAL STATISTICS, *Civil Registration: Vital Change. White paper*, London: HMSO, 2002.

OFFICE FOR NATIONAL STATISTICS (2003): OFFICE FOR NATIONAL STATISTICS, *Civil Registration: Delivering Vital Change. Consultation paper*, London: HMSO, 2003.

OOSTEROM-STAPLES (2004): H. OOSTEROM-STAPLES, "Burgerschap van de Unie. Een vrije keuze voor de achternaam van de eigen kinderen na het arrest *Garcia Avello*?", *NTER*, 2004, p. 57-61.

OTHENIN-GIRARD (1999a): S. OTHENIN-GIRARD, *La réserve d'ordre public en droit international privé. Personnes - Famille - Successions*, Zurich: Schulthess, 1999.

OTHENIN-GIRARD (1999b): S. OTHENIN-GIRARD, "Quelques observations sur le for de nécessité en droit international privé suisse (art. 3 LDIP)", *RSDIE*, 1999, p. 251-285.

OVERBECK (1972): A.E. OVERBECK, "Chapter 15: Persons", in: K. LIPSTEIN, *International Encyclopaedia of Comparative Law. Volume III: Private International Law*, Mouton: The Hague, 1972.

PALMER (2003): A. PALMER, "Discrimination on grounds of sexual orientation", *New LJ*, 2003, p. 1829-1830.

PÅLSSON (1978): L. PÅLSSON, "Chapter 16: Marriage", in: K. LIPSTEIN, *International Encyclopaedia of Comparative Law. Volume III: Private International Law*, Mouton: The Hague, 1978.

PANSIER (1999): F-J. PANSIER, "De la contractualisation du droit de la famille en général et du droit du mariage en particulier", *Gaz. Pal.*, 1999, p. 287-289.

PAOLO/GEEROMS (2004): G. PAOLO ROMANO and S. GEEROMS, "La loi belge du 13 février 2003 et le droit international privé: de la circulaire ministérielle du 23 janvier 2004 à l'alienéa 2 de l'article 46 du nouveau code", in: A. BONOMI and B. COTTIER (eds.), *Aspects de droit international privé des partenariats enregistrés en Europe*, Zurich: Schulthess, 2004, Volume N°. 49, p. 105-136.

PATOCCHI/GEIZINGER (1995): P.M. PATOCCHI and E. GEIZINGER, *Code de droit international privé Suisse annoté*, Lausanne: Éditions Payot, 1995.

PELLIS (1996): L.TH.L.G. PELLIS, *Alimentatie. Praktijkreeks IPR. Deel 6*, Deventer: Kluwer, 1996.

PELLIS (2002): L.TH.L.G. PELLIS, "Het homohuwelijk: een bijzonder nationaal product", *FJR*, 2002, p. 162-168.

PERTEGÁS SENDER (2003): M. PERTEGÁS SENDER, "Huwelijk tussen personen van hetzelfde geslacht in België: internrechtelijke en internationale implicaties", in: P. SENAEVE and F. SWENNEN (eds.), *De hervorming in het personen- en familierecht 2002-2003*, Antwerp: Intersentia, 2003, p. 257-280.

PIASTRA (2000): R. PIASTRA, "Loi relative au PACS", *D*, 2000, p. 203-208.

PICHONNAZ (2004): P. PICHONNAZ, "Le partenariat enregistré: sa nature et ses effets", *RDS*, 2004, p. 389-433.

PILLEBOUT (2000): J-F. PILLEBOUT, *Le PACS. Pacte civil de solidarité*, Paris: Litec, 2000.

PINTENS (1981): W. PINTENS, *Naam*, Ghent-Leuven: E. Story, 1981.

PINTENS (1999a): W. PINTENS, *Inleiding tot de rechtsvergelijking*, Leuven: Universitaire Pers Leuven, 1999.

PINTENS (1999b): W. PINTENS, "Over de europeanisatie van het familierecht", *FJR*, 1999, p. 238-243.

PINTENS (2001): W. PINTENS, "Partnerschaft im belgischen und niederländischen Recht", *FamRZ*, 2001, Vol. 2, p. 69-77.

PINTENS (2001b): W. PINTENS, *Casebook. European Family Law*, Leuven: Leuven University Press, 2001.

PINTENS (2003): W. PINTENS, "Europeanisation of family law in Europe", in: K. BOELE-WOELKI (ed.), *EFL Series: Volume 4. Perspectives for the harmonisation and unification of family law in Europe*, Antwerp: Intersentia, 2003, p. 3-33.

PINTENS/VAN DER MEERSCH/VANWINCKELEN (2002): W. PINTENS, B VAN DER MEERSCH and K. VANWINCKELEN, *Inleiding tot het familial Vermogensrecht*, Leuven: Universitaire Pers Leuven, 2002.

PINTENS/VANWINCKELEN (2001): W. PINTENS and K. VANWINCKELEN, *Casebook: European family law*, 2001, Leuven: Leuven University Press.

PIRRUNG (1999): J. PIRRUNG, "Europäische justitielle Zusammenarbeit in Zivilsachen – insbesondere das neue Scheidungsübereinkommen", *ZEuP*, 1999, p. 834-848.

PLANT (1986): R. PLANT, *The pink triangle. The Nazi war against homosexuals*, New York: Henry Holt & Co., 1986.

PLASSCHAERT (1998): J.N.E. PLASSCHAERT, *Het geregistreerd partnerschap*, The Hague: Elsvier, 1998.

PLASSCHAERT (1999): J.N.E. PLASSCHAERT, "Anderhalf jaar geregistreerd partnerschap in de praktijk", *FJR*, 1999, Vol. 9, p. 182-189.

PLASSCHAERT (2002): J.N.E. PLASSCHAERT, *Burgerlijke Stand*, Amsterdam: Stadsdrukkerij Amsterdam, 2002.

POLAK/EECKHOUT (2000): M.V. POLAK and V. VAN DER EECKHOUT, "Kroniek van het international privaatrecht" *NJB*, 2002, p. 573-580.

POULTER (1976): S. POULTER, "*Hyde v. Hyde* – a reappraisal", *ICLQ*, 1976, p. 475-508.

POULTER (1979): S. POULTER, "Definition of marriage in English law", *MLR*, 1979, p. 409-429.

PROBERT/BARLOW (2000a): R. PROBERT and A. BARLOW, "Cohabitation and the law: recent European reforms", *DEuFamR*, 2000, p. 76-81.

PROBERT/BARLOW (2000b): Displacing marriage – diversification and harmonisation within Europe", *CFLQ*, 2000, p. 153-165.

RAAPE (1934): L. RAAPE, "Les rapports juridiques entre parents et enfants comme point de départ d'une explication pratique d'anciens et de nouveaux problèmes fondamentaux du droit international privé", *Hague Recueil*, 1934, Vol. 50.IV, p. 401-544.

RABEL (1933): E. RABEL, "Le problème de la qualification", *Revue de Droit International Privé*, 1933, p. 1.

RABEL (1958): E. RABEL, *Conflict of laws: A comparative study*, Ann Arbor: University of Michigan Press, 1958, 2nd Edition.

RAULT (2003): W. RAULT, "The best way to court. The French mode of registration and its impact on the social significance of partnerships", Presentation at INED Conference in Stockholm, Sweden, 25th-26th September 2003 entitled "Same-sex couples, same-sex partnerships and homosexual marriages".

RAYMOND (1999): G. RAYMOND, *Ombres et lumbières sur la famille*, Paris: Bayard, 1999.

REED (2000): A. REED, "Essential validity of marriage: the application of interest analysis and dépeçage to Anglo-American choice of law rules", *New York Law School Journal of International and Comparative Law*, 2000, p. 387.

REGISTRAR GENERAL (2002): REGISTRAR GENERAL FOR ENGLAND AND WALES, *Registration: Modernising a Vital Service*, London: GRO, 2002.

REINHARTZ (2002a): B.E. REINHARTZ, "Flitsscheidingen in Nederlands-Duits verhoudingen" in: H.F.G LEMARIE and P. VLAS (eds.), *Liber Amicorum I.S. Joppe*, Deventer: Kluwer, 2002, p. 155-166.

REINHARTZ (2002b): B.E. REINHARTZ, "Gehuwd in Law Vegas of Thailand, wat nu?", *WPNR*, 2002, Vol. 6487, p. 346-348.

REINHARTZ (2004): B.E. REINHARTZ, "Het wetsvoorstel Wet conflictenrecht geregistreerd partnerschap", *WPNR*, 2004, Vol. 6583, p. 491-498.

RENCHON (1998): J-L. RENCHON, "Mariage, cohabitation légale et union libre", in: (ed.), *Liber Amicorum M. Meulders-Klein*, Brussels: Bruylant, 1998, 549-573.

RENCHON (2003): J-L. RENCHON, "L'avènement du mariage homosexuel dans le Code civil belge", *Rev. trim. dr. fam.*, 2003, Vol. 3, 439-469.

REVILLARD (2000): M. REVILLARD, "Le pacte civil de solidarité en droit international privé", *Rép Not.*, 2000, p. 337.

REVILLARD (2002): M. REVILLARD, "Les unions hors mariage. Regards sur la pratique de droit international privé" in: J. RUBELLIN-DEVICHI and L. BALESTRA (eds.), *Des concubinages, droit interne, droit international et droit compare. Études offertés à J. Rubellin-Devichi*, Paris: Litec, 2002, p. 579.

VAN RHEE (1990): R. VAN RHEE, "Een bijzonder gezin", *NJB*, 1990, p. 1670-1675.

RICHARDS (2002): C. RICHARDS, "The legal recognition of same-sex couples – The French perspective", *ICLQ*, 2002, p. 305-324.

RICHEZ-PONS (2005): A. RICHEZ-PONS, "Habitual residence considered as a European harmonisation factor in family law (regarding the Brussels IIbis regulation", in: K. Boele-Woelki (ed.), *EFL Series: Volume 10. Common core and better law in European family law*, Antwerp: Intersentia, 2005, p. 355-360.

RIGAUX (1956): F. RIGAUX, *La théorie des qualifications en droit international privé*, Brussels: F.Larcier, 1956.

RIGAUX (1987): F. RIGAUX, *Droit international privé. Tome I: Théorie générale*, Brussels: Larcier, 1987.

RIGAUX (2000): F. RIGAUX, "The law applicable to non traditional families", in: J. BASEDOW *et al.* (eds.), *Liber Amicorum Kurt Siehr*, The Hague: T.M.C. Asser Press, 2000, p. 647.

RIGAUX/FALLON (1993): F. RIGAUX and M. FALLON, *Droit international privé. Tome II. Droit positif belge*, Brussels: Larcier, 1993.

RIX (2000): B. RIX, "State of the union: The States' interest in the marital status of their citizens", *University of Miami Law Review*, 2000, Vol. 55, p. 1

RIX (2002): B. RIX, "Choice of law and marriage: A proposal", *FLQ*, 2002, p. 255.

ROBERTS (2000): N. ROBERTS, "Fitzpatrick v. Sterling – A case with wider implications?", *Fam. Law*, 2000, p. 417-422.

ROBERTSON (1940): A.H. ROBERTSON, *Characterisation in the conflict of laws*, Cambridge: Harvard University Press, 1940.

ROCA (2001): E. ROCA, "Same-sex relationships in Spain: family, marriage or contract", *EJLR*, 2003, p. 365-382.

ROES (2001): S. ROES, "De scheiding van Kerk en Staat en het huwelijk", *FJR*, 2001, p. 111-113

ROLAND (1998): R-M. ROLAND, "Du mariage sans contrat au contrat sans mariage", *Les Petites Affiches*, 1998, Vol. 28, p. 12-16.

RÖTHEL (2000): A. RÖTHEL, "Registrierte Partnerschaften im internationalen Privatrecht", *IPRax*, 2000, p. 74-79.

ROTHENBACHER (1998): F. ROTHENBACHER, "Social change in Europe and its impact on family structures", in: J. EEKELAAR and T. NHLAPO (eds.) *The changing family. Family forms and family law*, Oxford: Hart, 1998, p. 3-23.

ROY (2002): A. ROY, "Le partenariat civil, d'un continent a l'autre", *Rev. int. dr. com.*, 2002, p. 759.

RUBELLIN-DEVICHI (1999): J. RUBELLIN-DEVICHI, "Présentation de la loi adoptée le 13 octobre 1999 relative au PACS", *JCP Éd G*, 1999, p. 1909.

RUBELLIN-DEVICHI (2000): J. RUBELLIN-DEVICHI, "How matters stand in relation to family law reform", in: A. BAINHAM (ed.), *International survey of family law 2000 Edition*, Bristol: Jordans, 2000, p. 143-164.

Rubellin-Devichi (2001): J. Rubellin-Devichi (ed.), *Droit de la famille. 2001-2002,* Paris: Dalloz, 2001.

de Ruiter (1993): J. De Ruiter, *Manipuleren met leven. Handelingen Nederlandse Juristen Vereniging,* Zwolle: Tjeenk Willink, 1993.

Rutten (1999): S. Rutten, "Consulaire huwelijken: wijziging Wet conflictenrecht huwelijk", *FJR,* 1999, p. 114-121.

Saalden (1980): M. Saalden, "Artikel 248-bis wetboek van strafrecht de geschiedenis van een strafbaarstelling", *Groniek,* 1980, Vol. 66, p. 38-47.

Salomon (1933): R. Salomon, *Het qualificatie probleem in het internationaal privaatrecht,* Amsterdam: Menno, 1933.

Sandoz (1995) : S. Sandoz, "Régime matrimonial de la participation aux acquêts. Acquisition d'un bien à crédit avec constitution de gage", *RNRF,* 1995, p. 201-214.

Sandoz (1999): S. Sandoz, "Le point sur le droit de la famille", *RSJ,* 1999, Vol. 6, p. 118-121.

Sandoz (2000a): S. Sandoz, "Le contrat de partenariat stable", in: F. Guillaume and R. Arn (eds.), *Cohabitation non maritale. Evolution récente en droit suisse et étranger,* Geneva: Librairie Droz, 2000, p. 148-162.

Sandoz (2000b): S. Sandoz, "Le point sur le droit de la famille", *RSJ,* 2000, Vol. 6, p. 135-139.

Sandoz (2001a): S. Sandoz, "Partenariats enregistrés. La situation en Suisse de lege ferenda: tendances et options", *RSDIE,* 2001, Vol. 1, p. 61-70.

Sandoz (2001b): S. Sandoz, "Le point sur le droit de la famille", *RSJ,* 2001, Vol. 5, p. 93-98.

Sandoz (2002): S. Sandoz, "Le point sur le droit de la famille", *RSJ,* 2002, Vol. 6, p. 150-157.

Sandoz (2003): S. Sandoz, "Le point sur le droit de la famille", *RSJ,* 2003, Vol. 6, p. 145-152.

Sandoz (2004): S. Sandoz, "Le point sur le droit de la famille", *RSJ,* 2004, Vol. 6, p. 133-139.

Sandoz (2005): S. Sandoz, "Le point sur le droit de la famille", *RSJ,* 2005, Vol. 6, p. 138-144.

Sandoz/Terrier (1997): S. Sandoz and C. Terrier, "Participation aux acquêts et acquisition d'un bien à credit", *RNRF,* 1997, p. 73-83.

Šarčević (1999): P. Šarčević, "Private international law aspects of legally recognised regulated forms of non-marital cohabitation and registered partnerships", *Yearbook of Private International Law,* 1999, p. 37-48.

Sauveplanne (1990): J.G. Sauveplanne, "Chapter 6: Renvoi", in: K. Lipstein, *International Encyclopaedia of Comparative Law. Volume III: Private International Law,* Mouton: The Hague, 1990.

Savolainen (2003): M. Savolainen, "The Finnish and Swedish partnership acts – Similarities and divergencies", in: K. Boele-Woelki and A. Fuchs (eds.), *EFL Series: Volume 1. Legal recognition of same-sex couples in Europe,* Antwerp: Intersentia, 2003, p. 24-40.

Scappucci (2000): G. Scappucci, "Court of First Instance refuses to recognise Swedish 'registered partnership' rights and duties", *EPL,* 2000, p. 355-366.

Schelhaas *et al.* (2002): H. Schelhaas *et al., The Principles of European Contract Law and Dutch Law,* Nijmegen: Ars Aequi Libri, 2002.

Scherf (1999): Y. Scherf, *Registered partnership in The Netherlands,* The Hague: Ministry of Justice, 1999.

Scherpe/Yassari (2005): J.M. Scherpe and N. Yassari (eds.), *Die Rechtsstellung nichtehelicher Lebensgemeinschaften. Beiträge zum ausländischen und internationalen Privatrecht. Teil 81,* Tübingen: Mohr Siebeck, 2005.

SCHIMDT (2004): H. SCHIMDT, "Nog drie maanden een dilemma voor de ambtenaar van de burgerlijke stand (de omzendbrief over homohuwelijken)", *Ipr.be*, 2004, Vol. 3, p. 93-102.

SCHMITTHOFF (1945): C.M. SCHMITTHOFF, *A textbook of the English conflict of laws (Private international law)* London: Pitman & Sons, 1945.

SCHNEIDER (1987): B. SCHNEIDER, "Le concubinage et la loi", *RSJ*, 1987, Vol. 83, p. 288-290.

SCHRAMA (1998): W. SCHRAMA, "De Raad van Europa en het familierecht", *FJR*, 1998, p. 54-59.

SCHRAMA (1999a): W. SCHRAMA, "Registered partnership in The Netherlands", *IJLPF*, 1999, p. 315-327.

SCHRAMA (1999b): W. SCHRAMA, "Niet-huwelijske leefvormen en het IPR", *FJR*, 1999, p. 131-133.

SCHRAMA (2002): W. SCHRAMA, "Reforms in Dutch family law during the course of 2001: Increased pluriformity and complexity" in: A. BAINHAM (ed.), *International survey of family law*, Bristol: Jordans, 2002, p. 277-303.

SCHRAMA (2004): W. SCHRAMA, *De niet-huwelijkse samenleving in het Nederlandse en Duitse recht*, Amsterdam: Ars Notariatus, Kluwer, 2004.

SCHUTTE HEIDE-JØRGENSEN (1997): L. SCHUTTE HEIDE-JØRGENSEN, "Recht op homohuwelijk?", *AA*, 1997, Vol. 46, p. 86-92.

SCHWANDER (1993): I. SCHWANDER, "Entscheidungen/Jurisprudence", *PJA*, 1993, p. 1265-1268.

SCHWANDER (2001): I. SCHWANDER, "Registrierte Partnerschaften im Internationalen Privat- und Zivilprozessrecht", *PJA*, 2001, p. 350-356.

SCHWENZER (2001): I. SCHWENZER, "The evolution of family law – From status to contract and relation", *EJRL*, 2001, Vol. 3, p. 199-202.

SCHWENZER (2002): I. SCHWENZER, "Registrierte Partnerschaft: Der Schweizer Weg", *FamPra.ch*, 2002, Vol. 2, p. 223-237.

SCHWENZER (2003): I. SCHWENZER, "Methodological aspects of harmonisation of family law", *FamPra.ch*, 2003, p. 318-331.

SCOLES/HAY/BORCHERS/SYMEONIDES (2001): E.F. SCOLES, P. HAY, P.J. BORCHERS and S.C. SYMEONIDES, *Conflict of laws*, St. Paul, Minnesota: West Group, 2001, 3rd Edition.

SCOTTISH EXECUTIVE (2003a): SCOTTISH EXECUTIVE, *Civil partnership registration: A legal status for committed same-sex couples in Scotland*, Edinburgh: Scottish Executive, 2003.

SCOTTISH EXECUTIVE (2003b): SCOTTISH EXECUTIVE, *Adoption policy review group. Choices for children in fostering and adoption*, Edinburgh: Scottish Executive, 2003.

SCOTTISH EXECUTIVE (2004a): SCOTTISH EXECUTIVE, *The consultation on civil partnership registration: Analysis of the responses*, Edinburgh: Scottish Executive, 2004.

SCOTTISH EXECUTIVE (2004b): SCOTTISH EXECUTIVE, *Family matters: Improving family law in Scotland*, Edinburgh: Scottish Executive, 2004.

SCOTTISH LAW COMMISSION (1989): SCOTTISH LAW COMMISSION, *Report No. 116. Report on reform of the ground for divorce*, Edinburgh: HMSO, 1989.

SCOTTISH LAW COMMISSION (1990): SCOTTISH LAW COMMISSION, *Report No. 124. Report on succession*, Edinburgh: HMSO, 1990.

SCOTTISH LAW COMMISSION (1992): SCOTTISH LAW COMMISSION, *Report No. 135. Report on family law*, Edinburgh: HMSO, 1992.

SCOTTISH REGISTRAR (2001): REGISTRAR GENERAL OF BIRTHS, DEATHS AND MARRIAGES FOR SCOTLAND, *Civil registration in the 21st Century. A consultation paper*, Edinburgh: General Register Office for Scotland, 2001.

Scoular (2001): J. Scoular (ed.), *Family dynamics. Contemporary issues in family law*, Edinburgh: Butterworths LexisNexis, 2001.

Scyboz/Gillieron (1999): G. Scyboz and P-R. Gillieron, *Code civil Suisse et Code des obligations annotés*, Lausanne: Editions Payot, 1999, 6th Edition.

Senaeve (1992): P. Senaeve, "Rechtswaardering van het concubinaat", in: P. Senaeve (ed.), *Conbubinaat. De buitenhuwelijkse tweerelatie*, Leuven: Acco, 1992, p. 19-71.

Senaeve (1996): P. Senaeve, "Familierechtelijke aspecten van ongehuwd samenwonen", in: W. Pintens and B. Van Der Meersch (eds.), *Ongehuwd Samenwonen*, Antwerpen: Kluwer, 1996, p. 62-118.

Senaeve (1998): P. Senaeve, "De wettelijke samenwoning en het geregistreerd partnerschap in het Belgisch recht", *FJR*, 1998, Vol. 11, p. 254.

Senaeve (2000): P. Senaeve, "De Belgische 'wettelijke samenwoning' en het Franse 'pacte civil de solidarité'. Enkele rechtsvergelijkende beschouwingen", in: A. Verbeke and F. Bouckaert (eds.), *Liber Amicoram Bouckert*, Leuven: Universitaire Pers, 2000, p. 451.

Senaeve (2002): P. Senaeve, "Naar de invoering van het homohuwelijk in het Belgische recht?", *EJ*, 2002, Vol. 4, p. 50-52.

Senaeve (2003a): P. Senaeve, *Compendium van het Personen- en Familierecht. Deel 1*, Leuven: Acco, 2003, 6th Edition.

Senaeve (2003b): P. Senaeve, *Compendium van het Personen- en Familierecht. Deel 2*, Leuven: Acco, 2003, 6th Edition.

Senaeve (2003c): P. Senaeve, *Compendium van het Personen- en Familierecht. Deel 3*, Leuven: Acco, 2003, 6th Edition.

Senaeve (2003d): P. Senaeve, "De Wet van 13 februari 2003 tot invoering van het homohuwelijk in het Belgische recht", *EJ*, 2003, Vol. 4, p. 50.

Senaeve (2005): P. Senaeve, "Harmonisatie van het familierecht binnen Europa: noodzaak en/of utopie?", *JF*, 2005, Lustrumnummer/Jubelium Number (to be published).

Senaeve/Coene (1998a): P. Senaeve and E. Coene, "De wet van 23 november 1998 tot invoering van de wettelijke samenwoning", *EJ*, 1998, p. 156.

Senaeve/Coene (1998b): P. Senaeve and E. Coene, *Geregistreerd Partnerschap*, Antwerp/Appeldoorn: Maklu, 1998.

Seriaux (1998): A. Seriaux, "Être et ne pas être: les ambiguïtés juridiques de la constitution légale d'un contrat d'union civile", *Droit de la Famille Chronique*, 1998, Vol. 4.

Shah (2003): P.A. Shah, "Attitudes to polygamy in English law", *ICLQ*, 2003, p. 369-400.

Siehr (1982): K. Siehr, "Domestic relations in Europe: European equivalents to American evolutions", *AJCL*, 1982, p. 37-53.

Siehr (1989): K. Siehr, "Private international law at the end of the twenieth century – progress or regress?", *AJCL*, 1989, p. 193.

Siehr (2002): K. Siehr, *Das Internationale Privatrecht der Schweiz*, Zurich: Schulthess, 2002.

Siehr (2003): K. Siehr, "Family unions and private international law", *NILR*, 2003, p. 419-435.

Simons (2004): N. Simons, "Adoptie door personen van gelijk gelsacht", *FJR*, 2004, p. 152-155.

Sinclair (2004): J. Sinclair, "Embracing new family forms, entrenching outmoded stereotypes: building the rainbow nation", in: P. Lødrup and E. Modvar (eds.), *Family life and human rights*, Oslo: Gyldendal, 2004, p. 801-838.

Smits (2003): J. Smits, "Scotland as a mixed jurisdiction and the development of European private law", *EJCL*, 2003, Vol 7.5, http://www.ejcl.org/75/art75-1.html.

SNIJDERS/RANK-BERENSCHOT (2001): H.J. SNIJDERS and E.B. RANK-BERENSCHOT, *Studiereeks burgerlijk recht: Goederenrecht*, Deventer: Kluwer, 2001, 3rd Edition.

SOONS (1999): A.L.M. SOONS *et al.* (eds.), *Het Nederlandse huwelijksvermogensrecht*, Deventer: Gouda Quint, 1999, 3rd Edition.

SÖRGJERD (2005): C. SÖRGJERD, "Neutrality: The death or the revival of the traditional family? Regulating informal partnerships in Sweden", in: K. BOELE-WOELKI (ed.), *EFL Series: Volume 10. Common core or better law*, Antwerp: Intersentia, 2005, p. 335-352.

STAATSCOMMISSIE (1995): STAATSCOMMISSIE VOOR HET INTERNATIONAAL PRIVAATRECHT, *Brief omtrent Wet Conflictenrecht Echtscheiding van 28 maart 1995*, The Hague: Staatscommissie, 1995.

STAATSCOMMISSIE (1998): STAATSCOMMISSIE VOOR HET INTERNATIONAAL PRIVAATRECHT, *Geregistreerd partnerschap*, The Hague: Staatscommissie, 1998.

STAATSCOMMISSIE (2001a): STAATSCOMMISSIE VOOR HET INTERNATIONAAL PRIVAATRECHT, *Voorontwerp van het codificatie van regelgeving betreffende het international privaatrecht*, The Hague: Staatscommissie, 2001.

STAATSCOMMISSIE (2001b): STAATSCOMMISSIE VOOR HET INTERNATIONAAL PRIVAATRECHT, *Advies van de Staatscommissie voor het Internationaal Privaatrecht inzake het internationaal privaatrecht in verband met de openstelling van het huwelijk voor personen van hetzelfde geslacht*, The Hague: Staatscommissie, 2001.

STAATSCOMMISSIE (2002): STAATSCOMMISSIE VOOR HET INTERNATIONAAL PRIVAATRECHT, *Rapport aan de Minister van Justitie. Algemene bepalingen wet internationaal privaatrecht*, The Hague: Staatscommissie, 2002.

STAATSCOMMISSIE (2004a): STAATSCOMMISSIE VOOR HET INTERNATIONAAL PRIVAATRECHT, *Brief over artikel 5a lid 1, wet conflictenrecht namen*, The Hague: Staatscommissie, 2004.

STAATSCOMMISSIE (2004b): STAATSCOMMISSIE VOOR HET INTERNATIONAAL PRIVAATRECHT, *Advies van de Staatscommissie voor het internationaal privaatrecht in verband met de uitvoering van verordening (EG) Nr. 2201/2003 betreffende de bevoegdheid en de erkenning en tenuitvoerlegging van beslissingen in huwelijkszaken en Inzake de ouderlijke verantwoordelijkheid ('Brussel II-bis')*, The Hague: Staatscommissie, 2004.

STAATSCOMMISSIE (2005): STAATSCOMMISSIE VOOR HET INTERNATIONAAL PRIVAATRECHT, *Brief over administratieve ontbinding*, The Hague: Staatscommissie, 2005.

STEENHOFF (2005): G. STEENHOFF, "Nieuwe IPR-regels voor het partnerschapsvermogensregime in de WCGP", *JBN*, 2005, p. 9-11.

STEINER (2002): E. STEINER, "The spirit of the new French registered partnership law – promoting autonomy and pluralism or weakening marriage?", *CFLQ*, 2002, p. 1-14.

STETTLER (1987): M. STETTLER, *Le droit Suisse de la filiation. Traité de droit privé Suisse. Volume III. Tome II.1*, Fribourg: Editions Universitaires, 1987

STETTLER/GERMANI (1999): M. STETTLER and L. GERMANI, *Droit Civil III. Effets généraux du marriage*, Fribourg : Editions Universitaires, 1999, 2nd Edition.

STONE (1995): P. STONE, *The conflict of laws*, London/New York: Longman, 1995.

STORME (2005): H. STORME, "Brussel IIbis Vo van toepassing met ingang van 1 maart 2005", *Ipr.be*, 2005, Vol. 1, p. 50-65.

STORY (1834): J. STORY, *Commentaries on the conflicts of law*, Boston: Little Brown & Co., 1834, 1st Edition.

STORY (1857): J. STORY, *Conflict of laws*, Boston: Little Brown & Co., 1857, 8th Edition, p. 32.

STRIKWERDA (2002): L. STRIKWERDA, *Inleiding tot het Nederlands internationaal privaatrecht*, Deventer: Kluwer, 2002, 7th Edition.

STÜBER (2005): S. STÜBER, "Gesetz zur überarbeitung des Lebenspartnerschaftsrechts", (2005) *Fam RZ*, p. 574-578.

SUMNER (2002a): I. SUMNER, "Comparative analysis and assessment of the gradual recognition of homosexuality with respect to The Netherlands and England", *MJ*, 2002, p. 29-55.

SUMNER (2002b): I. SUMNER, 'Will the sky fall in above England? The proposed registered partnership bill', *FJR*, 2002, Vol. 1, p. 24-28.

SUMNER (2002c): I. SUMNER, "The Charter of Fundamental Rights of the European Union and sexual orientation", *IFL*, 2002, p. 156-165.

SUMNER (2003a): I. SUMNER, "Transformers: Marriages in disguise?", *IFL*, 2003, p. 15.

SUMNER (2003b): I. SUMNER, "Legal position of same-sex couples in English law" in: K. BOELE-WOELKI and A. FÜCHS (eds.), *European family law in action. Volume I: Legal recognition of same-sex couples*, Antwerp: Intersentia, 2003, p. 99.

SUMNER (2004a): I. SUMNER, "Dissolution of Registered Partnerships. An excursion in Conversion!", *IFL*, 2004, Vol. 4, p. 231-237.

SUMNER (2004b): I. SUMNER, "Happy ever after? The problems of terminating registered partnerships", in: M. DIGOIX and P. FETSY (eds.), *Same-sex couples, same-sex partnerships and homosexual marriages. A focus on cross-national differentials*, Paris: INED, 2004, Report N°. 124, p. 35-46.

SUMNER (2004c): I. SUMNER, "Private international law aspects of registered partnerships: Great Britain and The Netherlands compared", in: A. BONOMI and B. COTTIER (eds.), *Aspects de droit international privé des partenariats enregistrés en Europe*, Zurich: Schultess, 2004, Volume N°. 49, p. 29-59.

SUMNER/FORDER (2003): I. SUMNER and C. FORDER, "Bumper Issue: All you ever wanted to know about Dutch family law (and were afraid to ask)" in: A. BAINHAM (ed.), *International Survey of Family Law. 2003 Edition*, Bristol: Family Law, 2003, p. 263-321.

SUMNER/FORDER (2004): I. SUMNER and C. FORDER, "Proposed revision of matrimonial property law, a new inheritance law and the first translation of the Dutch Civil Code, Book 1 (Family Law) into English", in: A. BAINHAM (ed.), *International Survey of Family Law. 2004 Edition*, Bristol: Family Law, 2004, p. 337-369.

SUMNER/WARENDORF (2003): I. SUMNER and H. WARENDORF, *EFL Series: Volume 5. Family Law Legislation of the Netherlands,* Antwerp: Intersentia, 2003.

SUMNER/WARENDORF (2005): I. SUMNER and H. WARENDORF, *EFL Series: Volume 9. Inheritance Law Legislation of the Netherlands*, Antwerp: Intersentia, 2005.

SVERDRUP (2005): T. SVERDRUP, "Maintenance as a separate issue – the relationship between maintenance and matrimonial property", in: K. BOELE-WOELKI (ed.), *EFL Series: volume 10. Common core and better law in European family law*, Antwerp: Intersentia, 2005, p. 119-134.

SYKES (1955): E.I. SYKES, "The essential validity of marriage", *ICLQ*, 1955, p. 159.

VAN TEEFLEN (2001): P. VAN TEEFFELEN, "Sociaal en biologisch ouderschap", *FJR*, 2001, p. 133-137.

TEN WOLDE (2001): M.H. TEN WOLDE, "De uitgangspunten van het Voorstel voor een aantal IPR-bepalingen over het geregistreerd partnerschap nader beschouwd", *EB*, 2001, p. 141-143.

TERRE (1999): F. TERRE, "Historie d'une loi", *Hors série. Droit de la Famille. Décmebre 1999*, 1999, p. 28.

TERRE/FENOUILLET (1996): F. TERRE and D. FENOUILLET (eds.), *Droit Civil. Les personnes; la famille; les incapacités*, Paris: Dalloz, 1996, 6th Edition.

TERRE/LEQUETTE (1997): F. TERRE and Y. LEQUETTE, *Les successions, les libéralités*, Paris: Dalloz, 1997, 3rd Edition.

TERRE/SIMLER (2001): F. TERRE and P. SIMLER, *Les régimes matrimoniaux*, Paris: Dalloz, 2001, 3rd Edition.

THERY (1998): I. THERY, *Couple, filiation et parenté aujourd'hui, en droit face aux mutations de la famille et de la vie privée*, Paris: Ministry of Justice and Ministry of Employment and Solidarity, May 1998.

THÉRY/SCHULZ (1997): I. THÉRY and M. SCHULZ, "Le contrat d'union sociale en question", *Esprit*, 1997, Vol. 236, p. 159-211.

THOMPSON (1996): J.M. THOMSON, *Family Law in Scotland*, Edinburgh: Butterworths/LexisNexis, 1996, 3rd Edition.

THOMSON (2003): H. THOMSON, "Met elkaar gehuwde vrouwen en naamskeuze", *Burgerzaken & Recht 2003*, Vol. 10, p. 390.

THORN (2003a): K. THORN, "The German conflict of laws rules on registered partnerships", in: K. BOELE-WOELKI and A. FUCHS (eds.), *Legal recognition of same-sex couples in Europe*, Antwerp: Intersentia, 2003.

THORN (2003b): K. THORN, "The German law on same-sex partnerships", in: K. BOELE-WOELKI and A. FUCHS (eds.), *Legal recognition of same-sex couples in Europe*, Antwerp: Intersentia, 2003, p. 84-98.

TOBLER (2001): C. TOBLER, "Europe: same-sex couples under the law of the EU", *PJA*, 2001, p. 269-286.

TRAEST (2001): M. TRAEST, "Buitenhuwelijkse samenlevingsvormen in het international privaatrecht: een materie in volle evolutie", *AJT*, 2000-2001, p. 384-388.

TREITEL (1999): G. TREITEL, *The law of constract*, London: Sweet & Maxwell, 1999, 10th Edition.

TRUEX (2001): D. TRUEX, "Brussels II – It's here", *IFL*, 2001, p. 7-9.

UNGER (1937): J. UNGER, "The place of classification in private international law", *Bell Yard*, 1937, Vol. 19, p. 3.

VALETAS (2001): M.-F. VALETAS, "Le nom des femmes mariées dans l'Union européenne", *Population et Sociétés*, 2001, N°. 367.

VAN DE WOESTEYNE (2001): I. VAN DE WOESTEYNE, "De hervorming van de personenbelasting door de Wet van 10 augustus 2001: Wijzigingen in de gezinsfiscaliteit", *EJ*, 2001, p. 150-162.

VAN DEN EECKHOUT (2001): V. VAN DEN EECKHOUT, "Nieuw internationaal echtscheidingsprocesrecht: Brussel II", *TCR*, 2001, p. 25-31.

VAN DEN EECKHOUT (2004): V. VAN DEN EECKHOUT, "Communitarisation of private international law: Tendencies to "liberalise" international family law", *Ipr.be*, 2004, Vol. 3, p. 51-70.

VAN DEN PLAS (2000): U. VAN DEN PLAS, "Wettelijke samenwoning procedures", *De Schakel*, 2000, p. 11-14.

VAN GERVEN/COVEMAKER (2001): W. VAN GERVEN and S. COVEMAKER, *Verbintenissenrecht*, Leuven: Acco, 2001.

VAN HECKE/LENAERTS (1989): G. VAN HECKE and K. LENAERTS, *Internationaal Privaatrecht*, Ghent: Story Scientia, 1989, 2nd Edition.

VANDER ELST (1983): R. VANDER ELST, *Droit international privé belge et droit conventionnel international*, Brussels: Bruylant, 1983.

VAN DER VELDEN (1996): F.J.A. VAN DER VELDEN, "Nationaliteit als Europese jurisdictiegrond", in S.C.J.J. Kortmann *et al.* (eds.), *Op recht. Bundel opstellen, aangeboden aan prof. mr. A.V.M.Struycken ter gelegenheid van zijn zilveren ambtsjubileum aan de Katholieke Universiteit Nijmegen*, Zwolle: W.E.J. Tjeenk Willink, 1996, p. 357-365.

VAN DER VELDEN (2000): F.J.A. VAN DER VELDEN, "Een Europese Verordening betreffende bevoegdheid, erkenning en tenuitvoerlegging in familierechtelijke zaken", *WPNR*, 2000, Vol. 6421, p. 753-763.

VERBEKE (2002a): A. VERBEKE, "Belgisch reservatair erfrecht", *Fiscaal Tijdschrift Vermogen*, 2002, Vol. 2, p. 30.

VERBEKE (2002b): A. VERBEKE, "Chapter 3: Belgium", in: D. HAYTON (ed.), *European Succession Laws*, London: Jordans, 2002, p. 37-78.

VERBREEK (2000): M. VERBREEK, "De wet tot invoering van de wettelijke samenwoning", *De Burgerlijke Stand*, 2000, p. 120-124.

VERHELLEN (2000): J. VERHELLEN, "Enkele IPR-aspecten voor het huwelijk en niet-huwelijkse samenwoningsvorm", in: W. DE MULDER *et al.* (eds.), *Tot de dood ons scheidt?*, Antwerp: Maklu, 2000.

VERSCHELDEN (2004): G. VERSCHELDEN, *Afstamming*, Ghent: Story Scientia, 2004.

VERSCHRAEGEN (1995): B. VERSCHRAEGEN, "Huwelijk tussen personen van hetzelfde geslacht in rechtsverglijkend perspectief", *FJR*, 1995, Vol. 10, p. 229-231.

VERSTAPPEN (1997): L.C.A. VERSTAPPEN, "Het geregistreerd partnerschap", *FJR*, 1997, p. 277.

VERSTAPPEN (2002): L.C.A. VERSTAPPEN, "Renovatiewerkzaamheden aan het Nederlandse huwelijksvermogensrecht", *Themsis*, 2002, Vol. 6, p. 307-318.

VERWILGHEN (1985): M. VERWILGHEN, *Le Code de la Nationalité Belge*, Brussels: Bruylant, 1985.

VIVIER (2001): J.-L. VIVIER, *Le pacte civil de solidarité. Un nouveau contrat*, Paris: L'Harmattan, 2001.

VLAARDINGERBROEK (1995): P. VLAARDINGERBROEK, "Marriage, divorce and living arrangements in the Netherlands", *FLQ*, 1995, p. 635-644.

VLAARDINGERBROEK (2000): P. VLAARDINGERBROEK, "Adoptie door paren van gelijk geslacht", *FJR*, 2000, Vol. 9, p. 198-202.

VLAARDINGERBROEK (2004): P. VLAARDINGERBROEK *et al.*, *Het hedendaagse personen- en familierecht*, Deventer: W.E.J. Tjeenk Willink, 2004, 4th Edition.

VLAS (2001): P. VLAS, "Nieuw internationaal scheidingsprocesrecht: de Verordening 'Brussel II'", *WPNR*, 2001, Vol. 6444, p. 440-448.

VLAS (2003): P. VLAS, "De Algemene Bepalingen als sluitstuk van de codificatie van het Nederlandse IPR", *WPNR*, 2003, p. 443-449.

VLAS (2004): P. VLAS, "De codificatie van het Nederlandse IPR", *IPR.be*, 2004, p. 106-114.

VON BAR (1986): C. VON BAR, "Chapter 17: Personal Effects of Marriage", in: K. LIPSTEIN, *International Encyclopaedia of Comparative Law. Volume III: Private International Law*, Tübingen/Dordrecht: C.B.Mohr/Maritinus Nijhoff, 1986.

VON SAVIGNY (1880): F.C. VON SAVIGNY, *A treatise on the conflict of laws and the limits of their application in time and space. Translated by W. Guthrie*, Edinburgh: T&T Clark, 1880, 2nd Edition.

VONK (2003): M. VONK, "Een, twee of drie ouders?", *FJR*, 2003, Vol. 6, p. 122.

VONK (2004): M. VONK, "One, two or three parents? Lesbian co-mothers and a known donor with "family life" under Dutch law", *IJLPF*, 2004, Vol. 18, p. 103-117.

VRANKEN (2005): J. VRANKEN, *Mr. C. Asser's handleiding tot de beoefening van het Nederlandse burgerlijk recht. Algemeen deel. Een vervolg*, Deventer: Kluwer, 2005.

WAALDIJK (1991): K. WAALDIJK, "De heteroseksuele exclusiviteit van het huwelijk na Hoge Raad 19 oktober 1990", *AA*, 1991, Vol. 40, p. 47-56.

WAALDIJK (1992): K. WAALDIJK, "Vrij samen", *Regel Maat*, 1992, Vol. 2, p. 43-49.

WAALDIJK (1995): K. WAALDIJK, "Naar een gelijkgeslachtelijk huwelijk", *FJR*, 1995, p. 223-228.

WAALDIJK (1996): K. WAALDIJK, "Free movement of same-sex partners", *MJ*, 1996, p. 271-285.

WAALDIJK (1999): K. WAALDIJK, "De voorgestelde wet openstelling huwelijk", *FJR*, 1999, p. 198-213.

WAALDIJK (2000a): K. WAALDIJK, "Partnerschapsregistratie en huwelijk: toenemende rechtsgelijkheid voor geslachtsgelijke partners en hun kinderen" in: H. LENTERS *et al.*, *De familie geregld. Preadvies voor KNB*, Lelystad: Vermande, 2000, p. 178.

WAALDIJK (2000b): K. WAALDIJK, "Civil developments: Patterns of reform in the legal position of same-sex partners in Europe", *Canadian Revue of Family Law*, 2000, Vol. 17, p. 63-88.

WAALDIJK (2001): K. WAALDIJK, "Small change: How the road to same-sex marriage got paved in the Netherlands", in: R. WINTEMUTE and M. ANDENÆS (eds.), *Legal recognition of same-sex partnerships*, Oxford: Hart, 2001, Appendix VI.

WAALDIJK (2004): K. WAALDIJK, "Others may follow: the introduction of marriage, quasi-marriage and semi-marriage for same-sex couples in other European countries", *New Eng. LR*, 2004, p. 569-590.

WAALDIJK/CLAPHAM (1993): K. WAALDIJK and A. CLAPHAM (ed.), *Homosexuality: A European Community Issue*, Dordrecht: Martinus Nijhoff, 1993.

WAGNER (2001): R. WAGNER, "Das neue Internationale Privat- und Verfahrensrecht zur eingetragenen Lebenspartnerschaft", *IPRax*, 2001, p. 281-293.

WALKER (2001): D.M. WALKER, *The Scottish legal system*, Edinburgh: W. Green, 2001, 8th Edition.

WAMELEN (2000): C. WAMELEN, "Gezamenlijk gezag van rechtswege bij geregistreerd partnerschap", *FJR*, 2000, p. 155-156.

WARDLE (1995): L. WARDLE, "International marriage and divorce regulation and recognition: a survey", *FLQ*, 1995, p. 497-515.

WARDLE (1998): L. WARDLE, "Same-sex marriage and the limits of legal pluralism", in: J. EEKELAAR and T. NHALPO (eds.), *The changing family*, Oxford: Hart, 1998.

WASHINGTON/ALEXANDER (2005): J. WASHINGTON and S. ALEXANDER, "Civil partnership made easy", *Fam. Law*, 2005, p. 243-247.

WAUTELET (2004): P. WAUTELET, "Note sur l'ouverture du mariage aux ressortissants étrangers de même sexe", *Ipr.be*, 2004, p. 97-105.

WELLENHOFER (2005): M. WELLENHOFER, "Das neue Recht für eingetragene Lebenspartnerschaften", *NJW*, 2005, p. 705-709.

WERRO (2000): F. WERRO, *Concubinage, mariage et démariage*, Bern: Stämpfli, 2000, 5th Edition.

WHEELER (2003): D. WHEELER, "Brussels II: Forum disputes in England and Wales", *IFL*, p. 96-100.

WILKINSON/ MCK.NORRIE (1993): A.B. WILKINSON and K. MCK.NORRIE, *The law relating to parent and child,* Edinburgh: W. Green, 1993.

WILLEKENS (1998): H. WILLEKENS, "Long term developments in family law in Western Europe: an explanation", in: J. EEKELAAR and T. NHLAPO (eds.), *The changing family*, Oxford: Hart, 1998, p. 47-71.

WILLEMS (1999): A.W.M. WILLEMS, "Het homohuwelijk: een te hoge prijs?", *FJR*, 1999, p. 217.

WILLEMS (2000): A.W.M. WILLEMS, "Adoptie door homo-ouders en de positie van de spermdonor", *FJR*, 2000, p. 226-229.

WINTEMUTE (2000): R. WINTEMUTE, "Lesbian and Gay Inequality 2000: the potential of the Human Rights Act 1998 and the need for an Equality Act 2002", *EHRLR*, 2000, p. 603-632.

WINTEMUTE (2001): R. WINTEMUTE, "Conclusion" in: R. WINTEMUTE and M. ANDENÆS (eds.), *Legal Recognition of Same-Sex Partnerships*, Oxford: Hart Publishing, 2001, p. 759-773.

WOELKE (2004): A. WOELKE, "International aspects of civil partnerships", *IFL*, 2004, p. 111-114.

WOLFF (1950): M. WOLFF, *Private international law,* Oxford: Scientia, 1950, 1st Edition.

WOLFF (1977): M. WOLFF, *Private international law*, Oxford: Scientia, 1977, 2nd Edition.

WOMEN AND EQUALITY UNIT (2003a): WOMEN AND EQUALITY UNIT, "Civil Partnership: A framework for the legal recognition of same-sex couples", London: Department of Trade and Industry, 2003.

WOMEN AND EQUALITY UNIT (2003b): WOMEN AND EQUALITY UNIT, "Responses to Civil Partnership. A framework for the legal recognition of same-sex couples", London: Department of Trade and Industry, 2003.

WOODS (2004): U. WOODS, "Rights for cohabitees – who should qualify?", *NILQ*, 2004, Vol. 55, p. 8-32.

WORTMANN (1998): S.F. WORTMANN, *Als een eigen kind,* Inaugural Speech on the appointment to Professor in Youth Law, Family Law and the Law of Persons at the University of Groningen, 30th June 1998.

WORTMANN (2001): S.F.M. WORTMANN, "Sekseneutraal afstammingsrecht?", *FJR*, 2001, p. 231-236.

WORTMANN (2002): S.F.M. WORTMANN, "Rechtsontwikkelingen in het personen- en familierecht: flitsscheidingen en verrekenbedingen", *WPNR*, 2002, Vol. 6477, p. 165.

WORTMANN (2003): S.F.M. WORTMANN, "Kroniek van het personen- en familierecht", *WPNR*, 2003, p. 1665-1671.

WORTMANN/VAN DUIJVENDIJK-BRAND (2002): S.F.M. WORTMANN and J. VAN DUIJVENDIJK-BRAND, *Compendium van het Personen- en Familierecht*, Deventer: Kluwer, 2002, 8th Edition.

WRAGG (1996): D. WRAGG, "Constructive trusts and the unmarried couple", *Fam. Law*, 1996, p. 298-300.

YEW (2003): J. YEW, "A new dawn?", *NLJ*, 2003, p. 1226-1227.

YTTERBERG (2001): H. YTTERBERG, "Additional regulations besides the registered partnership", *PJA*, 2001, p. 291.

VAN ZEBEN (1998): C.J VAN ZEBEN *et al.* (ed.), *Compendium bijzondere overeenkomsten*, Deventer: Kluwer, 1998, 9th Edition.

ZWEIGERT/KÖTZ/WEIR (1998): K. ZWEIGERT and H. KÖTZ (Translated by T. WEIR), *Introduction to comparative law*, London: Clarendon, 1998, 3rd Edition.

CASE LIST

AUSTRIA

AUSTRALIA

BELGIUM

Cour de Cassation (Supreme Court)

Hof/Cour d'Appel (Court of Appeal)

Tribunal d'instance/Rechtbank van eerste aanleg (District court)

Arbitragehof (Constitutional Court)

CANADA

FRANCE

ITALY

THE NETHERLANDS

Hoge Raad (Supreme Court)

Hof (Court of Appeal)

Other Courts

UNITED KINGDOM

UNITED STATES OF AMERICA

Federal Courts

State Courts

EUROPEAN COURTS

European Court of Justice (European Union)

CURRICULUM VITAE

Ian Sumner was born on the 15th September 1978 in Liverpool, England. In 1997 he obtained five grade A 'A'-Levels from Merchant Taylors' School Crosby, after which he began his law degree at the University of Cambridge. In 1999, he spent a year at Utrecht University as an Erasmus student. In 2001, he obtained a First Class degree from Christ's College, Cambridge and was awarded the De Hart Law Prize for outstanding achievement. In September 2001, he began work at the Molengraaff Institute for Private Law at Utrecht University, first as a PhD researcher and from the 1st April 2005 as a junior lecturer/researcher. In conducting his research he spent time at the Law Faculty of the Catholic University of Leuven, the Swiss Institute for Comparative Law in Lausanne, the Institute of Advance Legal Studies in London and Washburn Law School in Topeka, Kansas, United States of America. His research at the Swiss Institute for Comparative Law was made possible due to the generous financial support of the Netherlands Organisation for Scientific Research (NWO). Together with Mr. Hans Warendorf, he has also translated Books 1 and 4 of the Dutch Civil Code into English.

EUROPEAN FAMILY LAW SERIES

1. *Legal Recognition of Same-Sex Couples in Europe*
   K. Boele-Woelki and A. Fuchs (eds.)

2. *European Family Law in Action. Volume I: Grounds for Divorce*
   K. Boele-Woelki, B. Braat and I. Sumner (eds.)

3. *European Family Law in Action. Volume II: Maintenance Between Former Spouses*
   K. Boele-Woelki, B. Braat and I. Sumner (eds.)

4. *Perspectives for the Unification and Harmonisation of Family Law in Europe*
   K. Boele-Woelki (ed.)

5. *Family Law Legislation of the Netherlands*
   I. Sumner and H. Warendorf

6. *Indépendance et interdépendance patrimoniales des époux dans le régime matrimonial légal des droits néerlandais, français et suisse*
   B. Braat

7. *Principles of European Family Law Regarding Divorce and Maintenance Between Former Spouses*
   K. Boele-Woelki, F. Ferrand, C. González Beilfuss, M. Jänterä-Jareborg, N. Lowe, D. Martiny and W. Pintens

8. *Inheritance law legislation of the Netherlands*
   I. Sumner and H. Warendorf

9. *European Family Law in Action. Volume III: Parental Responsibilities*
   K. Boele-Woelki, B. Braat and I. Curry-Sumner (eds.)

10. *Common core and better law in European Family law*
    K. Boele-Woelki (ed.)

Lightning Source UK Ltd.
Milton Keynes UK
UKOW05f0826111217
314238UK00006B/91/P

9 789050 955324